LOGIC

second edition

ROBERT BAUM Rensselaer Polytechnic Institute

with
David T. Wieck Rensselaer Polytechnic Institute

*Author of chapters on Quantification and
The Predicate Calculus*

Holt, Rinehart and Winston
New York   Chicago   San Francisco
Dallas   Montreal   Toronto

Cover: Robert Morris, *Labyrinth,* 1974. Painted plywood, masonite and two-by-fours, 8' high, 30' diameter, created expressly for the Institute of Contemporary Art, University of Pennsylvania, Philadelphia, on the occasion of the exhibition *Robert Morris/Projects,* March 23 to April 27, 1974. Photo credit: Will Brown
Portraits pp. 9, 11, 29, 32, 33, 64, 66, 134, 143, 155, 231, 245, 247, 267, 277, 281, 363, 394, 395, 397, 417, 503 courtesy The Granger Collection. Biorhythm chart, p. 480, reprinted from *Psychology Today,* © 1978 Ziff-Davis Publishing Company; photo of Reggie Jackson, courtesy Wide World Photos.

Library of Congress Cataloging in Publication Data

Baum, Robert, 1941–
Logic.

    Includes index.
    1. Logic. I. Wieck, David T., joint author. II.
Title.
BC108.B29   1981   160   80-11084

ISBN: 0-03-046396-3

Preface

I have always been puzzled and frustrated by the fact that introductory formal logic texts have traditionally been modelled on graduate mathematics or linguistics texts, particularly with regard to style and format. It is almost as if logicians assumed that "real" logic cannot be presented in a clear and interesting way, and that a logic text cannot have an aesthetic dimension that goes beyond the inclusion of several "elegant" abstract proofs. It seemed as though it would be intolerably heretical for a logic text to resemble in style and appearance recent texts in physics or psychology. Even the first edition of this text was subject to this criticism.

That others share my feelings about this problem with previous logic texts is clearly evidenced by the proliferation over the last five years of texts and courses dealing with "informal" logic. Some of these texts present their material in an interesting manner. Several even utilize a few illustrations or "real life" arguments, although for the most part even the informal logic texts are inexplicably austere in style and content.

The trend towards informal logic texts and courses is even more frustrating to me because it involves throwing out the baby with the bathwater. Students in such courses now get no significant exposure to the concepts of formal logic. They can get credit for a logic course without being able to test an argument for validity or even being able to define 'valid', just as they can get credit for an English course without being able to write a grammatically correct sentence or to distinguish a participle from an infinitive. I firmly believe that there is much of value in traditional formal logic, that formal logic can be related to "real" arguments in interesting and useful ways, and that all of this can be done in an aesthetically satisfying way which has not been approximated in any previous text.

In this edition of *Logic,* I have tried to retain that which is of basic value from the first edition and at the same time to present it in a way which makes a radical break with traditional formal logic texts. I have retained the clear and *rigorous* presentation of the various concepts and methods of formal logic and increased the flexibility of the text, which permits the instructor to select and order the presentation of the various topics to fit her or his classroom needs. I have substantially expanded the explicit treatment of the ways in which formal logic relates to the analysis of everyday arguments, so that this *formal* logic text now provides more numerous and more thorough analyses of "real" arguments than most informal logic texts. And, what should be most readily apparent to even the most casual peruser of this volume, I have presented all of this in a package which has an aesthetic dimension never before attempted in a logic text.

A major effort has been made in this revision to integrate the consideration of the problems of applying the concepts and methods of formal analysis to statements and arguments as they occur in everyday contexts. This has been accomplished in part by incorporating discussions of new examples into the treatments of the technical material and by doubling the number of exercises to almost 2,000—with most of the new examples and exercises being in ordinary language from everyday contexts. But the most significant change, and one that is unique to this book, is the

iii

presentation of four ordinary language arguments which are analysed as examples in five different chapters—2, 5, 7, 9, and 10. This is done in such a way as to not only develop basic skills and intuitions for analysing ordinary language statements and arguments, but also to give students a sense of the differences between and the relative strengths and weaknesses of the various modes of analysis. This approach gives the student a working awareness of the extent to which the application of formal logic to ordinary language arguments is an art involving critical judgment. It also makes students particularly sensitive to the extent to which arguments expressed in ordinary language in everyday contexts can be interpreted in a variety of different ways and in a variety of different logical systems with quite different results, e.g., that a single argument in ordinary language can (not unreasonably) be evaluated as a syllogism, an argument in propositional logic, an argument in quantificational logic, and an inductive argument with quite different results. This method of repeatedly analysing the same arguments in five different chapters also has the effect of developing a sense of the similarities as well as the differences between the various systems of formal and informal, inductive and deductive, and traditional and modern logic.

The basic layout and design of the first edition of this book represented a modest breakthrough in the tradition of dull and unattractive logic texts, but it still was only a token gesture towards providing a recognition of the noncognitive—especially the aesthetic—elements of the learning experience. The physical appearance of this book speaks for itself better than any written description or explanation. The inclusion of almost 100 cartoons and other illustrative materials is designed not only to increase student interest and motivation, but also student understanding of a variety of technical concepts. The illustrations have been selected and integrated into the text to disprove the tacit assumption among many logic teachers that logic can be made interesting only at the sacrifice of rigor and substance.

Although users of the first edition were generally pleased with the presentation of the technical material, several major changes have been made to improve the treatment of both the syllogistic logic and the quantificational logic. The presentation of syllogistic logic has been simplified in two ways. First, the new edition focuses on only one system of syllogistic logic (the traditional Aristotelean approach) rather than the potentially confusing dual system approach of the first edition, which presented the Boolean as well as the Aristotelean approach. Also, the Aristotelean rules for determining validity have been condensed from the five in the original edition to three in the present volume. The original chapter on quantificational logic, written for the first edition by my colleague David Wieck, has been almost completely rewritten and expanded into two chapters for the present edition by Professor Wieck. The new longer explication not only makes the material much more fully and clearly explained, but it also integrates it more closely into the rest of the text, particularly the chapters on propositional logic. The distinction between inductive and deductive logic has also been reworked in Chapter 2 to make it more understandable and usable for the average student while at the same time maintaining its technical precision.

The first edition was broken into four sections and was flexible to the extent that instructors could go from the Introduction directly to any one of the four sections. The present edition is even more flexible. After completing the Introduction and first two chapters, it is now possible to go directly to any one of six chapters—3, 4, 6, 10,

12, or 13. It is also possible to go to any of these six chapters from any other chapter in the book. Eight chapters are also developed as pairs, with Chapters 1, 4, 6, and 8 dealing with statements and Chapters 2, 5, 7, and 9 dealing with arguments. Thus, it is even possible for an instructor to go through the four chapters on statement analysis first and then go through the chapters on argument analysis.

It is impossible to acknowledge by name in this limited space all those who have contributed to this book. Perhaps my greatest debt is to my students, who probably have provided me with as much of a learning experience as I have been able to provide for them. It is, of course, impossible to identify the precise source of the many ideas, concepts, and methods contained in an introductory text such as this one, but certainly, whatever their historical origins, they have been transmitted to me, consciously or otherwise, by my own teachers, colleagues, and the authors of the numerous texts I have used and studied over the years.

Many individuals contributed directly to this edition, and many others to the first edition, but only one has made major contributions to both. My friend and colleague, David T. Wieck, wrote the chapter on Quantificational Logic for the first edition, which not only enabled me to meet an otherwise impossible publication deadline but also provided an exceptionally clear yet rigorous presentation of the topic which enhanced the overall value of the book. He has rewritten this material in an expanded and even more teachable form for the present edition. In addition, he has been of great help in providing critical comments and raising important questions about my drafts of both editions.

Others who have provided helpful comments on the first edition or drafts of this new edition include Professors Nelson Pole, Allen Harder, Philip Pecorino, Robert Ellis, Russell McIntire, Jr., Richard Oliver, John Lincourt, Robert Long, John Sertic, William Prior, Manuel Davenport, John Schumacher, and Robert Gurland. David P. Boynton and Jeanette Ninas Johnson provided patient and highly professional editorial support for this revision. The exercises were prepared by William Briel, Terri Nally, and Donald Kieffer. Nicholas Falletta and Sarah Parker served as editors of the first edition, and they deserve recognition for their contributions to the writing of the portions of that edition which have been carried over. Others who contributed in various ways to the writing of the first edition include Myron Jefka, Joseph Jackson, Jo Kaufman, Deborah Kransberg, Rose Slomowitz, Marlin Thomas, and John Rotondo. As always, responsibility for errors and matters of judgment rests entirely with me.

Troy, N.Y.   R. J. B.
October 1980

Contents

Introduction

*If you are reading this page, you are probably taking
a logic course, and if you are taking such a course
you will probably get a grade in it. Since you are
reading this page, you will probably get a grade in
a logic course.*

These two sentences provide an example of an argument. Logic involves the study of arguments and their components—words and statements—for the purpose of assessing the relations that hold among these components.

To get a sense of how common arguments are in everyday life, let's construct some others concerning the logic course you are taking. You probably have some idea now, even before you have started, what grade you will ultimately receive in the course. Even if you're one of the exceptional few who has not thought at all about your possible grade, for the purposes of this exercise, plug some letter into the blank in the following sentence.

I will get a(n) _____ in this logic course.

Judgments such as this normally can be supported by reasons of one sort or another. Certainly all kinds of reasons could be given in support of such a prediction about a grade in a logic course. For example, it may be the case that the grading in the course is going to be based on a system which will permit you to retake each test as often as is necessary to get the grade you want, and also that you are determined to retake the tests until you get a B. Or, it may be that you have learned from other students that while the person who is teaching the course gives very few A's, this instructor also *never* gives less than a C to anyone who attends all class sessions and takes all the exams. Or, it may be that you are basically quite intelligent and hard-working, with high verbal and quantitative aptitude scores and a straight-A average to date, and you intend to work hard to get an A in this course. Or, you may have a "foolproof" plan for cheating in this course, or you may want to fail it for some other reason or . . . . The list of possible reasons to support the judgment that a certain person will get a specific grade in this course could be extended indefinitely, but enough possibilities have been offered to give you an idea as to how to construct your own argument.

In the most general sense of the term, an argument is any set of statements that is such that one or more of them support (or provide evidence for) the truth of another statement. The statement being supported is the conclusion; the statement(s) offered in support of it are the premises. Thus, in the argument that you have just constructed, the statement 'I will get a(n) ___ in this logic course' is the conclusion; the statements giving the reasons you think you will get this grade constitute the premises of your argument. We can see this more clearly by looking at the following argument offered by Pat, a fictional student.

> *I will get at least a C in this logic course because I*
> *know that the instructor is a fair grader, that I am*
> *not dumb, and that I intend to work very hard in*
> *this course.*

The conclusion of this argument is 'I (Pat) will get at least a C in this logic course'. And although they are all part of the same sentence, the three reasons offered in support of this belief comprise three distinct premises for the argument. They are: 'The instructor is a fair grader', 'I am not dumb', and 'I intend to work very hard in this course'.

We should note here that some things could have been inserted in the blank above that would have given us a statement which would not have required any argument for its support. For example, had we inserted 'A or less', we would have had the statement 'I will get an A or less in this logic course'. It should be clear that this statement is true and that no further proof is necessary, but it may not be clear as to why this is so. The study of the logic of statements in this book will provide an explanation as to why and how such statements can be known to be true without any arguments being given to prove their truth. Such study will also explain the basic logical difference between statements such as 'I will get an A or less in this logic course' and statements such as 'I will get an A in this logic course, or I will not get an A in this logic course', which also requires no further proof—but for different reasons.

EXERCISE 1 *Construct arguments by giving at least three reasons (premises) in support of each of the following judgments (conclusions).*

---

1. I will probably enjoy this logic course.
2. This logic course will probably be my least interesting course this semester.
3. I will never be involved in an automobile accident.

4. I will get a good job when I graduate from college.
5. I am as intelligent as most of the other students in this class.

LOGICAL FORM AND STRUCTURE   Each reader who inserted a letter in the sentence in the previous section, 'I will get a(n) ____ in this logic course', made a unique statement different from that made by anyone else insofar as each statement had a different meaning from the others. Even if Pat, Lee, and Jan all inserted the same letter in the blank, they were each making different statements because the 'I' in each case refers to a different person; that is, when Pat says 'I will get a B in this logic course', it is the same as saying 'Pat will get a B in the particular logic course that Pat is taking', while Lee's statement will have the meaning 'Lee will get a B in the particular logic course that Lee is taking', and, of course, Jan's statement will be about Jan's grade. If we write all three sentences together, we can see that, even though they clearly have different meanings, they also look very similar. To simplify our discussion, let us consider the following sentences.

Pat likes logic.
Lee likes logic.
Jan likes logic.

Once again, these three statements have quite different meanings since they are about three different persons, but they also resemble one another in a basic way. One way of describing this similarity among the three statements is to say that *they have the same logical structure or form.* The statement 'Pat likes calculus' also shares this form, even though it, too, has a different meaning. The similarity of form can be most clearly shown by using blanks as follows:

_____ *likes* _____ .

Any sentence we might construct by putting appropriate nouns in the blanks would have the same logical form as our original three statements. Thus, 'Rover likes dog food' and 'Pat likes Jan' also share the same logical form. This concept of logical form will be discussed in much greater detail in later chapters.

EXERCISE 2   *Put nouns in the blanks to create five different sentences with the same logical form.*

---

1. _____ runs _____ .
2. All _____ are _____ .
3. _____ believes that _____ .
4. Not every _____ is a _____ .
5. _____ causes _____ .

LOGIC VERSUS
PSYCHOLOGY
As a discipline, logic dates back more than two thousand years to the Greek philosopher Aristotle, who first developed the syllogistic logic that will be studied in Chapters 4 and 5 of this book. For over two thousand years, Aristotelian logic was regarded as the only possible kind; it was not until the nineteenth and twentieth centuries that alternative systems were developed. Yet, in all this time, no simple, precise, universally accepted definition of logic has ever been formulated. Of the various definitions that have been offered, a good many have been more confusing than helpful. Nevertheless, it is worthwhile to examine some of them, so as to gain a clear insight into the nature of the discipline.

One common definition is that logic is the study of the laws of thought. The problem with such a definition is that it is too inclusive. Many mental activities— for example, imagining a two-headed man, or daydreaming about being a millionaire—would qualify as thought. However, none of these activities would be of interest to the logician. Logic is concerned primarily with the type of thinking called *reasoning,* the process by which an inference or conclusion is drawn from a statement or series of statements. Perhaps, then, can logic be properly defined as the study of the laws of reasoning? This is certainly more specific, but it is still too broad. The discipline of psychology is also concerned with what can properly be called laws of reasoning; and yet logic is not a branch of psychology but of philosophy.

If this is confusing, it is probably because there are two quite different senses in which we commonly use the term 'law'. A law may be a **descriptive** statement about the way something in fact happens; or it may be a **prescriptive** statement about how something should be done.

When we speak of the laws of nature or scientific law, we are using the term 'law' in its descriptive sense. The law of gravitation, the laws of motion, the laws of heat exchange were not created by a human legislature, and they cannot be repealed. They simply *are*—or rather, they describe the way in which the components of the universe, by their nature, always behave under given conditions. Nothing and no one can choose to obey or not to obey these laws. If I drop a brick from the top of the Empire State Building, my knowledge of several descriptive laws would enable me to predict rather accurately the ensuing course of events. And if, instead of dropping a brick, I myself step off the top of the Empire State Building, I will thereafter behave according to those same descriptive laws, whether I choose to or not.

Laws of behavior may also be descriptive; that is, they may purport to describe the ways in which individuals or groups of people tend to react to given conditions, on the basis of biological structure or social conditioning. If a person maintains that hungry people are more likely than well-fed people to riot against a corrupt government, he is stating what he believes to be a descriptive law. He is describing a way in which people do frequently tend to act.

Prescriptive law, on the other hand, is concerned with the way people ought to act. Moral laws are prescriptive; the laws of a political entity such as a nation or a city are prescriptive; the constitution and bylaws of an organization are prescriptive. Such laws are usually established by someone's deliberate choice, as a means of attaining a desired goal, and they can be broken. If a motorist sees a street sign setting forth the prescriptive law, "Speed limit 20 mph," it is possible for her to ignore it and push the speedometer up to 50. The consequences may be unfortunate, or they may not: she may arrive at her destination in one piece, having skidded off no cliff, struck no pedestrian, and picked up no speeding ticket.

To return now to our comparison of logic and psychology: we can see that, insofar as psychology is concerned with the laws of reasoning, it is concerned with describing the ways in which people actually do tend to reason. For instance, a psychologist may seek to discover the ways in which people form generalizations. To do so, he or she observes, interviews, and tests a number of subjects. One subject may be a college student who, after struggling with three difficult mathematics courses, has concluded that all mathematics courses are difficult. Another may be a person who has purchased meat twice from a particular store, found it tough on both occasions, and concludes that all meat sold by that store is of poor quality. Still others may report similar experiences. On the basis of this information, the psychologist concludes that all people tend to form generalizations on the basis of fewer than one hundred specific instances. The psychologist's conclusion says nothing about whether this is a good or a bad way to reason; it merely describes a way in which people do reason.

In contrast, the laws of reason with which logic is concerned are more of the prescriptive type. Logic seeks to set standards for the ways in which people ought to reason if they wish to reason well. Like speed limits, the prescriptive laws of reason may sometimes appear to be founded on a "because I tell you to" kind of authority, but, in fact, they are based on the logician's perception that certain ways of reasoning are, by their very nature, better than other ways of reasoning, or that adherence to certain methods of reasoning produce better results than alternative methods. Therefore, like speed limits, the prescriptive laws of logic can be ignored, but the ignorer is likely to find himself saddled with the results of mistaken conclusions. For example, a politician running for reelection in a district where school busing is a major issue might poll a sample of fifty residents and conclude from their responses that a pro-busing stand will ensure his victory. But if the fifty people he talked to are all members of a small liberal segment in a district which is generally working-class and conservative, he is probably in for a rude shock when he sees the election returns. In arriving at his conclusion, he indeed reasoned according to the process described by psychologists. However, from a logical point of view, his reasoning was poor—not because he was relying on other people's opinions, but because the opinions were drawn from a very small and unrepresentative sample of voters.

Thus, we can say that, whereas psychology is concerned with describing the way people reason, logic is concerned with evaluating this reasoning. In this text, we shall focus on methods for distinguishing good reasoning from bad and present formal criteria for evaluating inferences and arguments as well as techniques and procedures for applying these criteria to concrete cases. These criteria, techniques, and procedures are of value not only to logicians, but also to psychologists, students, businessmen, politicians, detectives, farmers, athletes, and anyone else who uses a variety of reasoning processes to make inferences and reach conclusions. In truth, we all require standards for determining which of these processes are good and which are poor; which is the same as to say that our reasoning and arguments are subject to logical evaluation.

Logic can also be characterized as the study of arguments in a descriptive sense. On this account, logic provides descriptions of basic logical structures of statements and of the relations that hold among them. For example, logic tells us that the statement 'The sun is shining or it is not shining' is true because of its logical structure. Logic also tells us that the statement 'The sun is shining' implies the statement 'It is not the case that the sun is not shining'. These statements are exemplars of some basic laws of logic which are at least as true (descriptively) as the laws of physics and which are more valid than most if not all of the descriptive "laws" of psychology. Thus, in this respect, logic is similar to psychology, but it differs in that it is descriptive of the logical structures of and logical relations among statements, not of human minds or reasoning processes.

FORMAL AND INFORMAL LOGIC

We have already indicated that logic involves the study of arguments and their components—words and statements—for the purpose of evaluating the relations that hold among the components. One way of approaching this task is by focusing on the basic logical structure or form of statements and arguments, with no consideration of their nonlogical content. To illustrate this briefly, we can go back to our hypothetical student Pat's argument concerning her grade in logic, which went as follows:

> *The instructor in this course is a fair grader.*
> *I am not dumb.*
> *I intend to work very hard in this course.*
> *Therefore, I will get at least a C in this logic course.*

The basic logical structure of this set of statements can be exhibited in a variety of ways using different systems of logic. One possible way is the following:

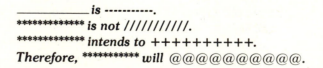

Because we are concerned only with the form or structure of these statements, it is not at all important (or even relevant) what terms might be plugged into the various blanks. *When the meanings of the nonlogical terms are not being con-*

sidered and only the logical form is of interest, we are working in the domain known as **formal logic.**

Some professional logicians study only formal logic; that is, they work only with abstract models which have purely logical substance and content. While such an activity can be as intellectually challenging and interesting as the game of chess, it has additional value in that it can be applied to the analysis and evaluation of statements and arguments which are part of our everyday lives. It is for this reason that logic courses are part of most college curricula while chess is not. Relating the abstract systems of formal logic to "real" statements and arguments is not part of formal logic itself; it requires the consideration of many issues and factors beyond the basic logical forms of the statements and arguments. *The study of the factors other than logical form relevant to the analysis and evaluation of statements and arguments of the kind that occur in everyday situations* is known as **informal logic.** This study includes consideration of such things as: the identification and clarification of vague or ambiguous statements; making explicit unstated assumptions, presuppositions, or biases; recognition of frequently used but highly questionable premises; and assessment of the strength of analogies between more or less similar cases.

In dealing with "real" arguments in everyday situations, it is difficult if not impossible to separate the consideration of logical form and structure from consideration of the various *nonlogical* aspects of statements and arguments. Thus, even though it is possible to discuss formal logic quite independently of informal logic (and vice versa), and this, in fact, is done in many books, the two sets of topics will be discussed here in as integrated a way as possible to make clear and explicit the ways in which the two forms can be used to assist in the analysis and evaluation of statements and arguments in everyday contexts.

A variety of systems have been developed over the last 2,000 years for analyzing the structure of and relations between statements. We shall be studying only a few of the more widely known and widely used systems in this volume. In Chapters 4 through 9, we will present three different *formal* systems for analyzing statements and arguments comprised of sets of statements. In dealing with each of these systems, we will deal first with their respective concepts and methods for analyzing the logical structures of individual statements and the relatively simple logical relations between pairs of statements (Chapters 4, 6, and 8). After the techniques and procedures for dealing with individual statements have been mastered, we will study the more complex logical relations that hold among sets of statements, particularly the relation known as 'deductive validity'.

Although the discussion of informal factors and methods will be incorporated as appropriate and necessary into the chapters on formal deductive logic, informal logic will also be discussed in more general and detailed ways in *several* separate chapters. Chapter 1 will focus on methods and concepts for the informal analysis of the logical structure of individual statements, with particular focus on the different kinds of statements that do not require arguments in their support. Chapter 2 will present the general principles of informal analysis of arguments, particularly as this is relevant to the application of formal techniques dealt with in Chapters 4 through 9. Chapter 3 presents a method of informal analysis for identifying certain kinds of common fallacious or defective arguments.

Inductive logic, as discussed in Chapters 10 through 13 might be most accurately described as *semi*-formal insofar as its formal elements are not as completely abstracted from its informal elements as is the case for deductive logic. Although the formal structure of inductive arguments can be and is presented in this text, it is of minimal value in assessing the quality of inductive arguments, at least as compared with the value of formal analysis of deductive arguments.

THE VALUE AND USES OF LOGIC

Although logic has been claimed by some of its proponents to be one of the most valuable and useful specialties within the general field of philosophy, it is not much more *directly* usable nor of any greater *immediate* value than philosophy in general. This is not to say that it is of little or no value or use. It only means that it is not as easy to describe or explain the value and uses of logic as it is for subjects like accounting, medicine, or engineering. Part of its value is, in fact, its use in these more directly applicable fields— logical analysis is an integral part of the practice of accounting, medicine, engineering, and most other fields. Thus, although philosophers who specialize in logic are not in great demand for jobs other than teaching logic and doing academic research, persons with training in logic can make important contributions to dealing with problems in more practical areas such as accounting or medicine. It is perhaps most directly applicable to fields such as computer programming and law, but knowledge of the concepts and methods of logic presented in this book can also be of considerable use and value in dealing with a wide range of situations that we all encounter in *everyday* life.

Two inescapable facts of human existence as we all must live it today are (1) the realities of *conflicts*, much too often hostile and even violent, between individuals and groups of individuals and (2) the necessity to make difficult *judgments and decisions* that affect our own lives and well-being as well as the lives and well-being of others. When confronted by conflicts, we often try to determine which side is in the right before taking sides or working to resolve the conflict. When faced with a difficult decision having a potentially significant effect on us and others, we usually want to make every effort to consider the pros and cons of the various alternatives from which we must ultimately choose.

The study of logic can help us in various ways to deal with conflicts and decisions in a more reasonable and satisfactory way than we might be able to do without the understanding and skills provided by such study. Unfortunately, it is impossible to explain or demonstrate briefly here how this can be; indeed, the primary objective of this entire book is to only *begin* to give some idea of the ways in which the study of logic can be relevant to and useful in dealing with

"I'm reading Philosophy on the basis that it will help me to accept not being able to get a job when I've graduated."

Since argument is not recognized as a means of arriving at truth, adherents of rival dogmas have no method except war by means of which to reach a decision. And war, in our scientific age, means, sooner or later, universal death.

—BERTRAND RUSSELL

If Russell's judgment is correct, the acceptance of logical analysis of arguments could be of far-reaching significance.

conflicts and decisions. Not everything learned in a logic course is necessarily useful for such tasks; nor is everything learned in the study of logic adequate for evaluating every statement or argument you will ever encounter. There are, in fact, many different systems of logic, each of which is useful for dealing with certain kinds of statements and arguments in certain ways. Only a few of the more frequently used systems of logic will be discussed in this book. In fact, a careful study of just two or three of the different systems presented in this book would be sufficient to give you a pretty good idea of the nature of logic in general and of its uses and limitations.

In brief, you should be prepared to find some things in your study of this book that will be of relatively immediate use and value, both to your other areas of study and to various everyday situations you may encounter. But much of what you will learn in logic will be only indirectly useful and sometimes only in the long run. Thus, you should approach the subject with patience and the understanding that its lack of apparent "relevance" to your current interests and concerns does not mean that it is not worth studying as part of your overall educational program. Every effort has been made in this book to make explicit the ways in which logic relates to many aspects of life and human activity, and it can be stated with confidence that the student who pursues the study of logic conscientiously will discover many other interesting and useful ways in which the methods and concepts to be discussed here relate to other areas of his or her life.

The life of the law has not been logic; it has been experience. The felt necessities of the time, the prevalent moral and political theories, intentions of public policy, avowed or unconscious, even the prejudices which judges share with their fellow men, have had a good deal to do with the syllogism in determining the rules by which men should be governed.

—OLIVER WENDELL HOLMES

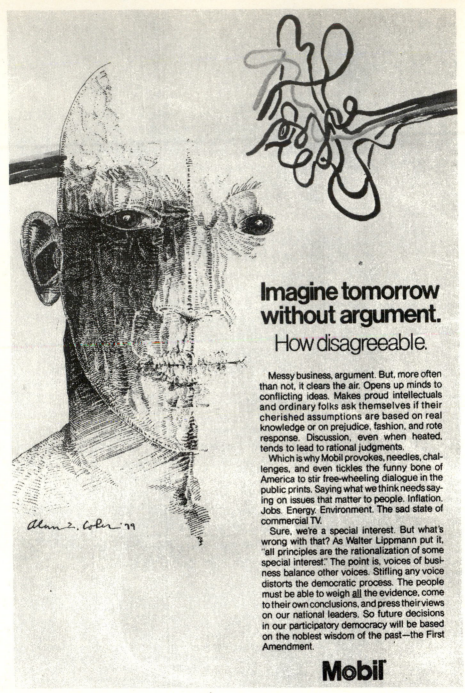

Imagine tomorrow without argument.
How disagreeable.

Messy business, argument. But, more often than not, it clears the air. Opens up minds to conflicting ideas. Makes proud intellectuals and ordinary folks ask themselves if their cherished assumptions are based on real knowledge or on prejudice, fashion, and rote response. Discussion, even when heated, tends to lead to rational judgments.

Which is why Mobil provokes, needles, challenges, and even tickles the funny bone of America to stir free-wheeling dialogue in the public prints. Saying what we think needs saying on issues that matter to people. Inflation. Jobs. Energy. Environment. The sad state of commercial TV.

Sure, we're a special interest. But what's wrong with that? As Walter Lippmann put it, "all principles are the rationalization of some special interest." The point is, voices of business balance other voices. Stifling any voice distorts the democratic process. The people must be able to weigh all the evidence, come to their own conclusions, and press their views on our national leaders. So future decisions in our participatory democracy will be based on the noblest wisdom of the past—the First Amendment.

Mobil

The above advertisement provides an argument in support of arguments. Do you think this is a good argument? Why or why not? Return to this argument after you have studied various parts of this book and reevaluate it.

Courtesy The Mobil Corporation.

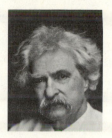

In the space of one hundred and seventy-six years the Lower Mississippi has shortened itself two hundred and forty-two miles. That is an average of a trifle over one mile and a third per year. Therefore, any calm person, who is not blind or idiotic, can see that in the old Oolitic Silurian Period, just a million years ago next November, the Lower Mississippi River was upward of one million three hundred thousand miles long, and stuck out over the Gulf of Mexico like a fishing-rod. And by the same token any person can see that seven hundred and forty-two years from now the Lower Mississippi will be only a mile and three-quarters long, and Cairo and New Orleans will have joined their streets together, and be plodding comfortably along under a single mayor and a mutual board of aldermen. There is something fascinating about science. One gets such wholesale returns of conjecture out of such trifling investment of fact.

—MARK TWAIN,
Life on the Mississippi (1875)

Although your intuitions are probably (correctly) strong that Mark Twain's argument is mistaken somewhere, it may be fairly difficult for you to specify precisely what is wrong with it. The study of logic should help you deal with such problems— and also with more practical ones—if you work at it conscientiously.

EXERCISE 3   *Each of the following articles, cartoons, and advertisements contains at least one argument. Try to identify the arguments and make an "educated guess" as to whether each is "good" or "bad." Save your written guesses. We will return to these arguments several times in the course of this book to give you a chance to assess the extent to which you will have increased your skills at argument analysis.*

1.

Final report on assassination:

Conspiracy likely in Kennedy death

WASHINGTON (AP) — President John F. Kennedy's death was probably due to a conspiracy, according to the final report of the House Assassinations Committee. The panel also says it cannot rule out the possibility of involvement by organized crime figures or Cubans.

The final report, to be released later this summer, says the two-year House investigation could not determine who the conspirators were, but it spells out evidence and allegations it gathered on the organized crime figures and on the possibility that they or Cubans were involved.

The committee concluded the assassination was probably a conspiracy because of evidence from accoustics experts who said they are 95 percent certain a shot was fired at Kennedy in Dallas on Nov. 22, 1963, from a location other than the nearby building from where Oswald is alleged to have fired three shots at the president's motorcade.

2.

"Fair enough—let's give them a cut out of what we take tonight"

Copyright 1975 by Herblock in The Washington Post.

3.

George F. Will

Commentary

Anyone with a small child feels as Cardinal Wolsey felt about Henry VIII: "Be well advised and assured what you put in his head, for ye shall never pull it out again." The aim of advertising directed at children, especially on Saturday morning, is not just to set visions of sweets dancing in small heads. The aim also is to make children even less like angels than it is their natural inclination to be. The aim, a candid assessment has said, is to turn them into "very successful naggers."

Conclusive evidence that advertising achieves this aim is the hundreds of millions of dollars spent each year on such advertising. Advertisers are not fools; they would not spend so much if they did not have hard evidence that it pays to bombard little people, even though little people have no money. Little people successfully belabor big people.

THE DISPOSABLE HUMANS?

SHOULD EVERY HUMAN LIFE BE RESPECTED? OR ARE SOME LIVES DISPOSABLE? IS THERE A DIFFERENCE BETWEEN A HUMAN LIFE AND A LEGAL PERSON?

THESE QUESTIONS ARE NOW ASKED WITH REGARD TO UNBORN BABIES. BUT DIDN'T OUR SOCIETY ASK THESE SAME QUESTIONS ONCE BEFORE . . . IN THE 19th CENTURY . . . WITH RESPECT TO BLACK PEOPLE? *(PERHAPS THIS IS WHY, OUT OF ALL GROUPS, IT IS THE BLACK COMMUNITY — NOT THE CATHOLIC COMMUNITY — THAT TODAY SHOWS LEAST SUPPORT FOR PERMISSIVE ABORTION . . . ACCORDING TO A 1970 HARRIS POLL AND A 1971 POPULATION COMMISSION POLL.)*

WHY NOT COMPARE TODAY'S RHETORIC WITH THAT OF THE LAST CENTURY AND SEE WHETHER THERE ARE SIMILARITIES?

SLAVERY 1857	*ABORTION* 1972
Although he may have a heart and a brain, and he may be a human life biologically, a slave is not a *legal person*. The Dred Scott decision by the U. S. Supreme Court has made that clear.	*Although he may have a heart and a brain, and he may be a human life biologically, an unborn baby is not a legal person. Our courts will soon make that clear.*
A black man only becomes a *legal* person when he is set free. Before that time, we should not concern ourselves about him because he has no legal rights.	*A baby only becomes a legal person when he is born. Before that time, we should not concern ourselves about him because he has no legal rights.*
If you think that slavery is wrong, then nobody is forcing you to be a slave-owner. But don't impose your morality on somebody else!	*If you think abortion is wrong, then nobody is forcing you to have one. But don't impose your morality on somebody else!*
A man has a right to do what he wants with his own property.	*A woman has a right to do what she wants with her own body.*
Isn't slavery really something merciful? After all, every black man has a right to be protected. Isn't it better never to be set free than to be sent unprepared, and ill-equipped, into a cruel world? *(Spoken by someone already free)*	*Isn't abortion really something merciful? After all, every baby has a right to be wanted. Isn't it better never to be born than to be sent alone and unloved into a cruel world? (Spoken by someone already born)*

Will the unborn baby become the modern Dred Scott?
Or will our country use its great resources to respect every human life
. . . black or white . . . poor or rich . . . woman or man . . .
unborn baby or octogenarian?

In Henry Aaron's Footsteps: The Man Who Isn't There Yet

(c) 1974 New York Times News Service

NEW YORK — Okay: Hank Aaron has overtaken Babe Ruth. who's next?

Anyone? Ever? In the foreseeable future?

It is safe enough to say that no one currently recognized as a major league homerun hitter has much chance of reaching 700, let alone whatever figure beyond that Aaron finally establishes. And anyone starting now would need, as Aaron and Ruth did, 20 years of averaging 35 homers a year to get three — which would be 1994.

The two players who come closest to having even a million-to-one chance of catching Aaron are Johnny Bench and Reggie Jackson. But, assuming each plays to the age of 40, Bench would have to average 83 homers a year for the next 14 years and Jackson would need 40 a year for the next 13 years to pass 700.

So even if Jackson did it, that would be in 1987 and it can be flatly asserted that Halley's Comet, due back in 1986, will return before anyone challenges Aaron's mark.

And it is extremely unlikely that anyone will threaten it during the rest of the 20th century.

Such projections are simple enough to make, because while no one can predict any man's actual career homerun total, it is quite possible to calculate a "maximum probable" total that a player will not exceed.

For example: Of all active players, Harmon Killebrew has hit homeruns with greatest frequency: 546 in 7,502 at-bats, or one homer every 13.74 times at bat. (These and all other figures are as of the start of this season.) It is reasonable to assume that he will not play past the age of 40, and that he will not average more than 500 at-bats a season in the remaining three years.

(Actually, Killebrew has averaged 394 at-bats the last three years, and Aaron 445, so 500 is a safe "outside limit" for players that age.)

Well, if Killebrew hit homers at his career pace for another 1,500 at-bats, he would add 109 to his total and finish with 655.

The same kind of estimate can be made for all players, young and old, and the results underline the magnitude of Aaron's achievement.

There are three categories for comparison: those players, still active, who already have high totals (like Killebrew); those who have established their slugging credentials but are much younger (like Bench and Jackson); and those who have acknowledged potential but are so young — under 25 — that they haven't yet produced a reliable form chart.

The first category is startling: there are only five players with even half the number of homers Aaron has: Frank Robinson 552, Killebrew 546, Willie McCovey 413, Al Kaline 386, and Billy Williams 376. All are 35 or over, so they simply don't have time to catch up.

In the second group, the tasks confronting Bench and Jackson have already been mentioned. Assuming age 40 as a cutoff, Earl Williams would have to average 41 homers for 15 years, Bobby Bonds 45 for 12 years, Darrell Evans 45 for 14 years, Nate Colbert 46 for 12 years and Dick Allen would have to average 52 for eight years. They won't make it.

John Milner of the Mets and John Mayberry of Kansas City are 24-year-olds with proven power. To reach 700, Mayberry would have to average 40 homers and Milner 42 for the next 16 years.

Cesar Cedeno of Houston, Greg Luzinski of Philadelphia and Jeff Burroughs of Texas are 23-year-olds with just as much power. For the next 17 years, Cedeno would have to average 38 homers a year and the other two 39 to reach 700.

Ruth's mark lasted 39 years. If Aaron's should last as long, that would bring us to the year 2013. Don't bet against it.

6.

Listen Smokers:
You don't have to wait 20 years
for cigarettes to affect you.
It only takes 3 seconds.

In just 3 seconds a cigarette makes your heart beat faster,
shoots your blood pressure up, replaces oxygen in your blood with
carbon monoxide, and leaves cancer-causing chemicals
to spread through your body.
All this happens with every cigarette you smoke.
As the cigarettes add up, the damage adds up.
Because it's the cumulative effects of smoking—adding this
cigarette to all the cigarettes you ever smoked—
that causes the trouble.

And tell that to your dog, too.

U.S. DEPARTMENT OF HEALTH, EDUCATION, AND WELFARE • This Space Contributed as a Public Service

Courtesy Committee Against Racism

8.

Pick a Color

Several months ago, I was required to complete a typical prying federal form, one which, among other things, inquired of my "minority status." Now that the courts have decided to implement "racial balance," the bureaucrats are right there demanding racially "mixed" neighborhoods, even apartment buildings, and "hire by quota" is the thing in the building trades.

After all, if you're going to bus kids or hire apprentices, you must know which is the "right" race, and in what correct proportion, to use, lest you fail to create that great magical amalgam "race harmony."

But what *is* race? What are those things which comprise "racial characteristics?" Was I (check one): a) white (nonminority); b) Negro/black; c) American Indian; d) Spanish-American; e) Oriental; f) Other minorities not under above.

Well, what the hell. I *felt* like being a "Negro/black" that day, and checked the box.

The forms attendant noticed the discrepancy as my white hands moved the pen on to another section of the form, and called my attention to my "error."

"It's no error," I replied. "I *am* Negro."

Still doubtful, the HUD bureaucrat said, "Bullshit!"

Being newly Negro/black, and not about to take any crap from a government employee, I returned his remark with, "You don't know my mother." That stopped him dead in his pencil pushing, the specter of my Negro/black mother haunting him.

Somewhere, some federal form now lists me as Negro/black. Next time, maybe, I'll choose "Oriental," or perhaps "Other" and insist I'm a Basque.

All of which makes me ask: how does anyone, anywhere, *know* who is black, or who is white, or who is whatever?

The answer is that the labels are applied on the basis of how the labeler *thinks* a black, a white, an Oriental, or an "Other" looks, whether appropriate or inappropriate. I have been assured by the more conscientious pickers and choosers of race among local school personnel that they assess "cultural differences" in determining category. Fine. When asked to define that, I get no coherent reply.

Underneath it all is the ultimate racist thought: *we* are talking about and labeling *them,* and everybody knows who *they* are. Indeed, *they* know who they are.

At what point on the chromatic scale, or whatever is used, does a person cease being "Negro/black" and become "white (nonminority)"? Or cease being "white" and become "Oriental"? Is there, deep in the recesses of HEW's Washington headquarters, a model of "whiteness" and "blackness"?

No, there are no models, because there are no legal definitions of what it takes to be "Negro/black," "Spanish-American," or "Other." There are no guidelines either. There are only prejudices and assumptions.

Actually, anyone may legally claim to be whatever nice color he wants to be. He may, under present laws, even choose to be of the opposite sex, if he/she so desires.

There are no United States equivalents to the Nazi Nuremberg Laws of Racial Purity.

Which means that if a community faced with some HEW massive busing plan should just claim that 50 per cent of its group is already black, or white, what official would oppose it? Or *could* oppose it?

Some citizen might go to court over the matter, but short of exhuming long-dead ancestors to check for coloration, no court could solve the question, unless a color code were formulated. That would be an American dilemma.   —LARRY MAY

Reprinted with permission of National Review, *150 East 35th St., New York, N.Y. 10016.*

Which Side Do You Believe?

There are two sides to the issue of nuclear power. Both sides feel strongly that their position is correct—which makes it difficult for Americans to form a responsible position on whether our country needs this source of energy.

Americans are bombarded with conflicting views and statements from numerous self-proclaimed energy experts. Some have even said that nuclear power—which currently provides 12% of the nation's electricity—should be halted altogether.

But consider the *sources* of the loudest anti-nuclear noise. Among those leading the attack on nuclear power are a host of actors and actresses, rock stars, aspiring politicians and others who think America has grown enough.

The Issue Isn't Just Nuclear

Nuclear power is not the only thing they oppose. These are often the same people who have been against development of geothermal energy in California . . . stopped new hydro-electric plants in Maine and Tennessee . . . blocked a new oil refinery for southern California . . . opposed new pipelines to deliver natural gas to the East . . . fought the building of more coal-fired plants. And they're the same people opposed to President Carter's plan for developing a synthetic fuels.program. One wonders what they are *for*, and how they propose meeting America's energy needs?

For many of these people, stopping nuclear power is but one part of a political objective to slow growth across the board in America. This no-growth philosophy of the anti-nuclear leadership was clearly expressed by Amory Lovins, one of the world's leading nuclear critics, when he admitted, "If nuclear power were clean, safe, economic . . . and socially benign per se, it would still be unattractive *because of the political implications . . .*"

Support For Nuclear Widespread

On the other hand, consider the many organizations that have *endorsed* nuclear power for America's future. They include: the AFL-CIO . . . the NAACP . . . the National Governor's Conference . . . Consumer Alert . . . and many more. These groups recognize that America's need for electric power is growing at a rate of 4% each year.

Consider also that the health and safety record of nuclear power has been endorsed by a vast majority of the *scientific* community—including such organizations as the National Academy of Sciences, the World Health Organization, the American Medical Association, and the Health Physics Society.

We're not saying that nuclear power is risk free. The truth is that risks are involved in *all* energy technologies. However, the overwhelming scientific evidence is clear: nuclear power is at least as clean and safe as any other means available to generate electricity—more so than most.

Where will Americans get the electricity that is needed if not, in part, from nuclear power? That's the real question in the nuclear debate. It's the one for which the anti-nuclear leaders have no answer.

Nuclear Power. Because America Needs Energy.

America's Electric Energy Companies, Department E, Post Office Box 420, Pelham Manor, New York 10803

Courtesy Committee for Energy Awareness

10.

THE DOORS OF INJUSTICE

SENECA FALLS, New York—In 1976, an ex-policeman disappeared while fishing on Seneca Lake in Upstate New York. Two men were arrested and accused of his murder, even though the body was never found.

Carol Ritter, court reporter for Gannett Rochester Newspapers, went to cover the pretrial hearing for the accused.

When she arrived at the courtroom, Ritter and other reporters were barred from the hearing on the pretext that the accused would not be able to get a fair trial if the pretrial hearing was covered by the press.

The Gannett Rochester Newspapers strongly disagreed and challenged the judge's right to close the doors of justice to the people, including the press. They took that challenge to the Supreme Court of the United States.

Gannett believes no judge should have the right to shut the people and their free press out of such pretrial hearings, where an overwhelming majority of criminal prosecutions are resolved.

Can you imagine up to 90 percent of all court cases being settled in secret? Gannett could not. But on July 2, 1979, the Supreme Court ruled it could happen.

Gannett protests vigorously this abridgment of the First Amendment. Not only has the Court limited journalists' access to gathering and reporting the news for the public, but it has also

trampled on the people's freedom to know, the cornerstone of our rights as a free people in a free society.

The freedoms of the First Amendment must be cherished, not shackled.

At Gannett, we have a commitment to freedom in every business we're in, whether it's newspaper, TV, radio, outdoor advertising or public opinion research.

And so from Burlington to Boise, from Fort Myers to Fort Wayne, every Gannett newspaper, every TV and radio station is free to express its own opinions, free to serve the best interests of its own community in its own way.

Gannett
A world of different voices where freedom speaks.

CHAPTER ONE

Informal Analysis of Statements

Logic should be a required course for all students.
Logic is similar to mathematics.
Logic is an art, not a science.
Logic is very interesting to many people.

Statements, such as those presented above, contain basic expressions of thoughts, ideas, and beliefs. They can, and often do, stand alone. But they also occur frequently in contexts where they stand in relation to other statements. Sometimes, a statement can provide evidence in support of the truth of another statement. Sometimes a statement can provide evidence against other statements. In this chapter we will focus on the nature of statements and on their logical structures and relations to one another. This study will provide the necessary basis for studying in the next chapter the complex sets of statements which comprise arguments. The study of statements, however, is also important because some statements don't require arguments to support their truth, and logical analysis can help us identify such statements.

Whether we are concerned with statements whose truth can be established without any further proof or with statements whose truth remains to be proved, we must have special conceptual and methodological tools for analyzing both their *meaning* and *logical structure*. This chapter will present some of the basic informal concepts and methods for getting at the meaning and structure of statements.

SENTENCES   Statements and sets of statements are generally expressed or communicated in the form of sentences. Strictly speaking, a **sentence** *is a physical entity*—a collection of ink marks on a page or sound waves traveling through the air; *and it is also a linguistic entity*—a collection of letters or words, organized according to grammatical rules.

Sentences of any kind, when taken as mere physical or linguistic entities, are of little value or interest to most people. However, like hammers and forks and pens, sentences can be of significant value when they are used in appropriate ways in certain contexts. Some of the many uses of sentences include—but certainly are not limited to—praying, cursing, greeting friends, deceiving, asking questions, thanking, giving orders, presenting facts, expressing anger, making jokes, and reporting on an event.

EXERCISE 1–1 *Compile a list of at least twenty-five additional uses of sentences.*

COGNITIVE AND NONCOGNITIVE USES OF SENTENCES The almost limitless number of uses of sentences might be overwhelming to anyone trying to study them in any systematic way. Fortunately, to help sort out the uses of language relevant to the logician, philosophers have developed a method of classification that distinguishes between just two fundamental uses of sentences—cognitive and noncognitive. A sentence is said to be **cognitive** when it is being used to express or assert something about which it makes sense to say that it is true or false. The following sentences, as commonly used in everyday contexts, provide examples of sentences being used cognitively:

> *Logic is easy for Heather.*
> *Bill forgot to study for today's exam.*
> *The sun will rise at 7:02 A.M. tomorrow.*
> *The sun revolves around the earth.*
> *Whales are mammals.*
> *I believe that the moon is made of green cheese.*

When uttered in ordinary contexts by native-English speakers, sentences such as these can be used to do a variety of things, such as to declare, report, classify, assert, inform, deny, predict, explain, argue, and admit. However, these sentences all have one use in common: each is normally used to express a statement or proposition of which it is proper to say that it is true or false. It does not matter whether the statement being expressed is, in fact, true or false. The sentence 'The sun revolves around the earth' can be used cognitively just as much as can the sentence 'Whales are mammals'.

A sentence is said to be **noncognitive** *when it is being used to do something other than express a true or false statement.* Noncognitive uses of language include issuing commands or giving orders, making requests, asking questions, and arousing emotions. As used in everyday situations, each of the following sentences or phrases is being used noncognitively:

> *Shut the door.*
> *Do you know where they hid the money?*
> *Please pass the salt.*
> *Wow!*
> *Right on, sister!*
> *Echhhh!*

It is never proper to ask of any question, command, or expression of feelings "Is it true or false?" For instance, with regard to the sentence 'Shut the door', insofar as it is being used in its normal way, to express a command, we may ask, "Is the command appropriate or inappropriate?" or "Should the command be obeyed or not obeyed?" but we cannot appropriately ask of the command itself, "Is it true or false?" Similarly, it is normally inappropriate to ask whether the question 'Do you know where they hid the money?' is true or false. Once again, we may challenge the appropriateness of the question, ask whether or not one ought to respond to it, and debate the answer given to it, but we cannot properly ask, "Is it true or false?" of the question itself. It is equally improper, assuming ordinary context, to ask, "Is it true or false?" of such expressive utterances as 'Wow!' 'Right on, sister!' and 'Echhhh!'

The subtlety and complexity of natural languages make it difficult to determine whether many sentences are being used in a cognitive or noncognitive way. One whole category of sentences has been the subject of debate among philosophers for many years, and no agreement has yet been reached as to whether such sentences are normally used cognitively or noncognitively. This category is the set of sentences used to make value judgments such as:

> *Everyone ought to study logic.*
> *Valid arguments are better than invalid arguments.*
> *Cheating on a logic exam is wrong.*
> *You have a responsibility to yourself to do your best.*

Some philosophers have argued that such sentences are only used to express positive or negative feelings about the subjects being referred to. Others claim that these are used essentially to make commands or give orders. On both of these views, such sentences are being used noncognitively. Other philosophers have asserted that such sentences are normally used cognitively, although they do not all agree as to exactly what kind of true or false statement they might be expressing. In the context of this book we will assume that sentences being used to express value judgments *are* being used *cognitively,* but we will not impose any specific cognitive interpretation on them.

EXERCISE 1–2   *In an everyday context, would each of the following sentences most likely involve cognitive, noncognitive, or mixed use of language? Explain each of your answers.*

1. The Second World War ended in 1945.
2. Thank God Hitler was defeated in the Second World War!
3. Take your umbrella with you today.
4. Take your umbrella with you today because the weatherman says it's going to rain.
5. More than half a million human beings speak Mandarin Chinese.
6. The original *Webster's Dictionary* was written by Noah Webster, not Daniel Webster.
7. What time is it?
8. Aha!
9. Be sure to sign your tax return before mailing it.
10. The melting point of lead is 327.5° C.
11. Do you know if she did it?
12. Are you sure that *she's* the one who did it?
13. It's Greek to me.
14. The atmospheric reactions leading to smog production are highly complex and not fully understood.
15. Why is it difficult to prove direct causal relationships between levels of specific pollutants and incidence of disease?
16. Workers of the world, unite; you have nothing to lose but your chains!
17. The best-laid plans of mice and men will ofttimes go astray.
18. Do you mean to tell me that you still haven't taken out the garbage? (You still have not taken out the garbage.)
19. Who says I'm not a good poker player? (I am a good poker player.)
20. If you tough my little brother again, you're going to end up with a mouth full of loose teeth!

EXERCISE 1–3   *The following sentences could be using language cognitively or noncognitively, depending on the context. For each sentence provide: (a) a context in which the speaker would be using language cognitively; (b) a context in which the speaker would be using the language noncognitively.*

1. Close the window, you polar bear!
2. George, wasn't that Barbara I saw you with last night?
3. Do you *really* believe in Santa Claus?
4. Drive with care.
5. Kill the umpire!
6. Don't try to tell me that Lincoln wasn't a great president!
7. You mean you're not going to go out drinking with us like you said you would?
8. Are women fickle?
9. Ladies and gentlemen of the jury, could any reasonable person really believe that a man of such outstanding character as my client could commit such a heinous crime?
10. Get out of here!

11. You are not going to wear *that* again?
12. Why do brave women die young?
13. Should tax credits be allowed for those who send their children to private schools?
14. Are high levels of hemoglobin-carbon monoxide complex a major cause of increased incidence of cardiovascular diseases among cigarette smokers?
15. Professor Adams, have a heart!

STATEMENTS   It is somewhat awkward and inconvenient to have to use repeatedly the lengthy phrase "sentences being used cognitively." There is also disagreement among philosophers as to whether it is correct or proper to speak of sentences (being used cognitively) as true or false. Many philosophers, for example, assert that it is not the sentence which is true or false; rather, it is the meaning or thought conveyed or statement expressed by the sentence which is true or false. Because we cannot elaborate on this problem here, we will simply announce the following rule: For the remainder of this book we shall use the term **statement** to refer to *the (true or false) thought which is being conveyed by a sentence which is being used cognitively.* We shall use the term **proposition** as being synonymous, and therefore interchangeable, with the term 'statement'. We shall restrict the term **sentence** to refer essentially to *the physical or linguistic entities—that is, the marks on the paper* and the *grammatical entities—used to convey the meanings.* Thus, in the remainder of this book, we will not talk about sentences as being true or false.

In brief, the key test of whether a sentence is expressing a statement* is if that which is being expressed can be said to be true or false. Note that falsity, just as well as truth, qualifies the sentence as expressing a statement. The important point is whether the question of truth or falsehood can properly be raised. Both the sentence 'The moon is made of geological materials' and the sentence 'The moon is made of green cheese' express statements. The first, however, happens to be true, whereas the second is patently false: nevertheless, both sentences express statements.

In recent years, logicians have begun investigating the nature of and relations among sentences used in various noncognitive ways. We are thus beginning to see the development of new fields such as the logic of questions and the logic of commands. However, we will not be studying these topics in this book and thus will stick to the more traditional definition of logic as being restricted to sentences being used cognitively to express arguments.

---

* Technically, sentences do not convey or express anything in and of themselves; they must be used by someone to communicate information (or express feelings or anything else). For the sake of brevity, we shall take the liberty in the remainder of this book of talking about 'the sentence which expresses the proposition such-and-such' in place of the technically correct but more lengthy formulation, 'the sentence which is being used by so-and-so to express the proposition such-and-such.' Similarly, the introduction to any statement ought to be phrased, 'the proposition (or statement) *expressed by the sentence* "such and such." ' For the sake of simplicity, however, in the remainder of this text we will often use 'the proposition (or statement) "such and such" ' as an abbreviation for the proper wording.

Recognizing Sentences Although the basic distinction between cognitive and noncognitive
Used To Express Statements uses of sentences can be formulated quite concisely and straight-
forwardly, it is not always easy to determine how a particular sen-
tence is being used in ordinary discourse. While grammatical structure can
provide valuable clues as to whether a sentence is being used cognitively or noncognitively, the structure is all too often misleading. Declarative sentences, with a
subject term followed by a verb and ending with a period are commonly used
cognitively. Interrogatives (ending with question marks) and imperatives (with
the verb preceding the subject) *usually* are used noncognitively to ask questions
and issue commands, respectively. However, the *context* in which the sentence
is being used plays a significant role in determining how the sentence is being
used. Thus, *depending on the context,* the same sentence can be used to
express two or more different statements, or it can be used to perform some
noncognitive function, or it can do several different things at once. Also, and
equally significant, different sentences can be used in appropriate contexts to
express the same true-or-false statement or to perform some other function in
common. These facts about sentences explain why it is not always easy to
determine how a particular sentence is being used in a specific context. Some
examples will help to illustrate how this occurs in ordinary discourse.

As an example of the fact that nondeclarative sentences may express statements, let us consider the following sentence:

> ### Didn't I see Linda with you today?

The sentence is interrogative in form, but in a certain context it could just as well
be expressed by:

> ### I saw you with Linda today.

This sentence more clearly expresses something which can be said to be true or
false: either the speaker saw Linda with the person to whom she is speaking, or
she did not. Thus, an interrogative sentence may be used to make an assertion;
in fact, negative interrogatives very often are used to do this.

The context of a sentence may have much to do with whether it expresses a
statement. 'Duuhhh!' does not by itself appear to convey a true-or-false assertion. But if it is uttered in response to the question "Did you understand the
lecture on atomic physics?" it might reasonably be translated as expressing the
same meaning as:

> ### I did not even remotely begin to understand the
> ### lecture on atomic physics.

Now this sentence expresses or asserts something which is either true or false.
Such an exclamation can express a statement *in this context.*

Again, the sentence 'I'm beat' is declarative in form, but does it express a
statement? If it is uttered to a group of people who want you to go skiing, it
conveys information, and does indeed express a statement. If it is uttered to an

empty room as you come in and collapse on the bed, it is probably exclamatory, and questions of truth or falsehood are quite irrelevant; so it does not express a statement.

Context, then, is at least as important as grammatical form in determining whether a sentence expresses a statement. All propositions *can* be expressed by declarative sentences, but not all of them are so expressed, and a declarative sentence does not invariably express a statement.

Even the context is not always sufficient for determining what the intended use of a particular expression might be, as Linus reveals to Charlie Brown in the comic strip below.

A single statement may also be expressed by different sentences either in the same or different languages. For example:

> *The house is very lovely.*
> *La maison est très belle.*
> *La casa es muy bella.*

These are clearly three different physical and linguistic entities—they are composed of different sets of letters and words, they occupy different spaces on the page—yet if uttered in the same context, the sentences express the same statement. Of course, the flexibility of each language makes it possible to express the same statement through different sentences:

> *Jane was the one who put jelly donuts on that windowsill.*
> *The jelly donuts on that windowsill were put there by Jane.*
> *On that windowsill are jelly donuts which Jane put there.*

In our everyday life we all too often encounter instances of lengthy sentences containing highly technical vocabulary being used to express relatively simple ideas, as in legal documents and contracts. Fortunately steps have been taken

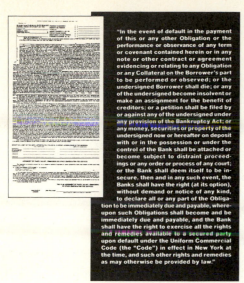

Form 1

Citibank's
former consumer
loan note.

"In the event of default in the payment of this or any other Obligation or the performance or observance of any term or covenant contained herein or in any note or other contract or agreement evidencing or relating to any Obligation or any Collateral on the Borrower's part to be performed or observed; or the undersigned Borrower shall die; or any of the undersigned become insolvent or make an assignment for the benefit of creditors; or a petition shall be filed by or against any of the undersigned under any provision of the Bankruptcy Act; or any money, securities or property of the undersigned now or hereafter on deposit with or in the possession or under the control of the Bank shall be attached or become subject to distraint proceedings or any order or process of any court; or the Bank shall deem itself to be insecure, then and in any such event, the Banks shall have the right (at its option), without demand or notice of any kind, to declare all or any part of the Obligation to be immediately due and payable, whereupon such Obligations shall become and be immediately due and payable, and the Bank shall have the right to exercise all the rights and remedies available to a secured party upon default under the Uniform Commercial Code (the "Code") in effect in New York at the time, and such other rights and remedies as may otherwise be provided by law."

Form 2

Citibank's
present consumer
loan note.

I'll be in default:
1. If I don't pay an installment on time; or 2. If any other creditor tries by legal process to take any money of mine in your possession.
You can then demand immediate payment of the balance of this note, minus the part of the FINANCE CHARGE which hasn't been earned, calculated as stated in the Prepayment paragraph. You will also have other legal rights, for instance, the right to repossess, sell and apply security to the payments under this note and any other debts I may then owe you.

recently by the government and some businesses to use briefer and technically less-difficult sentences to express statements that were previously expressed in almost unintelligible form. The example in the Citibank forms provides a particularly vivid illustration of the way in which the same statement can be expressed by two totally different sets of sentences.

Finally, though it may seem right now to be rather hairsplitting, consider these:

The sky is cloudy.
The sky is cloudy.

Even here, there are two different sentences expressing the same statement. One of them can be cut out of the page and thrown away, but the other would remain. Philosophers have introduced additional terminology to explain such cases; but it is sufficient to note for the purposes of this text that these are two distinct sentences, both of which can be used to express the same statement.

It is also important to note that different propositions can be expressed by the same sentence, insofar as a change in context changes the statement expressed by a given sentence. Consider the following sentence:

The official candidate of the Democratic party in last year's presidential election was a senator at that time.

If asserted in 1973, this would have been expressing a true statement about George McGovern. But in 1965 it would have expressed a false statement about Lyndon Johnson, since Johnson was the incumbent president during the 1964 campaign.

Contextual factors other than time may also determine what is being expressed by a given sentence. For example, the sentence 'This lake is quite large' may express a statement about Lake Superior, Lake Pontchartrain, or the Great Salt Lake, depending on the location of the speaker.

> REMEMBER!
>
> 1. *A sentence is a physical and linguistic entity which can be used to perform a variety of tasks, such as asking questions, issuing commands, and making assertions.*
> 2. *A statement or proposition is that which is expressed by certain sentences in certain contexts, and of which it is proper to say that it is true or false.*
> 3. *Different statements can be expressed by the same sentence.*
> 4. *Different sentences can express the same statement.*

BURDEN OF PROOF   It is not uncommon to encounter situations in which we are asked to provide reasons in support of statements we make in various contexts. Thus, if we assert that "George Washington wore wooden false teeth," someone might very well ask "How do you know that to be true?" We could answer this in a variety of ways. For example, we could respond that we were taught this in a history class in grade school. If pressed to give a reason for saying that what we were taught in a history course is true, we might give an answer to the effect that we have found over a period of time that most of what we were taught in that class (or even most of what we were taught in school in general) has proved to be true in subsequent experience. And we could then go on, if pressed further, to explain how the other things we were taught have been confirmed or to show how this general experience with things taught in school supports our belief that George Washington, in fact, wore wooden false teeth. Of course, we must always keep an open mind and be ready to recognize and willing to admit that our reasons may not be good ones. But it is also important to recognize that our inability to give good reasons in support of some of our judgments is not always a bad thing. Indeed, it is generally recognized that it is not possible to give reasons for or proofs in support of *every* one of our beliefs, even though someone may demand such justifications.

By demanding proof (and tacitly questioning the truth of our assertion) that Washington wore wooden false teeth, the person who asked how we knew this was attempting to place what is known as the **burden of proof** on us. In giving our reasons, we were accepting the burden of proof, but we could have refused to do so. We could also stop with the reasons that we have given up to this point

and refuse to accept the claim that it is up to us to further prove the truth of the reasons already offered. One of the most common strategies for shifting the burden of truth is that used by children as displayed in the Trudy cartoon—sheer stubborn persistence. However, there are other more reasonable strategies and rules that are part of various cultures for determining on whom the burden of proof should be placed.

It is possible to give various kinds of reasons in support of one's position concerning burden of proof, although the reasons are not necessarily going to be more effective than Trudy's effort in the cartoon. One good example of the utilization of the strategy of shifting the burden of proof is provided by George Bernard Shaw's response to persons who wanted him to prove why it is wrong to kill and dissect and otherwise use animals in biological research.

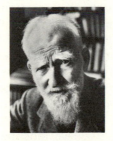

I decline altogether to explain why I am not a vivisectionist. It is for the vivisectionists to explain their conduct, not to challenge mine. I am on the jury, not in the dock. We have not yet reached a pass at which normal sanity, kindliness and regard for the honor of science can be waylaid and called to account by sadism, ethical imbecility, and invincible ignorance.

GEORGE BERNARD SHAW

There are many areas in our culture where informal conventions and sometimes even formal rules exist that specify on whom falls the burden of proof of a given statement. Thus, it would generally be agreed that it is the responsibility of the person who is asserting that Martians exist or that New York City is not in the United States to prove the truth of such assertions rather than to require others to prove that they are false. In a more formal way, as part of our legal system, we recognize that it is the responsibility of others to prove the truth of a charge that a person is guilty of a criminal offense. The principle "innocent until proven guilty" places the burden of proof on the accuser; the accused does not have to prove that the charges are false, a fact which is central to lawyer Perry Mason's strategy in the case described in the accompanying box.

Judge Fisk left the bench.

Mason turned to where Paul Drake and Della Street were seated beside him.

"Well," he said, "this is a lawyer's nightmare. I'm going to listen to the evidence without having the faintest idea of what the prosecution is holding up its sleeve until they start throwing punches."

"You can't get a word out of the defendants?" Drake asked, looking over to where Morley Eden and Vivian Carson were seated between two officers.

"Not a word," Mason said.

"Well, the prosecution has got something all right," Drake said. "They're keeping it buttoned up, but Ormsby is as snug as a bug in a rug."

"I know." Mason said, "but he doesn't want to be *too*

sure. I'm going to use every psychological trick that I can. I'm going to keep within the letter of the law but I'm going to make him prove these defendants guilty beyond all reasonable doubt.

"This is a case that is going to depend almost entirely on circumstantial evidence. It is a rule of circumstantial evidence, a rule of law in this state, that if the circumstances can be explained by any reasonable hypothesis other than that of guilt, the jurors are bound on their oaths to accept that hypothesis, and acquit the defendants.

"That is of course merely another way of stating the rule of law that a defendant can't be convicted unless the evidence proves him guilty beyond all reasonable doubt. If there is a reasonable doubt in the minds of the jurors they must resolve that doubt in favor of the defendants, and acquit.

From Erle Stanley Gardner, The Case of the Fenced-In Woman, 1972.

SELF-SUPPORTING AND SUPPORTING STATEMENTS   We have already made one major distinction—between sentences being used cognitively (that is, to express statements) and sentences being used noncognitively. It is now necessary to examine a basic distinction between two different kinds of statements: statements whose truth or falsity is dependent on the truth or falsity of certain related statements, and those whose truth or falsity is in some way self-evident or self-contained. Statements that require evidence (i.e., arguments) in their support will be referred to as **supported statements.** Statements that can stand on their own and that require no further evidence or support are **self-supporting statements.** (Technically, some statements are actually self-refuting, but they can be subsumed under the general category of self-supporting statements, using concepts to be developed later in this book, so we won't discuss them as a separate category of statement.)

Self-supporting statements are essentially those for which the burden or proof is recognized as falling on persons who question their truth. That is, they are statements that should be accepted as true unless a compelling proof to the contrary is provided. In everyday discourse, it is not always clear which statements fall into this category, but we can begin to get some guidance by briefly considering a few examples. More-formal and more-technical methods for identifying self-supporting statements will be presented in detail in later sections of this chapter and in several later chapters.

In general, we can characterize self-supporting statements as those for which the burden of proof is recognized as falling on persons who consider them to be false. That is, they are statements that most people will accept as being true unless someone can provide a compelling proof to the contrary. Statements of this kind are designated as *axioms* in both formal and informal systems—that is, statements that can be used to prove other statements but that don't require proof themselves. There are many theories as to what exactly qualifies a statement for this category and what exempts it from the need to be itself proved or supported. The consideration of this question and the study of these theories belongs for the most part not to the subject matter of logic but instead of the subfield of philosophy known as *epistemology* or the *theory of knowledge*. We shall, therefore, examine briefly only two of the most common types of self-supporting statement that relate most directly to the study of logic.

In CONGRESS, July 4, 1776.

The unanimous Declaration of the thirteen united States of America.

When in the Course of human events it becomes necessary for one people to dissolve the political bands which have connected them with another, and to assume among the powers of the earth, the separate and equal station to which the Laws of Nature and of Nature's God entitle them, a decent respect to the opinions of mankind requires that they should declare the causes which impel them to the separation. —— We hold these truths to be self-evident, that all men are created equal, that they are endowed by their Creator with certain unalienable rights, that among these are Life, Liberty and the pursuit of Happiness—that to secure these rights Governments are instituted among men, deriving their just powers from the consent of the Governed, That whenever any form of government becomes destructive of these ends, it is the right of the people to alter or to abolish it, and to institute new government laying its foundation on such principles and organizing its powers in such form, as to them shall seem most likely to effect their safety and happiness.

In their choice of wording for the declaration of their independence from the king of England, Thomas Jefferson and his colleagues presented their case as a set of self-supporting statements. The absence of alternative procedures for agreeing on whom the burden of proof rested resulted in the Revolutionary War. The possibility of mutual nuclear destruction today puts even more importance on the need for finding more reasonable means of resolving conflicts and for increasing our tolerance of positions different from our own even if we don't accept them.

One important class of self-supporting statements is the class of subjective **self-reports.** If I make a statement to the effect that I feel or believe or hope something, the statement is generally accepted as being true with no further demand for proof. Although someone might question whether I really feel a sharp pain in my side when I say "I feel a sharp pain in my side" but exhibit

"I have an inalienable constitutional and natural right to love whom I may, to love as long or as short a period as I can, to change that love every day if I please!"

VICTORIA WOODHULL

What kind of a self-supporting statement does this appear to be? In the nineteenth-century American society in which it was made, on whom did the burden of proof on this issue probably fall? On whom would it fall today? How, if at all, could the burden of proof for this statement be shifted from what it is today in this country?

none of the normal behavioral manifestations of pain, it would usually be sufficient for me to merely reiterate my statement (possibly more emphatically) without providing any additional evidence that I am feeling such a pain. Similarly, when I report that I believe that little green creatures inhabit Mars, it is possible to question whether such creatures actually do inhabit that planet, but it would be impossible to prove that I don't believe that they do. The burden of proof is always on others to demonstrate that our self-reports are false. One of the few things that would count as sufficient evidence to *prove* that a person doesn't believe or feel something that they say they believe or feel is for that person to admit that they were lying or mistaken in their original report.

The second important type of self-supporting statement is a type known in logic as an **analytic statement.** Actually, there are two types of analytically true statements: those that are true by virtue of their logical structure or form, and those that are true because of the meanings of key words in them. For example, the truth of statements such as 'It is raining or it is not raining' and 'If some widowers are men, then some men are widowers', is based on their logical forms—that is, it is impossible for any statement having these forms to be false. Likewise, the falsity of the statement 'It is false that if some widowers are men, then some men are widowers' is based on its logical form. Statements which are true or false by virtue of their logical form are called **syntactically analytic propositions** or statements. (This concept of analyticity is further discussed in Chapter 6).

Statements which are true or false by virtue of the meanings of the words in the statements are called **semantically analytic propositions** or statements. For instance, the statement 'All widowers are men' is a true semantically analytic statement, since the concept 'men' is part of the ordinary meaning of the word 'widower'. By the same token, 'All circles are squares' is a false semantically analytic statement, assuming the ordinary meanings of 'circle' and 'square'. To describe them in slightly different but equivalent terms, semantically analytic propositions are true (or false) **by definition.**

"When more and more people are thrown out of work, unemployment results."

This "immortal remark," attributed to President Coolidge, is a good example of a statement whose truth results directly from the meanings of the words comprising it —that is, it is semantically analytic.

A statement which is neither syntactically nor semantically analytic is called a **synthetic** or **contingent proposition** or statement. In other words, a synthetic or contingent proposition is one which is not true either by virtue of its logical form or by definition: its truth or falsity must be ascertained by other means. To determine the truth or falsity of the synthetic statement 'The lights are on in this room', one would probably be inclined to open one's eyes and look.

Given that a statement *is* analytic, there is no way that its truth can be challenged. It is *necessarily* true. It is not always possible, however, to prove that a particular sentence in a specific context is being used to express an analytic statement, especially a semantically analytic statement. For example, the sentence 'All spiders are creatures with eight legs' might be interpreted as being true

Is Churchy's "discovery" that Friday the thirteenth falls on Friday this month the discovery of an analytic truth? How could it be interpreted as nonanalytic?

by definition. On this interpretation, it is impossible to prove the statement false by any observations of spiders. If we produced one or even a million creatures with six legs, this would prove nothing. The person for whom 'having eight legs' is part of the definition of 'spider' would simply reply that any creature with fewer than eight legs is not a spider, by definition. The only way to attack this kind of an assertion is to challenge the definition. And to do this, we need to have a better understanding of the nature of definitions.

EXERCISE 1–4   *Examine each of the following sentences and decide whether the statement expressed is syntactically analytic, semantically analytic, or synthetic (contingent).*

---

1. My pet beagle is a dog.
2. The moon revolves around the earth.
3. The moon is made of green cheese.
4. All elephants are gray.
5. It is snowing or it is not snowing.
6. All actresses are women.
7. All blind persons are humans.
8. If all cheese is made from milk, then some cheese is made from milk.
9. All bachelors are men.
10. Some men are bachelors.
11. Some humans are blind persons.
12. Some liars never tell the truth.
13. No circles are squares.
14. Either John is dead or he is not dead.
15. George Washington was the first president of the United States.
16. Either that gem is a diamond or it is not a diamond.
17. No males are females.
18. If some swans are white, then all swans are white.
19. If some businessmen are poets, then some poets are businessmen.
20. If all coral snakes discovered to date are poisonous, then all coral snakes are poisonous.
21. If all persons are mortal, then some persons are mortal.
22. If no squares are circles, then no squares are round.
23. If some trees are taller than twenty feet, then some things which are taller than twenty feet are trees.
24. If it is raining, then it is pouring.

DEFINITIONS   A very significant kind of statement—one we have already used and will use much more, and one used frequently in arguments of the type to be studied in this book—is the **definition.** It is, therefore, important to delay the consideration of our primary subject of interest—arguments—until after a brief examination of the nature of definitions.

Definitions are significant to the study of logic and of arguments for several reasons. First, they provide us with a very important tool for getting at the meanings of words and statements, and understanding the meaning of a particular word can often be the critical part of analyzing and evaluating a statement or argument. Second, definitions often appear as premises, or need to be added as premises, in all types of arguments, and it is very important to be able to recognize them when they occur, to be able to supply the proper ones when needed, and to be able to determine whether they are "good" or "bad" in these various contexts. Also, many definitions comprise statements that are interesting and significant for their own sake, and it is important to recognize and appreciate them when we encounter them.

There are many different kinds of definitions, and they can each be used for a variety of different purposes. So our discussion of them will be fairly long. However, without this information, it would be almost impossible to analyze and evaluate the logical structures of and relations between many other statements that we encounter in arguments and other contexts.

"*What do you mean by 'innocent'? Are you innocent as charged, innocent with extenuating circumstances, or innocent with a plea for clemency? Are you innocent of anything you are not charged with? We demand precision here.*"

© 1973 Punch-Rothco.

KINDS OF DEFINITION
The technical term for a word that is to be defined is **definiendum.** The symbols or words used to define it are called the **definiens.** Thus, in the definition:

'square' =df. 'rectangle with four equal sides'

'square' is the definiendum and 'rectangle with four equal sides' is the definiens. In the definition:

'rectangle' =df. 'parallelogram all of whose sides are at right angles'

'rectangle' is the definiendum; 'parallelogram all of whose sides are at right angles' is the definiens.

In this book, definitions are used primarily to define words, not concepts or ideas. It is important, as always, to specify the context in which the definiendum is being used. For instance, the noun 'rest' may mean either 'repose', or a 'measured period of silence in music', or a 'written symbol which denotes this silence', or a 'prop', or a 'shelter', according to the context in which it is used.

There are several different methods by which the same word may be satisfactorily defined. That is to say, one may use various types of definiens to define a given definiendum. Depending on the type of definiens provided, a definition may be classified as one of several kinds, four of which will be discussed here: synonymous, enumerative, connotative, and operational.

Synonymous Definitions A **synonymous definition** is one in which the definiens consists of only one word or phrase which, in appropriate contexts, can be used interchangeably with the definiendum. The following are examples of synonymous definitions:

'freedom' = df. 'liberty'
'conceal' = df. 'hide'
'quoted' = df. 'cited'
'intentionally' = df. 'on purpose'

As the term 'synonymous' is usually used in everyday discourse, any adequate definition is such that its definiens is synonymous with its definiendum. Thus, it is important to note that we are using the term with a special, technical meaning, such that only those definitions whose definiens consist of exactly one word (with the exception of cases such as 'on purpose') qualify as synonymous definitions.

Synonymous definitions are the shortest and most direct of all definitions one can give—for example, to a child, or to a foreigner who is familiar with the definiens but not with the definiendum. If we choose a synonym with a Latin root for a definiendum with an Anglo-Saxon root, or vice versa, an intelligent foreigner who speaks a Romance or a Teutonic language may guess what the definiendum means, even though he has never heard either the definiens or the definiendum before, provided the definiens bears a resemblance to the equivalent word in his own language. It is likely that the meaning and usage of the English word and its foreign cognate will overlap without being identical. That, however, is also the case with many English synonyms for English words. They usually share some, but not all, of their meanings. As long as there is a significant overlap in meaning between two such words, it may be convenient to use one of them to define the other, although strictly speaking this would not be a synonymous definition in the sense we have stipulated (that is, if the two cannot always be interchanged in appropriate contexts).

Enumerative Definitions   In an **enumerative definition,** the definiens lists words referring to or presents actual examples of things, properties, relations, concepts, and so on to which the definiendum may be correctly applied. For instance, the enumerative definiens 'father, mother, son, daughter, uncle, aunt, grandparent, grandchild' may be given to clarify the sense in which the word 'relative' is being used in a particular context.

It has been said (and not without justification) that enumerative definitions make only slight demands on the intellect of the person who formulates them, while they often require considerable inductive leaps from the person whom they are supposed to enlighten. According to the manner in which the definiens is presented, enumerative definitions are divided into two categories, which one might characterize as 'show' and 'tell': ostensive (show) and denotative (tell) definitions.

Ostensive Definitions   In an **ostensive definition,** the meaning of the definiendum is presented by means of concrete examples. You point to your nose, to the child's nose, to the nose of anyone else present, while you repeat the word 'nose' until a child gets the idea what a nose is. Similarly, the concept 'yellow' may be defined by pointing to a daffodil, a lemon, and a grapefruit. Instead of using one's finger to point to a visible definiens, one may point out the definiens verbally. One could point one's finger and say: "That is a three-toed sloth," or one might merely say: "That rather dirty-looking animal which is hanging upside down in this tree is a three-toed sloth."

The definiens need not be perceivable merely or solely by the eyes. One can provide ostensive definitions for terms such as 'hard', 'fugue', 'sweet', and 'stink' by providing the appropriate nonvisual sensory experiences.

There are certain advantages to the use of ostensive definitions. They are easy to formulate. They can, as when noses are pointed out to babies, help to teach concepts that were previously unknown to the other person. They can also be understood in the absence of preexisting language, which makes them suitable for conveying meaning to small children or others whose vocabulary is limited.

Ostensive definitions also have disadvantages. They depend on the physical presence of the definiens. It would be impossible to give an ostensive definition of a seashell where none is at hand (unless one made a drawing of a seashell, which some logicians admit as a legitimate form of ostensive definition). The most serious disadvantage of ostensive definitions, perhaps, is that they are more easily subject to misinterpretation than other kinds of definition. The child, for

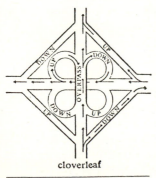

cloverleaf

An ostensive definition. Webster's Seventh New Collegiate Dictionary, 1976, p. 157.

instance, may conclude that 'nose' is the equivalent of 'face'. Or if one were trying to provide an ostensive definition of 'face' and happened to point to the middle of someone's face, the child might conclude that the word 'face' signified what most people call a nose. In other words, a person may associate the definiendum with the whole of the ostensive definiens when it was intended for her to associate it with only a part, and vice versa. Furthermore, even a randomly chosen definiens may have more than one set of common characteristics, and so an unintended set may be presumed to be the intended set. For example, all the noses pointed to may be Roman noses. In this case, a child might conclude that a pug nose is not a nose.

Denotative Definitions   Unlike ostensive definitions, **denotative definitions** do not require the physical presence of the definiens; rather, they list examples of things, or types or classes of things, to which the definiendum applies. The list comprising the definiens specifies what is known as the **denotation** or **extension** of the definiendum. Suppose the word 'carnivore' to be the definiendum, then the denotative definiens 'dogs and cats' would be correct; but it would not be adequate since the listener might well infer that the definiendum is 'pets'. To rectify this, let us add 'tigers, wolves, foxes, and hyenas'. The listener may now come up with 'carnivore'; he may, on the other hand, infer the concept 'mammal'. To prevent any further misunderstanding, we may add 'sharks, owls, and vultures' to the definiens. Had we left out 'dogs, cats, and hyenas', the listener might well have inferred that our definiendum was synonymous with 'predator'.

After demonstrating the nature as well as the pitfalls of denotative definitions, it should be noted that they are easy to formulate, and that they may be easily and correctly understood, especially when the listing in the definiens is exhaustive—that is, if it names *all* the things to which the definiendum refers. A case in point would be the definiendum 'gender', which is well served by the denotative definiens 'masculine, feminine, or neuter'.

A definition of the 'United States' as 'Alabama, Alaska, Arizona, Arkansas, California, etc.' would be a useful denotative definition only if the reader or listener is able to supply the meaning of the 'etc.' in this particular case. There are, moreover, some words for which it is not only difficult, but practically impossible to provide adequate denotative definitions. What kind of denotative definition could one give for words such as 'being', 'understand', 'infinity', and 'infer'?

Connotative Definitions   In everyday language, a set of terms such as 'bastards, whores, and fags' might be contrasted with the set 'illegitimate children, prostitutes, and male homosexuals' by explaining that, while both sets refer to the same groups, the terms in the first set have more of a pejorative connotation than those in the second set. Here, as in many contexts, the word 'connotation' carries approximately the same meaning as 'overtones', and is often used in conjunction with evaluative terms, such as 'favorable', 'negative', or 'neutral'. In logic, however, it has a different and technical meaning; the term **connotation** is used only to refer to the essential characteristic, or set of characteristics, of the thing(s) named or referred to by the definiendum.

The definiens in a connotative definition pinpoints the meaning of the definiendum by listing the set of properties common to all the things to which the definiendum can be correctly applied and common only to those things. The definitions of 'argument' and 'sentence' given earlier in this chapter, as well as the definition of 'connotation' just provided constitute an ostensive definition (i.e., examples) of 'connotative definition'. To give another example, 'hospital' might be defined connotatively as 'An institution staffed and equipped to provide the sick or the injured with diagnosis, medical or surgical treatment, temporary accommodation, and temporary custodial care'. Each property narrows down the possible meanings of the definiendum until, ideally, the sum total of the properties given applies not only entirely, but also exclusively, to the particular definiendum. The sum total of a definiendum's essential properties is variously called the **intension** or the 'connotation' of the definiendum.

clo·ver·leaf \-ˌlēf\ *n* : a road plan passing one highway over another and routing turning traffic onto connecting roadways which branch only to the right and lead around in a circle to enter the other highway from the right and thus merge traffic without left-hand turns or direct crossings

A connotative definition. Webster's Seventh New Collegiate Dictionary, *1976,* p. 157.

In the definiens above, the component 'institution' gives a broad location of the concept area in which the things referred to by the definiendum are to be found. For instance, it excludes the possibility that the term 'hospital' could apply to any living creature, natural occurrence, or manufactured article. Stating the purpose of the things named by the definiendum (rendering services to the sick and the injured) now eliminates all institutions that are primarily financial, political, punitive, or educational in their purpose. By addition of the statement that anything called 'hospital' provides accommodation, clinics, too, are eliminated; and specifying that the accommodation is temporary disqualifies homes for the aged and homes for the chronically infirm from the class of things to which the word 'hospital' can be correctly applied. On the other hand, if all references to sickness and medicine had been omitted from this definiens, there would be no reason to reject 'hotel' or 'boarding house' as synonyms of 'hospital'. The reference to 'custodial care' prevents the application of the term 'hospital' to some institutions in certain parts of the world, in which all other services are provided, but custodial care is not—members of each patient's family do his or her cooking, laundry, and so on. If we want to call such facilities hospitals, the reference to custodial care in the definiens must be removed.

It should be obvious at this point that an increase in the intension of a definition (the adding of properties) cannot result in an increase in the extension (or denotation) of the definiendum. Any properties added to the connotation will either diminish the denotation (extension) or leave it unchanged. Conversely, if there is a decrease in the connotation (intension)—that is, an elimination of some of the properties named by the definiens—the denotation of a term can only increase or remain unchanged; it cannot thereby be diminished. Thus, the word 'female' denotes slightly more than half the world's population. Expand this connotation to 'young female', by adding the property of youth, and you have decreased the denotation by about two-thirds. If you now add the property 'intelligent' to the others, the extension shrinks again. By the time you have increased your intension to 'intelligent young female scientist', the extension has undergone a drastic shrinkage, and this expression denotes a much smaller population than the original word 'female', which had a lesser connotation.

We have stated above that connotative definitions list the **essential attributes** or characteristics of a definiendum. To see how this works in practice, we might ask: "Essential to whom, and essential for what?"

Since we are concerned here with the definition of words, rather than of things, it is important to understand that an attribute is considered essential not by virtue of being essential to the thing itself, but by virtue of being essential to the definition of the word. The concept of essentiality should, however, be qualified even further, for the term 'essential attributes' is not an absolute, but a relative term. It might be defined as 'those attributes which, when included in the definiens, are most informative, most characteristic of the definiendum, and least open to misinterpretation'.

Definition by Genus and Difference   A **definition by genus and difference** is a type of connotative definition which consists of specifying the general class of things to which the definiendum belongs and then further specifying the properties by which the definiendum can be distinguished from other things belonging to the same general class. Traditionally, the general class is known as the *genus* and the distinguishing properties are called either the *differentia* or the *difference.*

Definitions by genus and difference are commonly used to define concepts pertaining to the natural sciences, though their use is not restricted to scientific contexts. In biology, a definition of 'gorilla' by genus and difference might begin by stating that the gorilla is an anthropoid ape. Then, because the genus 'anthropoid ape' includes not only gorillas, but chimpanzees, orangutans, and gibbons, it is necessary to point out the characteristic or set of characteristics distinguishing the species 'gorilla' from the other species of the same genus. In this case, one might specify that the gorilla is the largest of the anthropoid apes.

In any field of study which, like biology, has been exhaustively classified, definitions by genus and difference offer a concise and convenient method of pinpointing a definiendum. Moreover, to someone who is not familiar with either the word or the concept represented by the definiendum, but who knows the classification system of the particular subject matter, a definition by genus and difference offers a great deal of information in capsule form. Such a person could trace the gorilla back through ever more inclusive divisions in the hierarchy of biological classifications: from the genus 'anthropoid ape' to the class 'mammals' to the phylum 'vertebrates'. Since it is a requirement that the properties pertaining to the larger group must be shared by all its subgroups, the definition by genus and difference can provide a considerable amount of indirect, as well as direct, information about the anatomy and lifestyle of gorillas, with a great economy of words.

The method of definition by genus and difference can be used to define terms which are not part of such highly formalized systems as biology. In fact, it can be used for many words in our everyday vocabulary. 'Frying-pan' might be defined as a 'cooking utensil, consisting of a shallow metallic bowl attached to a long handle.' 'Bed' might be defined as a 'common piece of furniture, constructed to support the human form while asleep'.

There are some words for which it is quite possible to give a connotative definition, but quite impossible to give a denotative definition. 'Dragon', 'werewolf', 'unicorn', and 'cherubim' are cases in point. The fact that most people may not believe that these creatures do, or ever did, exist does not prevent us from explaining what it is that people have in mind when they mention these creatures. One can, for example, define 'unicorn' as 'a horselike creature with a single, pointed horn in the middle of its forehead', without implying that any such creature ever existed. (Remember, it is important to distinguish clearly between a picture of a unicorn and a real unicorn. One can readily give an ostensive definition of 'picture of a unicorn'.)

Operational Definitions   An **operational definition** is one whose definiens provides a test or a formal procedure which is to be followed to determine whether or not the definiendum applies to a certain thing. An operational definition of 'alkaline liquid' might read: 'If you immerse a piece of litmus paper in a liquid, and the litmus paper turns blue thereupon, the liquid is alkaline'. Similarly, an operational definition of 'brain activity' might read: 'Brain activity produces visible oscillations on an electroencephalograph that has been properly attached to the head'.

The following example of an operational definition is taken from a physical science textbook: "If the substance fails to break down upon being heated to

Was the King of Id entrapped by a definition? If so, what kind? How might he have avoided this predicament?

"The Wizard of Id" by permission of Johnny Hart and Field Enterprises, Inc.

1,000°, having an electric current passed through it, being treated with acid, etc., it is an 'element'." The behavioral sciences also make frequent use of operational definitions, setting up testing procedures to determine, for instance, whether certain behavior patterns are innate or learned, which aspects of motherhood signify 'mother' to baby chimpanzees, or by what features the feared and detested cuckoo is recognized as a cuckoo by other birds.

Household instructions routinely include operational definitions. A cake is ready to be taken out of the oven when a toothpick we insert in it comes out dry and clean; spaghetti is to be rinsed when it has been cooked to the point of looking opaque and feeling semisoft to the touch; an avocado can be considered ripe if the pit inside rattles when you shake it. And, in the nursery, we are told to judge whether or not a baby is hungry by whether it does or does not drink its milk.

EXERCISE 1–5   *Decide whether each of the following definitions is synonymous, enumerative (ostensive or denotive), connotative (possibly by genus and difference), or operational.*

---

1. "Herbivorous" means "feeding on plants."
2. A copy is a reproduction.
3. Prime numbers: 1, 2, 3, 5, 7, 11, 13, 17, 19, 23, etc.
4. The piece of music we are listening to now is an example of a string quartet.
5. An icosahedron is a polyhedron having twenty faces.
6. Alcoholic beverage: If, as you drink more and more of a beverage, you become more and more drunk, the beverage is an alcoholic beverage.
7. Free trade: As applied to international trade, the absence of export and import duties and of regulations which are clearly designed to reduce or prevent such trade (Sloan and Zurcher, *Dictionary of Economics*).
8. Aleph is the first letter of the Hebrew alphabet.
9. *Quercus alba* is the scientific name for the American white oak.
10. A prevaricator is a liar.
11. The face cards in a deck of playing cards are all the Jacks, Queens, and Kings.
12. Allergy: If a substance is placed on a person's skin and the person develops a rash, then that person has an allergy to that substance.
13. Stamina is the same thing as endurance.
14. An iguana is a large herbivorous tropical American lizard.
15. Noon (local time) is that time of day at which the sun is equidistant between the eastern and western horizons.
16. "Wireless" means "radio."
17. Right triangle: Given any triangle, construct a circle around the triangle, using the longest side of the triangle as the diameter of the circle. If all three vertices of the triangle lie on the circle, the triangle is a right triangle.
18. The principal parts of a Latin verb: amo, amare, amavi, amatus.
19. The principal parts of a Latin verb are the first person singular present indicative active, the present infinitive active, the first person singular perfect active, and the perfect passive participle.
20. The principal parts of a Latin verb are those verb forms from which all other possible verb forms can be derived.

21. An object is fluorescent if, when you put it under an ultraviolet lamp, it gives off light, whereas it did not before.
22. The provinces of Canada are British Columbia, Alberta, Saskatchewan, Manitoba, Ontario, Quebec, Newfoundland, New Brunswick, Nova Scotia, Prince Edward Island, the Northwest Territories, and the Yukon Territories.
23. The gross national product is the total value at current market prices of all the goods and services produced by a nation in a given year, prior to the deduction of depreciation charges and other allowances.
24. The constellation *Ursa Major* is the Big Dipper.
25. A full house is a poker hand consisting of three of a kind and a pair.
26. (An experienced poker player to a beginner) See, there you have a full house in your hand: three aces and two tens.
27. "Myopia" means "nearsightedness."
28. Myopia is a condition of the eye in which images come to a focus in front of the retina because the eyeball is elongated or the lens too convex, resulting in an inability to see distant objects well, if at all.
29. That's Nova Scotia over there off the bow, the only piece of land visible on the horizon.
30. Marsupials are an order of mammals in which the females have an abdominal pouch for carrying their young.
31. Marsupials are animals such as kangaroos, wombats, bandicoots, and opossums.
32. Man is a rational animal.
33. A tango is a modern ballroom dance in 4/4 time which originated in Buenos Aires and is characterized by syncopated rhythm, long pauses, and stylized body positions.
34. The Pleiades is that cluster of seven stars over there in the eastern sky where I'm pointing.
35. Lambda is the eleventh letter of the Greek alphabet.
36. Alcoholic beverages are beer, wine, hard liquors (bourbon, scotch, gin, vodka, rum), and liqueurs.
37. A person has an addiction to a drug or an activity if he manifests high anxiety reactions when deprived of the drug or prevented from engaging in the activity.
38. Phytohormones are the same thing as plant hormones.
39. Grimm's law is a linguistic law, formulated by Jacob Grimm, describing a pattern of consonant changes in words as they passed from primitive Indo-European languages into early Germanic languages.
40. A series of numbers is a geometric progression in which the same answer results from dividing the second number by the first, the third by the second, the fourth by the third, and so on to the end of the series.

EXERCISE 1–6   *Write (a) a synonymous definition (when possible), (b) an enumerative (ostensive or denotative) definition, and (c) a connotative definition (perhaps by genus and difference) for each of the following. Choose only one of the meanings of words with multiple meanings.*

---

1. Metropolis
2. Movie
3. Insect
4. Cat
5. Car

6. War
7. Exploit
8. Freedom
9. Play
10. Tyrant

EXERCISE 1–7   *Write an operational definition for each of the following.*

1. Magnet
2. Buoyant
3. Flammable
4. Contagious
5. Poison (n.)

6. Even number
7. Genius
8. Acid
9. Transparent
10. Definition

USES OF DEFINITIONS   Although our shorthand method of writing definitions (as 'defininiendum =df. definiens') may tend to obscure the fact, all definitions are indeed sentences. As such, like other sentences, they can be used in many ways to perform a variety of tasks. Definitions can be used to express statements, but they are not always used in this manner. And even when they are used propositionally (i.e., to express statements), the criteria for determining their truth or falsity can differ quite markedly from case to case. It is, therefore, important to briefly examine some of the more common uses of definitions.

To Report Meaning   Sometimes a definition is used to report the meaning of a term as it is normally used and understood by most members of a specific group (such as all Americans and all biologists). Such a definition is known as a **reportive** or **lexical definition.** It is the kind of definition one would expect to find in a dictionary ('lexicon' is a synonym for 'dictionary').

Lexical definitions can be enumerative, connotative, synonymous, or operational. 'Dandelion', for instance, may be defined as 'a yellow-flowered composite plant (genus *Taraxacum*): *esp.:* an herb (*T. officinale*) sometimes grown as a potherb and nearly cosmopolitan as a weed' (Webster), or as 'one of those plants growing out there in the lawn'. The first definition is connotative, the second enumerative (ostensive). 'Bachelor' may be defined as 'a member of the group which includes A, B, C, D, and E'—naming a number of bachelors known to the hearer—enumerative (denotative). Although each of these is a different kind of definition, they are all being used to do the same thing: namely, to report the generally accepted meaning of a word.

A lexical definition is propositional: it can be judged as being true or false, according to whether it accurately reports the way the word is actually used by members of a specific group. Thus, ' "bachelor" means "unmarried male" ' is a true lexical definition, for 'unmarried male' is the meaning generally given to 'bachelor' in ordinary use by native-English speakers.

A lexical definition is false only if the meaning it attributes to a word is one not normally associated with that word by the members of a specific group. But it may be true and yet flawed; that is, it may fail to give *all* the meanings normally associated with the word, or fail to indicate the context within which the word has a particular meaning. Thus, to define 'key' as 'a usually metal instrument by which the bolt of a lock is turned' (Webster) is true as far as it goes; but it would be of little help to the student wanting to understand the use of the term 'key' in his music appreciation book, or in the answer key at the back of this text. To be complete, the lexical definition must deal also with these and other common uses of the term 'key', and must indicate the context within which each applies. In fact, Webster's *Seventh New Collegiate Dictionary* lists many separate categories of meaning for the term 'key', some of them with several subdivisions, as shown below.

¹key \'kē\ *n* [ME, fr. OE *cæg;* akin to MLG *keige* spear] **1 a :** a usu. metal instrument by which the bolt of a lock is turned **b :** any of various devices having the form or function of such a key **2 :** a means of gaining or preventing entrance, possession, or control **3 a :** something that gives an explanation or provides a solution **b :** a list of words or phrases giving an explanation of symbols or abbreviations **c :** an arrangement of the salient characters of a group of plants or animals or of taxa designed to facilitate identification **d :** a map legend **4 a** (1) : COTTER PIN (2) : COTTER **b :** a keystone in an arch **c :** a wedge used to make a dovetail joint **d :** a small parallel-sided piece that fits into a groove and prevents relative motion between rotating parts; *also* **:** a wedge for drawing or holding parts together **5 a :** one of the levers of a keyboard musical instrument that actuates the mechanism and produces the tones **b :** a lever that controls a vent in the side of a woodwind instrument or a valve in a brass instrument **c :** a depressible digital that serves as one unit of a keyboard and that works usu. by lever action to set in motion a character or an escapement (as in some typesetting machines) **6 :** SAMARA **7 :** a leading individual or principle **8 :** a system of seven tones based on their relationship to a tonic; *specif* **:** the tonality of a scale **9 a :** characteristic style or tone **:** STRAIN **b :** the tone or pitch of a voice **c :** the predominant tone of a photograph with respect to its lightness or darkness **10 :** a decoration or charm resembling a key **11 :** a small switch for opening or closing an electric circuit

²key *vt* **1 :** to lock with a key: as **a :** to secure (as a pulley on a shaft) by a key **b :** to finish off (an arch) by inserting a keystone **2 :** to regulate the musical pitch of **3 :** to make conformable **:** ATTUNE **4 :** to identify (a biological specimen) by a key **5 :** to insert in (an advertisement) matter intended to identify answers **6 :** to make nervous or tense — usu. used with *up* ∼ *vi* **:** to use a key

³key *adj* **:** of basic importance **:** FUNDAMENTAL

⁴key *n* [Sp *cayo,* fr. Lucayo] **:** a low island or reef; *specif* **:** one of the coral islets off the southern coast of Florida

keys 1a

Are there any meanings of the word 'key' that are not reported in this dictionary listing? Do you disagree with any of the definitions reported here? If so, how would you go about determining what the "correct" definition is?

A lexical definition need not report the way an entire language group (such as all English-speakers) uses a word; it may properly be limited to reporting the way a term is used in a technical or otherwise limited context. For instance, a word may be defined in terms of the meaning which it carries in the context of a particular theory, in which case we have a **theoretical definition.*** Such

* In a very real way, ordinary, everyday language can itself be said to embody, contain, or presuppose a "theory." In this sense, *every* lexical definition is a theoretical definition. The concept of a theory need not be restricted to scientific theories in the narrow sense of the term; there are theories of other kinds as well—such as ethical, religious, esthetic, and metaphysical—which also give special meanings to certain words. We shall use the term 'theoretical' in a relatively broad sense which allows it to be applied to any "special" language group insofar as that group is also distinguished by any characteristics other than shared language. Thus, a definition reporting the way in which English-speakers use a particular word would not be theoretical, but a definition reporting the way in which it is used by all (and only) Satanists, or by all (and only) Abstract Expressionists, would be theoretical.

> color, colour. (1) The visual sensation caused by light. (2) Light of a definite wavelength or group of wavelengths which is emitted, reflected, refracted, or transmitted by an object. A c. is defined by three properties; *hue*, the wavelength of the monochromatic light, i.e., shade; *saturation*, the percentage of the light of the above wavelength present, i.e., strength; *brightness*, the amount of light reflected as compared with a standard under the same conditions, i.e., luminosity.

> collision. Interaction between material systems (molecule, atom, or electron), or electromagnetic induction, resulting in a change in molecular energy.

Could anyone besides a trained chemist judge the accuracy or adequacy of these theoretical definitions?

Hackk's Chemical Dictionary, *4th ed., 1969.*

definitions are useful when, as is often the case in scientific usage, the meaning of a term as used in a particular theory does not correspond in intension or extension to its ordinary lexical meaning. Thus, when used as a psychoanalytical term 'ego' requires a theoretical definition, for its meaning in the context of Freudian theory is different from that which it has in common usage. In point of fact, 'ego' has several quite different meanings within different psychoanalytic theories, and has still other meanings in various philosophical systems.

Other words, such as 'proton' and 'mitochondria', have *only* theoretical definitions, for they have been conceived in connection with particular theories, and whatever common usage they have has evolved out of their use in connection with those theories.

A theoretical definition, when contained in a textbook or presented in a classroom lecture, is being used propositionally and is either true or false, depending on whether or not it accurately gives the meaning of the word as used in the particular theory. However, prior to its incorporation into textbooks and other standard uses, the definition must go through an evolutionary evaluational process for one to determine its usefulness and appropriateness in the particular theory. During this process of introduction into the theory, the definition is being used *stipulatively*—a kind of use which will be discussed shortly.

Another case of a limited reportive definition is the **legal definition.** This is a definition specified in the laws as formulated by a legislative, judicial, or executive body. If a motorist is stopped on the highway and given a summons for 'speeding', the verb 'to speed' is not being used in the same sense as in the proverbial injunction 'to speed the departing guest' or in that of the drug addict who 'speeds' on amphetamines. In the context of traffic law, as pertaining to any particular stretch of road, 'to speed' is defined as meaning 'to drive at a rate exceeding *x* miles per hour'. The definition of 'valid' from a legal dictionary (see p. 48), is very different from the theoretical definition of 'valid' given later in this book.

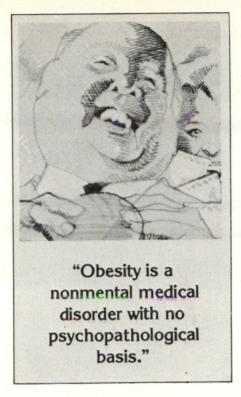

"Obesity is a
nonmental medical
disorder with no
psychopathological
basis."

*Can you translate this theoretical definition into "ordinary"
language? What is the theoretical content in this definition
given in the basic psychology reference work,* Diagnostic
and Statistical Manual of Mental Disorders, *3d ed.?*

Reprinted from Psychology Today. *Copyright © 1978 Ziff-Davis Publishing Company.*

When used in court, or in some other situation with reference to a law which already exists and a definition which is generally accepted, a legal definition is being cited in a reportive and therefore propositional way. However, when a proposed law is being debated for passage, the use of definitions in it may not be propositional.

To Introduce New Meaning   Occasionally, it is necessary to introduce new meanings. Sometimes this is done by "coining words." For instance, in his book, *Without Guilt and Justice,* philosopher Walter Kaufman analyzes the strategies people employ to avoid making fateful decisions, and suggests that the reason for this avoidance is the individual's fear of autonomy. "The fear of autonomy," he writes, "is a nameless dread, which leaves me free to coin a name for it: *decidophobia.*"* In thus defining and then naming a new concept, Kaufman formulated what is known as a **stipulative definition.**

* Walter Kaufman: *Without Guilt and Justice.* New York: Wyden Press, 1973.

VALID. Having legal strength or force, executed with proper formalities, incapable of being rightfully overthrown or set aside. Edwards v. O'Neal, Tex.Civ.App., 28 S.W.2d 569, 572. Of binding force; legally sufficient or efficacious; authorized by law. Anderson, L.Dict.; Morrison v. Farmers' & Traders' State Bank, 70 Mont. 146, 225 P. 123, 125. Good or sufficient in point of law; efficacious; executed with the proper formalities; incapable of being rightfully overthrown or set aside; sustainable and effective in law, as distinguished from that which exists or took place in fact or appearance, but has not the requisites to enable it to be recognized and enforced by law. Thompson v. Town of Frostproof, 89 Fla. 92, 103 So. 118; United States v. McCutchen, D.C.Cal., 234 F. 702, 709.

A deed, will, or other instrument, which has received all the formalities required by law, is said to be valid.

Meritorious; as a *valid* defense. Berringer v. Stevens, 145 Ark. 293, 225 S.W. 14, 15.

Compare this legal definition with the logical definition given at the top of p. 97 of this book, and with the definition(s) of "valid" given in any standard English dictionary.

Black's Law Dictionary, *Rev. 4th ed., 1968.*

A word that is stipulatively defined need not be a newly coined word. It may be a word which has a generally accepted meaning, but which the speaker wants to use in a new sense, and therefore stipulates that he or she will be using in that sense. Legislatures sometimes stipulate new meanings in the writing of new laws; courts sometimes expand the meaning of terms in existing laws to cover new situations. Thus, according to the stipulated legal definition of "contract," if a doctor stops by the roadside to assist an unconscious accident victim, the law recognizes a contract between them entitling the doctor to payment for his or her services and exposing the doctor to certain liabilities, even though no signed piece of paper, nor even a verbal agreement, exists.

The sciences often provide even clearer examples of stipulative definitions, for they are likely to develop new concepts which need to be named. Psychoanalytical terminology was originally introduced through stipulative definitions by Freud and some of his followers. Some of these terms, such as 'neurosis' and 'sublimation', were new coinages; others, such as 'transference' and 'repression', were words already in the language, to which new meanings were assigned.

Once a new word, or a new meaning for an old word, has been introduced, it may be absorbed into general usage or into the standard vocabulary of a particular discipline. What began as a stipulative definition then becomes a reportive definition, and can properly be cited as such.

To Remove Ambiguity or Vagueness

Ambiguity is said to exist when a word or phrase having two or more distinct meanings is used in such a way that it is not obvious from the context which meaning is intended. When we are told that a person is 'funny', we may not be immediately certain whether the speaker

It's time to hatch a better word.

When the world's top tennis professionals fought their way through the recent U.S. Open tennis tournament, the courts they played on caused almost as much comment as their drives and lobs. For the first time, the green grass of Forest Hills was gone, replaced by a clay-like composition that gave the ball a truer bounce.

Forest Hills' innovation is just one more example of a trend all of us now take for granted—toward synthetic products that are actually better than the real thing. Little ones, like synthetic vitamins. Big ones, like flood gates of rubber-coated nylon that may save Venice from a repetition of the 250 floods the medieval city has suffered in the past 15 years.

It occurs to us that the word "synthetic" no longer fits, because it somehow implies a pallid imitation, not something better. *Webster's New Collegiate Dictionary* defines "synthetic" as "devised, arranged, or fabricated for special situations to imitate or replace usual realities." But where's the "imitation" in an inflatable nylon body brace that allows paraplegics to walk on crutches? (It's a third as heavy as a regular metal brace.) And clothes made from synthetics mixed with cotton and wool go beyond the "usual." Wrinkle-free with no ironing, they represent a true revolution to the housewife.

Today's heat-resistant silicon carbides combine the best properties of ceramic and metal. Lush artificial furs, now being perfected, promise to save Africa's wild beasts from extinction. Plastics do everything now from brightening lives with long-playing records to saving them with blood-storage bags. The list goes on and on, but the bottom line never changes: developing products of the highest quality which improve on nature itself.

At Mobil, we market a line of synthesized hydrocarbon fluids that industry uses as circulating and gear oils. Our scientists spent 10 years perfecting them. They last three to five times as long as conventional lubricants. And they perform over a much broader temperature range. They're oil we never drilled for, and in these days of energy conservation, that's a big plus.

The line includes an auto engine lubricant which Mobil introduced abroad two years ago and is now test marketing in eight areas around the U.S. Without going into a commercial, extensive tests show this new lubricant can increase gasoline mileage for the average car as much as 10 miles per tankful, by drastically reducing engine friction. Additionally, it reduces oil consumption dramatically and facilitates starting down to 40 degrees below zero.

The thousands of new products developed through science are certainly more than just "synthetic," as Americans have come to understand the word. They're not only better than nature's products, but they conserve nature's resources in the process.

And they deserve a better name.

Mobil

Although it is possible to stipulate a new meaning for an existing word in a totally arbitrary way (e.g., 'logic' =df. 'orange peel') or an arbitrary meaning for a new word, we almost always have some reason for offering a new definition. Sometimes we can and do offer quite elaborate and carefully reasoned justifications for introducing new words or changing meanings of existing words. The accompanying Mobil ad provides a good example of the kind of argument that can be given in support of a new definition. What additional reasons can you think of for inventing a new word for the kinds of object mentioned for which "synthetic" is inappropriate? What arguments might be given for continuing to refer to such objects as "synthetic"? Since no new word is suggested in the ad, can you think of a new word that might be used to refer to these objects?

Courtesy The Mobil Corporation.

One of these characters is stipulating his own definition for the word "struthious," while the other wants to use the reportive definition.

Viewing ends of Pope's body

Galesburg (Ill.) Register-Mail 8/9/78

Pope's Death Stuns World, Brief Reign Cheered Many

Pittsburgh Post-Gazette 9/30/78

Ambiguities in newspaper headlines sometimes convey strange ideas.

means 'funny-haha' or 'funny-peculiar'. 'There's a rook on the patio' might refer to a large black bird or to a chess piece.

Vagueness exists when the meaning of a term is sufficiently imprecise that it is impossible to tell whether or not it applies to certain borderline cases. For example, the term 'hill' may seem clear enough, but at what point does a rise in the surface of the ground become a hill? Suppose I add one grain of sand at a time to a small mound; eventually the mound will become a hill, but where is the dividing line? If 4,987,523 grains of sand to not make a hill, do 4,987,524 grains make a hill? How about 4,987,525? There is a range of size within which most people will agree that the mound does not fit the definition of 'hill'; there is another range of size within which most will agree that it does; but there is a third, in-between range within which it is essentially impossible to obtain agreement. Instances which fall in this last range are known as borderline cases. Thus, a word is vague if it has borderline cases.

Color words are often imprecise: is such-and-such a particular shade of blue or green, red or orange? So are many other sensory words—loud and quiet, hard and soft, bright and dim—as well as terms of degree in general—at what precise point on a continuum of possible waistline measurements does a person cease to be plump and become fat?

In a sense, as we pointed out earlier in this chapter, almost all words in ordinary language are somewhat vague. If they were not so, everyday communication would be almost unmanageably overburdened with precision. One could not say, "I had scrambled eggs for breakfast." One would need to use different words according to whether the eggs were large, small, or medium-sized; fresh or less than fresh; brown or white; scrambled hard or soft. One would also have to specify what other foods the meal included, at what precise time it was eaten, and so on. As it is, we can add these details to the account if we wish to, but the vagueness of the terms 'eggs', 'scrambled', and 'breakfast' enables us to leave them out if they are not relevant to what we want to communicate at the moment. A certain degree of vagueness and imprecision, then, is valuable to the general usefulness of ordinary language. But in some situations it becomes a handicap, and then definitions must be offered to make the meanings of key words more precise.

Definitions used to eliminate ambiguity or vagueness are called **precising definitions.** They may be synonymous, connotative, or any of the other kinds discussed previously. They can also simultaneously serve the purpose of reporting accepted general or theoretical meanings, or they can be stipulative. Frequently, but not always, they are explicitly limited to specific contexts:

> *Throughout this book the word 'type' will be used to mean 'metal printing type'. (Removes ambiguity of 'type', which otherwise has several distinct meanings.)*
> *For the purposes of this discussion, the word*

If the universe were like this, there would be very few vague concepts.

"B.C." by permission of Johnny Hart and Field Enterprises, Inc.

> **'old' will be used to mean 'at least seventy-five years of age'. (Removes vagueness of 'old', which otherwise has borderline cases.)**

Precising definitions are not evaluated strictly in terms of truth or falsity. They are to be judged by whether they adequately eliminate ambiguity or vagueness and whether they do it without distorting the generally accepted meaning of the word. A definition that significantly changes the accepted boundaries of the definiendum—that is, that allows the word to be applied in cases where it was *clearly* inapplicable before, or excludes it in cases where it was clearly allowed before—can be said to be false, *if* it is being offered as a precising definition. For this reason the following definition can be considered to be false:

> **The word 'old' in ordinary English usage means 'at least ten years of age'.**

While this definition certainly eliminates vagueness, it also distorts the generally accepted meaning of the word 'old' in our culture, for it allows it to be applied in cases to which it is clearly not applicable under general usage.

On the other hand,

> **When I say 'old' I mean 'at least ten years of age'.**

may be true, for the speaker explicitly applies this definition only to the context of his or her own usage; but for this very reason it is not likely to prove a very useful definition. That is, it probably would not do much to facilitate clarity of communication between the speaker and anyone else. Such a definition is purely stipulative.

"Man, you can't get away from the Drug Squad even in the park these days . . ."

Ambiguity in language is the basis of much good humor.

© 1972 Punch-Rothco.

To Persuade Synonymous, enumerative, connotative, and operational definitions may also be used persuasively. **Persuasive definitions** are used to change the attitudes or feelings of people toward specific things. Thus, one may connotatively define 'chiropractor' as 'someone who claims to be able to treat illness by messing around with your spine, although he is not a licensed M.D.' or as 'a highly trained manipulative practitioner, who frequently succeeds in curing persons whom conventional medicine has been unable to help'. The first of these definitions is probably intended to persuade one *not* to consult a chiropractor; the second is quite possibly intended to persuade one to do so. 'The unemployed' may be defined enumeratively as 'bums, cripples, people too lazy to work, and people who got fired', or as 'people between jobs, and people for whom the capitalist economy fails to provide job opportunities'. The first definition might be cited to persuade someone to oppose an increase in welfare benefits, the second to arouse support for a socialistic economic program. Thus, persuasive definitions are usually geared to implanting in someone else's mind one's own evaluation of the definiendum and to affecting other people's behavior in some significant way.

It is generally inappropriate to evaluate persuasive definitions in terms of truth or falsity. Rather, a persuasive definition can be said to be *good* if it succeeds in doing what it was intended to do, and *bad* if it fails.

To Serve Social or Political Purposes   It is not at all uncommon for words to be defined or redefined to serve certain social or political purposes. Definitions used for such purposes can be of any of the several kinds and can also serve other purposes as well. To take one relatively simple and straightforward example, the U.S. government provides support for research on "significant" medical problems. It took many people many years to convince legislators and administrators that allergies are a "significant" disease. One argument given was the following by a clinician-researcher:

> If you agree that a significant disease is one that affects the victim's life significantly, then allergies are significant. I have a truck-driver patient who needs antihistamines but is so affected by them that he cannot drive. And there's a lawyer patient who was ruining his practice by continually cancelling appointments. He had nocturnal asthma. . . . Those things are "significant."

Once it was agreed that allergies are included among the denotata of 'significant disease', millions of dollars were made available for setting up new research centers around the country to study the disease. It is not at all clear whether this process involved a redefinition or a precising of the original definition (it might have even been the meaning of 'allergy' that was changed), but the effect of this change in definition is quite apparent and significant.

Many people in our society are very much concerned with the problem of alcoholism, either because it affects them directly and personally or because of its impact on society as a whole. There are two fundamental problems related to the definition of "alcoholism." One problem is that the definition is far from precise, and there is much disagreement as to who is an alcoholic. Many definitions have been offered. The Women's Christian Temperance Union, which wants to make the consumption of any and all alcoholic beverages illegal, defines an alcoholic as "anyone who drinks alcohol. As soon as they start to drink they're on that road downward." The Rutger's University Center of Alcohol Studies defines an alcoholic as "one who is unable consistently to choose whether he shall drink or not, and who, if he drinks, is unable consistently to choose whether or not he shall stop." The National Council on Alcoholism gives an operational definition. The council has constructed a checklist of twenty-six questions, and then defined a "*potential* alcoholic" as anyone who gives an affirmative answer to any one question. Their questions include "Do you drink heavily after a disappointment?" and "Are you secretly irritated when your family or friends discuss your drinking?" Other researchers don't believe it is possible to formulate a very precise definition. Which if any of these positions is correct?

Is there some way that 'energy crisis' could be defined that would prevent the bureaucrat/politician from being justified in announcing the end of the energy crisis?

The second difficult problem associated with the definition of 'alcoholism' is that of deciding whether it should be categorized as a mental illness, a physical illness, or a moral weakness. The way in which it is defined can have a very significant impact. For example, if alcoholism is defined as a physical illness, the costs of treatment for one illness would have to be covered by regular medical insurance policies. If it is defined as a mental illness, its treatment costs would be covered only by policies that provide for the treatment of mental illnesses. And, if it is defined as a manifestation of moral weakness, its treatment would not be covered by any kind of health insurance policy. In addition, societal attitudes toward the alcoholic would be quite different depending on whether the alcoholic is assumed to be suffering from a physical disease or that he or she is a weak-willed moral degenerate. A third significant effect of the definition of "alcoholism" is in the area of governmental support for research. If alcoholism is defined as a physical illness, most of the research funds would be channeled to physiologists and internists. If it is defined as a mental illness, most of the funds would go to psychologists and psychiatrists. If it is considered to be a moral

You're old enough to drink. But are you mature enough?

The legal voting age has been lowered recently.

So has the legal drinking age in many areas.

Both trends show growing confidence in the maturity of our young citizens.

But with every privilege comes a responsibility.

Young men and women who choose to exercise the privilege of social drinking, should learn to exercise a sense of responsibility. Above all, they should not pressure friends who choose not to drink.

This new generation is the best-informed, best-educated in our history. We hope it will drink responsibly. The vast majority of older Americans do.

If you choose to drink, drink responsibly.

What definition of 'alcoholism' is implicit in this advertisement sponsored by the liquor industry?

Distilled Spirits Council of the United States.

weakness research funds would not be justified at all. Thus, the debates over the definition of concepts such as "alcoholism" ultimately can turn out to be about very real and significant social and political policy issues.

The social goals and purposes to be served by certain definitions are sometimes as questionable as they are real. For example, in the Soviet Union, many kinds of political dissent that are tolerated in some other countries are defined as symptoms of mental illness, thus permitting the government to put dissidents in mental institutions. This has the same effect as imprisonment, but does not require any kind of a trial or public hearing. In contrast, there have been debates in recent years in the United States as to whether the definition of 'mental illness' in U.S. law is too liberal in that it may allow "real criminals" to escape imprisonment by claiming that they are mentally ill.

Most parties involved in discussions of definitions such as those mentioned in this section would be hard-pressed to categorize what they are doing in terms of our concepts of stipulating, precising, reporting, and so forth. Some may even consider that they are not discussing definitions at all, but are only concerned with "facts" about such conditions as mental illness, disease, and crime. Almost all would probably agree, however, that their primary interest and concern is with achieving certain social and political goals. The article at the bottom of page 57 provides one final example of this kind of definition.

Mixed Usage   It is not always clear what kind of definition is being used in a particular situation. The Supreme Court ruling on abortion offers a case in point. On January 22, 1973, the Court handed down a decision in two important cases, in which it held that the right to abortion could not be restricted by the

Label wrong all along, says author of change

by **DAVID L. AIKEN**

WASHINGTON—The psychiatrist who prepared the rationale for the American Psychiatric Association's removal of homosexuality from its list of disorders admits that it shouldn't have been there in the first place.

Dr. Robert L. Spitzer, a member of the APA's Task Force on Nomenclature and a psychiatrist at New York's Columbia University College of Physicians and Surgeons, said he felt homosexuality never met the criteria for defining a condition as a disorder: That it cause continual discomfort and interfere continually with ability to function in society.

Instead, he said, the main reason homosexuality was in the list of disorders was simply that society disapproved of it. This, he said, "is not in my view a scientific basis for having a nomenclature."

The primary reason for the APA's turnabout, he admitted, was persuasion from the gay activist movement.

ADVOCATE: Does this decision to change signify that times have changed and the APA is changing with them, or were you wrong all along?

SPITZER: I would have to say we were wrong. Since this is not getting wide circulation, I can say that. Of course, in some sense a mental disorder is whatever the profession says it is, but I think one can have certain criteria which make more sense than other criteria. The old criterion really was, anything that society very much disapproved of was grounds for being in the nomenclature. Society continues to disapprove of homosexual behavior, although certainly not to the extent it

did, but that is not in my view a scientific basis for having a nomenclature. So I would have to say, yes, it never should have been there, by itself.

ADVOCATE: Will the APA's decision help change the attitudes of society toward homosexuality?

SPITZER: I think so, and I guess you people have been telling us all along that it will . . . . Of course, psychiatry doesn't have the same currency that it did 10 or 20 years ago. I don't know how much people even care what psychiatrists have to say, but to the extent that they still do, it will have some effect. My impression is that people are not that interested in what psychiatrists have to say anymore.

The theoretical definition of mental disorder discussed here has ramifications extending far beyond the "experts" who have the political power to stipulate the definition.

states in the first three months of pregnancy; that it could be regulated to some extent, in the interest of maternal health, in the second three months; and that only in the last three months could it be prohibited altogether except to safeguard the life and health of the mother. Two important considerations entered into the Court's ruling. The first was whether or not the right to privacy (not explicitly stated in the Constitution, but recognized in previous Supreme Court decisions) ought to be regarded as including a woman's right to end her pregnancy. The second was the question of whether or when the fetus, or unborn child, can properly be said to be a person, and therefore entitled to the constitutional rights of a person—including the right to life. The Court decided the first question in the affirmative, but noted that the state may have a "compelling interest" which permits it to regulate, to some extent, the exercise of the right to privacy. One such compelling interest, the Court said, is concern for the protection of potential life.

The question, thus, was: at what point does the state's interest in protecting the fetus' life outweigh the woman's right to privacy in the control of her own body? If the fetus could properly be regarded as a person, this would influence the answer. Several considerations were cited in the Court's decision:

1. Constitutional usage: "The Constitution does not define 'person' in so many words. The usage of the term is such that it has application only postnatally."
2. Legal precedent: "The unborn have never been recognized in the law as persons in the whole sense."
3. Historical circumstances: "Throughout the major portion of the nineteenth century, prevailing legal abortion practices were far freer than they are today." "When most criminal abortion laws were first enacted, the procedure [abortion] was a hazardous one for the woman."

On these bases, the Court concluded that "the word 'person', as used in the Fourteenth Amendment, does not include the unborn." Therefore, presumably, the constitutional rights of persons do not apply to the fetus. The Court went on to hold, however, that the state acquires a compelling interest in protecting the life of the fetus at the time of viability—the point when the fetus "presumably has the capability of meaningful life outside the mother's womb."* Does this mean that, at the time of viability, the fetus does become a person? Or is viability another consideration altogether, independent of personhood but of

---

* This and the preceding quotations are cited from the majority opinion of the Court, written by Justice Harry A. Blackmun.

DEPRESSIONS: Inflation fighter Alfred E. Kahn has taken to calling that unmentionable economic downturn a "kumquat" rather than a "banana." Reason: a letter from United Brands Co. asserting Chiquita Banana's patriotism and claiming that banana price rises are now within the anti-inflation guidelines.

Shortly after he was appointed to head the anti-inflation program established by President Carter in 1978, economist Alfred E. Kahn stated in a press conference that a serious economic depression was quite possible if the anti-inflation guidelines were not followed. After newspaper headlines reported that Kahn had said that a depression was possible, the president told Kahn not to use the word depression again. Kahn complied, and told the press that he would only talk about "bananas" from then on. Shortly thereafter, the following item appeared in Business Week *(December 25, 1978).*

What kind of a definition did Kahn give? What uses did this definition have?

practical interest to the state? This question the Court appears to have left unanswered.

What sort of definition was the Supreme Court offering here? There have been various opinions. Was the Court merely reporting an existing meaning—saying, in effect, "This is what the Constitution means (or does not mean) by the term 'person'"? This might be a lexical definition, if the Constitution is presumed to be using the word 'person' in its ordinary sense. Or was the Court reporting the accepted legal definition, as suggested by its citation of past legal usage?

Some opponents of the abortion ruling have accused the Court of "legislating"—that is, of usurping the lawmaking function of Congress and the state legislatures under cover of interpreting the Constitution. In that case, perhaps we are faced with a stipulative definition, as if the Court had said: "The Constitution does not specify whether the fetus is a person, but we will define 'person' to include also 'a fetus which has reached the point of viability'." Or perhaps, instead, there is a precising definition: "The Constitution leaves unclear at what point on the continuum of development the fetus becomes a person. For purposes of this decision, 'person' will be held to mean 'a human being after the moment of birth' (or 'after the point of viability')."

Any of these is a possible interpretation of the Court's understanding of 'person'. Finally, it has been pointed out that the definition may well have a persuasive effect; referring to a twenty-week-old unborn human being as a 'fetus' rather than as a 'person' may tend in itself to persuade some hearers that abortion is morally permissible in addition to being constitutional.

EXERCISE 1–8   *Each passage below is concerned with the definition of a word, and in some cases a particular context has been supplied. Read each passage carefully and then determine the use to which the definition has been put. Is it* (a) *reportive;* (b) *limited reportive (perhaps theoretical or legal);* (c) *precising;* (d) *stipulative; and/or* (e) *persuasive?*

---

1. A physics teacher defining 'gravity', stating Newton's law of universal gravitation: Every body of matter in the universe attracts every other body with a force directly proportional to the product of their masses and inversely proportional to the square of the distance between them.
2. A professor to her graduate philosophy seminar: To eliminate confusion in this discussion, I propose that we define 'intuition' as 'unmediated knowledge' and find other words to express the other meanings that some of those involved in the discussion are attaching to the word 'intuition'.
3. A statement by Irving S. Shapiro, chairman of E. I. duPont de Nemours & Co., describing effective training programs for persons who will be working for industrial companies: Nearly 80 percent of the people who will be of working age in the year 2000 are already on the job or are now in school. These people are the direct bridge to the twenty-first century. They're what we might call our "people connection" with the future. (*New York Times*, Dec. 15, 1974)
4. Walter Lippmann, on the duty of public officials: Those in high places are more than the administrators of government bureaus. They are more than the writers of laws. They are the custodians of a nation's ideals, of the beliefs it cherishes, of its permanent hopes, of the faith which makes a nation out of a mere aggregation of individuals.
5. A music teacher to the class: Quality is one of the attributes of a note. By their quality, notes of the same pitch and volume may be distinguished. Quality depends on the extent to which overtones are present with the fundamental.
6. In addition, the newly discovered subatomic particle may be the first to possess a combination of mathematical properties rather unscientifically known as "charm" (a term first coined by Harvard physicist Sheldon Glashow and Stanford's James Bjorken), that involves such basic characteristics as the way in which the particle is produced and the means by which it breaks up into other particles. (*Newsweek*, Dec. 2, 1974)
7. A law school professor to his class: Escrow is defined as property placed by one person in the hands of a second person, usually a trust company, for the delivery to a third person upon the fulfillment by the latter of certain specific obligations.
8. A lobbyist who is against repealing marijuana laws: Marijuana is the devil's weed; it weakens the mind of the user and destroys the fabric of American society.
9. A social problems instructor to his class: "There are many varying definitions of poverty. By 'poverty', I mean any family unit of two or more persons which has a yearly $4,800 or less, or any individual living alone who has a yearly income of $2,000 or less."
10. A musician teaching his daughter to play the piano: "A natural is a note which is neither a sharp nor a flat."

11. A speaker at a Communist Party Convention: "Capitalism is the system whereby the worker is not given his equal share of return for his productivity. It is the system which enslaves men, women, and children with the hope of future happiness, but which provides them only with economic and social suffering."

12. An Israeli spokesman, arguing against establishing diplomatic relations between his country and Germany: "The noble gentlemen in this forum who seek diplomatic relations with Germany have a short memory. Have they forgotten what Germany is? Germany is the country that put Adolf Hitler in power and murdered six million Jewish people! That is what Germany is!"

13. A judge to a lawyer defending a thirteen-year-old charged with burglary: "In this district all charged persons under sixteen years of age are juveniles, and hence are subject not to the jurisdiction of this court, but rather to the jurisdiction of the juvenile court."

14. A sociologist in a paper about juvenile sexual attitudes: "In my study, 120 juveniles, which we shall consider to mean persons between the ages of eleven and sixteen, were interviewed to determine their attitudes toward sex roles, premarital sexual activity, masturbation, and other sexual matters."

15. A teacher to her class of sixth-graders: "The word 'juvenile' which you just came across in this book means 'a young person.' "

16. A chemistry professor to his students: "In chemistry, the term 'sublimation' refers to the process whereby a solid changes directly to the gaseous state without liquefaction."

17. A tour guide at the New York Stock Exchange to tourists: "That area with the circular steps on which all those frantic people are standing is the pit, the place where traders buy and sell futures in goods such as wheat, soybeans, and other commodities."

18. From an article on the status of railroads in the United States: "Railroads—as a system of transportation, not as companies—should begin to get equal treatment with the subsidized highway system. . . . If the railroads are dying, it is partly because our mental images equate 'railroad' with 'company', and so see dangers of socialism in a mix of public and private finance and ownership. Yet we have long ago accepted that mix as a fact of life in our street and highway system."

19. One businessman to another: "We work under a 'contract system' with the federal penitentiary in Smithsville. We sign a contract with the federal government for the use of convict labor. It's a way of keeping costs down and it's a socially valuable system as well, since we provide convicts with job training."

20. A science major to a friend: "The steady state universe is really a theory which states that the universe is infinite and eternal and that new material is formed to fill the gaps that occur as the universe expands."

21. A certain lunatic is convinced that all dons [Oxford professors] want to murder him. His friends introduce him to all the mildest and most respectable dons that they can find and after each of them has retired, they say, "You see, he really doesn't want to murder you; he spoke to you in a most cordial manner; surely you are convinced now?" But the lunatic replies "Yes, that was only his diabolical cunning; he's really plotting against me the whole time, like the rest of them." . . . Let us call that in which we differ from this lunatic, our respective *bliks*. He has an insane *blik* about dons; we have a sane one. (R. M. Hare, in Anthony Flew and Alasdair MacIntyre, *New Essays in Philosophical Theology*).

22. A high school teacher to her students: "The word 'revere' which the poet uses means 'to worship or adore someone.' "

EXERCISE 1–9   *Next to each word listed below is a use to which a definition for that word might be put. Write a definition for each word which functions according to the use indicated. Provide a context for each definition where necessary.*

---

1. Forecast (reportive)
2. Closed shop (limited reportive-legal)
3. Politician (persuasive)
4. Pornographic (precising)
5. Z-ray (stipulative)
6. Acceleration (limited reportive-theoretical)
7. Recent (precising)
8. Coup d'etat (reportive)
9. Socialism (persuasive)
10. Bail (limited reportive-legal)
11. Vase (reportive)
12. Good teacher (precising)
13. Gimbit (stipulative)
14. Transmission (limited reportive—theoretical)
15. Counsel (limited reportive—legal)
16. Rich (precising)
17. Velocity (limited reportive—theoretical)
18. Religion (persuasive)
19. Friend (reportive)
20. Lover (precising)

CRITERIA FOR GOOD DEFINITIONS   For any word you care to think of, there is no one definition that will be the best for all purposes and under all circumstances. Definitions are not made in a void. They are a part of the process of human communication and must, therefore, be formulated to suit the purpose for which they are given as well as the audience to which they are addressed.

It would be as inappropriate to list all the known properties of copper in answer to a small child's question, "What is copper?" as it would be to define 'copper' by its looks, tarnished and untarnished, when a chemistry major asks the same question in the classroom. Neither definition would be appropriate if the question were asked by a visiting professor of chemistry who had only a scant knowledge of English. Here, the detailed connotative definition would be needlessly cumbersome; the definition in terms of its appearance would be unnecessarily vague; and both might overtax the professor's knowledge of English. For the professor, the preferred definition would probably be 'Cuprum; Cu'—the synonymous scientific word and the internationally recognized chemical abbreviation for the element copper.

While the type of definition appropriate in a given context is determined by that context itself, there are some general criteria for good definitions which can be applied to any definiens, be it synonymous, enumerative, connotative, operational, or of any other kind.

Noncircularity   To be satisfactory, a definition must bridge the gap between the unfamiliar and the familiar, by relating the unfamiliar definiendum to something that is already known and understood. When a definiens contains the word that is to be defined, or contains a grammatical variation of this same word, this definition is said to be **circular.** One can compare it to a dog chasing its own tail instead of catching the rabbit.

Defining 'feoffer' as 'one who makes a feoffment', is circular and unenlightening; for it can be presumed that people who do not know the term 'feoffer' are equally ignorant of the word 'feoffment'. The only thing this circular definition reveals about 'feoffer' is that the word refers to a person. This leaves us with an infinite number of choices as to what the word actually means. For reasons of space, this kind of definition appears in dictionaries. But in a good dictionary, this circular definition would be supplemented by the entry, 'feoffment: the granting of a fee'. The conjunction of the two definitions eliminates the circularity.

Affirmativeness   Assume there are a thousand sweaters in a department store, and you know which one you want to buy. You could either tell the salesperson that the sweater you want is medium-sized, green, made of orlon, and with a boatneck collar, or you could say: "The sweater I want is not extra small, small, large, etc.; not blue, pink, white, etc.; not wool, cotton, dacron; I don't want a turtleneck, V-neck, etc., etc."

For almost any word you want to define, there are thousands of attributes or denotations that do not apply, and only a few that do apply. Consequently, an **affirmative** definiens, which states the applicable, is generally far more efficient at pinpointing a definition than a negative definiens, which states what is inapplicable.

One exception to this rule are definiens for words that in themselves signify an absence of something: baldness (no hair), broke (no money), spinster (no marriage), dead (no life).

One might at first think that a negative definition which consists of saying 'the word's antonym is not applicable' would point straight to the definiendum. But the result is ambiguous. By defining 'optimist' as 'someone who is not a pessimist' or (assuming that whoever does not know 'optimist' will also be unfamiliar with 'pessimist') as 'one who is not a despairing person and does not habitually perceive or expect the worst', we have not precluded the inference that 'optimist' means 'someone who sees both good and bad in everything and expects that some things will go well and others will go badly'.

When there are only two mutually exclusive categories into which the definiendum can fall, as whole numbers must be either odd or even, a negative definition of 'odd' as 'not even' is a satisfactory definition *if* one has already positively defined 'even'.

Accuracy   A definition should be neither too broad nor too narrow. If it is too broad, it applies not only to the things referred to by the definiendum, but to other things also. If it is too narrow, some concepts or things normally referred to by the definiendum will not be referred to by the definiens.

Defining 'pianoforte' as 'a musical instrument that has a keyboard' is too broad; for it fails to eliminate organs, harpsichords, and accordions. The definition 'a three-legged musical instrument which produces sound by means of a keyboard connected to hammers that activate strings by striking them' does

"No *man*, not even a doctor, ever gives any other definition of what a nurse should be than this—'devoted and obedient'. This definition would do just as well for a porter. It might even do for a horse. It would not do for a policeman."

FLORENCE NIGHTINGALE

On what grounds is the definition of 'nurse' being criticised? What are the social and political implications of the definition and what is the political message of the criticism?

successfully eliminate organs, harpsichords, and accordions. Unfortunately, it also eliminates upright pianos.

It is possible to fail on both counts simultaneously, especially with short definitions, such as 'eating implement' as a definition of 'knife'. This definition is too narrow, since it rules out woodcarving knives, penknives, and so forth; and it is also too broad, because it includes forks and spoons. Such errors result when a definition fails to mention the most telling characteristic of the thing named by the definiendum, which, in the case of the knife, is that it is an instrument used for cutting. This criterion applies not only to reportive definitions, but also to stipulative, precising, and other kinds of definition. For example, the precising definition of 'old' as meaning 'at least thirty years of age' is too broad.

In content and phrasing, the definiens should be as similar as possible to the definiendum. If the definiendum carries certain positive or negative overtones, these should be conveyed or described by the definiens, unless the definition is a persuasive definition, in which case, for obvious reasons, entirely different overtones may be used.

Clarity   The following definition of the concept of deception is taken from an excellent dictionary and observes all the criteria for good definitions we have mentioned so far:

> Die arglistige Erregung oder Erhaltung eines Irrtums in einem anderen durch bewusste Angabe falscher oder Unterdrückung wahrer Tatsachen.*

It has just been demonstrated that a definition, however good it is in all other respects, must also be understandable to those for whom it is intended. One must try to gauge the knowledge and the vocabulary of the intended audience and then frame the definition accordingly. A definiens couched in unknown or unfamiliar terms is as unenlightening as the definiens of a circular definition.

---

* Knaurs Konversationslexikon.

EXERCISE 1–10   *Indicate which criterion or criteria (noncircularity, affirmativeness, accuracy, clarity, or neutrality) is violated by each of the following definitions.*

1. A teacher to his fifth-grade students: "A protester is a person who protests."
2. A student in a college physics course to another student in the course: "Velocity is how fast something travels."
3. A science teacher to his fifth-grade students: "Velocity is equal to acceleration times time."
4. A logic student to another logic student: "Valid means justifiable or well-founded."
5. A doctor to a patient: "A depressant is not a stimulant."
6. A logic professor to his students: "Vagueness is the quality or state of being vague."
7. A prosecutor to a jury: "A defendant is one who is on trial because he has committed a crime."
8. A biology student to another student: "Genetics is the science that deals with inheritance."
9. A science teacher to his sixth grade students: "A layman is someone who is not trained as a scientist."
10. An English major to another student: "Vainglorious refers to someone who is characterized by vainglory."
11. Father to his teenage son: "A jury is a group of people at a criminal trial."
12. A member of a sailing club to a new member: "A schooner is a large sailing ship."
13. A craft enthusiast talking to a friend who knows nothing about weaving: "A warp is the opposite of woof."
14. A worker at an international currency exchange to a visiting German tourist: "A penny is one-hundredth of a dollar."
15. A San Franciscan to a French visitor who speaks little English: "A church is an edifice used as a place of worship by a religious group, usually Christian."

CONSISTENCY AND KINDS OF DISAGREEMENT

Although we have indicated that the primary concern of logic is with arguments, defined as sets of statements asserted as premises in support of specific conclusions, logic also deals with a fundamental relation between two statements known as 'consistency'. Two statements are **consistent** when it is possible for both to be true at the same time. Two statements are thus **inconsistent** if it is impossible for them both to be true. For example, assuming that they are being used in their normal way in the same context, the following two sentences express *inconsistent* propositions:

> *Oxygen is a basic chemical element.*
> *Oxygen is not a basic chemical element.*

If one of these statements is true, the other must be false. In contrast, the following two statements are consistent because the truth or falsity of one says nothing about the truth or falsity of the other, and it is possible for both to be true.

> *Oxygen is a basic chemical element.*
> *Hydrogen is a basic chemical element.*

Logicians traditionally have placed a high value on consistency, and it is widely accepted that, if an individual holds two beliefs which are logically inconsistent, one or the other must ultimately be rejected. Some people argue, however, that there is nothing wrong with inconsistencies and that they must not only be tolerated but must be recognized as accurately reflecting the "nature of reality." Although such a view has recently been presented as a "new contribution" to Western cultures from Oriental traditions, the significance and value of strict adherence to consistency has been critically questioned throughout the history of the Western intellectual tradition.

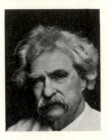

"I am persuaded that the world has been tricked into adopting some false and most pernicious notions about consistency—and to such a degree that the average man has turned the rights and wrongs of things entirely around, and is proud to be 'consistent,' unchanging, immovable, fossilized, where it should be his humiliation that he is so."

The Complete Essays of Mark Twain. Charles Neider, ed. (Garden City, N.Y.: Doubleday, 1963), p. 583.

It is important to recognize that the logical concept of consistency is not the same as, and in some ways is quite at odds with, one everyday notion of consistency—that of constancy or unchangeability. This is the concept which Mark Twain is attacking in the quotation in the box and which is being used by the drowning ant in the cartoon. In contrast to the everyday concept, the logical concept of consistency requires flexibility and change insofar as, whenever two statements are determined to be logically inconsistent, one of them must be rejected as false, as the King of Id is asserting in the cartoon. A person who does

"The Wizard of Id" by permission of Johnny Hart and Field Enterprises, Inc.

The concept of consistency, as used in this cartoon, is that of lack of change. It can be related to the logical concept of consistency only by positing a general principle such as 'Everything that happens to this ant is bad'. Then the two statements describing his predicaments—'He is drowning' and 'He is about to be eaten by an anteater'—are not only logically consistent with one another (which is a trivial fact) but they are also logically consistent with the general principle. The logical relations between such particular and general statements are discussed in detail in Chapters 10 and 12.

"B.C." by permission of Johnny Hart and Field Enterprises, Inc.

The inconsistency in this cartoon is grounded in the fact about the world that it is impossible to press down and pull up on something simultaneously. It is not clear that the situation may involve a logical inconsistency or impossibility.

"Freddy" by Rupe. Copyright 1974 Field Enterprises, Inc. Courtesy of Field Newspaper Syndicate.

not apply the logical concept of consistency essentially never has to change his or her position, since both a proposition and its denial can be accepted. Nothing can require such a person to reconsider any of his beliefs, since they are all simultaneously acceptable. Such a person could never even become involved in a disagreement with another person, because he would have no real grounds for challenging another's position. Few people, if any, actually place no value on the concept of logical consistency.

It is a basic fact that most of us do find ourselves involved in disagreements with other persons from time to time and also experience "inner conflicts" within ourselves. Therefore, it is important for us to be able to distinguish between real disagreements and conflict situations resulting from various kinds of misunderstanding.

EXERCISE 1–11   *Indicate which of the following pairs of statements are logically consistent and which are logically inconsistent. Assume A and B are expressed by different persons.*

1. *A:* I think strawberry tastes better than any other flavor of ice cream.
   B: I think chocolate tastes better than any other flavor of ice cream.
2. *A:* Strawberry is better than any other flavor of ice cream.
   B: Chocolate is better than any other flavor of ice cream.
3. *A:* Strawberry tastes better to me than any other flavor of ice cream.
   B: Chocolate tastes better to me than any other flavor of ice cream.
4. *A:* This van Gogh painting of sunflowers in a vase is a famous piece of modern art.
   B: It's famous, yes, but it's not modern. It was painted in 1888.
5. *A:* Zebras are more white than black.
   B: No, zebras are more black than white.

6. *A:* I think zebras are white.
   B: I think zebras are black.
7. *Fred:* I am a careful, conscientious worker.
   John: Fred is neurotically fussy about his work.
8. *A:* Senator Fulbright was a liberal: he opposed the war in Vietnam.
   B: Senator Fulbright was not a liberal: he was slow to support civil rights legislation.
9. *Amos:* Now, Clem, you've lived all your life in the state of Maine.
   Clem: Not yet.
10. *A:* Thoreau's book *Walden* is interesting.
    B: Thoreau's book *Walden* is boring.
11. (Police getting descriptions of a robber from two witnesses)
    Six-foot-eight basketball player: He was a short, chubby, middle-aged man with a beard.
    Five-foot-two grandmother: He was a big, fat, youngish man with a beard.
12. (Around a campfire at night in the woods)
    A: I saw something moving in the woods: I think it was a bear!
    B: I think you only saw the moving shadows cast by the campfire.
13. (Campfire again)
    A: There's a *bear* out there in the woods! I *saw* it!
    B: You're crazy, there's no bear in these woods!
14. *A:* I hate Tom! How could he do a thing like that to me?
    B: You don't really mean it; you're just very upset right now.
15. *A:* The sun looks larger when it's close to the horizon than when it's overhead.
    B: No, it's not any larger. It has an angular width of half a degree, no matter where it's located in the sky.

Real versus Apparent Disagreements

The first thing that must be done in trying to analyze, evaluate, and resolve disagreements in ordinary language is to agree on what is really being said. Otherwise, we are likely to waste time, energy, and tempers in knocking down claims our opponent never intended to make or in passionately defending a position that is not the one being attacked. Such a procedure may score us points for verbal cleverness, but it probably will not be very effective in convincing our opponent that we are right.

To begin with, then, we need to formulate the positions of both (or all) disputants as fully, clearly, and sympathetically as possible. Once the position of each disputant is accurately stated, it is possible to determine whether the disagreement is real or only apparent. A **real disagreement** is one in which the statements of the disputants' positions are logically inconsistent—that is, one in which it is logically impossible for both to be true at the same time. For example, assume that persons A and B make the following assertions:

> *A:* ***The moon is made of green cheese.***
> *B:* ***The moon is not made of green cheese.***

Obviously, if either of these statements is true, the other must be false. Therefore, this is a case of real disagreement between A and B.

On the other hand, if the statements of the disputants are not logically inconsistent—if it is possible for both of them to be true at the same time—we have an **apparent disagreement** or **pseudo-disagreement:**

> A: *I believe the moon is made of green cheese.*
> B: *I don't believe the moon is made of green cheese.*

Here the statements are not logically inconsistent. They are statements about the speakers' beliefs, not about the composition of the earth's satellite; and it is perfectly possible for A to believe one thing and B to believe its opposite. So long as the argument remains in these terms, it is a pseudo-disagreement.

This is not to say that A and B are really in perfect harmony. Their beliefs are diametrically opposed to one another, so they are clearly in conflict over the matter. But so long as each one merely describes what he or she believes, and does not assert that belief as a fact, the conflict is not one that can be dealt with logically. This is what we mean by calling it an apparent disagreement or pseudo-disagreement.

It is quite possible, though, to have a real disagreement about what a particular individual believes:

> A: *I believe the moon is made of green cheese.*
> B: *A does not really believe the moon is made of green cheese.*

Here we have two logically inconsistent statements about a single person's belief, and hence a real disagreement.

Some of life's more useless arguments are waged over statements which may appear on the surface to be logically inconsistent and are not:

> A: *That ball is red.*
> B: *That ball is blue.*

A request for clarification could result in reformulations such as the following:

> A: *I am receiving a sensation of a red spherical object here and now.*
> B: *I am receiving a sensation of a blue spherical object here and now.*

Since we now are talking about sensations received by two individuals, it is easier to see that the argument might be a pseudo-disagreement, because the statements now deal with individual perceptions and not with assertions of fact. It is when each party draws, from his or her sensations about part of the ball, an inference about the "real" color of the *whole* ball that a genuine disagreement arises. In a situation such as this, when two inconsistent statements are inferred from two consistent statements, there must be something wrong with the mode of inference, and the logician may be able to help by pointing out the error in reasoning. In the present case, a more correct pair of inferences would be from the reconstructed statements to the following:

> A: *The part of the ball that I see is red.*
> B: *The part of the ball that I see is blue.*

These statements are still logically consistent, and would probably suggest to their speakers the solution of the "disagreement"—that the ball is half red and half blue.

The distinction between perception and reality is especially important in the area of group dynamics and interpersonal communication. For example, consider the following:

> A: *B is always trying to pick a fight.*
> B: *That's not so! I never try to pick a fight.*

If A and B can be induced to examine the matter from a different perspective, they might restate their positions as follows:

> A: *I perceive B's behavior as an attempt to pick a fight.*
> B: *I do not intend my behavior as an attempt to pick a fight.*

The statements expressed by these sentences, unlike the original ones, are not logically inconsistent. What appeared to be a real, and rather nasty, disagreement about B's intentions has been revealed as a pseudo-disagreement stemming from two different perceptions of his behavior. We are not yet told why these perceptions differ—perhaps A and B come from two different cultural backgrounds which put different interpretations on certain kinds of language and gesture. But once both parties recognize that what A perceives may not be what B intends, there is considerably more chance that each can at least learn to understand accurately what the other is trying to say.

Verbal Disagreements   As with all logical analyses, it is important to make sure in any dispute that the words are being used with the same meaning by both sides. This must be done before we can tell whether we are dealing with a real or a pseudo-disagreement. For instance:

> A: *Half the people in the United States are poor.*
> B: *One-fifth of the people in the United States are poor.*

This may or may not be a real disagreement. If it turns out that A interprets 'poor' to mean 'receiving less than the median income', and B interprets it to mean 'receiving less than $1,000 per person per year', it is possible that both statements may be true. Logicians have given to this kind of pseudo-disagreement—one in which a key word or phrase is being used with different meanings—the name **merely verbal disagreement.**

A merely verbal disagreement is resolved—or dissolved—as soon as it is recognized that the two parties are using a key word or phrase with different meanings. However, the recognition of such a merely verbal dispute can lead to another sort of dispute—this time over the meanings themselves. Note the difference between the following pairs of statements:

> *A:* **I am using the word 'poor' to mean 'receiving less than the median income'.**
> *B:* **I am using the word 'poor' to mean 'receiving less than $1,000 per person per year'.**
>
> *A:* **The word 'poor' means 'receiving less than the median income'.**
> *B:* **The word 'poor' means 'receiving less than $1,000 per person per year'.**

In the first case there is only a pseudo-disagreement, for both statements can be true; but in the second case, there ia a real disagreement, if both A and B are asserting that their definition is a factual report of *the* meaning that most native-English speakers associate with the word 'poor'. (But since the word 'means' itself has several meanings, even this could still be a merely verbal dispute.)

EXERCISE 1–12   *Indicate whether each of the following pairs of sentences exemplifies a real or apparent disagreement, and if apparent, whether the disagreement is merely verbal. If you regard a disagreement as apparent rather than real, explain why.*

---

1. *Mike:* I have strong opinions about politics.
   Pete: I am not very interested in politics.
2. *Person A:* I think *Rhoda* is a boring show.
   Person B: I think *Rhoda* is a very entertaining show.
3. *Person A:* The Smiths are a poor family.
   Person B: The Smiths are not a poor family.
   (Persons A and B agree that the total income of the Smith family is $4,800 per year.)
4. *Person A:* President Nixon was impeached, since charges were brought against him by the House Judiciary Committee.
   Person B: President Nixon was not impeached, since he was not tried in the Senate and found guilty of the charges made against him.
5. *Pete:* When I see Bob, I'm going to punch him in the nose for what he told Susan about me.
   Mike: You don't really mean that; you're just upset right now; you'll get over it.

6. *Father:* Listen, son, would you shut off that blasting radio. I can't think with all that noise.
    Son: That's not noise, dad. That's the Eagles' new hit.
7. *Person A:* A straw looks bent when it is placed in a glass of water.
    Person B: No, the straw isn't bent. It's just as straight as it was before.
8. *Person A:* I saw Fred with Marsha last night.
    Person B: You saw Bob, Fred's identical twin, with Marsha last night.
9. *Person A:* Cairn terriers are the smallest dogs.
    Person B: Scotties are the smallest dogs.
10. *Person A:* I saw a strange object in the sky; I think it was a flying saucer.
    Person B: What you saw was a space satellite.
11. *Person A:* There was a flying saucer in the sky five minutes ago; I saw it with my own eyes.
    Person B: You're out of your mind; there are no such things as flying saucers.
12. *Person A:* Federico Fellini's first film was *Juliet of the Spirits.*
    Person B: Federico Fellini's first film was *Amarcord.*
13. *Person A:* Duchamp's painting *Nude Descending the Staircase* is a masterpiece.
    Person B: It's not a masterpiece; it's not even a hundred years old.
14. *Person A:* Dr. Jekyll and Mr. Hyde were really the same person; the physical appearance of the body is all that changed.
    Person B: No, Dr. Jekyll and Mr. Hyde were two different persons; they both lived in the same body and the body changed appearance when one person was dominant.
15. *Person A:* The sun looks like it revolves around the earth.
    Person B: No, the earth revolves around the sun.
16. *Person A:* Mercury is smaller than Venus in circumference.
    Person B: Mercury is larger than Venus in circumference.
17. *Person A:* John is an excellent student; he got an A in English last semester.
    Person B: John is a terrible student; he got a D in Biology last semester.
18. *Person A:* Robert is a very well-educated person.
    Person B: Robert is not a very well-educated person.
    (Persons A and B agree that Robert has only a high school diploma.)
19. *Person A:* I think *The Tempest* is a great play.
    Person B: I think *The Tempest* is a terrible play.
20. *Person A:* President Ford was a conservative because he opposed school busing.
    Person B: President Ford was not a conservative because he favored a tax rebate.

IMPLICATION

A second fundamental logical relation between statements, and one that is of equal importance with consistency, is that of **implication.** In logic, one statement is said to *imply* another if and only if it is impossible for the first statement to be true and the second false. To illustrate this relation, let us look at the following two statements:

> **All dogs are beagles.**
> **Some dogs are beagles.**

A moment's thought should make it clear that, if statement 1 is true, then statement 2 must also be true. That is, it is impossible for it to be true that all dogs are beagles *and* false that some dogs are beagles. Thus, by our definition, the first statement *implies* the second statement. However, the second statement does *not* imply the first statement, because it is possible for it to be true that some dogs are beagles and also be false that all dogs are beagles.

LOGICAL EQUIVALENCE Although in our example in the previous section, the first statement implied the second but the second did not imply the first, it is possible for two statements to imply one another, as in the following example.

No cats are dogs.
No dogs are cats.

These statements are such that, if the first statement is true, the second must also be true and vice versa. That is, it is impossible for either one of these statements to be true while the other is false. One definition of **logical equivalence** is that two statements are logically equivalent if and only if they are such that, whenever one is true then the other must be true, and whenever one is false then the other must be false.

It is important to recognize that two logically equivalent statements do not necessarily have exactly the same meaning. This concept refers only to certain similarities in logical structure between the two statements. Thus, for example, the following two statements are logically equivalent, but they clearly do not have exactly the same meanings.

This animal is either a horse or not a horse.
Lee Harvey Oswald did not both kill John
Kennedy and not kill John Kennedy.

INDEPENDENCE A final significant logical relation that can hold between two statements is that of *independence*. Two statements are logically **independent** of one another if and only if the truth or falsity of one has no relation whatsoever to the truth or falsity of the other. That is, neither statement implies the other, *and* the statements are not inconsistent. Thus, if we know that one statement is true, this tells us nothing about the truth or falsity of the other. And, if we know that one is false, we likewise know nothing about the truth or falsity of the other.

This animal is not a horse.
Lee Harvey Oswald killed John Kennedy.

All the logical relations between statements discussed above will be dealt with again in later chapters of this book.

EXERCISE 1–13 *Determine for each of the following pairs of statements whether A implies B, B implies A, A is logically equivalent to B, or A and B are independent.*

---

 1. A: All students share the spirit of learning.
   B: Some students share the spirit of learning.

2. A: All sailboats are powered by the wind.
    B: Some boats are powered by outboard motors.
3. A: That equation is not a physical law.
    B: Calculus is useful when expressing physical laws.
4. A: All dogs are mammals or not mammals.
    B: All autos are four-wheeled or not four-wheeled.
5. A: Some nonprofessionals are dedicated.
    B: All nonprofessionals are dedicated.
6. A: That tire is brand-new.
    B: That tire is flat.
7. A: All atoms have protons.
    B: Some atoms have electrons.
8. A: No elements are chemical compounds.
    B: No chemical compounds are elements.
9. A: No existential philosophers are people who dismiss the notion of Being.
    B: Some existential philosophers are not people who dismiss the notion of Being.
10. A: Snowshoes are designed only for walking on snow.
    B: Snowshoes are made much larger than the average foot.
11. A: No poems are prose.
    B: No prose is a poem.
12. A: All sports activities have had increased participation.
    B: Sales on new hockey equipment has increased sharply.
13. A: All photons have mass or do not have mass.
    B: All photons are associated with electromagnetic radiation and not associated with electromagnetic radiation.
14. A: Buddhism cannot be expressed in terms of a comprehensive philosophy.
    B: Most Buddhist ideas lack any connection with Western philosophy.
15. A: The Greek mathematician Pythagorus did not derive the Pythagorean theorem.
    B: Johannes Kepler believed that Pythagorus did derive the Pythagorean theorem.

EXERCISE 1–14

Consider and discuss the following statements with other students in the class. In particular, try to determine which statements are analytic and which synthetic, and, among those that are synthetic, decide how if at all the burden of proof might be placed on opponents to prove their falsity. Also, discuss how one might prove the truth of each of the synthetic statements, and, finally, construct an argument that you believe is the most reasonable that can be given in support of each statement.

---

1. The real difference between democracy and oligarchy is poverty and wealth. Wherever men rule by reason of their wealth, whether they be few or many, that is an oligarchy, and where the poor rule, that is a democracy. (Aristotle)
2. When a white man governs himself, that is self-government. But when he governs himself and also governs some other men, that is worse than self-government—that is despotism. What I do mean to say is that no man is good enough to govern another man without that other's consent. (Abraham Lincoln)
3. Enslave the liberty of but one human being and the liberties of the world are put in peril. (William Lloyd Garrison)

4. To be governed is to be watched, inspected, spied, directed, law-ridden, regulated, penned up, indoctrinated, preached at, checked, appraised, seized, censured, commanded by beings who have neither title nor knowledge nor virtue. (Pierre Joseph Proudhon)

5. Every great advance in natural knowledge has involved the absolute rejection of authority. *Lay Sermons, 1870.* (Thomas Huxley)

6. If the poor man is not able to support his suit according to the vexations and expensive manner established in civilized countries, has not the rich as great an advantage over him as the strong has over the weak in a state of nature? (Edmund Burke)

7. When great changes occur in history, when great principles are involved, as a rule the majority are wrong. The minority are right. (Eugene V. Debs)

8. If Negro freedom is taken away, or that of any minority group, the freedom of all the people is taken away. (Paul Robeson)

9. If the welfare of the living majority is paramount, it can only be on the ground that the majority have the power in their hands. (Oliver Wendell Holmes)

10. *Homo sapiens,* the only creature endowed with reason, is also the only creature to pin its existence on things unreasonable. *Two Sources of Morality and Religion,* (Henri Bergson)

11. The ignorance of the working-class and the superior intelligence of the privileged class are superstitions—are superstitions fostered by intellectual mercenaries, by universities and churches, and by all the centers of privilege. (George D. Herron)

12. You can always get the truth from an American statesman after he has turned seventy, or given up all hope of the Presidency. *Speech, November 7, 1860.* (Wendell Phillips)

13. All life is an experiment. (Oliver Wendell Holmes)

14. He who is unable to live in society, or who has no need because he is sufficient for himself, must be either a beast or a god; he is no part of a state. (Aristotle)

15. Freedom is the absolute right of all adult men and women to seek permission for their action only from their own conscience and reason, and to be determined in their actions only by their own will, and consequently to be responsible only to themselves, and then to the society to which they belong, but only insofar as they have made a free decision to belong to it. (Mikhail A. Bakunin)

16. If reason is a universal faculty, the decision of the common mind is the nearest criterion of truth. (George Bancroft)

17. For I do not seek to understand that I may believe, but I believe in order to understand. For this I believe—that unless I believe, I should not understand. (Saint Anselm)

18. Wages is a cunning device of the devil, for the benefit of tender consciences, who would retain all the advantages of the slave system, without the expense, trouble, and odium of being slave-holders. (Orestes A. Brownson)

19. The history of mankind is a history of repeated injuries and usurpations on the part of man toward woman, having in direct object the establishment of a tyranny over her. (Women's Rights Convention), *Manifesto, Seneca Falls, 1848.*

SUMMARY

1. Language has many uses. In this book we will be concerned only with sentences that are being used to express propositions which appear in arguments. To determine what, in ordinary language, is within the domain of the logician, systems have been developed for classifying ordinary language usage. One such classification is to categorize the uses of ordinary language as cognitive or noncognitive.

2. A sentence is **cognitive** when it is being used to express a proposition. Cognitive uses of language in everyday contexts include explaining, classifying, asserting, and so on. Statements of personal beliefs, attitudes, and feelings may also involve a cognitive use of language.

3. A sentence is said to be **noncognitive** when it is used to do something other than express a statement or proposition. Noncognitive uses of language involve such acts as issuing commands or giving orders, making requests, asking questions, and arousing emotions.

4. The context in which language is used is the most important criterion for determining whether or not it is being used to express a statement or proposition and is, therefore, logically analyzable. However, it is possible to have language which has mixed uses within a particular context.

5. A **sentence** is a physical and linguistic entity which can be used to convey meaning and perform a variety of tasks in different contexts. A **statement** or **proposition** is an assertion, description, or piece of information about which it can properly be said that it is true or false. A statement can be expressed by certain sentences in certain contexts; different statements can be expressed by the same sentence; and different sentences can express the same statement. Logical analysis can not only identify the logical relations between statements, but it can also identify special kinds of statements whose truth or falsity is determined entirely by their internal logical structure.

6. When we insist that someone give reasons in support of a particular statement, we are trying to place the **burden of proof** on that person. Informal conventions and sometimes even formal rules exist in every culture which help to determine where the burden of proof for various kinds of statements normally rests.

7. **Supported statements** are statements which require evidence in their support. Statements which require no additional proof are **self-supporting statements;** the burden of proof concerning such statements falls on persons challenging their truth. Axioms and self-reports are examples of self-supporting statements.

8. Analytic statements are an important kind of self-supporting statement. There are two types of **analytic statement:** those which are true or false by virtue of their logical form are called **syntactically analytic** propositions; and those which are true or false by definition (that is, by virtue of the meanings of the words in the statements) are called **semantically analytic** propositions. A statement which is neither syntactically nor semantically analytic is called a **synthetic** or **contingent proposition.** Such statements are used as statements about the world, and their truth or falsity is usually ascertained through empirical observation.

9. Definitions enable us to identify and deal with statements whose truth or falsity is determined by the meanings of the words which comprise them. They are also important in evaluating arguments in everyday contexts; in determining whether a given sentence expresses a proposition and is thus analyzable; and in determining whether two or more expressions have the same meaning. Meaning and the definition of words may also have a powerful effect on the practical course of people's lives.

10. In logic, all definitions are primarily used to define words, not concepts or

ideas. The term that is to be defined is called the **definiendum.** The word or words used to define it are called the **definiens.** When formulating a definition, it is important to specify the context in which the definiendum is being used. A definition may be classified as one of several kinds, depending on the type of definiens being used.

11. A **synonymous definition** is one in which the definiens consists of only one word or phrase which in appropriate contexts can be used interchangeably with the definiendum. We are thus using a special meaning of the term 'synonymous', since, as it is used in everyday discourse, any adequate definition is such that its definiens is synonymous with its definiendum.

12. **Enumerative definitions** are divided into two categories, according to the manner in which the definiens is presented; **ostensive definitions,** which present the meaning of the definiendum by providing concrete examples or appropriate sensory experiences; and **denotative definitions,** which name examples of things to which the definiendum applies, without requiring the physical presence of the definiens.

13. The definiens in a **connotative definition** pinpoints the meaning of the definiendum by listing a set of properties common to all the things to which the definiendum can be correctly applied, and common only to those things. The sum total of a definiendum's essential properties is variously called the **intension** or the **connotation** of the definiendum. An increase in the intension of a definition (the adding of properties) will either diminish the **denotation (extension)** or leave it unchanged; a decrease in the intension of a definition (the elimination of some of the properties named by the definiens) will either increase the denotation or leave it unchanged.

14. A **definition by genus and difference** is a type of connotative definition which consists of specifying the general class of things to which the definiendum belongs (the genus), and then further specifying the properties (the differentia or difference) by which the definiendum can be distinguished from the other things that belong to the same class. This type of definition is especially useful in any field of study which has been exhaustively classified.

15. Connotative definitions must list the **essential attributes** of a definiendum. 'Essential attributes' is a relative term which can be defined as 'those attributes which, when included in the definiens, are most informative, most characteristic of the definiendum, and least open to misinterpretation'. An attribute is essential if it is judged to be essential to the thing itself.

16. In an **operational definition,** the definiens provides a test or a formal procedure which is to be followed in order to determine the applicability of the definiendum.

17. Definitions can serve a variety of functions. A **reportive** or **lexical definition** is used to report the meaning of a term as it is used and understood by a specific group. It can be enumerative, connotative, synonymous, or operational; and it can be judged as being true or false according to whether it accurately reports the way the word is actually used and interpreted by the group in question. A limited reportive definition reports the way a term is used in a technical or otherwise limited context; for instance, a **theoretical definition** defines a word in terms of the meaning which it carries in a particular scientific theory. Some words have both lexical and theoretical

definitions; others are used and understood only in terms of their theoretical definitions. A **legal definition** is one that is specified in laws as formulated by a legislative, judicial, or executive body. It serves a limited reportive function when it is used in reference to a law that already exists and to a definition which is generally accepted.

18. A **stipulative definition** introduces new meaning. It may define either a newly coined word or a word which has a generally accepted meaning, but which is now being used in a new sense. Since there is no precedent for the newly stipulated use of a word, a stipulative definition cannot be true or false. It can be judged good if it achieves the specific purpose for which it was introduced and bad if it does not.

19. **Ambiguity** is said to exist when a word or phrase having two or more distinct meanings is used in such a way that it is not obvious from the context which meaning is intended. **Vagueness** exists when the meaning of a term is sufficiently imprecise that it is impossible to tell whether or not it applies to certain **borderline cases.** Definitions which are used to eliminate ambiguity or vagueness are called **precising definitions** and can be of any of the kinds of definition previously mentioned. They are evaluated according to how well they eliminate ambiguity or vagueness without distorting the generally accepted meaning of the word.

20. Synonymous, enumerative, connotative, and operational definitions may also be used persuasively. **Persuasive definitions** usually reflect the beliefs or persuasive intent of the speaker; they are usually intended to influence someone else's evaluation of the definiendum and to affect other people's behavior in some significant way. They are thus often used to achieve various social and political goals.

21. There are some general criteria for good definitions which can be applied to any definiens. A good definition is not **circular;** that is, the definiens does not contain the word that is to be defined, nor does it contain a grammatical variation of the same word. An **affirmative** definiens (one which states those attributes applicable to the word being defined) is generally more efficient at pinpointing a definiendum than a negative definiens (one which states what is inapplicable to the word being defined). A definition should be **accurate**—neither too broad nor too narrow. The definiens must also be **clear**—free from any vagueness or ambiguities which can reasonably be removed; and, unless the definition is a persuasive one, the definiens should convey or describe any positive or negative overtones carried by the definiendum.

22. There are several significant logical relations which can hold between just two statements. Two statements are **consistent** when it is possible for both of them to be true at the same time; if they can't both be true, then they are **inconsistent.** One statement logically **implies** another statement if and only if it is impossible for the first statement to be true and the second false. Two statements are **logically equivalent** if and only if each implies the other; that is, if one is true then the other must be true and if one is false then the other must be false. Two statements are logically **independent** of one another if and only if the truth or falsity of neither statement implies the other *and* the statements are not inconsistent.

23. A **real disagreement** is one in which the statements of the disputants' positions are logically inconsistent—that is, one in which it is logically impossible for both to be true at the same time. An **apparent disagreement** or **pseudo-disagreement** is one in which the statements of the disputants' positions are not logically inconsistent—that is, one in which it is logically possible for both to be true at the same time. A **merely verbal disagreement** is a type of pseudo-disagreement in which a key word or phrase is being used with different meanings.

CHAPTER TWO

Informal Analysis of Arguments

The Introduction to this book began with an example of an argument as follows:

> *If you are reading this page, you are probably taking a logic course, and if you are taking such a course you will probably get a grade in it. Since you are reading this page you will probably get a grade in a logic course.*

A second argument related to it is:

> *If you are taking a logic course for a grade, then you will have to take at least one exam. You are taking a logic course for a grade, so you will have to take at least one exam.*

It is to be hoped that, if you are indeed in such a situation, you will not find yourself in the predicament of the student in the "Mad Morality" cartoon on the next page.

Although it may appear at first glance that the father is presenting an argument, a more careful analysis indicates that he is probably only making an assertion or command to the effect that the son should spend more time studying for the exam (and perhaps also less time worrying about it) so that he will do better on it. In contrast, it may appear at first as if the son is only asking questions, whereas reconsideration makes it seem likely that he is expressing an argument which might be reformulated as

> *If I'm very upset, then I can't study for my exam.*
> *I'm very upset.*
> *Therefore, I can't study for my exam.*

This example should be sufficient to suggest that it is important to spend more time developing our skills for identifying arguments, which is the primary objective of this chapter.

It was indicated in the Introduction that, in the most general sense of the term, an argument is any set of statements such that one or more of them support or provide evidence for the truth of another statement. In clarifying and elaborating on this rough definition, it is necessary to begin by indicating some senses of the term 'argument' with which you are probably already familiar and which are quite distinct and different from the sense of the term as we will be using it in this book.

When two persons assert logically inconsistent statements, that is, when they are involved in a real disagreement as discussed at the end of the previous chapter, it would be quite proper in ordinary English discourse to say that they are involved in an argument. Thus, if person A were to assert that 'The government should pay for abortions for women on welfare who want them', and person B asserted that 'The government should not pay for abortions for anyone', we could correctly say that they were arguing. However, in the context of this book, we will *not* be using the term 'argument' to refer to such disagreements.

In pursuing their disagreement, persons A and B might each resort sooner or later to giving *reasons* in support of their positions. For example, person A might state that the government should pay for abortions for women on welfare *because* women who can afford them can have them at will, and thus women on

The Mad Morality. *Abingdon, 1970, p. 227.*

welfare are victims of economic discrimination if they can't afford abortions. Person B might assert that the government should not pay for abortions for women on welfare *because* abortion is morally wrong and, in paying for them, the state would be supporting an immoral practice. In providing reasons in support of their conflicting statements, the two can be said to be presenting arguments. The sense in which we will be using the term 'argument' in this text is closely related to but not identical with this everyday notion of an argument.

A slightly more detailed specification of the ordinary everyday definition of 'argument' is that given in *The American Heritage Dictionary.*

> **ARGUMENT** — *A course of reasoning aimed at demonstrating the truth or falsity of something.*

This definition certainly qualifies our examples above as arguments, insofar as reasons were being given to support or prove the truth (or falsity) of the position that the government should pay for abortions of women on welfare. But the definition needs several refinements to fit the use of the term 'argument' in formal logic, as we will be studying it in this book.

Formal logic is not concerned with reasoning processes in general, for the study of most reasoning is the domain of psychology. Logicians are not concerned with the psychological process of reasoning; rather they are concerned with relations among statements. Definite connections exist between the psychological processes and the relations among statements, and we will discuss these in more detail here.

INFERENCES AND ARGUMENTS   Notice that the dictionary definition of 'argument' above specifies that an argument is "aimed at" proving something or other. It is important to recognize right away that arguments themselves don't aim at anything. Arguments are sets of statements which can be used by persons towards a variety of ends. The definition does *not* say that the argument aims at anything; it states quite clearly and explicitly that an argument is aimed by someone. You or I or any other person can intend (or believe or hope) that a particular argument can or does prove something; the argument, as a set of statements can intend (or believe or hope) nothing.

The dictionary definition states that an argument is "a course of reasoning." Although this may sound okay at first hearing, it is as mistaken as saying that an argument intends or hopes or believes something. This point can be understood better by considering an example. While walking from her apartment to the library, Susan looks at her watch and notices that it shows the same time as it did when she looked at it earlier in the day. Having made this observation, let us also assume that Susan reacts by saying to herself, "Oh, my watch needs winding." She then winds it, the second hand of the watch begins to move, and she continues on her way, adjusting the time after arriving at the library and checking with the clock in the main entrance hall. In this instance, Susan used nonverbal cues to make an inference. **Inference** is the psychological process of moving from one thought to another presumably related thought; Susan inferred from the observation that the hands had not moved that her watch needed winding. An inference is *not* in itself an argument, but an argument can be constructed that corresponds to any inference. For example, the following argument corresponds to the inference made by Susan:

> *In most instances in the past, if my watch hands did*
> *not move, then my watch needed winding.*
> *The hands of my watch are not moving.*
> *Therefore, probably my watch needs winding.*

Strictly speaking, and logicians try to speak as strictly and precisely as possible, it is only correct to say that persons (or rational beings—possibly chimpanzees, dolphins, and others) make inferences. It is technically incorrect to say that the premises of an argument infer its conclusion. It is correct to say that the premises of an argument imply or support its conclusion. An argument can be constructed which corresponds to every inference, and the inference is only as good as its corresponding argument. The preceding example is both a good inference and a good argument.

REMEMBER

Persons make inferences; they don't imply anything.
Premises imply or support conclusions; they don't
*   infer anything.*

We make inferences almost continually in our everyday life. Using the techniques of formal logic presented in this text to evaluate the arguments corresponding to these inferences can be very helpful in determining whether our reasoning processes are good or bad. One common kind of inference made by students occurs in the context of answering multiple-choice questions on exams (including logic exams!). One of the kinds of reasoning that is often used in answering multiple-choice questions is the process of elimination. Consider how you might think your way through the following multiple-choice question.

> *Sentences being used to express definitions:*
> 1. *are always true.*
> 2. *sometimes are used to express premises of*
>   *arguments.*
> 3. *can never contain more than three words.*
> 4. *appear only in dictionaries.*

Assuming that we can't directly recognize the correct answer, there are a number of ways in which we might try to infer the right answer. For example, we might reason that since one and only one of the four answers can be correct, and since we know from Chapter 1 that some definitions can be false, can contain many words, and can appear in nondictionaries (such as this book), we can reasonably infer that the correct answer is 2. The argument corresponding to this inference is as follows:

> *One and only one of the four answers can be correct.*
> *Answer 1 can't be correct because . . .*
> *Answer 3 can't be correct because . . .*
> *Answer 4 can't be correct because . . .*
> *Therefore answer 2 must be correct.*

If you have not studied Chapter 1 carefully enough to know immediately that 1, 3, and 4 are false, you might reason in a somewhat different way. For example, you might consider that, in your past experience, universal generalizations (that is, statements that something is *always* or *never* the case) are true less often than statements that assert that something is *sometimes* the case (known as a particular statement). You could then infer from this that since 1, 3, and 4 are universal generalizations, the correct answer is probably 2. The argument corresponding to this inference is:

> *One and only one answer can be correct.*
> *Universal generalizations are usually true less often*
> *than "sometimes" statements.*
> *1, 3, and 4 are universal generalizations, and 2 is a*
> *"sometimes" statement.*
> *Therefore, 2 is most probably the correct answer.*

A third way of trying to select the correct answer would be to formulate some kind of a hypothesis about the pattern of answers in the test as a whole. We might, for example, feel fairly confident that our answers to all of the other questions are correct, and we might also notice that of the other 24 answers, 10 are 1s, 6 are 2s, 2 are 3s, and 6 are 4s. We might then reason that, insofar as the person who made up the exam should have tried to distribute the answers as evenly as possible among the four letters, the correct answer should be 3. However, we could also reason that the person who made up the exam had a preference (conscious or unconscious) for 1s and infer from this that the correct answer is most likely 1. The arguments corresponding to these inferences or reasoning processes would be as follows:

> *One and only one answer can be correct.*
> *The correct answers should be distributed fairly*
> *evenly among the four possible letters.*
> *All but one of the questions has been answered, and*
> *there are disproportionately few 3s among them.*
> *Therefore, it is most probable that the remaining*
> *answer is a 3.*

> *One and only one answer can be correct.*
> *The person who made up the exam apparently had a*
>   *conscious or unconscious tendency to make 1 the*
>   *correct answer.*
> *Therefore, it is most likely that the answer to this*
>   *question is 1.*

We will be studying methods for evaluating the quality of such arguments (and their corresponding inferences) in much of the rest of this book.

EXERCISE 2–1   *For each of the following multiple-choice questions, (a) choose one answer, and (b) construct an argument that illustrates the inference you used in your choice of answer.*

---

1. Rugged individualism
   a. is one of the qualities that has contributed to the nation's greatness.
   b. is an outmoded characteristic which cannot be found in our current totalitarian regime.
   c. was coined by T. Veblen.
   d. is a strategic play in rugby.
2. New Orleans' increased use of police to control behavior is an indicator of
   a. societal breakdown.
   b. a police state.
   c. overstaffed police force.
   d. likelihood of disorder during the festivities.
3. Future nuclear energy policies will be best determined by
   a. the public and legislators.
   b. an elitist team of experts.
   c. big business interests.
   d. a combination of the above.
4. Nuclear energy
   a. is dead.
   b. is an issue that remains debatable.
   c. is unquestionably hazardous.
   d. is the only viable answer to the energy shortage.
5. The split-brain theory
   a. is a well-proven scientific fact.
   b. is used to explain the differences between males and females.
   c. explains the duality in humans.
   d. is simply an interpretive metaphor.
6. Chemotherapy
   a. is a recognized cure for cancer.
   b. is recognized by the AMA as a viable treatment for cancer.
   c. is used as an immunosuppressant to cure cancerous growth.
   d. all of the above.
7. Vitamin supplements are
   a. essential to everyone's health.
   b. necessary when one is body building.

    c. proven as cancer cures.
    d. none of the above.
  8. The ecosystem
    a. is limited in its ability to remain stable.
    b. can absorb all pollutants with little repercussion.
    c. does not include rational beings, such as man, as its denizens.
    d. all but one of the above.

[handwritten margin note: Qualification: Statements or propositions are the materials of arguments. Thus, one intention always accompanies an arg.: getting one to believe that such & such is the case]

THE LOGICAL SENSE OF 'ARGUMENT'

Now that we have clarified the distinction between reasoning as a psychological process and as formulating arguments, we are ready to present the formal logical definition of 'argument' with which we will be working in the remainder of this book. In the context of logic, an **argument** is defined as *a set of statements which is such that one of them (the **conclusion**) is supported or implied by the others (the **premises**).* It is important to recognize that this sense of the term 'argument' differs from the dictionary definition discussed earlier insofar as it involves no psychological factors like "aiming at" or "intending" anything. An argument is an argument if it satisfies the above definition, even if no one has ever thought of it, let alone intended that it be used to prove something. Similarly, even if someone intends that a certain set of statements be used to prove something, that set of statements does not constitute an argument unless it satisfies the definition.

[handwritten margin note: To have effective, sound arg., at least two things hold? Go to p. 4 in lecture notes.]

We are in a difficult position at the moment because it is not possible to provide an adequate explanation of the formal logical concept of an argument without actually presenting one or more formal logical systems. Just as our understanding of the everyday concept depends on our understanding of and ability to use the whole system of ordinary English (or some other "natural" language), our understanding of the formal concept of an argument depends on our understanding of a system of formal logic. We have given the formal definition above, but you should not expect to fully understand it until after you have studied some of the later chapters in this book.

Because the dictionary definition of 'argument' (and presumably also the sense in which most of us use the term in everyday life) are quite different from the logical sense, it will be useful to supply a way for talking about the everyday use without confusing it with the logical sense of 'argument'. We shall do this by making explicit the distinction between what a person asserts or intends or believes to be an argument and what is, in fact, an argument. We shall always talk of the latter—which is essentially the same as the dictionary definition—as something that *appears to be* or that *is asserted or intended to be* an argument. We shall reserve the term 'argument' in the remainder of this book to refer only to sets of statements that satisfy our formal definition—that is, to sets of statements which are such that one of them is *in fact* supported or implied by the others. Much of what we will be doing in this book is studying ways of determining whether sets of statements that *appear* to comprise arguments or that are *asserted* to be arguments are *in fact* arguments.

Because of the "looseness" of ordinary languages, it is not always easy to determine when a set of statements is being asserted or intended as an argument in everyday contexts, let alone whether they actually comprise an argument. We have all encountered situations such as that in the accompanying Doonesbury cartoon where it is not at all clear whether a statement or statements are intended to give reasons in support of a conclusion, and where it is even less clear whether they provide any real support. In the cartoon, does the energy administrator's response in any way support or contradict the statement that the energy priority rating system discriminates against the little person? Is it even *intended* to be an argument? Or is it simply an attempt to avoid the question and change the subject?

While this is certainly an extreme example, each of us encounters situations daily where the connection (intended or actual) between statements is not clear, or where the logical relations are not what we thought they were at first glance. To adequately evaluate whether sets of statements in everyday contexts actually comprise arguments, we must use the methods and concepts of formal logic. But there is no simple and direct process for doing this; it is more an art than a science. What is needed is a basic intuitive "feel" for both ordinary language and for formal logic.

We will work on developing this "feel" by discussing in some detail the ways in which people assert in ordinary language that sets of statements are arguments. Once we are able to recognize when a set of statements is being asserted as an argument, we will go on to study some of the different methods for determining whether a given set of statements in fact constitutes an argument in the formal logical sense.

PREMISES AND CONCLUSIONS   It follows directly from our definition of 'argument' that every argument contains one and only one conclusion. So it is reasonable to expect that any set of statements that someone intends or offers as an argument in everyday contexts should also have exactly one conclusion. The following sets of statements all satisfy this requirement. How is it possible to determine which statements are intended as the conclusions and which are intended as the premises?

> 1. Since Sue has always done well in science courses, she will probably do well in logic.
> 2. The negotiations will probably fail, because neither the union nor management is willing to compromise.
> 3. All mammals nurse their young; hence all giraffes nurse their young, for all giraffes are mammals.

[handwritten margin notes: Pick out premises & Conclusions. Key words. Order of premise & conclusions. Read indicators on p. 90.]

In 1, the intended conclusion is 'she will probably do well in logic'; in 2, it is 'the negotiations will probably fail'; in 3, it is 'all giraffes nurse their young'. Identifying the intended conclusions in these examples may seem a simple task, but how was it done? Not in terms of the position of the statement, for the first conclusion follows its premise, the second precedes it, and the third sits squarely between two premises. Nor is there anything in the conclusion statements themselves that differentiates them in kind from the other statements or premises. Rather, the conclusion was recognized by its relation to the other statements, the way in which it is used in the purported argument. It is the statement the others seem to be leading up to.

Consequently, the identification of a particular statement as an intended conclusion is relative to the context in which it is being used. The next time we come across the same statement it may be serving a different function:

> 4. Given that all giraffes nurse their young, and that a baby giraffe has just been born at the zoo, it can be inferred that the mother giraffe will nurse it.

Now the conclusion of 3 has become a premise in 4. The same statement may be a conclusion in one context and a premise in another.

An important clue to the identification of premises and conclusions is sometimes provided by the use of **indicator words.** Not all arguments or purported arguments contain them, but when they are present they are a fairly reliable guide to the intended relationships between statements. The four examples above do contain such words.

> 1. Since *Sue has always* . . .
> 2. . . . because *neither the union* . . .
> 3. . . . hence *all giraffes nurse* . . . for *all giraffes are mammals.*
> 4. Given that *all giraffes* . . . it can be inferred *that the mother* . . .

'Since', 'because', 'for', and 'given that' usually indicate that the statement which follows is a premise; 'hence' and 'it can be inferred that' usually signal the approach of a conclusion.

An indicator word, then, is one which tells us the function that the following (and sometimes preceding) statement is intended to serve. There are many other indicator words, of course, in addition to those already mentioned. Common ones include:

Conclusion indicators: *thus, as a result, consequently, accordingly, it follows that, implies that, therefore*
Premise indicators: *due to, insofar as, inasmuch as, in view of, as shown by, on the assumption that, can be inferred from*

EXERCISE 2–2   *Identify (a) the conclusion, and (b) the premise(s) of each of the following sets of statements which you can assume are intended as arguments.*

---

1. Spiders are not insects, because insects have only six legs.
2. $X + Y = 6$ and $X = 4$, therefore $Y = 2$.
3. Frank could never become a policeman. He is only five feet two inches tall and weighs only 120 pounds.
4. This cannot be Pinot Chardonnay, for it is a red wine.
5. Tom will never be able to climb the face of that cliff. He has had no training in rock climbing.
6. The defendant is insane. Therefore, he is not guilty.
7. Some mammals can fly, since bats can fly.
8. Since Mr. Scott is a judge, it follows that he is a lawyer.
9. This figure is a pentagon, so the sum of its interior angles is 540 degrees.
10. The Vietnam War was futile, since neither side really won.
11. That is not a good French dictionary, because it does not show how each word should be pronounced.
12. The flu is caused by a virus; consequently it can't be cured with antibiotics.
13. Coffee keeps people awake; hence it must contain a stimulant.
14. Tom will not be able to go to the New Year's Eve party at the club, due to the fact that he is not a member.
15. It will take two seconds for that rock to fall, since it is going to fall a distance of sixty-four feet.
16. The housing bill will never come to a vote on the floor of Congress, since the opposition has enough votes to kill it in committee.
17. That this solution is an acid can be inferred from the fact that it turns litmus paper red.
18. Composers do not have to be able to hear music in order to write it, as can be shown by the fact that Beethoven was deaf.
19. Starvation will inevitably occur somewhere in the world, inasmuch as the expanding world population will eventually increase beyond the capacity of the total world agricultural resources to feed it.

20.   This flint knife we found at our excavation site has to be older than 2500 B.C., for it was found three layers below the layer we dated at 2500 B.C.

21.   The functioning of an expanding industrial system depends on an abundance of raw materials; hence our industrial system will eventually cease to expand since raw materials are running out.

22.   A square circle is a logical contradiction; thus, not even an infinitely powerful being could make one.

23.   Given that the defendant was not present at the scene of the crime, it can clearly be inferred that he did not commit the crime.

24.   We can expect the home opener to be cancelled, due to the fact that is raining and has been for the past two days.

25.   The fact that men are free implies that they are responsible.

26.   Oil is becoming more expensive and plastics are made from oil; therefore, plastics are becoming more expensive.

27.   It takes three seconds to operate the bolt of this rifle; consequently, no one could have gotten off three shots in a span of five seconds, as it has been alleged the defendant did.

28.   Oak is a course-grained wood. Walnut is a dark-colored wood. Willow is not a very strong wood. Therefore, since this chair is strong and made of light-colored, fine-grained wood, it is not make of oak, walnut, or willow.

29.   No statement can be proven with absolute certitude. Therefore, the statement, 'No statement can be proved with absolute certitude' cannot be proved with absolute certitude.

30.   As a body approaches the speed of light, its mass becomes infinite. Therefore, it cannot travel faster than the speed of light, since an infinite force would be needed to accelerate it.

PROBLEMS IN RECOGNIZING INTENTIONS

Even when a person definitely intends to be offering an argument, it is not always easy for us to recognize that this is the case or to determine precisely what the intended argument is. Thus, for example, New York State Senator Donovan apparently intended to give an argument in support of the death penalty in the letter cited in the news report on page 92, but it is not at all clear what the intended argument, particularly the premises, might be. The problem in this case is probably careless wording or simply bad logic on the part of the senator, but in other cases (as in the Doonesbury cartoon on page 88) the intentions of the speaker (or author) may be intentionally disguised or obscured. It is also possible that in some cases the intention is to make it appear that there is an argument when, in fact, none is really being presented at all.

It is important to recognize that not every set of statements is offered as an argument. Some, for example, are presented only as descriptions of states of affairs with no intention to use them as support for any conclusion.

The school was built in 1890. It is of red brick, with a columned portico in front. The main door and the first-floor windows are arched. A limestone cornice creates a horizontal line to balance the vertical thrust of the white columns.

Senator links death penalty, Christianity

ALBANY, N.Y. (AP — "Where would Christianity be if Jesus got eight to 15 years, with time off for good behavior?"

That question was posed by state Sen. James Donovan, an advocate of the death penalty, in a letter to a religious group which had written him that it was opposed to capital punishment "as a matter of faith."

"There would be no Christianity if it were not for the death penalty, which gave us the cross and the resurrection," Donovan replied.

The senator, a Republican from Oneida County, made his comment in a March 1 letter to the Council of Churches of the Mohawk Valley Area, which is opposed to the death penalty.

Copies of Donovan's letter were sent to news organizations, along with a handwritten note saying "local churches are shocked at Donovan's logic." The note was not signed.

Donovan confirmed Tuesday that he had written the letter.

Courtesy The Associated Press.

Here there are several statements, but none of them is offered as a conclusion or evidence for a conclusion. Such a series of statements constitutes exposition rather than argument.

The absence of indicator words is not sufficient for one to conclude that a particular set of statements is being intended as an exposition rather than an argument. In such cases, we have to look for other clues, such as the ways in which the various statements are phrased or presented in relation to each other.

> *That movie is going to be a great commercial success. It has plenty of sex and violence.*

> *High-rise apartments would destroy the character of our town. The rezoning plan ought to be rejected.*

In both of these cases, it is reasonable to assume that an argument is being intended, for a connection is certainly suggested between sex, violence, and commercial success, and between high-rise apartments, civic destruction, and the proper fate of the rezoning plan. Likewise, our knowledge of the context—of the speaker, the audience, the motivation, the background, the previous discussion—all may help us in determining whether a conclusion and supporting premises are being offered.

No definitive formal rules or procedures can be given that will guarantee that we will always make a correct judgment as to whether a set of statements is being offered as an argument. However, practice and thoughtful consideration of specific cases can definitely improve our ability to identify intended arguments when they are given.

One other factor that makes identification of intended arguments difficult is the fact that some indicator words have other functions. 'Since' is particularly tricky, for it can indicate temporal sequence as well as logical relation, and it is not always easy to determine which of these possible meanings is intended in a context. "We have not heard from her since she went away" is probably not intended as an argument, but what about "Since he left the company, many things must have changed"? For this, some knowledge of the context is needed. 'Because' is another tricky term because it is often used to indicate a causal relation between two events rather than a premise—conclusion relation between two statements. For example, "Congressman Jones was reelected because of his positions on school busing and abortion" is a proposition explaining the cause of Congressman Jones' reelection; it is probably not intended as an argument.

EXERCISE 2–3

Examine each sentence or group of sentences carefully. (a) Assuming ordinary context, would each sentence or group normally be used to express an argument? (b) If not, why not? (c) If so, identify the conclusion and premises.

1. If a rock is quartz, it will scratch glass.
2. That could not have been Helen you met last night. Helen has short brown hair.
3. If you want a ride to Chicago for Thanksgiving, give Joan a call.
4. Take your umbrella, because it's raining.
5. Since his company went bankrupt, he has never been the same.
6. Since his company went bankrupt, he lost all his money.
7. Please don't pick the flowers. They are here for all those who use the park to enjoy.
8. Spiders are not insects, because insects have only six legs.
9. Of course, you are an idealist. All Sagittarians are idealists.
10. Lee Harvey Oswald must have been crazy to shoot President Kennedy.
11. Since the fall of the Roman Empire, there has never been a single government for most of Western Europe.
12. A rolling stone gathers no moss.
13. All men are mortal. Socrates is a man. Therefore, Socrates is mortal.
14. If sugar is placed in water, it will dissolve.
15. All our citizens must be allowed to express their opinions freely; otherwise, their freedom of speech will be violated.
16. If sugar is placed in water, it will dissolve. This white crystalline substance is not sugar, since it did not dissolve when I placed it in water.
17. Hydrofluoric acid dissolves glass; consequently, it is stored in lead containers.
18. Logic is distinct from psychology for logic deals with prescriptive laws whereas psychology deals with descriptive laws.
19. Nothing interesting has happened since you went away.
20. It could not have rained, because the streets are completely dry.
21. If I pass today's examination, I will graduate.
22. President Nixon was impeachable because he was involved in obstruction of justice.
23. French is called a romance language because it is derived from Latin.
24. Your car was losing power because one of the spark plug wires had come loose.
25. The United States has always been governed by a president, Congress, and Supreme Court since it first came into existence as a nation.
26. No dimes made since 1964 are made of silver.
27. Don't use that book when you write your paper because Professor Brown doesn't agree with the person who wrote it.
28. If a rock is quartz, it will scratch glass. This rock is made of quartz. Therefore, it will scratch glass.
29. If a rock is quartz, it will scratch glass. This rock will not scratch glass, so it can't be quartz.
30. The United States has always been governed by a president, Congress, and Supreme Court, as that is the form of the government specified in the Constitution.
31. Skinner is a determinist, so I don't think you will agree with his conclusions in *Beyond Freedom and Dignity*.
32. Lake Erie is dead. People kept pouring pollutants into it beyond its capacity to absorb them, without thinking about the long-range consequences of their actions.
33. Since the turn of the century, commencement exercises were held on Wednesday afternoons. In the late sixties, administrators changed the day to Saturday, possibly because of a desire for better attendance.
34. "Scientific method, although in its more refined forms may seem complicated, is in essence remarkably simple. It consists in observing such facts as will enable the observer to discover general laws governing facts of the kind in question."—Bertrand Russell.

SUPPLYING MISSING STATEMENTS   Many, and perhaps most, sets of statements intended as arguments are not expressed in a fully explicit way. The intended conclusion and/or one or more of the premises may not be stated. Such arguments, with parts only implicitly suggested, are known as **enthymemes.** If a series of statements clearly tends toward a certain conclusion without ever quite getting there, the conclusion can be assumed to be implicitly stated, and we are justified in adding it to complete the intended argument:

> *High-rise apartments will destroy the rural character of our town. Studies have shown that the presence of such developments tends to increase the crime rate. Besides, we don't have the facilities to provide necessary services to such an enlarged population.*

The conclusion, implicit though not stated, is clearly, 'High-rise apartments should not be permitted in our town'.

If premises rather than conclusions are left out, it is often because the intended audience is assumed to be aware of them already. Thus, almost anyone can supply the implicit premises in the preceding example—'Anything that will destroy the rural character of our town should not be permitted', 'Nothing that tends to increase the crime rate should be permitted in our town', and 'If facilities to provide necessary services to such an enlarged population are unavailable, then high-rise apartments should not be permitted'. A general rule of thumb for supplying missing premises is to add whatever premises are needed to make the intended argument as good as possible. This rule is sometimes referred to as the **principle of charity,** and we will discuss it in more detail after discussing what constitutes a good argument.

To illustrate the importance of knowledge of context for identifying arguments, let's consider these three sentences.

> *The sun is shining today.*
> *Today is Wednesday.*
> *Tom will get an A in logic.*

Assuming that these sentences do express propositions, we do not have sufficient information to determine whether they might be intended as part of an argument. To even make an educated guess, we should know who is making these statements, where, when, to whom, and for what purpose. Let's consider two possible sets of circumstances in which these statements might be made.

If Linda wakes up on Monday, looks out the window, and says, "Oh, good, the sun is shining today"; two days later Professor Piffle looks at his calendar and says, "That's right, today is Wednesday"; and on Friday Bob, Tom's roommate, relaxes in the dorm and assures a friend, "Oh, yeah, Tom'll get an A in logic. I don't dare start an argument with him any more"—in this case, we can safely conclude that there is no argument. But if Linda, who is Tom's girl friend, meets

Bob in the library on Wednesday morning and makes all three of these statements, and if both of them already know certain other facts, there may be an argument intended after all. With the missing premises added, it might look like this:

> *The sun is shining today.*
> *Today is Wednesday.*
> *The final exam in logic is on Wednesday.*
> *The exam counts for 10 percent of the final grade.*
> *Tom has a 90 average going into the exam.*
> *Tom has always done well on sunny days.*
> *The cutoff point for an A is 89.5 percent.*
> *Therefore, Tom will get an A in logic.*

Knowing Tom and knowing the school—that is, knowing the relevant context—Linda and Bob can take all but the first two premises and the conclusion for granted, and perceive that these three original statements could be intended as comprising part of such an argument.

COMMON PROBLEMS IN IDENTIFYING ARGUMENTS

1. *A set of sentences each of which expresses a proposition may constitute an exposition rather than an argument.*
2. *Indicator words may be missing from an argument, in which case the premises and conclusion can often be recognized by other linguistic cues or by knowledge of the context.*
3. *Indicator words may be present when there is no argument.*
4. *The conclusion may be implicit rather than stated.*
5. *Premises may be omitted, in which case it may be necessary to examine the context to determine exactly which premise(s) should be supplied.*

DEDUCTIVE AND INDUCTIVE ARGUMENTS

We have already seen that it is not always easy to determine whether a person intends a particular set of statements to function as an argument or not. It is even more difficult, and often impossible, to even make an educated guess as to how strong an argument might be intended in any given case. Given that an argument is intended, the premises could be offered as providing anything from very weak support to very strong or even absolute support for the conclusion. Because the basic distinction between inductive and deductive arguments depends entirely on the degree of support the premises provide for the conclusion, and since it is so difficult to determine what degree of support is intended in specific cases, we will focus our discussion of the inductive/deductive distinction on actual arguments (i.e., those in which the premises in fact support the conclusion) rather than on sets of statements intended or offered as arguments.

The distinction between inductive and deductive can be grasped quite quickly at an intuitive level by considering a few examples. Returning to the argument about Tom and his logic grade, it should be clear that the premises offer only partial support for the conclusion. It is certainly *possible,* even though improbable, that Tom could get an 80 on the final exam and thus not get an A in the course. This is an example of an *inductive* argument.

For the moment, let us consider the effect of changing one of the premises. If instead of a 90 average, Tom had achieved a 100 average, the argument would read as follows:

> *The sun is shining today.*
> *Today is Wednesday.*
> *The final exam in logic is on Wednesday.*
> *The exam counts for 10 percent of the final grade.*
> *Tom has a 100 average going into the exam.*
> *Tom always does well on sunny days.*
> *The cutoff point for an A is 89.5 percent.*
> *Therefore, Tom will get an A in logic.*

Assuming that all the premises are true, is it possible for the conclusion to be false? Obviously not. Given the mathematics of the situation as stated, Tom is sure to end up with a final grade of 90 even if he gets a 0 on the exam. This is an example of what is known as a valid *deductive* argument.

The relation between inductive and deductive arguments can be graphically represented as follows:

	NONARGUMENTS	INDUCTIVE ARGUMENTS			DEDUCTIVE ARGUMENTS
DEGREE OF PREMISES' SUPPORT OF CONCLUSION	none	weak	moderate	strong	absolute

In a deductive argument, the premises must give absolute support for the conclusion. Any argument in which the premises provide anything less than absolute support is by definition an inductive argument. Any set of statements which is such that none of them provide any support at all for any of the others is not an argument at all—either inductive or deductive.

Deductive Arguments   Validity is an important concept in deductive logic. It is not the same thing as truth, though in ordinary speech we sometimes assert that a particular statement or belief is valid—meaning that it is true. We have already seen that in logic a statement is defined as that of which it can be properly said that it is true or false. Likewise, logicians have stipulated that the term **valid** is to be applied only to those *arguments* which are such that *if* the premises are true, the conclusion *must* also be true.

Consider the following examples. Are the premises true or false? The conclusions? Which arguments are valid; that is, in which cases do the premises necessarily lead to the conclusion?

1. *The Eiffel Tower is in London.*
   London is in Germany.
   Germany is in Africa.
   Therefore, the Eiffel Tower is in Africa.
2. *Plato was a Greek.*
   Plato was a philosopher.
   Therefore, all Greeks are philosophers.
3. *If Richard Nixon's name was on the ballot in the 1972 presidential election, then John voted for him.*
   Richard Nixon's name was on the ballot in the 1972 presidential election.
   Therefore, John voted for Richard Nixon.
4. *Dolphins are a kind of shark.*
   Sharks have breathing holes.
   Therefore, dolphins have breathing holes.
5. *Either the moon is made of green cheese, or it is not.*
   Therefore, Hawaii was the fiftieth state admitted to the Union.

The only arguments that are invalid are 2 and 5. It is easy to see that even though the premises of 2 are true—Plato really was a Greek and a philosopher—this does not imply or necessitate that all his fellow Greeks were also philosophers. In example 5 the premise about the moon is true, and the conclusion about Hawaii also happens to be true; but the premise does not in itself lend support for the conclusion. It is *impossible* to have a valid argument in which true premises lead to false conclusions. But, as example 5 illustrates, even having true premises and a true conclusion is no guarantee that the argument is valid.

In the other three examples, if the premises were true, then necessarily the conclusion would be true. That is, if the Eiffel Tower were really in London, and London were really in Germany, and Germany were really in Africa, then the Eiffel Tower would have to be in Africa. Similarly, we know that dolphins are not sharks, and sharks do not have breathing holes; but *if* they were and did, the conclusion that dolphins have breathing holes would have to be true. So it is possible to have a valid argument in which one or more of the premises are false or even one in which all the premises and the conclusion are false. It is also possible to have an argument with true premises and a true conclusion that is invalid. The point is that in a valid argument the premises necessarily imply the conclusion. So long as this is so, you can be certain that *if* the premises are true, the conclusion will be true as well.

A **valid deductive argument,** then, can be defined as one in which:

> **if** *the premises are true, the conclusion* **must** *be true;*
> *that is, it is* **impossible** *for all of the premises to be*
> *true and the conclusion false; or, the premises*
> **imply** *the conclusion.*

Valid deductive arguments have an additional significant characteristic. Look again at argument 4. Suppose a few more premises were added—'Dolphins communicate by means of a system similar to radar', 'Dolphins were considered omens of good luck by ancient sailors', 'Sharks have fusiform bodies', and 'Sharks are carnivorous'. Do these facts increase or decrease support for the conclusion? Clearly not, for so long as the original premises remain true, they are sufficient to guarantee the truth of the conclusion. Similarly, no premises we add to the other two valid arguments (1 and 3) will change the truth value of their conclusions. In fact, for any valid deductive argument, given that the original premises are true, the addition of any information whatsoever to this set of premises will not affect the truth of the conclusion. All this can be summed up in a phrase by saying that a valid deductive argument is one in which the premises provide *absolute* support for the conclusion.

Let us consider two more arguments.

> *All silamons are wistacious.*
> *Piliute is a silamon.*
> *Therefore, piliute is wistacious.*

> *If carnips are tumbulous, then iliks are quirkles.*
> *Carnips are tumbulous.*
> *Therefore, iliks are quirkles.*

Both these examples contain nonsense words; yet the logical form of each is deductively valid. If all silamons are wistacious, and if piliute is a silamon, it follows that piliute is wistacious. Likewise if the conditional statement 'If carnips are tumbulous, then iliks are quirkles' is true and if carnips are in fact tumbulous, then it necessarily follows that iliks are quirkles. In each example, a logical relationship exists between the premises and the conclusion that is independent of the content of these statements; it is a relationship that is based on the *form* of the argument. Thus, it is possible to evaluate the validity of both arguments solely on the basis of their logical form.

Counterexamples Consider now these two examples;

> *Some furnaps are spenels.*
> *Tursid is a furnap.*
> *Therefore, Tursid is a spenel.*

> *All surpids are rustids.*
> *All turnfers are rustids.*
> *Therefore, all surpids are turnfers.*

With a little thought, it should become evident that neither of the two examples above is a valid deductive argument. One way to prove this is to provide counterexamples. In constructing a **counterexample,** one keeps the same argument *form* but changes the factual content in such a way as to make the premises of the argument true and the conclusion false. Thus, we might provide the following counterexamples for the arguments above:

> *Some automobiles are Cadillacs.*
> *That Pinto is an automobile.*
> *Therefore, that Pinto is a Cadillac.*

> *All flies are insects.*
> *All ants are insects.*
> *Therefore, all flies are ants.*

Although providing a counterexample is sufficient to prove that an argument is *invalid*, the failure to construct an appropriate counterexample for a particular argument is *not* sufficient to prove that an argument is valid. Other procedures are necessary for proving validity.

EXERCISE 2–4 *Each of the following deductive arguments is invalid. Provide a counterexample for each.*

---

1. If man is mortal, then he must eat food to survive. Man must eat food to survive. Therefore, man is mortal.
2. Some women are courageous. Some women are considerate. Therefore, some women are courageous and considerate.
3. All paramecia are single-celled organisms. No sea urchins are paramecia. Therefore, no sea urchins are single-celled organisms.
4. All marigolds are plants. All flowers are plants. Therefore, all marigolds are flowers.
5. All cats are felines. A polar bear is not a cat. Therefore, a polar bear is not a feline.
6. Some Englishmen are Protestants. Winston Churchill was a Protestant. Therefore, Winston Churchill was an Englishman.
7. Orange juice is a delicious drink. Pineapple juice is a delicious drink. Therefore, orange-pineapple juice is a delicious drink.
8. All industrialists are rich. Henry Ford was rich. Therefore, Henry Ford was an industrialist.
9. No cats are dogs. No cats are canines. Therefore, all dogs are canines.
10. If an animal is a mammal, then it bears its young live. A gorilla bears its young live. Therefore, a gorilla is a mammal.
11. If an animal is a mammal, then it bears its young live. A bluebird is not a mammal. Therefore, a bluebird does not bear its young live.

12. If you studied hard, then you got an A in logic. You did not study hard. Therefore, you did not get an A in logic.
13. All men are mortal creatures. Some mortal creatures are toolmakers. Therefore, some men are toolmakers.
14. Some Greeks are philosophers. Socrates was a Greek. Therefore, Socrates was a philosopher.
15. Bronze is a metal. Bronze is made of copper and tin. Therefore, copper is a metal and tin is a metal.

Inductive Arguments   Now let us return to the original version of the Tale of Tom in which he had a 90 average going into the last exam. Given these premises, the conclusion that he will get an A in the course does not *necessarily* follow: with a 90 average, Tom needs an 85 in the final exam to get an 89.5 in the course. Even if all of the premises are true, it is still possible for the conclusion to be false. The premises do not provide absolute support for it. Thus, this is not a valid deductive argument. However, the premises do provide some support for the conclusion. That is, given the truth of the premises, a reasonable person would be more justified in accepting the truth of the conclusion than he or she would be without the premises. *Any argument whose premises provide some, but not absolute, support for the conclusion* is known as an **inductive argument.**

The concept of an inductive argument covers a broad range of arguments—from those that provide very strong (but not absolute) support for their conclusions to those whose premises provide very little support for the conclusions. Remember, a set of statements which does not in fact provide any support whatsoever for another statement does not comprise an argument at all in the formal logical sense. Any set of statements which does not comprise a deductively valid argument is either an inductive argument or not an argument at all (in the formal logical sense). Thus, even if someone *asserts* that a set of statements does support some conclusion, if the premises do not in fact provide any support for the conclusion, this is neither a deductive nor an inductive argument (in the formal logical sense).

As stated earlier, there is no simple method for determining on direct inspection whether a set of statements constitutes an argument in the formal logical sense, let alone whether they comprise an inductive or deductive argument. The only methods that can be used with absolute certainty are several formal techniques for determining whether certain kinds of statements constitute a deductively valid argument. Thus, what is necessary is to develop the ability to make intuitive or educated guesses as to whether a set of statements constitutes an inductive or deductive argument, and, whenever there is some doubt, to assume that it may be a deductively valid argument and test it using the methods to be presented in later chapters. It is not always necessary to guess whether a set of statements in fact constitutes a deductive or inductive argument in the formal sense, as in situations where we are presented with what is explicitly asserted to be deductive or inductive. If a set of statements is explicitly asserted to be a deductive argument, we can proceed directly to testing it, using the formal procedures, and we may be able to prove that it is or is not deductively valid in the logical sense. Before going into the formal procedures for testing arguments for validity, we should take a little time to look at some examples of deductive and inductive arguments for the purpose of beginning the development of the intuitive sense that is useful for making educated guesses before formally testing sets of statements for deductive validity.

It often has been said that in deductive arguments we reason from general to particular, whereas in inductive arguments we reason from particular to general. A typical example of a deductive argument is:

> *All mammals have eyes.*
> *Flipper is a mammal.*
> *Therefore, Flipper has eyes.*

And one pattern for an inductive argument is:

> *Animal A is a swan and is white.*
> *Animal B is a swan and is white.*
> *Animal C is a swan and is white.*
> *Animal D is a swan and is white.*
> *Therefore, probably all swans are white.*

In the deductive argument, we began with the universal statement 'All mammals have eyes' and concluded with a particular statement, 'Flipper has eyes'. In the inductive argument, each premise was particular, but the conclusion was general. However, it is quite possible to have arguments that do not fit these patterns. For example, consider the following:

1. *All mammals have eyes.*
   All dolphins are mammals.
   Therefore, all dolphins have eyes.
2. *If Flipper is a mammal, then he has eyes.*
   Flipper is a mammal.
   Therefore, Flipper has eyes.
3. *All robins are birds and build nests.*
   All sparrows are birds and build nests.
   All bluejays are birds and build nests.
   All pigeons are birds and build nests.
   Therefore, all birds build nests.
4. *Senator Jones is a politician and a liar.*
   Representative Smith is a politician and a liar.
   Mayor Great is a politician and a liar.
   Vice-President Padook is a politician.
   Therefore, Vice-President Padook is a liar.

Arguments 1 and 2 above are deductive, for if the premises are true the conclusion must also be true. Yet, in both these examples, the reasoning is not from general to particular: in argument 1 the reasoning goes from general premises to a general conclusion, and in argument 2 from particular premises to a particular conclusion. Arguments 3 and 4 are inductive since the premises provide some but not absolute support for the conclusion, but in both examples the reasoning is not from particular premises to general conclusions. In argument 3, the premises and conclusion are general, and, in argument 4, both the premises and the conclusion are particular. Consequently, it is evident that the general/particular rule is unreliable in practice as a way of distinguishing between deductive and inductive arguments.

EXERCISE 2–5   *Examine each argument below, assuming that each premise is true. (a) Is the argument deductive or inductive? (b) Explain.*

---

1. All birds can fly. I've never seen one that can't. *I*
2. A = B and B = C; therefore, A = C *D.*
3. No Vulcans are Clingons. Mr. Spock is a Vulcan. Therefore, he is not a Clingon. *D*
4. My three swans are white; therefore, some swans are white. *D,*
5. My three swans are white; therefore, all swans are white. *I* *Sagi → Nov 23 - Dec 21*
6. Bill is a Sagittarian, so his birthday is in December. *I.*
7. Bill is a Sagittarian; therefore, he is impulsive.
8. John must have a toothache again. He is not looking very cheerful. *I.*
9. 3X + Y = 10 and Y = 4; therefore X = 2.
10. One of these statements must be false, because if two statements contradict each other, they cannot both be true, and these two statements do contradict each other. *D.* (*modus ponens*)
11. The average college-educated person has a higher yearly income than the national average. Helen has a college education, so her yearly income is above the national average.
12. According to the polls, 54 percent of the voters favor Senator Erskine. Therefore, Senator Erskine will probably win the election. *I.*
13. Today is Wednesday. You came four days ago, so that means you came on Saturday, which was four days ago.
14. I sent her the letter three weeks ago and still have received no answer; therefore, my letter must have been lost in the mail. *I. Persons receiving could be on vacation.*
15. All human choices are determined, since all events in the universe are determined and all human choices are events in the universe.
16. Spot always comes home by dark. It's dark and he hasn't come home yet. Therefore, he must have been run over by a car. *I.*
17. Bob and Kay both have blue eyes. Therefore, the child they are expecting will have blue eyes.
18. Rick must be a conservative, since most supporters of Barry Goldwater are conservatives and Rick is a Goldwater supporter. *I*
19. If J. Paul Getty wrote *Love Story,* he would be rich. J. Paul Getty is rich, so he must have written *Love Story.*

20. The game will be cancelled, since if it rains the game must be cancelled, and it's raining. D.
21. Among the suspects, only the butler and Sir Chisholm knew how to shoot accurately at a distance with a .38 revolver. Lady Lawford was shot at a distance of 100 feet at nine o'clock Tuesday night. Sir Chisholm was a hundred miles away from the scene of the crime at nine o'clock Tuesday night. Therefore, the butler did it.
22. The electric company says that, if the demand for electricity continues to grow at the present rate, a new power station must be operational by 1980. The company predicts that demand will continue to grow at the present rate. Therefore, construction must start immediately. I.
23. No species of animal observed to date except man is capable of rational thought. Therefore, man is the only rational animal.
24. The United States, England, France, and Germany all underwent great cultural change during industrialization. Consequently, Japan will undergo great cultural change as it industrializes. I.
25. The sea painter is now toggled at the thwart. Only one thing can be toggled at the thwart at one time. Therefore, nothing else is toggled at the thwart.

CRITERIA FOR GOOD ARGUMENTS

So far, we have discussed what an argument is, ways to recognize arguments, and the two different types of argument; we have not touched on the subject of what constitutes a *good* deductive or inductive argument. It is to this subject that we now turn.

Good Deductive Arguments

A good deductive argument—one whose conclusion can be trusted to be true—is called a sound argument. To be **sound,** *a deductive argument* must satisfy two conditions: it *must be valid, and the truth of all its premises must be reasonably well established.* It was noted earlier that a valid deductive argument may contain false premises and a true conclusion as well as false premises and a false conclusion. Consider again two examples of valid argument offered earlier:

> *Dolphins are a kind of shark.*
> *Sharks have breathing holes.*
> *Therefore, dolphins have breathing holes.*

> *The Eiffel Tower is in London.*
> *London is in Germany.*
> *Germany is in Africa.*
> *Therefore, the Eiffel Tower is in Africa.*

In the first example, both premises are false, yet the conclusion is true. In the second, all of the premises and the conclusion are false. Both arguments are valid, though neither one is sound. Soundness refers to only one type of deductive argument: one which is valid and which contains premises whose truth is well established. In such instances, the truth of the conclusion must necessarily be well established, since a valid argument is such that, *if* its premises are true, its conclusion must be true, and we are told that the premises are in fact well established.

Let us consider now a deductively valid argument with more problematic premises.

> *Any person who smokes cigarettes runs a higher risk*
> *of developing lung cancer than a person who does*
> *not smoke.*
> *Tom smokes two packs of cigarettes a day and Bill*
> *does not smoke.*
> *Therefore, Tom is running a higher risk of developing*
> *lung cancer than Bill.*

Determining the truth value of the second premise to a reasonable degree of certainty is a relatively simple task: one could ask Tom and Bill if they smoke, or one could directly observe their behavior for several days. Making a determination about the truth value of the first premise, however, is much more difficult; it is a task best left to a medical researcher rather than a logician. Ordinarily, the logician has no special qualifications to decide if the proposition expressed by a premise is true or false. In any case, the logician's primary concern when examining a set of statements is determining whether it constitutes a valid deductive argument, an inductive argument, or no argument at all.

A final criterion for determining whether a deductive argument is good is that of noncircularity. A **circular argument** is one whose conclusion merely re-states, in different words, something that is already stated explicitly in the premises. In one sense, every valid argument is circular, since its conclusion must be contained in the premises. However, the term 'circular' will be reserved for arguments such as the following, which we will assume is being presented by a native-English speaker to an audience of native-English speakers:

> *All bachelors are unhappy.*
> *Therefore, all unmarried men are unhappy.*

Assuming that we already know that a bachelor is by definition an unmarried man, the conclusion of this argument is essentially nothing more than a restatement of the premise. We are left just where we began. The circularity of an argument is not as easily established as its validity, since it depends on what the hearer already knows. Consequently, an argument may be circular for one person and not for another. If the above argument about bachelors and unmarried men were presented to a Russian with a limited knowledge of English, it might not be circular to him, if he was not aware that 'bachelor' means 'unmarried man'. In fact, he might not perceive that any argument existed, until someone supplied him with the missing definition.

EXERCISE 2-6 *Each of these deductive arguments is valid. (a) Is the truth of each premise well established? (b) Is the argument sound?*

1. All flowers are plants. All roses are flowers. Therefore, all roses are plants.
2. All birds can fly. Some fish are birds. Therefore, some fish can fly.
3. All rectangles are four-sided figures. All squares are rectangular. Therefore, all squares are four-sided figures.
4. No apes can write novels. All orangutans are apes. Therefore, no orangutans can write novels.
5. All skyscrapers are tall buildings. The Empire State Building is a skyscraper. Therefore, the Empire State Building is a tall building.
6. All conservatives are wealthy. Some Republicans are conservatives. Therefore, some Republicans are wealthy.
7. All women are wise. Dr. Smith is a woman. Therefore, Dr. Smith is wise.
8. No socialist is a democrat. All liberals are democrats. Therefore, no liberals are socialists.
9. Some aliens are English speakers. All aliens are foreigners. Thus, some foreigners are English speakers.
10. No dead person can hear. Some living persons can hear. Some living persons are not dead persons.
11. No professional wrestler is well educated. Some well-educated persons are college professors. Some college professors are not professional wrestlers.
12. All solicitors are irritating. All petitioners are solicitors. Therefore, all petitioners are irritating.
13. All species of fish are cold-blood animals. All whales are a species of fish. Therefore, all whales are cold-blooded.
14. Either all insects have wings or all ants are insects. It is not the case that all ants are insects. Therefore, all insects have wings.
15. If man is mortal, then he must eat food to survive. Man is mortal. Therefore, he must eat food to survive.
16. If a man is a good husband, then he loves his wife. Ed is a good husband. Therefore, Ed loves his wife.
17. Either all dogs are canines or all cats are canines. It is not the case that all cats are canines. Therefore, all dogs are canines.
18. If Willis Reed is a basketball player, then he's taller than six feet. Willis Reed is a basketball player. Therefore, Willis Reed is taller than six feet.

Good Inductive Arguments As with deductive arguments, inductive arguments, to be good, should have premises whose truth is well established. Beyond that, it is necessary to consider the relative strength of support which the premises provide for the truth of the conclusion.

Because its premises do not provide absolute support for its conclusion, an inductive argument, unlike a deductive one, can be strengthened or weakened by the addition of new premises. In the previously discussed example of an inductive argument about Tom and his 90 average, we saw that he still has a reasonable chance to get his A. If we now add that Tom has studied hard for this exam and that he had a good night's sleep, the conclusion becomes even more likely. The new argument is stronger than the original. On the other hand, if we were to add the information that only two of the twenty exams Tom has taken thus far in college were taken on sunny days and that the harder Tom studies the more he tends to "go blank" on an exam, the premises give less support for the truth of the conclusion.

Insofar as terminology is concerned, neither the term 'sound' nor the term 'valid' will be applied to inductive arguments. Instead, we will usually say that an inductive argument is stronger or weaker than some other argument. When we assert that an inductive argument is strong (or weak), it should be interpreted as an assertion that of all possible arguments that could be given in support of this conclusion, this particular argument is stronger (or weaker) than most.

DEALING WITH ENTHYMEMES   We saw in our discussion of the problems of recognizing which sets of statements are intended as arguments that, in everyday contexts, not all of the parts of intended arguments are stated explicitly. It was also explained that such an argument (or set of statements intended as an argument) is known as an enthymeme. We further indicated that we should adhere to the principle of charity when we supply the missing premises—that is, we should add whatever premises are needed to make the argument as good as possible. We can now elaborate further on this by indicating that the 'best' argument is a sound argument, a valid argument with premises whose truth is well established.

This is an example of an enthymeme:

> *If Paris is in France, then Paris is in Europe.*
> *Therefore, Paris is in Europe.*

Although this set of statements does not comprise a valid argument as stated, it seems reasonable to assume that it was intended as an argument, and we should thus try to find other well-established truths that might be added as premises which would result in a valid (and sound) argument. For this example, the obvious missing premise (in brackets) can be supplied to give a valid argument as follows.

> *If Paris is in France, then Paris is in Europe.*
> *[Paris is in France.]*
> *Therefore, Paris is in Europe.*

In this example, the truth of the premise that was added seems to be quite well established, and it also made the argument valid.

Although everything worked out simply and well in this example, in many cases adherence to the principle of charity cannot result in a sound argument. Consider, for example, the following:

> *Shakespeare was an Englishman; consequently, all*
> *Englishmen are great playwrights.*

If we add the well-established truth, 'Shakespeare was a great playwright', as a premise, we still do not have a valid argument; at best, the resulting argument is a weak inductive argument.

> *Shakespeare was an Englishman.*
> *[Shakespeare was a great playwright.]*
> *Therefore, all Englishmen are great playwrights.*

It is not at all clear what additional premises would have to be added to make the argument valid, but they would have to be highly questionable statements such as, 'If one Englishman has ever been a great playwright, then all Englishmen must be great playwrights'.

In cases such as this, where one must choose between adding well-established true premises that will produce an invalid argument (with some degree of inductive strength) and adding questionable premises that will make the argument valid, logicians usually prefer to try to make the argument valid, since their expertise is in determining validity rather than in establishing factual truth. However, there are some situations in which adding a premise whose truth is well established does not result in a deductively valid argument but rather a strong inductive argument. In such cases, we would probably want to opt for the interpretation that results in the strong inductive argument with premises whose truth is quite well established rather than the validly deductive argument with false or highly questionable premises.

EXERCISE 2–7   *Assuming ordinary context, examine each of the following purported arguments.* (a) *Identify the conclusion.* (b) *Identify the stated premises.* (c) *Supply a missing premise that might make the argument deductively valid.*

---

1. That is not a rose bush because it doesn't have thorns.
2. There is no reason to vote, since all politicians are corrupt.
3. The end of a thing is the perfection of life, so death is the perfection of life.
4. Bats are not birds, because birds have feathers.
5. This wine is not Chablis, for it is red wine.
6. Gregory is not a Turkish Cypriot; therefore, he is a Greek Cypriot.
7. The baseball game was dull, since both teams played poorly.
8. Susan will not get the job. She has no experience.
9. All metaphysicians are eccentric, so Karl is eccentric.
10. All trees are plants and all oaks are trees. Therefore, all oaks are living things.
11. Mr. Poindexter did not work for the company, so he could not have stolen the money.
12. Since he just received a pay raise, he must be competent at his job.
13. All men make mistakes; consequently, so does John.
14. Peter is not my friend, because he told lies about me.
15. He passed the examination; therefore, he must have lied.
16. This liquid is not acid, for the litmus paper we placed in it did not turn red.

17.   Senator Brandt is a major party candidate and he is not a Republican. Therefore, he is a Democrat.
18.   If the demand for sugar exceeds the supply, the price of sugar will go up. Therefore, the price of sugar will go up.

THE PRINCIPLE
OF INDUCTION

We have emphasized earlier that it is usually difficult and often impossible to determine whether a particular set of statements is intended as an inductive or deductive argument. We have also pointed out that, in supplying missing premises in an enthymeme, we must exercise judgment in applying the principle of charity since it is usually possible to formulate any argument as a valid deductive argument *or* as a strong inductive argument. This can be illustrated clearly by considering the following example:

> **The Republicans have always controlled the council in this city in the past so they will do so again next year.**

It is reasonable to assume that this is being offered as an argument with 'The Republicans will control the council next year' being the intended conclusion, and 'The Republicans have always controlled the council in the past' being a premise. With only this one premise, we have what is a reasonably strong inductive argument with what we can only presume to be a well-established truth for the premise. If we add another premise such as, 'The same candidates are running next year as ran last year', the argument may even be stronger, although it is still inductive. However, if we add certain other new premises, we can make the argument deductively valid, as in the following case.

> **The Republicans have always controlled the council in this city in the past.**
> **[All similar events occur similarly in similar circumstances.]**
> **[The circumstances surrounding the city council election next year will be similar in all relevant respects to last year's election.]**
> **Therefore, the Republicans will win control in the election next year.**

The first of the premises we supplied is a version of a basic principle known as the **principle of induction.** When used in arguments (as in the above example), it can make most arguments deductively valid, but often, if not always, at the cost of introducing a premise or premises of questionable truth.

From a strictly logical point of view, such arguments are deductively valid, since the truth of their conclusions necessarily follows from the truth of their premises. Remember, too, that, from a strictly logical point of view, we are not concerned either with the factual truth of the premises of an argument or with any temporal relation between the premises and the conclusion. As logicians, we are concerned only with the relationship between the premises and the conclusion—that is, with the support which the premises offer for the conclusion. Quite clearly, both arguments above, with the suppressed premises added, are logically stronger than the original arguments. Nevertheless, there are serious obstacles to carrying out this reduction of an inductive argument to deductive form.

The first such obstacle is the problem of establishing the truth of the principle of induction itself. Although from a strictly logical point of view we need not be concerned with the truth of the premises of an argument, from a practical point of view this matter is of great concern, since as human beings we are interested in determining the best possible arguments. The "obvious" justification for the principle of induction may seem to be that it does, in fact, work. For instance, from past observations of voter behavior, poll-takers regularly predict the outcome of the next election. From past observations concerning the attraction of iron to a magnet, we correctly infer that in the next instance in which iron is placed near a magnet, it will be attracted to the magnet. But this seemingly well-founded pragmatic justification of the principle of induction has been criticized as being circular, since it can be formulated as follows:

> *In the past, similar things behaved similarly under*
> *similar circumstances.*
> *Therefore, all similar things behave similarly under*
> *similar circumstances.*

What has happened here is that an inductive argument has been used to justify the principle of induction. (Some philosophers have argued that *in this case* we are dealing with a special type of self-supporting argument, and that the circularity is legitimate. This claim is not universally accepted.)

Putting aside, for the moment, the problem of justifying the principle of induction, we find that the reduction of inductive arguments to deductive form faces another serious obstacle—that of resemblance. No two states of affairs resemble each other exactly; if they did they would be the same state of affairs. Such an objection may seem trivial, but it points out a significant flaw in the principle of induction—one with practical importance for many arguments which involve "less similar" things. For instance, the social sciences often make predictions about human behavior based on observed cases, yet no one would argue that two human beings resemble each other in every way. Quite obviously, since no two states of affairs (whether they be objects, human beings, plants, events, or whatever) are identical, a judgment must be made as to whether or not two cases resemble each other in *relevant* ways.

A deductive argument, it will be remembered, is such that no matter what premises we add to the original, the argument remains valid. But when the principle of induction is used as a premise, it usually remains possible to add other premises that will affect the strength of the inference from the premises to the conclusion. This is so because, as we have seen, it is difficult to determine *absolutely* that the observed and unobserved cases are similar in *all* relevant respects.

Numerous other arguments have been offered in support of the principle of induction, but none has been generally accepted. This has led some philosophers to suggest that, in fact, there is no justification for the principle of induction. Proponents of this view sometimes support their position by means of an argument based on an analogy between logic and branches of mathematics. They assert that just as there is no way, without circularity, to justify the axiom in geometry that the whole must be equal to the sum of its parts, so too it is impossible, without circularity, to justify a fundamental principle of logic such as the principle of induction. This argument may seem sound on the surface, but it is itself inductive, since it is based on an analogy. Although certain principles of reasoning in mathematics may not be provable, the argument from this analogy does not itself prove that the principle of induction cannot be justified. Here, again, an inductive argument has been used to support a conclusion about the principle of induction—in this case, the conclusion that no justification for it can be given.

In summary, no one has yet been able to provide a satisfactory justification for the principle of induction, but it would be pessimistic to conclude, on this ground, that no such justification will ever be provided.

EXERCISE 2–8   *Assuming ordinary context, evaluate each of the following as inductive arguments. (a) Identify the conclusion. (b) Identify the stated premise(s). (c) Add a premise that will make the argument stronger. (d) Add a premise that will make the argument weaker. (e) Discuss how adding the principle of induction as a premise might change the argument.*

---

1. I liked the 1969 Beaujolais wine that I drank. I liked the 1970 Beaujolais wine that I drank. I liked the 1971 Beaujolais wine that I drank. Therefore, I will like the 1972 Beaujolais wine that I am going to drink.
2. The guests our family has to dinner always like my mother's pot roasts. The Karlans are coming to dinner and my mother is serving pot roast. Therefore, the Karlans will like her pot roast.
3. John has done very well on all of his algebra tests, so he will do well on his algebra final today.
4. All swans observed to date have been white. Therefore, the chances are that any swan observed in the future will be white.
5. We will be able to see the partial eclipse of the sun, since the weatherman says we will have a clear day tomorrow, the same as today.
6. Sluggo Jones has hit more home runs this season than any other player on the team. Therefore, he is likely to hit a home run today.
7. I walked under a ladder and then a black cat crossed my path, so something terrible is going to happen to me.
8. No runoff will be necessary. The polls say 52 percent of the voters favor the mayor for reelection.

9.   Most east coast newspaper editors are liberals. Mr. Harrison is an east coast newspaper editor. Therefore, Mr. Harrison is probably liberal.
10. You will live to be at least seventy years of age. The life expectancy of someone your age is seventy years and your health has been better than average.
11. Most members of the Veterans of Foreign Wars condemn draft evaders. Mr. Robinson is a member of the Veterans of Foreign Wars. Therefore, he will probably condemn draft evaders.
12. Since it's not supposed to rain, and enough people to make two teams have promised to come, and we reminded them to bring their gloves and bats and balls, we should have a good baseball game at the picnic.
13. I just know I'm going to win some money at the race track today, because five of the horses I've picked fit the system I've worked out for picking winners.
14. There has been an outbreak of the Asian flu in the United States this month. You are more likely to catch the flu than I am because I have had a flu vaccination but you have not.
15. The automobile as we know it will eventually have to be replaced with other means of transportation, since at the present rate of consumption the known world petroleum reserves will be exhausted by 2005.

ANALYZING SAMPLE ARGUMENTS

Although logic can be studied as an abstract set of rules and procedures no more closely related to other aspects of human interest and activity than games such as chess or bridge, it does have useful applications, and we will be concerned in this book to focus as much as possible on these applications. In addition to being useful in helping us to understand the logical structure of statements and to identify logical relations between pairs of statements (as discussed in Chapter 1), logic is also useful for helping us to determine which sets of statements that are asserted to support or imply conclusions are in fact valid or inductively supportive of the conclusion. We have now introduced enough basic concepts to be able to present a general preliminary procedure for analyzing arguments in the ordinary language sense as they appear in everyday contexts to determine whether they are good arguments in the formal logical sense.

Let us begin with a relatively simple example:

Susan should do well in this logic course, because she always does well in science courses.

It is reasonable to interpret this sentence as asserting that the statement 'she always does well in science courses' supports in some way the apparent conclusion that 'Susan will do well in this logic course'. We should be able to see intuitively that the one statement does not imply the other, although it does seem to provide some support for it. As a second step in our analysis, therefore, let us see if there are any other statements which could be added as premises which might make this a valid argument. A likely candidate might be 'This logic course is a science course'. (*Webster's Twentieth Century Dictionary* defines 'logic' as 'the science of correct reasoning', so this premise can reasonably be said to be well supported.) Adding this premise, the argument now reads:

> [*This logic course is a science course.*]
> *Susan always does well in science courses.*
> *Therefore, Susan will do well in this logic course.*

Although it is stronger than the original version, this argument is still not deductively valid, because of an additional premise to the effect that Susan is not taking this logic course. That premise would be sufficient to make it false that Susan will do well in the course. Thus, one more premise must be added to make the argument valid.

> [*This logic course is a science course.*]
> [*Susan is taking this logic course.*]
> *Susan always does well in science courses.*
> *Therefore, Susan will do well in this logic course.*

This is about as far as we can go in analyzing the original argument without using any of the techniques of formal logic to test the argument for validity. However, we could also have pursued the analysis along a somewhat different route.

Instead of interpreting the sentence 'Susan always does well in science courses' in its broadest sense as applying to all courses—past, present, and future—that Susan might ever take, we could interpret it in the narrower sense as referring only to courses that Susan has taken in the past. Such a statement could be easily verified, whereas a statement about present and future courses could never be established as absolutely true (at least not until after Susan dies, in which case it would still be only about past courses which she has already taken). On this interpretation, the argument would now read:

> [*This logic course is a science course.*]
> [*Susan is taking this logic course.*]
> *Susan has always done well in science courses in the*
>   *past.*
> *Therefore, Susan will do well in this logic course.*

In this form, the argument is now an inductive argument. We won't be able to evaluate its strength until we have studied the general principles of induction in Chapters 10 and 11.

One other possible analysis of this example is worth noting. The addition of one more premise to the version just presented could turn that inductive argument into a valid deductive argument as follows.

> [*This logic course is a science course.*]
> [*Susan is taking this logic course.*]
> *Susan has always done well in science courses in the*
>   *past.*
> [*If Susan has always done well in science courses in*
>   *the past, she will always do well in them in the*
>   *future.*]
> *Therefore, Susan will do well in this logic course.*

The analyses given here are but three of many possible analyses that could be given of the same initial statements that comprised an argument in the ordinary language sense. Each of the three is plausible, but it might be difficult to arrive at a consensus even among professional logicians as to which of them, if any, is more plausible or reasonable. Such a judgment depends in part on assumptions about the relative value of such things as induction or deduction and true or only probable premises. No set of generally accepted formal criteria exists that can be appealed to if there is disagreement as to which of several analyses of an argument is "best." Such agreement, if it is to be attained at all, must be the result of open-minded discussion and negotiation among all of the parties.

Not only are many different analyses possible besides those given above, but these are only *preliminary* analyses. These analyses are only sufficient for preparing the original argument in the ordinary language sense to be analyzed using the techniques of formal logic to determine whether it is deductively valid or inductively weak or strong. And each of the different analyses above can be formally analyzed in a number of different ways. Although we can't explain this any further here, we will return to this example in Chapters 5, 7, 9, and 10 to show some of the different kinds of formal analysis that could be done on it.

Rather than pursue the theoretical limits of analysis of our first example, let us do partial preliminary analyses of several more examples, turning first to the argument (in the ordinary language sense) by Edwin A. Roberts, Jr., reprinted below.

Mainstreams

. . . Thoughts on the 10 Greatest Liars

By Edwin A. Roberts, Jr.

It fell to me the other week, in connection with a story assignment, to ask a dozen or so motel operators in a Florida town how business was. They all said business was just fine, the gasoline shortage wasn't hurting them at all, and if they were making any more money the local bank couldn't accommodate their deposits.

Oddly under such happy circumstances, the motel parking lots were practically empty. So I asked an officer of the local bank how the cashing of travelers' checks this year compared to last. As a matter of fact, said the banker, such check cashings were "way below" 1973. This information suggested that the motel operators

---

Comment

---

were dissembling, and so I am putting motel owners in resort towns on my list of The 10 Greatest Liars.

Courtesy National Observer, *April 6, 1974.*

The apparent conclusion of Roberts' argument is that resort motel operators are among the ten greatest liars. However, since nothing is said about how the comparison is made between resort motel operators and other groups concerning their reliability, no support seems to be given for the conclusion in this form. Reconsideration of this example might lead us to suspect that the reference to the "list of the 10 Greatest Liars" is a literary or rhetorical device that should not be taken literally. On this interpretation, the conclusion would read something like 'Resort motel operators lie a lot about their business'. Taking the statements presented that are relevant to this conclusion, we have the following:

> *The resort motel operators in one Florida town all said that their business was fine.*
> *The parking lots of these motels were practically empty.*
> *The local bank reported that it had cashed many fewer travelers' checks than in the previous year.*
> *Therefore, resort motel operators lie a lot about their business.*

To have a valid deductive argument, we must add a number of presumably suppressed premises. The following version is more complete but still not valid.

> *The resort motel operators in one Florida town all said that their business was fine.*
> *The parking lots of these motels were practically empty.*
> *The local bank reported that it had cashed many fewer travelers' checks than in the previous year.*
> *[If a motel's parking lot is almost empty and its bank has not cashed many travelers' checks, then the motel's business is not good.]*
> *[If someone says business is good when it is not, then they are lying.]*
> *[If all of the resort motel operators interviewed in one Florida town lie about their business, then all resort motel operators lie about their business.]*
> *Therefore, resort motel operators lie a lot about their business.*

Making all these premises explicit, or supplying all of the premises necessary to make the argument valid, brings out some new difficulties. One difficulty is that it is no longer entirely clear what the conclusion asserts. Does it say that all (that is, each and every one) of the resort motel owners in the country (or world) are liars, or only that as a group they are liars? Certainly it is a very strong claim that all of them are liars. To apply the principle of charity to this example, it would probably be fair to interpret the conclusion as referring to resort motel owners as a group rather than as individuals. Also, this formulation seems so strained that it increases the possibility that the argument should be analyzed as inductive rather than deductive. A possible alternative interpretation is the following:

> *All the resort motel operators interviewed in one Florida town reported that their business was good.*
>
> *The parking lots of these motels were practically empty, and the bank reported it had not cashed as many travelers' checks as in previous years.*
>
> *[If a motel's parking lot is almost empty and its bank has not cashed many travelers' checks, then the motel's business is not good.]*
>
> *[If someone says business is good when it is not, then they are lying.]*
>
> *Therefore, it is probable that most (or many) resort motel owners lie about their business.*

It is also possible to divide this example into two arguments—one that is deductive and one that is inductive. The deductive argument would consist of a version of the first four premises and its conclusion would be 'All the resort motel operators interviewed in one Florida town were lying about their businesses'. This conclusion could in turn be used as the premise of an inductive argument in support of the conclusion. Therefore, most (or many) resort motel owners in this country lie about their business'.

One other direction in which an analysis of this example could go is worth mentioning. Up to this point we have been interpreting the sentence expressing the intended conclusion more or less literally. This may not, however, be a fair reading of the intentions of the author. The sentence, 'I am putting motel owners in resort towns on my list of The 10 Greatest Liars' may instead be read as a recommendation or command, similar to that expressed by a sentence like 'Take statements by motel owners in resort towns with a grain of salt', or 'Don't always believe everything you are told by motel owners in resort towns'. Such an interpretation would put this argument outside the scope of the methods of formal logical analysis to be discussed in this book, although it could still be further analyzed using other methods. It certainly would not be unreasonable to take this as the most plausible interpretation, even though we would not be able to deal with it further in this book. However, we shall still consider the alternative interpretations as not unreasonable, so we can use this example to illustrate certain features of the various systems of logic to be presented in later chapters. Now, let us go on to do a preliminary analysis of another example.

In October 1977, the World Health Organization announced that the last "natural" case of smallpox had been treated and declared that this highly infectious disease had been eliminated from the earth. In August 1978, Mrs. Janet Parker, an employee in the Medical School of Birmingham, England, died of what was diagnosed as smallpox. An investigation was launched immediately to try to determine how she had contracted this apparently extinct disease.

The investigators concluded that Mrs. Parker had been infected by a virus transmitted through the air from a laboratory in the building where she worked. Their conclusion was based on the following evidence: Medical examiners isolated the smallpox virus from Mrs. Parker's body and identified it as a strain known as 'Abid'. It was determined that stocks of this strain were being kept and studied in a laboratory directly below the office where Mrs. Parker worked. Although it had long been believed that the smallpox virus could not be transmitted by any means other than direct physical contact, one case occurred in 1970 in a German hospital where it was concluded that smallpox had been transmitted by airborne viruses. Thus, even though Mrs. Parker had no known physical contact with anyone from the lab in which the smallpox virus was being kept, it was considered possible that the virus could have been transmitted through the air to her office. Since no other possible source existed of the virus from which she died, the investigators were certain that it must have come from the lab beneath her office. The tragedy was compounded when the director of that lab committed suicide a short time later.

The argument contained in this case could reasonably be expressed as follows:

> *Mrs. Parker was infected with the 'Abid' strain of smallpox virus.*
>
> *A quantity of the 'Abid' smallpox virus was being stored and studied in the lab directly below Mrs. Parker's office.*
>
> *It is possible for smallpox virus to be transmitted through the air.*
>
> *There was no other possible source of the 'Abid' virus than the downstairs lab.*
>
> *Mrs. Parker had not been in direct contact with any person or object from the downstairs lab.*
>
> *Therefore, Mrs. Parker must have been infected by a virus transmitted through the air from the downstairs lab.*

The argument in this form appears intuitively to be deductively valid. That is, it is structured in such a way that, *if* the premises are all true, then the conclusion must be true. In other words, there is no information that could be added to the premises—other than an assertion that at least one of the premises is false—that would make it possible for the conclusion to be false.

It would not be implausible to extract a somewhat different argument from the same case. For example, consider the following version:

> *The medical examiner reported that Mrs. Parker was infected with the 'Abid' strain of smallpox virus.*

> *A quantity of the 'Abid' strain of smallpox virus was being stored in the lab directly below Mrs. Parker's office.*
> *Of all of the millions of cases of smallpox examined over the years, there was only one in which it appeared that the virus was transmitted through the air.*
> *Mrs. Parker was not known to have been in contact with any person or object from the downstairs lab.*
> *The investigators could find no other source of the 'Abid' virus than the downstairs lab.*
> *Therefore, Mrs. Parker must have been infected by a virus transmitted through the air from the downstairs lab.*

On this interpretation, the argument is not deductively valid. Numerous premises could be added that would not challenge the truth of the given premises but that would make the conclusion false or at least doubtful. For example, Mrs. Parker might have been in physical contact with someone from the downstairs lab, even though the investigators had no knowledge of this. Or the medical examiner might have made a mistake. It would still be true that the medical examiner had diagnosed the case as one of 'Abid' smallpox, but it would be false that Mrs. Parker in fact had 'Abid' smallpox.

This kind of example helps us to see the extent to which our individual judgments affect the ways in which arguments are interpreted. Almost every argument can be qualified to a greater or lesser degree in such a way as to make it deductive or inductive. Thus, all generalizations about the world can be formulated as assertions about the *beliefs* of specific individuals or groups. For example, we can choose to formulate the third premise in the smallpox argument to say something about the transmitability of the virus through the air, but we can also formulate it as a statement describing the beliefs of medical experts.

We will conclude this chapter with the consideration of one final example, namely, the argument (in the ordinary language sense) expressed in the *Punch* cartoon on page 118. As with the two preceding examples, we will outline only a few of the possible preliminary analyses that might be made of it.

The simplest and most literal interpretation of the argument in the cartoon would seem to be something like the following.

> *You didn't bring me any flowers.*
> *If you don't bring me flowers, then you want me to think that you haven't got a guilty conscience.*
> *[Therefore, you want me to think that you haven't got a guilty conscience.]*

Such an argument is, in fact, valid, but it may not be an adequate analysis since it ignores much of the humor contained in a more subtle way in the situation. An

"No flowers. That means you want me to think you haven't got a guilty conscience."

© 1973 Punch-Rothco.

alternative conclusion that could be read out of this example is 'You have got a guilty conscience'. Another not implausible conclusion is 'You have done something that should cause you to have a guilty conscience'. Others are also possible. Let's only follow through a bit further with the first alternative. One possible set of premises that could be supplied in support of this conclusion would give the following argument.

> *You didn't bring me any flowers.*
> *If you don't bring me flowers, then you want me to*
>   *think that you haven't got a guilty conscience.*
> *[If you want me to think that you haven't got a guilty*
>   *conscience, then you must have a guilty*
>   *conscience.]*
> *[Therefore, you must have a guilty conscience.]*

This analysis has resulted in what can be shown to be a valid argument, but an inductive argument could also be read out of the same cartoon, as follows.

> *You didn't bring me any flowers.*
> *[In the past, whenever you didn't want me to think*
>   *you had a guilty conscience, you didn't bring me*
>   *flowers.]*
> *Therefore, you now want me to think that you don't*
>   *have a guilty conscience.*

While any of these interpretations is not entirely unreasonable, several more layers of subtle complexity could be read out of the cartoon that increase its humor as well. One possible analysis of the example is as a dilemma or Catch-22 situation, which might be formulated as follows:

> *You didn't bring me any flowers.*
> *[If you bring me flowers, then you must have a guilty*
>   *conscience.]*
> *If you don't bring me flowers, then you want me to*
>   *think that you don't have a guilty conscience.*
> *[If you want me to think that you don't have a guilty*
>   *conscience, then you must have a guilty*
>   *conscience.]*
> *[Therefore, you must have a guilty conscience.]*

Such an analysis not only makes it fairly apparent that the argument is deductively valid, but it makes explicitly clear that the conclusion is true, no matter what the husband has done, i.e., the first premise is essentially irrelevant and unnecessary.

Other interpretations are certainly possible. This discussion should be sufficient, however, to make the point that even a fairly simple and concise set of statements can be analyzed in a variety of plausible and quite different ways.

SOME BASIC ELEMENTS OF ARGUMENT ANALYSIS   The following listing of factors to be considered in the analysis and evaluation of arguments is in no way intended to be complete either in substance or detail. These are at most some of the more important and significant factors, and it must be recognized that there are many other factors that are more or less frequently relevant to the evaluation of particular arguments. It is also hoped that the preceding discussion of the sample argument has made it clear that a simple task description does not always mean that the task is simple. For example, it is easy to stipulate that the main conclusion should be identified and clearly and precisely formulated; it is all too often the case in dealing with actual arguments that this can be a very lengthy and complex task. In part, this complexity is the result of the requirement to adhere to the principle of charity, that is, to always try to interpret and formulate an argument in its strongest possible form. Since the strength of an argument is a function of the relation between the premises and conclusion, we cannot really know which formulation of a conclusion will make an argument stronger or weaker unless we already have some idea what the premises are. This also serves, therefore, as a reminder that the following list should not be understood to represent any kind of a fixed, necessary order for considering the specified factors. In actual practice it is not uncommon and often is even necessary to consider several factors simultaneously and to go from one to another and then back again to the first in some kind of a cyclic pattern. With these disclaimers and warnings, we now present the following list of significant factors in the analysis and evaluation of arguments:

- Identify and reformulate as necessary the main conclusion of the argument.
- Identify and reformulate as necessary the premises of the argument, making explicit any implicit premises.
- Determine whether the argument is most appropriately and strongly formulated in an inductive or deductive form.
- Identify and evaluate (using these same procedures) any subarguments offered in support of premises.
- Test the main argument for deductive validity or inductive strength.
- Identify the different kinds of premises, that is, those that are definitions, those that are statements of scientific fact or theory, metaphysical theory, ethical theory, and so on.
- Determine the degree of truth or plausibility of each of the premises.

EXERCISE 2–9   *Identify the conclusion in each of the following intended arguments and specify all explicitly stated premises. Add whatever premises you think are necessary to put the argument into its strongest form—whether inductive or deductive. Compare your analyses with those of other students in your class. Save these analyses!* You will need to use them later.

---

1. We are here to claim our rights as women, not only to be free, but to fight for freedom. It is our privilege, as well as our pride and our joy, to take some part in this militant movement, which, as we believe, means the regeneration of all humanity. Nothing but contempt is due to those people who ask us to submit to unmerited oppression. We shall not do it. (Christabel Pankhurst)
2. An aggressive war is the great crime against everything good in the world. A defensive war, which must necessarily turn to aggressive at the earliest moment, is the necessary great counter-crime. But never think that war, no matter how necessary, nor how justified, is not a crime. Ask the infantry and ask the dead. (Ernest Hemingway)
3. If I were a factory employee, a working man on the railroads, or a wage earner of any sort, I would undoubtedly join the union of my trade. If I disapproved of its policy, I would join in order to fight that policy; if the union leaders were dishonest, I would join in order to put them out. I believe in the union and I believe that all men who are benefitted by the union are morally bound to help to

the extent of their powers in the common interests advanced by the union. (Theodore Roosevelt)

4. Our government rests on public opinion. Whoever can change public opinion can change the government practically as such. (Abraham Lincoln)

5. From this arises the question whether it is better to be loved rather than feared, or feared rather than loved. It might perhaps be answered that we should wish to be both: but since love and fear can hardly exist together, if we must choose between them, it is far safer to be feared than loved. (Niccolò Machiavelli)

6. I would like to see the proletariat rule for a while . . . Through all the past this world has been ruled by property, and if there can ever come a time when the workingman can rule it, I will say he ought to have that chance to see what he can do; and yet to tell you that is to believe in the "dictatorship of the proletariat"—well, why not? (Clarence Darrow)

7. All amassing of wealth or hoarding of wealth above and beyond one's legitimate needs is theft. There would be no occasion for theft and no thieves if there were wise regulations of wealth, and social justice. (Mohandas Karamchana Gandhi)

8. All censorships exist to prevent any one from challenging current conceptions and existing institutions. All progress is initiated by challenging current conceptions, and executed by supplanting existing institutions. Consequently the first condition of progress is the removal of censorships. (George Bernard Shaw)

9. There are but three ways for the populace to escape its wretched lot. The first two are by the route of the wine-shop or the church; the third is by that of the social revolution. (Mikhail A. Bakunin)

10. The root problem is very simply stated: if there were no sovereign independent states, if the states of the civilized world were organized in some sort of federalism as the states of the American Union, for instance, are organized, there would be no international war as we know it . . . (Sir Norman Angell)

11. Freedom is not worth fighting for if it means no more than license for everyone to get as much as he can for himself. And freedom *is* worth fighting for. Because it does mean more than unrestricted grabbing. (Dorothy Canfield Fisher)

12. There is no safety where there is no strength; no strength without Union; no Union without justice; no justice where faith and truth are wanting. The right to be free is a truth planted in the hearts of men. (William Lloyd Garrison)

13. Marx predicted that the great industrial countries would be the first to advance, or collapse, into communistic socialism. His success as an economist in Russia was, in effect, his annihilation as a prophet. (Gilbert Seldes)

14. No reform, moral or intellectual, ever came from the upper class of society. Each and all came from the protest of martyr and victim. The emancipation of the working people must be achieved by the working people themselves. (Wendell Phillips)

15. Conventionality is not morality. Self-righteousness is not religion. To attack the first is not to assail the last. (Charlotte Bronte)

16. The truth is, as everyone knows, that the great artists of the world are never puritans, and seldom ever ordinarily respectable. No virtuous man—that is, virtuous in the YMCA sense—has ever painted a picture worth looking at, or written a symphony worth hearing, or a book worth reading, and it is highly improbable that the thing has ever been done by a virtuous woman. (H. L. Mencken)

17. The dictum that truth always triumphs over persecution is one of those pleasant falsehoods which men repeat after one another till they pass into commonplaces, but which all experience refutes. History teems with instances of truth put down by persecution. If not suppressed forever, it may be thrown back for centuries. (John Stuart Mill)

18. The Industrial Union grasps the principle: "No Government, no organization; no organization, no cooperative labor; no cooperative labor, no abundance for all without arduous toil, hence, no freedom." (Daniel DeLeon)

19. The chief end of man is to frame general propositions and no general proposition is worth a damn. (Oliver Wendell Holmes)

20. It is proof of a base and low mind for one to wish to think with the masses or majority, merely because the majority is the majority. Truth does not change because it is, or is not, believed by a majority of the people. (Giordano Bruno)

EXERCISE 2–10   *Return to the arguments which you analyzed in Exercise 3 of the Introduction and reanalyze them according to the instructions in Exercise 2.9. Compare your new analyses with those you did originally in the Introduction to determine the extent to which the concepts of logic which you learned in Chapters 1 and 2 have enabled you to make more sophisticated analyses. Save all of these answers for comparison with analyses you will be asked to do later.*

SUMMARY

1. In the context of logic, an **argument** is defined as a set of statements which is such that one of them (the **conclusion**) is supported or implied by the others (the **premises**). Although an argument is quite distinct from the psychological process (known as **inference**) of moving from one thought to another, an argument can be constructed that corresponds to every inference. Not all sets of statements which are asserted or intended to be arguments are in fact arguments; that is, the apparent premises do not provide any actual support for the conclusion.

2. Every argument or intended argument by definition contains one and only one conclusion, but it can have any number of premises. Identification of a conclusion may be facilitated by the presence of conclusion indicators such as 'therefore', 'hence', and 'it can be inferred'. Words such as 'since', 'because', 'for', and 'given that' indicate that the statement which follows is intended as a premise. In the absence of such **indicator words,** the function of a statement in a given argument often must be determined from its contextual use, since conclusion and premise statements in themselves are not inherently different (a conclusion in one argument may serve as a premise in another) nor do they occupy fixed positions in an argument (a conclusion may precede, follow, or come between premises).

3. Intended arguments may be difficult to identify for several reasons. A series of statements may be asserted as true but may not offer a conclusion or provide support for one. Indicator words are sometimes present when no argument is intended, or they may serve functions other than that of signifying the logical relationship between a given set of statements. We are then obliged to search for other linguistic clues or examine the context in order to determine whether an argument is intended or not.

4. It is possible that a series of statements intended as an argument may lack a conclusion and/or one or more premises but would qualify as an argument if the missing propositions were supplied. **Enthymemes,** as such intended

arguments are called, may strongly imply a certain conclusion or they may take for granted that the missing premises are already known by the intended audience. In the former case, we are justified in providing the missing conclusion. In the latter situation, we would examine the context and apply the **principle of charity** in adding the missing premise(s). This principle stipulates that whatever premises are added to the argument should make the argument as good as possible.

5.   There are two types of argument: **deductive** and **inductive.** In a **valid** deductive argument, the premises provide absolute support for the conclusion, whether or not they themselves are true. That is, if the premises *were* true, the conclusion would necessarily be true. The validity of a deductive argument, therefore, can be evaluated on the basis of its logical form, rather than its content. An argument which is not deductively valid constitutes an inductive argument. The premises of an inductive argument do not provide absolute support for the conclusion. A set of statements asserted or intended as a deductive argument may in fact be inductive (or not an argument at all) and vice versa.

6.   In order to qualify as a good argument of its type, a deductive argument must be **sound;** that is, it must be valid and the truth of all its premises must be well established. However, since determining the truth value of a given proposition often requires specialized knowledge of a subject, the logician is primarily concerned with evaluating the validity, rather than the soundness, of a deductive argument. A good deductive argument is not **circular:** it implies (and thus in effect contains) the conclusion in its premises, but its conclusion does not simply give an alternate wording of a statement that has already been expressed in the premises.

7.   Soundness, validity, and other absolute terms cannot be used in evaluating an inductive argument. In determining whether or not such an argument is good, we must consider the truth of its premises and the probability of its conclusion. We can say that an inductive argument is strong (or weak) if, compared with all possible arguments which could be given in support of its conclusion, this particular argument is stronger (or weaker) than most. Unlike a deductive argument, an inductive argument can be strengthened or weakened by additional information.

8.   In dealing with enthymemes (intended arguments with one or more statements implicit) it is usually possible to add statements that will result in a deductively valid (but possibly not sound) argument and also to add different statements that will make it a (strong or weak) inductive argument. One premise that can be added to many sets of statements to make them deductively valid is the **principle of induction** which states in one way or another that the future will resemble the past, that similar things behave similarly under similar circumstances.

9.   There are many factors which must be considered in analyzing intended arguments in everyday contexts, including identifying and reformulating the premises and conclusion, identifying and evaluating subarguments, and testing for deductive validity or inductive strength.

CHAPTER THREE

Informal Fallacies

In Chapter 2 it was pointed out that for an argument to be a good argument it must satisfy three conditions:

1. It must be valid or, if it is an inductive argument, the premises must provide a reasonable amount of support for the conclusion.
2. The truth of the premises must be well established.
3. It must not be circular.

Chapters 4 through 13 of this book present rather rigorous formal procedures, usually grounded on precisely defined concepts, for determining the validity or inductive strength (or weakness) of certain kinds of argument. However, such sophisticated techniques are not always necessary, or even adequate, for identifying many of the bad arguments each of us encounters frequently in everyday life. In this chapter we shall discuss a variety of kinds of bad argument that can be recognized as such without reliance on the methods of formal logic given in Chapters 4 through 13.

Logicians traditionally have used the term 'fallacy' as a synonym for 'bad reasoning'. Although some arguments are so blatantly fallacious that at most they can be used to amuse us, many are more deceptive and can be difficult to recognize. A conclusion often *appears* to follow logically and non-trivially from true premises, and only careful examination can reveal the fallaciousness of the argument. In this chapter we will be concerned only with such deceptively fallacious arguments, which are often accepted as good by persons in everyday situations—fallacies that are used, knowingly or unknowingly, by writers, advertisers, politicians, lawyers, and all those whose goal it is to persuade an audience to accept their conclusions. Such deceptively fallacious arguments, which can be recognized as such with little or no reliance on the methods of formal logic, are known as **informal fallacies.** Logicians and others have identified or defined literally hundreds of informal fallacies in the 2,300 years since Aristotle wrote the first treatise on logic. We will be able to present here only a small, though representative, sampling of some of the kinds of informal fallacy.

THE GENERAL METHOD OF INFORMAL ANALYSIS It is obviously much more valuable to have a general methodology for identifying fallacious arguments than to have memorized a very incomplete list of ten or even several dozen common fallacies. Thus, our discussion of informal fallacies in this chapter is designed to give you the sense of a method that can be used to identify not only the relatively few kinds of fallacies to be explicitly treated here but that you will be able to use for the whole range of fallacious arguments.

This general method is grounded in the basic fact that all sets of statements asserted as arguments in ordinary language can be analyzed in a variety of different ways. In particular, any set of statements can be interpreted as being both inductive and deductive arguments, as explained in Chapter 2, depending in part on the kinds of premises we choose to supply. We have seen that it is a matter of judgment as to which of many possible interpretations we should use in evaluating a particular set of statements, and that we should usually use the principle of charity to guide us in making those judgments. For the purpose of identifying informal fallacies, however, it is necessary to make some exceptions to this procedure, and instead to always begin our analysis by putting the argument in a deductively valid form. This procedure makes it easy to identify fallacies, since they must then be explicitly stated as clearly false or highly questionable premises. This general method will become clear if we apply it to some specific examples.

ARGUMENT FROM IGNORANCE At one time, most scientists believed that because the phenomenon of psychokinesis, or the ability to move physical objects with no devices or assistance other than one's mind, could not be scientifically proven, it obviously did not exist. That is, they made their inability to verify the phenomenon a justification for labeling all claims of its occurrence as false. In doing so they were using a fallacious mode of argument called *argumentum ad ignorantiam, or* **argument from ignorance.** The fact that a proposition has not been conclusively proved to be true or false establishes nothing but one's inability to prove or disprove it. In the case of our example, methods are now being devised to test psychokinesis, and there may one day be sufficient data to formulate a sound argument for or against its existence. Until then, the reasonable way of arguing about it is to say that existing evidence has not conclusively proved anything one way or the other.

The basic form of an *argumentum ad ignorantiam* is:

> *There is no evidence (or proof) that it is the case that X.*
> *Therefore, it is not the case that X.*

By substituting 'cigarette smoking causes cancer' for 'X', we produce the following argument:

> *There is no proof that cigarette smoking causes*
> *cancer.*
> *Therefore, cigarette smoking does not cause cancer.*

This argument is invalid as it stands, for the conclusion could be false while the premise is true. In fact, the truth of the premise is itself somewhat open to debate, since some people (e.g., the Surgeon General) assert that it has been proved that smoking causes cancer, whereas others (e.g., presidents of tobacco companies) deny this. For the purpose of this discussion, it is sufficient that the premise *may* be true. But it is not unreasonable to treat the argument as an enthymeme and add a premise to make it valid, as follows:

> *If there is no proof that something is the case, then*
> *that something is in fact not the case.*
> *There is no proof that cigarette smoking causes*
> *cancer.*
> *Therefore, cigarette smoking does not cause cancer.*

Although the argument is now, indeed, deductively valid, this new premise is far from being obviously true. In fact, it is highly questionable, and may be downright false. It is important to note that the weakness of the argument now rests in this questionable premise rather than in the validity of the argument.

Some arguments may appear on the surface to commit the *ad ignorantiam* fallacy, but on closer inspection can be seen to be legitimate. In particular, certain inductive arguments are quite good, even though they appear to have the same form as an *ad ignorantiam* fallacy:

> *Every possible attempt has been made to prove that*
> *such-and-such is the case.*
> *Not one attempt to prove that such-and-such is the*
> *case has been successful.*
> *Therefore, it is probable that such-and-such is not*
> *the case.*

This is essentially the type of reasoning that some physicists used at the end of the nineteenth century in arriving at the conclusion that a gravitational aether does not exist. It is probably also the kind of reasoning that led to the demise of alchemy. The conclusion that a base metal, such as lead, probably cannot be turned into gold was not unreasonable in the seventeenth or eighteenth centuries, even though present-day theories indicate that such a transmutation is at least theoretically possible. In any case, when confronted with an argument that appears to involve the *ad ignorantiam* fallacy, we should make sure that it cannot reasonably be interpreted as being a possibly good inductive argument.

FALSE DILEMMA A fallacy that is often very convincing when used in public debates is the **false dilemma,** which consists of presenting an argument as if there were fewer possible solutions of the problem than is actually the case. Usually only two alternatives are offered, in an either/or fashion. For example:

*If the new highway is built along the recommended
    route, the park will be destroyed.
If it is built along the alternate route, a residential
    neighborhood will be destroyed.
It will be built along either one route or the other.
Therefore either the park or a residential
    neighborhood will be destroyed.*

This argument is formally valid. If the premises are true, the conclusion will also be true. But it is probable that the either/or premise is not true. Very likely, there are other possible routes for the highway which would destroy neither park nor homes. Or, possibly, the highway may not be built at all (which may be precisely what the speaker of the above argument is trying to accomplish). If there are in fact such other alternatives, the argument as given above commits the fallacy of false dilemma.

In the case of the above argument, it was the either/or premise that was false. But one or both of the 'if . . . then . . .' statements might also be false; for example, consider the following argument:

*If coal miners work, they inhale coal dust and
    develop black-lung disease.
If they don't work, they can't earn any money.
Either they work or they don't.
Therefore either they develop black-lung disease or
    they don't earn any money.*

Again, this argument is formally valid. But the first 'if . . . then . . .' statement is false, for, although miners may indeed develop black-lung disease as a consequence of inhaling coal dust, it is not necessary for them to inhale the dust. The use of proper safety equipment in the mines can prevent it. Thus, again, the two alternatives offered are not the only ones, and the dilemma is a false one. There are conditions under which miners can both earn money and avoid contracting an incurable disease.

Actually, true either/or situations are very rare, and whenever a speaker, columnist, lobbyist, or advertiser confronts us with one we would do well to examine it carefully. Unless one alternative amounts to a direct contradiction of the other ('either X or not-X'), and both of the 'if . . . then . . .' statements are true, there are probably other choices available—choices which the arguer does not want his hearers to notice.

Dilemmas—false or valid—do not always have to be simple either/or problems; they sometimes are quite complex, as in the *Ms.* item at the left. What

Few firms have had formal policies against women traveling, but the unwritten obstacles are something else again. They are generally rationalized this way: if a woman travels alone, she might not be safe. If she travels with a single man, it might not look proper. If she travels with a married man, his wife might be jealous. If a customer makes a pass at her and she declines, he might be embarrassed and never deal with the company again. If she accepts, she might be embarrassed and never call on the customer again. And, worries one major corporation president, who will take care of the traveling woman's husband while she's gone?

DEE WEDEMEYER IN *Ms.*

FEIFFER

The executive in the above cartoon commits the fallacy of false dilemma. Explain what is wrong with his formulation of the alternative courses of action.

makes a dilemma fallacious is the implicit suggestion that all of the options are listed, when in fact one or more are not given. This example *is* fallacious. Can you identify some of the omitted options?

FALLACY OF FALSE CAUSE   If a person lives in an apartment with damp walls and roaches, he may conclude that damp walls cause roaches or that roaches cause damp walls, but he has no proof for either contention. Republicans claim that the Democrats cause wars, and Democrats say that the Republicans cause depressions. All that is known for certain is that Democratic presidents were in office when two world wars broke out, and that Republican presidents were in office when two major depressions occurred. These are examples of one of the most widespread and insidious of fallacies, the fallacy of **false cause.**

A special type of false cause fallacy is the *post hoc ergo propter hoc,* meaning 'after this, therefore because of this.' If a person arrives at a bus stop ten seconds before a bus pulls up, and believes that it has come, like a taxicab, because he or she is there to board it, he or she commits the fallacy of *post hoc ergo propter hoc.*

So does the person who steps into an empty elevator and, after it has filled up, says, "I know you're all wondering why I called this meeting."

There are, of course, many difficulties surrounding the entire concept of causality, some of which are outlined in Chapter 12. Still, it is easy enough to recognize that the conjunction in space and time of two events or states of affairs is not sufficient to establish the existence of a causal relation between them. Coincidences do happen, and one must not draw the conclusion that, just because something occurs in time after something else, the earlier was the cause of the later.

This fallacy can be formulated as involving inductive arguments whose premises really provide little or no support for their conclusions, although at first glance the argument may appear strong. However, it can also be formulated as a valid deductive argument—with an obviously false premise—as follows:

> *Any event which immediately precedes another*
>   *event is the cause of that event.*
> *Event X immediately preceded event Y.*
> *Therefore, event X is the cause of event Y.*

Thus, as with arguments in general, this kind can be formulated as both an inductive and a deductive argument, and the addition of the premise(s) necessary to make it deductively valid makes the weakness of this argument perfectly obvious.

FALLACY OF HASTY GENERALIZATION   The fallacy of **hasty generalization** involves forming a generalization from a sample that is too small or poorly selected, thus allowing the possibility that all the cases may be exceptional rather than typical. The basic premise necessary to make valid an argument committing the fallacy of hasty generalization is the following statement, which is certainly less than plausible:

> *If something is true of a few members of a group,*
>   *then it is true of all of the members of that group.*

This is, at best, a very weak version of the principle of induction discussed in Chapter 2.

Formal criteria for constructing good generalizations are spelled out in some detail in Chapter 10, but there are several informal commonsense rules that we all recognize and use regularly in everyday situations. The most obvious is that, to make a reasonably safe generalization and avoid the fallacy of hasty generalization, it is necessary to collect enough data about the matter at hand to distinguish the typical from the accidental. Consider the person who wants to be governor of Louisiana and, therefore, decides that to win he should be like Jimmy Davis, a former governor who, before his election, had been a professional guitar player and singer. But, if he did the proper research, he would discover that Davis was the only governor in the history of the state who had also been a professional musician—hence an exception to the general rule. Like other states, Louisiana tends to elect lawyers as its public officials, and any listing of qualifications for governor would more reasonably include being a lawyer—not being a musician—among its essentials.

The Irish poet W. B. Yeats and many of his friends and colleagues were agnostics and admirers of the aristocracy, but their case cannot be used to generalize about all Irish people. Yeats and his circle were a small minority and were thus exceptions, not the rule. Most of the Irish were then, as now, Catholic and republican. To generalize about the Irish on the basis of what one knows about Yeats would be "jumping to a conclusion" on the basis of inadequate evidence. This type of fallacious thinking characterizes many forms of prejudice. Poles are stupid; Jews are avaricious; Latin lovers are sexy; women are catty, and so on. In part, our tendency to make hasty generalizations may be psychologically grounded. A considerable amount of research supports the thesis that people tend to seek out examples that reinforce their beliefs. The old lady who is mugged by a Puerto Rican—even if she is a liberal old lady—is likely afterward to be particularly alert to other examples of crimes committed by Puerto Ricans, which then tend to support her conviction that all Puerto Ricans are dangerous lawbreakers. But the fact—if it is a fact—that we tend to think in this way provides in itself little if any justification for assuming that this is a good way to reason.

FALLACY OF COMPOSITION   The fallacy of **composition** is often confused with the fallacy of hasty generalization, although it is actually quite different. It does *not* involve generalizing from a few members of a group to all of the other members of the group. Rather, it involves an inference from something that is already known to be true of all members of the group to a conclusion concerning the group itself. In its deductively valid form, it looks like this:

> *All members (or parts) of X have property A.*
> *If all the members (or parts) of a group (or entity)*
>   *have a property, then the group (or entity) has that*
>   *property.*
> *Therefore, X has property A.*

We can see the weakness of the second premise by considering some examples representing two different forms of the same fallacy.

The first form of this fallacy occurs when a person falsely argues that a whole (considered as a single entity) has a certain characteristic because each of its parts has that characteristic. Thus, a person would commit the fallacy of composition if he concluded that, since each pane of glass in a geodesic dome is triangular, the dome itself must be triangular. Similarly, it would be fallacious to argue that if each individual member of an orchestra is an excellent musician, the orchestra will play excellently. The fallacy arises from taking an attribute common to all the parts and assuming that it is a characteristic of the whole, in a situation in which the whole operates under some principle different from that of the parts. In the case of the geodesic dome, the positioning of the glass triangles as they are joined results in a hemispherical shape for the dome. Likewise, the orchestra operates under a number of principles that do not affect the skill of the individual members, such as the ability of the musicians to play together and the competence of the conductor.

The first form of the fallacy of composition occurs in cases where the parts form a whole that is something more than the sum of the parts, as a geodesic dome is more than a heap of triangular pieces. The second form occurs when a person invalidly concludes that a *collection* of elements has a certain characteristic because each element in the collection has this characteristic. For example, every feather is light, but it is obviously erroneous to conclude that a ton of feathers is light. The fallacy here arises from a confusion between the distributive and collective uses of general terms. A word is used in its distributive sense when it refers to properties possessed by the individual members of a collection. When it refers to a property possessed by the totality of members of a collection, it is being used in its collective sense. Every feather is distributively light, but a ton of feathers is not collectively light. Similarly, a toaster uses more electricity than an ordinary light bulb, but it would be fallacious to conclude that all toasters together use more electricity than all light bulbs together. There are more light bulbs than toasters, and light bulbs are used more frequently. Thus, toasters use more electricity than ordinary light bulbs distributively, but not necessarily collectively.

FALLACY OF DIVISION   The fallacy of **division** is precisely the opposite of the fallacy of composition, in that it involves an inference from something that is known to be true of a group or entity to a conclusion concerning each member or component. Its deductively valid form also includes a highly questionable, if not blatantly false, premise.

> *X has property A.*
> *If some group (or entity) has a property, then all of its members (or parts) have that property.*
> *Therefore, each and every member (or part) of X has property A.*

Like the fallacy of composition, this fallacy also occurs in two forms. The first form occurs when it is falsely argued that because the whole has a certain attribute, a part also has that particular attribute. Sometimes the fallacy is obvious, as in the claim that because a joke is funny, every word in the joke is funny, or that because the jury is split over the decision, every juror must be split over the decision. Less obvious is the fallacy in the argument that George must be an excellent student because he went to Harvard, which has a high academic reputation. It is true that Harvard has a high reputation, but it is not necessarily true that *every* person who attended Harvard is a good student.

In the second form of the fallacy of division, one argues that what is true of a collection of items must be true of the items themselves. When the attribute being considered is a distributive attribute, the inference will be valid; but when it is a collective attribute, it will be invalid. Consider the following description of an entering class at Erehwon University:

> The class of '79 comes to us from 13 countries and 48 states. Their varied interests include archeology, Chinese, stamp collecting, filmmaking, physics, and basket weaving. They are unmarried, 60 percent female, and range in age from 15 to 24.

From this statement, it does not follow that a particular student in the class comes from 13 countries and 48 states, or is 60 percent female. To assume either of these would be to try to assign collective properties of the group distributively. The only one of these statements that is true of the group distributively as well as collectively is that any given student is single.

EXERCISE 3–1

Identify the informal fallacy, or fallacies—or at least one if there are several—involved in the following arguments. You may also find it useful to reformulate each example as a valid deductive argument, adding premises as needed, and then identifying which of the added premises are questionable or blatantly false.

---

1. One can see, from the number of unmarried women listed in the abortion statistics of states where abortion has been legalized, that the legalization of abortion has encouraged sexual activity outside marriage.
2. The Palace of Versailles gives us an idea of the elegance and luxury in which the people of France lived in the seventeenth and eighteenth centuries.
3. The counselor said I shouldn't have spanked Bennie for breaking the window; but isn't it better to do it right away rather than wait till my husband comes home and can do it in the evening?
4. Tests on the patient's blood and urine were performed at the hospital laboratory and have yielded negative results. The patient's illness can therefore be attributed to psychological rather than physiological causes.
5. We in America today are more fortunate than our ancestors in the Old World. While our present infant mortality rate is less than one percent, more than a third of my ancestors must have died during infancy, for they lived in a region where the rate of infant mortality was 39 percent until 1910.
6. It's not going to help the energy crisis to have people ride buses instead of cars. Buses use more gas than cars.
7. Faith healing is a fraud. There is no scientific evidence to suggest that any real medical healing takes place, although the power of suggestion may in some cases be great enough to make people think they are cured.
8. We will never have ideal rulers. If rulers are ambitious they will be willing to sacrifice the good of the people to their own private advantage. If rulers are not ambitious they will be ineffectual, even if well intentioned.
9. As TV watching has increased over the last ten years, so has the crime rate. The

more TV people watched, the more crimes they committed. So TV watching causes crime.

10. No one can prove that drivers who were drunk when they had accidents would not have the same accidents had they been sober. It is therefore unwarranted to claim that a driver's state of intoxication increases his likelihood of having an accident.

11. According to the latest figures from the Controller's office, the city's revenues have fallen off considerably. I suggest that the City Council immediately approve a 25 percent across-the-board budget cut for all departments. The people of the city will just have to learn to live with three-fourths of the services they have had up to this time.

12. With a *laissez faire* policy, each member of society acts in a way that will best advance his or her own economic interest. Consequently, all individuals and ultimately society as a whole achieves the maximum economic advantages.

APPEAL TO FORCE   Although it is one of the most obvious of the informal fallacies, the **appeal to force,** or *argumentum ad baculum,* is, nonetheless, one of the most effective. Literally translated, *argumentum ad baculum* means "argument toward the stick." Its power to persuade lies in its arousal of the listener's fear. Instead of obtaining agreement through cogent reasoning and the presentation of evidence, the appeal to force seeks to intimidate her or him into acquiescence.

The only possible premise that could be added to make an argument valid that commits this fallacy would be something to the effect of "might makes right." In complete form, it would have to look like the following:

> **Those who have the power to control other persons'
> health and welfare are always correct in their
> beliefs and opinions.
> X has the power to control other persons' health
> and welfare, and X believes that A is true.
> Therefore, A is true.**

The first premise may seem so obviously false that you might think that no one would ever commit this fallacy. Unfortunately, the history books and newspapers provide all too many examples of its use.

The success of the Spanish Inquisition in "defending" the Roman Catholic faith was largely due to its free use of the appeal to force. Dissident Catholics were told that they would spend eternity in Hell unless they recanted. And if their beliefs withstood this argument, there was the more immediate threat of torture or death. Although neither argument dealt directly with the religious doctrines under dispute, they both effected thousands of conversions. Such methods are by no means obsolete. In 1968, after the intelligence ship *USS Pueblo* was seized by North Korean gunboats, the commander admitted to spying activities when his adversaries told him, "You will sign this confession or we will begin to shoot your crew one at a time in your presence." The threat certainly gave the commander good grounds for signing the "confession," but it in no way proved that the statements therein were true.

The "force" appealed to need not be physical violence. Attempts to manipulate the views of a politician often include appeals to force, such as threats to withhold campaign financing unless the candidate reconsiders his position on some piece of proposed legislation. Here the appeal is to the politician's personal fear of financial embarrassment and loss of status, and it is used in place of arguments about the legislation itself. In the courtroom, a jury may be the target

"I long to hear that you have declared an independency. And in the new code of laws which I suppose it will be necessary for you to make, I desire you would remember the ladies and be more generous than your ancestors. . . . If particular care and attention is not paid to the ladies, we are determined to foment a rebellion and will not hold ourselves bound by any laws in which we have no voice or representation."

ABIGAIL (SMITH) ADAMS, LETTER TO JOHN ADAMS, 1774.

Was Abigail Adams committing the fallacy of appeal to force in her letter to her husband, or was she simply indicating that her position is a self-supported axiom and that she would not accept a shifting the burden of proof, just as her husband and his colleagues were doing with the king of England?

of the appeal to force. The prosecutor may say to them, for instance: "Will you be safe in the streets at night if this man is not convicted and put behind bars?" Without offering any additional evidence of the defendant's guilt, he has increased the chance of a "guilty" verdict by substituting the jurors' fears of being attacked for the proper criteria on which the guilt or innocence of the defendant should be determined. The defense, of course, will often respond in kind, "warning" the jury that "if you don't acquit this innocent person, you may some day be convicted of a crime you didn't commit."

The *ad baculum* is indeed so blatantly fallacious that it would not be a mistake to simply assert that it is not an argument at all. The premises that must be added to make it valid are certainly highly questionable. Thus, the response of the victim of the *ad baculum* in the cartoon at the top of page 135 is perhaps the best kind of analysis of such an "argument."

APPEAL TO AUTHORITY   A person makes an **appeal to authority** by citing the opinion of a purported expert to reinforce his own opinion. Because what is taken as fact is often derived from statements by an authority (particularly in scientific and technical matters), or from the consensus of several authorities, an argument that rests on such supporting opinion is not necessarily fallacious. An appeal to authority *is* fallacious, however, when the person appealed to is not truly an authority on the subject under consideration. It is such an illicit appeal to author-

"Sir, the logic of your argument is questionable, but your method of presentation is irrefutable."

Reprinted with permission of National Review, *150 East 36th St., New York, N.Y. 10016.*

ity, or pseudo-authority, which constitutes the *ad verecundiam* fallacy (literally, "argument toward reverence"). For instance, while it is legitimate to quote an internist's concurring opinion on the causes of appendicitis, it is hardly relevant to quote him as an authority on the stock market. Similarly, quoting a famous trial lawyer on the techniques of courtroom cross-examination might be appropriate, but using the attorney's political beliefs to support one's own is fallacious. Citing the attorney in the latter context amounts to an attempt to use the listener's presumed respect for her or his courtroom abilities to arouse similar respect for her or his political opinions, and there is no evidence that the latter are more authoritative than those of any other individual.

The basic form of arguments that commit the fallacy of the appeal to authority is something like this:

> **Person A is an expert on subject X.**
> **A says that such-and-such is the case about subject Z.**
> **Therefore, such-and-such is the case about subject Z.**

To make this argument deductively valid, we would have to add a premise such as the following, which is clearly false.

> **Everything that an expert on subject X says about subject Z is true.**

The only really plausible argument of this general form is the inductive one, which uses as its basic premise something like this:

Everything an expert on subject X says about subject X is probably true.

Who constitutes a genuine authority can be a matter of dispute, complicated by the fact that the evaluation of a particular authority may change with time. The arguments that Galileo's contemporaries marshaled against his contention that the sun stands still while the earth spins on its axis were based on the Bible, once accepted by Western society as the ultimate authority on everything. To-day, most of us would regard an attempt to refute astronomical measurements and calculations with the words of the Old Testament as a fallacious appeal to authority.

Nor does appealing to one authority in the appropriate field always prove an argument conclusively, for authorities in the same field often subscribe to conflicting theories. It is reasonable to quote a renowned psychologist as saying that premarital sexual relations between men and women have doubled in the past twenty years. But another renowned psychologist holds that it is the free-dom to discuss sex, not the incidence of premarital relations, that has grown. The opinions of the two authorities in this situation are contradictory, and it is impor-tant in such cases to acknowledge the controversial nature of the subject and the inconclusiveness of both arguments. It is even more important to recognize the need for going directly to the factual evidence whenever possible, rather than depending needlessly upon even legitimate authorities.

Advertisers frequently promote their products with the aid of pseudo-authorities. A favorite technique, until it was outlawed, was to dress an actor in a doctor's white coat and let him lecture the television audience on the benefits of some patent medicine. Advertisers also exploit the popularity of public figures whose only credentials as "authorities" are their fame as sports celebrities or television stars. They endorse products or services because they are paid to do so, not because they have made a study of all comparable products and found the ones they are endorsing to be superior. Thus, baseball pitcher Tom Seaver exhorts the television audience to buy a brand of gasoline which does not differ significantly from other gasolines. Willis Reed, in full basketball uniform, wordlessly eats a container of yogurt. His endorsement consists of smiling.

APPEAL TO THE PEOPLE   Another common mode of argument that is often persuasive, in spite of its manifest error in reasoning, is the *argumentum ad populum,* or **appeal to the people.** Perhaps calling it an "error in reasoning" is itself somewhat erroneous, for the source of the argument's persuasiveness often lies in the fact that it bypasses reasoning altogether, to manipulate the passions, prejudices, and identity of an audience.

Put into valid deductive form, most *ad populum* arguments look something like this:

> *If most people believe (or like, or want, etc.)*
> *something, then that something is true (or good, or*
> *valuable, etc.).*
> *Most people believe (or like, or want, etc.) X.*
> *Therefore, X is true (or good, or valuable, etc.).*

A common *ad populum* argument makes use of the "bandwagon effect" — "Everybody's doing it, so you should too." "Nineteen million people brush with Pearly Toothpaste." "It's all right to help yourself to a bit of the stuff in the stockroom now and then; all the guys do it." Bandwagon thinking is an important element in modern mass culture.

A relatively new version of the advertiser's favorite *ad populum* — the one that makes use of the desire "to be like everyone else" — is the appeal directed to the "individualist." One cigarette manufacturer, for example, challenges the consumer to identify which person in a group smokes its brand of cigarettes. The people in the photograph exhibit symptoms of everything from slavish conformity to mild insanity, except for the "right man" who poses as an island of untroubled tranquillity and independence. The appeal is direct: it's now "in" to be "out" and the right cigarette will help you get there.

It is interesting, and encouraging, to note that, when sound arguments and pertinent evidence are made available to the public, the persuasive power of an *ad populum* argument is noticeably reduced.

BEGGING THE QUESTION   It was pointed out in Chapter 2 that any argument that is circular is by definition deductively valid but is also a bad argument. It was also pointed out that it is difficult, if not impossible, to provide a definition that does not include all deductively valid arguments in the class of circular arguments, since one of the features of a deductively valid argument is that its conclusion must be contained in its premises. It was suggested that the definition of 'circular argument' must refer to psychological facts about the knowledge and beliefs of the hearer (or reader) of the argument rather than to any formal features of the argument itself. That is, an argument is circular if, for its intended audience, the conclusion is merely a restatement of something explicitly stated in the premises. Any argument that is bad because it is circular is said to commit the fallacy of **begging the question** or *petitio principii*. It is worth our while to look at several examples of this kind of fallacious reasoning.

Begging the question frequently follows a more circuitous pattern than in the example given in Chapter 2, and is then more aptly called a circular argument. For instance, someone may contend that public television is better than commercial television, the proof being that more-intelligent people prefer it.

And when questioned about how it is known that those who watch public television are more intelligent, he may reply that they are recognizable by their good taste and critical alertness, and then define people of good taste and critical alertness as those who appreciate the sort of program shown on public television.

Lucy's analysis of Charlie Brown's problem in the Peanuts cartoon also involves a common form of the fallacy of begging the question since she only offers synonyms for the original term in Charlie's question—weaknesses and failings are not the causes of faults, they are the same thing as faults!

The longer the circular argument, the more chance there is that the listener will lose track and be fooled into accepting the conclusion as having been proved true. Such was the strategy effectively employed by Ernst Huber, Nazi political scientist and prolific spokesman for Hitler:

> The Fuehrer is the bearer of the people's will; he is independent of all groups, associations, and interests, but he is bound by laws which are inherent in the nature of his people. . . . The Fuehrer is no "representative" of a particular group whose wishes he must carry out. . . . He is . . . himself the bearer of the collective will of the people. In his will the will of the people is realized. He transforms the mere feelings of the people into a conscious will. . . . Thus it is possible for him, in the name of the true will of the people which he serves, to go against the subjective opinions and convictions of single individuals within the people if these are not in accord with the objective destiny of the people. . . . He shapes the collective will of the people within himself.*

The point is made, but where is the proof? It clearly does not lie in repeating the same thing a half dozen times or more, which is all Huber has really done. In a sense, such a question-begging "argument" as this is not really an argument so much as it is a belabored exposition. But, as history has shown, such arguments have often proved very persuasive.

FALLACY OF EQUIVOCATION   Some fallacies are such that they cannot be identified by putting them into deductively valid form because they originally occur in what at least *appears* to be a valid form. To recognize these fallacies it is necessary to learn how to see through the appearances to the underlying problems. One such fallacy is that of **equivocation,** which involves the concept of ambiguity already discussed in Chapter 1. In brief, this fallacy occurs whenever the validity (or inductive strength) of an argument is dependent on the assumption (intentional or accidental) that an ambiguous term is being used with the same meaning throughout the argument when, in fact, it has at least two different meanings in different places in the "argument."

---

* Quoted in Raymond E. Murphy, Francis B. Stevens, Howard Rivers, and Joseph M. Roland, *National Socialism: Basic Principles, Their Application by the Nazi Party's Foreign Organization and the Use of Germans Abroad for Nazi Aims.* U.S. Government Printing Office, 1943, pp. 34–35.

Serious examples of the fallacy of equivocation are usually characterized by this similarity of meanings in the equivocal element. An example occurs in the following argument:

> *Man is an inventor.*
> *No woman is a man.*
> *No woman is an inventor.*

The argument seems deductively valid. Both premises are plausible. How, then, can the conclusion be false? The answer is that two different senses of the word 'man' are confused in the argument. 'Man' means 'mankind' in the first premise and 'member of the male sex' in the second. Both meanings are legitimate, but they are not interchangeable. (The feminists' efforts to remove the first sense of 'man' from our vocabulary may thus prevent people from committing this particular fallacy of equivocation.)

Some examples of the fallacy of equivocation are patently absurd, such as the following:

> *Somebody arrived at the party at six o'clock.*
> *Somebody left the party at nine o'clock.*
> *Somebody stayed at the party for three hours.*

The fallacy here lies in the ambiguous use of the word 'somebody'. The "validity" of the argument rests on the assumption that 'somebody' refers to the same person throughout.

It is not always as easy to identify a word or phrase being used equivocally as in the preceding examples. Equivocation is often concealed in the manipulation of statistics, as in the following hypothetical argument:

The war against crime has been highly successful in some areas of the nation. The increase in the number of crimes in New York City in 1973 was well below the increase in 1972. In 1972, the number of crimes increased 50 percent over 1971. In 1973, the number increased only 33.3 percent over 1972.

Mathematical substitution can be used to demonstrate that the conclusion cannot be drawn from the facts asserted in the premises. If, for example, there were 1,000 crimes in 1971 and the number of crimes increased by 50 percent in 1972, then there were 1,500 crimes in 1972. If that number increased by 33.3 percent in 1973, there were 2,000 crimes that year. Thus the number of crimes in 1973 increased by 500, just as it did in 1972. The equivocation in this example turns on the false assumption that the phrase '50 percent increase in crime' refers to a larger number than the phrase '33.3 percent increase in crime', when in fact the two phrases both refer to the same quantity—namely, 500.

A final prevalent form of the fallacy of equivocation involves the use of relative terms—terms of degree that have different meanings in different contexts. All terms that imply a degree of quantitative measurement such as 'heavy', 'small', and 'major', may be sources of equivocation. No one hesitates to pick up

SCOOPS   **by Doug Sneyd**

What is the critical ambiguity in this 1978 editorial cartoon? What definition might be used to clarify it? Is Senator Kennedy equivocating?

Sneyd Syndicate, Inc.

a heavy baby on the ground that he cannot lift a heavy car, because he knows that 'heavy' means something different when it describes a baby than when it describes a car. But reports of a heavy snowfall in Atlanta might deter a New Englander from driving there until he learned that 'heavy' in the South may mean 'two inches'. Similarly, the fallacy of equivocation may result from imprecise use of such words as 'good', 'bad', and 'difficult'. For instance, some people argue that good laws make good citizens, or that a student who is bad in science is a bad student.

The important lesson to be learned from this and similar fallacies is that what sometimes appears to be a valid or inductively strong argument, and what can even be *proved* to be deductively valid using the techniques of formal logic, is not always even an argument due to the ambiguities inherent in natural languages. We must *always* be alert for fallacies such as these. Because of the importance of this topic, let us look briefly at a second fallacy which underlies what appears to be a valid argument.

FALLACY OF AMPHIBOLY   An amphibolous statement contains imprecise grammar or syntax which permits two or more interpretations, only one of which is accurate. Dangling modifiers often produce amphiboly, as in the following example;

> The film is about a real person, Frank Serpico, who deals with equally real corruption in the New York City Police Department, and was shot this summer in New York, with full cooperation from the city and the police department.*

> * Quoted in *The New Yorker,* Dec. 3, 1973. P. 53. Originally published in the Long Beach (Calif.) *Independent Press-Telegram.* (*The New Yorker's* comment: "You can't fight City Hall.")

The fallacy of **amphiboly** occurs when a person draws an invalid conclusion from a faulty interpretation of a grammatically ambiguous statement. If a reader of this movie review concluded that Serpico was the victim of some official plot, his error would have resulted from the reviewer's use of amphiboly.

Amphiboly is usually given short shrift in logic texts as a fallacy that seldom occurs in serious modern arguments. It is true that formal invalid reasoning based on amphibolous statements is rare. However, the real issue with amphiboly is not erroneous reasoning, but erroneous interpretation of arguments presented in informal everyday contexts. Modern advertising is filled with examples of intentionally ambiguous statements which the advertiser wants the consumer to misinterpret. For instance, an advertisement may claim that the product

"I always promise them the good life. They always re-elect me and that's exactly what I get — the good life."

Although it may be debatable whether the politician in the above cartoon committed the fallacy of equivocation or the fallacy of amphiboly, it is certainly clear that he intentionally deceived his constituents in his choice of wording for his campaign pledge.

Reprinted Courtesy of *The Boston Globe*.

comes with a "lifetime guarantee." The consumer assumes that the product is guaranteed for as long as he lives, whereas the guarantee actually refers to the life of the product. Likewise, the manufacturer who claims that "nine out of ten doctors recommend the pain-relieving ingredients in our product" hopes that the consumer will misinterpret the statement to mean "nine out of *every* ten doctors recommend our product," rather than nine out of a particular and selected ten.

It is often difficult to determine whether a particular bad argument commits the fallacy of amphiboly or the fallacy of equivocation. Take, for instance, the classic tale of Croesus, King of Lydia, who asked the oracle if he could be assured of victory in going to war with Persia. When the oracle replied, "You will destroy a great kingdom," Croesus confidently set off to war, only to learn that the great kingdom to be destroyed was his own. Clearly, he was a victim of fallacious reasoning; but it is not clear whether it rested on the ambiguity in the term 'great kingdom' (in which case it would be the fallacy of equivocation) or on the ambiguity of the entire sentence (in which case it would be the fallacy of amphiboly). For practical purposes, what is important is to recognize that the reasoning *is* fallacious, whether or not we can decide precisely which fallacy it commits.

ARGUMENT AGAINST THE PERSON

Some fallacies arise primarily in the context of responding to or criticizing someone else's argument or position. Such counterarguments are fallacious when they fail to identify any weakness in the other person's argument or conclusion. The fallacy of **argument against the person** consists of attacking a person's beliefs or assertions by attacking the person himself in one way or another. It is often referred to by its Latin name, *argumentum ad hominem,* which, literally translated, means "argument toward the man." This fallacious argument appears most often in one of three forms: the abusive, the circumstantial, and the *tu quoque* ("you, too").

Abusive Argument

A disputant is unlikely to change his opinion because his opponent has dubbed him "an unrealistic fool." But it takes considerable independence of thought on the part of the listeners to support him in spite of such a label. Thus, an **abusive argument** leveled against one's opponents can have the effect of discrediting any statements they make—something former Vice-President Spiro Agnew recognized in his campaign against journalists and newscasters who criticized the Nixon administration. By calling them "an impudent corps of *effete* snobs" and "nattering nabobs of negativism," he tried to diminish their influence on the American public. Similar name-calling is equally common at the international level.

To make an *ad hominum* argument deductively valid, it is necessary to add a highly questionable premise such as the following.

> **Anything that a person with characteristic A says (or believes or advocates) is false.**

Person X has characteristic A and advocates P.
Therefore, P is false.

Unless characteristic A is something like "being a chronic liar" or "having an IQ of 10" *and* strong evidence is presented that X in fact has characteristic A, the counterargument is fallacious.

As well as using epithets, the abusive argument against the person can also operate with factual but irrelevant data about the opponent. It is, for instance, quite irrelevant to a debate about school appropriations that the opponent fought on the side of the Germans in World War II and that he is now living with another man's wife. Yet these facts may be so abhorrent to some hearers that they will not want to be associated with such a man, even on the issue of school appropriations. On the other hand, if the prosecution's key witness in a murder case can be shown to be a habitual liar, this is quite relevant, since his trustworthiness is a key factor in the worth of his testimony.

Circumstantial Argument   The **circumstantial argument** cites the opponent's personal circumstances as sufficient reason for dismissing a statement she has made. "Of course she favors highway construction: her biggest campaign contributor was a manufacturer of road-building machinery." "Why shouln't those welfare mothers support public day care? They're the ones who'll benefit from it, and they don't have to pay for it." These statements about an individual's personal circumstances may be perfectly true, but they do not by themselves constitute rational disproof of her position on the issues.

Other circumstantial *ad hominem* arguments may point out a contrast between the opponent's lifestyle and his expressed opinions, thereby suggesting that the opponent and his statements can be dismissed as hypocritical. For example: "This man who has just condemned all types of corporal punishment goes hunting every weekend and kills harmless animals," or, "If Mrs. Jones really believed that the hospital is understaffed, she would work there as a volunteer." Such assumptions are, by themselves, quite clearly insufficient to support any conclusions as to the real merits of corporal punishment or the true staff situation at the hospital.

Of course, we say that we do not believe in god. We know perfectly well that the clergy, the landlords, and the bourgeoisie all claimed to speak in the name of god, in order to protect their own interests as exploiters.
V. I. LENIN

Lenin is committing the ad hominem–circumstantial fallacy in this statement. Why?

Tu Quoque Argument   In a **tu quoque,** or "you, too," argument, a person does not address himself to the issue raised against him, but instead attempts to absolve himself by proving the guilt of his opponent. In response to objections or accusations, the *tu quoque* has several tactical advantages: it allows one to avoid answering to the substance of the charges; it may throw the opponent off guard; and it directs the attention to the opponent's weakness and away from one's own.

During the hearings of the Senate's special Watergate committee, for example, Senator Ervin criticized John Mitchell for directing President Nixon's reelection campaign while still serving as Attorney General. To this, White House speechwriter Patrick Buchanan replied that Robert Kennedy, while Attorney General, had been a political operative for President John F. Kennedy. "The fact that Bobby Kennedy may have done this," said Ervin, "does not justify John Mitchell doing it." "No, sir," Buchanan agreed, "the *tu quoque* is the weakest of all arguments." But Buchanan, whom many commentators regarded as the most sophisticated of all the Watergate witnesses, would not have used a *tu quoque* argument had he not thought that it would be effective.

A premise that can be added to make any *tu quoque* argument valid is 'If someone else did X, then it is all right for me to do X'. For this reason, the fallacy is also sometimes called the "two wrongs make a right" fallacy. Another premise that might be supplied is one to the effect that 'similar cases should be treated similarly'. One could validly deduce from this the subprinciple that 'if his doing X was not considered wrong, then my doing X should not be considered wrong'. But this leaves open a second possibility, namely, 'If my doing X is considered wrong, then his doing X should also be considered wrong'. Thus, although this seems to be a reasonable premise, it is not sufficient to derive validly the conclusion, 'My doing X should be considered right'.

THE STRAW PERSON FALLACY   One of the most commonly used ways of attacking an individual's position on a given matter is to interpret (or perhaps misinterpret) her statements in such a way as to make them most susceptible to attack and criticism. In other words, the strategy is to set up what can be called a "straw" person, who can be knocked down much more easily than the "real" person, and who can be counted on not to fight back. In effect, this fallacy is the exact opposite of the principle of charity, the use of which has been advocated throughout this book. Whenever we interpret an opponent's argument in a less than sympathetic way, we are committing the **straw person fallacy.** This is a tactic used widely in political campaigns and debates, but it can also be found in logic courses.

One of the basic ways of committing the straw person fallacy is to reduce a relatively complex argument to excessively simple form, in the process leaving out some of its key elements. For example, in some recent controversies over the requirements of social order and public safety versus the constitutional rights of prisoners and arrested persons, liberals have sometimes accused conservatives of favoring a repressive police state, while conservatives have accused liberals of wanting to turn hordes of dangerous criminals loose on unprotected communities. Both groups have thus distorted and caricatured the real arguments of their opponents, and have then gone on to refute these false arguments which no one really supports. In doing so, both have avoided coming to grips with the real complexity of the problem and with the many arguments that can reasonably be offered pro and con.

In summary, we are committing the straw person fallacy any time we fail to adhere to the principle of charity in evaluating an argument. We should always make sure, before branding an argument as fallacious, that we have interpreted it in the most favorable way possible, or else we shall be reasoning fallaciously ourselves.

FALLACY OF THE IRRELEVANT CONCLUSION

A young girl from a feuding mountain family has fallen in love with a son of the rival family. When her father forbids her to see him, she passionately defends her love. She argues that although the families have long been enemies, she and her beloved are not. Indeed, they believe they can stop the feud, by marrying and showing their parents that such fighting is unnecessary. When she finishes, her father looks at her coldly and says, "But his grandfather killed your grandfather."

The father's response is a clear example of the fallacy of **irrelevant conclusion.** He offers as proof, in criticism of his daughter's conclusion, evidence that actually establishes another conclusion—one that is psychologically related to, but does not refute, the one in question. The Latin name for the fallacy of irrelevant conclusion is *ignoratio elenchi,* meaning "ignorance of the refutation," an appropriate description because such a conclusion entirely misses the point of the argument. The girl argues that feuds are wrong, that she and the boy have no quarrel with each other, and that therefore they should be allowed to marry. Her father cites the killing of her grandfather, implicitly concluding that it is justification for continuing the feud unto the third generation. Even if this were so, the father has made no attempt to answer the argument that feuds are unnecessary, nor has he really explained why the two young people should not marry.

To take a second example of *ignoratio elenchi,* Bob may feel that rapists ought to be castrated to prevent them from doing further harm to society. Bill may argue that the trouble lies in their minds, not in their bodies, and that providing psychiatric help is a more reasonable way to prevent continued transgressions. Bob responds curtly, "My sister was raped." Bob's sister undoubtedly suffered a terrible experience, but to cite this as, in itself, justifying the castration of men who commit sexual crimes is beside the point.

Courtroom lawyers sometimes argue toward irrelevant conclusions because, if delivered passionately and cleverly, such arguments are often much more compelling than the relevant ones; they can also be used to obscure the lack of pertinent evidence. Some arguments commonly used to divert attention from the real issues are that rape is a heinous crime and that robbery causes the victim unwarranted deprivation. Most jurors obviously will agree with these statements, although the information is not relevant for determining whether the person on trial has committed the actual crime in question. And the experience of being able to agree with the prosecutor on a moral issue may lure jurors into accepting the argument and its conclusion and ignoring the actual question of the innocence or guilt of the defendant.

This is an appropriate fallacy with which to end this discussion, since it brings out very clearly the fact that a bad argument can actually involve more than one informal fallacy. In fact, most of our examples of the other kinds of fallacy also seem to involve the fallacy of irrelevant conclusion. Also, one should not be overly concerned by the fact that it is sometimes difficult to determine which particular informal fallacy is committed by a particular argument, since there are many borderline cases. For example, the *ad populum* argument from the John

CITIVIEWS

CITIVIEWS is distributed quarterly to Citicorp investors. It contains viewpoints on timely public issues. We believe the following may be of interest to you...

Is Capitalism Kaput?

Marx and Engels, writing at the inception of communism, gave capitalism great credit for its revolutionary role in history. One passage in their *Manifesto* is especially worth examining:

The bourgeoisie, wherever it has got the upper hand, has put an end to all feudal, patriarchal, idyllic relations. It has pitilessly torn asunder the motley feudal ties that bound man to his "natural superiors" and has left remaining no other nexus between man and man than naked self-interest, than callous "cash payment." It has drowned the most heavenly ecstasies of religious fervor, of chivalrous enthusiasm, of philistine sentimentalism, in the icy water of egotistical calculation. It has resolved personal worth into exchange value, and in place of the numberless indefeasible chartered freedoms, has set up that single, unconscionable freedom—Free Trade.

Since the authors of this statement clearly disapprove of the "motley feudal ties" that capitalism rent asunder, why does not capitalism emerge a hero? The clue is in that one word, *unconscionable*, which means "unrestrained by conscience." Why is Free Trade unconscionable? Because it is, by definition, free—and free means unrestrained. We are in the presence of a tautology, the absurdity of which can be shown by simply calling it Unrestrained Trade instead of Free Trade; thus capitalism is guilty of engaging in unrestrained Unrestrained Trade.

How many fallacies can you identify in the passage quoted from Marx and Engels and in the Citibank's counterargument? Which "argument" do you think is stronger and why?

MISTER PRESIDENT

We are a group of independent oil and gas men in Denver. Independent oil and gas men are a vital part of the oil and gas industry in America. We recognize the always difficult and sometimes awesome duties of the presidency. We share your concern over the many problems facing our nation, especially those concerning oil and gas.

We have looked to the White House for years in search of direction toward meeting the energy problem, some means of translating into understandable prose the sheaves of regulations, de-regulations, promises, threats and pure political expediency that make up government supervision of the economic metabolism of ALL the nations' industries, including the oil business. We are still looking.

In your address to the nation on April 5th, announcing your plan to de-control prices on crude oil, you promised the end of excessive government controls. You acknowledged that increased oil prices will insure more exploration, more refineries, more national petroleum production and less dependency on OPEC. That was all very good news.

However, the balance of your address of April 5th was a direct insult to the energy consuming public and to the oil industry in this country.

You made indelibly plain to the consumer that he can expect increased prices. Increases in the price of energy, Mr. President? This is hardly startling news.

Your White House statisticians spend endless hours tabulating surges in prices and in estimating future increases, not for oil products alone, but in other vital areas such as food, clothing, transportation, housing, health and government. That, Mr. President is your own in-house evidence of inflation. It is all-consuming; and it goes on at a runaway pace.

You acknowledged the ineptitude of government control of the oil industry. To quote you: …"the federal bureaucracy and red tape have become so complicated, it's almost unbelievable." **We** believe it, Mr. President.

You suggested that you will take away some of the pain of increased oil prices (gasoline prices) by the imposition of a windfall profits tax on the oil companies, and that this money will go to assist low income families, mass transportation and long range energy problems. Our Congress will determine this.

Some of the language in your address we find insulting, purely political and unnecessary. You called us cheats. You alleged that as the result of de-control the nation can expect the oil companies to reap "unearned" profits and "windfalls." You predicted price gouging of the public by oil companies. Your allegation was based on the valid premise that we must explore more, produce more and lessen our dependency on foreign oil imports.

You became prosecutor, judge and jury in your broad indictment of the oil industry. You then convicted us of terrible skulduggery even before your proposals are in effect. You plea bargained with the public in your distasteful announcement that our nation is in for price hikes. All before the fact.

Indeed, you emphasized your verdict against the oil and gas industry with this quote: "First, as surely as the sun will rise, the oil companies can be expected to fight to keep the profits which they have not earned."

You blamed part of the projected rise in consumer prices on the Congress. And you admonished the public to let the Congress know it favors the "windfall profit tax" … adding, "and that you do not want the need to produce more energy to be turned into an excuse to CHEAT the public and to damage our nation."

The oil industry in America is made up of millions of people from all avenues of commerce, including investors who receive yearly compensation from shares owned in oil companies and hundreds of thousands of farmers, ranchers and other individuals who receive a monthly royalty payment from oil and/or gas production. In fact, the largest single monthly oil and gas royalty payment recipient in America is the United States Government.

We resolutely and in the strongest terms object to you imprinting your presidential seal on broad-brush allegation that the oil industry is made up of "cheats," who rake in "unearned" profits on projected "windfalls" that might come from a not yet implemented White House proposal.

We know that other segments of American industry with which we are associated share our objection, our disbelief and resentment concerning your unrelenting and unjust public flogging of April 5.

How many informal fallacies do the oil producers accuse President Carter of committing? Do they appear to be committing any fallacies themselves in their ad?

Bill Callaway	Joe Bander	Tom Connelly	Al Hickerson
Paul Rothwell	Tom Jordan	Phil Anschutz	Bob Boekel
Ray Duncan	Bob Haynie	Vince Duncan	Ray Rader
Send inquiries to:	Fred Mayer		Dow and Marks

Bill Callaway, Denver Independent Oil Fund, 145 Security Life Bldg., Denver, Colo., 80202

Courtesy William O'Callaway, 145 Security Life Bldg., Denver 80202.

Birch Society might be interpreted as an *ad hominem* (abusive), and also as an irrelevant conclusion, while the irrelevant conclusion example concerning the young couple might be interpreted as an *ad hominem* (circumstantial). What is most important is that a fallacious argument be recognized as such, even if it cannot be comfortably pigeonholed in any of the categories we have listed.

EXERCISE 3–2

Identify the informal fallacy, or fallacies—or at least one if there are several—involved in the following arguments. You may also find it useful to reformulate each example as a valid deductive argument, adding premises as needed, and then identifying which of the added premises are questionable or blatantly false.

---

1. The theory of evolution cannot be true. The Bible says the world was created in seven days.
2. Blacks are better athletes and entertainers than doctors or lawyers. Look at Wilt Chamberlain and Sammy Davis, Jr.
3. A mother's protection of her young offspring does not primarily result from any reasoning process on her part, nor from behavior patterns she acquired by learning or imitation. It is primarily the manifestation of her maternal instinct, as one can see, for instance, by observing the instinctive way a cat will protect her kittens from danger.
4. There is no reason to enact new inheritance laws. The advocates of new inheritance laws believe that without laws to prevent children from inheriting their parents' money and property, we will, in a few generations, have a society in which people no longer work, based on the assumption that it is economic pressure which motivates people to work, and there is no economic pressure on a person who has inherited more money than he or she will ever need. And clearly this assumption is false.
5. Everyone must be allowed to speak his or her mind, because otherwise freedom of speech would be violated.
6. Of course UFOs are visitors from outer space. No one has ever been able to offer a shred of evidence to the contrary.
7. After murdering our lay-down Three No Trump contract in the last rubber, my bridge partner has no reason to criticise me because I went down in a partscore I could have made.
8. Take out a subscription to the *Investigator,* the nation's leading newsweekly, and be as well informed as your neighbors!
9. Insurance salesmen never tell you about the ways their company has to get out of paying insurance claims. You find out about those when you actually file a claim. So how can insurance companies blame people for padding their claims the next time they have an accident or a burglary?
10. If you drop a feather from a ten story building, it will float to earth very slowly. Therefore, if you drop that pillow from a ten story building, it too will float to earth slowly.
11. None of my grandchildren plays a musical instrument; it must be that young people today don't care about music anymore.
12. Doctors who favor the extermination of rats and mosquitoes do so in violation of their Hippocratic oath, which binds them to do all they can to preserve life and nothing to destroy it.

13. If by the end of class you are still convinced that I have not treated you fairly, you'll stay here in the classroom while the other students go out to the playground.

14. There will be a meteoric rise in food prices by the end of the year. I know this through a man who is a well-known meteorologist.

15. Salt is not poisonous, so neither of the elements of which it is composed, sodium and chlorine, is poisonous either.

16. The other executives find it helpful to do a few hours' work in the office on Saturday mornings. The person who was your predecessor never did; that's the reason we replaced him. We hope you won't find that your family can't spare you on weekends.

17. In 1972, Richard Nixon had the choice of fighting the Democrats by devious and sometimes unethical means or handing the Presidency over to George McGovern, whose foreign and domestic policies would, in Nixon's opinion, have spelled disaster for the country.

18. The guidebook must be mistaken. It says, "the shortest route to the other side of the hill is by the road that circles the base of the hill." There is a path on the map that runs in a straight line from here to the top of the hill and down the other side which must be the shorter route, because a straight line is the shortest distance between two points.

19. If he sent money to Biafra and to Bangladesh because the people there were starving, perhaps he'll send us money, too; because we are always starving by the time dinner is finally on the table.

20. You should begin a meal with a nourishing first course, such as soup. With tomato soup, which contains one part of vegetable solids, fat, flour, and spices for every three parts of water, three-quarters of the nourishment will actually be derived from its water content.

21. The only way to manage a company effectively is to instill fear in your workers. Either you treat employees kindly and they take advantage of you and goof off, or you are tough on them and they'll work hard for you.

22. Our cat died at the animal hospital, then on 65th Street in Manhattan. So, our cat died twice.

23. Things that are difficult to find cost a lot, and secret hiding places are difficult to find, so secret hiding places cost a lot.

24. John says that he loves me and he must be telling the truth, because a person who says that he loves someone would never lie to the person he loves.

25. Nothing has ever been discovered that travels faster than the speed of light; therefore, it is impossible to travel faster than the speed of light.

26. Two children playing monopoly:
Child A: I will throw the dice first.
Child B: No, I'll throw first.
Child A: No, it's only fair that I go first, because it's my game and I'll take it home if I can't go first.

27. The sixth commandment says "Thou shalt not kill." Yet you, Reverend Smith, claim that the United States was correct to send fighting men to Vietnam. Surely, you do not mean to contradict God's commandment!

28. President Kennedy died in office because, in this century, every man who was elected to the presidency in a year with a number which ended in zero has died while he was in office.

29. Mr. Ball's argument is exactly what one can expect from a racist like him!

30. The reviewer said that the cooking in this restaurant was especially well done, but he was wrong: I've never seen such a rare steak as this one.

31. *New York Times* Op-Ed articles, such as the one by Lieutenant Colonel King, have raised the question whether West Point ought not be abolished as "being irrelevant

to modern needs." What the articles lacked on objectivity, they made up for in apparent authority—no matter that both King and Lieutenant Colonel Herbert, another favorite of the *Times,* had turned anti-military only after being passed over for promotion. [*National Review,* March 1974]

32. How can we expect to get impartial coverage of political issues from the knee-jerk liberals of the East Coast journalistic establishment? Can you really trust the reports printed in a newspaper like *The New York Times,* with its long history of support for communist causes?

33. Tom is a very heavy smoker, so he'd better not sit in that chair—it's not strong enough to hold heavy people.

34. This must be a good toy: it is advertised on TV.

35. Is it not enough that Puerto Rican immigrants compete with native Americans for the declining number of unskilled jobs? Must we also extend welfare and unemployment benefits—which come out of the worker's taxes—to the Puerto Ricans who live in this country without working?

36. My opponent, who has so ably defended rent control, knows that there are more tenants who can give him their votes than there are landlords.

37. The process of playing a piano sonata consists of depressing the keys of the piano in the order and for the length of time which the printed score of the sonata indicates. If a person has no difficulty in depressing any one of the keys singly for any given length of time, and his hands are large and strong enough to depress simultaneously the keys of such chords as the sonata includes for any given length of time, he should have no difficulties in playing a piano sonata.

38. That woman admits she's an atheist, and atheists have no respect for the values on which this country was founded; so of course *she's* going to claim that we shouldn't have prayers in our schools.

39. The All Stars should be the best college football team in the country, for it is composed of all the best college players in the country.

40. You really should vote for this bill, Senator; our 50,000-member local union is in favor of it, and you are up for re-election this fall.

41. Uncle Homer says he has lived to celebrate his ninetieth birthday because all his life he ate a garlic clove and downed a shot of whiskey every day.

42. They want someone to fill potholes in the office of the Department of Highways. I think I'll apply for the job. I like to work indoors.

43. Freedom of the will is a myth; B. F. Skinner has pointed this out in *Beyond Freedom and Dignity.*

44. Allowing people to compete is a necessary condition for high achievement. The technical and economic progress of our free enterprise system are unique in the history of the world, and would not be possible without the advances motivated by competition.

45. Some oil company ads are heavyhanded, self-serving, and sprinkled with half-truths. Asks one Mobil ad: "Are oil profits big? Right. Big enough? Wrong. So says the Chase Manhattan Bank." That is like asking American Motors whether small cars have a future. [Adapted from *Time* magazine, February 11, 1974]

46. The peoples of the world necessarily face widespread and horrible death within the next century. If enough food is produced to feed the expanding world population, then water and air will be polluted beyond the tolerable limit by the amount of fertilizers and insecticides that are required. So people will die of water and air poisoning. If these fertilizers and insecticides are not used, not enough food will be able to be produced on the land available, and people will starve.

47. Why should we be so solicitous about protecting the legal rights of prisoners? They themselves have already chosen to disregard the law when they committed the crimes that brought them to prison.

48. For Liberals to denounce the Nixon Administration for aggrandizing the power of the presidency is enough to cause hollow laughter in hell; their own 40-year record on that subject is surely enough, in common decency, to strike them dumb forever. [*Time* magazine, April 15, 1974]

49. The nauseating Watergate scandal continues to drag along interminably with an incessant stream of leaks, innuendos, and accusations proved and unproved. Against the background of the hysteria prevailing among "the small willful men" in Congress and the critics in the media "out to get Nixon" it would seem that a more sober attitude prevails in countries outside the United States. King Faisal of Saudi Arabia has called on American citizens to be "wise enough" to "rally around you, Mr. President, in your noble effort, almost unprecedented in the history of mankind, the effort aimed at securing peace and justice in the world." [Adapted from *The New York Times,* June 30, 1974: letter to the editor]

50. There is no real energy crisis. The oil companies are just holding back their supplies to try to increase the demand, so they can raise their prices and increase their profits.

51. If you really want to be in the swing of things, read our magazine every week.

52. Diabetics should avoid things containing large amounts of sugar. Sugar maple trees are things containing large amounts of sugar. Therefore, diabetics should avoid sugar maple trees.

53. Continuing to disagree with my interpretation of *Hamlet* could be risky when it comes to exam time. After all, I am the teacher and a Shakespearean scholar.

54. The Swedes are 90 percent Protestant. Uncle Gustav is a Swede. Therefore, he is 90 percent Protestant.

55. The world of science contains numerous examples of great men and women who believed in a god, so a god must exist.

56. Of course, you realize that if you fail to vote against the gun control bill, our organization will not support your next reelection drive with a donation as it has done in the past.

57. As sure as I am talking to you, Bob Davis is guilty of embezzlement. You know he has a criminal record; he was convicted of income tax evasion and stock fraud five years ago.

58. A statement made by Richard M. Nixon in 1973: "Mr. Sparkman and Mr. Stevenson should come before the American people, as I have, and make a complete financial statement as to their financial history, and if they don't it will be an admission that they have something to hide."

59. Either Frank is poor or he is rich, and by looking at the car he drives, you can see that he is rich.

60. Great works of art are rare, so Joyce's *Ulysses* is rare.

61. Good roast beef is rare these days, so you shouldn't order yours well done.

62. Since this committee began investigating abuses in nursing home care of the elderly, it has received ten thousand letters from old people in homes, complaining of poor conditions. Quite obviously, every nursing home is filled with abuses.

63. The United States should not give aid to lesser-developed countries. It always causes trouble. We gave aid to India and they developed an atomic bomb. We gave aid to South Vietnam and the war there has continued. We gave aid to Turkey and they invaded Cyprus.

64. You shouldn't accept Mr. Jefferson's argument that high school English teachers should have fewer students in their classes since they have to grade so many compositions. After all, Mr. Jefferson is a high school English teacher; he stands to benefit.

65. In the latest poll, 60 percent of the American people favored the President's han-

dling of the economy. Therefore, of the ten Democrats on the Senate Finance Committee, exactly six favor the President's handling of the economy.

66. Me, I'm dead set against a national welfare plan. Why, when I drove through the so-called poor part of town the other day, I saw a bunch of guys standing on the corner drinking beer. Man, I'd love for someone to pay me to stay at home and spend the afternoon on the street corner drinking beer and shootin' the breeze.

67. Well Mr. Mayor, it's perfectly fine for you to say that the quality of education in our neighborhood schools is superior. But how do you explain the fact that you send your daughter to a private school?

68. A college debate team member arguing against legalization of marijuana: The only possible justification its proponents can give for legalizing marijuana is that marijuana laws cannot be absolutely enforced. Obviously this is a very weak argument, since no one claims that *any* law can be absolutely enforced.

69. Since Babe Ruth, Mickey Mantle, Lou Gehrig, and Joe DiMaggio were all great baseball players and members of the Yankees, it follows that all Yankees are great ballplayers and also that all great baseball players are Yankees.

70. All people who like the novels of Emily Bronte are persons with excellent literary taste, since persons with excellent literary taste are persons who like Emily Bronte's novels.

EXERCISE 3–3   *Reconsider the arguments for which you did preliminary analyses in Exercises 2–9 and 2–10 to determine which if any fallacies are commited in each one.*

SUMMARY

1. Commonly used and often highly persuasive arguments which *appear* to present a logical relationship between a conclusion and true premises sometimes prove to be bad arguments. Since they can be recognized with little or no reliance on the methods of formal logic, they are often referred to as informal fallacies. A bad argument may involve one or more informal fallacies. Most fallacies can be formulated as either inductive or deductive arguments. However, it is usually necessary to add at least one obviously false or highly questionable premise to an argument which involves an informal fallacy to make it deductively valid.

2. The fact that a proposition has not been conclusively proved to be true or false—especially when little or no real attempt has been made to verify it—often establishes nothing but one's inability to prove or disprove it. To treat this inability as establishing the truth or falsity of the proposition is to use a fallacious mode of argument known as the **argument from ignorance** (*argumentum ad ignorantiam*). The basic form of this fallacy is: There is no evidence (proof) that it is the case that X; therefore, it is not the case that X. When confronted with an argument which appears to have this form, we should make sure that it cannot be reasonably interpreted as a legitimate inductive argument before labeling it as fallacious.

3. The fallacy of **false dilemma** consists of presenting an argument as if there were fewer possible solutions of the problem than is actually the case. Usually two alternatives are offered in an either–or fashion; but unless both are

reasonably correct and one directly contradicts the other, there are probably other alternatives available.

4. Underlying the fallacy of **false cause** is the notion that the conjunction in space and time of two events or states of affairs is sufficient to establish the existence of a causal relation between them. A special type of false-cause fallacy, the *post hoc ergo propter hoc,* argues that because one event occurs after another, the earlier was the cause of the later.

5. Forming a generalization from a sample that is unrepresentative or too small constitutes the fallacy of **hasty generalization,** since the generalization is based on exceptional, or specially selected, rather than typical, or randomly selected, cases. To avoid this fallacy, one should collect enough data about a given situation to distinguish the typical from the accidental.

6. The fallacy of **composition** involves two forms of erroneous reasoning. The first occurs when a person falsely argues that a whole which is a single entity has a certain characteristic because each of its component parts has that characteristic. The second form occurs when a person invalidly concludes that a collection of elements has a certain characteristic because each element in the collection has this characteristic.

7. The fallacy of **division** also involves two forms of erroneous reasoning. The first form occurs when it is falsely argued that each part in a whole has a particular attribute because the whole itself has that attribute. The second form occurs when it is falsely argued that what is true of a collection of items must also be true of the items themselves. When the attribute being considered is a distributive attribute (i.e., refers to properties possessed by the individual members of a collection), the inference will be valid; when it is a collective attribute (i.e., refers to a property possessed by the totality of members of a collection), the inference will be invalid.

8. The **appeal to force** (*argumentum ad baculum*) constitutes one of the most effective informal fallacies, since it seeks to obtain the listener's agreement by arousing his fears and intimidating him into acquiescence. The appeal to force may involve threats of immediate physical violence or threats against a person's status and general well-being.

9. Citing the opinion of a pseudo-expert as reinforcement for one's own opinion constitutes the fallacy known as the **appeal to authority** (*argumentum ad verecundiam*). Identifying this fallacy may be difficult for several reasons: there may be disagreement over who is a genuine authority in a given field at a given time, and authorities in the same field often subscribe to conflicting theories and opinions.

10. The **appeal to the people** (*argumentum ad populum*) can be highly persuasive, since it manipulates the passions, prejudices, and identity of specific audiences and often bypasses reasoning altogether. However, when sound arguments and pertinent evidence are made available to an audience, the persuasive power of an *ad populum* may be weakened.

11. Any argument which is bad because it is circular—that is, because, for its intended audience, the conclusion is merely a restatement of something explicitly stated in the premises—is said to commit the fallacy of **begging the question** (*petitio principii*). Usually, the longer the circular argument, the more deceptive and persuasive it is likely to be.

12. The fallacy of **equivocation** involves the use of a word or phrase that can be interpreted in two or more different ways in the given context. The equivocal element may be used in one sense in the premise(s) and in another in the conclusion; or it may be used in different senses in different premises; or it may be used in such a way that it is impossible to determine the sense in which it is being used.

13. The fallacy of **amphiboly** occurs when a person tries to draw a conclusion from a faulty interpretation of a grammatically ambiguous statement. Amphiboly is not a matter of erroneous reasoning so much as of erroneous interpretation.

14. The fallacy of **argument against the person** (*argumentum ad hominem*) consists of attacking a person's beliefs or assertions by attacking the person himself in one way or another. This fallacy usually appears in one of three forms: the abusive, the circumstantial, and the *tu quoque*. Using epithets, or factual but irrelevant data about one's opponents, the **abusive** argument can have the effect of discrediting any statements they make. The **circumstantial** argument cites the opponent's personal circumstances as sufficient reason for dismissing a statement he has made; or it may point out a contrast between the opponent's lifestyle and his expressed opinions, thereby suggesting that the opponent's statements can be dismissed merely because the opponent himself is hypocritical. In a **tu quoque** ("you, too") argument, a person attempts to escape criticism of his position by attacking the position of his opponent, rather than by answering the charges directly.

15. When we interpret an individual's statements on a given matter in such a way as to make them most vulnerable to attack and criticism, we are violating the principle of charity and committing the **straw person fallacy.** This fallacy often involves reducing a relatively complex argument to simple form, thereby leaving out some of its key elements.

16. When one attempts to disprove a conclusion by presenting information that merely establishes another conclusion rather than refuting the one under criticism, he is committing the fallacy of **irrelevant conclusion** (*ignoratio elenchi*). Fallacious arguments of this sort are often used because they are more persuasive and compelling than those which present pertinent information or evidence.

CHAPTER FOUR

Aristotelian Logic: Statements

We noted in the Introduction that there are a number of different systems of logic and that we will only be able to study a few of them in this book. The system of logic we will be discussing in this chapter and the next is significant not only because it was developed as the first comprehensive system over 2,300 years ago, but also because it is still a useful system for analyzing statements and arguments even in comparison to most of the more "modern" theories. This system was originally formalized by the Greek philosopher Aristotle (384–322 B.C.). It was for all practical purposes the only formal logic in the Western world for over 2,000 years, and even though some of the logics developed in the twentieth Century are more powerful and sophisticated, Aristotelian logic is still as good or even better for dealing with certain kinds of statements and arguments. The fundamental restriction of Aristotelian logic is that it can deal only with the special class of statements known as categorical statements.

Aristotle

CATEGORICAL STATEMENTS

All statements can be expressed by sentences comprised at least of subject and predicate terms. In the sentence 'Tom will fail logic', 'Tom' is the subject term and 'will fail logic' is the predicate. It is possible to interpret any declarative sentence with a subject and predicate as expressing a relation between two classes of objects—one class named by the subject term and the other class designated by the predicate term. In our example, the subject term, 'Tom', can be interpreted as naming the class which has as its only member the person Tom, and the predicate refers to the class consisting of all of the people who will fail logic. To take another example, the sentence 'All students are intelligent' expresses a relation between the members of the class of students and the members of the class of intelligent beings.

Classes of things can be related to each other in several ways, and categorical statements assert such relationships. The statement expressed by the sentence 'All human beings are primates' asserts that all the members of the class of human beings are *included* in the class of primates. The statement 'No politicians are honest persons' asserts that all members of the class of things referred to by the subject term 'politicians' are *excluded* from the class of things referred to by the predicate term 'honest person'. Both these statements make assertions about *all* the members of the class referred to by the subject term and their inclusion or exclusion from the class referred to by the predicate term. Categorical statements may also make assertions about *some* of the members of the class referred to by the subject term and their inclusion in or exclusion from the predicate class. For instance, the statement 'Some persons in this room are politicians' asserts only that some of the members of the class of persons in this room are included in the class of politicians. Likewise, the statement 'Some persons in this room are not honest persons' excludes some of the members of the class of persons in this room from the class of honest persons.

Categorical propositions may be defined as statements which assert that some or all of the class of things named by the subject term are included in or excluded from the class of things named by the predicate term. We will also require that the classes referred to by both the subject term and the predicate term contain at least one member for a statement to qualify as categorical. According to this additional criterion, the sentence 'Gremlins are never more than four feet tall' does not express a categorical statement, since the class of gremlins has no members. Similarly, 'Pegasus is a flying horse' does not express a categorical statement because Pegasus does not exist and the class of flying horses has no members. It is important not to confuse such things as pictures or ideas of flying horses with the members of the class of flying horses. The class of flying horses has no members, but the class of pictures of flying horses does have members, as does the class of ideas of flying horses.

Quality and Quantity Each categorical proposition is said to possess a certain **quality,** the characteristic of asserting that some or all of the members of the subject class are *included in* or *excluded from* the predicate class. When a statement asserts that all or part of the subject class are *included* in the predicate class, it is said to be **affirmative** in quality. For instance, the statements 'All students are hard workers' and 'Some singers are dancers' are affirmative categorical statements or propositions. Categorical statements which assert that all or part of the subject class are *excluded* from the predicate class are said to be **negative** in quality. Categorical statements such as 'No birds are mammals' and 'Some paintings are not works of art' are readily identified as negative.

Categorical statements or propositions also are said to possess **quantity;** they refer to *all* or *some* of the members of the subject class. The terms 'all', 'some', 'few', 'every', and 'none' indicate the quantity of a categorical statement and are, for this reason, called **quantifiers.** Categorical statements which refer to *all* the members of the subject class are said to be **universal** in quantity. Statements such as 'All professors are college graduates' and 'No murderers are decent human beings' are examples of universal categorical statements. Categorical statements which only make assertions about some of the members of the subject class—for instance, 'Some corporation executives are embezzlers' and 'Many first novels are not good'—are called **particular** categorical statements.

The term 'some' in ordinary discourse is sometimes used as a synonym for 'several' and sometimes implies 'not all'. However, in logic, 'some' is *always* interpreted to mean 'at least one', and it does not exclude the possibility that the subject of the statement may refer to the entire class. In logic, the statement expressed by the sentence 'Some officers of the student government are women' does not imply that some officers of the student government are not women; they may all be women or some may be men. The particular statement only asserts that *at least one* member of the class of officers of the student government is a woman; it could be that two, three or more of them are women.

Statements about one individual person or thing—such as 'Jonathan got into a terrible mess today' or 'London is not a nice place to live'—are called **singular** statements. The subject of a sentence expressing a singular statement may be a proper name, such as 'Jonathan' or 'London', or it may be a descriptive phrase, such as 'the present mayor of Chicago' or 'this five dollar bill'; the point to be emphasized is that the subject term makes reference to *exactly one* individual entity. Logicians have developed a variety of ways to deal with such statements. For the moment, we shall interpret a singular statement as a statement that asserts that the only member of the one-member class named by the subject is included in or excluded from the predicate class. The statement 'Jonathan got into a terrible mess today' asserts that the class whose only member is Jonathan is included in the predicate class named by 'those who got into a terrible mess today', a class which probably has a good many members. On the other hand, the subject class whose only member is London is excluded from the predicate class of nice places to live in the statement, 'London is not a nice place to live'. Since the subjects of singular statements will be interpreted as referring to *all* members of single-member classes, these statements will be treated in this chapter and the following one as universal statements.

The Four Types of Categorical Proposition

Categorical statements can be either affirmative or negative in quality and particular or universal in quantity. These characteristics of quality and quantity may be combined to form four different types of categorical statements or propositions, as shown in Figure 4–1.

Universal affirmative statements, also called **A** statements, affirm that all members of the subject class are included in the predicate class. The following are examples of sentences that can be used to express universal affirmative statements:

> *Everyone in the room heard the piercing scream.*
> *All rises in prices are due to increased manufacturing costs.*
> *Cats are carnivorous animals.*
> *My cat, Dolly, will eat nothing but fish.*

Particular affirmative statements, also known as **I** statements, affirm at least one member of the subject class is included in the predicate class, as in the following examples:

> *Some professors are inclined to play politics.*
> *Half of the households surveyed own electric dishwashers.*
> *Many students at this university live at home.*

Universal negative statments, or **E** statements, affirm that all members of the subject class are excluded from the predicate class. The following are examples of sentences that can be used to express universal negative statements:

> *None of the candidates for mayor had campaigned before.*
> *Marcia is not in the best of spirits this morning.*
> *Mammals never have feathers.*

Particular negative statements, or **O** statements, affirm that at least one member of the subject class is excluded from the predicate class, as in the following examples:

> *Some women are not willing to accept inequality with men.*
> *Most vegetarians will not eat eggs.*
> *Nearly all the students in my dorm do not sleep eight hours.*

FIGURE 4–1

Quality \ Quantity	Universal (Including Singular)	Particular
Affirmative	**A** Universal Affirmative	**E** Particular Affirmative
Negative	**I** Universal Negative	**O** Particular Negative

typo !

EXERCISE 4–1   *Indicate whether each of the following sentences expresses an **A, E, I,** or **O** statement.*

---

1. All typewriters are noisy.
2. Some doctors are surgeons.

3. Some dodos are not extinct.
4. No newspapers are red.
5. Some Toyotas get thirty miles to the gallon.
6. All triangles have three sides.
7. Yon Cassius has a lean and hungry look.
8. No guitar has more than twelve strings.
9. Some cars do not have pollution control devices.
10. Some Frenchmen are Parisians.
11. No man is an island.
12. All seals have a smooth coat of fur.
13. No seals have a smooth coat of fur.
14. Some dolphins are not cetaceans.
15. Nobody waved goodby.

Standard-form Sentences The examples of the four types of categorical statement show that each type can be expressed in a variety of ways. In 'Everyone in the room heard the piercing scream', 'everyone' refers to all members of the class of persons in the room, just as 'all' in the statement 'All rises in prices are due to increased manufacturing costs' refers to all members of the class of rises in prices. The sentence 'Cats are carnivorous animals' may not seem on the face of it to specify whether all members of the class of cats are being referred to, or only some members. But any mature English speaker should recognize that in most contexts the statement asserts that *all* members of the class of cats are included in the class of carnivorous animals; thus, this is a universal affirmative proposition. Finally we have stipulated that singular statements, such as 'My cat, Dolly, will eat nothing but fish', are to be treated as universal categorical statements that refer to all members of a class containing exactly one member. These are only some of the many ways in which universal affirmative statements are expressed in ordinary language. And the same variety holds true for the other three types of categorical statement, as the examples given show. For practical considerations, logicians have agreed to use a single form of sentence to express each of the four different types of categorical statement. Categorical statements are easier to work with when each type is always expressed in what is known in logic as its *standard* sentence form. A **standard-form sentence** must begin with one of the three quantifiers—'All,' 'No', or 'Some.' It must also have as its principal verb a present tense form of the verb 'to be'; this term is known in logic as the **copula.** Each standard-form sentence also has a noun, a qualified noun ('carnivorous animals') or noun clause ('rises in prices') as its subject and as its predicate. A sentence which does not satisfy all of these requirements must be reformulated to be treated in syllogistic logic.

The following are examples of the standard-form expressions of the four types of categorical statement:

A—All cats are carnivorous animals.
E—No cats are carnivorous animals.
I—Some cats are carnivorous animals.
O—Some cats are not carnivorous animals.

ABBREVIATIONS AND SCHEMAS   As in everyday writing, it is often useful in logic to use abbreviations whenever possible rather than writing out entire words and clauses again and again when this is not necessary. Logicians have developed a variety of standard abbreviations. In this chapter and the next, we will be particularly concerned with abbreviating subject and predicate terms in sentences expressing categorical propositions. We will use the convention that such sentences can be **abbreviated** by replacing the subject and predicate terms with capitals of the first letters of the principal words in each term. Thus, 'All required courses are introductory surveys' is abbreviated 'All C are S', in which 'C' stands for 'required courses', and 'S' stands for 'introductory surveys'. Standard-form sentences expressing universal affirmative or **A** statements can be referred to as **A** sentences. Similarly, a standard-form sentence expressing an **E** proposition will be referred to as an **E** sentence, and the same will hold for **I** and **O** sentences.

Of course, it is possible for the key words in the subject and predicate terms to begin with the same letter, causing some problems in abbreviating the sentence. For instance, the **A** sentence expressing the universal affirmative statement 'All cats are carnivorous animals' could theoretically be abbreviated 'All C are C'. To avoid the obvious confusion that might result from such an abbreviation, we will follow the basic rule that *words with two different meanings should not be abbreviated by the same letter.* There are several alternative kinds of abbreviation that can be used when one is confronted with such cases. One possibility is to use more than one letter from a given word; for example, the **A** sentence above may be abbreviated 'All C are Car'. Another possibility is to use a letter other than the first to represent the term. Thus, the sentence 'All cats are carnivorous' might be abbreviated as 'All C are V', where 'V' represents the term 'carnivorous'. One should use common sense when faced with such abbreviating problems.

Whenever abbreviating sentences, one should provide a "dictionary" indicating the term which a particular letter represents. One handy method is to underscore the letter or letters that will be used to represent the term as is appears in the actual statement. For example, in the **A** sentence, 'All licensed doctors are medical school graduates', the letters 'd' in 'doctor' and 'm' in 'medical' are underscored to indicate that they will be used to represent these terms in the abbreviation 'All D are M'. Such a convention is particularly helpful when abbreviating troublesome sentences such as 'All Persians are procrastinators'. In this case, by underscoring the 'P' in 'Persians' and the 'c' in 'procrastinators', we are likely to avoid confusion. This convention will be used throughout this book.

Each type of categorical statement also has its own **schema** which is used to exhibit its *logical form.* It is formed by replacing both the subject and predicate terms in a standard-form sentence with blanks. Thus, for example, the schema for universal affirmative statements is

$$\textit{All} \ \_\ \_\ \_\ \_\ \_\ \_\ \_ \ \textit{are} \dots\dots\dots\dots$$

This notation is somewhat awkward and lengthy, so we will use symbols to represent the blanks rather than using blanks themselves. We will indicate the subject term blank with an 'S' and the predicate term blank with a 'P'. The lines under the letters have been placed there to indicate that they are *not* being used to abbreviate a particular subject or predicate term. This is a very important distinction! *Abbreviations and schemas are two quite different things.* When we speak of an abbreviation, we are talking about a shortened sentence, and thus abbreviations express statements that are true or false just as the original sentences do. However, schemata are *not* shortened sentences and consequently do not express statements; schemata only display the logical form of statements. The underscored letters only represent *blanks* into which *any* noun or noun clause can be placed to form a sentence. The single schema for a given type of proposition will fit any proposition of that type expressed in standard sentence form. *Any* nouns (or noun clauses) can be filled into the blanks of a schema. Once terms have been placed into the blanks in a schema, it is no longer a schema; it is now a sentence that is expressing a specific statement.

Universal Affirmative Statements

The following are examples of standard-form sentences used to express **A** or universal affirmative statements;

> *All hallucinogenic drugs are complex organic compounds.*
> *All required courses are introductory surveys.*
> *All gifts to nonprofit organizations are legitimate deductions for income tax purposes.*

It is quite easy to recognize a sentence expressing a universal affirmative statement if it is in standard form. It is more difficult to recognize such a sentence in everyday situations where it is not in standard form, and it is not always easy to put a sentence in nonstandard form into standard form, even when we know that it expresses an **A** statement. It requires some thought and practice to develop a facility for translating ordinary sentences into standard-form sentences. Consider the following examples:

> **Original:** *Every actor in the play is well chosen for the part.*
> **Standard form:** *All actors in the play are people well chosen for their parts.*
> **Abbreviation:** *All A are C.*

> **Original:** *Anyone who can't report for work should call his supervisor.*
> **Standard form:** *All persons who can't report for work are persons who should call their supervisors.*
> **Abbreviation:** *All R are C.*

Sentences expressing singular affirmative statements also are translated as universal affirmatives. For example:

> **Original:** *Prudence believes in extrasensory perception.*
> **Standard form:** *All persons who are members of the class of which Prudence is the only member are persons who believe in extrasensory perception.*

However, singular affirmative statements are often easy to work with as they stand. For our purposes, we will stipulate that such sentences can be written in the simpler form, 'S is P'. Thus, we would accept as being in standard form the sentence 'Prudence is a person who believes in extrasensory perception'. Singular propositions can be abbreviated quite easily in the normal way.

When translating ordinary sentences into standard form, one should be particularly careful to make certain that the predicate term is translated into a noun or noun clause. Frequently, ordinary-language sentences containing predicate terms expressed by adjectives are mistakenly assumed to be in standard form. For example, the **A** sentence 'All Republicans are conservative' on superficial examination may seem to be in standard form, but in fact it is not, because the predicate term is an adjective, not a noun. This sentence can be translated into standard form as 'All Republicans are conservative persons' or 'All Republicans are persons who are conservative'. Likewise, when dealing with ordinary-language sentences that contain predicate terms consisting of verb clauses, one may be tempted to think they are in standard form. Consider the following examples:

> **Original:** *All the rats are fleeing the sinking ship.*
> **Standard form:** *All rats are things that are fleeing the sinking ship.*
> **Abbreviation:** *All R are F.*

> **Original:** *All students are striking.*
> **Standard form:** *All students are persons who are striking.*
> **Abbreviation:** *All S are Sk.*

Notice, too, that it is possible to construct noun clauses in many ways when translating sentences into standard form. For example, the last sentence, 'All students are striking', might have been translated as 'All students are things that are striking' or as 'All students are animals that are striking'. All these translations are correct, but when dealing with an argument in which there are several sentences expressing categorical statements, it is important to make certain that the translation is the same throughout.

Universal Negative Statements   The following are examples of standard form sentences used to express universal negative statements or **E** statements:

> *No courses numbered over 330 are courses open to freshmen.*
> *No employees who work here are commuters.*

Every standard-form **E** sentence begins with the term 'No', has a subject and a predicate, each consisting of a noun, qualified noun, or noun clause, and contains a present tense form of the verb 'to be', its copula. Of course, each sentence should be interpreted as expressing a universal negative statement, affirming that all the members of the subject class are excluded from the predicate class.

The standard-form **E** sentence 'No employees who work here are commuters' may be abbreviated as 'No E are C'. As with universal affirmative statements, universal negative statements or **E** propositions have a schema which may be shown in one of two ways:

> *No _ _ _ _ _ _ _ _ are . . . .*

or

> *No S̲ are P̲.*

It is important to remember that the 'S̲' and 'P̲' represent *blanks* and are not abbreviations for specific nouns or noun clauses. When nouns or noun clauses are substituted in both blanks, the schema becomes a sentence.

Translation of sentences in ordinary English into standard form **E** sentences must be done carefully so that one is certain that the meaning is not changed. For example, a person is likely to interpret a sentence such as 'Employees who work here are not commuters' as expressing a universal negative statement. However, the correctness of this interpretation depends on the context in which the sentence is used. Note that the quantity of the subject is not clearly specified. The sentence could express either the **E** statement, 'No employees who work here are commuters', or the **O** statement, 'Some employees who work here are not commuters'. Likewise the sentence, 'All students are not lazy persons', at first may appear to be expressing a universal negative statement. With a little thought, however, it should be clear that this sentence is not necessarily expressing the statement, 'No students are lazy persons'. More likely the sentence is expressing the **O** statement, 'Some students are not lazy', or the **I** statement, 'Some students are lazy'. Here again, the context in which the sentence is used will be the important factor in determining what statement is being expressed.

Sentences expressing singular negative statements should be translated into **E** sentences, since we have chosen to interpret them as affirming that the only member of a one-member class named by the subject term is excluded from the class named by the predicate term. As with sentences expressing singular affirmative statements, sentences expressing singular negative statements usually present no translation or abbreviation problems. We will again permit them to be abbreviated without the quantifier. For example:

> **Original:** *This is not a universal affirmative statement.*
> **Standard form:** *No statements that are members of the class of which this statement is the only member are universal affirmative statements,* or more simply, *This statement is not a universal affirmative statement.*
> **Abbreviation:** *No S are U* or *S is not U.*

Particular Affirmative Statements

The following particular affirmative statements are expressed by standard-form sentences, or **I** sentences:

> *Some affirmative statements are particular statements.*
> *Some facial expressions are signs of emotions.*
> *Some floods are natural disasters that cause millions of dollars of damage.*

Each of these **I** sentences begins with the quantifier 'some', has a subject and predicate consisting of a noun, qualified noun, or noun clause, and contains a form of the verb 'to be'. Of course, each sentence should be interpreted as expressing an **I** statement or proposition that affirms the inclusion of part of the subject class in the predicate class. The method for abbreviating standard form **I** sentences is the same as that for **A** and **O** sentences. Thus, the sentence 'Some affirmative statements are particular statements' may be abbreviated as 'Some A are P'. All particular affirmative statements have the following schema:

> *Some* _ _ _ _ _ _ _ *are* ....

or

> *Some S are P.*

Just as with **A** and **E** sentences, one must be careful when translating ordinary sentences into **I** form.

> **Original:** *Students were among those joining in the festivities.*
> **Standard form:** *Some students are people who joined in the festivities.*
> **Abbreviation:** *Some S are F.*

Although the original sentence has no quantifiers, it is clear that in most contexts it would not be used to refer to all students. However, the ambiguity of the phrase 'among those' also makes it possible in appropriate contexts to translate the sentence as: 'Some nonstudents were among those joining in the festivities'. Depending on the argument in which this sentence appears, we might be interested in drawing out this second translation, or even the conjunction of the two translations—'Some students are people who joined in the festivities *and* some nonstudents are people who joined in the festivities'.

The sentence 'Logic students argue with facility' also lacks a quantifier, but it is not clear whether the subject term is referring to all or some members of the subject class. Usually the context in which such a sentence is found tells us whether it is expressing an **I** statement or an **A** statement. *When the context provides no clues, one should use the weaker interpretation,* that is, the one that provides less information. In this case, the **I** sentence, which refers to some of the students, is weaker than the **A** sentence, which refers to all of them. Thus, provided there are no contextual clues indicating otherwise, the sentence 'Logic students argue with facility' should be translated as follows:

> **Original:** *Logic students argue with facility.*
> **Standard form:** *Some logic students are people who argue with facility.*
> **Abbreviation:** *Some L are A.*

Notice what happens to the following ordinary sentences when they are translated into standard-form **I** sentences:

> **Original:** *Many Americans earn less than $5,000 per year.*
> **Standard form:** *Some Americans are persons who earn less than $5,000 per year.*
> **Abbreviation:** *Some A are E.*

> **Original:** *Most families own a television.*
> **Standard form:** *Some families are things that own a television.*
> **Abbreviation:** *Some F are T.*

Clearly, the meaning of each of these standard-form sentences is more restrictive than the original. This is particularly evident when we remember that the word 'some' in **I** sentences must be interpreted as meaning 'at least one'. This loss of meaning cannot be avoided in the system of logic we are now studying, and it is one of the reasons logicians have developed alternative systems that can deal with such statements without as much loss of meaning.

Particular Negative Statements

The following are examples of standard-form sentences expressing particular negative or **O** statements:

> *Some riots are not student protests.*
> *Some negative statements are not particular statements.*

> *Some houses in that neighborhood are not buildings*
> *that are made of brick.*

Each of these **O** sentences begins with the quantifier 'some', has a subject and a predicate consisting of nouns, qualified nouns, or noun clauses, and contains a copula consisting of some form of the verb 'to be'. Like other sentences expressing categorical statements, **O** sentences also may be abbreviated. For example, the sentence 'Some riots are not student protests' may be shortened to 'Some R are not P'. The schema for particular negative propositions is:

> *Some* _ _ _ _ _ _ _ _ *are not* . . . .

or

> *Some S̲ are not P̲.*

Examining the following examples will give you some insight into the way ordinary sentences that express **O** propositions may be translated into standard sentence form.

> **Original:** *Many Protestants are not Baptists.*
> **Standard form:** *Some P̲rotestants are not B̲aptists.*
> **Abbreviation:** *Some P are not B.*

> **Original:** *There are events in every person's life that*
>   *are not pleasant.*
> **Standard form:** *Some e̲vents in every person's life are*
>   *not pleasant events.*
> **Abbreviation:** *Some E are not P.*

One must pay close attention to context when translating ordinary sentences expressing **O** propositions into standard sentence form. For instance, 'All of the students in the class are not present' if uttered in a classroom, probably does not express the **E** proposition 'No students in the class are persons who are present'. Such a classroom would be empty, except for the lecturer who spoke. Thus, this sentence would be translated in the following way:

> **Original:** *All of the students in the class are not*
>   *present.*
> **Standard form:** *Some of the s̲tudents in the class are*
>   *not persons who are present.*
> **Abbreviation:** *All S are not P.*

In accordance with our rule that sentences with two or more possible meanings should always be translated in their weakest sense, statements with the form:

> *All* _ _ _ _ _ _ _ _ *are not* . . . .

should be translated into standard-form sentences expressing **O** statements unless the context clearly indicates otherwise. Thus, the sentence 'All students are not religious' should be translated into the **O** sentence, 'Some students are not religious persons', when sufficient contextual information is not available to justify any stronger interpretation.

Again, one must be particularly alert when translating sentences that contain quantifiers such as 'Not all', 'Almost all', 'Not quite everyone', and 'All but a few'. As mentioned earlier, in most contexts sentences beginning with these quantifiers express two propositions, one of which is an **O** statement. Thus, the sentence, 'Almost all students are hard workers' expresses both the **I** statement, 'Some students are hard workers', and the **O** statement, 'Some students are not hard workers'. Likewise, the sentence 'Hardly any club members attended the meeting' normally translates into 'Some club members are persons who attended the meeting' and 'Some club members are not persons who attended the meeting'. Sentences with such quantifiers do not express one categorical statement but rather the conjunction of two categorical statements.

Exceptive and Exclusive Statements

There are two kinds of statement that are particularly tricky and deceptive, and which therefore require a bit of special attention.

Exceptive Statements

One might assume that sentences such as 'Almost all of the students were at the game' or 'Not quite all his money was spent on women' express particular affirmative statements. But such **exceptive statements** expressed by sentences with quantifiers such as 'almost all', 'not quite all', and 'almost everyone' are actually complex propositions which in ordinary contexts usually make two assertions rather than one. In most contexts, 'Almost all of the students were at the game' expresses two statements: the **I** statement, 'Some students were at the game', and the **O** statement, 'Some students were not at the game'.

Not all exceptive statements are conjunctions of particular (**I** and **O**) statements: some of them involve conjunctions of two universal propositions. For example, when quantifiers such as 'all but', 'all except', or '_____ alone' are used in a sentence, it is necessary to translate the original sentence into a conjunction of **A** and **E** standard sentence forms. Thus, 'All but seniors are eligible for the scholarship' expresses both the **A** statement, 'All nonseniors are persons eligible for the scholarship' and the **E** statement 'No seniors are persons eligible for the scholarship'.

Exclusive Statements

Exceptive statements should not be confused with a linguistically similar but logically quite different kind of statement known as an *exclusive* statement. Statements expressed by sentences containing qualifiers such as 'only' or 'none but' often are **exclusive statements.** The following are examples:

> *Only friends are invited to my party.*
> *None but expert skiers can navigate Hell's Highway.*

The term 'exclusive' is used to describe such statements, since they usually affirm that the predicate applies exclusively to the subject. Thus, when translating such sentences into standard form **A** sentences, it is necessary to reverse the subject and predicate, as the following examples show:

> **Original:** *Only friends are invited to my party.*
> **Standard form:** *All persons invited to my party are friends.*
> **Abbreviation:** *All P are F.*

> **Original:** *None but expert skiers can navigate Hell's Highway.*
> **Standard form:** *All persons who can navigate Hell's Highway are expert skiers.*
> **Abbreviation:** *All N are S.*

One particularly confusing point needs clarification. Statements expressed by sentences beginning with the term 'the only' are *not* exclusive; therefore, there is no reversal of subject and predicate terms when translating them into standard form. Consider the following example:

> **Original:** *The only people who are invited to my party are friends.*
> **Standard form:** *All people invited to my party are friends.*
> **Abbreviation:** *All P are F.*

EXERCISE 4–2 (a) *If necessary, translate the following sentences into standard form.* (b) *Indicate whether each expresses an* **A**, **E**, **I**, *or* **O** *statement.* (c) *Write an abbreviation for each sentence, indicating which term each letter represents.* (d) *Write the schema for each statement.*

---

1. All Frenchmen are Europeans.
2. Lassie is not a cocker spaniel. No things id. w Lassie are cocker spaniels. No L are C. (E)
3. Some sailors are swarthy.
4. Most records cost less than five dollars. Some records are things costing less than $5. Some R are L. (I)
5. No ponderosas are shrubs.
6. Some hives do not have bees. Some hives are places w/out bees. *(Some hives are not places w/ bees)*
7. Kraters are Greek vases.
8. Panama hats are made in Ecuador. All pan. hats are things made in Ecuador. (A)
9. Many fans are not machines.
10. Man is a tool-making animal. All men are tool-making animals. (A)
11. All politicians are not dishonest.
12. No mussels are mammals. E.
13. Many European families do not own an automobile.
14. B. F. Skinner is a behavioral scientist. All persons id. to Skinner are beh. sc. (A)

[Handwritten top margin: All but S are P = All S are P or No S are P. Only S are P = All P are S. None but S are P = All P are S.]

15. Almost all paperbacks are inexpensive.
16. War is not healthy for children and other living things. *[handwritten: No wars are things healthy... E]*
17. Only members of the club are invited.
18. All but automotive unions have settled. *[handwritten: All AU's are Os which have settled (A) or]*
[left margin handwritten: E, No Aus are Os which have settled]
19. Sixty percent of all college students work part-time to pay for their education.
20. Blessed are the peacemakers. *[handwritten: All peacemakers are blessed.]*
21. Almost all professional basketball players are over six feet four inches tall.
22. The only road to success is hard work. *[handwritten: All roads are hard work roads. (A)]*
23. None but his friends were invited to the party. *[handwritten: (All P are S.)]*
24. Nothing is certain except death and taxes. *[handwritten: All deaths and taxes are certain things (A)]*
[left margin handwritten: E: No things that are DT are certain things. No DT are C.]
25. Only those who bought tickets in advance were able to get seats.

EXERCISE 4–3   *Using the instructions given for Exercise 4–2, return to Exercise 4–1. Translate each sentence into standard form where necessary. Give an abbreviation and schema for each sentence.*

VENN DIAGRAMS AND CATEGORICAL STATEMENTS

Each of the four types of categorical statement has a schema which displays the *logical form* of that particular kind of proposition. It is also possible to display the logical form of categorical statements by means of diagrams. One of the most frequently used methods for doing this is the Venn diagram technique, named for John Venn, the nineteenth-century British logician who developed it.

Before showing how the different types of categorical statements can be diagrammed, it is necessary to explicate some of the principles of the method.

1. Two overlapping circles are used to represent the classes of things referred to by the subject and predicate terms of the categorical statement (see Figure 4–2).
2. If an area of a circle is shaded, this indicates that it is empty: that is, the class that it represents contains no members.
3. If an 'X' appears in an area of a circle, then the designated class contains at least one member.
4. If an 'X' appears on a line between two circles, one or the other of the designated classes contains at least one member, but it is undetermined which class it is. An 'X' on a line does *not* mean that *both* classes contain members, although it does not rule out this possibility.
5. If an area is *completely* blank, that is, if it is not shaded and it does not contain an 'X' or part of an 'X', this means that we have *no information* about that area. It does *not* mean that the class represented by that area has no members.
6. The circles representing the subject and predicate classes of a categorical proposition are placed within a rectangle which represents the **universe of discourse.** It is possible and sometimes desirable to limit

FIGURE 4–2

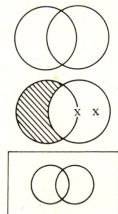

the universe of discourse to a specific class such as the class of all physical objects or the class of all human beings, but in this book we shall stipulate that the universe of discourse is everything that exists—both physical and nonphysical entities. The area inside the rectangle and outside of both circles represents the class of all things which are not contained in either or both of the two classes referred to by the subject and predicate terms of the categorical statement.

7. Since we are operating with the principle that both terms of a categorical proposition must name classes which have at least one member, there must be an 'X' in some area of both circles in the Venn diagram for every categorical proposition.

FIGURE 4–3

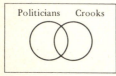

Using these principles, let us proceed to diagram the **A** statement, 'All politicians are crooks'. The first thing that must be done is to label each circle to indicate the class it represents, as in Figure 4–3. The circle on the left represents the class of politicians and the circle on the right represents the class of crooks, and the area common to both circles represents the class of things that are both politicians and crooks. The area outside the circles but within the rectangle represents everything else that is neither a politician nor a crook. It is also possible to label circles with abbreviations, using just letters to represent the full names of the classes. When doing this, one should follow the rules for abbreviation presented in the first part of this chapter.

To return to our example, we know that the class of politicians contains a member, so an 'X' must be placed within the circle representing this class. It is difficult to determine exactly where the 'X' should go since it could be placed in the area common to P and C, or in the area of P outside of C, or on the line between them. However, the proposition, 'All politicians are crooks' clearly asserts that there are no members of the class of politicians that are not contained in the class of crooks. Therefore, the area of the P circle that is outside of C can be shaded to indicate that the class it represents contains no members, as in Figure 4–4.

FIGURE 4–4

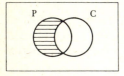

The only remaining area in which an 'X' can be placed to indicate that the class of politicians contains a member is the area that is common to both P and C. Why can't the 'X' be placed on the line between the P and C circles? The area that is shaded indicates that there are no members in the class of politicians that are not contained in the class of crooks. An 'X' is placed on the line only when there is uncertainty as to which class contains a member. In this instance, it is known that the area of P outside of C, representing politicians who are not crooks, definitely does not contain a member, so the 'X' must be placed in the area common to both, as in Figure 4–5.

FIGURE 4–5

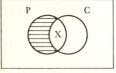

A: All P are C.

Our definition of a categorical proposition also requires that the class referred to by the predicate term contain at least one member. It can be seen in Figure 4–5 that the C circle already contains an 'X'; it is in the area common to both P and C. This tells us that at least one crook does exist, since the member or members of the class of politicians named by the subject term also happens to be a crook. The **A** proposition 'All politicians are crooks' does not assert explicitly that there are any members in the class of crooks that are not politicians. There may in fact be crooks who are not politicians, but the proposition says nothing about them. Therefore, since there is already an 'X' in one part of the C circle, it would be incorrect to place an 'X' in the area of C outside the area common to both P and C. Thus, the diagram presented in Figure 4–5 is a complete representation of the information contained in the **A** proposition 'All politicians are crooks'.

Let us diagram another **A** proposition: for example, 'All spiders are insects'. Once again, we begin with two overlapping circles, of which one represents the class of things referred to by the subject term, 'spiders', and the other represents the class of things which are referred to by the predicate term, 'insects'. The area outside the circles but within the rectangle represents the remainder of the universe of discourse, which includes everything that is neither a spider nor an insect (Figure 4–6).

Since the proposition does not tell us where to place the 'X' that represents the member of the class of spiders, the area that we know contains no members is shaded first, as in Figure 4–7. The statement 'All spiders are insects' asserts that there are no spiders that do not belong to the class of insects; hence the area of the S circle that is outside the area common to the S and I circles is shaded. This procedure will be followed throughout the remainder of this discussion. *Whenever Venn diagrams are used to represent categorical statements, the area containing no members should be shaded before placing 'Xs' where needed.* An 'X' is then placed in the area common to both S and I to indicate that the class of spiders contains at least one member, as in Figure 4–8. This 'X' also indicates that the class of insects contains a member. As in the first **A** proposition that was diagrammed, it would be incorrect to place another 'X' in the area of the I circle that is outside the area common to both the S and I circles. Clearly, the proposition 'All spiders are insects' says nothing about members of the class of insects that are not spiders.

If you examine Figures 4–5 and 4–8, it is obvious that they are the same diagram, except for the labels on the circles since each refers to a different class of things. The fact that the Venn diagrams for two different **A** propositions look the same should come as no great surprise. Venn diagrams are a method for representing the *logical structure* of a categorical statement, and it has already been shown that all **A** statements have the same logical form. For this reason, it is possible to provide a diagram analogous to the schema of any **A** statement (see Figure 4–9). The labels S and P are again used as "blanks" for which any nouns or noun clauses can be substituted to create a diagram representing an **A** proposition.

The Venn diagram that represents the universal negative or **E** statement, 'No politicians are crooks' is shown in Figure 4–10. Since this statement asserts that there are no members of the class of politicians that are members of the class of

FIGURE 4–6

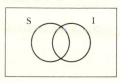

FIGURE 4–7

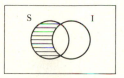

FIGURE 4–8

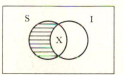

A: All S are I.

FIGURE 4–9

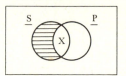

A: All S are P.

FIGURE 4–10

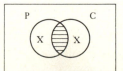

E: No P are C.

crooks, the area common to both classes is shaded to indicate that it contains no members. Also, since the subject class must contain at least one member, an 'X' is placed in the remaining area of the P circle. An 'X' is also needed in the C circle, since the proposition assumes the existence of at least one member in the predicate class. All universal negative (or E) statements are diagrammed in the same way.

The Venn diagram for I or particular affirmative statements such as 'Some politicians are crooks' is shown in Figure 4–11.

The 'X' in the area that is common to both circles indicates that at least one member of the class of politicians is included in the class of crooks. This proposition says nothing about any other members of the subject and predicate classes; that is, it does not assert that there are any politicians that are not crooks, or any crooks that are not politicians. Therefore, no 'Xs' are placed in these areas of the circles. Note that no shading is required for diagramming I propositions. All particular affirmative or I propositions are diagrammed in this manner.

Particular negative or O statements such as 'Some politicians are not crooks' are represented by the Venn diagram shown in Figure 4–12. An 'X' is placed in the area of P outside of C to indicate that at least one member of the class of politicians is excluded from the class of crooks; in other words, at least one politician exists who is not a crook. This O statement assumes that at least one crook exists, but it does not tell us whether that crook is a politician, so we must place the 'X' in the C circle on the line of the P circle. Once again, no shading is needed when diagramming O statements. All particular negative or O statements are diagrammed in the same way.

FIGURE 4–11

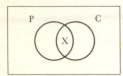

I: Some P are C.

FIGURE 4–12

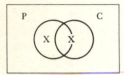

O: Some P are not C.

EXERCISE 4–4

(a) If necessary, translate each of the following sentences into standard form. (b) Write an abbreviation for each sentence. (c) Write the schema for each. (d) Draw a Venn Diagram to represent the categorical statement.

1. Some wine is made from dandelions.
2. No Beatles are bugs.
3. All beetles are bugs.
4. All oaks are hardwoods.
5. No termites are ants.
6. Some nebulae are not galaxies.
7. Not all Arabs are Moslems.
8. All harpies are mythological.
9. Some dancers can Charleston.
10. Many people in the world do not have enough to eat.
11. Only sophomores attend the Soph-ball.
12. No behaviorists tolerate idle speculation.
13. No one scored higher than 90 percent on the test.
14. Almost everyone at the Mardis Gras was drunk.
15. Only citizens can vote.

16. None but the freshmen are invited to the picnic.
17. Lightning never strikes twice in the same place.
18. All except exceptive statements are easy to translate into standard form.
19. Almost all art collectors are rich.
20. Some beetles do not have bugs.

EXERCISE 4–5   *Repeat Exercise 4–4 using the sentences that appear in Exercises 4–1 and 4–2.*

LOGICAL RELATIONS BETWEEN CATEGORICAL PROPOSITIONS

As with statements in general, there are a variety of logical relations which hold between different categorical propositions. We are now in a position to examine some of the more common and important relations that exist between certain categorical propositions.

The Traditional Square of Opposition

Assuming that each of the four types of categorical statement have the same subject and predicate terms, certain truth relationships among these different statements exist. Medieval logicians developed what is known as the traditional square of opposition to show these logical relationships. The four different categorical statements were arranged as shown in Figure 4–13. Assuming that the class named by the subject term of a categorical statement contains at least one member, one can use the square of opposition to exhibit a variety of kinds of immediate inference.

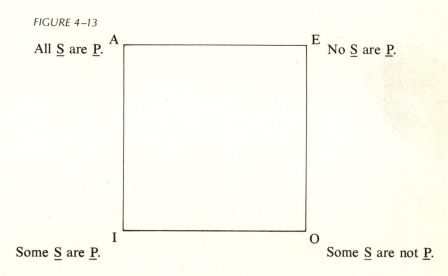

FIGURE 4–13

A   All S̲ are P̲.

E   No S̲ are P̲.

I   Some S̲ are P̲.

O   Some S̲ are not P̲.

Contradiction   **Contradictory propositions** are *statements that are related in such a way that if one is true, the other must be false, and if one is false, the other must be true.* Contradictory propositions cannot both be true at the same time; nor can they both be false at the same time. Consider the following pairs of statements:

All senators are women. (**A**)
Some senators are not women. (**O**)

If the **A** statement 'All senators are women' is true, then the **O** statement 'Some senators are not women' *must* be false. If 'All senators are women' is false, then the statement 'Some senators are not women' must be true. Likewise, given the truth of 'Some senators are not women', it follows that it is false that all senators are women. If it is false that some senators are not women, then 'All senators are women' must be true. In brief, knowing the truth or falsity of either statement we can always determine the truth or falsity of the other directly. A relation such as this—where the truth or falsity of a given statement can be determined directly from the truth or falsity of one other statement—is known as an **immediate inference.** All **A** and **O** propositions with the same subjects and predicates are contradictories, since it is impossible for both to be true or for both to be false, and, therefore, we can make immediate inferences from the truth or falsity of one to the truth or falsity of the other.

    A and **O** propositions differ in both quality and quantity as do **E** and **I** propositions. Like **A** and **O** statements, all **E** and **I** statements with the same subject and predicate terms are also contradictories. Consider, for example, the following pair of statements:

No senators are women. (**E**)
Some senators are women. (**I**)

    If the **E** statement 'No senators are women' is true, then the **I** statement 'Some senators are women' must be false. If the **E** statement is false, then the **I** statement must be true. If the **I** proposition is true, then the **E** proposition must be false, and if the **I** proposition is false, then the **E** must be true.

Contrariety   At first glance, the **A** statement 'All senators are women' might appear to be the contradictory of the E statement 'No senators are women', but further consideration will show this not to be the case. Although it is impossible for both statements to be true, it is possible for both to be false, as in the case where only one senator is a woman or exactly half of the senators are women. Such statements are known as *contraries.* Two statements are **contraries** if and only if *they are related in such a way that both cannot be true at the same time, but both may be false.* Let us consider another example:

All students are logicians. (**A**)
No students are logicians. (**E**)

FIGURE 4–14

A ——————— E

Contrariety

**If A is true, then
E is false.
If E is true, then
A is false.**

If the **A** statement 'All students are logicians' is true, then the **E** statement 'No students are logicians' must be false, given our assumption that the class of students contains at least one member. If it is true that every single student is included in the class of logicians, then obviously it is false that no member of the class of students is included in the class of logicians. Likewise, if the **E** statement 'No students are logicians' is true, then the **A** statement must be false. Both statements cannot be true at the same time. However, if the **A** statement 'All students are logicians' is false, what can be inferred about the truth or falsity of the **E** statement 'No students are logicians'? Knowing only that it is not the case that every student is a logician, can we validly infer that not even one student is a logician? Obviously not, for knowing that it is false that all students are logicians does not tell us how many are *not* logicians—it is possible that only one or five thousand of the students are not logicians, although it is also *possible* that none of the students are logicians. Thus, if the **A** statement is false, then the truth or falsity of the **E** statement cannot be determined. Similarly, if we know only that the **E** statement 'No students are logicians' is false, then the truth or falsity of the **A** statement is also undetermined.

Subcontraries   **A** and **E** propositions have the same quantity, but they differ in quality, one being affirmative and the other being negative. **I** and **O** propositions also have the same quantity and differ in quality. Are **I** and **O** propositions contraries? Let us consider the following pair of statements to determine the answer to this question:

> **Some dogs are terriers. (I)**
> **Some dogs are not terriers. (O)**

If the **I** statement 'Some dogs are terriers' is true, it is still possible for the **O** statement 'Some dogs are not terriers' to be true. Contrary statements, however, cannot both be true; therefore **I** and **O** propositions are not contraries. Another logical relationship known as subcontrariety exists between **I** and **O** statements.

Two categorical propositions are **subcontraries** if *both cannot be false, but both may be true.* Consider the following pair of statements:

> **Some women are ambitious persons. (I)**
> **Some women are not ambitious persons. (O)**

FIGURE 4–15

I ——————— O

Subcontratriety

**If I is false,
then O is true.
If O is false,
then I is true.**

Both statements cannot be false, given our assumption that at least one woman exists. If the **I** statement 'Some women are ambitious persons' is false, then the **O** statement 'Some women are not ambitious persons' must be true, and if the **O** statement is false, then the **I** statement must be true. However, if the statement 'Some women are ambitious persons' is true, then the truth or falsity of the **O** statement 'Some women are not ambitious persons' is undetermined. Knowing only that some members of the class of women are members of the class of ambitious persons, we cannot tell that some women are excluded from the class of ambitious persons; it may be that all women are ambitious. In a similar way, knowing only that 'Some women are not ambitious persons' is true, we cannot tell anything about the truth or falsity of the **I** statement 'Some women are ambitious persons'; it is still possible that no women are ambitious. Both statements cannot be false, but both may be true; this relationship of subcontrariety holds between all **I** and **O** propositions with the same subjects and predicates.

Subimplication and
Superimplication

The logical relationships of contradiction, contrariety, and subcontrariety involve immediate inferences in which the truth of one statement implies the falsity of the other statement, and/or the falsity of one statement implies the truth of the other statement. In none of the immediate inferences discussed so far did we infer the truth of one statement from the truth of the other, or the falsity of one statement from the falsity of the other. Such immediate inferences can be made with certain types of categorical statements through the processes of subimplication and superimplication.

Before explaining the immediate inferences of subimplication and superimplication, it is necessary to define some terms. Universal statements, both **A** and **E**, are called **superimplicants** (or **superalterns**), and particular statements, both **I** and **O** are called **subimplicants** (or **subalterns**). Strictly speaking, the **A** proposition is the superimplicant of the **I** proposition with the same subject and predicate terms, and the **I** is the subimplicant of the **A**. Likewise, the **E** proposition is the superimplicant of the **O** with the same subject and predicate terms, and the **O** is the subimplicant of the **E**.

Subimplication (or subalternation) is the *process by which the truth of a particular statement is inferred from the truth of its corresponding universal statement*. Thus, given the assumption that at least one corporation president exists, if the **A** statement 'All corporation presidents are millionaires' is true, then the **I** statement 'Some corporation presidents are millionaires' must be true. Likewise, if the **E** statement 'No corporation presidents are millionaires' is true, then the **O** statement 'Some corporation presidents are not millionaires' is also true. However, if the **A** statement is false, then the truth value of the **I** statement is undetermined; some corporation presidents may be millionaires or none may be millionaires. If the **E** statement 'No corporation presidents are millionaires' is false, then it is also impossible to determine the truth value of its corresponding **O** statement.

The immediate inference called 'superimplication' is the converse of subimplication. In **superimplication,** *the falsity of the universal statement is inferred from the falsity of its corresponding particular statement*. Thus, assuming at least one corporation president exists and knowing only that the **I** statement 'Some corporation presidents are millionaires' is false, we can infer that the **A** statement 'All corporation presidents are millionaires' must be false. If it is false that not even one member of the class of corporation presidents is contained in the class of millionaires, then it must be false that *every* member of the class of corporation presidents is contained in the class of millionaires. Similarly, if the **O** statement 'Some corporation presidents are not millionaires' is false, then the **E**

FIGURE 4–16

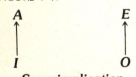

Subimplication
If A is true then
  I is true.
If E is true then
  O is true.

FIGURE 4–17

A   E

I   O

Superimplication
If I is false then
  A is false.
If O is false, then
  E is false.

statement 'No corporation presidents are millionaires' must be false. But if we know only that the **I** statement 'Some corporation presidents are millionaires' is true, then the truth value of the **A** statement 'All corporation presidents are millionaires' is undetermined. In this instance, all members of the class of corporation presidents may be members of the class of millionaires or only some may be members of the class of millionaires. Then too, if the **O** statement 'Some corporation presidents are not millionaires' is true, then the truth value of the corresponding **E** statement 'No corporation presidents are millionaires' is also undetermined.

REMEMBER!

In subimplication, only the truth *of the particular statement can be inferred from the* truth *of its corresponding universal statement.*

In superimplication, we can only infer the falsity *of the general statement from the* falsity *of its corresponding particular statement.*

The logical relationships that exist between certain pairs of categorical statements with the same subject and predicate terms are shown in the completed traditional square of opposition, which appears in Figure 4–18.

FIGURE 4–18
The square of opposition

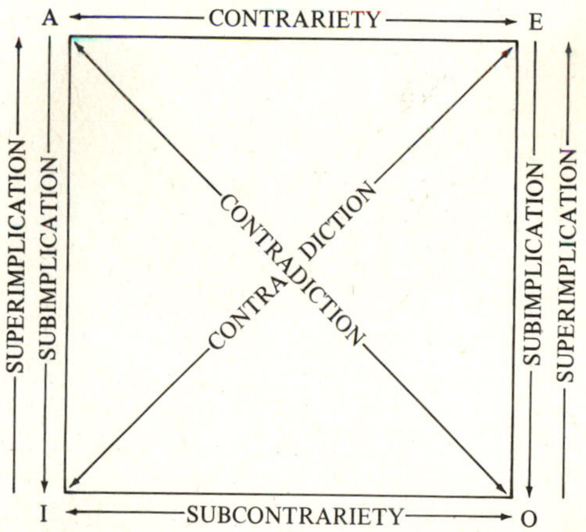

All of the immediate inferences that can be made from any given categorical statement, such as an **A** statement, on the square of opposition can now be brought together. For example, what can be immediately inferred from the statement 'All diamonds are precious gems'? If this **A** statement is true, then, by contradiction, the **O** statement 'Some diamonds are not precious gems' is false; by contrariety, the **E** statement 'No diamonds are precious gems' is false; and by subimplication, the **I** statement 'Some diamonds are precious gems' is true. If the **A** statement is false, then its contradictory 'Some diamonds are not precious gems' is true; the truth or falsity of its contrary 'No diamonds are precious gems' is undetermined; and the truth value of its subimplicant 'Some diamonds are precious gems' is also undetermined.

Immediate Inferences Valid on the Square of Opposition

If **A** is true	If **E** is true	If **I** is true	If **O** is true
E is false	**A** is false	**E** is false	**A** is false
I is true	**I** is false	**A** is undetermined	**E** is undetermined
O is false	**O** is true	**O** is undetermined	**I** is undetermined
If **A** is false	If **E** is false	If **I** is false	If **O** is false
O is true	**I** is true	**A** is false	**E** is false
E is undetermined	**A** is undetermined	**E** is true	**A** is true
I is undetermined	**O** is undetermined	**O** is true	**I** is true

EXERCISE 4–6   *Below you will find pairs of categorical statements. (a) Identify the relationship between each pair as contradiction, contrariety, subcontrariety, subimplication, or superimplication. (b) Assuming that the first statement of each pair is true, what can be inferred about the truth value of the second statement? (c) Assuming that the first statement is false, what can be inferred about the truth value of the second statement?*

1. All judges are lawyers.
   No judges are lawyers.
2. Some judges are lawyers.
   Some judges are not lawyers.
3. Some books are not dictionaries.
   No books are dictionaries.
4. Some wagons are not motor vehicles.
   All wagons are motor vehicles.
5. Some diseases are not fatal.
   No diseases are fatal.
6. No shrews are rodents.
   Some shrews are rodents.
7. No shrews are rodents.
   All shrews are rodents.
8. Some newspapers are biased things.
   All newspapers are biased things.
9. All men are mortal beings.
   No men are mortal beings.
10. All city police are city residents.
    Some city police are city residents.
11. No satellites are planets.
    Some satellites are not planets.
12. Some speed limits are reasonable things.
    Some speed limits are not reasonable things.
13. No members of the Little League are girls.
    Some members of the Little League are girls.
14. All Germans are beer drinkers.
    Some Germans are beer drinkers.
15. No UFOs are things that come from outer space.
    All UFOs are things that come from outer space.

EXERCISE 4–7   *Below you will find several sets of categorical statements. (a) What is the relationship between each statement and the original? (b) Assuming that the first is true, what can you infer about the truth value of the other statements? (c) Assuming that the first is false, what can you infer about the truth value of the other statements?*

1. All straight-A students in this school are women.
   (a) No straight-A students in this school are women.
   (b) Some straight-A students in this school are women.
   (c) Some straight-A students in this school are not women.
2. No computers are humans.
   (a) Some computers are humans.
   (b) Some computers are not humans.
   (c) All computers are humans.
3. Some horses are thoroughbreds.
   (a) Some horses are not thoroughbreds.
   (b) No horses are thoroughbreds.
   (c) All horses are thoroughbreds.
4. Some desserts are not fattening foods.
   (a) All desserts are fattening foods.
   (b) No desserts are fattening foods.
   (c) Some desserts are fattening foods.
5. All men are overburdened with wealth.
   (a) No men are overburdened with wealth.
   (b) Some men are overburdened with wealth.
   (c) Some men are not overburdened with wealth.
6. No toothless piranhas are threats.
   (a) Some toothless piranhas are threats.
   (b) Some toothless piranhas are not threats.
   (c) All toothless piranhas are threats.
7. Some people are basically insecure people.
   (a) Some people are not basically insecure people.
   (b) All people are basically insecure people.
   (c) No people are basically insecure people.

CONSISTENCY AND INDEPENDENCE   Before proceeding with our discussion of categorical statements and the logical relations between them, it is necessary to review the two basic concepts of *consistency* and *independence*. As we saw in Chapter 1, two statements are **consistent** if it is possible for both of them to be true. Let us look at the four kinds of categorical proposition to determine which are consistent with which others. The **A** statement 'All dogs are canines' and the **I** statement 'Some dogs are canines' are consistent because both may be true at the same time. The **E** statement 'No flowers are things made of inorganic material' and the **O** statement 'Some flowers are not things made of inorganic material' are also logically consistent. Likewise, the **I** statement 'Some students are scholarship holders' and the **O** statement 'Some students are not scholarship holders' may both be true at the same time. All **A** and **I** statements with the same subject and predicate terms, **E** and **O** statements with the same subject and predicate terms, and **I** and **O** statements with the same subject and predicate terms are logically consistent. However, the **A** statement 'All wines are alcoholic beverages' is not consistent with the **E** statement 'No wines are alcoholic beverages', because it is impossible for both statements to be true. Similarly, contradictory statements are also logically inconsistent. The consistency relation can be superimposed on the square of opposition, as shown in Figure 4–19.

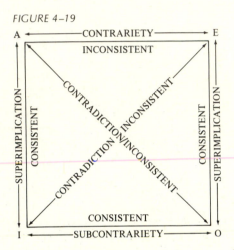

FIGURE 4–19

Two statements are said to be logically **independent** if knowledge of the truth value of one (either true or false) tells us nothing about the truth value of the other and vice versa. The concept of logical independence can cause some confusion, so some additional clarification is required. Let us consider these two statements:

1. *Some horses are stallions.* **(I)**
2. *Some horses are pintos.* **(I)**

If we know only that statement 1 is true, we know nothing about the truth value of statement 2; and if we know only that statement 1 is false, then the truth value of statement 2 still remains undetermined. Likewise, if we know only that statement 2 is true, then we know nothing about the truth value of statement 1; and if we know only that statement 2 is false, then the truth value of statement 1 is still undetermined. Thus, the statements are said to be logically independent, since the truth value of each tells us nothing about the truth value of the other.

The relationships of contradiction, contrariety, subcontrariety, subalternation, and superalternation should make it obvious that it is impossible for the four types of categorical statement with the same subject and predicate terms to be logically independent. If two statements are inconsistent, then if one is true the other must be false, but this means that inconsistent statements are not independent. Therefore, from this we can conclude that if two statements are independent, they must be consistent.[1]

EXERCISE 4–8　　　*Examine each pair of sentences. (a) Indicate whether statements are logically consistent or inconsistent, and (b) whether they are logically dependent or independent.*

---

1. All machines are man-made things. Some machines are man-made things.
2. Some devices are machines. Some devices are not machines.
3. Some devices are machines. Some devices are clever.
4. No chimpanzees are striped animals. Some chimpanzees are striped animals.
5. Some cigarettes are not things made of tobacco. No cigarettes are things made of tobacco.
6. All cats are felines. Some lions are felines.
7. All factories are buildings. All dogs are pets.
8. Some Frenchmen are great lovers. Some Frenchmen are not great lovers.
9. No Americans are vegetarians. Some Americans are not vegetarians.
10. Some minors are voters. No minors are voters.

EQUIVALENT STATEMENTS　　　The logical relations discussed so far—those of contradiction, contrariety, subcontrariety, subalternation, and superalternation—have been concerned only with propositions that contain the same subject and predicate terms and that vary in quantity, quality, or both. There are other kinds of relations that hold between categorical propositions that have different subject and predicate terms. These relations involve categorical propositions that are logically equivalent. Two categorical propositions are **logically equivalent** if and only if they both necessarily have the same truth value; that is, if one statement is true, it follows that the other statement is true, and if one statement is false, it follows that the other is false. Thus, the two **I** propositions, 'Some bus drivers are poets' and 'Some poets are bus drivers' are logically equivalent. If 'Some bus drivers are poets' is true, then 'Some poets are bus drivers' must be true, and vice versa. And if 'Some bus drivers are poets' is false, then 'Some poets are bus drivers' must also be false, and vice versa. The logical equivalence of two categorical propositions can be tested by means of Venn diagrams. If their Venn diagrams are identical, that is, if both propositions are diagrammed in *exactly* the same way, they are logically equivalent. The Venn diagram for the statement 'Some bus drivers are poets' is shown in Figure 4–20. The diagram in

FIGURE 4–20

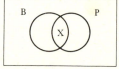

I: Some B are P.

FIGURE 4–21

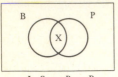

I: Some P are B.

Figure 4–20 is identical to the diagram in Figure 4–21 which represents the proposition 'Some poets are bus drivers'.

Knowing that two statements are logically equivalent is important because it enables us to make inferences about the truth value of one statement from the truth value of the other statement. Thus, if we know that two statements are logically equivalent and that one statement is true, then we can immediately infer that the other must be true. Or, if we know that one statement is false, then we can infer that any logically equivalent statement must be false.

COMPLEMENTARITY Another important concept is that of complementary classes. The **complement of a class** is the class of all things or beings in the universe of discourse that do not belong to the class. Thus, the complement of the class of lovers is the class of all those things that are not lovers. The complement of any class is expressed by joining the prefix 'non' to the name of the class, so the complement of the class of lovers is referred to as the class of nonlovers. The complement of the class of lovers is not the class of haters, for there are people who are nonlovers who are not haters. Furthermore, the complements of terms such as 'nonlovers' and 'nonhaters' are simply expressed as 'lovers' and 'haters', respectively, to avoid having more than one prefix. One must be particularly careful when dealing with qualified terms, that is, those containing adjectives or adverb clauses. For example, the complement of the term 'lazy student' is not 'nonlazy students' but 'non(lazy students)'. The class referred to by the term 'nonlazy students' contains all those students who are not lazy, whereas the class which is referred to by the complementary term 'non(lazy students)' contains all things in the universe of discourse which are not lazy students. When forming the complement of any qualified term, always enclose the entire expression in parentheses and then add the 'non' in front of the parentheses.

To deal most simply with the equivalence relations we will be introducing shortly, we will add to our assumption that the subject and predicate classes of a given statement must each contain at least one member the new requirement that *the complement of every class must have at least one member* as well. This is actually a very plausible assumption, because the only class whose complementary class is empty is the class which is identical to the entire universe of discourse, a situation which is generally quite trivial and uninteresting. This new stipulation must be taken into account in drawing Venn diagrams for the remainder of this chapter.

OBVERSION Having defined the concepts of logical equivalence and complementary class, we can now consider *obversion*. **Obversion** is the mechanical process of changing the quality of a categorical statement and replacing the predicate term with its complement. Is the obverse of a categorical statement logically equivalent to its original statement? That is, is one true whenever the

FIGURE 4–22

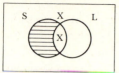

A: All S are L.

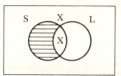

E: No S are nonL.

FIGURE 4–23

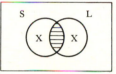

E: No S are L.

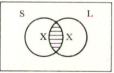

A: All S are nonL.

FIGURE 4–24

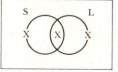

I: Some S are L.

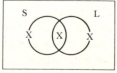

O: Some S are not nonL.

other is true and false whenever the other is false? Consider, for example, the following statements:

All senators are lawyers. (A)
No senators are nonlawyers. (E)

Here, the first statement, or *obvertend,* is a universal affirmative statement. By changing the quality of this proposition from affirmative to negative and then replacing the predicate term with its complementary term, we arrive at its *obverse,* which is a universal negative proposition. To test whether these two statements are logically equivalent, we can examine Figure 4–22, which shows the Venn diagrams for both propositions. The X outside the L circle not only indicates the existence of a nonL but also of a nonS. Thus another X is not necessary to indicate a nonS.

The Venn diagrams for both propositions are exactly the same. The **E** statement asserts that there are no members of the subject class that are members of the predicate class, and that at least one senator exists. In this instance the **E** statement, 'No senators are nonlawyers', is asserting that there are no members of the class of senators who are members of the class of nonlawyers. The class of nonlawyers is represented by the area outside the L circle, so the area outside the L circle and inside the S circle must be empty. Since all **A** statements and their obverses have the same form, which can be represented by the same schema, the Venn diagrams for **A** statements and their obverses are all the same with the exception of the labels on the circles. Thus, the obverse of any **A** statement is logically equivalent to its original statement. This means that the **A** statement implies its obverse, *and* the obverse implies the **A** statement. Now let us consider whether or not the obverses of **E, I,** and **O** propositions also are logically equivalent to their original statements.

The obverse of the **E** statement 'No senators are lawyers' is the **A** statement 'All senators are nonlawyers'. The Venn diagrams representing these statements are shown in Figure 4–23. Note that the X in the S circle not only indicates the existence of an S but also the existence of a nonL, and the X in L indicates the existence of a nonS.

Because the Venn diagrams for both statements are identical, we can say that the obverse of this **E** statement is logically equivalent to its original statement. Again, because all **E** statements and their obverses have the same logical form and, therefore, are represented by the same Venn diagrams, we may say that all **E** statements are logically equivalent to their obverses.

The obverse of the **I** statement 'Some senators are lawyers' is the **O** statement 'Some senators are not nonlawyers'. The Venn diagrams for these propositions appear in Figure 4–24 and are clearly identical to each other. Since we don't know whether the nonL is an S or a nonS, we must place an X on the line of the S circle. Likewise, the X for the nonS must be on the line of the L circle. Therefore, the obverse of this **I** statement and, of course, of any **I** statement, is logically equivalent to its original statement.

Similarly, the obverse of the **O** statement 'Some senators are not lawyers' is the **I** statement 'Some senators are nonlawyers'. The Venn diagrams for these statements, which are shown in Figure 4–25, make it evident that these statements are also logically equivalent.

FIGURE 4–25

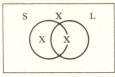 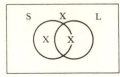

O: Some S are not L.   I: Some S are nonL.

Thus, the obverses of all four types of categorical propositions are logically equivalent to their original statements.

EXERCISE 4–9   (a) *Write the obverse of each of the following statements.* (b) *Determine whether the original statement and its obverse are logically equivalent, using Venn diagrams to test for equivalence.*

---

1. No oaks are maples.
2. Some books are dictionaries.
3. All madrigal singers are musicians.
4. Some of Shakespeare's works are not plays.
5. Some gifts are expensive things.
6. All senators are politicians.
7. No biscuits are muffins.
8. Some vampire bats are dangerous animals.
9. Some members are not lawyers.
10. No numbers are integers.

CONVERSION   **Conversion** is the mechanical process of interchanging the subject and predicate terms of a categorical proposition. The **I** proposition 'Some buildings are things designed by Marcel Breuer' is converted into another **I** proposition 'Some things designed by Marcel Breuer are buildings'. The statement with which we start is usually called the **convertend,** and the statement formed from it by the process of conversion is called the **converse.** Thus, in the example above, the **I** statement 'Some buildings are things designed by Marcel Breuer' is convertend, and the **I** statement 'Some things designed by Marcel Breuer are buildings' is the converse. The Venn diagrams representing these two propositions are presented in Figure 4–26.

FIGURE 4–26

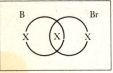

I: Some B are Br.

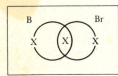

I: Some Br are B.

Since all **I** propositions and their converses have the same logical form, they can be represented by the same Venn diagrams as those shown above, except for a change in the letters which abbreviate the subject and predicate terms. Hence, all **I** statements and their converses are logically equivalent statements.

FIGURE 4–27

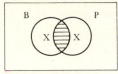

E: No B are P.

FIGURE 4–28

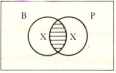

E: No P are B.

Likewise, all **E** propositions are logically equivalent to their converses. Consider, for example, the **E** statement 'No businessmen are poets' which is represented by the Venn diagram that appears in Figure 4–27. This **E** statement is converted by interchanging the subject and predicate terms, giving us another **E** proposition 'No poets are businessmen' which is represented by the Venn diagram in Figure 4–28.

On examination, it is easy to see that the Venn diagrams in Figures 4–27 and 4–28 are exactly the same. Again, since we know that all **E** statements have the same form, the Venn diagrams for these statements demonstrate that any **E** statement is logically equivalent to its converse.

A propositions, however, are not logically equivalent to their converses. Consider, for example, the **A** statement 'All gorillas are primates.' By interchanging the subject and predicate terms, we obtain its converse, which is 'All primates are gorillas'. Clearly, these two statements are not logically equivalent, since the original **A** statement or convertend is true, whereas its converse is obviously false. The Venn diagrams for these two propositions, shown in Figure 4–29, are

FIGURE 4–29

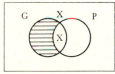 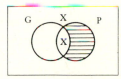

A: All G are P.   A: All P are G.

different, thereby demonstrating that the propositions are not logically equivalent. This single counterexample is sufficient to prove that no **A** statement is logically equivalent to its converse, since it shows that it is *possible* for an **A** statement to be true and its converse false.

An **O** statement is not logically equivalent to its converse for similar reasons. For example, the converse of 'Some trees are not oaks' is 'Some oaks are not trees', and, while the first is true, the second is false. The Venn diagrams for these statements are also different, as shown in Figure 4–30.

FIGURE 4–30

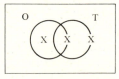 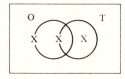

O: Some O are not T.   O: Some T are not O.

In summary, we have shown that all **E** and **I** propositions are logically equivalent to their converses, while no **A** or **O** propositions are equivalent to their converses.

EXERCISE 4–10   (a) *Write the converse of each of the following statements.* (b) *Determine whether the converse is logically equivalent to the original statement by using Venn diagrams.*

1. All salmon are fish.
2. No gnus are auks.
3. Some Americans are Californians.
4. Some songs are not ballads.
5. All pens are writing instruments.
6. All asps are vipers.
7. No women are four-star generals.
8. Some tables are marble things.
9. Some representatives are not elected persons.
10. No pollutants are beneficial things.

CONTRAPOSITION   The last immediate inference involving logically equivalent statements is contraposition. **Contraposition** is the process of interchanging the subject and predicate terms of a categorical statement and then replacing each with its complement. In other words, the subject term of the original statement is replaced by the complement of the predicate term, and the predicate term of the original is replaced by the complement of the subject term. Thus, the contrapositive of the **A** statement 'All fish are vertebrates' is the **A** statement 'All nonvertebrates are nonfish'. Contraposition may also be considered in light of our discussion of obversion and conversion. For example, examine the following steps:

FIGURE 4–31

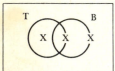

A: All F are V.

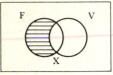

A: All nonV are nonF.

Original statement: *All fish are vertebrates.* (A)
By obversion: *No fish are nonvertebrates.* (E)
By conversion: *No nonvertebrates are fish.* (E)
By obversion: *All nonvertebrates are nonfish.* (A)

FIGURE 4–32

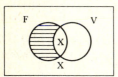

O: Some T are not B.

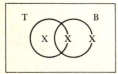

O: Some nonB are not nonT.

Thus, contraposition is not actually a new process, since we can obtain the contrapositive of a statement by obverting the original, then converting the resulting statement, and then obverting the resulting statement. Of course, our main concern is whether the contrapositive of a statement is logically equivalent to the original statement. In the case of the **A** statement in the example above, this seems to be the case, since each step produces a statement that is logically equivalent to the previous statement. It is possible to check whether the contrapositive of an **A** statement is logically equivalent to the original statement by means of Venn diagrams. The Venn diagrams representing the original **A** statement 'All fish are vertebrates' and its contrapositive 'All nonvertebrates are nonfish' are shown in Figure 4–31.

Since the Venn diagrams for the two statements are identical, they demonstrate that this **A** statement and its contrapositive, and therefore that *any* **A** statement and its contrapositive, are logically equivalent.

Any **O** statement and its contrapositive are also logically equivalent. For example, consider the **O** statement 'Some teachers are not bachelors' and its contrapositive 'Some nonbachelors are not nonteachers'. The Venn diagrams representing both these statements are shown in Figure 4–32.

Clearly, both diagrams are identical, and, since all **O** statements and their contrapositives have the same form, we can assert that any **O** statement and its contrapositive are logically equivalent. The logical equivalence of the **O** statement and its contrapositive may also be seen in the following series of operations:

> Original statement: *Some teachers are not bachelors.* **(O)**
> By obversion: *Some teachers are nonbachelors.* **(I)**
> By conversion: *Some nonbachelors are teachers.* **(I)**
> By obversion: *Some nonbachelors are not nonteachers.* **(O)**

Because the statement derived by each operation is logically equivalent to the preceding statement, the original **O** statement 'Some teachers are not bachelors' is logically equivalent to its contrapositive 'Some nonbachelors are not nonteachers'.

An **I** statement is not logically equivalent to its contrapositive. Consider, for example, the **I** statement 'Some relatives are friends' and its contrapositive 'Some nonfriends are nonrelatives'. The Venn diagrams representing both these statements appear in Figure 4–33.

The Venn diagrams for the two statements are different; this one counterexample shows that the contrapositive of an **I** statement is not logically equivalent to its original statement.

The contrapositive of an **E** statement also is not logically equivalent to its original. Consider, for example, the **E** statement 'No dogs are cats' and its contrapositive 'No noncats are nondogs'.

The Venn diagrams representing these statements are shown in Figure 4–34. Since the Venn diagrams are different from each other, the two statements are not logically equivalent.

FIGURE 4–33

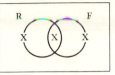

I: Some R are F.

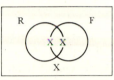

I: Some nonF are nonR.

FIGURE 4–34

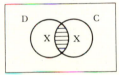

E: No D are C.

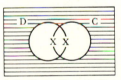

E: No nonC are nonD.

10. Some V are G ⊃ Some V are not G̅ ⊂→ Some G̅ are not V ⊃→ Some G̅ are V̅   unequiv.

Some P are G ⊃ Some P are not G̅ → Some G̅ are not P ⊃→ Some G̅ are P̅   not equiv.

EXERCISE 4–11　(a) *Write the contrapositive of each of the following statements.* (b) *Use Venn diagrams to test whether the contrapositive is logically equivalent to the original statement.*

1. All hammers are tools.
2. No pencils are pens.
3. Some drinks are nonalcoholic beverages.
4. Some cars are not Fords.
5. No mice are men.
6. All members are graduates of Harvard.
7. No elephants are carnivores.
8. Some bicycles are valuable objects.
9. Some kettles are not deep things.
10. Some unpleasant obligations are good obligations.

1. No Pe are P ⊃ All Pe are P̅ ⊂→ All P are P̅e → No P are P̅e   not equiv.

4. Some C are not F ⊃ Some C are F̅ ⊂→ Some F̅ are C ⊃→ Some F̅ are not C̅   equiv.

6. All M are G ⊃ No M are G̅ ⊂→ No G̅ are M ⊃→ All G̅ are M̅   equiv.

8. Some B are V ⊃ Some B are not V̅ ⊂→ Some V̅ are not B ⊃→ Some V̅ are B̅   not equiv.

Summary of Equivalences of Categorical Statements

OBVERSION

Original Statement		Obverse
A: All S are P	equivalent	**E:** No S are nonP
E: No S are P	equivalent	**A:** All S are nonP
I: Some S are P	equivalent	**O:** Some S are not nonP
O: Some S are not P	equivalent	**I:** Some S are nonP

CONVERSION

Original Statement		Converse
A: All S are P	not equivalent	**A:** All P are S
E: No S are P	equivalent	**E:** No P are S
I: Some S are P	equivalent	**I:** Some P are S
O: Some S are not P	not equivalent	**O:** Some P are not S

CONTRAPOSITION

Original Statement		Contrapositive
A: All S are P	equivalent	**A:** All nonP are nonS
E: No S are P	not equivalent	**E:** No nonP are nonS
I: Some S are P	not equivalent	**I:** Some nonP are nonS
O: Some S are not P	equivalent	**O:** Some nonP are not nonS

SEQUENCES OF EQUIVALENT STATEMENTS

Using a combination of obversion, conversion, and/or contraposition, it is sometimes possible to perform a *sequence* of immediate inferences by which we arrive at a statement which is logically equivalent to its original, but which is neither the obverse, converse, nor contrapositive of the original. This process is based on the **principle of equivalence** which asserts that if one proposition is logically equivalent to a second proposition, and the second is logically equivalent to a third, then the first statement is logically equivalent to the third. This can be explained most simply by noting that all three such statements will have identical Venn diagrams. To take one example, if we began with the **O** statement 'Some fish are not mackerels', we could obtain its obverse, which is the **I** statement 'Some fish are nonmackerels'. The original statement and its obverse are logically equivalent statements. It is then possible to convert the obverse 'Some fish are nonmackerels', thereby deriving the **I** statement 'Some nonmackerels are fish'. We also know that the converse of an **I** statement is logically equivalent to its original statement. Therefore, since the statement 'Some fish are not mackerels' is logically equivalent to 'Some fish are nonmackerels', which is logically equivalent to 'Some nonmackerels are fish', we know that the original statement 'Some fish are not mackerels' must be logically equivalent to the new statement 'Some nonmackerels are fish'. Note that this new statement is neither the obverse, converse, nor contrapositive of the original statement; yet it is still possible to infer the truth value of this new statement from the truth value of the original.

EXERCISE 4–12 (a) *How is each of the following statements related in terms of logical equivalences and the square of opposition to "All dinosaurs are reptiles"? Note that in some cases it is a two-step sequential relation. (b) If the original statement above is true, what can be validly inferred about the truth value of each statement following? Is the following statement true, false, or undetermined?*

All D are R – No D are R

1. No dinosaurs are nonreptiles.
2. No dinosaurs are reptiles.
3. Some dinosaurs are not reptiles.
4. Some dinosaurs are reptiles.
5. All reptiles are dinosaurs.
6. No reptiles are dinosaurs.
7. Some reptiles are not dinosaurs.
8. Some reptiles are dinosaurs.
9. Some nonreptiles are dinosaurs.
10. Some nonreptiles are nondinosaurs.
11. All nonreptiles are nondinosaurs.
12. No nonreptiles are nondinosaurs.

EXERCISE 4–13 (a) *How is each of the following statements related in terms of logical equivalences and the square of opposition to "No Navahos are Apaches"? Note that in some cases it is a two-step sequential relation. (b) If the original statement above is true, what can be validly inferred about the truth value of each succeeding statement? Is the succeeding statement true, false, or undetermined?*

No N are A

1. All Navahoes are non-Apaches.
2. All Navahos are Apaches.
3. Some Navahos are Apaches.
4. Some Navahos are not Apaches.
5. No Apaches are Navahos.
6. All Apaches are Navahos.
7. Some Apaches are Navahos.
8. Some Apaches are not Navahos.
9. Some non-Apaches are non-Navahos.
10. Some non-Apaches are Navahos.
11. No non-Apaches are Navahos.
12. No non-Apaches are non-Navahos.

EXERCISE 4–14 (a) *How is each of the following statements related in terms of logical equivalences and the square of opposition to "Some Englishmen are women"? Note that in some cases it is a two-step sequential relation. (b) If the original statement above is true, what can be validly inferred about the truth value of each succeeding statement? Is the succeeding statement true, false, or undetermined?*

1. Some Englishmen are not nonwomen.
2. Some Englishmen are not women.
3. No Englishmen are women.
4. All Englishmen are women.
5. Some women are Englishmen.
6. No women are Englishmen.
7. All women are Englishmen.
8. All nonwomen are non-Englishmen.
9. No nonwomen are non-Englishmen.
10. Some women are not Englishmen.
11. Some nonwomen are non-Englishmen.
12. No women are non-Englishmen.

EXERCISE 4–15

(a) *How is each of the following statements related in terms of logical equivalences and the square of opposition to "Some rock is not granite"? Note that in some cases it is a two-step sequential relation. (b) If the original statement above is true, what can be validly inferred about the truth value of each succeeding statement? Is the succeeding statement true, false, or undetermined?*

1. Some rock is nongranite.
2. Some rock is granite.
3. All rock is granite.
4. No rock is granite.
5. Some granite is not rock.

6. Some nongranite is rock.
7. No nongranite is rock.
8. No rock is nongranite.
9. All granite is rock.
10. All nongranite is nonrock.

EXERCISE 4–16

Reconsider the statements of which you did preliminary analyses in Exercise 1–13. Symbolize each one with as little loss of meaning as possible, using the methods of this chapter. Also use the methods given in this chapter to try to determine which of the statements (as symbolized) is analytic and which is synthetic.

SUMMARY

1. **Categorical propositions** are statements that assert that part or all of the class of things named by the subject term are included in or excluded from the class of things named by the predicate term. The classes referred to by both the subject and predicate terms must each contain at least one member in order for a statement to qualify as categorical. Categorical propositions can be either **affirmative** or **negative** in quality and **particular** or **universal** in quantity. **Universal affirmative** statements, also called **A** statements, affirm that all members of the subject class are included in the predicate class. **Particular affirmative** statements, also known as **I** statements, affirm that at least one member of the subject class is included in the predicate class. **Universal negative** statements, or **E** statements, affirm that all members of the subject class are excluded from the predicate class. **Particular negative** statements, or **O** statements, affirm that at least one member of the subject class is excluded from the predicate class.

2. Though categorical propositions may be expressed in a variety of ways, it is helpful to use a standard form sentence to express each of the four types. Standard form sentences can be referred to as **A, E, I,** or **O** sentences, depending on the type of categorical statement being expressed. **Abbreviations** of standard-form sentences express statements that are true or false. However, **schemata** are not abbreviations and do not express statements. Schemata only exhibit the logical form of statements. The schema of each type of categorical statement is formed by removing both the subject and predicate terms and retaining only the quantifier and copula; then the letters S̲ and P̲ (underscored to indicate that each represents a blank for which a noun or noun clause may be substituted) are appropriately inserted. Thus the schema

for any **A** proposition is 'All S̲ are P̲', for any **I** proposition 'Some S̲ are P̲', for any **E** proposition 'No S̲ are P̲', and for any **O** proposition 'Some S̲ are not P̲'.

3. Translating sentences into standard form may present problems. One should make certain that the predicate term is translated into a noun or noun clause and that the same noun clause construction is used throughout. When translating **exclusive statements** into standard **A** sentences, it is necessary to reverse the subject and predicate terms; but sentences beginning with 'the only' do not express exclusive statements and therefore do not require a reversal of subject and predicate terms. Sentences expressing singular affirmative statements are translated as universal affirmatives. When one is translating sentences expressed in ordinary language, context is often an important factor in determining what type of statement is being expressed. When context provides no clues, one should use the translation that provides less information. In ordinary context, an **exceptive statement** usually expresses two propositions, both of which are either universal or particular, and therefore must be translated into a conjunction of **A** and **E**, or **I**, and **O**, standard sentence forms.

4. The traditional square of opposition exhibits a variety of types of immediate inference and illustrates the logical relationships that exist among the four types of categorical statements. **Contradictory** propositions are categorical statements with the same subject and predicate terms which cannot both be true nor both be false at the same time. All **A** and **O** propositions and all **E** and **I** propositions with the same subject and predicate terms are contradictories. Two categorical statements are contraries if they are related in such a way that both cannot be true, but both may be false, at the same time. All **A** and **E** propositions with the same subject and predicate terms are contraries. However, all **I** and **O** statements with the same subject and predicate are subcontraries; that is, both cannot be false, but both may be true, at the same time. **Subimplication** (or **subalternation**) is the process by which the truth of a particular statement is inferred from the truth of its corresponding universal statement. **I** and **O** statements are subimplicants of **A** and **E** propositions (respectively) with the same subject and predicate terms. **Superimplication** is the process by which the falsity of the universal statement is inferred from the falsity of its corresponding particular statement. **A** and **E** propositions are superimplicants of **I** and **O** propositions (respectively) with the same subject and predicate terms.

5. Two statements are said to be **consistent** if both can be true at the same time. All **A** and **I** statements with the same subject and predicate terms, **E** and **O** statements with the same subject and predicate terms, and **I** and **O** statements with the same subject and predicate terms are logically consistent. Two statements are said to be logically independent if knowledge of the truth value of one (either true or false) tells us nothing about the truth value of the other, and vice versa. It is impossible for the four types of categorical statement with the same subject and predicate terms to be logically independent.

6. Two propositions are **logically equivalent** if the truth of one statement necessitates the truth of the other, and vice versa, or if the falsity of one statement necessitates the falsity of the other, and vice versa. The mechanical processes of obversion, conversion, and contraposition can produce logically equivalent statements with different subject and predicate terms.

7. **Obversion** is the mechanical process of changing the quality of a categorical statement and replacing the predicate term with its complement. (The **complement of a class** is the class of all things or beings in the universe of discourse that do not belong to the class and is expressed by joining the prefix 'non' to the name of the class.) The obverses of all four types of categorical proposition are logically equivalent to their original statements.

8. **Conversion** is the mechanical process of interchanging the subject and predicate terms of a categorical proposition. All **E** and **I** propositions, but no **A** or **O** propositions, are logically equivalent to their converses. *No* **A** or **O** statements are logically equivalent to their converses, and **E** and **I** statements *are* logically equivalent to their converses.

9. **Contraposition** is the process of interchanging the subject and predicate terms of a categorical statement and then replacing each with its complement. Any **O** statement is logically equivalent to its contrapositive; any **A** statement is logically equivalent to its contrapositive *only if* the additional requirements that the complementary classes must each contain at least one member are satisfied; and no **I** or **E** statements are logically equivalent to their contrapositives.

CHAPTER FIVE

Aristotelian Logic: Arguments

Each group below contains three sentences, each of which expresses a categorical statement or proposition.[1] Examine each set of statements carefully to determine whether it is an argument, and, if it is an argument, whether it is a valid one. An argument, it will be recalled, is a group of statements, one of which (the conclusion) is supported by the other statements. An argument is *valid* when the truth of the premises necessitates the truth of the conclusion; that is, it is such that it is impossible for all of the premises to be true and the conclusion false.

1. *All college graduates are educated persons.*
    All employees of this company are college graduates.
    Therefore, all employees of this company are educated persons.

2. *No students who are on the Dean's List are lazy, since no students on the Dean's List have poor grades, and all lazy students have poor grades.*

3. *Some physical exercises are not dangerous activities.*
    All physical exercises are sports.
    It follows that some sports are not dangerous activities.

---

[1] As in the previous chapter, we will be following the two stipulations previously specified. Since no specific context is given for any of these sentences, the reader should interpret them as expressing the statements that they would normally be used to express in ordinary usage. Also, we will usually abbreviate the technically accurate expression 'The statement expressed by the sentence "such and such" ' as 'The statement "such and such." '

> **4.** *No people who never make mistakes are*
> *instructors.*
> *Perfect teachers never make mistakes.*
> *Therefore, no instructors are perfect teachers.*

Each of these groups of sentences expresses an argument; each has an indicator word ('therefore', 'it follows that', or 'since') which enables us to distinguish the premises from the intended conclusion, and the premises do provide support for the conclusion in each case. For example, in the second group, the word 'since' indicates that the second and third statements are being offered in support of the first statement, or the conclusion. Arguments presented in everyday contexts are often formulated in this way.

Your logical intuition guided you correctly if you concluded that each of these groups of statements comprises a *valid* argument. Each argument is such that, if all of the premises are true, then the conclusion must be true. In this chapter, we will present several methods for testing arguments of this kind for validity, methods that are more reliable than intuition.

In Chapter 4 we were concerned only with logical relations between pairs of statements, some of which were such that, from the truth or falsity of one of the statements, we could directly infer the truth of falsity of the other. Such inferences were referred to as immediate inferences. In this chapter we shall be concerned with arguments such as those above which consist of *exactly three* statements, of a form known as the 'syllogism'. In arguments such as these, where the truth of the conclusion must be inferred from two or more premises, we are dealing with what is called **mediate inference.**

In such instances, the conclusion is drawn from the first premise through the *mediation* of the second premise; or, alternately, the conclusion is drawn from the two premises through a mediating or middle term which appears in both premises. In each of the arguments above, the two premises have a term in common, such as 'college graduates' in the first argument and 'physical exercises' in the third.

THE CATEGORICAL SYLLOGISM   The **categorical syllogism** is composed of exactly three categorical statements containing three different terms, each of which appears twice, but only once in any one statement. In light of this definition, we can determine whether the arguments presented at the beginning of this chapter are categorical syllogisms. Each argument does consist of three statements, but are they all categorical statements? Examine them carefully, identifying each as an **A, E, I,** or **O** categorical statement. Do the arguments fit the requirements concerning the number of terms, their placement within the argument, and their appearance within each statement? Consider the first argument. Its three categorical statements contain only three terms—' employees of this company', 'college graduates', and 'educated persons'. Each term appears only twice in the argument, and only once in any one statement. Because the first argument is composed of three categorical statements, all universal affirmative or **A** statements, and because it also satisfies the requirements concerning terms, it is a categorical syllogism. In the same manner, the other arguments presented above can be shown to be categorical syllogisms. We will continue to appeal to the assumption that all categorical statements assert the existence of at least one member in each of the classes referred to by both the subject and predicate terms (but *not* by their complements).

Standard Form Syllogisms
We have found that using a standard form for the sentences expressing each type of categorical statement is quite useful when studying immediate references. This is also true when dealing with categorical syllogisms. When a syllogism is composed of three categorical statements expressed by standard-form sentences and when these statements are presented in a given order, then the syllogism is said to be in *standard form*. For obvious reasons, when a syllogism is in standard form, the conclusion *follows* the two premises. The order of the premises is determined by the subject and predicate terms of the conclusion.

Major and Minor Premises
The predicate term of the conclusion is called the **major term,** and the subject term of the conclusion is called the **minor term.** The remaining term is called the **middle term** of the syllogism; it does not appear in the conclusion, but appears once in each premise. The premise containing the major term is called the **major premise;** the premise containing the minor term is called the **minor premise.** By definition, a syllogism is in **standard form** when its three categorical statements, expressed by standard form sentences, follow the order of major premise, minor premise, and conclusion.

For the remainder of this chapter we will use the symbol 'P' (for predicate) to represent the major term in the schema of any syllogism, 'S' (for subject) to represent the minor term, and 'M' to signify the position of the middle term.

> *The standard form syllogism can be outlined as follows:*
> *Major premise — must contain P and M.*
> *Minor premise — must contain S and M.*
> *Conclusion — S must be the subject and P must be the predicate.*

Let us return to the first argument presented at the beginning of this chapter to determine whether it is in standard form.

> *All college graduates are educated persons.*
> *All employees of this company are college graduates.*
> *Therefore, all employees of this company are educated persons.*

All three statements are expressed by standard-form sentences. The predicate term of the conclusion, 'educated persons', is by definition the major term, and thus the premise containing it (the major premise) should appear first in the syllogism, as it does. 'Employees of this company' is the minor term, since it is the subject of the conclusion, and the premise containing it (the minor premise) appears second, followed by the conclusion. The middle term in this example is

"If the coach and horses and the footmen and the beautiful clothes all turned back into the pumpkin and the mice and the rags, then how come the glass slipper didn't turn back, too?"

Has the child in this cartoon formulated a valid syllogism that punches a hole in the classic fairy tale about Cinderella? The methods to be presented in this chapter will help you to evaluate this argument.

Drawing by H. Martin; © *1974 The New Yorker Magazine.*

'college graduates', which appears once in each premise, as it should. Therefore, this categorical syllogism is in standard form.

We have already indicated that the second argument is not in standard form:

> *No students who are on the Dean's List are lazy,*
> *since no students on the Dean's List have poor*
> *grades, and all lazy students have poor grades.*

The first thing that must be done is to put each sentence into standard form, making certain that each subject and predicate term contains a noun or a noun clause. Thus, the first sentence, 'No students who are on the Dean's List are lazy' should be translated into 'No students who are on the Dean's List are lazy students'. Note that the subject term of the conclusion is 'lazy students'; therefore, this premise should not be translated as 'No students who are on the Dean's List are lazy persons'. To use this second translation would violate our definition of a categorical syllogism, since the argument would then contain four terms. The second sentence can be translated into 'No students who are on the Dean's List are students with poor grades', in which case the third sentence would read 'All lazy students are students with poor grades'. If the second premise had been translated as 'No students who are on the Dean's List are *persons* with poor grades', then the third premise would have to be translated as 'All lazy students are persons with poor grades'.

Of course, merely translating each sentence into standard form does not make this argument a standard-form syllogism. Its conclusion, 'No students who are on the Dean's List are lazy students', comes first, when it should come last. The predicate term of the conclusion, 'lazy students', makes the statement 'All lazy students are students with poor grades' the major premise, which should come first. This should be followed by 'No students on the Dean's List are students with poor grades' as the minor premise, since it contains the minor term, 'students on the Dean's List', which is the subject term of the conclusion. Written in standard form, the argument would read as follows:

> *All lazy students are students with poor grades.*
> *No students on the Dean's List are students with*
> *   poor grades.*
> *Therefore, no students on the Dean's List are lazy*
> *   students.*

The third argument is already in standard form, but the fourth argument must be rewritten.

> *No people who never make mistakes are instructors.*
> *Perfect teachers never make mistakes.*
> *Therefore, no instructors are perfect teachers.*

The sentence 'Perfect teachers never make mistakes' must be translated into standard form, keeping in mind that its subject and predicate terms should be expressed in the same way as the corresponding terms in the other sentences. Consequently, this sentence would be translated as 'All perfect teachers are people who never make mistakes'. The predicate term of the conclusion, 'perfect teachers', is the major term, and 'instructors', the subject term, is the minor term. Therefore, 'All perfect teachers are people who never make mistakes' is the major premise and should come first, not second. 'No people who never make mistakes are instructors' is the minor premise, since it contains the minor term, 'instructors'. In standard form, the argument now reads:

> *All perfect teachers are people who never make mistakes.*
> *No people who never make mistakes are instructors.*
> *Therefore, no instructors are perfect teachers.*

> *When putting a categorical syllogism in standard form, one should follow this procedure:*
>
> 1. *Translate each of its three sentences into standard categorical form, if they are not already so.*
> 2. *Determine which sentence expresses the conclusion.*
> 3. *From the predicate and subject terms of the conclusion, determine the major and minor terms.*
> 4. *Place the major and minor premises in that order before the conclusion.*

1-7, 10

EXERCISE 5-1   *Examine each of the following arguments. (a) Determine if it is a categorical syllogism. (b) If it is a categorical syllogism, determine whether it is in standard form. (c) If it is not, put it in standard form.*

---

1. All bees can sting.   *All B are S*
   Some bees are insects.   *Some B are I ∴ Some I are S*   AII-3
   Therefore, some insects can sting.
2. All Vulcans are completely logical persons.   *All V are L*   *∴ All S are L*   AAA-1
   Mr. Spock is a Vulcan.   *All S are V*
   Therefore, Mr. Spock is a completely logical person.
3. No fluorescent lights are incandescent lights.   *No F are I*   *no syllogism*
   Some electric lights are incandescent lights.   *Some E are I ∴ Some E are not I*
   Therefore, some electric lights are not incandescent lights.
4. No sloops are motorboats.
   All hydroplanes are motorboats.   *No S are M*   EAE-2
   Therefore, no hydroplanes are sloops.   *All H are M*
   ∴ No H are S

[handwritten top margin:]
5: Some D are DR → All DR are A
All DR are A → Some D are DR   AII-1
∴ Some D are A   ∴ Some D are A

5. Some drinkers are drunkards.
   All drunkards are alcoholics.
   Therefore, some drinkers are alcoholics.
6. All documentaries are educational.   *[handwritten:]* All D are E   A II-1
   Some films are documentaries.   *[handwritten:]* 6: Some F are D
   Therefore, some films are educational.   *[handwritten:]* Some F are E
7. All cats are mammals.
   All mammals are vertebrates.   *[handwritten left margin:]* No syllogism
   All vertebrates are animals.
   Therefore, all cats are animals.
8. If this painting is a Rembrandt, then it must be an expensive thing.
   This painting is a Rembrandt.
   Therefore, this painting must be an expensive thing.
9. Some men do not have the use of reason; therefore, some rational animals do not
   have the use of reason, since all men are rational animals.

[handwritten left margin:] EAE-2
No S are C
All H are C ←
No H are S

10. No hyperbolas are squares, since all hyperbolas are conic sections, but no squares
    are conic sections.
11. Some revolutionaries are not Marxists, but all communists are Marxists, so some
    revolutionaries are not communists.
12. Some food additives should not be allowed, because some food additives are
    dangerous to human health, and no substances dangerous to human health should
    be allowed.
13. No generals are kangaroos, since all generals are soldiers, and no kangaroos are
    soldiers.
14. Some insects are bees; therefore, some insects can sting, since all bees can sting.
15. Some coaches are teachers, so some teachers are coaches.
16. No toadstools are edible things, so some mushrooms are not toadstools, for some
    edible things are mushrooms.
17. If there is no God, then everything is permissible.
    Everything is permissible.
    Therefore, there is no God.
18. Some respectable citizens are not Democrats, because all mayors are respectable
    citizens, but some mayors are not Democrats.
19. All congressmen are citizens, so all noncitizens are noncongressmen.
20. No public officials are dishonest persons; therefore, no dishonest persons are public
    officials.

Abbreviating Syllogisms   Syllogisms can be represented in shortened form by using the methods of abbreviation presented in the previous chapter. However, two additional procedures are required: first, a line should be placed between the premises and the conclusion to separate them, and second, the symbol '∴' should be used as an abbreviation of the word 'therefore' or any other conclusion indicator. Thus, the third argument presented at the beginning of this chapter:

> *Some physical exercises are not dangerous activities.*
> *All physical exercises are sports.*
> *It follows that some sports are not dangerous*
>   *activities.*

can be abbreviated as follows:

Some E are not D	*(O statement)*
All E are S.	*(A statement)*
∴Some S are not D.	*(O statement)*

Consider another categorical syllogism:

> *No well-illustrated books are dull books.*
> *Some textbooks are well-illustrated books.*
> *Therefore, some textbooks are not dull books.*

This syllogism can be abbreviated in the following way, which also makes it easier to see that the syllogism is in standard form.

No I are D.	*(E statement)*
Some T are I.	*(I statement)*
∴Some T are not D.	*(O statement)*

Syllogistic Schemata   As we saw in Chapter 4, each type of categorical proposition has a logical form which can be represented by a schema. The logical form of a categorical syllogism may also be represented by a schema. Let us consider the last example, about textbooks. As with all categorical syllogisms, it contains three terms: a major term, a minor term, and a middle term. If we remove the terms and fill the remaining blanks with different symbols, we have the following:

> *No ✱✱✱✱✱✱✱ are ....*
> *Some – – – – – – – – are ✱✱✱✱✱✱✱.*
> *Therefore, some – – – – – – – – are not..........*

What we have done is to present a schema for each proposition, substituting the same symbol for each term when it appears. Thus, any three nouns or noun clauses can be substituted in the above schema to produce a syllogism with the same form as the preceding syllogism about textbooks. For the sake of clarification, let us consider for a moment the following example:

No friends are enemies.	*(E statement)*
Some relatives are friends.	*(I statement)*
Therefore, some relatives are not enemies.	*(O statement)*

Using the symbols 'S', 'P', and 'M' as stipulated earlier to represent the minor, major, and middle terms, respectively, the schema of any syllogism can be presented more concisely. It should be recognized that these symbols are *not* abbreviations; rather, they function as blanks into which any noun or noun clause can be inserted to produce sentences expressing categorical statements. Thus, the following schema:

> No *M* are *P*.
> Some *S* are *M*.
> ∴Some *S* are not *P*.

displays the logical form of these syllogisms:

No well-illustrated books are dull books.	*(E statement)*
Some textbooks are well-illustrated books.	*(I statement)*
Therefore, some textbooks are not dull books.	*(O statement)*
No friends are enemies.	*(E statement)*
Some relatives are friends.	*(I statement)*
Therefore, some relatives are not enemies.	*(O statement)*

and any other syllogism with the same logical form.

The process of substituting nouns or noun clauses for the symbols (or blanks) in a schema to produce a syllogism is called the **interpretation** of the schema. For example, consider the following schema:

> No *P* are *M*.
> Some *M* are *S*.
> ∴Some *S* are not *P*.

Suppose the term 'poets' is substituted for '*P*', 'students' for '*S*', and 'unimaginative people' for '*M*' in the schema above. This interpretation (that is, substitution of nouns or noun clauses) would produce the following categorical syllogism:

No poets are unimaginative people.	*(E statement)*
Some unimaginative people are students.	*(I statement)*
Therefore, some students are not poets.	*(O statement)*

This syllogism and the preceding one are both in standard form and both consist of **E, I,** and **O** statements in that order. However, these two syllogisms have different schemata, because the middle term is in a different position in each premise. Such similarities and differences between syllogisms are traditionally discussed in terms of the concepts of mood and figure.

EXERCISE 5–2   *Write (a) an abbreviation of the syllogism and (b) its corresponding schema for each of the arguments in Exercise 5–1 that is a categorical syllogism. Make certain the syllogism is in standard form before writing an abbreviation and schema for it.*

MOOD AND   Note that each of the three preceding categorical syllogisms has an **E**
FIGURE   statement for the major premise, an **I** statement for the minor premise, and an **O** statement for the conclusion. This, of course, does not
hold true for all syllogisms in standard form. Look back at the arguments at the
beginning of this chapter. The first consists of three **A** statements, and the third
argument has an **O** statement for the major premise, an **A** statement for the
minor premise, and an **O** statement for the conclusion. Thus, standard form
categorical syllogisms can be comprised of various combinations of categorical
statements. The **mood** of a standard form syllogism is the particular combination
of categorical statements of which the syllogism is composed, expressed in terms
of the statement names **A, E, I,** and **O.** The first letter in the mood description
indicates the form of the major premise, the second that of the minor premise, and
the third that of the conclusion. Thus, the mood of the first is expressed as **AAA,**
and the mood of the third as **OAO.** The three syllogisms for which schemata
were given in the previous section all have the same mood, namely, **EIO.**

Syllogisms having the same mood do not necessarily have the same form.
Therefore, the description of the mood of a syllogism is not sufficient for revealing its exact form. Although the last two syllogisms have the same mood, **EIO,**
note that their schemata are different:

E	No <u>M</u> are <u>P</u>.		*E*	No <u>P</u> are <u>M</u>.
I	Some <u>S</u> are <u>M</u>.		*I*	Some <u>M</u> are <u>S</u>.
O	∴Some <u>S</u> are not <u>P</u>		*O*	∴Some <u>S</u> are not <u>P</u>.

How do these two schemata differ? The difference is in the placement of the
middle term. In the schema on the left, the middle term is the subject of the
major premise but the predicate of the minor premise. In the schema on the
right, the middle term is the predicate of the major premise and the subject of the
minor premise. The **figure** of a standard form categorical syllogism is determined
by the placement of the middle term in the two premises of the syllogism. There
are two other possible locations for the middle term besides those given. The
middle term could also be the subject of both premises, or it could be the
predicate of both premises. These four arrangements of the middle term give the
four figures for categorical syllogisms; they have traditionally been numbered as
follows:

Figure 1	*All observant people are expert drivers.*	*M–P*
	All students are observant people.	*S–M*

	Therefore, all students are expert drivers.	$S-P$
Figure 2	All expert drivers are observant people.	$P-M$
	Some students are not observant people.	$S-M$
	Therefore, some students are not expert drivers.	$S-P$
Figure 3	Some observant people are expert drivers.	$M-P$
	All observant people are students.	$M-S$
	Therefore, some students are expert drivers.	$S-P$
Figure 4	No expert drivers are observant people.	$P-M$
	Some observant people are students.	$M-S$
	Therefore, some students are not expert drivers.	$S-P$

Observe that the placement of the middle term affects only the figure of the syllogism and *not* its mood.

The **form** of a syllogism is determined by the combination of its figure and its mood. It is conventional to express the form of a syllogism by placing the number of its figure after the letters that state its mood. Thus the form of the figure 1 syllogism above is **AAA**-1. For the figure 2 syllogism, the form is **AOO**-2. For the figure 3 syllogism, the form is **IAI**-3, and for the figure 4 syllogism, **EIO**-4. (Note that the form of a syllogism symbolized in this way is actually an abbreviation of the schema.)

A standard mnemonic, or memory, device will help you relate the placement of the middle term to the proper number of the figure of a syllogism. A line is drawn through the middle terms with the figures arranged in order, as follows:

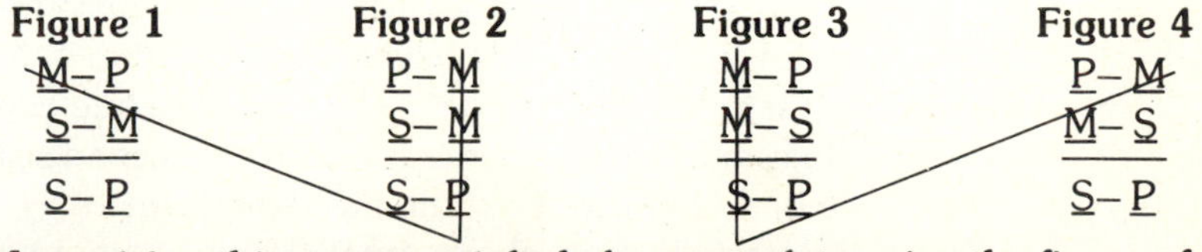

Figure 1	Figure 2	Figure 3	Figure 4
M– P	P– M	M– P	P– M
S– M	S– M	M– S	M– S
S– P	S– P	S– P	S– P

Memorizing this pattern might help you to determine the figure of a syllogism or to construct a syllogism in any given figure.

EXERCISE 5–3   *Give the form (the mood and figure) of each of the arguments in Exercise 5–1 that is a categorical syllogism. Again, make certain that the syllogism is in standard form.*

TESTING
THE VALIDITY
OF SYLLOGISMS

The form of a categorical syllogism is completely specified when its mood *and* figure are given. Not all syllogisms are valid arguments. The validity or invalidity of a syllogism does not depend on the terms used in it, that is, on its content, but solely on its form. Syllogisms with certain forms are valid, whereas those with other forms are invalid. This is true regardless of the actual terms in the statements and regardless of the truth or falsity of the statements of which the syllogisms are composed. Consider, for example, the following syllogisms:

All bacteria are organisms visible through a light microscope.	*All $\underline{P}$ are $\underline{M}$.*
No viruses are organisms visible through a light microscope.	*No $\underline{S}$ are $\underline{M}$.*
Therefore, no viruses are bacteria.	*∴No $\underline{S}$ are $\underline{P}$.*

All bacteria are organisms invisible through a light microscope.	*All $\underline{P}$ are $\underline{M}$.*
No viruses are organisms invisible through a light microscope.	*No $\underline{S}$ are $\underline{M}$.*
Therefore, no viruses are bacteria.	*∴No $\underline{S}$ are $\underline{P}$.*

Both syllogisms have the same form, **AEE**-2. Since bacteria, in fact, are microorganisms visible through a light microscope and viruses are not thus visible, the premises of the first syllogism are both true; the conclusion is also true, for viruses are distinct from bacteria. But the premises of the second syllogism are both false, for bacteria, in fact, are not invisible through a light microscope, but viruses are invisible. However, the conclusion of the second syllogism, the same as that for the first, is true. Thus, the same true conclusion was drawn in the first syllogism from true premises and in the second syllogism from false premises by use of syllogisms of exactly the same form.

Both syllogisms above are valid, since an argument is valid when, *if* its premises are true, then its conclusion *must* be true. Logicians define the necessity of this 'must' by pointing to the concept of the form of the argument, as exhibited by the schema. An argument is valid if and only if *no* argument with that *form* can have true premises and a false conclusion—that is, the truth of the conclusion follows necessarily from the truth of the premises.

The schema of a statement or proposition cannot properly be said to be true or false; only the statement itself can be so described. Thus, the schema of the true statement, 'All bacteria are organisms visible through a light microscope', is 'All $\underline{S}$ are $\underline{P}$', which is not true or false until terms are substituted for the symbols '$\underline{S}$' and '$\underline{P}$'. However, an argument schema, which shows the form of a syllogism, can be characterized as valid or invalid. A **valid argument schema** is an argument schema for which there is no possible interpretation—that is, no substitution of terms—that would create an argument with true premises and a false conclusion. For example, no terms substituted for the symbols in the valid argument schema

> *All $\underline{P}$ are $\underline{M}$.*
> *No $\underline{S}$ are $\underline{M}$.*
> *∴No $\underline{S}$ are $\underline{P}$.*

would produce a syllogism with true premises and a false conclusion. Thus, it follows that an argument is valid if and only if its schema is valid. Consequently, the two syllogisms above are valid because their argument schema is valid. If a schema is not valid, then no argument that is an interpretation of that schema can be valid either. Several methods have been developed for testing the validity and/or invalidity of argument forms. One such method involves the use of counterexamples.

Testing by Counterexample   A **counterexample** is an interpretation of an argument schema that makes all the premises true and the conclusion false. An interpretation, as you may recall, is the substitution of terms (nouns or noun clauses) for the blanks $\underline{S}$, $\underline{P}$, and $\underline{M}$ of the argument schema. Therefore, this method of testing syllogisms involves constructing a syllogism with a particular logical form, which is clearly invalid. Suppose, for example, the following syllogism—all of whose statements we will assume to be true—is to be tested by the method of counterexamples:

> *All women are good*
> *   administrators.*   *All $\underline{P}$ are $\underline{M}$.*
> *Some officers of the council*
> *   are good administrators.*   *Some $\underline{S}$ are $\underline{M}$.*
> *Therefore, some officers of*   *∴Some $\underline{S}$ are $\underline{P}$.*
> *   the council are women.*

You may think there is something wrong with this syllogism; you may suspect that it is not valid, but you may be uncertain. If you can construct a counterexample—that is, if you can find an argument with the same logical form (i.e., an interpretation of the same schema) which makes both premises true and the conclusion false—then the schema and all arguments with this form will have been proved to be invalid. The following argument would seem to provide such a counterexample:

<table>
<tr><td>*All <u>apples</u> are <u>fruits</u>.*</td><td>*All <u>P</u> are <u>M</u>.*</td></tr>
<tr><td>*Some <u>berries</u> are <u>fruits</u>.*</td><td>*Some <u>S</u> are <u>M</u>.*</td></tr>
<tr><td>*Therefore, some berries
   are apples.*</td><td>*∴Some <u>S</u> are <u>P</u>.*</td></tr>
</table>

Because the conclusion of this interpretation of the schema seems to be false while the two premises appear to be true, the schema has been shown to be invalid. Therefore, the original syllogism is also invalid, as are any syllogisms of this form (**AII**-2).

Providing a counterexample with true premises and a false conclusion proves the invalidity of a particular syllogistic form, but failing to provide counterexamples, or providing examples with true premises and a true conclusion, *does not* prove the validity of a syllogistic form. Examine the following syllogisms:

All Cadillacs are large cars.
No Cadillacs are cars that get good mileage.
Therefore, no cars that get good mileage are large
   cars.

All cats are felines.
No cats are canines.
Therefore, no felines are canines.

Both syllogisms seem to have true premises and true conclusions. Both also fit the argument schema **AEE**-3:

All <u>M</u> are <u>P</u>.
No <u>M</u> are <u>S</u>.
∴No <u>S</u> are <u>P</u>.

Many more examples of syllogisms of this form with true premises and true conclusions could be given. This syllogistic form might seem to be valid, but in fact it has not been proved that there is *no* interpretation of the **AEE**-3 schema which results in an argument with true premises and a false conclusion. The substitution of 'lilacs' for '<u>S</u>', 'things that are violet' for '<u>P</u>', and 'flowers in this bouquet' for '<u>M</u>' does produce such a counterexample:

All flowers in this bouquet are things that are violet.
No flowers in this bouquet are lilacs.
Therefore, no lilacs are things that are violet.

We can easily conceive of a situation that would make both premises true, but the conclusion, 'No lilacs are things that are violet', is false, since many lilacs are violet in color. This single counterexample has shown that *all* syllogisms of the form **AEE**-3 are invalid. A thousand examples of arguments of this form with true premises and true conclusions would not have proved its validity.

Counterexamples can be used only to prove the *invalidity* of an argument schema. Even at this task they are not very effective, since counterexamples are often difficult to think up, and the failure to think up a counterexample is not sufficient to prove an argument valid. There is also the problem that the truth or falsity of any specific statement can be challenged in one way or another. Thus, no counterexample can be taken as absolute, since someone could always argue that an apparently true premise is actually false, or a seemingly false conclusion is really true. What is really needed is a definite **decision procedure,** a mechanical procedure that can be used to prove the validity *or* invalidity of any particular argument schema or intended argument in a finite number of steps. An *ideal* decision procedure would also avoid the problem of determining the truth or falsity of specific statements, as is necessary in the method of counterexamples. Two other techniques, one using Venn diagrams and the other syllogistic rules, provide such "ideal" decision procedures.

EXERCISE 5–4   *Write counterexamples for each of the following invalid syllogisms, all of which are in standard form.*

---

1. All Frenchwomen are Europeans.
   Some Europeans are college-educated persons.
   Therefore, some college-educated persons are Frenchwomen.
2. Some conservatives are Republicans.
   No Republicans are Democrats.
   Therefore, some Democrats are not conservatives.
3. No lions are tigers.
   No tigers are cheetahs.
   Therefore, no lions are cheetahs.
4. Some humans are not musicians.
   All New Yorkers are humans.
   Therefore, some New Yorkers are not musicians.
5. All Chicagoans are citizens.
   Some citizens are beer drinkers.
   Therefore, some beer drinkers are Chicagoans.
6. All flowers are plants.
   All roses are plants.
   Therefore, all roses are flowers.
7. No sergeants are generals.
   All sergeants are officers.
   Therefore, no officers are generals.

8. All falcons are hawks.
    Some birds are hawks.
    Therefore, some birds are falcons.
9. All primates are mammals.
    No primates are egg-bearing animals.
    Therefore, no egg-bearing animals are mammals.
10. All addicts are persons to be pitied.
    All addicts are unhappy persons.
    Therefore, all unhappy persons are persons to be pitied.
11. No rocks are intelligent things.
    No clouds are rocks.
    Therefore, no clouds are intelligent things.
12. Some animals are extinct species.
    No animals are perennial flowers.
    Therefore, some perennial flowers are not extinct species.
13. Some animals are stray animals.
    All dogs are animals.
    Therefore, some dogs are stray animals.
14. All Nazis are culpable persons.
    Some Germans are not Nazis.
    Therefore, some Germans are not culpable persons.

Testing with Venn Diagrams

Venn diagrams were used in Chapter 4 to exhibit the logical forms of **A, E, I,** and **O** statements and to test whether two statements are logically equivalent. One circle was used to represent each of the two terms of any statement. Venn diagrams also can be used to represent categorical syllogisms and to test for their validity or invalidity. Because the standard-form syllogism has three terms—subject, predicate, and middle term—each of which designates a different class of things, three circles are required to represent the classes to which these three terms refer. In Chapter 4, it was noted that all categorical statements with the same schema are represented by the same Venn diagram, except for the labels on the circles. It is possible to use the symbols $\underline{S}$ and $\underline{P}$ to represent blanks to be filled in by the subject and predicate terms of a particular statement. Likewise, all categorical syllogisms with the same schema are represented by the same Venn Diagram, except for the labels on the circles. Consequently, we shall discuss the techniques for diagramming argument schemata before actually using the Venn diagram technique to test the validity or invalidity of actual categorical syllogisms.

Venn Diagrams and Syllogistic Schemata

The three terms of the standard-form syllogism are conventionally diagrammed using the symbol $\underline{S}$ to stand for the blank to be filled by the minor term, $\underline{P}$ for the major term blank, and $\underline{M}$ for the middle term blank, as shown in Figure 5–1. The three circles are labeled $\underline{S}$, $\underline{P}$, and $\underline{M}$ with the labels placed outside the circles. The $\underline{S}$ circle in the upper left portion of the box represents the class of things referred to by whatever minor term might be supplied; the $\underline{P}$ circle represents the class of things referred to by the major

FIGURE 5–1

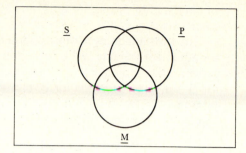

term; and the <u>M</u> circle represents the class of things referred to by the middle term.

Each of the distinct areas in the box represents a distinct class, as shown in Figure 5–2.

FIGURE 5–2

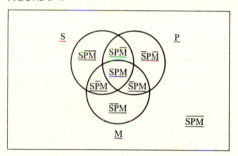

The center area labelled <u>SPM</u> contains all those things that are members of all three classes whose names might be substituted for <u>S</u>, <u>P</u>, and <u>M</u>. A bar above a symbol in a section indicates that anything contained in that section is *not* a member of the class signified by that symbol. The notation $\overline{\text{SPM}}$ outside the circles, but within the box, signifies that this area contains all those things that do not belong to any of the three classes. The area labelled $\overline{\text{SPM}}$ contains all those

FIGURE 5–3

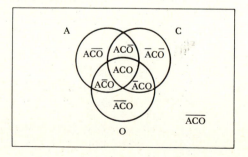

things that are members of the S class (without a bar), but that are not members of the P and M classes, for the P and M classes do not cover this section of the S circle.

The substitution of nouns or noun clauses for S, P, and M in the diagram of an argument schema will give us the diagram of a specific argument. Let us provide an interpretation of an argument schema by substituting the term 'artists' for S, the term 'creators' for P, and the term 'original thinkers' for M. In this instance, the various areas of the Venn diagram shown in Figure 5–3 would represent the following classes:

> $A\overline{CO}$ *is the class of artists who are neither creators nor original thinkers.*
>
> $AC\overline{O}$ *is the class of artists and creators who are not original thinkers.*
>
> $\overline{A}C\overline{O}$ *is the class of creators who are neither artists nor original thinkers.*
>
> *ACO is the class of artists who are creators and original thinkers.*
>
> $A\overline{C}O$ *is the class of artists who are original thinkers but are not creators.*
>
> $\overline{A}CO$ *is the class of creators who are original thinkers but not artists.*
>
> $\overline{A}\,\overline{C}O$ *is the class of original thinkers who are neither artists nor creators.*
>
> $\overline{ACO}$ *is the class of those who are neither artists, nor creators, nor original thinkers.*

This last class, $\overline{ACO}$, will not be of concern to us in this chapter; therefore, we will not hereafter place the circles of the Venn diagram within a box.

Diagramming Categorical Syllogisms

In using Venn diagrams to represent standard-form syllogisms, we will continue to assume that all of the classes named by the subject and predicate terms in every statement contain at least one member. However, since it is not relevant for determining the validity or invalidity of a syllogism, we will *not* make any assumptions about the existence of members in the complements of these classes.

Following the rule given for diagramming categorical syllogisms (see box), let us diagram the following categorical syllogism of the form **AAA**-1.

All original thinkers are creators.	*All T are C.*
All artists are original thinkers.	*All A are T.*
Therefore, all artists are creators.	*∴All A are C.*

> *The rules for diagramming a categorical syllogism are an extension*
> *of those for diagramming categorical statements, as follows:*
>
> 1. *If a statement asserts that a particular class is empty, the area*
>   *of the diagram representing that class is shaded.*
> 2. *An area of the diagram representing a class that is asserted to*
>   *contain at least one member is marked with an 'X'.*
> 3. *When a proposition does not specify in which of two adjacent*
>   *areas a thing exists, the 'X' is placed on the line between the*
>   *sections.*
> 4. *An area that has been shaded cannot have an 'X' placed in it.*
> 5. *Universal statements are always diagrammed first, before any*
>   *particular statements. No Xs should be put in the diagram until*
>   *after all necessary shading has been done for* both *premises.*
> 6. *Only the major and minor premises of the syllogism are dia-*
>   *grammed. If the syllogism is valid, the diagram of the conclusion*
>   *will already be contained in the diagram of the premises.*

FIGURE 5–4

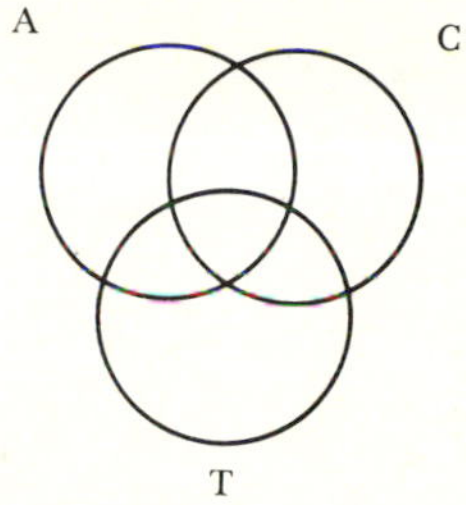

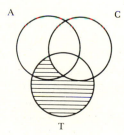

First it is necessary to draw a Venn diagram for the three terms of this syllogism. The circle representing the class of things referred to by the minor term is labelled 'A'; the circle representing the major term class is labelled 'C'; and the circle representing the middle term class is labelled 'T', as shown in Figure 5–4.

The major premise, 'All original thinkers are creators', since it is universal, can be diagrammed first. All of the T circle that is not within the C circle should be shaded to indicate that it is empty, since all members of T must also be in the class C, as shown in Figure 5–5. We must wait to place the Xs until after we have completed whatever shading is necessary for the minor premise, 'All artists are original thinkers'. Because this proposition asserts that all of the members of the class of artists are contained in the class of original thinkers, we must shade all sections of the A circle outside the T circle to show that they are empty, as shown in Figure 5–6.

FIGURE 5–5

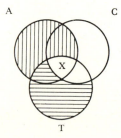

In using Venn diagrams to test a syllogism for validity, we *never* diagram the conclusion. Thus, we can now place the Xs in the diagram for the premises to indicate the existence of at least one member in each of the classes of original thinkers (T), creators (C) and artists (A). In the case of this argument, the X placed in the only nonshaded part of the A circle also happens to be in the C and T circles, and therefore no additional Xs are necessary.

FIGURE 5–6

Figure 5–6 represents the information contained in both the major and the minor premises of the syllogism. To test the validity of this syllogism, we must determine whether the diagram of the conclusion is already contained in the diagram of the premises. The conclusion of this syllogism, 'All artists are creators', asserts that all members of the class of artists are also members of the class of creators. In terms of the diagram, 'All A are C' tells us that there is nothing inside the A circle that is not also inside the C circle. Looking at the diagram in Figure 5–6, we can note that all of the sections of the A circle outside of the C circle are already shaded, and there is an X in both the A circle and the C circle. Therefore, the diagram of the premises tells us that 'All artists are creators'. Nothing more needs to be added to the diagram for the conclusion to be shown in this way. The conclusion is already contained in the premises, as it must be in a valid syllogism.

Let us consider another standard form syllogism, also with the form **AAA**-1:

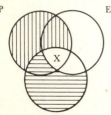

FIGURE 5–7

All scientists are experimenters.	*All S are E.*
All physicists are scientists.	*All P are S.*
Therefore, all physicists are experimenters.	*∴All P are E.*

The major premise, 'All scientists are experimenters', tells us that the area of the S circle outside the E circle must be empty. Thus, the sections of the S circle outside the E circle are shaded, as shown in Figure 5–7. Similarly, the minor premise, 'All physicists are scientists', tells us that the area of the P circle outside the S circle is also empty, and should be shaded, as it is in Figure 5–7. The conclusion, 'All physicists are experimenters', is already diagrammed, for the only section of the P circle remaining unshaded is within the E circle.

Examining the Venn diagrams in Figures 5–6 and 5–7, you will observe that they are identical except for the labeling of the circles. This is not surprising, for we already know that all arguments with the same form (these are both of the form **AAA**-1) have the same schema, and we know that the Venn diagram displays the form of the argument. Consequently, all arguments which are interpretations of the same schema must have the same diagram. We have also seen that an argument is valid if and only if its schema is valid. Thus, the validity or invalidity of an argument can be tested by testing its schema. However, when testing an argument *schema,* one must use the symbols S, P, and M to represent the minor, major, and middle terms, respectively. In diagramming the schema of a specific syllogism (that is, one of its interpretations) we will put the abbreviations of the specific terms in parentheses, to make it easier to read the diagram.

Identifying Valid Syllogisms   Thus far, we have worked only with Venn diagrams for **AAA**-1 syllogisms. To sharpen our skills, let us diagram some valid categorical syllogisms with different forms. Another valid form of categorical syllogism is **AEE**-2, exemplified in the following argument in which the term 'artists' is substituted for the minor term (S), 'creators' for the major term (P), and 'original thinkers' for the middle term (M).

All creators are original thinkers.	*All P are M.*
No artists are original thinkers.	*No S are M.*
Therefore, no artists are creators.	*∴No S are P.*

FIGURE 5–8

S (A)   P (C)

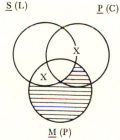

M (T)

This form is valid, even though one might consider all the statements in this particular interpretation to be false. As shown in Figure 5–8, the major premise, 'All creators are original thinkers', tells us that all of the P class is included in the M class, or that the part of the P circle outside the M circle contains no members. Therefore, these sections of the P circle are shaded. The minor premise, 'No artists are original thinkers', tells us that all sections of the S circle that fall within the M circle should be shaded. Checking the conclusion, 'No artists are creators', you will see that all of the S circle that is inside the P circle has been shaded on the basis of the information given in two premises. Nothing more needs to be added to the diagram in Figure 5–8 to represent this conclusion; thus the diagram exhibits the validity of the argument form.

A third valid form of syllogism is **OAO**-3, which can be illustrated by the following syllogism and schema:

FIGURE 5–9

S (L)   P (C)

Some politicians are not crooks.	**Some M are not P.**
All politicians are liars.	**All M are S.**
Therefore, some liars are not crooks.	**∴Some S are not P.**

In this particular syllogism, the major premise and the conclusion seem to be true, and the minor premise is probably false, but nevertheless the syllogism is valid, as are any syllogisms with this form. According to rule 5, universal statements must be diagrammed before particular statements. In this syllogism, the minor premise is universal and the major premise is particular, so the minor premise must be diagrammed first. 'All politicians are liars' asserts that there are no politicians who are not also liars, so the sections of the M circle not in the S circle are shaded, as in Figure 5–9.

M (P)

Once the shading for this universal premise has been put in the diagram, the particular major premise, 'Some politicians are not crooks', can be diagrammed by placing an 'X' in the section of the M circle outside of the P circle, indicating that at least one politician exists who is not a crook. This 'X' is also in the S circle. To complete the diagram for the minor premise, we must also place an 'X' in the P circle. To check the conclusion, 'Some liars are not crooks', note that the 'X' in Figure 5–9 is in a section of the S circle that is outside the P circle. Thus, the diagram of the conclusion is already contained in the diagram of the two premises of the syllogism.

FIGURE 5–10

S (L)   P (C)

What would have happened if the particular major premise had been diagrammed before the universal minor premise? In this instance, the 'X' representing the major premise, 'Some M is not P', would have been placed directly on the line between the two sections of the M circle outside of the P circle, as in Figure 5–10. The 'X' would be placed on the line because the premise does not specify in which section it belongs: it could be either or both. Then, in diagramming the universal minor premise, 'All M is S', one of the sections containing the 'X' on the line would have been shaded, thus covering half of the 'X'. Since this,

M (P)

in effect, tells us that there is no 'X' in the shaded area and that the half-'X' should be replaced by a full 'X', there is a good reason for the rule that a universal premise is always diagrammed before a particular premise.

Another valid syllogistic form is **IAI-4**, illustrated by the following syllogism and schema:

FIGURE 5–11

S (A)   P (M)

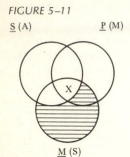

M (S)

Some mammals are sharks.   Some P are M.

All sharks are dangerous
    animals.   All M are S.

Therefore, some dangerous
    animals are mammals.   ∴Some S are P.

Again, the universal minor premise of this syllogism is diagrammed before the particular major premise. 'All sharks are dangerous animals' asserts that there are no sharks who are not dangerous animals, so the sections of the M circle outside the S circle are shaded, as shown in Figure 5–11.

'Some mammals are sharks' tells us to place an 'X', representing at least one mammal, in the remaining section of the P circle which is also in the M circle, as shown in Figure 5–11. Is the conclusion, 'Some dangerous animals are mammals', shown in the diagram? Yes, since the 'X' indicates that at least one member of S is included within P.

Identifying Invalid Syllogisms   In the previous section, we dealt only with valid syllogisms. In each example, nothing had to be added to diagram the conclusion, once the premises had been diagrammed. The diagrams of the conclusions of these syllogisms were already contained in the diagrams of their two premises. This proved the validity of each of the forms discussed, for a valid argument is one whose conclusion is contained in its premises, or one whose conclusion must be true if its premises are true. On the other hand, if the conclusion has not been completely diagrammed when the premises have been diagrammed, then the argument is invalid. Thus, this Venn diagram technique provides us with a decision procedure for determining the validity *or* invalidity of a syllogism. After the two steps of diagramming the premises in accordance with the rules, the one additional step of checking to see if the diagram of the conclusion is contained within the diagram of the premises is sufficient to determine whether the argument is valid or invalid. Let us now show how Venn diagrams can be used to prove that certain syllogistic forms are invalid.

We will begin by discussing the following **AII-2** syllogism, which was considered earlier in the chapter. The argument and its schema appear below.

All women are good
    administrators.   All P are M.

Some officers of the council
    are good administrators.   Some S are M.

Therefore, some officers of
    the council are women.   ∴Some S are P.

FIGURE 5–12

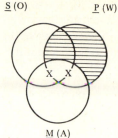

S (O)   P (W)

M (A)

The major premise, 'All women are good administrators', tells us that all sections of the P circle outside the M circle are to be shaded, as shown in Figure 5–12. Also, we should place an 'X' in the unshaded area of the P circle to indicate the existence of at least one woman. This 'X' must be on the line of the S circle, and since it is also in the M circle, no other 'X' is needed for this premise. The minor premise, 'Some officers of the council are good administrators', tells us to place an 'X' on the line between the two sections of the S circle that is included in the M circle, for we do not know which section is referred to. Now all the information given in the two premises has been included in the diagram shown in Figure 5–12. Finally, checking the conclusion, 'Some officers of the council are women', against the diagram, we see that the diagram of the conclusion is not contained within the diagram of the premises. The 'X' on the line indicates that there *may* be one member in the section of the S circle within the P circle, but it also may be entirely outside of the P circle. The conclusion, which specifies that there must be an 'X' entirely in the area common to the S and P circles, is not shown in the diagram, and so this syllogism and all syllogisms with the form **AII-2** are invalid.

We have already demonstrated that a syllogism with the form **AAA**-1 is valid. Let us examine another syllogism with the same mood but with a different figure. In the following example, we are dealing with a syllogism with the form **AAA**-2:

FIGURE 5–13

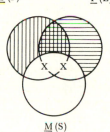

S (P)   P (E)

M (S)

All experimenters are scientists.	*All P are M.*
All physicists are scientists.	*All S are M.*
Therefore, all physicists are experimenters.	*∴All S are P.*

The major premise, 'All experimenters are scientists', tells us to shade all areas of the P circle that are not included within the M circle, as shown in Figure 5–13. The minor premise, indicating that all physicists are included in the class of scientists, tells us to shade all sections of the S circle outside of the M circle. This is also shown in Figure 5–13. We must also place an 'X' in the unshaded part of the P circle, and an 'X' in the unshaded part of the S circle to indicate the existence of at least one scientist, one physicist, and one experimenter.

Looking at the resulting diagram in terms of the conclusion, 'All physicists are experimenters', one can see that it is not contained in the diagram of the premises, for one section of the S circle outside of the P circle remains unshaded. Therefore, although the **AAA** mood is valid for figure 1, it is invalid for figure 2, and any syllogisms of the form **AAA-2** are invalid, since we have shown one syllogism with this form to be invalid.

Let us consider another syllogism and its schema, this one with the form **EAE**-4:

No elephants are primates.	*No P are M.*
All primates are bipeds.	*All M are S.*
Therefore, no bipeds are elephants.	*∴No S are P.*

FIGURE 5–14

S (B)   P (E)

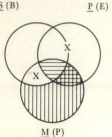

M (P)

The Venn diagram that represents this syllogistic form appears in Figure 5–14. The shading in the area common to the M and P circles means, of course, that there is nothing which is both P and M, that is, no elephants are primates. The shading in the M circle outside S tells us that all primates are bipeds. A section of the S circle common to the P circle is still unshaded, which indicates that it is *possible* that some bipeds are elephants. Therefore, this **EAE-4** syllogism is invalid, as are all syllogisms with the same form.

Another syllogism and its schema, this one with the form **AOO**-1, is shown as:

All *bears* are *mammals*.   All *M* are *P*.
Some *animals* are not
   bears.   Some *S* are not *M*.

Therefore, some *animals*
   are not *mammals*.   ∴Some *S* are not *P*.

"GEE, YOU'RE *LOTS* OF FUN! ARE YOU *SURE* YOU'RE A GIRL?"

Formulate Dennis' argument as a syllogism and test it for validity using Venn diagrams.

FIGURE 5–15

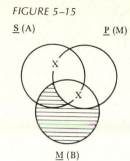

S (A)   P (M)

M (B)

The major premise, 'All bears are mammals', tells us that all sections of the M circle outside the P circle must be shaded, as shown in Figure 5–15. The minor premise, 'Some animals are not bears', tells us that an 'X' should be placed on the line between the two sections of the S circle outside the M circle, for it does not specify whether the animal who is not a bear is or is not a mammal. The conclusion, 'Some animals are not mammals', is not completely diagrammed in Figure 5–15, for the 'X' on the line means that information given by the two premises does not specify that at least one thing exists in the area inside S but outside P. Therefore, this **AOO**-1 syllogism is invalid, as are all syllogisms of this form.

Although the Venn diagram technique provides a simple and effective decision procedure for determining the validity and invalidity of syllogisms, it does require the use of writing materials and can, therefore, be inconvenient. There is an alternative decision procedure which enables us to determine the validity or invalidity of any syllogism in three steps or fewer and which can be performed by direct inspection of the syllogism without the need for writing materials.

EXERCISE 5–5

Test the validity of the following categorical syllogisms with Venn diagrams. Where the syllogisms are not in standard form, put them in standard form first.

---

1. No pot smokers are law-abiding citizens.
    All hippies are pot smokers.
    Therefore, no hippies are law-abiding citizens.
2. All hippies are pot smokers.
    No pot smokers are law-abiding citizens.
    Therefore, no law-abiding citizens are hippies.
3. All hallucinogens are dangerous things.
    Some drugs are hallucinogens.
    Therefore, some drugs are dangerous things.
4. All hallucinogens are dangerous things.
    All hallucinogens are drugs.
    Therefore, all drugs are dangerous things.
X 5. All hallucinogens are dangerous things.
    All hallucinogens are drugs.
    Therefore, some drugs are dangerous things.
6. Some reactionaries are powerful men.
    All dictators are powerful men.
    Therefore, some dictators are reactionaries.
7. Some dictators are reactionaries.
    All dictators are powerful men.
    Therefore, some powerful men are reactionaries.
8. Some actors are rich persons.
    Some actors are egoists.
    Therefore, some rich persons are egoists.

9. Some Buddhists are monks, so some Buddhists are ascetics, since all monks are ascetics.
10. Some Buddhists are not ascetics, because some Buddhists are not monks, and all monks are ascetics.
11. No oak trees are pine trees, so no conifers are oak trees, since all pine trees are conifers.
12. All zinnias are roses, since all zinnias are flowers, and all roses are flowers.
✗ 13. No cats are canines; therefore, some wolves are canines, since no cats are wolves.
14. Some mushrooms are edible things, but no edible things are toadstools; therefore, some mushrooms are not toadstools.
15. Some mushrooms are not toadstools, because no edible things are toadstools, but some edible things are mushrooms.

Testing by Rules   The form of a categorical syllogism can be completely specified by giving its mood and its figure. Neither mood alone, such as **AAA,** nor figure alone, such as figure 1, will give the precise form of a syllogism. However, together, as in **AAA**-1, the mood and figure do provide a complete specification of the form of a syllogism. With this in mind, one can determine the number of possible syllogistic forms. Each change in mood and each change in figure yields a different form of syllogism. There are sixty-four possible moods and four different figures for each, which produce two hundred and fifty-six different possible forms of syllogism. However, only 24 of these are valid on the interpretation we are presently using. An examination of the valid forms of the syllogism—as determined by using the Venn diagram test, for example—shows that they have three characteristics in common which distinguish them from the invalid forms. Any syllogisms that satisfy all three criteria are valid, and any syllogisms that fail to satisfy one or more of these three criteria are invalid. Two of the criteria used to distinguish valid from invalid syllogistic forms are dependent on an understanding of the concept of the distribution of terms.

Distribution of Terms   The terms of a categorical proposition are not distributed in and of themselves; rather, terms are distributed by the propositions in which they occur. A term is **distributed** if it occurs in a position in a categorical statement such that *every* term which appears in that position in *every* statement of that form refers to all members of the class named by the term. Thus, the subject of any **A** statement is distributed, since, in every **A** statement whatsoever, the subject term refers to every member of the class named. However, the predicate term in an **A** proposition is not distributed. Although 'unmarried males' in the statement 'All bachelors are unmarried males', happens to refer to all of the members of the class it names, the term is not distributed by the proposition, since terms appearing in the same position in other **A** statements do not refer to all members of the class named. For example, 'dogs' in the **A** statement 'All terriers are dogs' does not refer to the entire class of dogs.

Both subject and predicate terms are distributed in **E** statements such as 'No pens are musical instruments'. In excluding all of the class of pens from the class of musical instruments, this **E** statement must refer to the whole class of pens as well as to the whole class of musical instruments. In contrast, both subject and predicate terms of **I** statements are always undistributed. In the statement, 'Some pens are black things', the whole class of pens is not referred to, for there are pens of many colors other than black, nor is the entire class of black things referred to, for many black things exist which are not pens. In the statement, 'Some terriers are dogs', 'terriers' in fact happens to refer to the entire class of terriers, but, since in other **I** statements the subject term does not refer to all members of the class named, we cannot say that 'terriers' is distributed by this **I** statement.

The subjects of **O** statements are always undistributed, but their predicate terms always refer to *every* member of the class named and, therefore, are distributed. In the **O** statement, 'Some pens are not black things', for example, the subject term 'pens' refers to only a part of the whole class of pens, so it is undistributed. However, the proposition excludes these pens from the *whole* class of black things, thereby referring to the whole class and thus distributing the predicate term. The subject term in 'Some dogs are not cats' happens to refer to the entire class of dogs, but it is not distributed by the proposition, since the subject terms in some **O** propositions do not refer to every member of the class named.

A summary of the distribution of terms in the four types of categorical proposition is presented in the following table:

TYPES OF STATEMENT		SUBJECT TERM	PREDICATE TERM
A	All S are P.	distributed	undistributed
E	No S are P.	distributed	distributed
I	Some S are P.	undistributed	undistributed
O	Some S are not P.	undistributed	distributed

Having explained the concept of distribution, we can state the characteristics or criteria that distinguish valid and invalid syllogisms in terms of three rules that syllogisms must satisfy to be valid. *An argument that violates any one of these rules* is said to be **fallacious,** and *a fallacious syllogism is invalid.* However, when a syllogism satisfies all the rules, it is valid. It must be emphasized that these rules apply only to standard form categorical syllogisms. Thus, any argument that has a different form cannot be tested for validity using these rules. In particular, no argument that contains more than three terms can be tested, since, by our definition, a categorical syllogism must contain just three terms. Sometimes an argument may seem to contain only three terms when, in fact, it contains more. Consider, for example, the following:

> *All criminal actions are morally wrong acts.*
> *All trials for crimes are criminal actions.*
> *Therefore, all trials for crimes are morally wrong*
>   *acts.*

The surprising conclusion in this argument is a consequence of the ambiguous middle term, 'criminal actions'. In the major premise, this term means 'behavior of criminals', but in the minor premise it has shifted in meaning to 'court process dealing with those indicted for crimes'. Because the argument actually has four terms it is not a standard form syllogism and so cannot be tested for validity by Venn diagrams or by the rules we are about to present.

EXERCISE 5–6   *Test the validity of the following syllogistic schemata with Venn diagrams:*

---

1. **AEE**-4	6. **AEE**-1	11. **AOO**-2
2. **EAE**-2	7. **IAI**-2	12. **III**-1
3. **EAE**-3	8. **IAI**-3	13. **III**-2
4. **EIO**-3	9. **AII**-1	14. **EIO**-4
5. **IEO**-4	10. **AOO**-4	15. **EAO**-2

Rule One   **The middle term of a valid standard form syllogism must be distributed in at least one premise.** Breaking this rule is referred to by logicians as the *fallacy of the undistributed middle*.

The middle term, 'persons with long hair', is distributed once in the following syllogism with the form **AAA**-1:

> **All persons with long hair are**
> **radicals.**   All <u>M</u> are <u>P</u>.
> **Ed is a person with long hair.**   All <u>S</u> are <u>M</u>.
> **Therefore, Ed is a radical.**   ∴ All <u>S</u> are <u>P</u>.

Since the middle term, 'persons with long hair', is distributed in the major premise, although undistributed in the minor premise, this syllogism does not commit the fallacy of the undistributed middle. The two terms of the conclusion are related to each other through the middle term in the premises. If all the members of the class named by the middle term are not related to some or all of the members of one of the other classes referred to by the premises, then it is possible that the major and minor classes may be related to different members of the class named by the middle term and, consequently, may not be related to each other at all. Since a term must be distributed by a proposition for us to be certain that it refers to all the members of a class, the middle term of a syllogism must be distributed at least once. The major premise of this syllogism asserts that all the members of the class named by the middle term, 'persons with long hair', are contained in the class named by the predicate term, 'radicals'. The minor premise asserts that all members of the class of which Ed is the only member are contained in the class of persons with long hair. Since *all* the members of the class of persons with long hair are contained within the class of radicals, Ed must also be a member of the class of radicals.

The following invalid syllogism with the form **AAA**-2 illustrates what happens when the middle term is undistributed in both premises:

All *radicals are people with long hair.*	All *P* are *M*.
Ed is a person with long hair.	All *S* are *M*.
Therefore, Ed is a radical.	∴All *S* are *P*.

FIGURE 5–16

S (E)   P (R)

M (H)

In this syllogism, the middle term, 'people with long hair', is undistributed in both premises, since in both it is the predicate term of an **A** statement. Both the major and the minor terms are related to the middle term in the premises, but neither the major nor the minor class is related to the entire class referred to by the middle term, so their relationship to each other is not known. The first premise does not rule out the possibility that the class of people with long hair contains members who are not radicals, and the second premise would permit Ed to be such a person. The Venn diagram representing an **AAA**-2 syllogism is shown in Figure 5–16. The diagram visually displays the invalidity of this syllogistic form, since it is possible that something exists inside S but outside P.

Rule Two **A term that is distributed in the conclusion of a valid categorical syllogism must also be distributed in the premise in which the term occurs.** Breaking this rule involves committing what is known as the *fallacy of the illicit major* or the *fallacy of the illicit minor,* depending on which term is not distributed in its premise. When a term is distributed in the conclusion it refers to the whole class, and generalization to a whole class cannot be made from statements that refer to only part of the class, since it is possible that something that is true of part of the class may not be true of the entire class. Thus, whatever term is distributed in a conclusion must also be distributed in its premise.

The following **AEE**-1 syllogism illustrates the *fallacy of the illicit major:*

All lawyers are logicians.	All *M* are *P*.
No engineers are lawyers.	No *S* are *M*.
Therefore, no engineers are logicians.	∴No *S* are *P*.

In the conclusion, 'No engineers are logicians', both terms are distributed, each referring to all members of its class. The minor term, 'engineers', is also distributed in the minor premise, in which it is again the subject term of an **E** statement. However, the major term, 'logicians', is not distributed in the major premise, in which it appears as the predicate of an **A** statement. Since the undistributed term occurs in the major premise, the fallacy being committed is that of illicit *major.* The invalidity of this syllogism is demonstrated by the Venn diagram in Figure

FIGURE 5–17

S (E)   P (Lo)

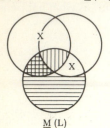

M (L)

5–17. Examining this diagram makes it evident that the conclusion, 'No engineers are logicians', is not represented. The unshaded area common to both S and P indicates that some engineers *could* be logicians. Thus, all syllogisms of the form **AEE**-1 are invalid.

The following **AAA**-3 categorical syllogism exemplifies the *fallacy of the illicit minor.*

All lawyers are well-paid people.	**All M are P.**
All lawyers are logicians.	**All M are S.**
Therefore, all logicians are well-paid people.	**∴All S are P.**

In the conclusion of this syllogism, the subject term, 'logicians', is distributed, but the same term is undistributed as the predicate term of an **A** statement in the minor premise. This invalid syllogism is diagrammed in Figure 5–18. The unshaded section in the S circle outside the P circle leaves open the possibility that at least one logician may not be a well-paid person. Therefore, the diagram of the conclusion is not contained in the diagram of the premises, and all syllogisms of the form **AAA**-3 are invalid.

FIGURE 5–18

S (Lo)   P (W)

M (L)

Rule Three   **A valid standard form categorical syllogism cannot have a negative premise unless it has a negative conclusion, in which case it must have exactly one negative premise.** Violating this rule involves committing one of three different fallacies. The *fallacy of two negative premises* is exemplified by the following syllogism.

No Sundays are good days to study logic.	**No M are P.**
No Sundays are weekdays.	**No M are S.**
Therefore, all weekdays are good days to study logic.	**∴All S are P.**

FIGURE 5–19

S (W)   P (G)

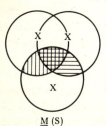

M (S)

Note first that this argument does not violate either rule one or rule two, but its Venn diagram shows it to be invalid (see Figure 5–19). Because negative premises simply affirm the exclusion of the members of one class from another class, the major premise here excludes all Sundays from the class of good days to study logic, and the minor premise excludes all Sundays from the class of weekdays. But these exclusions do not in any way specifically relate the members of the class of weekdays to the class of good days to study logic. The way members of the S class (weekdays) and members of the P class (good days to study logic) are related, whether by partial or total inclusion or exclusion, is not specified in the premises. Therefore, the premises do not support the conclusion that all members of the S class, in fact, are contained in the P class.

The following syllogism with the form **OAI**-2 breaks rule three, thus committing the *fallacy of affirmative conclusion from a negative premise.*

FIGURE 5-20

S (B)   P (M)

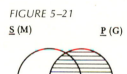
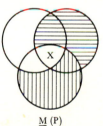

M (A)

*Some **men** are not good **a**thletes.*
*All **b**aseball players are good **a**thletes.*
*Therefore, some **b**aseball players are **m**en.*

Some M are not G. Rule 4
All B are G
Some B are M.

This argument violates none of the first three rules, but its Venn diagram (Figure 5–20) shows that it is indeed invalid. The conclusion, 'Some baseball players are men', is not shown in the diagram of the two premises, since there is no 'X' in the unshaded area common to the S and P circles, thus leaving open the possibility that the class of men baseball players may be empty.

We noted previously that nothing can be derived validly from two negative premises, since each premise asserts that two classes are partially or totally excluded from each other. With *one* negative premise (which also asserts that some or all of the members of one class are excluded from the other class), we are not given any information that would support the assertion of class inclusion in the conclusion statement. However one positive and one negative premise together *may* give enough information to support a conclusion asserting class exclusion—that is, a negative conclusion—provided none of the other rules is violated.

The third fallacy that can be committed under rule three is the *fallacy of a negative conclusion from affirmative premises,* illustrated by the following syllogism with the form **AAO**-4.

FIGURE 5-21

S (M)   P (G)

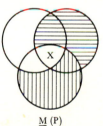

M (P)

*All **g**orillas are primates.*   *All **P** are **M**.*
*All primates are **m**ammals.*   *All **M** are **S**.*

*Therefore, some **m**ammals are*
*   not **g**orillas.*   *∴Some **S** are not **P**.*

This syllogism does not violate rule one, since the middle term, 'primates,' is distributed in the minor premise. Nor does it violate rule two, since the term 'gorilla' is distributed in both the conclusion and the major premise. The syllogism also does not have any negative premises. Yet, if we examine the Venn diagram that represents this syllogism, we will see that it is clearly invalid, since the diagram of its premises does not contain the diagram of its conclusion (see Figure 5–21). The conclusion, 'Some mammals are not gorillas', asserts that at least one member of the class of mammals is not a member of the class of gorillas. For this conclusion to be represented by the Venn diagram, there must be an 'X' inside the S circle but outside the P circle. This is obviously not the case. Thus, this syllogism does not violate the first two rules, but it violates rule three, and its Venn diagram shows it to be invalid.

These three rules are sufficient for providing a decision procedure for testing categorical syllogisms. It is possible to add other rules—in fact, some other texts do—but any such additional rules would be redundant. For example, one could stipulate as a rule that 'No valid syllogism can have two **I** statements as premises'. However, any argument that violates this rule would also violate rule one, since both the subject and predicate terms of **I** statements are undistributed, and the middle term appears only in the premises. It is also possible to stipulate that no syllogism can have two **O** premises, but any such syllogism would violate rule three, since a syllogism with two **O** premises would have two negative premises. One additional rule commonly found in other texts is that a categorical syllogism can only contain three terms. This rule is unnecessary, since it is part of our *definition* of a categorical syllogism. Having shown that only three rules are needed, let us test the validity of some additional sample syllogisms, using this decision procedure.

Testing Sample Syllogisms   Let us begin by considering the following argument:

> **Some connoisseurs of food are men.**
> **All good cooks are connoisseurs of food.**
> **Therefore, all men are good cooks.**

The first step is to check to see whether we are dealing with a categorical syllogism that is in standard form. The argument contains three categorical statements and three terms, each of which appears once in two of the statements. But the premise containing the subject term of the conclusion (the minor premise) appears first and the major premise second. Thus, this syllogism must be recast into standard form as an **AIA**-4 syllogism:

> **All good cooks are connoisseurs of food.**   *All P are M.*
> **Some connoisseurs of food are men.**   *Some M are S.*
> **Therefore, all men are good cooks.**   ∴*All S are P.*

Construct a syllogism corresponding to the reasoning Mark's mother used to trick him into a position where he could not get angry at her for damaging his motorcycle, and test it for validity using the three rules.

Now it is possible to check to see if one or more of the three rules have been violated. Under rule one, it is necessary to determine if the middle term is distributed in at least one of the premises. The middle term is undistributed in the major premise, for it is the predicate term of an **A** statement. The middle term is also undistributed in the minor premise, since **I** statements have undistributed subject and predicate terms. This syllogism thus commits the fallacy of the undistributed middle term, and this is sufficient to show that the argument is invalid. However, for practice let us proceed through the rest of the rules. According to rule two, any term distributed in the conclusion of the argument must also be distributed in the premises. The predicate term of the conclusion, 'good cooks', is undistributed, but the subject term, 'men', is distributed. Since the term 'men' is undistributed in the minor premise, where it appears as the predicate of an **I** statement, this syllogism also commits the fallacy of the illicit minor, and is invalid on two counts. The syllogism does not violate rule three, since it contains no negative propositions at all.

Let us consider one more argument to sharpen our skills in using these rules.

No common stocks are good investments.	*No P are M.*
All bonds are good investments.	*All S are M.*
Therefore, no bonds are common stocks.	*∴No S are P.*

Again the first thing to determine is whether we are dealing with a standard-form syllogism. There are three statements and three terms. Each term appears only once in two statements. Furthermore, the major premise, containing the predicate term of the conclusion, appears first, followed by the minor premise and the conclusion. The argument is a standard-form categorical syllogism of the form **EAE**-2.

The middle term, 'good investments', is distributed in the major premise, so the syllogism does not violate rule one. Both the subject and predicate terms of the conclusion are distributed; consequently, both these terms must be distributed in the premises to satisfy rule two. The term 'bonds' appears as the subject

VALID SYLLOGISTIC FORMS*			
FIGURE 1	*FIGURE 2*	*FIGURE 3*	*FIGURE 4*
AAA	AEE	AII	AEE
EAE	EAE	IAI	IAI
AII	AOO	EIO	EIO
EIO	EIO	OAO	AEO
AAI	AEO	AAI	EAO
EAO	EAO	EAO	AAI

* Each class referred to by the syllogism must contain at least one member.

term of the minor premise, an **A** statement. Since the subject terms of **A** statements are distributed, the syllogism does not commit the fallacy of the illicit minor. The predicate term of the conclusion, 'common stocks', appears as the subject term of the major premise, an **E** statement. Because the subject term of an **E** statement is distributed, the syllogism also does not commit the fallacy of the illicit major. The syllogism satisfies rule three, for it has exactly one negative premise to go with its negative conclusion. Because none of the three rules is violated, it follows that this argument, and thus *all* **EAE**-2 syllogisms, are valid. A Venn diagram would confirm this judgment.

EXERCISE 5–7   *Test the validity of each of the following categorical syllogisms by determining which rule(s), if any, it violates. Where the syllogism is not in standard form, put it in standard form.*

---

1. All basketball players are athletes.
   Some men are not basketball players.
   Therefore, some men are not athletes.
2. All drunkards are alcoholics.   *A II-1 valid*
   Some drinkers are drunkards.
   Therefore, some drinkers are alcoholics.
3. All falcons are hawks.
   All hawks are birds.
   Therefore, some birds are not falcons.
4. All addicts are persons to be pitied.   *AAA-3 illicit minor*
   All addicts are unhappy persons.
   Therefore, all unhappy persons are persons to be pitied.
5. Some reactionaries are powerful men.   *IEO-4 il*
   All dictators are powerful men.
   Therefore, some dictators are reactionaries.
6. Some conservatives are Republicans.
   No Republicans are Democrats.   *IEO-4 illicit major*
   Therefore, some Democrats are not conservatives.
7. All interpreters are bilingual persons.
   Some bilingual persons are persons with good memories.
   Therefore, all persons with good memories are interpreters.
8. No fish are animals with lungs.
   All guppies are fish.   *EAO-1 valid*
   Therefore, some guppies are not animals with lungs.
9. All Nazis are culpable persons.
   Some Germans are not Nazis.
   Therefore, some Germans are not culpable persons.
10. No friends are enemies.   *EEO-1   two neg. premises*
    No relatives are enemies.
    Therefore, some relatives are not friends.
11. No maples have gangrenous limbs, because all maples are trees and no trees have gangrenous limbs.

13: No P are U
All A are U
∴ Some A are not P

EAO-2
valid

14: All human beings are fallible.
All persons id. to Jane are human beings.

All persons id. to Jane are fallible.

12. All amoebae are unicellular organisms, so some amoebae are not primates, since no primates are unicellular organisms.
13. Some intelligent people are sensitive people who will, therefore, suffer a lot in life.
14. Jane is fallible because she is a human being, and everybody makes mistakes.

All H are F
All P are H
All P are F

AAA-1
valid

ARGUMENTS IN ORDINARY LANGUAGE

Some of the problems of translating sentences expressed in ordinary language into standard-form sentences were discussed in Chapter 4, in connection with the four different types of categorical statements. We noted then that the context in which a sentence is uttered or written often provides a clue as to the statement it is expressing. For example, the sentence, 'Cars are a good investment', is ambiguous, since it lacks a quantifier. It may be taken to express either the statement, 'All cars are good investments', or 'Some cars are good investments', depending on the context in which it is used. If it were uttered in the context of the sales pitch of a used-car dealer, in conjunction with the following statements, one could be reasonably certain that it was expressing a *universal* affirmative statement:

> *Cars are good investments. After all, no car owner has to pay transportation fares, and the time a driver saves going from one place to another is also worth money.*

However, if the same statement appeared in the context of a consumer publication, in conjunction with the following statements, one could reasonably assume that it was being used to express a *particular* affirmative statement:

> *Considering the average lifespan of cars such as the Mercedes-Benz, Rolls Royce, and Austin Healy, and the minimal repairs they require, it is obvious that cars are good investments.*

The way in which statements are translated can make a difference in whether the argument is valid or invalid. Consider, for example, the following argument, uttered at a college track meet:

> *Tom is a real athlete, for all persons who run here are real athletes, and Tom runs here.*

This argument may be translated into the following standard-form syllogism:

> *All persons who run here are real athletes.*
> *Tom is a person who runs here.*
> *Therefore, Tom is a real athlete.*

The only statement that requires translation into standard form is 'Tom runs here', since its predicate term is a verb instead of a noun or noun clause. Of course, it is necessary to place each statement within the syllogism in its proper order, with the major premise first and the minor premise next, followed by the conclusion. Now let us consider another argument expressed in ordinary language. This one is being uttered by a tour guide who is taking visitors through a completely automated factory in which robots are used on the assembly line:

> *Tom is a machine, for all things that run here are*
> *machines, and Tom runs here.*

Translated into standard form, this argument would read as follows:

> *All things that run here are machines.*
> *Tom is a thing that runs here.*
> *Therefore, Tom is a machine.*

Now, if the original formulation of the argument is uttered by the guide as he points to a robot labeled Tom, the premises of the argument would seem to be reasonably true, and the truth of its conclusion follows validly from the premises. However, if the guide utters the comment while pointing to the plant superintendent who happens to be a person named Tom and who also happens to be running, then it would be incorrect for us to translate the statement, 'Tom runs here', as 'Tom is a thing that is running'. In this rather bizarre context, such a translation produces an argument with four terms, since, in the major premise, 'things that are running here' means 'things operating here', whereas in the minor premise, 'thing that is running here', means 'person who is moving rapidly on foot'. Thus, in this last instance, we are not even dealing with a syllogistic argument.

While the example above may seem a bit outrageous, one should not assume that translating ordinary language arguments is a simple task. Translation can be tricky, especially when one must supply missing premises for syllogistic arguments expressed in ordinary language.

Enthymemes   As we noted in Chapter 2, an **enthymeme** is an argument in which one or more of the premises and/or the conclusion are not explicitly stated. In everyday discourse, syllogisms are sometimes expressed enthymematically. People seldom state explicitly all of the premises they are assuming as true and as providing support for their conclusions. When we speak or argue with others, we assume that the other people possess a considerable body of knowledge that will enable them to fill in the gaps in our abbreviated arguments. Any type of argument can be expressed as an enthymeme, but our concern in this chapter is only with syllogistic arguments.

When supplying missing premise or conclusion statements in a syllogistic argument, one should adhere to the **principle of charity,** which stipulates that one should supply statements that make the argument as good as possible. When possible, the supplied statements should make the argument valid, *and* their truth should be reasonably well established.

For the moment, let us consider the following ordinary language argument:

> *Children cannot be expected to know when to be*
> *quiet, for they do not possess a wide range of*
> *social experiences.*

The conclusion of the argument is explicitly stated: 'Children cannot be expected to know when to be quiet'. However, this sentence is not in standard form. One reasonable translation would be 'No children are persons who can be expected to know when to be quiet'. The expressed premise, 'they do not possess a wide range of social experiences', may be reasonably translated as 'No children are persons who possess a wide range of social experiences'. Since the term 'children' appears as the subject term of the conclusion, we know that this statement is the minor premise. To complete the argument we must supply the missing major premise. From the context, one reasonable premise which might be added is 'All persons who have a wide range of social experiences are persons who know when to be quiet'. With this major premise, the argument, expressed in standard form, would be:

> *[All persons who possess a wide range of social*
> *experiences are persons who can be expected to*
> *know when to keep quiet.]*
> *No children are persons who possess a wide range of*
> *social experiences.*
> *Therefore, no children are persons who can be*
> *expected to know when to keep quiet.*

Expressed in this way, this argument has the form **AEE**-1. However, the problem with this formulation is that it makes the argument invalid. The term 'persons who can be expected to know when to keep quiet' is distributed in the conclusion, but it is not distributed in the major premise. Consequently, this syllogism violates rule two, which stipulates that any term that is distributed in the conclusion of a syllogism must be distributed in the premise in which it occurs. However, if we add a different suppressed premise, it is possible to make the argument valid. Consider this formulation of the original argument:

> *[All persons who can be expected to know when to*
> *keep quiet are persons who possess a wide range*
> *of social experiences.]*
> *No children are persons who possess a wide range of*
> *social experiences.*
> *Therefore, no children are persons who can be*
> *expected to know when to keep quiet.*

The new major premise does not seem any less reasonable than the first one we tried, which made the argument invalid. But, formulated in this new way, the argument has the form **AEE**-2, which is valid. In this new formulation, the term 'persons who can be expected to know when to keep quiet' is distributed in the conclusion and also in the supplied major premise.[2]

Let us consider the argument implicit in Rex Stout's endorsement of the book, *Mother of Her Country*. The conclusion of this intended argument can be formulated as the standard form sentence, 'Rex Stout is a person who loves this book'. The explicitly stated premise has as its standard form wording, 'Rex Stout is a person who loves the First Amendment and who loves to laugh'. Since 'person who loves this book' is the predicate of the conclusion, it must also appear in what we can assume to be the suppressed major premise, which can be expressed in standard form **as** 'All persons who love the First Amendment and who love to laugh are persons who love this book'. (This is, of course, the message the publishers hoped would get across to readers.) The syllogism, a valid **AAA**-1, can be written out in complete standard form as follows:

> *All persons who love the First Amendment and who*
> *love to laugh are persons who love this book.*
> *Rex Stout is a person who loves the First*
> *Amendment and who loves to laugh.*
> *Therefore, Rex Stout is a person who loves this book.*

Sometimes the minor premise of a syllogism is suppressed. For example, consider the following argument:

> *Since all cats are felines, so are all tigers.*

The conclusion of this argument may be translated as the standard form sentence, 'All tigers are felines'. The premise statement, 'all cats are felines', is already in standard form, and, since the predicate term of the conclusion is 'felines', we know that this must be the major premise. The minor premise must be supplied to complete this argument. One premise whose truth is well established and which also makes the argument valid is 'All tigers are cats'. In standard form, the syllogism now reads:

> *All cats are felines.*
> *[All tigers are cats.]*
> *Therefore, all tigers are felines.*

It is also possible for the conclusion of a syllogistic argument to be suppressed. For example, consider the following argument, spoken by a lawyer who is summing up a case for the jury in a trial for theft:

> *Only a person who knew the combination to the safe*
> *could have stolen the bonds, and only Mr.*
> *Snodgrass knew the combination.*

Courtesy Random House.

---

[2] It should be remembered that there is no single 'correct' way to deal with an enthymeme. In the case of this example, one could also apply the principle of charity by adding a premise whose truth is better established than that of the premise added in the example and which makes the argument inductively strong (rather than deductively valid).

The conclusion, although unstated, is clearly 'Only Mr. Snodgrass could have stolen the bonds'. However, this statement is not in standard form. The word 'only' indicates that it is an exceptive statement which is really expressing a universal affirmative proposition. This proposition may be expressed in standard form as 'All persons who could have stolen the bonds are members of the class of which Mr. Snodgrass is the only member'. The premise statement, 'Only a person who knew the combination to the safe could have stolen the bonds', is also an exceptive statement, which may be translated reasonably as 'All persons who could have stolen the bonds are persons who knew the combination to the safe'. The other premise statement, 'Only Mr. Snodgrass knew the combina-

"God is Mind, and God is infinite; hence all is Mind."
MARY BAKER EDDY

The above argument provides the foundation of the religion of Christian Science. Discuss what assumptions must be made about the meanings of the terms in it for it to be interpreted as a syllogism. Test the syllogistic form of this argument for validity using the three rules and also using Venn diagrams. Could this argument be treated as an enthymeme and would doing so make it any stronger?

tion', is also exceptive. Given the formulations of the conclusion and the given premise, we know that the major term is 'members of the class of which Mr. Snodgrass is the only member' and that the middle term is 'persons who knew the combination to the safe'. This means that 'All persons who knew the combination to the safe are members of the class of which Mr. Snodgrass is the only member' is the major premise. The other statement, 'All persons who could have stolen the bonds are persons who knew the combination to the safe', is the minor premise, since it contains the subject term of the conclusion. In standard form, this **AAA**-1 argument reads as follows:

> ***All persons who knew the combination to the safe are members of the class of which Mr. Snodgrass is the only member.***
> ***All persons who could have stolen the bonds are persons who knew the combination to the safe.***
> ***[Therefore, all persons who could have stolen the bonds are members of the class of which Mr. Snodgrass is the only member.]***

EXERCISE 5–8   *Each of the arguments below is an enthymeme. (a) Supply the missing premise or conclusion that would make the enthymeme a valid categorical syllogism. (b) Translate the syllogism into standard form.*

1. All mushrooms are fungi; therefore all toadstools are fungi.
2. Some judges are not elected officials, because some judges are appointed.
3. Some mushrooms are not edible; some are poisonous.
4. No soaps are cleansing agents, because all detergents are cleansing agents.
5. Soybeans are nutritious; they contain a lot of protein.
6. All whiskeys are liquors; therefore some whiskeys are bourbons.
7. No operas are understandable, because they're all written in foreign languages.
8. Some people jog five miles every day, and all people who jog five miles every day are in good physical condition.
9. All foreign-language dictionaries are reference books, and no reference books can be taken out of the library.
10. Cyclamates should be banned from use as food additives, since they may cause cancer.
11. All the students in her class always get good grades; therefore she must be a terrific teacher.
12. Since diamonds are rare, they must be valuable.
13. That movie is sure to make a lot of money; it has plenty of violence and sex.
14. Jack cannot practice law; he never passed the bar examination.
15. All members of the American Bar Association must be college graduates, since all lawyers are college graduates.
16. Ed cooks well, so he must be a connoisseur of good food.
17. Mary is a very intelligent person; after all she is a member of Phi Beta Kappa.
18. Some paintings are good investments since some of them increase in value.
19. There must be fire for I smell smoke.
20. Willis Reed is a basketball player, so he must be over six feet tall.
21. There must be water near here; there's grass growing.
22. John can't own a car because he doesn't have a driver's license.
23. Many countries are not democratic, since not all of their citizens are allowed to vote.
24. Most hand-made items are expensive because they require so much labor.

Sorites   Many of the intended arguments we encounter in everyday contexts are composed of three or more premises and a single conclusion. The method of the syllogism clearly cannot be used directly to test such arguments, since a syllogism, by definition, must have exactly two premises. For example, the following premises:

> *All dancers are agile persons.*
> *Some secretaries are dancers.*
> *All secretaries are good typists.*

will not, by a single syllogistic inference, yield the conclusion:

> *Some good typists are agile persons.*

Although this is not a single syllogism, it can be treated as a chain of interlocking syllogisms. If we combine two of the premises and derive a conclusion from them, then combine this with the remaining premise, we can validly derive the final conclusion:

> *All dancers are agile persons.*
> *Some secretaries are dancers.*
> _____
> *[Therefore, some secretaries are agile persons.]*
> *All secretaries are good typists.*
> _____
> *Therefore, some good typists are agile persons.*

FIGURE 5–22

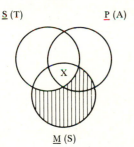

S (S)   P (A)

M (D)

S (T)   P (A)

M (S)

A set of more than three categorical statements, one of which is designated as the conclusion, is known as a **sorites** (from the Greek word for 'pile' — presumably a pile of propositions). Although special kinds of Venn diagram can be constructed for dealing with arguments having four or more terms (that is, Venn diagrams with four or more circles), the construction of such diagrams can be very tricky; thus, it is wise to test sorites by constructing separate three-circle diagrams for each of the component syllogisms. *The sorites is invalid if any one component syllogism is invalid.* Venn diagrams for the preceding sorites are shown in Figure 5–22.

The premises, of course, may not be in standard form or in the most useful order. Thus:

> *Dogs cannot reason.*
> *Anyone who can read can get into college.*
> *Creatures that cannot reason cannot get into college.*
> _____
> *Therefore, dogs cannot reason.*

To have a syllogism, we need a middle term, and the combination of premises 1 and 2 does not provide it. So we rearrange the premises to form the following chain of valid syllogisms:

> *All creatures that can read are creatures that can get into college.*
> *No creature that cannot reason is a creature that can get into college.*
> _____
> *[Therefore, no creature that cannot reason is a creature that can read.]*
> *All dogs are creatures that cannot reason.*
> _____
> *Therefore, no dogs are creatures that can read.*

EXERCISE 5–9   *The following groups of sentences* are sorites. Determine whether the argument is valid by constructing a chain of syllogisms, supplying the intermediate conclusions, and testing each component syllogism by the method of rules or Venn diagrams.*

---

1. All comets are wanderers in the zodiac.
    No terriers are wanderers in the zodiac.
    All curly-tailed creatures are terriers.
    Therefore, no curly-tailed creatures are comets.
2. All my poultry are ducks.
    Some officers are not creatures that waltz.
    No ducks are creatures that waltz.
    Therefore, none of my poultry are officers.
3. All shade-grown fruit is unripe fruit.
    No unripe fruit is wholesome fruit.
    All apples in this basket are wholesome fruit.
    Therefore, no apples in this basket are shade-grown fruit.
4. All really well-informed people are good company.
    All showy talkers are people who think too much of themselves.
    No people who think too much of themselves are good company.
    Therefore, no showy talkers are really well-informed people.

ANALYZING SAMPLE ARGUMENTS   Although there is quite a bit more that can be presented concerning syllogistic logic, enough has been said for our purposes in this book.

It remains now only to discuss further the ways in which this system of logic can be used to evaluate arguments of the kind that are encountered in everyday life. We will do this by considering again the sample arguments that were given a preliminary analysis at the end of Chapter 2, beginning with the example concerning Susan and this logic course.

In our preliminary analysis, we added a variety of possible suppressed premises and came up with three different formulations of the original argument. The formulation that appears to be most amenable to testing for validity using the methods of syllogistic logic is the following.

> *This logic course is a science course.*
> *Susan is taking this logic course.*
> *Susan always does well in science courses.*
> *Therefore, Susan will do well in this logic course.*

The first step in dealing with any argument in syllogistic logic is to express each proposition in standard form. This gives us:

> *This logic course is a science course.*
> *Susan is a person who is taking this logic course.*

---

* These examples are adapted from Lewis Carroll, *Symbolic Logic* (New York: Dover Publications, Inc.), pp. 112–120.

Susan is a person who always does well in science courses.
Therefore, Susan is a person who will do well in this logic course.

We must now try to break the premises into a sequence of valid syllogisms that will ultimately lead to the desired conclusion. Unfortunately, the only term that appears twice in the three premises, and thus the only candidate for a middle term, is 'Susan', and there is only one valid syllogism that can be constructed with two **A** premises in the third mood (i.e., the middle term in the subject of each premise), namely the **AAI**-3. This would give us one of two intermediate conclusions: 'Some persons who are taking this logic course are persons who always do well in science courses' and its converse, neither of which could be used to support the **A** proposition in the principal conclusion. Thus we must write the argument off as invalid or find another plausible interpretation of the original argument that would test out favorably in syllogistic logic. The following reformulation would seem to satisfy this requirement.

Susan is a person who always does well in science courses.
All persons who always do well in science courses are persons who will do well in this logic course if they take it.
Therefore, Susan is a person who will do well in this logic course if she takes it.

This argument (which is not quite in standard form because the minor premise is first) is an **AAA**-1 syllogism and is valid because it violates none of the three rules.

Notice that in this reformulation we are unable to include the suggestion implicit in the original argument that Susan is, in fact, taking this logic course. We had to add the qualifier, 'if they take it', to the supplied premise to make it more plausible. Even so, such a qualified generalization is still not highly probable. In putting the original argument into a valid syllogistic form, we did not necessarily make it into a very good argument, since it does not carry the full meaning of the original and includes a premise whose truth is questionable.

If we are to do much at all with the second sample argument—that concerning resort motel operators—in the syllogistic logic, it is necessary to simplify it considerably from the form in which it appears in the original essay. The following is one interpretation that fits fairly well into syllogistic form, although it is invalid in this form.

All persons who say that their business is good when it isn't are liars.
All resort motel owners interviewed in one Florida town are persons who said that business was fine when it wasn't.

By Edwin A. Roberts, Jr.

It fell to me the other week, in connection with a story assignment, to ask a dozen or so motel operators in a Florida town how business was. They all said business was just fine, the gasoline shortage wasn't hurting them at all, and if they were making any more money the local bank couldn't accommodate their deposits.

Oddly under such happy circumstances, the motel parking lots were practically empty. So I asked an officer of the local bank how the cashing of travelers' checks this year compared to last. As a matter of fact, said the banker, such check cashings were "way below" 1973. This information suggested that the motel operators

---

Comment

---

were dissembling, and so I am putting motel owners in resort towns on my list of The 10 Greatest Liars.

From "Mainstreams . . . Thoughts on the 10 Greatest Liars," The National Observer.

> *All resort motel owners who were interviewed in one*
> *Florida town were resort motel owners.*
> *Therefore all resort motel owners are liars.*

This can be broken into a sequence of syllogisms as follows:

> *All persons who say that their business is good when*
> *it isn't are liars.*
> *All resort motel owners interviewed in one Florida*
> *town are persons who said business was fine when*
> *it wasn't.*
> *Therefore, all resort motel owners interviewed in one*
> *Florida town were liars.*
>
> *All resort motel owners interviewed in one Florida*
> *town were liars.*
> *All resort motel owners interviewed in one Florida*
> *town were resort motel owners.*
> *Therefore, all resort motel owners are liars.*

The first of these syllogisms, an **AAA**-1, is valid, since it violates none of our three rules. The second syllogism, an **AAA**-3, is invalid, since the minor term is distributed in the conclusion but is not distributed in the premise, thus violating rule two. The argument could be made valid by replacing the minor premise in the second syllogism with its converse, but such a statement—'All resort motel owners are resort motel owners interviewed in one Florida town'—is blatantly false.

The difficulties encountered thus far in analyzing this example should not be interpreted as indicating anything more than that we have not been able to find a plausible formulation of the original argument that can be proved to be valid in the system of syllogistic logic. It is possible that, if we were to keep trying, we might eventually find a valid syllogistic formulation. Even if such a formulation were not forthcoming, it is also possible that this example could be proven to be deductively valid in some other system of logic, such as those to be presented in the next few chapters. And of course, the argument could be shown to be a good inductive argument, in the event that it can't be shown to be valid in any system of deductive logic. Thus, although our failure to prove this example valid in the syllogistic system has some significance, there are many other possibilities that should be considered before arriving at any definite conclusions about the goodness or badness of the original argument. We will consider this example further in later chapters. For now, let us turn to the third example for which we provided a preliminary analysis in Chapter 2.

The general argument concerning the cause of Mrs. Parker's death is too complex to even try to put into syllogistic form here. What we will do instead is to analyze a simplification of it which still relates quite closely to the original.

> *Mrs. Parker's death was caused by the 'Abid' strain*
> *of smallpox virus.*
> *The only source of the "Abid" strain of virus was the*
> *lab directly below Mrs. Parker's office.*
> *The only way in which the virus could have been*
> *transmitted to Mrs. Parker was through the air.*
> *Therefore, Mrs. Parker's death was caused by a virus*
> *transmitted through the air from the lab below her*
> *office.*

Each of the statements in this formulation were expressiable in standard form as follows.

> *Mrs. Parker's death was a death caused by the*
> *"Abid" strain of smallpox virus.*
> *All sources of the "Abid" strain of virus were the lab*
> *directly below Mrs. Parker's office.*
> *All ways in which the virus could have been*
> *transmitted to Mrs. Parker were the way of*
> *transmission through the air.*
> *Therefore, Mrs. Parker's death was a death caused*
> *by a virus transmitted by air from the lab below*
> *her office.*

Even in this simplified formulation, where the connections among the premises and between the premises and conclusion are intuitively apparent, it is still not clear what more might be done to make these connections explicit in the form of a sequence of standard-form syllogisms. Rather than take the time or effort to try to do this here, we will instead write this example off as a case which does not fit very "naturally" into syllogistic logic and which would probably be better dealt with in one of the other systems of logic. (Insofar as this example is theoretically analyzable in syllogistic logic, it is left as a challenge to the ambitious reader to work it all the way through in this system.)

The fourth, and final, sample argument was formulated in our preliminary analysis primarily in terms of 'if . . . then . . .' premises about the specific individual in the cartoon who had failed to bring flowers to his friend/spouse. 'If . . . then . . .' statements about individuals are usually expressions of universal propositions, so we can reformulate the example in standard form as follows:

> *You are a person who didn't bring me any flowers.*
> *All persons who don't bring me flowers are persons*
> *who want me to think they don't have a guilty*
> *conscience.*
> *All persons who want me to think they don't have a*
> *guilty conscience are persons who have a guilty*
> *conscience.*

"No flowers. That means you want me to think you haven't got a guilty conscience."

> *Therefore, you are a person who has a guilty conscience.*

This can be broken into a sequence of two syllogisms without having to add any more premises.

> *All persons who don't bring me flowers are persons who want me to think they don't have a guilty conscience.*
> *You are a person who didn't bring me any flowers.*
> *Therefore, you are a person who wants me to think they don't have a guilty conscience.*
>
> *All persons who want me to think they don't have a guilty conscience are persons who have a guilty conscience.*
> *You are a person who wants me to think they don't have a guilty conscience.*
> *Therefore, you are a person who has a guilty conscience.*

The first syllogism is an **AAA**-1. It violates none of the three rules, so it is deductively valid. The second syllogism is also an **AAA**-1 and valid. Thus, the primary conclusion, 'You are a person who has a guilty conscience', has been proven to follow validly from the reformulated premises. Determining whether the argument is a good one or not requires additional considerations concerning the truth of these premises and also of the extent to which this reformulation accurately reflects the original argument contained in the cartoon. Because these considerations are not part of formal logic, we will leave them to interested readers to work out for themselves.

EXERCISE 5–10   *Reconsider the arguments for which you did preliminary analyses in Exercise 2–9. Find one version of each argument that seems more appropriate for analysis, using the methods of the present chapter, and carry out such analyses. Compare your analyses here with those of the same arguments you may have done in Exercises 3–3, 7–9, 9–9, and 10–7.*

EXERCISE 5–11   *Reconsider the arguments for which you did preliminary analyses in Exercise 2–10. Apply the instructions for Exercise 5–10 to these arguments and compare these analyses with those of the same arguments that you might have done in Exercises 3–3, 7–10, 9–10, and 10–8.*

SUMMARY

1. A **categorical syllogism** is an argument composed of exactly three categorical statements and containing three terms, each of which appears twice in the argument but only once in any one statement. The predicate term of the conclusion of a syllogism is called the **major term,** and the subject term of the conclusion is called the **minor term.** The **middle term** does not appear in the conclusion but appears once in each premise. The premise containing the major term is called the **major premise,** and the premise containing the minor term is called the **minor premise.**

2. A syllogism is said to be in **standard form** when it is composed of three categorical statements expressed by standard-form sentences and when these statements follow the order of major premise, minor premise, and conclusion. When abbreviating syllogisms, one should use the methods discussed in Chapter 4 and the following additional procedures: (1) place a line between the premises and the conclusion to separate them; (2) use the symbol '∴' as an abbreviation of the word 'therefore' or any other conclusion indicator.

3. The logical form of a categorical syllogism can be represented by a schema using the symbols $\underline{S}$, $\underline{P}$, and $\underline{M}$, which represent the major term, minor term, and middle term, respectively. These three symbols function as blanks in which nouns or noun clauses may be substituted to produce sentences expressing categorical statements. When such substitutions are made in an **argument schema** to produce an argument, the process is called the **interpretation** of the argument schema.

4. The **mood** of a standard-form syllogism is the particular combination of statements of which the syllogism is composed, expressed in terms of the letters **A, E, I,** or **O** which signify the different types of categorical statement. The first letter in the mood indicates the form of the major premise, the second that of the minor premise, and the third that of the conclusion. Syllogisms having the same mood do not necessarily have the same form. The **figure** of a standard form syllogism is determined by the placement of the middle term in the two premises of the syllogism. There are four possible arrangements, traditionally numbered as follows: figure 1, in which the middle term appears as the subject term of the major premise and the predicate term of the minor premise; figure 2, in which the middle term appears as the predicate term in both the major and the minor premises; figure 3, in which the middle term appears as the subject term in both the major and the minor premises; and figure 4, in which the middle term appears as the predicate term in the major premise and the subject term in the minor premise. The **form** of a syllogism is determined by the combination of its mood and figure, and is usually expressed by placing the number of the figure after the letters that state the mood.

5. The validity or invalidity of a syllogism does not depend on its terms or on the truth or falsity of its statements but solely on its form. A **valid argument schema** is one for which there is no possible interpretation or substitution of terms that would create an argument with true premises and a false conclusion. Accordingly, a valid argument is one whose schema is valid. A **counterexample** is an interpretation of an argument schema that makes all the premises true and the conclusion false. Counterexamples can be used only to prove the invalidity of an argument schema. More useful are two techniques—one using Venn diagrams and the other syllogistic rules—which provide definite decision

procedures; that is, mechanical procedures that can be used to prove the validity or invalidity of any particular argument schema or argument in a finite number of steps.

6. Venn diagrams display the form of an argument and thus can be used to test syllogisms for their validity or invalidity. All arguments with the same form have the same schema, and all arguments that are interpretations of the same schema have the same Venn diagrams except for the labels on the circles. A syllogism is valid if and only if the diagram of its conclusion is already contained in the diagram of its two premises.

7. A term of a categorical proposition is **distributed** if it occurs in a position in the proposition such that *every* term that appears in that position in *every* statement of that form refers to all members of the class named by the term. The subject term but not the predicate term is distributed in any **A** statement; both subject and predicate terms are distributed in **E** statements; both subject and predicate terms are undistributed in **I** statements; and the predicate term but not the subject term is distributed in any **O** statement.

8. Syllogistic rules provide a three-step decision procedure that can be used to test the validity of standard form categorical syllogisms. Violation of *any* of these rules makes an argument **fallacious** and, therefore, invalid. Rule one: The middle term of a standard form syllogism must be distributed in at least one premise. Breaking this rule results in the fallacy of the undistributed middle. Rule two: A term that is distributed in the conclusion of a categorical syllogism must also be distributed in the premise in which the term occurs. Breaking this rule results in the fallacy of the illicit major or the fallacy of the illicit minor, depending on which term (predicate or subject term of the conclusion) is not distributed in its premise. Rule three: A standard-form categorical syllogism cannot have a negative premise unless it has a negative conclusion, in which case, it must have exactly one negative premise. Violating this rule results in one of the following fallacies: (1) negative conclusion from affirmative premises, (2) two negative premises, or (3) affirmative conclusion from a negative premise.

9. The manner in which the statements of a syllogistic argument are translated from ordinary discourse into standard form can affect the validity or invalidity of the argument. In translating, one should examine the context to clarify any ambiguous terms. An **enthymeme** is an argument with one or more missing premises and/or a missing conclusion. When supplying missing premises or conclusions in enthymematical syllogisms, one should adhere to the **principle of charity;** that is, the supplied statements should make the argument as good as possible on the Aristotelian interpretation, and their truth should be reasonably well established. In some cases, an apparently single syllogism is actually a chain of syllogisms, and the conclusion cannot be derived directly from the premises as they are given. An argument of this type, known as a **sorites,** must be put into standard form and the intermediate conclusions drawn. It can be tested with a series of Venn diagrams, one for each syllogism; if any one of the syllogisms proves to be invalid, the sorites is invalid.

CHAPTER SIX

Propositional Logic: Statements

It has already been indicated that a proposition is that about which it makes sense to say that it is true or false. It is technically improper to say that a sentence is true; rather, one should say that the proposition being expressed by that sentence is true. It has been shown that declarative sentences do not always express propositions or statements and that interrogative, imperative, and other sentences can be used to express propositions in certain contexts. In logic we are interested essentially in propositions and in arguments composed of propositions; so, insofar as we are interested in sentences at all, we are interested only in those sentences which express propositions.

Instead of saying that a proposition is that about which it makes sense to say that it is true or false, logicians often make the equivalent assertion that *every proposition has a* **truth value.** Although this is essentially another way of saying the same thing, it is both shorter and, for our purposes in the next few chapters, more convenient.

COMPOUND PROPOSITIONS AND LOGICAL OPERATORS

In this chapter and the next, we will be dealing with a particular kind of proposition, known as a **truth-functional proposition.** A truth-functional proposition is a *compound* statement which is such that, *if we know (1) the truth value (the truth or falsity) of each of its component statements and (2) the meanings of the logical terms in the sentence expressing the compound statement, we can determine precisely the truth or falsity of the compound statement.* In other words, the truth value of the compound proposition is a *function* of the truth values of the component statements.

To illustrate, let us look at some examples. Take, for instance, the proposition expressed by the following sentence:

It is not the case that logic is interesting.

This proposition contains within it the simple proposition 'Logic is interesting', which itself has a truth value (that is, it is either true or false). The sentence also contains the expression 'it is not the case that', which, taken by itself, cannot be used to express a proposition.

Insofar as expressions (logical terms) such as 'it is not the case that' "operate" on propositions to create new propositions with different logical structures, they are called **logical operators.** A logical operator is thus *an expression such that if it is correctly used with an appropriate number of propositions, a new proposition is produced, with a different logical structure.* No logical operator by itself is or expresses a proposition.

Take another example:

> *Logic is interesting, and all students enjoy logic.*

Here, we can separate out 'Logic is interesting' and 'All students enjoy logic' as each by itself expressing a proposition. The word 'and' functions as a logical operator, because it serves to connect the two propositions in such a way that a new compound proposition is formed—a proposition that has a different logical structure than the component propositions taken by themselves.

In our first example, if you know that 'Logic is interesting' is true, you can infer that the resulting compound is false. Similarly, if you know that 'Logic is interesting' is false, you can infer that the compound is true. That is, if you know the truth value of the proposition and the meaning of the logical operator 'it is not the case that', you can determine the truth value of the compound proposition produced by combining them.

Similarly, in the second example, if you know that each of the component propositions is true, and you know the meaning of the logical operator 'and', you can tell that the compound is true. Both these examples, therefore, satisfy our definition of a truth-functional proposition.

Truth-Functional Operators   Certain logical operators belong to the type known as **truth-functional operators.** A truth-functional operator is *a logical operator such that when it is correctly used with the appropriate number of propositions, a truth-functional proposition is produced.* Both the logical operators we have considered so far are thus truth-functional operators.

However, this does not mean that truth-functional operators, such as 'it is not the case that' and 'and', can appear *only* in sentences expressing truth-functional propositions. For example:

> *Wash your face and brush your teeth.*

This is a compound sentence whose component sentences are connected by the logical operator 'and'. However, the component sentences, 'Wash your face' and 'Brush your teeth', ordinarily express commands, which are neither true nor false, rather than propositions. Thus, the resulting compound also does not express a truth-functional proposition. Operators such as 'and' and 'it is not the case that' are *truth-functional* operators only when they form component parts of a truth-functional proposition.

There are many other compound propositions which are not truth-functional. The following compounds appear similar to 'It is not the case that logic is interesting'; but are they truth-functional?

> *Tom does not believe that logic is interesting.*
> *Susan ought to know that logic is interesting.*
> *It is necessarily the case that logic is interesting.*

None of these examples satisfies the definition of a truth-functional proposition. Each is a compound, and each contains one simple proposition, 'logic is interesting'. But none of them contains a truth-functional operator. '_____ does not believe that' **is** a *logical* operator, for it does operate to produce a new proposition with a changed logical structure; but it is *not truth-functional*, because knowing what this phrase means and knowing the truth value of 'Logic is interesting' is not enough to tell us anything about the truth or falsity of the compound statement 'Tom does not believe that logic is interesting'. We still need to know what Tom in fact believes. Knowledge of the truth value of 'Logic is interesting' is not sufficient for determining the truth value of this compound statement, for the statement is no longer about logic but about Tom's belief. Tom may not believe that logic is interesting, whether it is, in itself, really interesting. Thus, the compound cannot be a truth-functional proposition. A similar analysis can be made of the other two examples.

Another kind of compound proposition which is also not truth-functional would be:

> *John failed the exam because he did not sleep well*
> *last night.*

Here, the component sentences 'John failed the exam' and 'He did not sleep well last night' both express propositions, but the word 'because' that connects them does not function as a truth-functional operator. 'Because' is a logical operator, since its inclusion as part of a compound certainly creates a new

The basic simple truth-functional proposition in the above cartoon is 'You knew that'. Can you explain why all of the other 'knows' can be considered to be logical operators? Given that they are interpreted as logical operators, are they truth-functional operators? Explain why or why not.

proposition with a different logical structure. However, unlike 'and', which plays a similar connecting role, 'because' is not truth-functional, since knowing its meaning and the truth value of both propositions does not tell us for certain whether the compound statement is true or false. We might know that it is true both that John failed the exam and that he did not sleep well last night without knowing that he failed *because* he did not sleep well. It is possible that he failed the exam because he did not study for it and would have failed even if he had slept well last night. Thus, the causal relationship asserted by 'because' is not truth-functional.

EXERCISE 6–1

For each of the following sentences, indicate whether (a) *it expresses a compound proposition. If so,* (b) *identify all component propositions and* (c) *logical operators.* (d) *Indicate whether the proposition is truth-functional.*

---

1. Pines are evergreens and oaks are hardwoods.
2. Oaks are evergreens and pines are hardwoods.
3. It is not true that the earth is flat.
4. It is not the case that ice melts at 32° Fahrenheit.
5. Do good and avoid evil.
6. The sky is blue and the grass is green.
7. You ought to know that the earth is not flat.
8. It is not true that Thomas Jefferson was the second president of the United States.
9. I don't think that Thomas Jefferson was the second president of the United States.
10. Come on out and help me shovel snow.
11. Joseph came out and helped me shovel snow.
12. Are you a Republican or are you a Democrat?
13. Ronald Reagan is a liberal and Edward Kennedy is a conservative.
14. Ronald Reagan is a Republican or Edward Kennedy is a Conservative.
15. Ronald Reagan is a Republican and Edward Kennedy is a Democrat.
16. The woods are full of rattlesnakes; therefore, wear your snake boots.
17. Is Maureen coming to dinner or does she have to stay home and study?
18. Maureen is not coming to dinner because she has to stay home and study.

PROPOSITIONAL ABBREVIATIONS AND SCHEMATA

We will be dealing in the next four chapters with what is known as 'symbolic logic'. A **symbol** is *a sign which can be used to abbreviate or schematize any of the components in a given system,* such as the propositions and logical operators we have been talking about. Any logical system can be reduced to symbolic form. But, mainly for historical reasons, the name 'symbolic logic' is usually reserved for the logical systems developed since the latter part of the nineteenth century, particularly by Gottlob Frege and Bertrand Russell.

In symbolic logic, the use of certain abbreviations has become conventional to shorten the space and time necessary to express propositions. By this means,

Bertrand Russell

long sentences expressing complicated propositions can be condensed into less than a single line, and their logical structure can be more clearly displayed. These techniques are particularly useful for dealing with arguments composed of several compound propositions.

Before we can present and analyze the various truth-functional operations that will be covered in the rest of this chapter, it will be necessary to introduce a number of new concepts.

Constants and Abbreviations   The first is the notion of a **propositional constant,** which is essentially *an abbreviation for a sentence expressing a proposition.* These abbreviations can be used to express the same propositions as are expressed by their corresponding sentences.

We will adopt the convention of using capital letters as propositional constants.[1] Thus we can abbreviate:

> **It is not the case that logic is interesting.**

as:

> **It is not the case that A.**

where **A** stands for 'Logic is interesting'. Similarly, we can abbreviate:

> **Logic is interesting and grammar is boring.**

as:

> **A *and* B.**

Whenever the component propositions of a compound statement are different, we will need a different propositional constant for each one. However, if one or more propositions are repeated in the same compound statement or in the same group of compound statements, we should use the same letters for them each time they appear, since the proposition expressed by each constant remains the same each time we use it in a given context.

Thus, in the two compound sentences under consideration, since the proposition[2] 'Logic is interesting' is expressed by each one, we can use the same propositional constant '**A**' in abbreviating that sentence in each compound. And since the sentence 'Grammar is boring' expresses a different proposition, we use a different propositional constant '**B**' in the second sentence.

---

[1] There is little danger of confusing capital letters used as abbreviations for propositions with capital letters used as abbreviations for nouns and noun clauses in the syllogistic logic treated in Chapters 4 and 5. In syllogistic logic, the letters occur only in the subject and predicate positions of statements such as 'All A are B', while propositional constants can never occur in such contexts.

[2] We shall resume use of the convention stipulated in Chapter 1 to simplify our discussion, by sometimes speaking of 'The statement (or proposition) . . .' instead of the more accurate, but more complicated, 'The statement expressed by the sentence . . . .'

Sometimes, as we saw in Chapter 1, different sentences are used to express the same proposition. For example, the German sentence:

Karl Marx lebt.

can be used to express the same proposition as the English sentence:

Karl Marx lives.

We can use the same propositional constant to abbreviate two different sentences, so long as both sentences are being used to express the same proposition. Thus, the propositional constant 'C' can be used to abbreviate both of these sentences.

'A' will not always signify 'Logic is interesting' and 'C' will not always signify 'Karl Marx lives', since, if they did, the number of propositions that could be so symbolized would be limited to the number of symbols we could invent. However, in the given context of analysis of the present logical problem, 'A' and only 'A' will be used as an abbreviation for the sentence 'Logic is interesting'. In a different context, we could abbreviate a sentence expressing some other proposition with the letter 'A' and the meaning of that symbol would remain constant *throughout that context.* (That is why we call a propositional constant a 'constant'.)

Variables and Schemata   A **propositional variable** is *a symbol which functions as a blank into which we can insert a sentence expressing any proposition whatever.* Since the blank can be filled in by a sentence expressing any proposition, it has no truth value in itself. We use propositional variables to bring out the logical structure of a compound proposition. *A formula containing only propositional variables and logical operators* is called a **propositional schema.**

The symbols normally used for propositional variables are the small letters from the middle to the end of the alphabet, starting with p (p, q, r, s, t, and so on). If we need more than these eleven variables, we can use p', q', r', and so on and even, if necessary, with p'', q'', . . . , p'', etc. Using these symbols, we can display the logical form of the proposition expressed by 'A and B' (and any other propositions with the same logical structure, such as 'A and C' or 'D and E') with the propositional schema

p *and* q

The logical form of all the above abbreviations could also be displayed as:

_ _ _ _ _ _ _ _ *and* . . . .

However, it is customary to use letters instead of blanks, so that more complex logical operations can be symbolized and handled more easily and with less confusion.

If the blanks or propositional variables are filled in or replaced by sentences expressing propositions, or by their abbreviations, then we have added a content

If a man will begin with certainties, he will end in doubts; but if he will be content to begin with doubts, he will end in certainties.
—FRANCIS BACON

This statement is about only two things—doubts and certainties—but it requires four different propositional constants in its symbolization. Can you explain why?

to the form. In doing this we have changed a propositional schema into a sentence expressing a proposition. Given that '**A**' is an abbreviation of 'Logic is interesting' and '**B**' is an abbreviation of 'Grammar is boring', the formula:

> **A** *and* **B**

expresses a proposition with a specific truth value, whereas the formula:

> **p** *and* **q**

merely displays the form or logical structure of an infinite set of propositions and has no further meaning and no specific truth value.

EXERCISE 6–2   *Given the formulas '**A** and **B**' and 'p and q':*

1. Explain the differences between propositional variables and propositional constants.
2. (a) Which contains propositional variables and (b) which contains propositional constants?
3. (a) Which is normally used to represent a particular compound proposition and (b) which to represent an infinite set of compound propositions?
4. (a) Which normally has a determinate truth value and (b) which normally does not?
5. Explain why one formula has a specific truth value and the other does not.

CONJUNCTION   A truth-functional proposition has been defined as a compound statement which is such that, if we know the truth or falsity of each of its component statements and the meanings of the logical terms in the sentence expressing the compound proposition, then we can determine precisely the truth or falsity of the compound proposition. So, to determine the truth value of a compound proposition, we must know not only the truth value of each of its component propositions but also the meaning of the logical operator(s).

We have defined the logical operator which creates a truth-functional proposition as a truth-functional operator, and have given 'and' as an example of such an operator. The meaning of the truth-functional operator 'and' is essentially that of the term 'and' as it is commonly used in ordinary English. So let us examine its meaning in the following truth-functional propositions:

> *Chemistry is a science and termites cannot read.*
> *Cats can talk and humans can talk.*
> *Washington was the first U.S. president and Lincoln*
>   *is still alive.*
> *Trout are mammals and beagles are reptiles.*

A truth-functional proposition whose component statements are connected by the truth-functional operator 'and' is called a **conjunction;** the component statements of a conjunction are called **conjuncts.** All four of these truth-functional propositions are thus conjunctions whose component statements are their conjuncts.

Each of the above compound propositions consists of two component statements connected by the truth-functional operator 'and'. In the first, the truth of both components is well established. In the second, it is reasonable to assume that the first component is false and the second true. In the third example, the first component is true and the second false. Finally, in the fourth example, both components are presumably false. The question before us is: What effect does the truth-functional operator 'and' have on the truth value of each of these compound propositions?

To simplify analysis, we can use the letter 'A' as a propositional constant to abbreviate 'Chemistry is a science' in our first example. Similarly, we can use the propositional constant 'B' to abbreviate 'Termites cannot read'. Thus, the compound proposition 'Chemistry is a science and termites cannot read' and can be abbreviated as 'A and B'.

We can abbreviate the second example by symbolizing 'Cats can talk' with the propositional constant 'C' and 'Humans can talk' with 'D'. The two remaining propositions can be similarly abbreviated:

Washington was the first U.S. president and Lincoln *is still alive.*	*E and F*
Trout are mammals and beagles are reptiles.	*G and H*

To determine the truth values of these four compound propositions, we have to consider the truth value of each of their components. Since 'A' is true and 'B' is true, anyone who understands the meaning of 'and' as it is used in this sentence would probably agree that the compound 'A and B' is true. Most people would also recognize that since 'C' is false and 'D' is true, 'C and D' is false. By the same reasoning, 'E and F' is false; and since 'G' is false and 'H' is false, 'G and H' is false as well.

Only the first of our conjunctions above, whose conjuncts were *both* true, turned out to be true. The other three, in each of which one or both conjuncts were false, all turned out to be false. By way of an informal definition, then, we can say that conjunction is a logical operation in which an operator is used to connect exactly two propositions in such a way that the resulting compound proposition is true if and only if both component propositions are true, and false if either or both of the conjuncts are false.

The Truth-Table Definition of Conjunction

The logical structure of any conjunction can be displayed by the propositional schema 'p and q'. In themselves, the propositional variables 'p' and 'q' have no truth values, since they can be replaced by any proposition whatever.[3] Therefore, the schema for conjunction has several possible truth values, for 'p' can be replaced by either a true or a false proposition, and 'q' can also be replaced by either a true or a false proposition.

If we adopt the convention of using the capital letter '**T**' to stand for the truth value 'true' and the capital letter '**F**' to stand for the truth value 'false', we can assign the values '**T**' or '**F**' to any of the four possible instances of 'p and q' exhibited by our examples. We shall also adopt the convention of abbreviating the 'and' of conjunction by the symbol '·'. (There are other abbreviations commonly used for 'and', including '∧' and '&'; some logicians simply use no symbol at all between the two propositional variables or constants. In this case our first sentence would be abbreviated '**AB**'.)

The propositional schema of any simple conjunction can thus be symbolized as:

p · q

just as the particular conjunction '**A** and **B**' can by symbolized as:

A · B

With these conventions, the truth values of the four conjunctions we have already abbreviated by propositional abbreviations can be represented by replacing each of their component propositions with its respective truth value. This gives us:

A · B	**T · T**
C · D	**F · T**
E · F	**T · F**
G · H	**F · F**

These are the *only* four possible combinations of **T**'s and **F**'s that a conjunction with the form 'p · q' can have.

---

[3] Remember that this is not the same as '**A** and **B**', which is an abbreviation of a *specific* conjunction and therefore represents components with definite truth values.

We saw earlier that, of these four compound propositions, only the first, both of whose components are true, can be regarded as itself true. We can now summarize all of this information symbolically by means of the following table, called a **truth table.** A truth table can be used to define a truth-functional operator (in this case, conjunction) in terms of all possible combinations of truth values of statements that could be substituted for the variables 'p' and 'q' in a compound using this operator.

p	q	p · q
T	T	T
F	T	F
T	F	F
F	F	F

That is, if the proposition substituted for 'p' is true and the one substituted for 'q' is also true, then the compound 'p · q' is true; if the proposition substituted for 'p' is true and the one substituted for 'q' is false, the compound 'p · q' is false; and so on. The table defines the dot symbol for conjunction in such a way that a **conjunction** *is true if and only if both conjuncts are true; otherwise it is false.* This corresponds with the informal definition we established above.[4]

It is important to recognize that 'and' is often used in ordinary English in ways that are not truth-functional. If an 'and' in an ordinary language sentence is not being used truth-functionally, it cannot be adequately symbolized with the dot. For example:

Tom and Mary have been married for three years.

In this case, 'and' is being used to conjoin two subjects in the same sentence rather than to conjoin two separate sentences. If we reformulate the sentence as a conjunction of two sentences, we get:

Tom has been married for three years and Mary has been married for three years.

This is not equivalent to the original, since it does not imply, as the other obviously does, that Tom and Mary are married to each other. In this case, symbolizing the compound by using the dot symbol would significantly change the meaning, and this should be explicitly noted.

On the other hand, a sentence such as:

Babe Ruth and Mickey Mantle were baseball players.

---

[4] It would be technically wrong to construct a truth table for a *proposition* such as '**A · B**' since '**A**' and '**B**' and '**A · B**' are abbreviations for specific propositions which have definite truth values, and thus correspond to only one particular line of the truth table of the schema 'p · q' (in this case the first line).

is merely a shorter way of expressing the conjunction:

> ***Babe Ruth was a baseball player and Mickey Mantle***
> ***was a baseball player.***

In such a sentence, 'and' functions truth-functionally, and the dot can be used to symbolize it with no loss of meaning.

Another case in which 'and' could not be adequately translated with a dot would be:

> ***Tom woke up and shut off the alarm.***

Here, the 'and' expresses a temporal sequence, meaning that Tom woke up *and then* shut off the alarm. If the word 'and' were truth-functional here, then reversing the sequence of the conjoined propositions would not affect the meaning of the conjunction. But this would give us:

> ***Tom shut off the alarm and woke up.***

which has hardly the same meaning as the original, since in the former he woke up first, whereas in the latter he allegedly shut off the alarm first (in his sleep?). Here, too, the 'and' is not truth-functional. The use of the dot symbol conveys the truth-functional meaning of 'and', so we should always watch out for losses of meaning when we use it and thus make it as explicit as possible.

There are many other words which in ordinary English are similar to 'and', such as 'but', 'although', 'yet', and 'moreover'. In appropriate contexts, these words can operate truth-functionally in the same way as 'and', and insofar as they do they can be symbolized by the dot in a truth-functional conjunction:

> ***The weather is bad, but we will go to the game.***
> ***The mayor was elected on a reformist platform, yet***
> ***the city government is still inefficient and corrupt.***
> ***The patient is suffering from severe cramps;***
> ***moreover, he has a rash on much of his body.***
> ***My father will help send me to graduate school,***
> ***although he would rather have me go into the***
> ***family business.***

As the examples show, these words are often used in such a way that they carry more meaning than that expressed in the truth-table definition of the dot. To take another instance:

> ***Muhammad Ali is big but fast.***

Here, 'but' is used to mean both that 'Muhammad Ali is big and fast' and that 'Muhammad Ali is fast despite being big'. The use of 'but' instead of 'and' serves to emphasize that one would not ordinarily expect a heavyweight boxer to be fast. If we translate 'but' into ' · ', the sentence would lose part of its meaning. In

Discuss whether there would be any loss of meaning if the 'but' in the above cartoon were symbolized with the dot—that is, the conjunction operator of truth-functional logic.

"B.C." by permission of Johnny Hart and Field Enterprises, Inc.

some contexts, this would be all right—as, for instance, if one wished to make a coldly objective assessment of Ali's chances against another fighter.

Similarly, if we translate:

> **Forego won the Widener Handicap although he carried 130 pounds.**

into a conjunction, we would still be asserting that he won the race and that he carried 130 pounds, but we would no longer be suggesting that horses that carry 130 pounds do not usually win handicaps—a suggestion that is conveyed by the original sentence with 'although'.

The decision as to whether or not to translate an 'and' (or similar expression such as 'but') in terms of the dot symbol must be made on a case-by-case basis, using common sense, our knowledge of the context, and our "feel" for the language. Since there are no rigorous formal criteria on which to base such decisions, there will be cases over which two intelligent persons will disagree as to whether or not a proposition can be symbolized using the dot. In any case, if we use the dot, any resulting loss of meaning should be noted.

EXERCISE 6–3

In each of the following sentences (a) indicate what meaning, if any, would be lost by translating the 'and' with the dot. If the dot cannot be used, explain why. (b) If the translation is possible, symbolize the sentence using the appropriate propositional constants; and indicate what each constant represents.

---

1. The gunmen robbed the bank and made their getaway.
2. The gunmen covered their faces with masks and wore gloves.
3. The Oakland Athletics and the Los Angeles Dodgers played in the world series.
4. The Oakland Athletics and the Los Angeles Dodgers are baseball teams.

5. The band played rock and roll.
6. The band played *Stardust* and *Moon River*.
7. Each prisoner wore a ball and chain.
8. The weather will be cloudy and cool tomorrow.
9. Sam was involved in a hit-and-run accident.
10. Jim mailed a letter and bought some books.
11. Jim climbed out of the water and dried himself off.
12. George and Martha are quarreling again.
13. George and Martha are characters in Albee's *Who's Afraid of Virginia Woolf.*
14. Wilt Chamberlain scored 20 points although he played only half the game.

TRUTH TABLES   As was illustrated in our last section on conjunction, truth-functional operators can be defined with the use of truth tables. A **truth table** is *an illustrative device which is used to display all of the possible combinations of truth values of propositions which could be substituted for the propositional variables in a given propositional schema.* Once we have displayed all the possible combinations of truth values for the propositions that could be substituted for the variables in a schema containing only a single operator, and have displayed the corresponding truth values for each of the compound statements formed by those propositions, we have provided a complete definition of the logical operator which is part of that schema. Truth tables, therefore, can be used to define truth-functional operators in terms of an exhaustive list of the possible combinations of truth values in compound statements using a given truth-functional operation.

If we invented an operation of 'truthation' whose operator could be symbolized by '$\mathbb{D}$', we could define the symbol by the following truth table:

p	q	p $\mathbb{D}$ q
T	T	T
F	T	T
T	F	T
F	F	T

From this truth table, it should be obvious that our truthational operator makes true any compound proposition in which it is the main operator, whatever the truth values of the component propositions. Therefore, any proposition with the form 'p $\mathbb{D}$ q' would be true by virtue of the definition of the '$\mathbb{D}$'.

In our last section we could just as well have defined the dot symbol for conjunction in the following way:

p	T	F	T	F
q	T	T	F	F
p · q	T	F	F	F

But it has become conventional to display the various possible combinations of propositions that could be substituted for 'p' and 'q' on a truth table in terms of four rows forming a column under each variable. The order of the T's and F's used is also a standard one. The T's and F's are alternated under the first variable, and pairs of T's and F's are alternated under the second variable. A little thought will make clear that this arrangement is bound to result in a table showing all possible combinations of T and F for a proposition containing only two variables. (Tables for propositions containing three or more variables will be discussed later in this chapter.)

NEGATION   If we wish to deny, or negate, the truth value of a simple proposition we can do so by forming a new compound statement conjoining the operator 'it is not the case that' to that proposition. Whatever the truth value of the proposition being denied, the new proposition which denies it will have the opposite truth value.

Negation is the name we give to *the logical operator that operates on a given proposition to form a new compound statement which has the opposite truth value from that proposition.* The standard abbreviation we will use for the negation operator is the curl or tilde symbol, '~'. The propositional schema for the negation of a proposition is '~p'.

We can define the negation operator in terms of the two possible propositions that could be substituted for the variable 'p' in the propositional schema '~p' with the following truth table:

p	~p
T	F
F	T

Thus, if a proposition is true, its negation is false and, if a proposition is false, its negation is true.

We have adopted the convention of translating the '~' operator into the English phrase 'it is not the case that . . .'[5] There are, however, various other ways of negating a statement in ordinary English usage. Take the statement:

Hitler is dead.

___

[5] Strictly speaking, 'it is the case that . . .' is also a truth-functional operator, but it is unnecessary to use it since when one says 'it is the case that **P**' one is saying nothing more than what is being said in the mere assertion of '**P**'. Thus, it would be redundant to have an additional symbol for the truth-functional operator 'it is the case that . . .' or 'it is true that . . .' (e.g., the symbol ⊃) for if '**P**' has the value 'true', then ⊃ **P** is also true and if '**P**' has the value 'false', then ⊃ **P** is false.

We can negate that statement in any of several ways, including the following:

> *It is not the case that Hitler is dead.*
> *It is false that Hitler is dead.*
> *Hitler is not dead.*
> *Hitler is alive.*

Because all four of these sentences can normally be used to express the same proposition, they can all be abbreviated in the same way, and they must also have the same schema. The important point to be noted is that the "obvious" symbolization for the first two is '~p', while the "obvious" symbolization for the last is 'p'. The symbolization for the third is perhaps not so "obvious." But, since all can be used to express the same proposition, is it not necessary that all be symbolized in the same way? The answer is both 'yes' and 'no'. The basic rule to be followed is that *once a particular symbol has been assigned to a sentence in a given context, the same symbol must be used for every other sentence that is being used in that context to express the same proposition.* Thus, if an argument contains both 'Hitler is not dead' and 'Hitler is alive' as components, then, if 'Hitler is not dead' is symbolized as '~p', 'Hitler is alive' must also be symbolized as '~p'. Alternatively, if 'Hitler is alive' is symbolized as 'p', then 'Hitler is not dead' must also be symbolized as 'p', even though it may appear at first to be expressing a negative proposition. (All of this assumes, of course, that the two sentences are really being used to express the same proposition.)

DISJUNCTION   **Disjunction** or **alternation** is *the logical operation which most closely corresponds to the connecting of two sentences by the word 'or' in ordinary English.* The two sentences being connected are called *disjuncts* or *alternatives.* However, in ordinary usage, the English word 'or' is ambiguous in that it is commonly used to express two different meanings. For example, consider the following sentence, uttered by Tom's psychiatrist:

> *Tom dreamt about sex or food last night.*

which is shorthand for the sentence:

> *Tom dreamt about sex last night or Tom dreamt*
> *about food last night.*

Both express the same compound statement. In both, the word 'or' is being used in what is known as the *inclusive* sense. The inclusive 'or' is used to assert that either the first disjunct or the second disjunct *or both* disjuncts may be true. Thus, the above sentence is true either if Tom dreamt about sex last night, or if Tom dreamt about food last night, or if Tom dreamt about both last night. An inclusive disjunction is true if the first, the second, or both disjuncts are true; it is false only if both disjuncts are false.

In contrast, when a customer in a restaurant asks the waiter 'What dessert comes with this dinner?' and the waiter answers 'You can have cake or pie', he almost certainly means that the customer is entitled to either cake or pie for dessert, but not both. In this situation, 'or' is being used in the *exclusive* sense. The exclusive 'or' is used in sentences where either the first disjunct, or the second disjunct, *but not both,* may be true. An exclusive disjunction is true if and only if the first disjunct is true and the second is false, or the first disjunct is false and the second is true.

An exclusive disjunction is stronger than an inclusive disjunction, since for it to be true an extra condition has to hold—namely, that both disjuncts cannot be true.

If we treat a disjunct such as:

He vacationed in Florida or California.

as an inclusive disjunction, then it could be false only if he did not vacation in either Florida or California. If we treat it as an exclusive disjunction, then it would be false if he did not vacation in either Florida or California, but it would also be false if he vacationed in both Florida and California. Thus, when we treat a disjunction as exclusive, we are making the extra assumption that both disjuncts cannot be true—an assumption that would be warranted only if the context made perfectly clear that this extra restriction was intended. Therefore, *logicians always assume every 'or' to signify inclusive disjunction, unless there is strong evidence that the 'or' is being used exclusively.* We will follow the practice, since it is always better to assume too little than too much.

Many disjunctions in ordinary language are vague, and only a thorough analysis of the specific contexts in which they are made can reveal for certain whether they are intended as inclusive or exclusive. In treating as inclusive all disjunctions which are not clearly exclusive, we are covering at least that part of their meaning that all disjunctions have in common, namely that both disjuncts are not false. And, as was stated before, and as will become clearer in the next chapter when we deal with arguments, it is always better to assume too little than to assume too much. Later in this chapter we will present the logical tools for dealing with cases where an exclusive disjunction is clearly stated or intended—tools, that is, to express the extra condition that both disjuncts cannot be true. In the meantime, we will interpret the 'or' of disjunction only in its weaker or inclusive sense.

The logical operator for inclusive disjunction is the wedge or 'vee' symbol '$\lor$'. We can define the '$\lor$' operator by means of the following truth table:

p	q	p $\lor$ q
T	T	T
F	T	T
T	F	T
F	F	F

"AND MAKE MR. WILSON'S ULCER BETTER.
OR ME, OR *ONE* OF US, ANYWAY...."

*What sense of 'or'—inclusive or exclusive—is being used in the above cartoon?
Would there be any significant loss of meaning if the truth-functional disjunction
operator—the "wedge"—were used in place of the 'or'?*

Dennis the Menace ® *cartoons* © *Field Enterprises, Inc.*

An inclusive disjunction is thus true if and only if either or both disjuncts are true
and is false if and only if both disjuncts are false.

MATERIAL IMPLICATION   For a number of reasons which are too complex to go into in this
book, most systems of symbolic logic include an operation known as
material implication. The logical operator for material implication is symbolized
by the horseshoe symbol '⊃' and is defined in terms of the following truth table:

p	q	p ⊃ q
T	T	T
F	T	T
T	F	F
F	F	T

From this table we can see that any proposition of the form 'p ⊃ q' is false if and only if the proposition substituted for 'p' is true and the proposition substituted for 'q' is false. In all other cases, a proposition with this form is true.

The symbol '⊃' is usually translated into ordinary English in terms of 'If . . . then . . .' sentences, or sentences with the form 'p implies q'. (The relation of material implication to the notion of valid arguments will be discussed in the next chapter.) Sentences of the 'If . . . then . . .' form are also called **conditionals.** The term preceding the horseshoe is known as the **antecedent,** and the term following it is known as the **consequent.**

Although logicians follow the convention that every formula containing the horseshoe symbol can be translated into an 'If . . . then . . .' sentence, it must be recognized that most 'If . . . then . . .' sentences in ordinary English carry more meaning than does the horseshoe of material implication. In fact, the truth-functional operator symbolized by the horseshoe has no real counterpart in ordinary English. However, it is sufficiently similar to certain ordinary-language terms that it can be used in the logical analysis of many (but not all) conditional statements. This can best be illustrated by concrete examples.

In the first row of the truth table for material implication, both the antecedent and the consequent are true. This is illustrated by the following interpretation of the schema 'p ⊃ q':

$$2 + 2 = 4 \supset \textit{George Washington was the first}$$
$$\textit{president of the United States.}$$

On the basis of the truth-table definition of the horseshoe, we would have to say that the above sentence expresses a true proposition, since the antecedent '$2 + 2 = 4$' and the consequent 'George Washington was the first president of the United States' are both true. Although the names for this operator—'material implication' and 'conditional'—both carry over from their everyday usages suggestions of some sort of meaningful relation between the antecedent and consequent, this is simply not the case with regard to the horseshoe. The sentence above containing the horseshoe symbol does not carry all of the meaning contained in the statement expressed by the following sentence in everyday usage:

$$\textit{If } 2 + 2 = 4\textit{, then George Washington was the first}$$
$$\textit{president of the United States.}$$

This sentence appears to assert that Washington's having been the first president is in some way related to the mathematical truth that $2 + 2 = 4$. This is a suggestion that we would reject on factual grounds, for the truth of this mathematical statement has nothing to do with the truth of this or any other historical statement. We might even want to say that the 'If . . . then . . .' statement is false, even though the horseshoe statement is true. In short, the expression 'If

. . . then. . . .' when used in the context of ordinary language, almost always carries more meaning[6] than does '⊃'.

The meaning of the horseshoe is given *entirely* in its truth table. Like all truth-functional operators, the horseshoe asserts no relationship between the component propositions other than that specified in its truth table. If 'p' and 'q' are both true, then 'p ⊃ q' is true no matter what other relations hold or do not hold between 'p' and 'q'. Once we know the meaning of the horseshoe symbol as a logical operator, then, to determine precisely the truth value of a material implication, we need ascertain only the truth values of the antecedent and the consequent. Any other relationship between antecedent and consequent is irrelevant from a strictly logical point of view.

Knowing this, we can avoid becoming confused about material implications in which the antecedent and the consequent are not only true but are asserted (in ordinary language) to be causally related. Take, for example, the sentence:

> **If you stop breathing, then you will die in a few**
> **minutes.**

In this case, the antecedent and the consequent do not merely both happen to be true; the antecedent is asserted to be the *cause* of the consequent. But when the same sentence is symbolized using the horseshoe, the assertion of a causal connection disappears.

Sentences expressing causal relations represent a kind of implication that is stronger than material implication, though it contains material implication within it. An exhaustive analysis of such sentences would take us beyond the bounds of truth-functional logic. (The topic is dealt with more fully in Chapter 12.) For our present purposes, it is sufficient to note that, by symbolizing such a statement with the horseshoe symbol, we cover at least that part of its meaning that is relevant for our present purpose, which is that of analyzing the logical structure of arguments containing such statements. Thus, if we ignore the suggested causal relationship between the antecedent, 'If you stop breathing', and the consequent, 'You will die in a few minutes', we can still subject the proposition to a truth-functional analysis by the use of the truth-table definition of the horseshoe. If we assume that it is true that you stop breathing but false that you will die in a few minutes—that is, if we affirm the antecedent and deny the consequent— then the original sentence expresses an obviously false proposition. We have, therefore, a situation corresponding to line 3 of the truth table: 'p' is true, 'q' is false, and 'p ⊃ q' is false. Whether we know that the cessation of breathing is the *cause* of dying in a few minutes, we can still know it to be true that, *if* you stop breathing, *then* you will die shortly thereafter. Only if it were in fact the case that

---

[6] As we saw in our discussion of the two senses of disjunction, statement **A** carries more meaning than statement **B** if and only if whenever **A** is true then **B** is also true, but when **B** is true it is possible that **A** might be false.

people who stopped breathing did not die shortly thereafter would it be false that a material implication holds between 'You stop breathing' and 'You will die in a few minutes'. Therefore we can treat such conditionals as if they were material implications, even though they are also much more; but we must recognize that, in so treating them, we sacrifice much of their meaning.

There are other ways in which material implication differs from our ordinary conception of the meanings of conditional sentences. Consider the following:

> *If the moon is made of green cheese, then I am*
> *Superman.*

Here the speaker evidently wants to deny the antecedent and adduces a patently false consequent ('I am Superman') to assert that the antecedent ('The moon is made of green cheese') is not only false but ridiculous. According to the truth-table definition of the horseshoe, we would have to accept the compound proposition as true, merely on the ground that both component propositions are false (see line 4 of the table), which is a much weaker and less interesting assertion than what was intended. To avoid this, the 'If . . . then . . .' statement might best be reformulated as a simple negation of the antecedent:

> *It is not the case that the moon is made of green*
> *cheese.*

Here too, however, some meaning would be lost from the original.

Whereas conditionals with false consequents are often used in ordinary language as a means of emphasizing the falsity of the antecedent, there are few, if

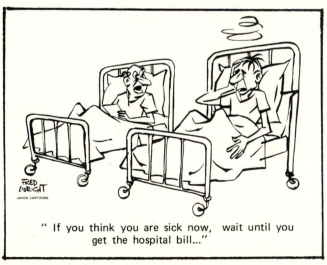

" If you think you are sick now, wait until you get the hospital bill..."

Discuss what meaning is lost when the 'If . . . then . . .' in the above cartoon is symbolized using the horseshoe.

Fred Wright, *UE News.*

any, ordinary-language contexts in which one would use a conditional with a false antecedent and a true consequent. To anyone other than a logician, the following assertion:

> *If tigers are reptiles, then* War and Peace *was written*
> *by Tolstoy.*

would naturally suggest either (a) that the speaker sincerely believed tigers to be reptiles (and probably also regarded this fact as good evidence for Tolstoy's authorship of *War and Peace*); or—assuming he knew that tigers are not reptiles—(b) that he believed Tolstoy was not the author of *War and Peace;* or (c) that the sentence was nonsensical and was not being used to express a proposition at all. But to the logician, this statement, if it were symbolized using the horseshoe, would simply be true, by virtue of the truth-table definition (line 2 of the table).

Ordinary language is laden with conditionals which are not truth-functional.[7] But we are here interested only in the one kind of conditional which is. Some material implications seem strange, or even patently absurd, when expressed in ordinary language. Nevertheless, material implication is a legitimate and extremely useful logical operation. Its usefulness will become more evident as we get further into the discussion of propositional logic.

It is always important to remember that the translation of the horseshoe into an ordinary-language 'If . . . then . . .' often results in the addition of new meanings, while the translation of the ordinary-language 'If . . . then . . .' into the horseshoe often results in a significant loss of meaning. Thus, if the form represented by the schema 'p ⊃ q' sometimes sounds very strange when the variables are replaced by ordinary English sentences expressing true or false propositions, we must bear in mind that the horseshoe symbol means *only* that the compound statement containing it is false if and only if the antecedent is true and the consequent is false.

There are other ordinary English expressions, as well as those of the form 'If . . . then . . .', that use the term 'if' in such fashion that they can justifiably be symbolized as material implications. For example:

> *I will go if you will go.*

Since the 'if' immediately precedes 'you will go', this sentence can be

---

[7] A not uncommon type of 'If . . . then . . .' statement in ordinary English which cannot be symbolized with the horseshoe is the *counterfactual conditional,* such as: 'If John Kennedy had not been assassinated, then the United States would not have gotten involved in Vietnam' and 'If John Kennedy had not been assassinated, then the United States would have got even more deeply involved in Vietnam'. Clearly, it is impossible for both of these sentences, as we normally interpret them, to express true statements. Yet, since both have a false antecedent, both would be true by definition if symbolized with the horseshoe of material implication. Counterfactuals are generally founded on causal relations, and thus will not be discussed here.

"Look at it like this, Father—if they're going to rebel against their upbringing, why not bring them up the wrong way?"

Discuss the loss of meaning that results when this cartoon is formulated using the horseshoe operator as follows: 'Children are going to rebel against their upbringing ⊃ Bring them up the wrong way.'

© 1968 Punch-Rothco.

symbolized—admittedly with loss of meaning—as:

<u>Y</u>ou will go ⊃ <u>I</u> will go.[8]

Its abbreviation and schema display its logical structure directly:

Y ⊃ I   *and*   **q ⊃ p**

The variable 'q' has been substituted for the proposition 'You will go', and 'p' has been substituted for 'I will go'. If we make the same substitutions in the original proposition, we get 'p if q'.

The slightly different sentence:

I will go only if you will go.

can be symbolized as:

I will go ⊃ you will go, or

I ⊃ Y

[8] For the remainder of this chapter and the next chapter, we will identify the letters to be used in abbreviating a sentence by underscoring them in their original context. Thus, in this example, the underscored '<u>Y</u>' indicates that '<u>Y</u>ou will go' is to be abbreviated as 'Y'.

To understand this more clearly, consider the original sentence as equivalent to the speaker's saying to a third party, "If you see me going, you can be sure Y is going, because if she doesn't go, I won't go either." (Also, look back at the truth table, which shows that in a true 'p ⊃ q' proposition, 'p' can be true *only* if 'q' is true.)

Substituting variables for the component sentences, we obtain a schema of the form:

p *only if* q

which, we therefore conclude, can legitimately be symbolized as 'p ⊃ q'.

Still another ordinary English locution using 'if' is:

I will go **even if** *you go.*

This is really a way of asserting simply:

I will go.

because in saying, 'I will go even if you go', I am not only asserting that I will go if you go, but am also asserting that I will go if you do *not* go. Thus, whether you go or not, I will definitely go.

Therefore, statements of the form 'p even if q' can be rendered into statements of the simpler form 'p', and do not fit the truth-table definition of material implication (because 'p' may be true even when 'q' is false).

Some general rules for the '⊃' are:

if **p** *then* q	*can be symbolized as*	p ⊃ q
p *if* q	*can be symbolized as*	q ⊃ p
p *only if* q	*can be symbolized as*	p ⊃ q
p *even if* q	*can be symbolized as*	p

MATERIAL EQUIVALENCE

Material equivalence is the same name given to *the logical operation which joins two propositions into a compound statement such that, if the two components have the same truth value, the compound statement is true, and if they have different truth values, the compound statement is false.* The logical operator for material equivalence is the symbol '≡'. We can define the '≡' symbol by means of the following truth table:

p	q	p ≡ q
T	T	T
F	T	F
T	F	F
F	F	T

A material equivalence is thus true if both of its component propositions are true or if both are false, and it is false if they have different truth values.[9]

The '≡' symbol for material equivalence can best be rendered into ordinary English as 'if and only if'. Thus, instead of saying:

> *'Caesar crossed the Rubicon' is materially equivalent*
> *to 'Shakespeare wrote Hamlet',*

we can say:

> **Caesar crossed the Rubicon if and only if**
> **Shakespeare wrote Hamlet.**

All we are asserting here is that both components have the same truth value—that either both are true *or* both are false. The translation of the '≡' into 'if and only if' might sometimes tempt one to read into it more meaning than it is actually intended to bear, just as 'if . . . then . . .' sometimes conveys more meaning than the horseshoe is defined to convey. Thus, it cannot be too strongly emphasized that the meaning of '≡' is *only* what is specified in its truth-table definition.[10]

EXERCISE 6–4

(a) Symbolize the truth-functional proposition expressed by each of the following sentences using propositional constants and the symbols for conjunction, negation, disjunction, material implication, and material equivalence. (b) Indicate precisely what part of the original sentence each constant symbolizes. (c) Indicate what meaning, if any, is lost in replacing the English word with the logical operator.

---

1. Roses are red and violets are blue.
2. Roses are red yet violets are blue.
3. It rained today and the mailman was late.
4. If I give you one, then everybody will want one.
5. It is not the case that hickory is a soft wood.
6. It is snowing in Detroit or else the weather report is inaccurate.
7. Joyce needs a kitchen table and some chairs for her apartment.

---

[9] We should not make the mistake of confusing the '≡' for material equivalence with the '=' symbol for identity. Material equivalence says *only* that both the component propositions have the same truth value, whereas an identity statement asserts that the two components not only have the same truth value but are identical in every other way as well. Actually, identity is a relation which is usually said to hold between events, things, or properties rather than between propositions.

[10] It should be noted that sometimes, in ordinary English, people use 'If . . . then . . .' sentences to express what is intended as a material equivalence. Thus, the instructor who says to a class, 'If you maintain an average of 90 or better on all your work in the course, then you will get an A', may in fact be telling the students that they will get A's *if and only if* they maintain a 90 average or better.

8. Thoreau was an American or a Frenchman.
9. Athens and Sparta fought in the Peloponnesian War.
10. Athens and Sparta were city states in ancient Greece.
11. Oil and water will mix if and only if they are emulsified.
12. If a total eclipse of the sun occurs, then the sky darkens.
13. If a total eclipse of the sun occurs, then the moon is positioned directly between the earth and the sun.
14. His battery went dead and his car wouldn't start.
15. It is not the case that sugar is a protein.
16. If this lump of sugar is placed in water, it will dissolve.
17. This object will float if and only if its specific gravity is less than 1.0.
18. You left the window open or the thermostat is turned down too low.
19. A geometrical figure is an equilateral if and only if all its sides have the same length.
20. It is not true that all triangles are right triangles.
21. I will take the job if it pays well.
22. I will take the job if and only if it pays well.
23. If an American president's last name was Johnson, then he was vice-president before he was president.
24. Carl drinks bourbon or scotch.
25. Most swans are white, although some are gray.
26. It is not true that Plato was Aristotle's disciple.
27. A conjunction is true if and only if both its component propositions are true.
28. If the stock market fails, then many people will lose fortunes.
29. Many people will lose fortunes if the stock market fails.
30. Candles can be made of tallow or beeswax.
31. Either he came after I left, or he didn't come at all.
32. You will pass this exam if you study hard.
33. You will pass this exam only if you study hard.
34. You will pass this exam if and only if you study hard.
35. It did not rain although the clouds were dark and ominous.

PROPOSITIONS WITH MORE THAN ONE LOGICAL OPERATOR   Many of the arguments with which we frequently wish to deal contain statements that include more than one logical operator—that is, they are compound statements whose components include other compound statements. For instance, the following compound might appear as either a premise or a conclusion in different arguments:

> **Either *the Democrats will not win the election* or, if**
> **they do, they will not have a very large majority.**

This proposition contains both a disjunction and a conditional (which can be treated as a material implication). We must therefore discuss the ways of dealing with truth-functional propositions containing two or more logical operators.

Grouping   In symbolic logic, when symbolizing compound statements that are parts of larger compound statements, we use additional symbols to group together the components to which a particular operator applies. **Grouping** is the setting off of compound propositions within a larger compound (usually by means of parentheses) in such a way that it is made clear to which variable or variables a particular operator applies.

Grouping is a familiar technique in mathematics, where parentheses are used to clarify ambiguous statements such as:

$$3 \times 5 + 4$$

which can mean either:

$$3 \times (5 + 4)$$

which is equal to 27, or:

$$(3 \times 5) + 4$$

which is equal to 19.

Certain words and/or punctuation marks (commas, semicolons, and so on) can serve the same purpose as such parentheses. In English, the ambiguity of the sentence:

It is not true that Chris will win or I will get sick

can be avoided by the appropriate use of the word 'either'. We can place 'either' before the operator 'it is not true that', which gives us:

**Either it is not true that Chris will win or I will get
    sick**

or we can place it immediately after the negation operator, which gives us:

**It is not true that either Chris will win or I will get
    sick**

which expresses a quite different proposition.

The original ambiguous sentence could be symbolized as '$\sim C \vee I$'. We could express the first alternative as:

$$(\sim C) \vee I$$

and the second alternative as:

$$\sim (C \vee I)$$

The former is a disjunction, the first component of which is a negation. Here the wedge is what is known as the **main operator.** The latter is a negation whose component compound proposition is a disjunction. In this case, the tilde is the main operator. In general, a statement with the form:

$$(\sim p) \vee q$$

clearly has a different logical structure than a statement with the form:

$$\sim (p \vee q)$$

For the sake of simplicity, we will adopt the convention that no parentheses are needed in symbolizing the negation of a simple proposition. That is, *when a propositional constant or variable is preceded by the tilde with no parentheses, the tilde should be understood to apply only to that one variable.* Thus, we will simply write '~p ∨ q' instead of the equivalent '(~p) ∨ q'.

Commas and other punctuation marks can also be used in ordinary English to clarify ambiguous groupings. Consider the sentence:

> *Susan will defeat Fran and I will defeat you or I will give up chess.*

This could mean either of the following:

> 1. *Susan will defeat Fran and I will defeat you, or I will give up chess.*
> 2. *Susan will defeat Fran, and I will defeat you or I will give up chess.*

The first alternative uses a comma to make a disjunction out of the whole compound (and a conjunction within the first disjunct) and should be symbolized as:

$$(S \cdot D) \vee G$$

In this case, the wedge is the main operator. The second alternative uses a comma to make the whole compound into a conjunction (whose second conjunct is a disjunction) and should be symbolized as:

$$S \cdot (D \vee G)$$

The main operator now is the dot. If Susan does not defeat Fran, but I do defeat you, and I do give up chess (which makes 'S' false, 'D' true, and 'G' true), the

". . . Either all of us are going to die together or we are going to learn to live together and if we are to live together we have to talk."
ELEANOR ROOSEVELT

Make sure that you get the grouping right when you symbolize this statement in the propositional logic.

first interpretation will turn out to be true, since a disjunction is true if one or both of its disjuncts is true. However, the second interpretation will turn out to be false, since a conjunction cannot be true unless both conjuncts are true. This one case is sufficient to demonstrate that the two interpretations are not the same, since the compound is true in one grouping and false in the other.

Sometimes we encounter a sentence composed of three or more conjuncts, or three or more disjuncts; for example:

> *I overslept and it was raining pitchforks and the*
>   *professor gave a surprise quiz.*
> *Susan is a plumber or Frank is a cook or Phil is a*
>   *carpenter.*

Sentences of this sort are not ambiguous, but they must still be grouped, because the definitions of the logical operators '·' and '∨' limit them to two component propositions. For this reason, 'p · q · r' must be grouped as either '(p · q) · r' or 'p · (q · r)'; and 'p ∨ q ∨ r' must likewise be grouped as '(p ∨ q)

To Take This Credit.—You must file Form 1040, not Form 1040A, and you meet **all** of the conditions listed below.

(1) It was necessary for you to make child and dependent care payments so you (and your spouse if you were married) could work or look for work.

(2) One or more qualifying persons lived in your home.

(3) You (and your spouse if you were married) paid more than half the cost of keeping up your home. This cost includes rent or mortgage payments; utility charges; maintenance and repairs; property taxes and property insurance; and food costs (but not dining out).

(4) You must file a joint return if you were married. There are two exceptions to this rule. You can file a separate return if:

(a) You were legally separated; or

(b) You were living apart and:

● The qualifying person lived in your home for more than 6 months; and

● You paid more than half the cost of keeping up your home; and

● Your spouse did not live in your home during the last 6 months of your tax year.

Child Custody Test.—If you were divorced, legally separated, or separated under a written agreement, your child is a qualifying person if you had custody for the longer period during 1978. The child must also have:

● Received over half of his or her support from the parents, and

● Been in the custody of one or both parents for more than half of 1978, and

● Been under 15, or physically or mentally unable to care for himself or herself.

(5) You paid someone, other than a dependent relative or your spouse, to care for the qualifying person.

You are allowed to pay a relative who was not your dependent if their services are considered employment for social security purposes. However, if the relative is your child, he or she must have been at least 21. If the relative is your parent, both of the following conditions must have been met for 4 continuous weeks during a calendar quarter:

(a) The qualifying person was your child under 18 or whose physical or mental condition required care by an adult.

(b) You were a widow(er) or divorced; or your spouse was physically or mentally unable to care for the child under 18.

Government documents and forms, despite efforts in recent years to simplify them, still contain some of the most complex statements ever formulated by the human mind (although some wags have suggested that they are in fact formulated by inhuman—and inhumane—minds). Can you interpret and then symbolize the two very complex statements reproduced above from the U.S. Income Tax Form 2441—Credit for Child and Dependent Care Expenses?

$\vee$ r' or as 'p $\vee$ (q $\vee$ r)'. The choice of grouping in such a case is completely arbitrary.

EXERCISE 6–5   (a) *Symbolize each of the following sentences. In all cases this requires using more than one logical operator. Use the underscored letters as propositional constants, and use parentheses where necessary to indicate correct groupings of propositional constants and logical operators.* (b) *Identify the main operator in each formula by underlining it.*

---

1. I am both going to San Francisco and I will stay with my relatives in Oakland, or else I will visit Don. $S \cdot (R \vee D)$ $(S \cdot R) \vee D$
2. I am going to San Francisco, and either I will stay with my relatives in Oakland or I will visit Don. $S \cdot (R \vee D)$
3. Either I am going to San Francisco, or I will stay with my relatives in Oakland and I will visit Don. $S \vee (R \cdot D)$
4. Either I am going to San Francisco or I will stay with my relatives in Oakland, and in either case I will visit Don. $(S \vee R) \cdot D$
5. I am going to San Francisco, and I will both stay with my relatives in Oakland and I will visit Don. $(S \cdot R) \cdot D$
6. I am going to San Francisco and will stay with my relatives in Oakland and I will visit Don.
7. It is not the case that if I am going to win then I will go home.
8. If it is not the case that I am going to win, then I will go home. $\sim W \supset H$
9. If I am going to win, then it is not the case that I will go home.
10. If I am going to win, then I will not go home. $W \supset \sim H$
11. If I am not going to win, then I will go home.
12. It is not the case that both Lassie is a collie and Spot is a mongrel. $\sim (C \cdot M)$
13. Lassie is a collie and Spot is not a mongrel.
14. Lassie is not a collie and Spot is a mongrel. $(\sim C \cdot M)$
15. Lassie is not a collie and Spot is not a mongrel.
16. It is not the case that both Lassie is not a collie and Spot is not a mongrel. $\sim (\sim C \cdot \sim M)$
17. It is not the case that both Lassie is a collie and Spot is not a mongrel.
18. It is not the case that both Lassie is not a collie and Spot is a mongrel. $\sim (\sim C \cdot M)$
19. If it snows and driving will be hazardous, then the Bakers will not come.
20. If it snows then both the driving will be hazardous and the Bakers will not come. $S \supset (H \cdot \sim C$
21. If it snows then either the driving will not be hazardous or the Bakers will not come.
22. If it snows then either the driving will be hazardous or the Bakers will come. $S \supset (H \vee C)$
23. If it snows then if the driving will be hazardous the Bakers will not come.
24. If it either snows or the driving will be hazardous then the Bakers will not come. $(S \vee H) \supset \sim$
25. If they run out of beer then everyone will stop dancing and the party will be a flop.
$*$ 26. If they run out of beer, then if everyone stops dancing the party will be a flop.
27. If they run out of beer, then either everyone will stop dancing or the party will be a flop.
28. If they run out of beer or everyone stops dancing, then the party will be a flop. $(B \vee D) \supset P$
29. Either Kurt is German and Marie is French or Harold is English.
30. Kurt is German and either Marie is French or Harold is English. $K \cdot (M \vee H)$
31. Kurt is German or Marie is French and Harold is English.
32. Kurt is German and it is not the case that either Marie is French or Harold is English.

$*$ $B \supset (D \supset P)$

$B \cdot (D \supset P)$ + Baum's answer?

33. It is not the case that either Kurt is German or both Marie is French and Harold is English.
34. It is not the case both that Kurt is German and that either Marie is French or Harold is English.
35. It is not the case that either Kurt is German and Marie is French, or Harold is English.
36. Kurt is German or it is not the case that both Marie is French and Harold is English.
37. Kurt is German or both Marie is French and Harold is not English.
38. Kurt is German or it is not the case that both Marie is French and Harold is not English.
39. Kurt is not German and either Marie is French or Harold is English.
40. Kurt is not German and it is not the case that either Marie is not French or Harold is not English. $\sim K \cdot \sim (\sim M \vee H)$

Truth-Table Construction

Having developed the logical punctuation procedures necessary to present propositional schemata with more than one operator, we can develop the techniques for constructing truth tables for those schemata. There are three basic rules involved in constructing truth tables for schemata with more than one operator.

The first rule follows from our basic requirement of including all possible combinations and permutations of truth values in the truth table for a particular propositional schema. Mathematicians have shown that, for the two truth values **T** and **F**, the number of possible combinations and permutations for a given compound propositional schema containing exactly n propositional variables is 2^n—that is, 2 times itself $n - 1$ times. We have already seen that each grouping of truth values requires a separate row in the truth table. Therefore, our first rule is that the truth table for a propositional schema should contain 2^n rows, where n is the number of propositional variables in the schema.

The cases we have dealt with thus far conform to this: the truth table for negation, with one variable, contained $2^1 = 2$ rows, while the others, with two variables, contained $2^2 = 4$ rows. A schema with three variables would have $2^3 = 8$ possible groupings of **T**'s and **F**'s, and thus eight rows in the truth table. For four variables there would be $2^4 = 16$ rows, for five variables $2^5 = 32$ rows, and so on.

The second rule is essentially an extension of the procedure we have already established for listing **T**'s and **F**'s in the columns under the propositional variables. As before, we alternate **T**'s and **F**'s in the first column, and alternate pairs of **T**'s and **F**'s in the second column. In addition, since we may now require three or more columns, we will alternate sets of four **T**'s and four **F**'s in the third column, and so on. Thus, if we need a fourth column for a fourth variable we would alternate sets of eight **T**'s and **F**'s, for a fifth column sets of sixteen, and so on. This will guarantee that every possible combination and permutation of **T**'s and **F**'s is included.

The final rule is that the part of the truth table under the operators in the schema should be filled in with the appropriate truth values, beginning from the "inside" of the parentheses out. This can best be explained in terms of the following example.

Step One   Suppose we wish to construct a truth table for the schema '~((p ∨ ~q) ⊃ r)'. Once the columns under the propositional variables have been filled in, we must *find any negation operators which are associated with single propositional variables,* and fill in the columns under them as stipulated in the truth-table definition of the tilde (that is, if 'p' is true, '~p' is false, and so on). In our example, the only tilde associated with a single propositional variable is the one in '~q'. We will fill in the column under it first.

p	q	r	~((p ∨ ~q) ⊃ r)
T	T	T	F
F	T	T	F
T	F	T	T
F	F	T	T
T	T	F	F
F	T	F	F
T	F	F	T
F	F	F	T
			(1)

Step Two   After we have filled in all columns of this sort, we *next fill in the columns under any operators which connect components that are not separated by parentheses,* using the truth-table definitions of those operators. In our example, the wedge connecting 'p' and '~q' is the only such operator.

p	q	r	~((p ∨ ~q) ⊃ r)
T	T	T	T F
F	T	T	F F
T	F	T	T T
F	F	T	T T
T	T	F	T F
F	T	F	F F
T	F	F	T T
F	F	F	T T
			(2) (1)

Step Three,   Next we fill in the columns under any tildes that precede exactly one
Step Four   parenthesis (there are none of these in our example). *Then we fill in the columns under operators connecting components at least one of which is contained in single parentheses,* but neither of which is contained in

double parentheses. In our example, the horseshoe is such an operator, as it connects 'r' with '(p ∨ ~q)'.

p	q	r	~((p ∨	~q) ⊃	r)
T	T	T	T	F	T
F	T	T	F	F	T
T	F	T	T	T	T
F	F	T	T	T	T
T	T	F	T	F	F
F	T	F	F	F	T
T	F	F	T	T	F
F	F	F	T	T	F
			(2)	(1)	(3)

Step Five   Next, *we will fill in the columns under any tildes which immediately precede* exactly two *parentheses.*

p	q	r	~	((p ∨	~q) ⊃	r)
T	T	T	F	T F	T	T
F	T	T	F	F F	F	T
T	F	T	F	T T	T	T
F	F	T	F	T T	T	T
T	T	F	T	T F	T	F
F	T	F	F	F F	F	T
T	F	F	T	T T	T	F
F	F	F	T	T T	T	F
			(4)	(2)	(1)	(3)

After this we would fill in the columns under any operators connecting components at least one of which is contained in double parentheses, then those under any tildes preceding exactly three parentheses, and so on.

The *last operator under which we fill in the column* is the **main operator**—in our example, the tilde preceding the first parenthesis. It is this column that provides the truth-table definition of the schema.

EXERCISE 6–6   *Construct truth tables for each of the following propositional schemata.*

---

1. p · ~q
2. ~p · q
3. p ⊃ ~q
4. ~p ⊃ q

5. ~p · ~q
6. ~(p · q)
7. ~(p ⊃ q)
8. ~(p · ~q)

9. $p \lor \sim q$
10. $\sim(p \lor q)$
11. $\sim(\sim p \lor q)$
12. $\sim(\sim p \lor \sim q)$
13. $(p \cdot q) \equiv p$
14. $(p \cdot q) \supset p$
15. $(p \cdot q) \supset q$
16. $(p \cdot q) \supset r$
17. $(p \lor q) \supset r$
18. $(p \supset q) \supset r$
19. $\sim(p \cdot q) \supset \sim r$

20. $\sim(p \cdot \sim q) \supset \sim r$
21. $((p \lor q) \cdot p) \supset r$
22. $((p \lor \sim q) \cdot p) \supset r$
23. $(\sim(p \lor \sim q) \cdot p) \supset r$
24. $\sim(\sim(p \lor \sim q) \cdot p) \supset r$
25. $((p \supset q) \cdot \sim q) \supset \sim p$
26. $(p \supset q) \equiv (\sim q \supset \sim p)$
27. $\sim(p \cdot q) \equiv (\sim p \lor \sim q)$
28. $\sim(p \cdot q) \equiv (\sim p \cdot q)$
29. $((p \cdot q) \supset r) \equiv (p \supset (q \supset r))$
30. $((\sim p \cdot q) \supset \sim r) \equiv (\sim p \supset (q \supset \sim r))$

LOGICALLY EQUIVALENT STATEMENTS Once we have a procedure for constructing truth tables for any truth-functional propositional schema, we can compare the propositional schemata of statements with different logical structures. We noted that, in a truth table for a schema with more than one operator, the final column filled in (the one under the main operator) is the one that defines that schema. *Any two schemata with the same truth-table columns under their main operators are* **logically equivalent.** (Of course, this presupposes that the truth tables for both schemata were constructed in accordance with the rules given in the preceding section.) Two propositions are logically equivalent if their schemata are logically equivalent.

Law of Double Negation An obvious pair of logically equivalent schemata is 'p' and '$\sim\sim$p'. If we set their truth tables side by side, it becomes apparent that they are clearly the same—or, to be more precise, the last column filled in is the same:

p
T
F

p	$\sim\sim$	$\sim$p
T	T	F
F	F	T

In the truth table on the left, the truth values of the propositional schema 'p' are displayed. This column comprises the entire truth table for this schema. In the table on the right, the schema '$\sim \sim$p' is defined by the column under the first tilde, which is the main operator of this schema. Since both of these columns are the same, with a **T** in the first row and an **F** in the second row, the two schemata are therefore logically equivalent.

In demonstrating the logical equivalence between 'p' and '$\sim\sim$p', we have proved what is known as the **law of double negation.** According to this law, whenever a negative sentence such as:

It is not the case that _meat_ is healthy.

whose abbreviation is:

$$\sim M$$

is itself negated, as in the sentence:

> **It is not the case that it is not the case that <u>meat</u> is healthy.**

whose abbreviation is:

$$\sim\sim M$$

the resulting statement is logically equivalent to the proposition with both negations removed:

> **<u>Meat</u> is healthy.**

whose abbreviation is:

$$M$$

De Morgan's Rules   Another important pair of logically equivalent schemata is '$\sim(p \lor q)$' and '$(\sim p \cdot \sim q)$'. The truth tables for these are:

p	q	~(p ∨ q)				p	q	(~ p · ~ q)			
T	T	F	T			T	T	F	F	F	
F	T	F	T			F	T	T	F	F	
T	F	F	T			T	F	F	F	T	
F	F	T	F			F	F	T	T	T	
		(2)	(1)					(1)	(2)(1)		

This logical equivalence holds, since the columns under the main operators have the same truth values.

Still another pair of logically equivalent schemata is '$\sim(p \cdot q)$' and '$(\sim p \lor \sim q)$'. Their truth tables are:

p	q	~(p · q)				p	q	(~ p ∨ ~ q)			
T	T	F	T			T	T	F	F	F	
F	T	T	F			F	T	T	T	F	
T	F	T	F			T	F	F	T	T	
F	F	T	F			F	F	T	T	T	
		(2)	(1)					(1)	(2)(1)		

These formulae are logically equivalent, since all the truth values under the main operators of the two schemata are the same.

The two equivalences we have just analyzed are known as **De Morgan's rules,** and state, in ordinary English, that:

1. The negation of the *disjunction* of two statements is logically equivalent to the *conjunction* of the negations of the statements.
2. The negation of the *conjunction* of two statements is logically equivalent to the *disjunction* of the negations of the two statements.

LOGICAL EQUIVALENCE AND MATERIAL EQUIVALENCE The concept of logical equivalence we are discussing here is not the same as but is closely related to the concept of material equivalence discussed earlier. It will be remembered that material equivalence was defined essentially in terms of its truth table, which assigns the value **T** to a compound statement where the two statements joined by the ≡-operator have the same truth values (either both true or both false) and assigns the value false in all other cases. Because two logically equivalent statements are such that their schemata have the same truth values in each row under their main operators, it follows that, if we connect the schemata of two logically equivalent statements with the material equivalence operator, the resulting truth table would have all **T**'s under the main operator—that is, it would be analytically true. For example, if we so connect the schemata of a proposition and its double negation, we get the following truth table:

p		p ≡ ~ ~ p
T		T T F
F		T F T
		(3)(2)(1)

Similarly, the truth table of the schemata of De Morgan's rules joined by the material equivalence operator gives us:

p	q		~ (p ∨ q)	≡	(~p · ~q)
T	T		F T	T	F F F
F	T		F T	T	T F F
T	F		F T	T	F F T
F	F		T F	T	T T T
			(3) (2)	(4)(1)	(2)(1)

Another logical equivalence, which incidentally throws further light on material implication, is:

(p ⊃ q) ≡ ~(p · ~q)

whose truth table is:

p	q	(p ⊃ q)	[≡]	~ (p · ~ q)
T	T	T	T	T T F F
F	T	T	T	T T F F
T	F	F	T	F F T T
F	F	T	T	T T F T
		(2)	(4)(3)	(2)(1)

The usual set of truth values for material implication, listed in the column under the horseshoe, is obviously the same as the set of truth values in the column under the first tilde, which is the main operator of the second component. This proves that the two components are logically equivalent. The component on the right also satisfies our intuitive understanding of material implication, since one possible English-language rendering of:

$$\sim(p \cdot \sim q)$$

is:

It is not the case both that p is true and q is false

which is one wording of the definition of material implication.

Biconditionals   A final example of a logical equivalence, which illuminates the concept of material equivalence, is expressed in the formula:

$$(p \equiv q) \equiv ((p \supset q) \cdot (q \supset p))$$

whose truth table is:

p	q	(p≡q)	[≡]	((p ⊃ q) · (q ⊃ p))
T	T	T	T	T T T
F	T	F	T	T F F
T	F	F	T	F F T
F	F	T	T	T T T
		(1)	(3)	(1) (2) (1)

This shows us that a material equivalence—that is, '(p ≡ q)'—is logically equivalent to the compound of a conditional—'(p ⊃ q)'—and its converse —'(q ⊃ p)'. This fact has led logicians to call it a '**biconditional**'. A biconditional is a statement in which the first component materially implies the second, *and the* second materially implies the first.

    The logical equivalence between material equivalence and the conjunction of the two material implications is also brought out in the English translation of '≡'

as 'if and only if'. It was pointed out in the section on material implication that 'p if q' should be symbolized as 'q ⊃ p', and that 'p only if q' should be symbolized as 'p ⊃ q'. Thus it should come as no surprise that 'p if and only if q' can be symbolized as '(p ⊃ q) · (q ⊃ p)' as well as 'p ≡ q'.

Similarly, it can be shown that 'p ∨ q' is logically equivalent to '~(~p · ~q)' and that 'p ≡ q' is logically equivalent to '~(p · ~q) · ~(q · ~p)'. Because, in each of these pairs, the two schemata have the same columns under their main operators, it is possible to symbolize every truth-functional proposition using only the tilde and the dot. Thus, the '∨', '⊃', and '≡' are theoretically eliminable from our system. However, since it is so much easier to write 'p ≡ q' than '~(p · ~q) · ~(q · ~p)' and so on, we will continue to use the wedge, horseshoe, and triple-line symbols for the operations of disjunction, material implication and material equivalence, respectively.

"I had reasoned this out in my mind: there were two things that I had a right to, liberty and death. If I could not have one, I would have the other, for no man should take me alive."
HARRIET TUBMAN

Harriet Tubman's statement eloquently expresses an exclusive disjunction in a logically complex and sophisticated form. Symbolize her formulation using the horseshoe (and any other necessary operators). Also, symbolize the exclusive disjunction without the horseshoe, and then test your two formulations for logical equivalence using truth tables.

EXERCISE 6–7   *Construct truth tables to determine whether the following pairs of propositional schemata are logically equivalent.*

1.	p · q	~(~p ∨ ~q)	8.	~(p ≡ q)	~p ≡ ~q
2.	p · q	~(~p ∨ q)	9.	~p ≡ q	p ≡ ~q
3.	~p · q	~(p ∨ ~q)	10.	~(p ⊃ q)	~p ⊃ ~q
4.	~(p · q)	~p · ~q	11.	~(p ⊃ q)	p · ~q
5.	~(p ∨ q)	~p ∨ q	12.	~(p ⊃ q)	p ∨ ~q
6.	p ≡ q	~p ≡ ~q	13.	~(p ∨ q)	~p ∨ ~q
7.	p ⊃ q	~p ∨ q	14.	~(p · ~q) · ~(q · ~p)	p ≡ q

TAUTOLOGIES   At the end of Chapter 1 it was pointed out that some statements are such that their truth or falsity can be determined solely by analyzing their logical structure. Such statements are known in logic as analytically true and false statements. Statements that are *analytically true* are also known as **tautologies.** In the context of truth-functional logic, a statement is a tautology if and only if its schema has only **T**'s under the main connective in its truth table; that is, it has a truth-functional form such that it is *impossible* for it to be false. Thus, all the logical equivalences connected by the material-equivalence operator in the preceding section comprise tautologies, because there are only **T**'s under the main (material-equivalence) operator. There are many other tautologies which are of special interest to logicians, several of which we will consider briefly here.

One schema represents a tautology known as the **law of excluded middle.** Its truth table is:

p	(p $\vee$ ~p)
T	T F
F	T T
	(2) (1)

An example of a proposition that shares this schema is the analytic truth:

> ***Either the lights are on in this room or the lights are not on in this room.***

We can see that it is impossible for a statement of this form to have the value **F**, since there are only **T**'s under the main operator in the truth table of its schema.

Any proposition with the schema:

> **~(p · ~p)**

is also a tautology. This schema expresses what is known as the **law of noncontradiction.** Its truth table is:

p	~	(p · ~p)
T	T	F F
F	T	F T
	(3)	(2)(1)

The propositions whose schemata are defined by the above truth tables are obviously tautologies, since in each one there are only **T**'s under the main connective.

CONTRADICTIONS   Certain propositional schemata are such that, unlike tautologies, whatever the truth values of the propositions that could be substituted for their variables, the resultant compound statements are false. Propositions with such schemata are false in virtue of their logical form and are known as **contradictions**. A contradiction is a statement whose schema has only F's under the main connective in its truth table—that is, it is a proposition which has a logical form such that it is *impossible* for it to be true.

The most obvious example of a contradiction is a statement such as:

>**Gladstone was the Prime Minister of England and**
>**Gladstone was not the Prime Minister of England.**

The schema for this is:

p · ~p

and the truth table is:

p	p	·	~p
T		F	F
F		F	T
		(2)	(1)

Another contradictory statement would be one such as:

>**Homer was blind if and only if Homer was not blind.**

The schema for this is:

p ≡ ~p

and its truth table is:

p	p	≡	~p
T		F	F
F		F	T
		(2)	(1)

A more complicated contradictory statement is:

>**If it is the case that John is bald if and only if it is not**
>**the case that John is not bald, then it is not the**
>**case that either Achilles was a hero or Achilles**
>**was not a hero.**

Here the schema is:

$$(p \equiv \sim\sim p) \supset \sim(q \supset \sim q)$$

and the truth table is:

p	q	(p ≡ ~ ~p)	⊃	~	(q ∨ ~q)
T	T	T T F	F	F	T F
F	T	T F T	F	F	T F
T	F	T T F	F	F	T T
F	F	T F T	F	F	T T
		(3) (2) (1)	(5)	(4)	(3) (1)

Since there are only **F**'s under the main connective in this truth table, the original proposition must be a contradiction.

Contradictions are also known as **analytically false statements** because their falsity can be determined solely by an analysis of their logical form. As with tautologies, there is no need to make any empirical observations to determine their truth values.

CONTINGENT STATEMENTS   Any statement which is neither a tautology nor a contradiction is said to be 'contingent'. A **contingent statement** is *one whose schema has both T's and F's under the main connective in its truth table.* For example, take the sentence:

The light in this room is on.

This expresses a simple (not compound) statement whose schema is 'p'. Its truth table is:

p
T
F

Since this truth table has both a **T** and an **F**, we cannot determine whether the statement is true or false simply by examining its logical form. We would have to use other means, such as going into the room and looking around.

Similarly, take the compound statement expressed by the sentence:

**If Joan is a physician, then it is not the case that
Joan is ten years old.**

Its truth table is:

p	q	p $\supset$	~q
T	T	F	F
F	T	T	F
T	F	T	T
F	F	T	T
		(2)	(1)

Again, this truth table has both **T**'s and an **F** under its main connective; so the mere analysis of its logical form is not sufficient for determining whether the statement is in fact true or false.

Contingent statements are thus neither analytically true nor analytically false; it is always *logically* possible for them to be either true or false. If a contingent statement turns out to be factually true, it could have been false without violating any *logical* law, and if it turns out to be false, it could have been true without violating any *logical* law. To determine the truth value of a contingent statement, it is necessary to do more than subject it to a logical analysis.

"If we had keen vision of all that is ordinary in human life, it would be like hearing the grass grow or the squirrel's heart beat, and we should die of that roar which is the other side of silence."
GEORGE ELIOT

You should be able to display the logical structure of the above passage from Middlemarch *quite adequately using the tools of propositional logic, but it would be difficult if not impossible to express in any other way the meanings packed into this single sentence by its creator. Construct a truth table to determine whether it is contingent, a tautology, or a contradiction.*

EXERCISE 6–8

(a) *Are propositions with each of the following schemata tautologies, contradictions, or contingent statements?* (b) *Construct a truth table to determine your answer in each case.*

1. p $\supset$ q
2. p $\supset$ p
3. p $\supset$ ~p
4. (p · q) $\supset$ p

5. p ⊃ (p ∨ q)
6. (p ∨ ~p) ⊃ (p ∨ q) *con., r. 4*
7. ((p ⊃ q) · ~q) · p
8. ((p ⊃ q) · ~q) ∨ p *con., r. 2*
9. (p ⊃ q) ≡ (~p ∨̄ q)
10. (p ⊃ q) ≡ (~p · q) *con., r. 1, 4*
11. (p ⊃ q) ≡ (p · ~q)

12. ((p ⊃ q) · p) ∴ q *con., r. 2–4*
13. ((p ⊃ q) · p) · ~q
14. ((p ⊃ q) · p) ⊃ q *taut.*
15. (p ∨ ~p) ⊃ (p · ~q)
16. (p ∨ ~p) ⊃ (p · ~p) *contradiction*
17. ~(p ⊃ q) ≡ (~p ⊃ q)
18. (~p ⊃ q) ≡ (p ∨ q) *taut.*

EXERCISE 6–9   *Reconsider the statements of which you did preliminary analyses in Exercise 1–13. Symbolize each one with as little loss of meaning as possible using the methods of this chapter. Also use the methods of this chapter to try to determine which of the statements (as symbolized) is analytic and which is synthetic.*

SUMMARY

1. To say that a proposition is that about which it makes sense to say that it is true or false is equivalent to saying that *every* proposition has a **truth value.** A **truth-functional proposition** is a compound statement which is such that, if we know (1) the truth value of each of its component statements and (2) the meanings of the logical terms in the sentence expressing the compound statement, we can determine precisely the truth or falsity of the compound statement: in other words, its truth value is a *function* of the truth values of the component statements. A **logical operator** is an expression such that if it is correctly used with the appropriate number of propositions, a new proposition is produced with a different logical structure. No logical operator by itself is or expresses a proposition. A **truth-functional operator** is a logical operator such that, when it is correctly used with the appropriate number of propositions, a truth-functional proposition is produced.

2. A **symbol** is a sign that can be used to abbreviate or schematize any of the components in a given system. A **propositional constant** is an abbreviation for a sentence expressing a proposition; the meaning of the symbol remains constant throughout a given context. A **propositional variable** is a symbol that functions as a blank into which we can insert a sentence expressing any proposition whatever. Like logical operators, propositional variables have no truth values in themselves. A formula containing only propositional variables and logical operators is a **propositional schema,** which displays the form or logical structure of a proposition. Propositional variables are normally symbolized by small letters from the middle to the end of the alphabet, starting with 'p'.

3. A truth-functional proposition whose component statements are connected by the truth-functional operator 'and' is called a **conjunction,** and its component statements are called **conjuncts.** Conjunction is defined in such a way that it is true if and only if both conjuncts are true; otherwise it is false. In appropriate contexts, such words as 'but,' 'although,' 'yet,' and 'moreover' can operate truth-functionally in the same way as 'and'. A customary abbreviation for conjunction is the dot symbol '·'.

4. A **truth table** is an illustrative device which is used to display all of the possible combinations of truth values of propositions that could be substituted for the propositional variables in a given propositional schema. Truth tables can be used to define truth-functional operators in terms of an exhaustive list of the possible combinations of truth values in compound statements using a given truth-functional operation.

5. **Negation** is the logical operator which operates on a given proposition to form a new compound statement which has the opposite truth value from that proposition. The standard abbreviation for the negation operator is the curl or tilde symbol '~'. Sometimes it is possible to symbolize a given proposition as either an affirmative or a negative statement (*i.e.,* as either 'p' or '~p'). However, once a particular symbol has been assigned to a sentence in a given argument, the same symbol must be used for every other sentence in that argument which is being used to express the same proposition.

6. **Disjunction** or **alternation** is the logical operation which most closely corresponds to the connecting of two sentences by the word 'or'. The two sentences connected are **disjuncts** or **alternatives.** However, 'or' is used in two senses in ordinary English. In the **inclusive** sense, it asserts that either the first disjunct or the second *or both* may be true. An inclusive disjunction is true under all circumstances except when both disjuncts are false. In the **exclusive** sense, it asserts that the first or the second disjunct, *but not both,* may be true. An exclusive disjunction is true if and only if one disjunct is true and one is false. Because exclusive disjunction is stronger than inclusive disjunction, logicians always assume that 'or' in ordinary English is being used inclusively, unless there is strong evidence otherwise. The logical operator for *inclusive* disjunction is the wedge or 'vee' symbol '$\vee$'.

7. **Material implication,** symbolized by the horseshoe symbol '$\supset$', is an operation according to which the compound proposition is false if and only if the antecedent is true and the consequent is false. The symbol '$\supset$' is usually translated in terms of 'If . . . then . . .' sentences, or sentences with the form 'p implies q'. Sentences of the form 'If . . . then . . .' are *conditionals,* and in ordinary English they often suggest a causal relation which is absent from the horseshoe of material implication. The meaning of the horseshoe is given entirely in its truth table, and it asserts no relationship between the components other than that specified in the table.

8. **Material equivalence** is the logical operation which joins two propositions into a compound statement that is true if and only if the two components have the same truth value. The logical operator for material equivalence is the symbol '$\equiv$', which is best translated as 'if and only if'.

9. **Grouping** is the setting off of compound propositions within a larger compound in such a way that it is made clear to which variable or variables a particular operator applies. The **main operator** is that operator in a compound proposition that operates on all the component propositions.

10. There are three basic rules for constructing truth tables for schemata with more than one operator: (1) the truth table for a propositional schema should contain 2^n rows, where n is the number of propositional variables in the schema; (2) under the variables, T's and F's should be alternated in the column under the first variable, pairs of T's and F's in the column under the

second, sets of four **T**'s and four **F**'s in the column under the third, and so on; (3) the part of the truth table under the operators in the schema should be filled in with the appropriate truth values beginning from the "inside" of the parentheses out. The last operator under which the column is filled in is the **main operator,** and this column provides the truth-table definition of the schema.

11. Any two schemata with the same truth-table columns under their main operators are said to be **logically equivalent.** According to the **law of double negation,** whenever a negative sentence is itself negated the resulting statement is logically equivalent to the proposition with both negations removed. **De Morgan's Rules** state that the *negation of the disjunction* of two statements is logically equivalent to the *conjunction of the negations* of the same statements, and that the *negation of the conjunction* of two statements is logically equivalent to the *disjunction of the negations* of the same statements.

12. Two statements are **logically equivalent** if and only if, when they are connected by the symbol '≡', the column under that symbol contains only **T**'s. A sentence expressing a material equivalence is sometimes called a **biconditional** in that its first component materially implies the second, *and* the second materially implies the first.

13. A proposition is a **tautology** if and only if its schema has only **T**'s under the main operator in its truth table; that is, its logical form makes it *impossible* for it to be false. Two tautologies are the schema 'p ∨ ~p', which expresses the **law of excluded middle,** and also the schema '~(p · ~p)', which expresses the **law of noncontradiction.** Tautologies are **analytically true statements** in that their truth can be determined solely by an analysis of their logical form.

14. A **contradiction** is a statement whose schema has only **F**'s under the main operator in its truth table; that is, its logical form makes it *impossible* for it to be true. Contradictions are **analytically false statements** in that their falsity can be determined solely by an analysis of their logical form.

15. A contingent statement is one whose schema has both **T**'s and **F**'s under the main operator in its truth table. Contingent statements are neither analytically true nor analytically false; their truth or falsity must be determined by extralogical means.

CHAPTER SEVEN

Propositional Logic: Arguments

In the preceding chapter we were concerned only with the logical structure of individual truth-functional propositions. It was noted there that a truth-functional proposition is a compound statement which is such that, if we know the truth value of each of its component statements and the meanings of the logical operators, the truth or falsity of the compound statement can be determined. Thus, the truth-functional proposition 'It is not the case that George Washington was the third president of the U.S.' consists of the statement 'George Washington was the third president of the U.S.', a false proposition, and the logical operator 'It is not the case that'. Consequently, we know that this particular truth-functional proposition is true. Similarly, the proposition 'All men are mortal and all women are mortal' qualifies as a truth-functional proposition, since knowing the truth value of its component statements ('All men are mortal'; 'All women are mortal') and the meaning of its logical operator ('and'), we can determine the truth value of the compound statement.

An individual truth-functional proposition is not an argument, at least not in the sense in which we are using the term 'argument' in this book. It should be recalled from Chapter 2 that an argument is a set of statements such that one of them is implied or supported by the others. It was also pointed out that it is important to recognize that some sets of statements which are offered or intended in everyday contexts as arguments are not in fact arguments in our formal sense of the term. That is, some sets of statements which are asserted or apparently intended to be deductively valid or inductively strong are such that the supposed premises do not in fact imply or provide any support for the conclusion.

In this chapter we are going to be concerned primarily with learning methods for determining which sets of statements do in fact comprise deductively valid arguments—that is, arguments in which the premises imply or provide absolute support for the conclusion. To see why special methods are useful and sometimes even necessary for determining which arguments are valid, consider the following sets of sentences which are being asserted as arguments. Which in fact express deductively valid arguments?

1. *Either John is lying or Bill is lying.*
   It is not the case that John is lying.
   So, don't listen to Bill.

2. *If Juan's car is a Cadillac, then it burns a lot of gas.*
   But Juan's car is not a Cadillac.
   Therefore, Juan's car does not burn a lot of gas.

3. *If Michael passes his exams, then Susan will be happy.*
   If Scott gives Michael his notes, then Michael will pass his exams.
   Consequently, if Scott gives Michael his notes, Susan will be happy.

4. *John loves Mary and Tom loves Sue.*
   Either John will marry Mary or Tom will marry Sue.

The first of these sets of sentences cannot comprise an argument on the purely technical ground that its "conclusion" is a command, not a statement. If the last sentence were interpreted as expressing the same proposition as the sentence 'So, Bill is lying', it would then qualify as a deductively valid argument. Each of the sentences in the other three sets would normally express statements, but it is not easy to determine by inspection or intuition which if any of them expresses a deductively valid argument. In fact, only set 3 is a valid deductive argument, but this can best be demonstrated using methods and concepts of formal logic.

TRUTH-FUNCTIONAL VALIDITY   In this chapter, we will present two procedures for identifying valid arguments, that is, arguments whose premises provide absolute support for their conclusions. The basic definition of validity we are using is that an argument is valid if and only if it is such that if the premises are true then its conclusion must be true. As we noted in Chapter 2, a valid deductive argument may have true premises and a true conclusion, false premises and a true conclusion, or false premises and a false conclusion. The only situation excluded by the definition of validity is one in which there are true premises and a false conclusion.

For the moment, let us reconsider purported argument 2 which was presented above:

If Juan's car is a Cadillac, then it burns a lot of gas.
But Juan's car is not a Cadillac.
Therefore, Juan's car does not burn a lot of gas.

This "argument" is not valid, since the truth of the premises does not guarantee the truth of the conclusion. Even if both premises are true, the conclusion could still be false. For example, Juan might own a Jaguar with a V-12 engine which is even less efficient than a Cadillac, in which case both premises would be true and the conclusion false, making it not valid by our definition. Let us now reconsider argument 3 above:

> *If Michael passes his exams, then Susan will be*
> *happy.*
> *If Scott gives Michael his notes, then Michael will*
> *pass his exams.*
> *Consequently, if Scott gives Michael his notes, Susan*
> *will be happy.*

This is a valid deductive argument since *if* its premises are true, then its conclusion *must* be true. Whether Susan will be happy if Michael passes his exams, and whether Michael will pass his exams if Scott gives Michael his notes, the conclusion logically follows from the premises. In point of actual fact, the premises in this argument may be false and the conclusion may be false, or the premises and the conclusion may all be true; nevertheless, *if the premises are true, then the conclusion must be true.* The argument, therefore, is valid.

Contradictory Premises and Tautologous Conclusions

Implicit in our discussion of contradictions and tautologies at the end of the preceding chapter are two consequences which relate directly to the concept of validity. Given our definition of validity, any argument at least one of whose premises is a contradiction is necessarily valid. This is not as peculiar as it may first sound if one considers that validity only rules out a situation in which an argument is such that *all* of the premises are true and the conclusion is false. If one of the premises of an argument is a contradiction (that is, it is necessarily false), we can never have the situation in which *all* the premises are true and the conclusion is false. Thus, the argument *must* be valid. This is also the case with an argument which is such that the conjunction of two or more of its premises results in a contradiction. Any set of premises which is such that it is logically impossible for all of them to be true at the same time is said to be **inconsistent.** Thus, any argument with an inconsistent set of premises must be valid. Consider, for instance, the following:

> 5. *The Empire State Building is the world's tallest*
>   *building and the Empire State Building is not the*
>   *world's tallest building.*
>   *Therefore, the Sears Building is the world's*
>   *tallest building.*

> 6. *The Empire State Building is the world's tallest*
>   *building.*

> *The Empire State Building is not the world's*
> *tallest building.*
> *Therefore, the moon is made of green cheese.*

Each of these arguments is deductively valid. In argument 5, we have a false premise and a true conclusion, and in argument 6, inconsistent premises and a false conclusion, but this, of course, is permitted by our definition of validity. In short, for reasons that were explained in Chapter 6, a contradictory statement is always false, so it is impossible for an argument with a contradictory premise or an inconsistent set of premises to have all true premises and a false conclusion.

It should be noted here that, in a valid argument, the premises have to provide support for the conclusion only in a purely formal and very abstract sense. In the second argument, there is no conceptual relation whatsoever between the premises and the conclusion, but the argument still satisfies the formal logical definition of 'valid'.

The other consequence of our discussion at the end of Chapter 6 is related to the concept of a tautology, which is defined as a statement that is always true by virtue of its logical form. Given our definition of validity, any argument whose conclusion is a tautology must be valid. If the conclusion of any argument can only be true, then it is impossible for its premises to be true and its conclusion false. So the argument must be valid. Consider the following examples of arguments with tautological conclusions:

7. *The Hancock Building is the world's tallest*
   building.
   Therefore, either the Empire State Building is the
   world's tallest building or the Empire State
   Building is not the world's tallest building.

8. *George Washington had wooden false teeth.*
   Therefore, either the Empire State Building is the
   world's largest building, or the Empire State
   Building is not the world's largest building.

In argument 7, we have a false premise and a true conclusion, whereas in argument 8, we have a true premise and a true conclusion. Both arguments are valid since validity is ruled out only by an argument in which it is possible for the premises to be true and the conclusion false. Because an argument with a tautology as a conclusion must always have a true conclusion, it is impossible for the premises to be true and the conclusion false. Such arguments must be valid.

ABBREVIATING TRUTH-FUNCTIONAL ARGUMENTS

In Chapter 6, we saw that it was possible to abbreviate truth-functional propositions by using propositional constants and symbols for the various logical operators. For instance, the statement "Either John will hit a home run or the other team will win the game" can be abbreviated as:

$$A \lor B$$

where 'A' stands for the proposition 'John will hit a home run', '∨' stands for the logical operator 'or', and 'B' stands for the statement 'The other team will win the game'.

Just as it is possible to abbreviate individual truth-functional propositions, it is also possible to abbreviate a group of statements which comprise an argument. As noted earlier, we must make certain that we use different propositional constants to represent each different proposition and the same propositional constant to represent the same proposition whenever it occurs in the argument. Thus, we can abbreviate the argument

> **9.** *If <u>w</u>hales are fish, then <u>c</u>ats are herbivorous.*[1]
> *<u>C</u>ats are not herbivorous.*
> *Therefore, <u>w</u>hales are not fish.*

in this way:

$$W \supset C$$
$$\frac{\sim C}{\therefore \sim W}$$

In the argument abbreviation above, 'W ⊃ C' stands for the compound proposition 'If whales are fish, then cats are herbivorous'. More specifically, in this first premise, 'W' represents the proposition 'Whales are fish', '⊃' represents the material implication operator, and 'C' represents the proposition 'Cats are herbivorous'. The second premise, '∼C', is an abbreviation for the compound proposition 'Cats are not herbivorous' which consists of the negation operator ('It is not the case that') and the statement 'Cats are herbivorous'. The conclusion, '∼W', is the abbreviation for the compound proposition 'Whales are not fish', which is also composed of the negation operator and a simple proposition, 'Whales are fish'.

SCHEMATIZING TRUTH-FUNCTIONAL ARGUMENTS   Just as it is possible to display the form of a truth-functional compound statement by using propositional variables and symbols for logical operators, so, too, it is possible to schematize a truth-functional argument. Using our example from the previous section, we can remove all the propositional constants and replace them with different symbols, in the following way.

> .... ⊃ – – – – – – –
> ∼ – – – – – – –
> *Therefore,* ∼...............

---

[1] Throughout this chapter, we will continue to use the convention introduced in the previous chapter to the effect that the letter to be used in the abbreviation of a given sentence will be indicated by underscoring it in its original occurrence.

Notice that we have used the same type of blank in place of the same statement each time it appears in the argument, but that we have used different types of blanks in place of each different statement. Together, the schemata for all of the propositions produce an argument schema.

Just as a propositional schema displays the logical structure of a particular truth-functional proposition, an argument schema displays the logical form of an argument composed of several propositions. The symbols used in the argument schema above are blanks which are understood to be such that any *proposition* may be substituted into any blank, so long as the same proposition is substituted into every blank of a certain type. For instance, we can place the proposition 'The money is missing' in each occurrence of the blank symbolized by '................', and the proposition 'John is a crook' into each occurrence of the blank symbolized by '_ _ _ _ _ _ _ _'. Translating the logical operators into English, we get:

> *10.   If the money is missing, then John is a crook.*
> *John is not a crook.*
> *Therefore, the money is not missing.*

Argument 10 above has exactly the same form as argument 9 and also the same form as argument 2. For convenience, propositional variables, such as those used in schematizing particular truth-functional propositions, are also used to schematize truth-functional arguments. The same convention of using small letters, starting with p and working toward the end of the alphabet, is followed. Thus, the following schema represents the logical form of both arguments 9 and 10 and any other argument with the same form:

$$p \supset q$$
$$\underline{\sim q}$$
$$\therefore \sim p$$

The propositional variables—'p' and 'q'—represent blanks into which any particular statements can be substituted. The process of substituting actual propositions for the propositional variables results in a **substitution instance** or an **interpretation** of the argument schema. When we substituted the propositions 'The money is gone' and 'John is a crook' into the argument schema, we were creating a substitution instance.

We are not restricted to substituting *simple* propositions for propositional variables. We could just as well substitute *compound* propositions into these "blanks," as in the following example, which is a substitution instance of the same schema as that of arguments 9 and 10.

> *If either Tom or Ann gets an A in logic, then Sue will*
> *be happy and Ed will be angry.*
> *It is not the case that Sue will be happy and Ed will*
> *be angry.*
> *Therefore, it is not the case that either Tom or Ann*
> *gets an A in logic.*

In this substitution instance, the disjunction 'Tom or Ann gets an A in logic' was put into the blank in the schema represented by the variable 'p'. The conjunction 'Sue will be happy and Ed will be angry' has been substituted for the propositional variable 'q' in the argument schema.

When providing substitution instances of a particular argument schema, we are restricted in two ways. We can substitute only propositions for propositional variables, and we must substitute the same proposition[2] for *every* occurrence of any given variable in a particular argument schema. Thus, we could even substitute the same proposition for *every* occurrence of *every* variable in a given schema. For example, the following is also a substitution instance of the schema we have been using above:

> *If it is raining, then it is raining.*
> *It is not raining.*
> *Therefore, it is not raining.*

As we noted in Chapter 6, a propositional schema for a particular truth-functional proposition—for instance 'p ⊃ q', the first premise in the schema above—has no truth value until we provide a specific substitution instance for it. However, it is proper to say that an argument schema is valid or invalid. A valid argument is one such that, if the premises are true, then the conclusion must be true. The necessity of the 'must' is best explained in terms of the form of the argument, as displayed by the schema. An argument is valid if and only if no argument with the same form can have true premises and a false conclusion. Consequently, a **valid argument schema** can be defined as an argument schema for which there is no possible substitution instance (or interpretation) that would result in an argument with true premises and a false conclusion. Several methods have been constructed to test the validity of argument forms. One such method involves a variation of the method of truth tables which was introduced in Chapter 6.

EXERCISE 7–1   (a) *Write an abbreviation for each of the following truth-functional arguments. Be sure to provide a dictionary for each abbreviation, indicating the proposition which each propositional constant represents.* (b) *Write an argument schema for each argument.*

---

1. If it is raining, then the ground is getting wet.
    It is raining.
    Therefore, the ground is getting wet.

---

[2] It must be remembered from Chapter 1 that the same proposition can be expressed by different sentences and that the same sentence can be used to express different propositions. One must always be careful when dealing with arguments expressed in ordinary English not to symbolize them simply in terms of similarities among or differences between the sentences involved. It is the propositions being expressed which are of primary interest to the logician in identifying the *logical* (as opposed to the grammatical) form of arguments.

2. If it is raining, then the ground is getting wet.
   The ground is not getting wet.
   Therefore, it is not raining.

3. Either there are clouds in the sky or the sun is shining.
   The sun is not shining.
   Therefore, there are clouds in the sky.

4. Either the television set is not plugged in or it is not working.
   The television set is plugged in.
   Therefore, it is not working.

5. If that artifact is from the Stone Age, then it will not be made of metal.
   That artifact is made of metal.
   Therefore, it is not from the Stone Age.

6. If all dogs are carnivores, then Fido is a carnivore.
   All dogs are carnivores.
   Therefore, Fido is a carnivore.

7. If all dogs are carnivores, then Fido is a carnivore.
   Fido is not a carnivore.
   Therefore, it is not the case that all dogs are carnivores.

8. If the law of noncontradiction does not hold, then logical thought is not possible.
   Logical thought is possible.
   Therefore, the law of noncontradiction holds.

9. Either this chair is made of walnut or it is made of mahogany or it is made of teakwood.
   It is not made of walnut.
   Therefore, it is made of mahogany or teakwood.

10. If the gross national product has decreased for three straight quarters, then the country is in a recession.
    The gross national product has decreased for three straight quarters and unemployment is high.
    Therefore, the country is in a recession.

11. If that glass you are holding contains nitroglycerin and you are dropping the glass, then the nitroglycerin will explode.
    That glass you are holding contains nitroglycerin and you are dropping it.
    Therefore, the nitroglycerin will explode.

12. If either the fuse blows or there is an electric blackout, then none of the appliances in the kitchen will operate.
    There is an electric blackout.
    Therefore, none of the appliances in the kitchen will operate.

13. If we are going to the state park for a picnic, then we will take Johnny or Billy along.
    We are going to the state park for a picnic.
    Therefore, we will take Johnny or Billy along.

14.   If we are going to the state park for a picnic, then we will take Johnny and Billy along.
      We are going to the state park for a picnic.
      Therefore, we will take Johnny and Billy along.

15.   If we are going to the state park for a picnic and we are taking Johnny along, then we will take Billy along.
      We are going to the state park for a picnic and we are taking Johnny along.
      Therefore, we will take Billy along.

16.   If we are going to the state park for a picnic or we are taking Johnny along, then we will take Billy along.
      We are going to the state park for a picnic.
      Therefore, we will take Billy along.

17.   If we are going to the state park for a picnic or we are taking Johnny along, then we will take Billy along.
      We are taking Johnny along.
      Therefore, we will take Billy along.

18.   If Harry needs help painting, then either Joan will take time off from work or Tom will postpone writing his paper.
      Harry needs help painting.
      Therefore, either Joan will take time off from work or Tom will postpone writing his paper.

19.   If you put topspin on the cue ball, then it will follow the six ball into the pocket and you will scratch.
      You put topspin on the cue ball.
      Therefore, it will follow the six ball into the pocket and you will scratch.

20.   Either it is raining, or it is snowing, or sleet is falling.
      It is not raining.
      Therefore, either it is snowing or sleet is falling.

21.   If we are having a heavy rain, the sewers will be overloaded.
      If the sewers are overloaded, the basement will flood.
      We are having a heavy rain.
      Therefore, the basement will flood.

22.   Either it is snowing or sleet is falling.
      If it is snowing, then we will go sled riding.
      Sleet is not falling.
      Therefore, we will go sled riding.

23.   If it is snowing, then we will go sled riding.
      Either it is snowing or sleet is falling.
      We will not go sled riding.
      Therefore, sleet is falling.

24.   If sleet is falling, then we will not go sled riding.
      Either we will go sled riding or we will stay at home.

Sleet is falling.
Therefore, we will stay at home.

25. If it is raining and the wind blows, then water will get in the tent.
It is raining.
The wind is blowing.
Therefore, water will get in the tent.

26. If it is raining, then if it is getting cold, my car won't start.
It is raining and it is getting cold.
Therefore, my car won't start.

27. If snow is falling, then it is getting cold.
If it is getting cold, then my car won't start.
Snow is falling.
Therefore, my car won't start.

28. If Peter is playing piano and Bob is playing bass and Don is playing drums, then our regular combo is here.
Peter is playing piano.
Bob is playing bass.
Don is playing drums.
Therefore, our regular combo is here.

29. If Peter is playing piano and Bob is playing bass and Don is playing drums, then our regular combo is here.
Our regular combo is not here.
Therefore, either Peter is not playing piano, or Bob is not playing bass, or Don is not playing drums.

30. Either Peter is playing piano and Bob is playing bass and Don is playing drums, or else our regular combo is not here.
Our regular combo is here.
Therefore, Peter is playing piano and Bob is playing bass and Don is playing drums.

31. If the statement under discussion is an equivalence, then it contains an implication.
Either the statement under discussion is a disjunction or it is an equivalence.
The statement under discussion is not a disjunction.
Therefore, the statement under discussion contains an implication.

32. Either the statement under discussion is a disjunction or it is an equivalence.
If the statement under discussion is an equivalence, then it contains an implication.
The statement under discussion does not contain an implication.
Therefore, it is a disjunction.

33. The statement under discussion is either a conjunction or it is a disjunction.
It is either a conjunction or an implication.
If it is a disjunction, then it is not an implication.
Therefore, it is a conjunction.

34. The statement under discussion is either a truth-functional proposition or it is a command.

Handwritten annotations in margin:

30: (P • (B • D)) V ~C
C /∴ P • (B • D)
Tautology (Disj. Syllogism)

32: D V E
E ⊃ I   Tautology
~I
∴ D

(for 31:) (E, I, D)

Handwritten at bottom right:

6. G → T   2,3 H.S
7. ~T   4,5 M.P.
8. ~G   6,7 M.T.
9. (G v R)   1,5 M.P
10. R

34:
$T \lor C$
$T \supset P$
$P \supset L$
$\sim L \ /\therefore C$
Tautology

If it is a truth-functional proposition, then it is a compound proposition.
If it is a compound proposition, then it contains a logical operator.
The statement under discussion does not contain a logical operator.
Therefore, it is a command.

35. The statement under discussion is either a truth-functional proposition or it is a command.
If it is a truth-functional proposition, then it is a compound proposition.
If it is a compound proposition, then it contains a logical operator.
The statement under discussion is not a command.
Therefore, it contains a logical operator.

36:
$Y \supset C$ 5. $Y \supset V$ 1,2 DS
$C \supset V$ 6. $Y \supset R$ 5,3 □
$V \supset R$ 7. R 4,6 M.P.
$Y \ /\therefore R$
Tautology

36. If the Cheshire cat is yellow, it is colored.
If it is colored, it is visible.
If it is visible, it is real.
The Cheshire cat is yellow.
Therefore, it is real.

37. If the Cheshire cat is yellow, it is colored.
If it is colored, it is visible.
If it is visible, it is real.
The Cheshire cat is not real.
Therefore, it is not yellow.

38:
$R \lor \sim V$ Tautology
$V \lor \sim C$
$C \lor \sim Y$
$\sim R \ /\therefore \sim Y$

38. Either the Cheshire cat is real or it is not visible.
Either it is visible or it is not colored.
Either it is colored or it is not yellow.
The Cheshire cat is not real.
Therefore, it is not yellow.

1. $R \lor \sim V \rightarrow \sim V \lor R \rightarrow V \supset R$ }
2. $V \lor \sim C \rightarrow \sim C \lor V \rightarrow C \supset V$ }

$$\frac{C \supset V}{\frac{V \supset R}{C \supset R}} \qquad \frac{C \supset R}{\frac{\sim R}{\sim C \ (M.T.)}}$$

$$\frac{C \lor \sim Y}{\frac{\sim C}{\therefore \sim Y}}$$

39. Either the Cheshire cat is real or it is not visible.
Either it is visible or it is not colored.
Either it is colored or it is not yellow.
The Cheshire cat is yellow.
Therefore, it is real.

40:
1. $P \lor D$
2. $P \supset G$ Tautology
3. $D \supset F$
4. $\sim D \ /\therefore G$

40. Either Plato was an Athenian or Descartes was a Parisian.
If Plato was an Athenian, then he spoke Greek.
If Descartes was a Parisian, then he spoke French.
Descartes was not a Parisian.
Therefore, Plato spoke Greek.

5. $\sim P \supset D$ 1, m.I.
6. $\sim G \supset \sim P$ 2, Contrap.
7. ($\sim G \supset D$ H.S. 5,6
   $\sim D \ /\therefore \sim \sim G$ M.T. 4,7
9. G 8, D.N.

41. If Herb is a Hoosier, he is from Indiana.
If Herb is a Buckeye, he is from Ohio.
If Herb is either from Indiana or Ohio, he is a U.S. citizen.
Herb is either a Hoosier or a Buckeye.
Therefore, Herb is a U.S. citizen.

1. $P \supset (G \lor R)$
2. $G \supset S$
3. $S \supset T$
4. $P \supset \sim T$
5. $P \ /\therefore R$
6. ~~C⊃F~~

42. If Pete can come tonight, then either Gary or Ralph can come.
If Gary can come, then Sam can come.
If Sam can come, then Ted can come.
If Pete can come, then Ted cannot come.

6. $\sim T$ 4,5 M.P.   10. R 7,9 D.S.
8. $G \lor R$ 1,5 M.P.
8. $\sim S$ 3,6 M.T.
9. $\sim G$ 2,8 M.T.

Pete can come.
Therefore, Ralph can come.

43. Either we will have red wine for dinner or we will have white wine.
     If we have roast beef, then we will have red wine.
     Either we will have roast beef or we will have fillet of sole.
     If we have fillet of sole then we will have fruit salad for dessert.
     We will not have red wine for dinner.
     Therefore, we will have fillet of sole for dinner, and we will have white wine, and
     we will have fruit salad for dessert.

44. Either Preston or Quincy is a member of the Safari Club.
     If either Quincy or Randolph is a member, then Stuart is not.
     Either Stuart is a member or both Trumbull is a member and Randolph is not.
     Preston is not a member.
     Therefore, Quincy and Trumbull are both members.

45. If Preston is a member of the Safari club, then Quincy is a member; or else, if
     Randolph is a member, then Stuart is a member.
     If Preston is a member, then Randolph is a member, and if Trumbull is a member,
     then Stuart is not a member.
     Preston is a member.
     Therefore, Quincy, Randolph, and Trumbull are all members.

$1. (P \lor Q)$ ~~~~

$2. (Q \lor R) \supset \sim S$

$3. S \lor (T \cdot \sim R)$

$4. \sim P \quad \therefore \quad Q \cdot T$

$5. Q \qquad 1,4$ D. Syll.

$6. Q \lor R \quad 5$ addition

$7. \sim S \quad 2,6$ M.P.

$8. T \cdot \sim R \quad 3,7$ D. Syll,

$9. T \qquad 8,$ Simp.

$10. Q \cdot T \quad 5,9$ Adjunction

TESTING VALIDITY BY TRUTH TABLES

In Chapter 6 we were able to define the meaning of a particular logical operator by means of a truth table which displayed all possible combinations of truth values that could be substituted for the propositional variables used in a propositional schema containing that operator. We noted there that it is technically incorrect to construct a truth table for a specific proposition (such as 'Chicago is in Illinois and San Francisco is in California'), since each component proposition in such a compound proposition has a specific truth value, thereby making it inappropriate to display other possible combinations of truth values. For the same reason, it is technically incorrect to construct a truth table for a particular argument or argument abbreviation since each component proposition also has a specific truth value. It is only proper to construct truth tables for an argument schema.

Basically, the truth-table method for testing the validity of arguments requires that we construct a truth table for each premise and the conclusion of an argument schema. Let us do this using the argument schema discussed in the last two sections:

$$p \supset q$$
$$\underline{\sim q}$$
$$\therefore \sim p$$

We begin by setting up the table, providing a column for each propositional variable ('p' and 'q') and for each premise and the conclusion. We then fill in all possible combinations of truth values for the propositional variables, using the rules presented in Chapter 6.

	p	q	(PREMISE 1) p ⊃ q	(PREMISE 2) ~q	(CONCLUSION) ~p
(1)	T	T			
(2)	F	T			
(3)	T	F			
(4)	F	F			

We then fill in each column under the logical operators for each premise and the conclusion.

	p	q	(PREMISE 1) p ⊃ q	(PREMISE 2) ~q	(CONCLUSION) ~p
(1)	T	T	T	F	F
(2)	F	T	T	F	T
(3)	T	F	F	T	F
(4)	F	F	T	T	T

Once we have constructed the truth table, we must check to see if there is any row in which there are **T**'s under the main operator of *each* premise *and* an **F** under the main operator of the conclusion. If there is such a row, then the argument schema is invalid, since this shows that there exists a *possible* substitution instance in which there are true premises and a false conclusion. Examining each row in the truth table above, it becomes apparent that the argument is valid. Any specific argument with this form is valid. This particular argument schema is called **modus tollens,** and it is one we will use later when we present a different system for testing truth-functional validity.

A schema that is strikingly similar to that of the *modus tollens* schema, but which is deductively invalid, is known as *the fallacy of denying the antecedent.* An example of this schema is provided in the cartoon on the next page.

The intended argument can be formulated as follows:

> **If the dollar is in trouble, then the dime is in trouble.**
> **The dollar is not in trouble.**
> **Therefore, the dime is not in trouble.**

This can be proven invalid using the following truth table:

p	q	p ⊃ q	~p	~q
T	T	T	F	T
T	F	F	F	T
F	T	T	T	F
F	F	T	T	T

"*I, for one, am glad the dollar's out of trouble, because if the dollar's in trouble, then the dime is certainly in trouble.*"

Drawing by Dana Fradon; © 1971 The New Yorker Magazine, Inc.

The invalidity of this schema is demonstrated in the third row which shows that it is possible for both premises to be true while the conclusion is false.

For practice, let us test the validity of another truth-functional argument:

> **If John is intelligent, he will know what to do.**
> **John is intelligent.**
> **Therefore, he will know what to do.**

The abbreviation and schema for this argument are:

ABBREVIATION	SCHEMA
J ⊃ K	p ⊃ q
J	p
∴ K	∴ q

The truth table for this argument schema follows:

	p	q	(PREMISE 1) $p \supset q$	(PREMISE 2) p	(CONCLUSION) q
(1)	T	T	T	T	T
(2)	F	T	T	F	T
(3)	T	F	F	T	F
(4)	F	F	T	F	F

As we can see by checking the rows, the argument is valid since there is no row in which there are **T**'s under each premise and an **F** under the conclusion. This particular argument schema is called **modus ponens.**

Of course, this means that any substitution instance of this argument schema is valid, even one that involves the substitution of compound propositions for propositional variables, provided our other restrictions have been satisfied. Consider, for example, the following argument:

> *If Peter bought a new Cadillac and remodeled his home, then either he got a large bonus at work or his recently deceased uncle left him a large inheritance.*
> *Peter bought a new Cadillac and remodeled his home.*
> *Therefore, either he got a large bonus at work or his recently deceased uncle left him a large inheritance.*

Using our underscored letters as a dictionary, we may abbreviate the above argument schema as:

$$(C \cdot H) \supset (B \lor I)$$
$$\underline{C \cdot H}$$
$$\therefore B \lor I$$

Translating the propositional constants in the abbreviation into propositional variables, we get the following schema for the argument:

$$(p \cdot q) \supset (r \lor s)$$
$$\underline{p \cdot q}$$
$$\therefore r \lor s$$

The truth table below demonstrates that this is a truth-functionally valid argument schema.

	p	q	r	s	(PREMISE 1) (p · q) ⊃ (r ∨ s)			(PREMISE 2) p · q	(CONSLUSION) r ∨ s
(1)	T	T	T	T	T	T	T	T	T
(2)	F	T	T	T	F	T	T	F	T
(3)	T	F	T	T	F	T	T	F	T
(4)	F	F	T	T	F	T	T	F	T
(5)	T	T	F	T	T	T	T	T	T
(6)	F	T	F	T	F	T	T	F	T
(7)	T	F	F	T	F	T	T	F	T
(8)	F	F	F	T	F	T	T	F	T
(9)	T	T	T	F	T	T	T	T	T
(10)	F	T	T	F	F	T	T	F	T
(11)	T	F	T	F	F	T	T	F	T
(12)	F	F	T	F	F	T	T	F	T
(13)	T	T	F	F	T	F	F	T	F
(14)	F	T	F	F	F	T	F	F	F
(15)	T	F	F	F	F	T	F	F	F
(16)	F	F	F	F	F	T	F	F	F

Upon careful examination of the argument schema, it will become evident that it is possible to show that it is truth-functionally valid without considering all its component statements. In effect, the argument schema is the same as modus ponens; only compound statements rather than simple statements have been substituted for the propositional variables.

Another valid argument schema is that known as the **hypothetical syllogism,** which appears as follows.

$$p \supset q$$
$$\underline{q \supset r}$$
$$\therefore p \supset r$$

An example of an argument with this form is:

> *If you study hard, then you will get an A on all the exams.*
> *If you get an A on all the exams, then you will get an A in this course.*
> *Therefore, if you study hard, then you will get an A in this course.*

The validity of this schema, and thus of any argument which has the same logical form, is demonstrated by its truth table which has no row in which both premises have the value **T** and the conclusion has the value **F**.

p	q	r	(PREMISE 1) $p \supset q$	(PREMISE 2) $q \supset r$	(CONCLUSION) $p \supset r$
T	T	T	T	T	T
F	T	T	T	T	T
T	F	T	F	T	T
F	F	T	T	T	T
T	T	F	T	F	F
F	T	F	T	F	T
T	F	F	F	T	F
F	F	F	T	T	T

Let us consider the following intended argument and its corresponding schema to deepen our understanding of the truth table method.

> If George **W**ashington is a national hero, then
>   Thomas **J**efferson is a national hero.
> If Alexander **H**amilton is a national hero, then Aaron
>   **B**urr is a national hero.
> Either George **W**ashington is a national hero, or
>   Aaron **B**urr is a national hero.
> Therefore, either Thomas **J**efferson is a national
>   hero, or Alexander **H**amilton is a national hero.

The abbreviation and schema appear as:

$$W \supset J \qquad\qquad p \supset q$$
$$H \supset B \qquad\qquad r \supset s$$
$$\underline{W \vee B} \qquad\qquad \underline{p \vee s}$$
$$\therefore J \vee H \qquad\qquad \therefore q \vee r$$

Examining the truth table below, we can see that this schema is truth-functionally invalid. When the propositional variables 'p', 'q', and 'r' are assigned the truth value **F** and the propositional variable 's' is assigned the truth value **T**, there are true premises and a false conclusion. Such a situation is shown in row 8.

	p	q	r	s	(PREMISE 1) $p \supset q$	(PREMISE 2) $r \supset s$	(PREMISE 3) $p \vee s$	(CONCLUSION) $q \vee r$
(1)	T	T	T	T	T	T	T	T
(2)	F	T	T	T	T	T	T	T
(3)	T	F	T	T	F	T	T	T
(4)	F	F	T	T	T	T	T	T
(5)	T	T	F	T	T	T	T	T
(6)	F	T	F	T	T	T	T	T
(7)	T	F	F	T	F	T	T	F
(8)	F	F	F	T	T	T	T	F
(9)	T	T	T	F	T	F	T	T
(10)	F	T	T	F	T	F	F	T
(11)	T	F	T	F	F	F	T	T
(12)	F	F	T	F	T	F	F	T

	p	q	r	s	(PREMISE 1) p ⊃ q	(PREMISE 2) r ⊃ s	(PREMISE 3) p ∨ s	(CONCLUSION) q ∨ r
(13)	T	T	F	F	T	T	T	T
(14)	F	T	F	F	T	T	F	T
(15)	T	F	F	F	F	T	T	F
(16)	F	F	F	F	T	T	F	F

Limits of Truth-
Functional Validity
It is of the utmost importance to recognize that the methods of testing arguments for validity in this chapter have one serious limitation. Any arguments that the methods in this chapter prove to be valid are definitely valid. However, if we test an argument using one of these methods and it is not proved to be valid, it is still possible that the argument could be proved to be valid using one of the other methods presented elsewhere in this book. For this reason, it is always wise to qualify judgments based on the methods of this chapter with the preface 'truth-functional', especially with regard to invalidity. If an intended argument is truth-functionally invalid, it *may* in some cases be proved to be valid using a different logical system. To get a better idea of what this means, let us consider another example:

> *All politicians are liars.*
> *Mayor Jones is a politician.*
> *Therefore, Mayor Jones is a liar.*

None of the statements in this argument contains any truth-functional operators, so they cannot be broken into any simpler truth-functional components. Also, each premise is a different proposition, and the conclusion is a different proposition. Thus, the abbreviation of this argument in truth-functional logic must consist of three different constants. The abbreviation and schema of this particular argument are:

$$\frac{\begin{array}{c}P\\J\end{array}}{\therefore L} \qquad \frac{\begin{array}{c}p\\q\end{array}}{\therefore r}$$

Following is a truth table for the above argument schema:

	p	q	r	(PREMISE 1) p	(PREMISE 2) q	(CONCLUSION) r
(1)	T	T	T	T	T	T
(2)	F	T	T	F	T	T
(3)	T	F	T	T	F	T
(4)	F	F	T	F	F	T
(5)	T	T	F	T	T	F
(6)	F	T	F	F	T	F
(7)	T	F	F	T	F	F
(8)	F	F	F	F	F	F

This cartoon provides an example of an argument which is deductively valid but which is very difficult to formulate in a way which makes it truth-functionally valid. For example, the following formulation can be proved valid using other methods, but is invalid using the methods of truth-functional logic.

> **If a beautiful woman kisses this frog, it will turn back into a prince.**
> **This woman kissed the frog and it did not turn back into a prince.**
> **Therefore, this woman is not beautiful.**

Can you reformulate this argument in a form which can be shown to be deductively valid using truth tables?

Once again we check the rows to see if there is any in which there are T's under the main operator of each premise and an **F** under the main operator of the conclusion. According to the truth table, this argument is invalid. In row 5, there are T's under the premises and an **F** under the conclusion. Now if you have already studied the syllogistic logic presented in Chapters 4 and 5, you probably know that the argument presented above ('All politicians are liars') is a valid syllogism. (Its validity also should be apparent on an intuitive level.) Why then does its truth table show it to be invalid?

The truth table indeed *proves* that the argument is *truth-functionally invalid*. But this should only be interpreted to mean that it is impossible to prove that the argument is valid using the truth-functional logic we have presented in this and the preceding chapter. Because this or any other argument has been shown to be truth-functionally invalid does not mean that it cannot be proved to be valid using the system of syllogistic logic presented in Chapter 5, and/or also using the system of quantificational logic presented in Chapter 9.

EXERCISE 7–2   *Test the truth-functional validity of each of the following argument schemata by the truth-table method.*

---

1. $p \cdot q$
     $\therefore p$

2. $q \supset p$
     $\therefore \sim p \supset \sim q$

3. $q \supset p$
     $\therefore \sim q \supset \sim p$

4. $p \supset q$
     $\therefore p \supset (p \cdot q)$

5. $(p \supset q) \supset (p \lor q)$
     $\therefore (p \lor q) \supset (q \lor p)$

6. $q \supset p$
     $\therefore p \supset (p \cdot q)$

7. $p \lor q$
     $\sim p$
     $\therefore q$

8. $p \lor q$
     p
     $\therefore \sim q$

9. $p \lor q$
     $\therefore q$

10. p
     $\therefore p \lor q$

11. q
     $\therefore p \cdot q$

12. $q \lor r$
     $p \supset q$
     $\therefore p \supset r$

13. $p \supset q$
     $p \supset r$
     $\therefore q \lor r$

14. $p \supset \sim q$
     $(q \cdot r) \lor p$
     $\therefore \sim q$

15. $p \supset q$
     $p \lor r$
     $\sim r$
     $\therefore q$

16. $p \supset (q \supset r)$
     $\sim r \lor \sim q$
     $\therefore p$

17. $p \supset q$
     $q \supset r$
     $\therefore p \supset r$

18. $(p \supset q) \cdot (r \supset s)$
     $\therefore p \supset q$

19. $p \supset (q \cdot r)$
      $(q \lor r) \supset \sim p$
      $\therefore \sim p$

20. $p \supset q$
      $q \supset r$
      $\sim r$
      $\therefore \sim p$

21. $p \supset q$
      $p \supset r$
      $\sim r$
      $\therefore \sim q$

22. $p \supset q$
      $p \lor r$
      $\sim p$
      $\therefore q$

23. $p \supset q$
      $p \lor r$
      $\sim q$
      $\therefore r$

24. $p \supset (q \supset r)$
      $p \supset q$
      $\therefore r$

25. $\sim q$
      $q \supset r$
      $\therefore r$

26. $(p \cdot q) \supset (p \lor r)$
      $p \lor r$
      $\therefore p \cdot q$

27. $p \supset q$
      $\sim p$
      $\therefore \sim q$

28. $p \supset q$
      $q \supset r$
      p
      $\therefore r$

29. $p \supset q$
      $r \cdot p$
      $\therefore q \lor r$

30. $p \supset (q \supset r)$
      $q \supset (p \supset r)$
      $\therefore (p \lor q) \supset r$

31. $(p \cdot q) \supset r$
      $p \cdot \sim r$
      $\therefore \sim q$

32. $p \supset q$
      $\sim (q \cdot \sim r)$
      $\therefore p \supset r$

33. $p \supset (q \supset r)$
      $p \supset q$
      $\therefore q \supset r$

34. $p \supset (q \supset r)$
      $p \supset q$
      $\therefore p \supset r$

35. $\sim p \supset (q \cdot r)$
      $\sim r$
      $\therefore p$

36. $p \lor (\sim q \cdot r)$
      $q \supset \sim p$
      $\therefore \sim q$

37. $p \supset q$
      $p \supset (q \supset r)$
      $q \supset (r \supset s)$
      $\therefore p \supset s$

38. $(p \lor q) \supset (p \cdot q)$
      $\sim (p \cdot q)$
      $\therefore \sim (p \lor q)$

39. $(\sim p \lor q) \supset r$
      $\sim r$
      $\therefore \sim p$

40. $(p \cdot q) \supset (r \lor s)$
      $r \supset p$
      $\sim r \lor \sim s$
      q
      $\therefore p \supset s$

Short Truth-Table Method   Truth tables provide a mechanical decision procedure by which we can test the truth-functional validity of an argument in a finite number of steps. However, as the number of propositional variables within a particular argument schema increases, the number of rows increases rapidly according to the formula 2^n, as we indicated in the previous chapter. An argument with two variables needs four rows (2^2), an argument with three variables needs eight rows (2^3), an argument with four variables needs sixteen rows (2^4), and so on. Of course, as the number of variables and premises in an argument increases, the number of columns necessary for the truth table also increases.

As we have just seen, when using a truth table to test an argument for truth-functional validity, we check to see if there is a situation in which the conclusion has an **F** under its main operator and the premises all have **T**'s under their main operators. If such a situation exists, then we know that the argument schema is truth-functionally invalid. The short truth-table method is based on this concept insofar as it involves an attempt to identify just one row with all true premises and a false conclusion. In using this method, we begin by assigning an **F** to the conclusion, and then backtrack to see if it is possible to assign the appropriate truth values to the component statements such that all the premises of the argument can be true while the conclusion is false. If we succeed, we have proved that the argument is truth-functionally invalid. The shortened truth-table method saves considerable time and energy since it is no longer necessary to construct elaborate truth tables with numerous rows and columns. However, because it is easy to make mistakes, we recommend that the shortened truth-table method should be used only to prove the truth-functional *invalidity* of an intended argument. A complete truth table should be constructed to prove an argument valid, or else the method of deductive proof that will be discussed later in this chapter can be used to prove validity. Let us reconsider the last example in the preceding section which had the schema:

$$p \supset q$$
$$r \supset s$$
$$\underline{p \lor s}$$
$$\therefore q \lor r$$

We begin our shortened truth table by laying out columns for each variable, all premises, and the conclusion of the argument as follows:

p q r s	(PREMISE 1) p ⊃ q	(PREMISE 2) r ⊃ s	(PREMISE 3) p ∨ s	CONCLUSION q ∨ r

We place an **F** under the main operator of the conclusion as shown below, since we are seeking to recreate a situation in which the premises are true and the conclusion false, if such a situation exists. For 'q ∨ r' to be false, both its components must be false. We therefore put **F**'s under each occurrence of the variables 'q' and 'r'.

p q r s	(PREMISE 1) p ⊃ q	(PREMISE 2) r ⊃ s	(PREMISE 3) p ∨ s	CONCLUSION q ∨ r
F F	F	F		F F F

Starting with the premise 'If money is God, then Stanley will defeat the giant', construct an argument based on this cartoon and test it for validity using the short truth-table method.

Given the truth values of 'q' and 'r', we then seek to assign to the variables 'p' and 's' those truth values that will make all the premises of the argument true, while the conclusion is false. If we assign the truth value **F** to the variable 'p' and the truth value **T** to the variable 's', all the premises of the argument take the value **T** as shown in the short truth table below.

p q r s	(PREMISE 1) p ⊃ q	(PREMISE 2) r ⊃ s	(PREMISE 3) p ∨ s	(CONCLUSION) q ∨ r
F F F T	F T F	F T T	F T T	F F F

Thus, we have succeeded in proving that the above argument schema is truth-functionally invalid since we have constructed a case in which all the premises are true and the conclusion is false. We have also done this without the need to fill in truth values for sixteen different rows as we did in the preceding section. If the conclusion had been a conjunction instead of a disjunction, there would have been three different assignments of truth values to 'p' and 'q', which would have made the conclusion false. Also, as the number of variables in an argument increases and as the premises and conclusion of an argument become more complex, using the shortened truth-table method becomes less practicable. When dealing with such arguments, it may be necessary to "play" with the short truth-table method. For instance, you might make some premises true and then determine whether on the basis of the truth values assigned to various component statements it is possible to create a false conclusion. Practice is the only way to learn when it is easier to use the short method and when the regular method would be at least as easy.

EXERCISE 7–3   *Using the short truth-table method, prove the invalidity of each of the following argument schemata.*

1. p ⊃ q   *p = F*
    q ⊃ r   *→ T*
    ∴ q ∨ r   *q r = f*

2. p ⊃ q
    q ⊃ r   *r = T, p = F, q = T or F*
    ∴ r ⊃ p   *q = F, p = F*

3. p ⊃ (q · r)   *, p = F*
    ~p
    ∴ ~r   *r = T*

4. p ⊃ (q ∨ r)
    (q · r) ⊃ s
    ∴ p ⊃ s

P	q	r	s
T	F	T	F
T	T	F	F

5. p · q
    p ∨ r
    ∴ r

6. p ⊃ q
    p ∨ r
    ∴ q

P	q	r
F	F	T

7. $p \supset q$
    $p \lor r$
    $\therefore q \supset \sim r$

8. $p \supset q$
    $p \lor r$
    $\therefore q \lor \sim r$

    $p \quad q \quad r$
    $F \quad F \quad T$

9. $p \supset (q \lor r)$
    $\sim q$
    $\therefore r \supset p$

10. $p \supset (q \lor r)$
    $(q \cdot r) \supset \sim p$
    $\therefore \sim p$

    $p \quad q \quad r$
    $T \quad F \quad T$
    $T \quad T \quad F$

11. $p \supset (q \lor r)$
    $q \supset s$
    p
    $\therefore r \supset s$

12. $(p \cdot q) \supset r$
    $r \supset s$
    $(p \cdot s) \supset q$
    $\therefore \sim r \lor q$

    $p \quad q \quad r \quad s$
    $F \quad F \quad T \quad T$

13. $p \supset (q \supset r)$
    p
    $\therefore r$

14. $p \supset q$
    $q \supset r$
    $\therefore p \cdot r$

    $p \quad q \quad r$
    $F \quad F \quad T$
    $F \quad F \quad F$
    $T \quad T$

15. $(p \supset r) \cdot (s \supset t)$
    $r \lor t$
    $\therefore p \lor s$

16. $(p \supset q) \lor (q \supset r)$
    $p \lor q$
    $\therefore q \cdot r$

    $p \quad q \quad r$
    $T \quad F \quad F$
    $T \quad F \quad T$
    $T \quad T \quad F$
    $F \quad T \quad F$

17. $p \supset q$
    $r \supset s$
    $\therefore (p \lor q) \supset (r \cdot s)$

18. $p \supset ((q \cdot r) \lor (s \cdot t))$
    $q \supset \sim (s \cdot t)$
    $\therefore p \supset \sim (q \cdot r)$

    $p \quad q \quad r \quad s \quad t$
    $T \quad T \quad T \quad F \quad T$
    $T \quad T \quad T \quad T \quad F$
    $T \quad T \quad T \quad F \quad F$
    F

TRUTH-FUNCTIONAL ARGUMENTS AND CORRESPONDING CONDITIONALS

In this chapter, we have been concerned thus far with testing the truth-functional validity and/or invalidity of arguments by means of truth tables or short truth tables. An important logical relationship— that between truth-functional arguments and their corresponding conditionals—has not been touched upon, and it is to this subject that we now turn. For every truth-functional argument, it is possible to construct a corresponding conditional statement. We saw in our discussion of material implication in Chapter 6 that a conditional statement is an 'if . . . then . . .' statement such that it is false if and only if its antecedent is true and its consequent is false. A **corresponding conditional** to a truth-functional argument is defined as a material implication whose antecedent consists of the conjunction of the premises of that argument and whose consequent is the conclusion of that argument. For example, consider the following argument:

> *Either Pat will pass this course or she will be*
> *ineligible for the varsity basketball team.*
> *Pat will not pass this course.*
> *Therefore, she will be ineligible for the varsity*
> *basketball team.*

The schema for this argument is:

$$p \lor q$$
$$\underline{\sim p}$$
$$\therefore q$$

We can create a corresponding conditional for this argument by conjoining its premises into the antecedent of a conditional statement, and using its conclusion as the consequent of the conditional, the schema of which is shown here:

$$((p \lor q) \cdot \sim p) \supset q$$

Using the phrasing of the original argument, its corresponding conditional would read:

> *If either Pat will pass this course or she will be ineligible for the varsity basketball team, and Pat will not pass this course, then she will be ineligible for the varsity basketball team.*

Of course, this corresponding conditional does not say precisely the same thing as the original argument. The corresponding conditional is only one compound statement, whereas the argument is composed of several statements. Also, the conditional is just that—the conclusion is asserted to be true only *on the condition* that the premises are true. In contrast to the corresponding argument, the conditional only asserts that, *if* the premises are true, then the conclusion is true. In the argument, the premises are asserted to be true; they are not hypothesized. However, a significant logical relationship exists between any truth-functional argument and its corresponding conditional statement. *If a truth-functional argument is valid, then its corresponding conditional is a tautology, and vice versa.* Let us first check to see if the argument schema above, known as the **disjunctive syllogism,** is truth-functionally valid by means of its truth table.

	p	q	(PREMISE 1) p ∨ q	(PREMISE 2) ~p	(CONCLUSION) q
(1)	T	T	T	F	T
(2)	F	T	T	T	T
(3)	T	F	T	F	F
(4)	F	F	F	T	F

From the truth table, it is obvious that the disjunctive syllogism is valid, since there is no row in which there is an **F** under the conclusion and **T**'s under both premises. Let us now construct a truth table for the corresponding conditional to this argument schema.

	p	q	((p ∨ q)	·	~p)	⊃	q
(1)	T	T	T	F	F	T	
(2)	F	T	T	T	T	T	
(3)	T	F	T	F	F	T	
(4)	F	F	F	F	T	T	

Examining column 4, we can see that there are all T's under the horseshoe, indicating that the statement is, in fact, a tautology.

Let us consider another argument schema and test its corresponding conditional to determine whether it is a tautology. Of course, if it is not a tautology, we know that the corresponding argument schema is truth-functionally invalid. The argument schema shown below is known as the **constructive dilemma**.

$$(p \supset q) \cdot (r \supset s)$$
$$\underline{p \lor r}$$
$$\therefore q \lor s$$

The corresponding conditional for this argument schema is:

$$(((p \supset q) \cdot (r \supset s)) \cdot (p \lor r)) \supset (q \lor s)$$

and its truth table appears as follows:

	p	q	r	s	(((p ⊃ q)	·	(r ⊃ s))	·	(p ∨ r))	⊃	(q ∨ s)
(1)	T	T	T	T	T	T	T	T	T	T	T
(2)	F	T	T	T	T	T	T	T	T	T	T
(3)	T	F	T	T	F	F	T	F	T	T	T
(4)	F	F	T	T	T	T	T	T	T	T	T
(5)	T	T	F	T	T	T	T	T	T	T	T
(6)	F	T	F	T	T	T	T	F	F	T	T
(7)	T	F	F	T	F	F	T	F	T	T	T
(8)	F	F	F	T	T	T	T	F	F	T	T
(9)	T	T	T	F	T	F	F	F	T	T	T
(10)	F	T	T	F	T	F	F	F	T	T	T
(11)	T	F	T	F	F	F	F	F	T	T	F
(12)	F	F	T	F	T	F	F	F	T	T	F
(13)	T	T	F	F	T	T	T	T	T	T	T
(14)	F	T	F	F	T	T	T	F	F	T	T
(15)	T	F	F	F	F	F	T	F	T	T	F
(16)	F	F	F	F	T	T	T	F	F	T	F

We can see that the statement is a tautology, since the column under its main operator contains all T's. This means that the argument schema known as the constructive dilemma is valid.

THE PROPOSITIONAL CALCULUS   As we have seen, the truth-table method described above provides a mechanical decision procedure by which to test the truth-functional validity of an argument. By the use of truth tables, the truth-functional validity or invalidity of any argument can be determined in a finite number of mechanical steps. However, suppose we had to test the validity of the following argument schema:

$$p \supset q$$
$$q \supset r$$
$$r \supset s$$
$$s \supset t$$
$$t \supset u$$
$$u \supset v$$
$$v \supset w$$
$$w \supset x$$
$$\underline{x \supset z}$$
$$\therefore p \supset z$$

Using truth tables to test this schema would require some 1,024 rows (2^{10})—hardly a very practicable arrangement. How might such an argument schema be tested for validity without requiring such an enormous amount of time and energy? The short truth-table method could perhaps be used; but this particular schema is valid, and we should follow our rule of thumb which recommends that the short truth-table method be used only to prove truth-functional invalidity. But there is another, simpler method to prove the validity of such arguments or argument schemata; this is called the **method of deductive proof.**

It is possible to construct a deductive proof system consisting of a set of rules and procedures which enable us to prove the validity of a deductive argument schema in step-by-step fashion. Since such deductive systems, in effect, allow us to "calculate" the validity of an argument at the propositional (truth-functional) level, they are sometimes referred to as **propositional calculi.**

Most deductive proof systems do not provide us with a decision procedure; that is, they do not offer a mechanical procedure such that, after a finite number of steps, we are sure to have a proof that a particular argument is truth-functionally valid or invalid. *Thus, if, when using such a system, we are unsuccessful in proving the validity of an argument, this does not mean that we have proven it to be invalid; it simply means that we have not been successful in proving its validity.* Although it is possible to construct a deductive system which does give us a decision procedure for determining truth-functional validity, we will not use such a system here. Instead, we shall present a system that provides us with a foundation for later constructing proofs for a more sophisticated type of argument—a type for which it has been shown to be theoretically impossible to provide a decision procedure.

The fundamental procedure underlying any deductive proof system is the use of a small number of rules or axioms, which are such that, when they are used in conjunction with the premises of a valid argument, it can be shown that, if all the premises are true, then the truth of the conclusion logically follows. The basic rules or axioms are such that it is inappropriate to ask that their validity (or, in some cases, their truth) be proved within the system itself.[3] In effect, we are using the rules of the deductive system in conjunction with the premises of a particular valid argument to draw out and make explicit the conclusion that was already implicitly contained in those premises.

Constructing a Formal Proof   Let us consider how we may construct a formal proof, using as our example the complex argument which was introduced at the beginning of this section. The schema for this argument reappears in slightly altered form below.

1.	p ⊃ q	*Premise*
2.	q ⊃ r	*Premise*
3.	r ⊃ s	*Premise*
4.	s ⊃ t	*Premise*
5.	t ⊃ u	*Premise*
6.	u ⊃ v	*Premise*
7.	v ⊃ w	*Premise*
8.	w ⊃ x	*Premise*
9.	x ⊃ z/∴p ⊃ z	*Premise/conclusion*

Notice that what we have done is list the schemata in order of their appearance in the original argument, numbering them consecutively and labeling each as a premise in the column on the right. The last line contains the last premise schema, a slash, the symbol for 'therefore', and the conclusion; in the right-hand column we have indicated that both a premise *and* the conclusion appear on this line. In the construction of a formal proof, this procedure for presenting the premises and conclusion of an argument should always be employed.

Earlier, we considered an argument schema we called 'hypothetical syllogism' and proved it valid by means of a truth table. We will now use the hypothetical syllogism as a basic deductive rule or axiom, to aid in proving the truth-functional validity of the argument schema above. It will be recalled that the schema for the rule of hypothetical syllogism is:

$$\frac{\begin{array}{c} p \supset q \\ q \supset r \end{array}}{\therefore p \supset r}$$

---

[3] Their validity can be proved using the method of truth tables, although some logicians consider their validity to be "intuitively obvious," and, thus, to not require any proof at all.

Using this schema as a deductive rule, we can deduce from lines 1 and 2 of the argument schema that 'p ⊃ r'. We write this information beneath line 9, as shown here:

1.	p ⊃ q	*Premise*
2.	q ⊃ r	*Premise*
3.	r ⊃ s	*Premise*
4.	s ⊃ t	*Premise*
5.	t ⊃ u	*Premise*
6.	u ⊃ v	*Premise*
7.	v ⊃ w	*Premise*
8.	w ⊃ x	*Premise*
9.	x ⊃ z ∴ p ⊃ z	*Premise/conclusion*
10.	p ⊃ r	*H.Syll., 1,2*

Note that we have numbered the line, written out the full schema we have deduced, and indicated at the right both the schemata from which this conclusion was deduced and the abbreviation of the rule (H. Syll. for hypothetical syllogism) by which we justify the deduction. The statement schema on line 10 then becomes part of the proof. We may use it to deduce other schemata, just as we may use any line of the original argument schema. Why is this possible? Since we know that the statement 'p ⊃ r' follows validly from lines 1 and 2, we know that if the premises are true then the statement with the schema 'p ⊃ r' must also be true. In other words, the truth of the original premises is being transmitted to this new premise. Since line 10 follows deductively from lines 1 and 2, the truth of the original premises is necessarily transmitted to the statement with the schema 'p ⊃ r'.

We still have not proved this particular argument schema to be valid, although we are clearly on the right track. It should be fairly obvious that using 'p ⊃ r' (our deduced schema) and 'r ⊃ s' (line 3 of the original argument schema), we can deduce 'p ⊃ s', as:

$$\begin{array}{c} p \supset r \\ \underline{r \supset s} \\ \therefore p \supset s \end{array}$$

One might object that this argument schema is not the same as that represented by the hypothetical syllogism schema four paragraphs back, since the present schema contains the variables 'p', 'r', and 's', whereas the hypothetical syllogism schema has the variables 'p', 'q', and 'r'. The objection, however, does not hold. A variable, it will be recalled, functions as a blank into which any particular statement can be inserted, so long as the same statement is substituted for the same variable every time it appears in a particular argument schema. Thus, if we substituted, in the previous argument schema, the statement 'Mary gets that job' for the variable 'p', the statement 'She will be happy' for the variable 'r', and the statement 'Her husband will be happy' for the variable 's', we would get the following argument:

> *If Mary gets that job, then she will be happy.*
> *If she is happy, then her husband will be happy.*
> *Therefore, if Mary gets that job, her husband will be*
>   *happy.*

If we return to our original formulation of the hypothetical syllogism and substitute the statement 'Mary gets that job' for 'p', 'She will be happy' for 'q', and 'Her husband will be happy' for 'r', we will get exactly the same argument. This illustrates how two argument schemata can be logically identical, even if they contain different variables. To clarify the point, consider the following three argument schemata, the third of which uses a new set of symbols as variables.

$$
\begin{array}{ccc}
p \supset q & r \supset s & \triangle \supset \bigcirc \\
\underline{r \supset q} & \underline{s \supset t} & \underline{\bigcirc \supset \square} \\
\therefore p \supset r & \therefore r \supset t & \therefore \triangle \supset \square
\end{array}
$$

The schema at the left is not the same as the one we call 'hypothetical syllogism'. Although it contains three material implication schemata and three propositional variables, the variables are not distributed in the same positions as in the hypothetical syllogism schema. However, the variables in the schemata in the middle and to the right are distributed exactly as they are in the hypothetical syllogism schema. The validity of the argument is due to its form, not to the particular variables used to display that form.

To continue constructing our formal proof of the argument schema under discussion, we add this new schema to our list, also providing the justification for it, as shown below:

1.	$p \supset q$	*Premise*
2.	$q \supset r$	*Premise*
3.	$r \supset s$	*Premise*
4.	$s \supset t$	*Premise*
5.	$t \supset u$	*Premise*
6.	$u \supset v$	*Premise*
7.	$v \supset w$	*Premise*
8.	$w \supset x$	*Premise*
9.	$x \supset z / \therefore p \supset z$	*Premise/conclusion*
10.	$p \supset r$	*H.Syll., 1,2*
11.	$p \supset s$	*H.Syll., 10,3*

Notice that for our justification we have used line 10 (a validly deduced intermediary statement) and line 3 (a premise of the original argument) and the inference rule hypothetical syllogism. It should now be obvious that by continuing to use the hypothetical syllogism in the same manner we will ultimately reach the conclusion of the original argument. The full proof is shown below:

1.	$p \supset q$	*Premise*
2.	$q \supset r$	*Premise*
3.	$r \supset s$	*Premise*
4.	$s \supset t$	*Premise*
5.	$t \supset u$	*Premise*
6.	$u \supset v$	*Premise*
7.	$v \supset w$	*Premise*
8.	$w \supset x$	*Premise*
9.	$x \supset z / \therefore p \supset z$	*Premise/conclusion*
10.	$p \supset r$	*H.Syll., 1,2*
11.	$p \supset s$	*H.Syll., 10,3*
12.	$p \supset t$	*H.Syll., 11,4*
13.	$p \supset u$	*H.Syll., 12,5*
14.	$p \supset v$	*H.Syll., 13,6*
15.	$p \supset w$	*H.Syll., 14,7*
16.	$p \supset x$	*H.Syll., 15,8*
17.	$p \supset z$	*H.Syll., 16,9*

The schema in line 17 ('$p \supset z$') is identical to the conclusion of the original argument schema. The final line of any deductive proof must be the conclusion of the original argument, if the proof is to demonstrate the validity of the argument schema.[4]

We have thus proved the validity of this argument schema in eight steps, using only one rule—a considerable saving of effort when compared to the 20,480 steps that would be required to construct a truth table for this particular schema.

Of course, one rule alone would not provide us with a very useful deductive proof system. In fact, when setting out to construct such a system, we have a multiplicity of options since the number of rules we choose to include within the system is somewhat arbitrary. Logicians have demonstrated that it is theoretically possible to have an adequate system of deductive proof with as few as three rules. However, such a system has its shortcomings since the fewer the rules, the greater the number of steps necessary to prove the truth-functional validity of most argument schemata. On the other hand, it would be possible to construct a system with a thousand or more rules, enabling us to test the truth-functional

---

[4] It is important to note that although it is inappropriate to construct truth tables for arguments or argument abbreviations (truth tables should only be constructed for schemata), it is permissible to construct deductive proofs using abbreviations rather than schemata. This is because our rules are applicable to all substitution instances of a given schema. It is only for reasons of stylistic consistency that all of the deductive proofs in this chapter are presented in terms of schemata rather than abbreviations. The use of abbreviations in the proofs would have been at least as appropriate from a logical standpoint.

validity of many complex arguments in a single step. However, such a system would be as inconvenient as one consisting of only three rules since we would be required to have facility with all the rules and would sometimes have to go through literally hundreds of rules to find the appropriate one for a particular proof. Consequently, we are faced with something of a pragmatic dilemma. The obvious solution is to compromise. The system we will employ consists of twenty rules and thus is relatively easy to use. It is also deductively complete: that is, any argument which can be proven truth-functionally valid using truth tables can be proven truth-functionally valid using this system's rules and procedures.

INFERENCE RULES   The rules of our system are known as **rules of inference.** Rules of inference are essentially basic argument schemata which can be proved valid using the truth-table method. We have already proved four of the inference rules in this way—modus tollens, modus ponens, hypothetical syllogism, and constructive dilemma. These and four other inference rules are presented below, with the standard abbreviations for their names. (Notice that two of the rules—disjunctive syllogism and simplification—have two variations each.)

[handwritten: don't forget principle of substitution!]

Modus tollens (M.T.)

p ⊃ q
~q
∴ ~p

Modus ponens (M.P.)

p ⊃ q
p
∴ q

Hypothetical syllogism (H.Syll.)

p ⊃ q
q ⊃ r
∴ p ⊃ r

Constructive dilemma (Dil.)

(p ⊃ q) · (r ⊃ s)
p ∨ r
∴ q ∨ s

Disjunctive syllogism (D.Syll.)

p ∨ q   p ∨ q
~p   ~q
∴ q   ∴ p

Simplification (Simp.)

p · q   p · q
∴ p   ∴ q

Conjunction (Conj.)

p
q
∴ p · q

Addition (Add.)

p
∴ p ∨ q

[handwritten: Valid Conj. Syll. ~(P·Q) P ∴ ~Q]

[handwritten: (P⊃Q)·(R⊃S) ~Q ∨ ~S ∴ ~P ∨ ~R]

The four rules we have not previously examined can easily be shown to be valid by the truth-table method, as was done with modus tollens, modus ponens, hypothetical syllogism, and constructive dilemma. These argument schemata are said to be "basic" because each is a fundamental valid argument form which can be used to construct a formal proof for other, more complex, truth-functional arguments (and also because we will regard as inappropriate any effort to prove the validity of any one of them using the other rules). A **formal proof** is the process (or result of the process) whereby the conclusion of an argument can be validly derived from a set of statements, each one of which either is a premise of the original argument or has been validly deduced using the rules of the system from the premises and/or other statements which have themselves been validly deduced using the rules of the system.

We sometimes encounter a complex argument which is really nothing more than a substitution instance of a particular inference-rule argument schema. For example, consider the following argument:

> *Either John will study hard, pass all his exams, and
>   graduate at the end of this term, or he will blow it
>   and be forced to go to summer school.*
> *It is not the case that John will study hard, pass all
>   his exams, and graduate at the end of this term.*
> _____
> *Therefore, he will blow it and be forced to go to
>   summer school.*

The abbreviation for this argument is:

$$((S \cdot P) \cdot G) \vee (B \cdot F)$$
$$\underline{\sim((S \cdot P) \cdot G)}$$
$$\therefore (B \cdot F)$$

and its schema is:

$$((p \cdot q) \cdot r) \vee (s \cdot t)$$
$$\underline{\sim((p \cdot q) \cdot r)}$$
$$\therefore (s \cdot t)$$

It should be fairly obvious that this is merely a complex version of the disjunctive syllogism argument schema. The first premise is a disjunctive statement, both disjuncts of which are compound statements; the second premise, although complex, is merely the negation of the compound statement which forms the first disjunct of the first premise.

Let us consider one other schema before using the rules to test the truth-functional validity of some sample argument schemata:

> *John will study hard and pass all his exams.*
> _____
> *Therefore, John will study hard or be lucky, and pass
>   all his exams.*

The abbreviation for this argument is as follows:

$$S \cdot P$$
$$\therefore (S \vee L) \cdot P$$

and its schema is:

$$\frac{p \cdot q}{\therefore (p \lor r) \cdot q}$$

One might be tempted to say that this is a truth-functionally valid argument schema, although it is certainly not identical to any of the inference rules given so far in our formal deductive system. Why not treat it as involving merely an application of the rule of addition, with the disjunction symbol and the variable 'r' added to the first conjunct of the compound premise? Unfortunately, such a use of the rules is not permissible. The rules of inference are valid *argument* schemata, and therefore cannot be applied to components of compound *propositional* schemata within a single step of an argument. In other words, *the eight*

"I DON'T CHEW BUBBLE-GUM, AND *YOU* DON'T CHEW BUBBLE-GUM......"

Mr. Wilson's reasoning in this cartoon can be expressed in an argument involving only a substitution instance of the inference rule, disjunctive syllogism. Write out the full argument, abbreviate it, and give its schema.

Dennis the Menace ® *cartoons* © *Field Enterprises, Inc.*

rules of inference so far given can be applied only to entire lines of a deductive proof.

Let us now consider several more complex argument schemata, using our first eight rules to prove their truth-functional validity.

A Sample Proof   The number of rules and steps required to prove the validity of a particular argument schema varies with the complexity of the argument and the facility of the person doing the proof. Consider, for example, the following schema:

$$(p \lor q) \cdot r$$
$$\underline{\sim p}$$
$$\therefore q$$

A formal deductive proof for this argument schema might be:

1.	(p ∨ q) · r	*Premise*
2.	∼p/∴q	*Premise/conclusion*
3.	((p ∨ q) · r) · ∼p	*Conj., 1,2*
4.	(p ∨ q) · r	*Simp., 3*
5.	p ∨ q	*Simp., 4*
6.	q	*D.Syll., 5,2*

The first thing we did here was conjoin the premises of the argument schema using the conjunction rule. Then we were able to remove the '∼p' from '((p ∨ q) · ∼p' by using simplification. Employing simplification again, we were able to remove the 'r' from '(p ∨ q) · r'. Then, employing disjunctive syllogism with the deduced statement 'p ∨ q' and the second premise of the original argument schema ('∼p'), we derived 'q', the conclusion of the original argument schema.

As shown below, it is also possible to prove the validity of this argument schema by means of a formal deductive proof which contains only two steps instead of four, and which uses only two rules instead of three:

1.	(p ∨ q) · r	*Premise*
2.	∼p/∴q	*Premise/conclusion*
3.	p ∨ q	*Simp., 1*
4.	q	*D.Syll., 2,3*

Both prove the validity of the argument schema. The second proof is certainly a bit simpler than the first, since it employs fewer rules and steps, but both are equally "good" from a logical point of view, since both *prove* that the argument schema is valid. A person who is thoroughly familiar with the rules of inference is probably less likely than a novice to begin the proof using conjunction as was done in the first proof above; but both can reach the desired conclusion.

These examples serve to highlight several features of our formal deductive proof system. First, an infinite number of correct formal deductive proofs can theoretically be constructed for any valid truth-functional argument. Second, given such an argument, the ability to construct a formal deductive proof is dependent on many subjective factors, such as one's knowledge of the rules, one's experience with using them, one's logical intuition, and one's psychological and physical state at the moment. These reasons suggest why failing to construct a formal deductive proof for a particular argument schema is not sufficient to prove that the schema is truth-functionally invalid; at most, it simply indicates that this person has not proved it valid. The fact that a person has just learned the rules, or got only two hours of sleep the night before, may be the cause of his or her inability to construct a formal deductive proof of the validity of an argument. And it cannot be too strongly emphasized that *there is no substitute for practice* in constructing formal proofs. Consequently, it will be worthwhile to present several more samples and, while doing so, to point out some generally helpful rules of thumb.

Rules of Thumb for Proof Construction   We are already familiar with two general maxims concerning ways of eliminating variables that appear in the premises but not in the conclusion. The first is that the hypothetical syllogism is helpful in removing middle terms when we have a sequence such as 'p ⊃ q' and 'q ⊃ r'. Second, as we saw in our last example, simplification is another inference rule which is helpful as a means of eliminating variables that appear as *conjuncts* in one or more premises of an argument but do not appear at all in the conclusion. But sometimes we encounter the opposite situation: we have variables in the conclusion that are not present in the premises. The following argument schema presents such a situation:

$$p \lor q$$
$$\sim p$$
$$\therefore q \lor (r \cdot s)$$

Because the last line of any formal deductive proof must be identical to the conclusion of the original argument schema, we must somehow add 'r · s', which appears in the conclusion but not in the premises. The addition rule permits this. Thus, we can prove the validity of this particular argument schema by means of the following proof:

1. **p ∨ q**   *Premise*
2. **∼p/∴q ∨ (r · s)**   *Premise/conclusion*
3. **q**   *D.Syll., 1,2*
4. **q ∨ (r · s)**   *Add. 3*

It should be noted that addition permits us to add a variable (or a compound) *only as a disjunct;* it does not permit adding anything by conjunction (that is, by means of the dot).

Sometimes it is helpful, in working out a proof, to examine the conclusion of a particular argument schema and try to work backward from it to the premises, still using the rules as we have given them. For example, consider one more argument schema:

$$\sim p$$
$$(q \lor p) \supset r$$
$$p \lor s$$
$$(s \lor t) \supset q$$

$$\therefore r$$

Starting from the conclusion, we look back to see if there are any premises from which this statement can be directly deduced. We find that there are none; and we also see that 'r' appears only in premise 2. We know that we could deduce 'r' from '$(q \lor p) \supset r$' by means of modus ponens if we had the premise '$q \lor p$'. Looking again at the premises, we can see that '$q \lor p$' appears only in the material implication of line 2. However, we know that we could derive '$q \lor p$' by addition if we had the premise 'q'. Examining the premises again, we see that 'q' appears in the material implication of line 4, '$(s \lor t) \supset q$'. Now we could derive 'q' from line 4 by means of modus ponens, if we could assert '$s \lor t$'. However, '$s \lor t$' appears only in line 4. Nevertheless, we know that we could derive '$s \lor t$' from 's' by means of addition if we had 's' by itself. And, by means of disjunctive syllogism, we can derive 's' from premises 3 and 1 ('$p \lor s$' and '$\sim p$'). Thus, our whole deductive proof falls into place, as shown here:

1.	$\sim p$	*Premise*
2.	$(q \lor p) \supset r$	*Premise*
3.	$p \lor s$	*Premise*
4.	$(s \lor t) \supset q / \therefore r$	*Premise/conclusion*
5.	s	*D.Syll., 3,1*
6.	$s \lor t$	*Add., 5*
7.	q	*M.P., 4,6*
8.	$q \lor p$	*Add., 7*
9.	r	*M.P., 2,8*

Using Inference Rules   Two points must be emphasized about the use of inference rules. The first, which we have already noted, is that *the eight inference rules so far presented can be applied only to entire lines of a deductive proof.* It is incorrect to apply any of these rules to only part of a line. Thus, the following proof misuses the simplification rule:

1.	$q \supset (p \cdot r)$	*Premise*	
2.	$q / \therefore p$	*Premise/conclusion*	
3.	$q \supset p$	*Simp., 1*	[error]
4.	p	*M.P., 2,3*	

In line 3 of this proof, simplification was applied to the compound consequent ('$p \cdot r$') of the conditional statement of line 1 ('$q \supset (p \cdot r)$'). This is impermissible, since an inference rule can be applied only to an entire line of a deductive proof. A correct deductive proof for the same argument schema, using simplification properly, is shown below:

1. $q \supset (p \cdot r)$ *Premise*
2. $q / \therefore p$ *Premise/conclusion*
3. $p \cdot r$ *M.P., 1,2*
4. p *Simp., 3*

In this proof, the inference rules are applied only to complete steps, thus satisfying our rule about their use.

Another important procedural rule, sometimes referred to as the **rule of rigor** (or sometimes, more feelingly, as the 'pain-in-the-neck principle'), requires that *we use only one rule in each step of a deductive proof, and that we use the rules only in the form in which they are given in the system.* The following proof violates the rule of rigor in line 3:

1. $p \lor (q \cdot r)$ *Premise*
2. $\sim p / \therefore r \cdot q$ *Premise/conclusion*
3. $r \cdot q$ *D.Syll., 1,2*   [error]

Although the schema 'r · q' in line 3 may appear to be the same as the schema 'q · r' in the second disjunct of line 1, the two are different in that the two component variables appear in opposite sequence; thus the proof violates the rule concerning the use of rules in their stated form.

One might try to get around this by using the following proof:

1. $p \lor (q \cdot r)$ *Premise*
2. $\sim p / \therefore r \cdot q$ *Premise/conclusion*
3. $q \cdot r$ *D.Syll., 1,2*
4. $r \cdot q$ *Simp., Simp., Conj., 3*   [error]

Here, in line 4, we deduce the statement 'r · q' from 'q · r' by employing simplification twice and then conjunction. In fact, we *can* derive 'r · q' from 'q · r' by using these rules, but only one rule may be used in each step. Thus, the acceptable proof for this argument schema is:

1. $p \lor (q \cdot r)$ *Premise*
2. $\sim p / \therefore r \cdot q$ *Premise/conclusion*
3. $(q \cdot r)$ *D.Syll., 1,2*
4. r *Simp., 3*
5. q *Simp., 3*
6. $r \cdot q$ *Conj., 4,5*

The rule of rigor may indeed seem like nothing more than a pain in the neck. Nevertheless, it should be adhered to, particularly by the novice, so that errors may be avoided in the construction of formal deductive proofs for complex argument schemata.

EXERCISE 7–4   *Using the eight rules of inference discussed thus far, construct a proof to demonstrate the validity of each of the following argument schemata.*

rule of rigor 323

1. 1. p ∨ ~q   4. ~q   1,3 D.Syll.
    2. r ⊃ q   ∴ 5. ~r   2,4 M.T.
    3. ~p
    ∴ ~r

2. p ∨ q
    q ⊃ r
    ~p
    ∴ r

3. 1. (p ∨ q) ⊃ r   4. p ∨ q   2, Add.
    2. p   ∴ 5. r   1,4 M.P.
    ∴ r

4. p
    (p ⊃ q) · (r ⊃ s)
    ∴ q ∨ s

5. 1. p   5. q · s   4,1 M.P.
    2. q ⊃ r   6. q   5, Simp.
    3. s ⊃ t   7. r   2,6 M.P.
    4. p ⊃ (q · s)   8. s   5, Simp.
    ∴ r · t   9. t   3,8 M.P.

★ 6. p ⊃ (q · r)   9. t   3,8 M.P.
    p   ∴ 10. r · t   7,9 Conj.
    ∴ r

7. p ⊃ ~r
    q ⊃ r
    p
    ∴ ~q

★ 8. p ⊃ ~r
    q ∨ r
    p
    ∴ q

9. (p · q) ⊃ (r · s)
    (r · s) ⊃ (t · u)
    ∴ (p · q) ⊃ (t · u)

★ 10. (p · q) ⊃ (r · s)
    (r · s) ⊃ (t · u)
    p · q
    ∴ t · u

11. p
    (p · q) ⊃ r
    s ⊃ (p ⊃ q)
    s
    ∴ r

★ 12. 1. p ⊃ q   5. ~p   1,4 MT
    2. ~p ⊃ (q ⊃ r)   6. (q ⊃ r)   2,5 MP
    3. r ⊃ s   7. q ⊃ s   3,6 H.Syll.
    4. ~q
    ∴ q ⊃ s

13. (p ⊃ q) ⊃ (r ⊃ s)
    (t ⊃ u) ∨ (p ⊃ q)
    ~(r ⊃ s)
    ∴ t ⊃ u

14. (p ⊃ q) ∨ (r ⊃ s)
    (r ⊃ s) ⊃ (t ⊃ u)
    q ⊃ r
    ~(t ⊃ u)
    ∴ p ⊃ r

15. p · s
    (p ∨ r) ⊃ (p ⊃ q)
    s ⊃ t
    ∴ q · t

16. (p · q) ⊃ (r · s)
    (r · s) ⊃ (t · u)
    p · q
    ∴ u

17. p ⊃ q
    q ⊃ r
    p
    ∴ p · r

18. p ⊃ q
    q ⊃ r
    ~r
    ∴ ~r · ~p

19. (p ⊃ q) · (r ⊃ s)
    (q ⊃ t) · (s ⊃ u)
    p ∨ r
    ∴ t ∨ u

20. p
    p ⊃ q
    (p · q) ⊃ (r · s)
    ∴ r · s

21. ~p
    (~p ∨ ~q) ⊃ ~(r ⊃ s)
    (r ⊃ s) ∨ (t ⊃ s)
    ~s
    ∴ ~t

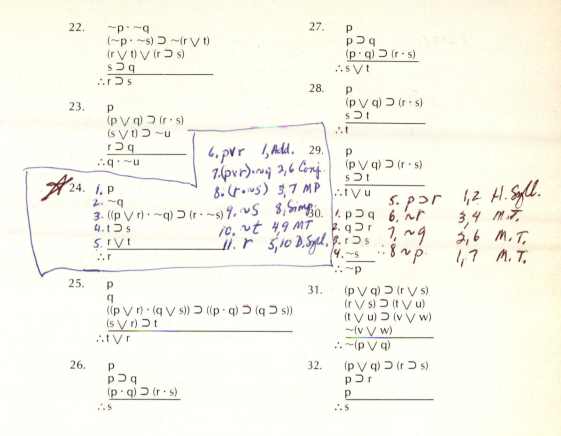

22. ~p · ~q
    (~p · ~s) ⊃ ~(r ∨ t)
    (r ∨ t) ∨ (r ⊃ s)
    s ⊃ q
    ∴ r ⊃ s

23. p
    (p ∨ q) ⊃ (r · s)
    (s ∨ t) ⊃ ~u
    r ⊃ q
    ∴ q · ~u

✗ 24. 1. p
    2. ~q
    3. ((p ∨ r) · ~q) ⊃ (r · ~s)
    4. t ⊃ s
    5. r ∨ t
    ∴ r

(handwritten)
6. p ∨ r   1, Add.
7. (p ∨ r) · ~q   2, 6 Conj.
8. (r · ~s)   3, 7 MP
9. ~s   8, Simp.
10. ~t   4, 9 MT
11. r   5, 10 D. Syll.

25. p
    q
    ((p ∨ r) · (q ∨ s)) ⊃ ((p · q) ⊃ (q ⊃ s))
    (s ∨ r) ⊃ t
    ∴ t ∨ r

26. p
    p ⊃ q
    (p · q) ⊃ (r · s)
    ∴ s

27. p
    p ⊃ q
    (p · q) ⊃ (r · s)
    ∴ s ∨ t

28. p
    (p ∨ q) ⊃ (r · s)
    s ⊃ t
    ∴ t

29. p
    (p ∨ q) ⊃ (r · s)
    s ⊃ t
    ∴ t ∨ u

30. 1. p ⊃ q
    2. q ⊃ r
    3. r ⊃ s
    4. ~s
    ∴ ~p

(handwritten)
5. p ⊃ r   1, 2 H. Syll.
6. ~r   3, 4 M.T.
7. ~q   2, 6 M.T.
∴ 8 ~p   1, 7 M.T.

31. (p ∨ q) ⊃ (r ∨ s)
    (r ∨ s) ⊃ (t ∨ u)
    (t ∨ u) ⊃ (v ∨ w)
    ~(v ∨ w)
    ∴ ~(p ∨ q)

32. (p ∨ q) ⊃ (r ⊃ s)
    p ⊃ r
    p
    ∴ s

EQUIVALENCE RULES

In the proof we just discussed, we were required to go through three steps to deduce 'r · q' from 'q · r'. These two statements are, of course, logically equivalent. As we saw at the end of Chapter 6, we can demonstrate their logical equivalence by writing the two statements as a biconditional statement and then using the truth-table method. If we find all **T**'s under the material equivalence operator, then the biconditional is a tautology, which means that the two statements are logically equivalent. This is shown in the following truth table:

q	r	(q · r)	≡	(r · q)
T	T	T	T	T
F	T	F	T	F
T	F	F	T	F
F	F	F	T	F

If we had an inference rule that allowed us to substitute logically equivalent statements in a deductive proof, we could save a considerable number of steps

SAMPLE PROOF

1. $S \equiv (T \lor V)$ P₍
2. $\sim(T \lor V) /\therefore \sim(S \cdot W)$ P./C.
3. $[S \supset (T \lor V)] \cdot [(T \lor V) \supset S]$ 1, Bi.Eq.
4. $[S \supset (T \lor V)]$ 3, Simp.
5. $\sim S$ 3,4 M.T.
6. $(S \cdot W) \supset S$ Taut.
7. $\sim(S \cdot W)$ 5,6 M.T.

PROPOSITIONAL LOGIC: ARGUMENTS

in arguments such as this one. In fact, we will introduce a rule into our deductive proof system, calling it the **rule of replacement**. The rule of replacement is much more complex than the previous eight inference rules. In symbolic language, it states:

The two following schemata are valid inference forms:

$$\frac{\ldots \Phi \ldots \quad \Phi \equiv \Psi}{\ldots \Psi \ldots} \qquad or \qquad \frac{\ldots \Psi \ldots \quad \Phi \equiv \Psi}{\ldots \Phi \ldots}$$

where '$\Phi \equiv \Psi$' is one of the equivalences listed below:

De Morgan's rules (De M.):	$\sim(p \cdot q) \equiv (\sim p \lor \sim q)$
	$\sim(p \lor q) \equiv (\sim p \cdot \sim q)$
✓ **Commutation (Comm.):**	$(p \lor q) \equiv (q \lor p)$
	$(p \cdot q) \equiv (q \cdot p)$
✓ **Association (Assoc.):**	$(p \lor (q \lor r)) \equiv ((p \lor q) \lor r)$
	$(p \cdot (q \cdot r)/) \equiv ((p \cdot q) \cdot r)$
✗ **Distribution (Dist.):**	$(p \cdot (q \lor r)) \equiv ((p \cdot q) \lor (p \cdot r))$
	$(p \lor (q \cdot r)) \equiv ((p \lor q) \cdot (p \lor r))$
✓ **Double Negation (D.N.):**	$p \equiv \sim\sim p$
Transportation (Trans.): ✓ — *Contraposition*	$(p \supset q) \equiv (\sim q \supset \sim p)$
Material Implication (Impl.):	$(p \supset q) \equiv (\sim p \lor q)$
	$(p \supset q) \equiv \sim(p \cdot \sim q)$
Material Equivalence (Equiv.):	$(p \equiv q) \equiv ((p \supset q) \cdot (q \supset p))$
	$(p \equiv q) \equiv ((p \cdot q) \lor (\sim p \cdot \sim q))$
Exportation (Exp.): ✗ *Prove Exportation*	$((p \cdot q) \supset r) \equiv (p \supset (q \supset r))$
Tautology ((Taut.): *any Taut. admissable*	$p \equiv (p \lor p)$ $(P \cdot Q) \supset P$
	$p \equiv (p \cdot p)$

Simply stated, the rule of replacement asserts that any propositional schema that is produced by replacing all or part of another schema with a schema which is equivalent to the replaced portion, according to one of the listed equivalences, is validly derivable from the original schema. This should not be surprising, since two statements which are logically equivalent have the same truth value in the same instances. If one statement is true in the original premises, then its logically equivalent statement is also true, and vice versa. Thus, a statement can be substituted for a logically equivalent statement anywhere in a proof, even in the middle of a line. It is not necessary to replace only whole lines with equivalent statements. Five of the basic logical equivalences—double negation, De Morgan's rules, material implication, material equivalence, and tautology—were in-

SAMPLE ID

1. p ⊃ q	P.	
2. r ⊃ ~q	P.	
3. ~(p ⊃ ~r) /∴ ~s·(q⊃~r)		
4. ~~q ⊃ ~r	2, Trans.	
5. q ⊃ ~r	4, DN	
6. (p ⊃ ~r)	1,5 H.Syll.	
7. (p⊃~r)v~s	6 Add.	
8. ~s	3,7 D.Syll.	
9. ~s·(q⊃~r)	5,8 Conj.	

troduced in Chapter 6. The other five can be proved to be logical equivalences by using truth tables.

Although we are formally introducing the rule of replacement as a single inference rule, we shall treat it—for reasons that should soon become obvious—as ten distinct rules in constructing proofs. Each of these rules consists of the original general formula, with Φ and Ψ, plus one of the ten equivalence statements. In our proofs, we shall use the names of the equivalences to state the justifications of steps. This is considerably more convenient and helpful than simply referring to the general rule of replacement.

Returning to the argument on p. 323 we can see that these additional rules can save us a number of steps, as shown in the following proof:

1. p ∨ (q · r) *Premise*
2. ~p/∴r · q *Premise/conclusion*
3. q · r   D.Syll., 1,2
4. r · q   Comm., 3

In this proof, we justified deducing 'r · q' from 'q · r' by commutation. Technically speaking, we employed a part of the rule of replacement; but we gave only the name of the appropriate equivalence as a justification.

Some Sample Proofs   The equivalence rules not only simplify some proofs, they also enable us to prove the validity of some argument schemata which cannot be proved valid using only the eight original rules of inference, although such schemata can be shown to be valid using the truth-table method. The following is such an argument:

If John is Peter's brother, then Mary is Peter's sister.
If Mary is John's sister, then Mary is not Peter's sister.
Therefore, If John is Peter's brother, then Mary is not John's sister.

The abbreviation and schema for this intended argument are:

ABBREVIATION	SCHEMA
J ⊃ P	p ⊃ q
M ⊃ ~P	r ⊃ ~q
∴ J ⊃ ~M	∴ p ⊃ ~r

By using the equivalence rules as well as our eight original rules, we can prove the validity of this argument schema:

1. p ⊃ q   *Premise*
2. r ⊃ ~q/∴p ⊃ ~r   *Premise/conclusion*
3. ~~q ⊃ ~r   *Trans., 2*
4. q ⊃ ~r   *D.N., 3*
5. p ⊃ ~r   *H.Syll., 1,4*

Notice that on line 4 we justified the statement 'q ⊃ ~r' by double negation, even though we applied it to only part of the statement in line 3 ('~~q ⊃ ~r'). As we indicated earlier, when using the replacement rule, we may substitute logically equivalent statements *whenever they occur,* either as a whole step or as part of a step—as cannot be done with the eight original inference rules.

Thus, the replacement rule further extends our formal deductive proof system, enabling us to test the truth-functional validity of many complex argument schemata. Consider one more example:

$$(p \supset q) \cdot (r \supset s)$$
$$p \lor r$$
$$\underline{(p \supset \mathord{\sim} s) \cdot (r \supset \mathord{\sim} q)}$$
$$\therefore s \equiv \mathord{\sim} q$$

Examining this schema to formulate a strategy, we can see that only the variables 's' and 'q' appear in the conclusion, thereby indicating that we must eliminate 'p' and 'r' which appear in the premises but not the conclusion. This can be accomplished most simply by using constructive dilemma, as shown below:

1.	$(p \supset q) \cdot (r \supset s)$	*Premise*
2.	$p \lor r$	*Premise*
3.	$(p \supset \mathord{\sim} s) \cdot (r \supset \mathord{\sim} q)/\therefore s \equiv \mathord{\sim} q$	*Premise/conclusion*
4.	$q \lor s$	*Dil., 1,2*
5.	$\mathord{\sim} s \lor \mathord{\sim} q$	*Dil., 3,2*

Working backward from the conclusion of the original argument schema ('s ≡ ~q'), we can see that it is a biconditional. In our list of equivalences, only the material equivalence rule has a component which is itself a biconditional. Quite obviously, in some way we need to invoke the material equivalence rule to prove the truth-functional validity of this argument. But this rule can be used only with a conjunction of two material implications—(p ≡ q) ≡ ((p ⊃ q) · (q ⊃ p))—or with the disjunction of two conjunctions—(p ≡ q) ≡ ((p · q) ∨ (~p · ~q)). We have reduced our argument to the two variables ('q' and 's') which appear in the conclusion, but they appear in disjunctive propositions (see lines 4 and 5). Consequently, we must somehow transform the disjunctions of lines 4 and 5 into either material implications or conjunctions. The material implication rule—(p ⊃ q) ≡ (~p ∨ q)—permits us to replace a disjunction with its logically equivalent material implication. Thus, we can complete our proof as below:

1.	$(p \supset q) \cdot (r \supset s)$	*Premise*
2.	$p \lor r$	*Premise*
3.	$(p \supset \mathord{\sim} s) \cdot (r \supset \mathord{\sim} q)/\therefore s \equiv \mathord{\sim} q$	*Premise/ conclusion*
4.	$q \lor s$	*Dil., 1,2*
5.	$\mathord{\sim} s \lor \mathord{\sim} q$	*Dil., 3,2*

PEANUTS ® By Charles M. Schulz

Write out the argument given in this cartoon and prove its validity using the rules of the propositional calculus. If you can't construct a proof of its validity, use the short truth-table method to see if it's invalid. If it's invalid, then reformulate your interpretation of the cartoon so that it becomes truth-functionally valid.

6.	$\sim\sim q \lor s$	D.N., 4
7.	$s \supset \sim q$	Impl., 5
8.	$\sim q \supset s$	Impl., 6
9.	$(s \supset \sim q) \cdot (\sim q \supset s)$	Conj., 7,8
10.	$s \equiv \sim q$	Equiv., 9

Note that, since the rule of rigor does not permit us to apply two rules in one step of a proof, it was necessary, in order that material implication might be applied to the statement in line 4 ('q ∨ s'), to apply double negation first.

Our explanation of this proof is intended as a guide, to show how one might go about constructing a formal deductive proof to test the truth-functional validity of a complex argument schema. While such strategies are important, it must be emphasized that there is no *one* correct formal deductive proof for a particular argument schema. As we noted earlier, an infinite number of different logically correct proofs could be constructed for any one schema such as the above, using the eighteen rules presented thus far—though most of them would be somewhat longer and more complex. The knowledge of how and when to use particular strategies can come only from extensive practice and experience with constructing such deductive proofs.

EXERCISE 7–5

Using the rules of inference discussed thus far, including the ten rules of replacement, construct a proof to demonstrate the validity of each of the following argument schemata.

---

1. $\sim p$
$\therefore \sim(p \cdot q)$

2. $\sim p \cdot \sim q$
$(p \lor q) \lor (r \lor s)$
$\therefore r \lor s$

3. p
$\sim q \supset \sim p$
$\therefore q$

4. p
$\sim p \lor q$
$q \equiv r$
$\therefore r$

5. p
$q \lor (r \cdot s)$
$\sim q \lor \sim p$
$\therefore s$

6. $p \lor q$
$(q \lor p) \supset (r \lor s)$
$(s \lor r) \supset \sim q$
$\therefore p$

7. $q \supset \sim p$
p
$\therefore \sim q$

8. $p \lor (q \lor r)$
$(p \lor q) \supset \sim s$
$\sim r$
$\therefore \sim s$

9. $\sim r \cdot \sim s$
$(p \lor q) \supset (r \lor s)$
$\therefore \sim(p \lor q)$

10. $\sim r \cdot \sim s$
$(p \lor q) \supset (r \lor s)$
$\therefore \sim p \cdot \sim q$

11. $p \supset (q \supset r)$
       $\sim r$
       ∴$\sim(p \cdot q)$

(handwritten:)
4. $\sim p \cdot \sim q$ 1,2 Conj.
5. $\sim(p \lor q)$ 4 De.M.
6. $(p \lor r)$ 3,5 M.P.
7. r 1,6 D.Syll.

12. *(marked with X)*
1. $\sim p$
2. $\sim q$
3. $\sim(p \lor q) \supset (p \lor r)$
∴r

13. $\sim p$
       $\sim(p \cdot q) \supset (\sim p \supset r)$
       ∴r

14. $\sim r$
       $(p \cdot q) \supset (r \cdot s)$
       ∴$\sim p \lor \sim q$

15. $\sim(p \lor q)$
       $r \supset p$
       $s \supset q$
       ∴$\sim(r \lor s)$

16. $\sim r \cdot \sim s$
       $(p \lor q) \supset (r \lor s)$
       ∴$\sim q$

(handwritten box:)
3. $\sim(r \lor s)$ 1, De M.
4. $\sim(p \lor q)$ 2,3 MT
5. $(\sim p \cdot \sim q)$ 4, De M.
6. $\sim q$ 5, Simp.
7. $\sim r$ 1, Simp.
8. $\sim q \cdot \sim r$ 6,7 ~~Simp~~ Conj.

17. $\sim r \cdot \sim s$
       $(p \lor q) \supset (r \lor s)$
       ∴$\sim q \lor t$

18. *(marked with X)*
1. $\sim r \cdot \sim s$
2. $(p \lor q) \supset (r \lor s)$
∴$\sim q \cdot \sim r$

19. $\sim r \lor \sim s$
       $(p \cdot q) \supset (r \cdot s)$
       ∴$\sim(p \cdot q)$

20. $\sim r \lor \sim s$
       $\sim(r \cdot s) \supset (p \cdot q)$
       ∴$q \lor t$

21. $\sim(q \lor \sim p)$
       $(p \cdot \sim q) \supset (p \supset r)$
       $r \supset s$
       ∴$p \supset s$

22. $p \supset q$
       $(r \lor s) \supset p$
       $(\sim p \lor q) \supset s$
       ∴q

23. $\sim(p \supset q)$
       $p \supset r$
       $s \supset q$
       $\sim(r \supset s)$

24. $\sim(p \cdot q)$
       $(p \supset \sim q) \supset (\sim(p \cdot q) \supset r)$
       ∴r

25. p
       q
       $p \equiv q$

26. $\sim p \lor q$
       $(p \supset q) \supset (p \supset r)$
       ∴$p \supset r$

27. $\sim p \lor q$
       $(p \supset q) \supset (p \supset r)$
       p
       ∴r

28. $\sim p \lor q$
       $(p \supset q) \supset (p \supset r)$
       p
       $q \cdot r$

29. $\sim(p \cdot \sim q)$
       $(p \supset q) \supset (p \supset r)$
       ∴$p \supset r$

30. $p \cdot \sim r$
       $(p \supset q) \supset (p \supset r)$
       ∴$p \cdot \sim q$

31. $p \cdot (q \lor r)$
       $\sim(p \cdot r)$
       ∴q

32. $p \cdot (q \lor r)$
       $\sim p$
       ∴q

33. $(p \cdot q) \supset r$
       $(p \cdot r) \supset q$
       p
       ∴$r \equiv q$

34. $(p \cdot q) \equiv (r \lor s)$
       r
       ∴$p \cdot r$ *(handwritten:)* $r \supset p$

35. $\sim p \lor (q \cdot r)$ *(handwritten:)* $p \supset (q \cdot r)$ + $r \supset (q \cdot r)$
       $r \supset p$
       ∴$p \equiv r$

(handwritten at bottom:)
$\sim(p \cdot \sim(q \cdot r))$ $\sim(r \cdot \sim(q \cdot r)$

$\sim(q \cdot r) \supset \sim r$ con.

CONDITIONAL PROOF   Not every argument that can be proved valid using truth tables can be proved valid using our eighteen rules of inference. Consider, for example, the following argument:

> *John is a doctor or Susan is a doctor*
> _____
> *Therefore, if John is not a doctor then John is not a doctor and Susan is a doctor*

The abbreviation and schema for this argument are:

ABBREVIATION	SCHEMA
$\mathbf{J \vee S}$	$p \vee q$
$\therefore \mathbf{\sim J \supset (\sim J \cdot S)}$	$\therefore \sim p \supset (\sim p \cdot q)$

We can show this particular argument schema to be valid by introducing a new rule called the rule of **conditional proof.** Notice that the conclusion of the argument schema above is a conditional proposition: Conditional proof is most commonly used in arguments with such conclusions. The method of conditional proof requires *assuming* an additional premise, which is actually the antecedent of a conditional statement that is necessary in the proof, and then deducing the consequent of the desired statement from the assumption and the original premises. Let us first present a conditional proof for the above argument schema and then discuss each step:

1.	$p \vee q / \therefore \sim p \supset (\sim p \cdot q)$	*Premise/Conclusion*
2.	$\sim p$	*Assumption*
3.	q	*D.Syll., 1,2*
4.	$\sim p \cdot q$	*Conj., 2,3*
5.	$\sim p \supset (\sim p \cdot q)$	*C.P., 2–4*

We set up the premise and conclusion in line 1 in exactly the same way as in our other deductive proofs. In line 2 we asserted our assumed premise, '$\sim p$', which is the antecedent of the conditional conclusion, and labeled it as an assumption. In line 3, we deduced the statement 'q' from lines 1 and 2 by means of disjunctive syllogism. In line 4, we used conjunction to deduce the statement '$\sim p \cdot q$', which is the consequent of the conditional conclusion. Then, in step 5, we deduced the conclusion statement '$\sim p \supset (\sim p \cdot q)$' from lines 2 and 4 by means of the rule of conditional proof (C.P.).

In the proof above, premises 2, 3, and 4 are marked off by a line with an arrow pointing to line 2 (the assumed premise) which then extends downward and finally crosses beneath line 4. This line indicates the **scope** of our assumption; that is, lines 3 and 4 can be validly deduced from the premises only assuming '$\sim p$' as an additional premise. As soon as we assert the rule of conditional proof, we end the scope of the assumption: that is, the assumption is said to be *discharged.* Line 5 of the proof is not dependent on our assumed premise; it is dependent only on the original premise of the argument.

In effect, the rule of conditional proof is a straightforward application of our definition of material implication. A formal statement of this new inference rule is:

The following procedure can be inserted at any point in a proof, **provided that none of the formulae derived within the lined-off area are used outside this portion of the proof:**

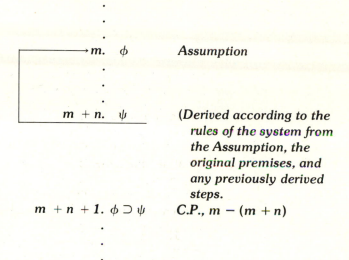

.
.
.

m. ϕ *Assumption*

.
.
.

m + *n.* ψ *(Derived according to the rules of the system from the Assumption, the original premises, and any previously derived steps.*

m + *n* + *1.* $\phi \supset \psi$ *C.P., m − (m + n)*

.
.
.

All that is being said in the last step shown is that, *if* ϕ is true, then ψ is also true.

The step ending the conditional proof *must* be a conditional statement with the assumed premise as its antecedent. Also, as the formal statement of the rule indicates, no step from inside the scope of the assumption—that is, from inside the line marking off the conditional proof—can be used *outside* that assumption. Thus, in our example, one could not use step 3 ('q') at any point in the proof after the line between steps 4 and 5, which discharges the assumption. Step 3 could be used after this only if it could be derived again, independently of the assumption '~p'—which, in this particular case, is impossible. Our proof demonstrates that, given p $\vee$ q, then *if* ~ p then ~p · q. In terms of the propositions of our original example, we have shown that given 'John is a doctor' or 'Susan is a doctor', then *if* 'John is not a doctor', is true, then 'John is not a doctor and Susan is a doctor' is also true.

The rule of conditional proof does more than enable us to prove the validity of arguments whose validity cannot be proved using only the eighteen rules discussed earlier. It is a powerful tool which also enables us to prove in relatively few steps the validity of complex arguments which require numerous steps when we use only the eighteen rules. For example, consider the conditional proof below:

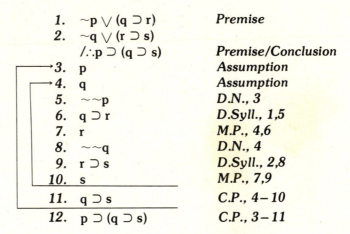

1.	(q ∨ r)·(s ∨ p)	
	/∴~s ⊃ (p·(q ∨ r))	*Premise/Conclusion*
2.	~s	*Assumption*
3.	s ∨ p	*Simp., 1*
4.	p	*D.Syll., 2,3*
5.	q ∨ r	*Simp., 1*
6.	p·(q ∨ r)	*Conj., 4,5*
7.	~s ⊃ (p·(q ∨ r))	*C.P., 2–6*

The reader may wish to try constructing a formal deductive proof for this same argument schema using only the eighteen rules, without conditional proof. The attempt should suffice to demonstrate the great convenience of this additional rule.

Of course, we are not limited to making only one assumption in a conditional proof. Any number of assumptions can be made, provided they are eventually discharged, leaving the conclusion dependent only on the premise(s) of the original argument schema. Consider, for example, the following conditional proof, which uses two assumed premises:

1.	~p ∨ (q ⊃ r)	*Premise*
2.	~q ∨ (r ⊃ s)	
	/∴p ⊃ (q ⊃ s)	*Premise/Conclusion*
3.	p	*Assumption*
4.	q	*Assumption*
5.	~~p	*D.N., 3*
6.	q ⊃ r	*D.Syll., 1,5*
7.	r	*M.P., 4,6*
8.	~~q	*D.N., 4*
9.	r ⊃ s	*D.Syll., 2,8*
10.	s	*M.P., 7,9*
11.	q ⊃ s	*C.P., 4–10*
12.	p ⊃ (q ⊃ s)	*C.P., 3–11*

Notice that the scope of the second assumption ('q') carries through line 10. What we have done in lines 4 through 10 is derive the consequent of the conclusion. The second assumption is contained within the scope of the first assumption, since we justified line 6 by lines 1 and 5, and line 5 is derived from our first assumption. Therefore, line 11, which was justified by lines 4 through 10, could not have been derived without the assumption of line 3 as well. Thus it was also necessary to discharge the first assumption to satisfy the requirements of the conditional proof rule.

In other words, the argument goes like this: If we don't have CRP, the Soviet Union could evacuate its cities, do something provocative, and dare us to attack, knowing that we couldn't evacuate our cities (except spontaneously and haphazardly) in preparation for their counterattack. If we do have CRP, and the Soviet Union evacuates its cities and does something provocative, then we could evacuate our cities, giving the Russians good reason to think we *would* dare to attack. However, since the Russians would be well aware that we have CRP and could match their evacuation with our evacuation, they would be less likely to evacuate in the first place, or, for that matter, to do something provocative. Thus, if we have CRP, it is unlikely that we will need it. We need it only if we don't have it. And we don't have it. So we need it.

Not everyone agrees with this logic. "It's a crazy way to spend money," Representative Aspin says. "If they evacuate, *we* have *them* in a blackmail situation. How long can they sit out in the countryside with their cities and all their industries sitting idle?"

—ED ZUCKERMAN, "Hiding from the Bomb Again," *Harper's,* July, 1979.

Use the propositional calculus to test the validity of the two arguments above—one in support of and one opposed to the U.S. Defense Department's program called Crisis Relocation Planning (CRP).

EXERCISE 7–6   *Prove the validity of the following argument schemata, using the rules of inference including the conditional proof.*

1. $\underline{p \supset q}$
    $\therefore p \supset (p \cdot q)$

2. $\underline{(p \supset q) \cdot (r \supset s)}$
    $\therefore (p \lor r) \supset (q \lor s)$

3. $(p \lor q) \supset (r \cdot s)$
    $\underline{\sim r}$
    $\therefore \sim s \supset \sim q$

4. $\underline{(p \lor q) \supset r}$
    $\therefore ((r \lor s) \supset t) \supset (p \supset t)$

5. $\underline{p \supset (q \supset r)}$
    $\therefore (\sim r \cdot s) \supset (q \supset \sim p)$

6. $\underline{q}$
    $\therefore p \supset (p \cdot q)$

7. $\underline{p \supset (q \supset r)}$
    $\therefore (p \cdot q) \supset r$

8. $p \supset (q \supset r)$
    $\underline{p \supset q}$
    $\therefore p \supset r$

9. $\underline{q \supset r}$
    $\therefore p \supset (q \supset (r \lor s))$

10. $\underline{p \supset r}$
    $\therefore p \supset (q \supset (r \lor s))$

11. $(p \lor q) \supset (r \equiv s)$
    $\sim (\sim s \cdot p)$
    $\underline{\sim t \supset \sim r}$
    $\therefore p \supset (t \cdot r)$

12. $\underline{\sim p \lor \sim (q \cdot r)}$
    $\therefore q \supset (r \supset \sim p)$

13. $\sim p \supset (q \supset r)$
    $\underline{s \supset q}$
    $\therefore s \supset (\sim p \supset r)$

14. $p \supset q$
    $\therefore (p \cdot r) \supset q$

15. $(p \cdot q) \supset r$
    $\therefore p \supset (q \supset r)$

16. $(p \cdot q) \lor (r \cdot s)$
    $\therefore \sim p \supset (r \cdot s)$

17. $p \cdot (q \lor r)$
    $\therefore \sim q \supset (p \cdot r)$

18. $r \equiv s$
    $p \lor r$
    $\therefore \sim p \supset (r \cdot s)$

19. s
    $\therefore p \supset (q \supset (r \supset s))$

20. r
    $\therefore p \supset (p \lor q)$

INDIRECT PROOF   The *indirect proof,* or, as it is sometimes called, the *reductio ad absurdum* proof, is a special case of conditional proof. Using the method of conditional proof, we can assert the negation of the conclusion as our assumed premise and then attempt to derive from it the denial of that assumption. This then allows us to derive the conclusion of the argument schema, as shown below:

1.	$q / \therefore p \supset (p \lor q)$	*Premise/Conclusion*
2.	$\sim(p \supset (p \lor q))$	*Assumption*
3.	$\sim\sim(p \cdot \sim(p \lor q))$	*Impl., 2*
4.	$p \cdot \sim(p \lor q)$	*D.N., 3*
5.	$p \cdot (\sim p \cdot \sim q)$	*De M., 4*
6.	$(p \cdot \sim p) \cdot \sim q$	*Assoc., 5*
7.	$p \cdot \sim p$	*Simp., 6*
8.	$\sim p$	*Simp., 7*
9.	$\sim p \lor (p \lor q)$	*Add., 8*
10.	$p \supset (p \lor q)$	*Impl., 9*
11.	$\sim(p \supset (p \lor q))$ $\supset (p \supset (p \lor q))$	*C.P., 2–10*
12.	$\sim\sim(p \supset (p \lor q))$ $\lor (p \supset (p \lor q))$	*Impl., 11*
13.	$(p \supset (p \lor q))$ $\lor (p \supset (p \lor q))$	*D.N., 12*
14.	$p \supset (p \lor q)$	*Taut., 13*

Our assumed premise in line 2 is the negation of the conclusion. Having made this assumption, we then seek to derive the conclusion itself, which we achieve in step 10 after applying several of our rules. We can now assert conditional proof, indicating also the scope of our assumed premise. Notice that, although the statement on line 10 is the conclusion we are seeking to derive, it falls within the scope of the assumption. But the assumption must be discharged *before* the conclusion is deduced, if our proof is to be correct. Therefore, we must again deduce the conclusion of the argument *after* discharging the assumption, so that the conclusion will be dependent only on the original premise of the argument. This we accomplish in lines 11 through 14.

Backtracking a little, we can see that on line 7 we deduced a contradiction ('p · ~p'). As we demonstrated earlier, any statement whatsoever is validly deducible from a contradiction. Each step after line 7 is really just a step in the process of deducing the conclusion ('p ⊃ (p ∨ q)') from the contradiction ('p · ~p'). Thus, we can bypass all these steps, discharge the assumption, and assert the conclusion immediately after deriving the contradiction. In justification, we cite our assumed premise (line 2), the contradiction (line 7), and the rule of indirect proof (I.P.) as shown below.

1.	q/∴p ⊃ (p ∨ q)	*Premise/Conclusion*
2.	~(p ⊃ (p ∨ q))	*Assumption*
3.	~~(p · ~(p ∨ q))	*Impl., 2*
4.	p · ~(p ∨ q)	*D.N., 3*
5.	p · (~p · ~q)	*De M., 4*
6.	(p · ~p) · ~q	*Assoc., 5*
7.	p · ~p	*Simp., 6*
8.	p ⊃ (p ∨ q)	*I.P., 2–7*

Although it is a straightforward variation of the rule of conditional proof, the rule of indirect proof can be formally stated on its own as follows:

The following procedure can be inserted at any point in a proof, provided that none of the formulae derived within the lined-off area is used outside this portion of the proof:

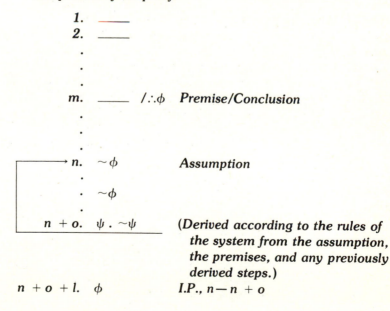

1.	——		
2.	——		
.			
.			
.			
m.	——	/∴φ	*Premise/Conclusion*
.			
.			
.			
n.	~φ		*Assumption*
.	~φ		
.			
n + o.	ψ · ~ψ		*(Derived according to the rules of the system from the assumption, the premises, and any previously derived steps.)*
n + o + l.	φ		*I.P., n — n + o*

Quite obviously, the rule of indirect proof is powerful, since it enables us to prove the validity of some argument schemata in fewer steps than does the rule of conditional proof. As one might expect, since indirect proof is a special case of conditional proof, it too can be used to prove the validity of arguments which could not be proved using only the eighteen rules of inference and equivalence. For example, consider the following, in which neither of the variables in the premise appears in the conclusion, but which is valid because the conclusion is a tautology:

1.	$r \lor s / \therefore p \supset (p \lor q)$	Premise/conclusion
2.	$\sim(p \supset (p \lor q))$	Assumption
3.	$\sim\sim(p \cdot \sim(p \lor q))$	Impl., 2
4.	$p \cdot \sim\sim(p \lor q)$	D.N., 3
5.	$p \cdot (\sim p \cdot \sim q)$	De M., 4
6.	$(p \cdot \sim p) \cdot \sim q$	Assoc., 5
7.	$p \cdot \sim p$	Simp., 6
8.	$p \supset (p \lor q)$	I.P., 2–7

Except for the first and last lines, the indirect proof above parallels our first indirect proof. This should not be surprising, since we can see that the conclusions of both argument schemata ('$p \supset (p \lor q)$') are the same. Thus, we negate the same conclusion in both proofs and derive the same contradiction in line 7 ('$p \cdot \sim p$'). From the contradiction, we can ultimately derive the desired conclusion statement. The fact that nowhere in our proof did we need to use the original premise tells us that, regardless of the premise(s), any argument with this conclusion can be proven valid in the same number of steps.

Deductive Completeness   So far, we have touched on the subject of the **deductive completeness** of our propositional calculus only in an incidental way. A deductive proof system for truth-functional arguments is said to be deductively complete when any argument schema that can be proved valid using truth tables can be proved valid using the system's rules and procedures. Thus, the original

Can you do any better than Charlie Brown in finding the error in this argument with the conclusion, "It doesn't matter how I act"? Is the propositional calculus at all helpful in analyzing this apparent argument?

eighteen rules of inference do not in themselves constitute a deductively complete system. As we have seen, certain argument schemata that can be proved valid by truth tables cannot be proved valid using these rules alone. However, the original eighteen rules in conjunction with the rule of conditional proof do constitute a complete deductive system, since any argument schema whose validity can be proved by truth tables can be proved valid using one or more of the eighteen rules and the conditional proof rule.

Indirect proof does not add anything to the deductive completeness of our system. Since it is a special case of conditional proof, any argument schema that can be proved valid using Indirect Proof can be proved valid using conditional proof. However, since both conditional proof and indirect proof are powerful tools for testing truth-functional validity, we will include both within our system.

In conclusion, it should be reiterated that the deductive system given in this chapter does not provide a decision procedure. True, it is theoretically possible, using our nineteen rules (or twenty, if we count indirect proof as a separate rule), to construct a proof of validity for every argument that can be proved valid using truth tables. However, these rules do not provide a mechanical method which *guarantees* that after a finite number of steps we will have proved that a given argument is valid *or invalid*. The system of rules cannot be used at all to prove invalidity. Failure to derive the desired conclusion after a specified number of steps could just as well indicate a failure on the part of the individual to find the proper sequence of steps as it could suggest the invalidity of the argument. Therefore, if, after trying for a reasonable length of time to construct a proof, one has not been able to do it, it would be appropriate to test the argument by the short truth-table method, which does enable us to prove invalidity.

EXERCISE 7–7   *Prove the validity of each of the following argument schemata using the method of indirect proof.*

---

1. $\sim q \supset (\sim p \cdot r)$
    $\underline{\sim r}$
    $\therefore q$

2. $p \supset (q \cdot r)$
    $\underline{\sim q}$
    $\therefore \sim p$

3. $p \lor (q \cdot r)$
    $p \lor t$
    $\underline{t \supset \sim(q \cdot r)}$
    $\therefore p$

4. $(r \lor q) \supset p$
    $p \supset (s \cdot t)$
    $\underline{\sim s \lor \sim t}$
    $\therefore \sim(r \lor q)$

5. $(p \supset q) \cdot (r \supset s)$
    $(q \lor s) \supset t$
    $\underline{\sim t}$
    $\therefore \sim(p \lor r)$

6. $p \lor q$
    $\underline{p \lor \sim q}$
    $\therefore p$

7. $p \supset (q \supset r)$
    $\sim s \supset (p \lor r)$
    $\underline{p \supset q}$
    $\therefore s \lor r$

8. $\sim p \supset q$
    $\underline{\sim(\sim p \cdot q)}$
    $\therefore p$

9. $(p \cdot q) \supset r$
     $\sim p \supset r$
     $\underline{q}$
     $\therefore r$

10. $p \equiv q$
      $\underline{\sim r \vee p}$
      $\therefore r \supset q$

11. $p \cdot q$
      $\underline{\sim (p \supset q)}$
      $\therefore r \supset s$

12. $\sim p \supset (q \cdot r)$
      $\underline{\sim r}$
      $\therefore p$

13. $p \supset (q \vee \sim (r \vee s))$
      $\underline{\sim r \supset s}$
      $\therefore \sim q \supset \sim p$

14. $(p \vee q) \supset (r \supset \sim s)$
      $\underline{(s \vee t) \supset (p \cdot r)}$
      $\therefore \sim s$

EXERCISE 7–8   *Using any of the methods discussed in this chapter, prove the validity or invalidity of the arguments presented in Exercise 7–1.*

ANALYZING
SAMPLE ARGUMENTS
Much more could be said about this system of the propositional calculus and about propositional logic in general, but enough has been said to give a sufficient understanding for the purposes of this book. Before turning to the discussion of a new logical system, however, we will return to the sample arguments for which we gave preliminary analyses in Chapter 2 to see how they can be tested for validity using the methods of this chapter.

The reformulation of the first example that we felt intuitively to be deductively valid was the following:

> **This logic course is a science course.**
> **Susan is taking this logic course.**
> **Susan always does well in science courses.**
> **Therefore, Susan will do well in this logic course.**

If we symbolize this in the propositional calculus, we get the following abbreviation and schema:

L	p
T	q
W	r
∴S	∴s

We can tell by inspection that the proposition in the conclusion is not contained in any of the premises, and we can also see that the premises are consistent and the conclusion is not a contradiction. We could, therefore, conclude immediately that this example is not truth-functionally valid. However, let us confirm this using the shorter truth-table technique. If we assign the value **F** to the conclusion, it is still possible to assign the value **T** to each of the three premises as follows.

$$p \; , \quad q \; , \quad r \quad \therefore s$$
$$T \qquad T \qquad T \qquad F$$

Although this is sufficient to prove that the example is not truth-functionally valid, remember that it does *not* prove that it is not deductively valid; this argument might still be proved to be valid using some other system of formal logic.

The second sample we discussed in Chapter 2 was considerably more complex, and our intuition was that even our most elaborate reformulation still was not valid. Let us try to symbolize it and test it in the propositional calculus.

> *The resort motel operators in one Florida town all said that their business was fine.*
> *The parking lots of these motels were practically empty.*
> *The local bank reported that it had cashed many fewer travelers' checks than in the previous year.*
> *[If a resort motel's parking lot is almost empty, and its bank has not cashed many travelers' checks, then the resort motel's business is not good.]*
> *[If someone says business is good when it is not, then he is lying.]*
> *[If all of the resort motel operators interviewed in one Florida town lie about their business, than all resort motel operators lie about their business.]*
> *Therefore, resort motel operators lie a lot about their business.*

The abbreviation and schema for this example are:

M	p
P	q
B	r
$(L \cdot \sim C) \supset \sim G$	$(s \cdot \sim t) \supset \sim u$
$S \supset T$	$v \supset w$
$I \supset O$	$x \supset y$
$\therefore O$	$\therefore y$

The symbolization of this example requires some explanation. At first glance, it may be thought that the antecedant of the fourth premise should be abbreviated as 'P · B' rather than 'L · ~C', since it appears to be a conjunction of the second and third premises. This certainly would give the set of premises greater coherence, but unfortunately does not represent the argument as we had formulated it in our preliminary analysis. The second premise is about the specific set of resort motels in a particular town, whereas the first part of the fourth premise is about a randomly selected motel anywhere—and is thus about *all* motels everywhere. Likewise, the second premise is about a specific bank in the one town in Florida, while the fourth premise is about banks in general. Similarly, premise 5 is about anyone who misrepresents their business, which is quite different from the first premise which is only about the motel operators in one town. It is for this reason that different symbols had to be used in the abbreviation and schema of this argument. On this basis, the argument can be shown to be truth functionally invalid using the shortened truth-table method.

$$p \ , \ q \ , \ r \ , \ (s \supset {\sim}t) \supset {\sim}u \ , \ v \supset w \ , \ x \supset y \ , \ \therefore y$$
$$T \quad T \quad T \quad T \ T \ TF \ T \ TF \quad T \ T \ T \quad F \ T \ F \quad F$$

Once again, it must be remembered that truth-functional invalidity does not imply that the argument is invalid in any absolute sense; it might still be proved to be valid using one of the other systems of logic.

As noted in the preliminary analysis of this argument in Chapter 2, only a few of the numerous possible interpretations of the original argument were given there. This is an appropriate point at which to consider one other formulation of this example, one that is more likely to test out as truth-functionally valid. Rather than formulate the added premises in a generalized form as we did originally, we can formulate them to refer to the same things as the explicit premises, so that the same symbols can be used in the abbreviations of two or more premises.

> *The resort motel operators in one Florida town all said that their business was fine.*
> *The parking lots of these motels were practically empty.*
> *The local bank reported that it had cashed many fewer travelers' checks than in the previous year.*
> *If the parking lots of these motels were practically empty, and the local bank reported that it had cashed many fewer travelers' checks than in the previous year, then the business of these motels was not good.*
> *If the resort motel operators in one Florida town all said that their business was fine and the business of these motels was not good, then these motel operators lie about their business.*
> *If the resort motel operators in one Florida town lie about their business, then all resort motel operators lie about their business.*
> *Therefore, all resort motel operators lie about their business.*

The abbreviation and schema for this formulation are as follows:

M	p
P	q
B	r
$(P \cdot B) \supset \sim G$	$(q \cdot r) \supset \sim s$
$(M \cdot \sim G) \supset L$	$(p \cdot \sim s) \supset t$
$L \supset O$	$t \supset u$
$\therefore O$	$\therefore u$

In this form, the argument schema has six variables, and thus its truth table would have 2^6, or 64 rows. It would, therefore, be most reasonable either to try to prove it to be invalid using the short truth-table method, or to go with our intuitive hunch that the argument in this form is valid and try to prove that it is using the method of deductive proof. Let us try the latter approach first. If after awhile we can't complete the proof, then we can test it for invalidity using the shorter truth-table method.

1.	p	*Premise*
2.	q	*Premise*
3.	r	*Premise*
4.	$(q \cdot r) \supset \sim s$	*Premise*
5.	$(p \cdot \sim s) \supset t$	*Premise*
6.	$t \supset u / \therefore u$	*Premise/conclusion*
7.	$q \cdot r$	*2,3 Conj.*
8.	$\sim s$	*4,7 M.P.*
9.	$p \cdot \sim s$	*1,8 Conj.*
10.	t	*5,9 M.P.*
11.	u	*6,10 M.P.*

Thus, we have proven that *in this formulation* the argument is truth-functionally valid. The difficult judgments, of course, are whether this formulation is sufficiently close to the author's intent and whether the truth of the premises is reasonably well established, and these judgments are beyond the scope of the methods of formal logic.

Let us look only briefly at the third sample analysis from Chapter 2 since the more interesting version of it is the inductive interpretation. The deductive formulation, it will be remembered is as follows:

> *Mrs. Parker was infected with the "Abid" strain of smallpox virus.*
> *A quantity of the "Abid" smallpox virus was being stored in the lab directly below Mrs. Parker's office.*
> *It is possible for smallpox virus to be transmitted through the air.*

> *There was no other possible source of the "Abid"*
> *virus than the downstairs lab.*
> *Mrs. Parker had not been in contact with any person*
> *or object from the downstairs lab.*
> *Therefore, Mrs. Parker must have been infected by a*
> *virus transmitted through the air from the*
> *downstairs lab.*

A bit of thought reveals that since there are no recurring simple propositions in this formulation, it could not be truth-functionally valid. We must, therefore, try to add some compound statements that connect the other premises. The following appears to be a reasonable possibility:

> *If Mrs. Parker was infected with the "Abid" strain of*
> *smallpox virus, and there was no other possible*
> *source of the virus than the downstairs lab, then*
> *either she had been in direct contact with some*
> *person or object from the downstairs lab, or she*
> *was infected by a virus transmitted through the air*
> *from the downstairs lab.*

With the addition of this premise, the second (Q) and third (A) premises become unnecessary. The argument can now be abbreviated and schematized as follows (eliminating unnecessary premises).

I	p
$\sim S$	$\sim q$
$\sim C$	$\sim r$
$(I \cdot \sim S) \supset (C \vee T)$	$(p \cdot \sim q) \supset (r \vee s)$
$\therefore T$	$\therefore s$

Since there are only four variables in the schema, the truth table would only have sixteen rows. However, a deductive proof would still probably be simpler, so we will try this method first:

1.	p	*Premise*
2.	$\sim q$	*Premise*
3.	$\sim r$	*Premise*
4.	$(p \cdot \sim q) \supset (r \vee s)/\therefore s$	*Premise/conclusion*
5.	$p \cdot \sim q$	*1,2 Conj.*
6.	$r \vee s$	*4,5 M.P.*
7.	s	*6,3 D.Syll.*

Once again, proving truth-functional validity for this formulation is not that difficult. The significant question is whether the argument that we ultimately proved to be valid is essentially the same as the argument with which we began. In this case, it is not at all clear that it is the same.

"No flowers. That means
you want me to think you
haven't got a guilty
conscience."

© 1973 Punch-Rothco.

The last of the four examples for which we gave preliminary analyses in Chapter 2 fits most naturally into the formal system of propositional logic. Its last formulation was as follows:

> *You didn't bring me any flowers.*
> *If you bring me flowers, then you must have a guilty*
>   *conscience.*
> *If you don't bring me flowers, then you want me to*
>   *think that you don't have a guilty conscience.*
> *If you want me to think that you don't have a guilty*
>   *conscience, then you must have a guilty*
>   *conscience.*
> *Therefore, you must have a guilty conscience.*

The abbreviation and schema for this example are as follows:

$\sim B$	$\sim p$
$B \supset G$	$p \supset q$
$\sim B \supset W$	$\sim p \supset r$
$W \supset G$	$r \supset q$
$\therefore G$	$\therefore q$

The argument can be proved to be truth-functionally valid quite directly, and the truth table only requires eight rows. For practice, we will use the method of deductive proof:

1.	$\sim p$	*Premise*
2.	$p \supset q$	*Premise*
3.	$\sim p \supset r$	*Premise*
4.	$r \supset q / \therefore q$	*Premise/conclusion*
5.	r	*3,1 M.P.*
6.	q	*4,5 M.P.*

EXERCISE 7–9

Reconsider the arguments for which you did preliminary analyses in Exercise 2–9. Find one version of each argument that seems more appropriate for analysis using the methods of the present chapter and carry out such analyses. Compare your analyses here with those of the same arguments you may have done in Exercises 3–3, 5–10, and 10–7.

EXERCISE 7–10

Reconsider the arguments for which you did preliminary analyses in Exercise 2–10. Apply the instructions for Exercise 7–9 to these arguments and compare these analyses with those of the same arguments that you might have done in Exercises 3–3, 5–11, and 10–8.

SUMMARY

1. A **truth-functional proposition** is a compound statement which is such that if we know the truth value of each of its component statements and the meanings of the logical operators, the truth or falsity of the compound statement can be determined.

2. Since we are concerned with the relationships between premises and conclusion, we want to know whether a particular deductive argument is valid or invalid. A valid deductive argument has previously been defined as one which is such that, *if* the premises are true, then the conclusion *must* be true. Given this definition of validity, two consequences result: any argument with an inconsistent set of premises is necessarily valid (because it is impossible for all its premises to be true at the same time), and any argument whose conclusion is a tautology must be valid (because it is impossible for the conclusion to be false, whatever the truth or falsity of the premises).

3. Just as it is possible to abbreviate and schematize a truth-functional compound statement by using propositional constants, propositional variables, and symbols for logical operators, so, too, it is possible to abbreviate and schematize a truth-functional argument by means of the same symbols. An **argument schema** displays the logical form of an argument. Once such a schema is set up, either a simple or a compound proposition may be substituted for the propositional variables in the schema. This produces a **substitution instance,** or an **interpretation** of the argument schema. But there are two restrictions: only *propositions* can be substituted for propositional variables, and the same proposition must be substituted for *every* occurrence of any given variable in a particular argument schema.

4. Unlike a propositional schema, an argument schema is valid or invalid. A **valid argument schema** is one for which there is no possible substitution instance that would result in an argument with true premises and a false conclusion.

5. The truth-table method for testing the truth-functional validity of arguments requires that we construct a truth table for each premise and the conclusion of an argument schema. If, in this table, there is any row in which there are **T**'s under the main operator of each premise and an **F** under the main operator of the conclusion, then the argument schema is truth-functionally invalid. However, such a schema may, in some cases, be proved valid when tested by the methods of other systems of logic such as the syllogistic and quantificational logic discussed in other chapters of this book.

6. Because using the full truth-table method becomes cumbersome as the number of propositional variables in an argument schema increases, a short method may be used in such cases. It is recommended that this method be used to prove only the invalidity, not the validity, of an argument schema. In using it, we begin by assigning an **F** to the conclusion and then backtrack to see if it is possible to assign truth values to the component statements, such that all of the premises can be assigned the truth value **T.** If so, the argument is truth-functionally invalid.

7. For every truth-functional argument, it is possible to construct a **corresponding conditional statement:** that is, a material implication whose antecedent consists of the conjunction of the premises of the argument and whose consequent is the conclusion of the argument. An argument and its correspond-

ing conditional differ in two respects: first, the argument is composed of several statements, whereas the corresponding conditional is a single compound statement; and second, whereas in the argument the premises are asserted to be true, they are not so asserted in the conditional. If a truth-functional argument is valid, then its corresponding conditional is a tautology, and vice versa.

8. The method of deductive proof supplies an alternative to the truth-table method of proving the validity of argument schemata. A **deductive proof system,** consisting of a set of rules and procedures that make it possible to prove the validity of a deductive argument schema in step-by-step fashion, is known as a **logical calculus.** Most deductive proof systems do not provide a decision procedure, and therefore cannot be used to obtain an unequivocal proof of *invalidity*; they can be used only to prove validity. Basically, a deductive proof system uses a small number of rules or axioms which are such that when they are used in conjunction with the premises of a valid argument, it can be shown that, if all the premises are true, then the truth of the conclusion logically follows.

9. A deductive proof system for truth-functional arguments is **deductively complete** if any argument which can be proved to be truth-functionally valid using truth tables can also be proved valid using this system's rules and procedures. The number of rules contained in such a system may vary from as few as three to infinitely many. A system of convenient size and substantial utility can be constructed of about twenty rules, and such a system is used in this book.

10. Each of the rules of this system is a **rule of inference:** that is, a basic argument schema which can be proven valid by the truth-table method, and which can be used in constructing a formal proof for other, more complex truth-functional arguments. It is considered inappropriate to try to prove the validity of any one of these rules of inference using the other rules.

11. The first eight rules of inference are **modus tollens, modus ponens, hypothetical syllogism, constructive dilemma, disjunctive syllogism, simplification, conjunction,** and **addition.** Because these rules are valid *argument* schemata, not propositional schemata, they can be applied only to entire lines of a proof and not to individual components of such lines.

12. A **formal proof** is the process whereby the conclusion of an argument can be validly derived, using the rules of the system, from a set of statements, each one of which either is a premise of the original argument or has been validly deduced from the premises and/or other statements which have themselves been validly deduced by means of the rules of the system. Theoretically, an infinite number of correct formal deductive proofs can be constructed for any truth-functionally valid argument. The ability to construct a formal deductive proof for a valid argument is dependent on many subjective factors. Thus, failure to construct a formal deductive proof for a particular argument schema is not sufficient to prove that the schema is truth-functionally invalid. Several rules of thumb for constructing proofs are provided in this chapter, but the most effective way to acquire the skills necessary for constructing proofs is continued practice.

13. A procedural rule, called the **rule of rigor,** requires that only one rule be used

in each step of a deductive proof and that the rules be used only in the form in which they are given in the system.

14. The **rule of replacement** allows us to substitute logically equivalent statements in a deductive proof. It asserts that any propositional schema that is produced by replacing all or part of another schema with a schema which is equivalent to the replaced portion according to one of the equivalences listed in the following paragraph is validly derivable from the original schema. Unlike the first eight rules of inference, the **rules of equivalence** included under the rule of replacement can be applied to parts of lines in a proof as well as to entire lines.

15. The ten equivalences contained in the rule of replacement are **De Morgan's rules, commutation, association, distribution, double negation, transportation, material implication, material equivalence, exportation,** and **tautology.**

16. Not every argument which can be proved valid using truth tables can be proved valid using these eighteen rules of inference. The addition of the rule of **conditional proof** makes our system deductively complete and enables us to prove the validity of such arguments. The method of conditional proof involves assuming an additional premise, which is actually the antecedent of a conditional statement that is necessary in the proof, and then deducing the consequent of the desired statement from the assumption and the original premises. The step ending the conditional proof must be a conditional statement, with the assumed premise as its antecedent.

17. Steps derived from the assumed premise are said to be within the **scope** of the assumption. As soon as the rule of conditional proof is asserted, the scope of the assumption is ended, and the assumption is said to be discharged. No formula that has been derived within the scope of the assumption (and that is therefore dependent on the assumption) may be used outside its scope. This is because conditional proof asserts only that, *if* the assumption (the antecedent of the conditional) is true, the consequent is also true; it does not assert that the assumption *is* true. Any number of assumptions can be made, provided they are eventually discharged, leaving the conclusion dependent only on the premise(s) of the original argument schema.

18. **Indirect proof,** or the *reductio ad absurdum* proof, is a special case of conditional proof. In this we assert the negation of the conclusion as our assumed premise and then derive a contradiction from it, which then permits us to derive the conclusion of the argument schema. Even with the addition of these two rules, this deductive proof system still does not provide a decision procedure.

CHAPTER EIGHT

Quantification

Many valid arguments cannot be proved by a truth table or the propositional calculus. An example is the following:

> **All felines are quadrupeds.**
> **All lions are felines and have tufted tails.**
> ∴**All lions are quadrupeds.**

Propositionally, this argument is of an invalid form: 'p', 'q', therefore 'r'. We can divide the second premise into its propositional components—'All lions are felines', 'All lions have tufted tails'—but there is still no repetition of propositions, and we know in advance that the truth table test of validity will turn out negative.

In the argument above, validity depends on the repetition of *terms* ('lions', 'felines', 'quadrupeds'); on the pattern of that repetition; and on the presence of quantifying terms ('all'). To prove validity, we have to "get inside" the individual statements and analyze their logical grammar, their internal structure. Syllogistic logic, presented in Chapters 4 and 5, does allow us to analyze term relationships, quite effectively, but only if each proposition contains exactly two terms. The possibility of a fruitful combination of propositional and term analysis suggests itself—a combination that is realized in **quantificational logic**.

The symbols and definitions of truth-functional logic serve as foundations for quantificational logic. We will see in the present chapter how truth-functional techniques are adapted to create an entirely novel analysis of the internal structure of statements. The way is prepared thereby for the predicate calculus (Chapter 9), which incorporates and goes beyond the propositional calculus; in our new calculus we will be able to prove the validity of numerous arguments that cannot possibly be solved by syllogistic or propositional means. A more powerful system is usually more difficult to master, and we warn that the generalization obtains here. We shall, of course, emphasize basic concepts and simpler applications, as is appropriate to an introduction to logic; but sharp attention to the "why" of the logical operations is essential to learning how to use them.

This chapter was written by David T. Wieck.

We start our investigation by considering the following statement:

1.   All of Harriet's children are unmarried.

For lack of a truth-functional operator, this statement can be treated, in propositional logic, only as a unit, as 'p'. But there is a pattern in the statement, a structure, that becomes visible when we blank out 'Harriet', 'children', and 'married':

2.   All of _____'s _____ are un-_____.

Into this pattern we can fit any number of other propositions. If we replace the blanks with 'Paula', 'brothers', and 'married', for example, we get:

3.   All of Paula's brothers are unmarried.

Substituting 'Jim', 'decisions', and 'wise', we get:

4.   All of Jim's decisions are unwise.

By concentrating on this pattern, and specifically on statement 1, we will be able to illustrate many features of quantificational symbolism.

What does it mean to say that *all of* Harriet's children are unmarried? One answer is that the proposition seems clearly to imply that if Amy, for example, is a child of Harriet's, then Amy is unmarried, and that the same is true of Carl and Fred and everyone else we can think of. The importance of this is that '*If* Amy is a child of Harriet's, *then* Amy is unmarried' can be analyzed truth-functionally as a material conditional, 'p ⊃ q'. This gives us an opening. We might now imagine our writing all those conditionals in a great conjunctive series. But as a way of symbolizing 'All of Harriet's children are unmarried', that would be absurdly inconvenient, if it had no other drawback.

Thinking further about the Amy-statement and all its companions, we may notice that they have an interesting logical feature in common. In each conditional, *the same individual* is the subject of both the antecedent and the consequent: If *Amy* is a child of Harriet's, then *Amy* is unmarried. In addition to being truth-functional, all these statements will have the following pattern:

*5.   If _____ is a child of Harriet's, then _____ is
unmarried.*

To make this form usable—and we shall use it—we replace the blanks by 'x's, as follows:

6.   If x is a child of Harriet's, then x is unmarried.

Now we have an expression that is almost statement-like—but it does not express a statement. It resembles an English sentence with an 'it' as its subject and with no referent or context by which to identify the 'it': in isolation from context, such sentences have no truth value.

We can, however, supply a context for those 'x's. We can do this by incorporating the whole expression into the following sentence:

> 7.   *Let x be anything whatever: if x is a child of*
>   *Harriet's, then x is unmarried.*

This means: Pick out anything you care to from the whole universe; if it's a child of Harriet's then it's unmarried. In this way, without mentioning a single individual, we cover the cases of Amy, Carl, Fred, and all the others. And of the greatest significance: We now have a *statement,* true if true for all individuals, false if false for one. We are, indeed, getting very close to the form in which we are going to express 'All of Harriet's children are unmarried'.

As a transition, we say next:

> 8.   *(x) (if x is a child of Harriet's, then x is*
>   *unmarried)*

At this point we have made use of a "universal quantifier," '(x)', to do the work of 'let x be anything whatever'. As a final preliminary we will rewrite 'x is unmarried' so that we can bring out the role that 'un-' plays in our statement.

> 9.   *(x) (if x is a child of Harriet's, then it is not the*
>   *case that x is married)*

Now we will express that statement in full symbolic form. For 'if, then' we will use the horseshoe. 'x is a child of Harriet's' we will abbreviate as 'Cx'. For 'it is not the case that' we use the tilde. And to abbreviate 'x is married' we use 'Mx'. Our result is the following:

> 10. $(x) (Cx \supset \sim Mx)$

As a way of explaining the quantifier, we said 'let x be anything whatever'. There are, however, many ways of paraphrasing statement 10, of which we give a few, beginning with logicians' quasi-English:

> 11.   *For any x, if x is a child of Harriet's, then it is*
>   *not the case that x is married.*
> 12.   *Everything (anything, any x, any given thing or*
>   *individual) that is a child of Harriet's is*
>   *unmarried.*
> 13.   *Whatever is a child of Harriet's is unmarried.*

And by no means least, with only a very slight reservation that we will discuss later on:

> 14.   *All of Harriet's children are unmarried.*

If we now want to symbolize 'All of Paula's brothers are unmarried', we can indicate 'Bx' as abbreviation for 'x is a brother of Paula's' and, once more, 'Mx' for 'x is married', and write:

   15.   (x) (Bx ⊃ ~ Mx)

To say that all of Jim's decisions are unwise we would abbreviate 'x is a decision of Jim's' by 'Dx' and 'x is wise' by 'Wx', with the result:

   16.   (x) (Dx ⊃ ~ Wx)

And of course if we thought that all of Jim's decisions *were* wise, we would write:

   17.   (x) (Dx ⊃ Wx)

Before going further we need to establish our terminology and explain certain points.

The letter 'x' we have been using is called an **individual variable.** When additional variables are needed, it is customary to follow with 'y' and 'z', and, if it comes to that, 'u', 'v', and 'w'. We first encountered these variables as replacements for the names of individuals. In symbolizing statements about individuals, we use **individual constants,** 'a' through 't', as abbreviations, usually for names, sometimes for a definite description of an individual. To symbolize 'If Amy is a child of Harriet's, then Amy is unmarried' we would use 'a' as an abbreviation for 'Amy' and write: 'Ca ⊃ ~ Ma'. To write a similar statement about 'the present mayor of Atlanta', we could use 'm' as abbreviation, with the result 'Cm ⊃ ~ Mm'. Statements about individuals are called **singular statements.**

The capital letters we have conjoined with individual variables and individual constants are called **predicate constants.** These are abbreviations for *predicates,* by which we mean such phrases as 'is a child of Harriet's', 'is married', 'is wise', 'likes strawberries', 'catches mice', and other statement-completing expressions. The sense of the term 'predicate' here, it may be observed, is slightly different from the ordinary grammatical sense; the copula 'is' or 'are', if present, is incorporated into the predicate.

Sentences such as 'Cx', 'Mx', 'Cx ⊃ Mx', and 'Cx ⊃ ~ Mx', are called **open sentences** to distinguish them from sentences that express statements. They may be *transformed into* statements by replacing their variables with constants; they may *appear in* statements when their variables are "bound" by a quantifier of the same letter. In 'Cx ⊃ ~ Mx' the 'x's are "free." In '(x) (Cx ⊃ ~ Mx)' the 'x's of the open sentence are "bound"; they are tied to the quantifier and read in the context of the quantifier. The parentheses around 'Cx ⊃ ~ Mx' in the quantified statement indicate that the variables are in the *scope* of the quantifier, hence bound by it. For scope we must be watchful: '(x)Cx ⊃ ~ Mx' remains an open sentence—does not express a statement—because, although the 'x' in 'Cx' is bound (its adjacency to the quantifier allows us to dispense with scope-indicating parentheses), the 'x' in '~Mx' remains entirely "free." The presence of an unbound variable will signify that we have not symbolized a statement correctly.

A **universal quantifier** means, roughly, 'anything', 'everything', 'any given thing', 'any x', or, somewhat awkwardly, 'any "it" '. To constitute it, we put an individual variable in parentheses. Such a quantifier functions to make a claim, a **universal statement,** about all the individuals in a universe. We say 'a universe' because it is sometimes convenient to limit the universe by stipulating that we are "talking" only about the universe of persons, or of animals, or of numbers. So far we have not restricted our universe, which explains why, in some of our paraphrases of '(x) (Cx ⊃ ~ Mx)', we used terms like 'everything' and 'whatever' when the reader might have expected 'anyone' and 'whoever'.

A quantified proposition has **instances.** All those statements about Amy and Carl and Fred and the rest (in the great series that we mentioned) are *instances* of '(x) (Cx ⊃ ~ Mx)'. They are formed by dropping the quantifier and replacing the variables of the open sentence with a constant. If a universal proposition is true, all its instances must be true. This has a surprising consequence. If '(x) (Cx ⊃ ~ Mx)' is true, and the universe is unlimited, then it must apply to my cat Sam and to the star Betelguese; in logic, stars as well as people are "individuals." Then the following "instances" must be true:

> **18. *If my cat Sam is a child of Harriet's, then my
> cat Sam is unmarried.***
>
> **19. *If the star Betelguese is a child of Harriet's,
> then the star Betelguese is unmarried.***

Restricting the universe to people won't rid us of these curious truths. For example:

> **20. *If Harriet's grandmother is a child of Harriet's,
> then Harriet's grandmother is unmarried.***

From familiarity with the "material conditional" of truth-functional logic, it is easy to understand why the singular statements, 18, 19, and 20, are true: each has a false antecedent. Such "truth" is peculiar but harmless. Actually, in this context, we are just not interested in Sam and Betelguese and Harriet's grandmother: they don't provide any kind of test for our universal proposition; they don't *confirm* it, they can't possibly *falsify* it. The only instances that can put the proposition to a test are those that identify someone who actually is a child of Harriet's—those instances, that is, that have true antecedents. If *they* have a false consequent, then the universal proposition is false.

Exceptions to the rule that universal propositions should be symbolized as *universally quantified conditionals* are rare. Those exceptions usually occur when the universe is limited by stipulation. Thus, if we want to write 'Everyone has a spinal column and a liver', we can abbreviate 'x has a spinal column' by 'Sx' and 'x has a liver' by 'Lx', *limit the universe to human beings,* and write a universally quantified conjunction:

> **21. *(x)(Sx · Lx)***

A single human case—but only a human case—of either 'no spinal column' or 'no liver' will falsify this proposition. In an unlimited universe, '(x)(Sx · Lx)' would not have a chance. For that universe, however, we could write an additional open sentence, 'x is human', 'Hx', and form a conditional:

22.   **(x)(Hx ⊃ (Sx · Lx))**

For an unlimited universe, this proposition would have the same meaning and truth value as statement 21 for a universe of human beings only.

As the last example suggests, we are by no means restricted in our symbolizing to the expression of statements with just two "terms." The truth function in the scope of a quantifier may be as complex as the statement to be symbolized requires. If we wanted to say that all players on our team are either fast and nimble or big and strong, we could express this by the abbreviations 'Px' for 'x is a player on our team', 'Fx' for 'x is fast', 'Nx' for 'x if nimble', 'Bx' for 'x is big', and 'Sx' for 'x is strong'. We would then write:

23.   **(x)(Px ⊃ ((Fx · Nx) ∨ (Bx · Sx)))**

The Principle of Least Analysis

The example at the end of the previous section is meant to show something of what we can do by quantificational analysis—when we have to. That proviso is something to keep in mind. So as not to complicate our task of symbolization, increase probability of error, and add labor to deductions, *we should never carry an analysis further than is needed for a specific purpose.* We call this the **principle of least analysis.**

Arguments that are valid propositionally cannot be invalid quantificationally; it is always best, therefore, to check the propositional form first. Imagine a truth-functionally valid argument in which statement 23 did no other "work" than to affirm the antecedent of a conditional (modus ponens). In that case, we should symbolize the statement by a propositional constant, say 'P', and be done with it. Quantificational notation would be foolish; we should avoid idle displays of logical virtuosity. One could also make up an argument where we need quantification but where detailed analysis of the consequent in statement 23 would not be necessary. Then we would simply write a single open sentence for that consequent, 'x is either fast and nimble or big and strong', abbreviate it as 'Ex', and symbolize our statement as '(x)(Px ⊃ Ex)'.

In short, don't do it the hard way. Do what the context calls for, and symbolic logic will be much easier to use. That is what the "principle of least analysis" tells us.

EXERCISE 8–1
1. Symbolize 'If John is an English teacher, then John speaks English', using 'j' for 'John', 'Tx' for 'x is an English teacher', and 'Sx' for 'x speaks English'.
2. Using the same definitions, symbolize 'All English teachers speak English'.
3. Suppose 'If John is an English teacher, then John speaks English' is true. What will be the truth value of 'All English teachers speak English'? Suppose that the 'John' statement is false; what will be the truth value of the universal statement?

4. Suppose that all English teachers do speak English. Will 'If John is an English teacher, then John speaks English' be true or false? If it is not the case that all English teachers speak English, will 'If John is an English teacher, then John speaks English' be true or false?

5. Which of the following are instances of 'All English teachers speak English'? (a) If Walter is an English teacher, then Walter speaks English. (b) If Walter is not an English teacher, then Walter does not speak English. (c) Walter is not an English teacher. (d) Karen is an English teacher. (e) If Karen's dog is an English teacher, then Karen's dog speaks English.

6. Symbolize 'My next-door neighbor is an English teacher and does not speak English'.

7. Suppose it is true that my next-door neighbor is an English teacher and does not speak English. What will be the truth value of 'All English teachers speak English'? What will its truth value be if the 'next-door neighbor' statement is false? If the universal proposition is true, what is the truth value of the 'next-door neighbor' statement? And what will be the truth value of the 'next-door neighbor' statement if the universal proposition is false?

8. Let 'Bx' be 'x has a brain'. Define a universe larger than the universe of humans for which '(x)Bx' will be true, and a universe for which it will be false.

9. Which of the following are singular statements; which are universally quantified statements; which are open sentences? On what basis do you arrive at your answers?
   a. $(x)((Fx \lor Gx) \supset Hx)$
   b. $(x)(Fx \lor Gx) \supset Hx$
   c. $Fa \supset Ga$
   d. $(x)Fx$

RELATIONS

We began by exhibiting the form of the English sentence 'All of Harriet's children are unmarried' as follows:

1. All of _____'s _____ are un-_____.

We have now seen how '(x)' does the work of 'all of'; how the tilde in front of an open sentence does the work of 'un-'; and how 'are' becomes incorporated into the predicate of an open sentence, while the horseshoe does the work of the copula in linking the components of the statement. So far, ''s' has remained buried in the phrase "Harriet's children," and, for most purposes, this would be fine. At times, however, the possessive needs special treatment.

For simplicity, we will consider first the singular statement 'Amy is a child of Harriet's'. Using the individual constant 'a' as abbreviation of 'Amy', we can write 'Ca', still ignoring the possessive 's'. By this symbolization, we are treating the sentence 'Amy is a child of Harriet's' as, in effect, a statement about *Amy*. But we can also look at it as expressing a *relation* between two persons. After all, Amy's mother is an individual, too. Proof of validity will depend sometimes on our expressing such a relation *as* a relation, by a **relational statement.**

The predicates of our 'Cx' and 'Mx' open sentences are called **monadic,** or one-place, predicates because a single variable is conjoined with the predicate constant. To express a *relation between* Amy and Harriet, we need a **dyadic,** or two-place, predicate, one that has a "place" for each individual. That predicate will be simply 'is a child of'. Assigning 'h' as abbreviation for Harriet, we can express 'Amy is a child of Harriet's' as 'Cah'.

Using this new predicate, we can symbolize 'All of Harriet's children are unmarried' as a relational statement. The open sentence for our antecedent will be 'x is a child of Harriet'—the ''s', of course, disappears—or 'Cxh'. We write:

$$2. \quad (x)(Cxh \supset \sim Mx)$$

By this symbolization we do not change the meaning of the Harriet statement in any way; we simply make it available for combination in deductions with statements that *require* relational treatment. From the two statements, 'All of Harriet's children are unmarried' and 'Amy is a daughter of Harriet's', we certainly understand that Amy is unmarried. To prove it, however, we would need a link between 'children' and 'daughter': 'Everyone who is a daughter of someone is a child of that person'. This last statement cannot be analyzed satisfactorily with monadic predicates. If we have the predicate 'is a child of Harriet's' in one statement, as in '$(x)(Cx \supset \sim Mx)$', and the predicate 'is a child of' in the children/daughter statement, we would have no repetition of predicates and no possibility of combining those statements logically.

A great deal of our reasoning involves relations: 'is larger than', 'lives next to', 'is unkind to', 'likes', and so on. When practical, we avoid introducing dyadic predicates because they usually bring with them a second variable and a second quantifier, as we shall illustrate below. But their ability to express relations, when necessary, is an important part of the power of quantificational logic.

There is one other relation that we can draw out of the Harriet statement, one that is implicit. A person cannot be married or unmarried except *to* someone or no one. Most times it would be unnecessary to make it explicit that 'unmarried' means 'not married to anyone'; in Chapter 9 we will analyze, and prove, an argument—really a rather ordinary one—that does make it necessary. Again, it will be a question of repetition of predicates.

What we need for relational symbolization is to expand 'it is not the case that x is married' to read 'it is not the case that x is married to anyone'. Speaking the language of quantification, 'It is not the case that x is married to anyone' means 'Think of any individual: it is not the case that x is married to that individual'. Using a second variable and a second quantifier, we write: '$(y) \sim Mxy$', or, 'For any y, it is not the case that x is married to y'. We then rephrase our Harriet statement as follows:

$$3. \quad (x)(Cx \supset (y) \sim Mxy)$$

Alternatively, of course, '$(x)(Cxh \supset (y) \sim Mxy)$'. To paraphrase this expanded statement, 'Harriet's children aren't married to anyone' would be reasonable, for the English sentence is quantified implicitly. (If we prefixed it with 'all' or 'all of' we would get a very ambiguous sentence.) Fully explicit would be 'None of Harriet's children is married to anyone', but it takes practice to recognize this.

EXISTENTIAL   Just as we sometimes assert the truth of universal propositions, we
QUANTIFIERS   often *deny* such propositions; we assert the truth of their negation.
To deny '(x)(Cx ⊃ ~ Mx)', or '(x)(Cxh ⊃ (y) ~ Mxy)' all *we have* to
say is 'It's not so' and write the tilde of negation in front of the symbolized
proposition. But the negation of a universal has an affirmative meaning: If it is
not the case that all of Harriet's children are unmarried, then it *is* the case that
there exists *at least one* child of Harriet's who is married.

To make 'at least one' claims is the function of the **existential quantifier.** We
write that quantifier as a variable preceded by '∃' and enclosed in parentheses:
'(∃x)', '(∃y)', and so on. In logicians' English, '(∃x)' is read as 'there is at least
one x such that' or 'there exists at least one x such that'. To symbolize 'At least
one child of Harriet's is married', we can write:

1.   **(∃x)(Cxh · Mx)**

or more simply '(∃x)(Cx · Mx)', if that is all the context requires. We don't want
a conditional. We want to assert *that there is* at least one individual of whom two
things are true—being a child of Harriet's and being married. As the conditional
is the rule for universal propositions, so the conjunction is for existentials.

The most direct use of the existential quantifier is to state in affirmative terms
what it means to say that a universal proposition is false. If someone proposes a
"law" that all lions are fierce, the proposition that there is a nonfierce lion, even
one, contradicts the "law." The existential quantifier does, however, also give us
a way to express that "someone" or "something" of which we often speak:
'someone objected', 'someone broke down the door', 'something hit me on the
head'. And it enables us to symbolize 'some', 'few', 'several', 'many', 'a whole
lot of' whenever it looks like interpreting these "quantifiers" as 'at least one' will
be sufficient to establish the validity of an argument. Obviously, there is a considerable loss of meaning in expressing 'a whole lot of' as 'at least one'. When
someone says that some lions are not fierce, they not only mean 'more than
one', or else they would not use the plural 'lions', they probably mean 'enough
worth mentioning'. Between 'at least one' and 'all', we do not have an intermediate quantifier. This is less of a drawback than it might seem. The English-
language quantifiers ('some', 'few', and so on) are imprecise and not meant to
be interpreted precisely. We have all witnessed futile arguments over whether
there were or were not "many" people at the ball game.

The existential quantifier has an interesting, and essentially simple, relationship to the universal quantifier. Consider the following, where 'Sx' abbreviates 'x
has a spinal column' and the universe is limited to humans:

2.   **(x)Sx**

This reads in English as 'Everyone has a spinal column'. We could write this also
by means of an existential quantifier, since 'everyone has' means the same as 'it
is not the case that someone does not have'. Thus:

3.   **~(∃x) ~ Sx**

Consider next the negation of statement 2:

4.   ~(x)Sx

'Not everyone has a spinal column' means that at least one person doesn't have one. Hence, it is logically equivalent to statement 5.

5.   (∃x) ~ Sx

To statements 2 and 3, and 4 and 5, we can add two further patterns of logical equivalence, and these patterns will cover all cases of "quantifier exchange":

'(x)Sx' is logically equivalent to '~(∃x) ~ Sx'
'~(x)Sx' is logically equivalent to '(∃x) ~ Sx'
'(x) ~ Sx' is logically equivalent to '~(∃x)Sx'
'~(x) ~ Sx' is logically equivalent to '(∃x)Sx'

These four equivalences can be subsumed under the single rule that, if we change the quantifier, and if we change the sign on each side (by adding a negation sign if there is none and deleting it if there is one), we get a logically equivalent statement, a statement with the same truth value.

Given the above equivalences, we could manage with just one kind of quantifier, existential or universal, if we were willing to put up with negation signs to an extent that would make deductions tedious and deduction rules complex. A little redundancy, in logic as in other matters, is usually not a bad thing. In practice, it is almost always advantageous to quantify affirmatively—that is, with no initial negation sign.

To illustrate our point that existential propositions, when they are compounds, should as a rule be symbolized as conjunctions, we will symbolize 'Some antelopes are elephants' as a conditional and see what happens. Suppose we abbreviated 'x is an antelope' by 'Ax' and 'x is an elephant' by 'Ex' and then wrote:

6.   (∃x)(Ax ⊃ Ex)

To make his peace with an unpleasant fact, Charlie Brown resorts to logic. Is his logic all mush? Does he start out well and go astray? Or does Charlie make more sense than he thinks? Symbolize his statements in frames 2 and 3 using quantifiers as appropriate.

© 1967 United Feature Syndicate, Inc.

Setting out to symbolize a proposition that we surely regarded as false, we have written a *true* one! 'p ⊃ q' is equivalent logically to '~p ∨ q'; hence, statement 6 is logically equivalent to:

7.   (∃x)(~Ax ∨ Ex)

But all that statement 7 says is that there is something, at least one thing, that is either a nonantelope *or* an elephant. There are lots of things that aren't antelopes and surely there are elephants. Statements 6 and 7 are true, therefore; they could be false only if *every* last thing in the world were an antelope (in disguise, no doubt) *and* there were no elephants.

REMEMBER!

In quantificational logic:

The main operator within the scope of a universal quantifier is normally the horseshoe.

The main operator within the scope of an existential quantifier is normally the dot.

EXERCISE 8–2   *In the sentences listed below, 'Ax' is an abbreviation for 'x is an albatross', 'Bx' for 'x is a bird', and 'Fxy' for 'x is a friend of y'. 'a' stands for 'Albert' and 'g' stands for 'George'. For each sentence, indicate whether it is: (a) a statement; (b) a singular statement; (c) an existentially quantified statement; (d) a universally quantified statement; (e) a truth-functional compound of quantified statements; and whether (f) its predicates are monadic or dyadic; (g) it contains any free variables; (h) it contains any constants.*

1. (∃x)(Ax · Bx)
2. (∃x)(Ax · Ba)
3. Ax ⊃ By
4. (x)(Ay ∨ Bx)
5. Aa ⊃ Ba

6. (x)(y)Fxy
7. (x)(Ax ⊃ Bg)
8. (x)(Ax ⊃ Bx)
9. (x)Ax ⊃ (∃x)Bx
10. Fga

EXERCISE 8–3   *Open sentences are called atomic if, like 'Ax' or 'Fxy', they contain no truth-functional operators. For each of the following, write the atomic open sentences that you would use in a quantificational analysis of the statement. Use letters only for variables; express predicates in words.*

---

1. All three-lane highways are dangerous.
2. Every proposition is expressible by a sentence.
3. Every sentence either expresses a proposition or does not express a proposition.

4. If an expression contains free variables, it is not a statement.
5. Open sentences become statements if their free variables are replaced by the name of an individual.
6. Some arguments that are valid are not truth-functionally valid.
7. Whatever is greater than something is neither less than nor equal to that other thing.
8. Not all books are hard-bound.
9. There are no vertebrates that are not animals.
10. A universally quantified statement is true if and only if every instance of it is true.
11. None but players of the first rank entered the tournament.
12. All the cheap goods in the store are either shoddily made or defective.
13. Emil is in the tournament and there is a player who is in the tournament whom Emil cannot beat.
14. Some actors who are award winners are not Academy Award winners.

Existential Import   In our opening discussion we said that symbolization of 'All of Harriet's children are unmarried' as '$(x)(Cx \supset \sim Mx)$' was correct except for one slight reservation. That reservation applies equally to our more elaborate Harriet symbolizations. The point we left dangling is that we would hardly make such a statement ('All . . . are . . .') *if Harriet did not have children*. Yet our symbolized statement, as will any universal conditional ('*If* anything is . . ,'), leaves that question open.

If there is no Amy, no Bill, nor anyone else who is a child of Harriet, then we say that the proposition has no **existential import.** Given our definitions, we will have to regard the proposition as *true*. Because every instance of the universal will be a conditional with a false antecedent, and therefore true, the universal will be true. Of such universals it is customary to say that they are *vacuously* true. A classic example is statements about square circles: 'All square circles are lawyers' and 'No square circles are lawyers' both come out true.

To call such statements true may go against our inclination. Unfortunately the alternatives are not wholly attractive. We could decide to reject such sentences altogether, that is, rule them "out of order," on the ground that they don't *say* anything, are meaningless. In the traditional syllogistic logic one main line of interpretation (the Aristotelian) is based on that option. But then consistency would seem to oblige us to say that the sentence 'All students who cut five or more classes will fail this course' does not express a statement if no students do cut that many classes. Intuitively, it doesn't seem that the statement—if it truly is a statement—loses its meaning just because students choose to attend class. We might also want to accept, as meaningful, scientific statements about ideal conditions that we believe not to exist. Well, then, suppose we do accept statements that lack "existential import"; what truth value would we *like* to assign to them? We might want to say 'false' for all square-circle statements, but we might not be so sure about the 'all students' case.

Given the way our logic handles universal propositions, those without existential import have to be evaluated as true, but no real harm results, save perhaps to our sensibilities. If the fancy takes us, we can add a "disclaimer"—

'~(∃x)Sx'—that asserts the nonexistence of square circles. Even more important, anyone who regards square-circle sentences as meaningless is free to have nothing to do with them. These are not the only sentences about which questions can be raised as to whether they express propositions: Some people will deny that value judgments have truth value; others say yes. A formal logic does not tell people which expressions have a truth value; it only presents a set of procedures for handling whatever people do accept as propositions.

With respect to propositions that have existential import, the silence of the universal conditional on that point matters only occasionally. When it does affect an argument, we can write an affirmation of existence—just the opposite of the square-circle "disclaimer." To '(x)(Cx ⊃ ~ Mx)', for example, we would simply conjoin '(∃x)Cx' with the result: '(x)(Cx ⊃ ~ Mx). (∃x)Cx'.

Symbolization and Translation

We have now reviewed the "machinery" of our logic—short of the deductive proof procedure to be presented in Chapter 9. In the remainder of this chapter, we shall explore further the "meanings" of quantified expressions.

One of the basic problems in becoming comfortable with quantificational reasoning is uncertainty about rendering quantified statements into English, and vice versa. So far, we have emphasized the alternatives that confront us. To make things a little easier, we will use for the remainder of our discussion, wherever possible, the standardized reading of symbolized statements given in the "Translation Dictionary" on the next page.

We give two kinds of reading: One, which we call the "logician's reading," retains the variables and the truth-functional syntax; the "suggested reading" approaches natural English so far as standardization permits. For purposes of example, we have used the open sentences 'x is black' and 'x is a crow', with obvious abbreviations. If we were making statements about human beings, and had limited the universe to humans, 'everyone' would replace 'everything'; if we were making statements about numbers, and had so limited the universe, 'every

Who can argue with the statement that criminals are criminals? (How would you symbolize it?—and why would you be obliged to agree with it?) But you will have trouble—more than you may think—in arguing with 'guilty or innocent, a criminal is a criminal'. Try symbolizing it and see if you can diagnose why it turns out to be necessarily true. Is there an alternative interpretation which would not necessarily be true?

© 1977 The Austin American Statesman.

number' would replace 'everything'. Not all open sentences, of course, include 'is': if the open sentence for the first statement were 'x surprises me', then the suggested reading would be 'Everything surprises me'. Truth-functional compounds of any of the statements will be read as such; the suggested reading for '(x)Bx $\lor$ (x) $\sim$ Bx' is 'Either everything is black or nothing is black'.

	TRANSLATION DICTIONARY	
Statement	*Logician's reading*	*Suggested reading*
(x)Bx	*For any x, x is black.*	*Everything is black.*
(x)(Bx · Cx)	*For any x, x is black and x is a crow.*	*Everything is both black and a crow.*
(x)(Bx $\lor$ Cx)	*For any x, either x is black or x is a crow.*	*Everything is either black or a crow.*
(x)(Bx $\supset$ Cx)	*For any x, if x is black then x is a crow.*	*Everything that is black is a crow.*
(x)(Bx $\equiv$ Cx)	*For any x, x is black if and only if x is a crow.*	*Everything is either black and a crow or neither black nor a crow.*
$\sim$(x)Bx	*It is not the case that: for any x, x is black.*	*Not everything is black.*
(x)$\sim$Bx	*For any x, x is not black.*	*Nothing is black.*
$\sim$(x)(Bx $\supset$ Cx)	*It is not the case that: for any x, if x is black then x is a crow.*	*Not everything that is black is a crow.*
(x)(Bx $\supset$ $\sim$Cx)	*For any x, if x is black then x is not a crow.*	*Nothing that is black is a crow.*
($\exists$x)Bx	*There is an x such that x is black.*	*Something is black.*
($\exists$x)(Bx · Cx)	*There is an x such that x is black and x is a crow.*	*Something is both black and a crow.*
$\sim$($\exists$x)Bx	*It is not the case that there is an x such that x is black.*	*Nothing is black.*
($\exists$x)(Bx $\supset$ Cx)	*There is an x such that if x is black then x is a crow.*	*Something is either nonblack or a crow.*

"In the United States there is more space where nobody is than where anybody is."
GERTRUDE STEIN

This deceptively simple statement is trickier to symbolize than it might at first appear to be. Be careful!

EXERCISE 8–4   *Using "suggested readings," translate the following into English.*

1. (x)(Mx ⊃ ~Vx)   x eats meat; x is a vegetarian; universe, people.
2. ~(x)(Gx ⊃ Wx)   x grows in my yard; x is a weed.
3. ~(∃x)Ux   x is a unicorn.
4. (∃x)(Px · Mx)   x is a physicist; x is a musician; universe, people.
5. ~(∃x)(Sx · Cx)   x is circular; x is square.
6. (x)(Sx ⊃ Ex)   x is for sale; x is too expensive.
7. (∃x)Ax ⊃ ~(x)Px   x is absent; x is present; universe, people.
8. (x)(Cx ⊃ ~Mx)   x is a child of Harriet's; x is married; universe, people.
9. (x)(Lx ⊃ Px)   John learned x; x proved useful.
10. (∃x)(Cx · ~Mx)   x is a child of Harriet's; x is married; universe, people.
11. (x)Fx ⊃ (∃x)Fx   x is a form of energy.
12. (∃x)(Cx · Dx)   x is a canine; x is a dog.
13. (x)(Ox ⋁ Ex)   x is odd; x is even; universe, integers.

EXERCISE 8–5   *Define open sentences and individual constants and symbolize, using monadic predicates only. Examples:*

Something is hard and smooth.
Hx = x is hard; Sx = x is smooth.
(∃x)(Hx · Sx)

John plays tennis and golf.
Tx = x plays tennis; Gx = x plays golf; j = John.
Tj · Gj

---

1. If all centipedes are nonmammals, then all mammals are noncentipedes.
2. Not all books are hardbound.
3. Every proposition is expressible by a sentence.
4. No one who is an atheist believes in God.

5. With no exceptions, three-lane highways are dangerous.
6. Some impulsive people make good decisions but some don't.
7. If Walter does his job, our plans will all work out.
8. Nearly everybody enjoyed the lecture.
9. Some players in the tournament are former champions.
10. There are no humans who aren't mammals.
11. If Jerry is a friend of Eliot's then Jerry lives in Detroit.
12. Everyone who lives in Detroit lives in Michigan.
13. Some arguments that are valid are not truth-functionally valid.
14. All three-lane highways are dangerous.
15. If an expression contains free variables, it is not a statement.
16. None but players of the first rank entered the tournament.
17. All the cheap goods in the store are either shoddily made or defective.
18. Every human is either alive or not alive.
19. Some actors who are award winners are not Academy Award winners.

LOGICAL RELATIONS BETWEEN QUANTIFIED STATEMENTS   To understand the meanings of statements more thoroughly, we can be helped by knowing what other statements they imply and which imply them. For the simpler kinds of quantificational statements, it is often possible to discover, by careful reasoning, the logical relations that hold, or do not hold, between them.

Initially we restrict ourselves to a universe of human beings and work with just two open sentences: 'Tx' for 'x is timid' and 'Nx' for 'x is nervous'. We begin with:

1. $(x)Tx$

or 'Everyone is timid'. Does anything follow logically from statement 1? Unless the universe has no members, whatever is true of everything is true, obviously, of at least one thing. Since the universe of human beings has members, statement 1 implies:

2. $(\exists x)Tx$

But we must be careful in applying the principle that what is true of everything is true of something. 'Everyone who is timid is nervous' does not imply 'Someone is both timid and nervous', as we can see by examining their symbolizations, statements 3 and 4:

3. $(x)(Tx \supset Nx)$
4. $(\exists x)(Tx \cdot Nx)$

Statement 3 does not say that timid people exist. It asserts only that *if* any members of the universe of humans are timid, then those people are also nervous. If there are no timid people, statement 3 will be true—vacuously true, because all instances of the universal will have false antecedents. But then statement 4 will be false, since it claims that there are timid people. Because we know that there is a circumstance under which statement 3 will be true and statement 4 false, the former does not imply the latter. To deduce statement 4 from statement 3, we would need an additional premise—in fact, statement 2 above—that affirms that at least one timid person exists. Statement 2 will tell us that someone is timid; statement 3 tells us that such people are nervous, hence statement 4.

In symbolic terms, the 'if everything then something' principle means this: A universal proposition implies an existential proposition with exactly the same open sentence. Such was the case with statements 1 and 2, and such is the case with statement 3 and statement 5 below:

5. $(\exists x)(Tx \supset Nx)$

For reasons discussed earlier, statement 5 is a very weak statement.

Statement 3 is worth a little more attention. It will be remembered from truth-functional logic that an English language 'if, then' statement normally conveys a sense of causal relation between antecedent and consequent and that this meaning is lost in symbolization. Exactly the same is true of universally quantified propositions. 'Everyone who is timid is nervous' may suggest a causal connection between timidity and nervousness. Its symbolization, statement 3, merely reports a dry 'it is the case that' about a certain correlation, with no causal overtones. Logically, it means nothing more than its equivalent:

6. $(x)(\sim Tx \vee Nx)$

The equivalence of statements 3 and 6 can be recognized by the equivalence of their open sentences, the one of the form 'p $\supset$ q'; the other of the form '$\sim$p $\vee$ q'.

For a moderately difficult exercise, let us compare the following pair of propositions:

7. $(x)Tx \vee (x)Nx$
8. $(x)(Tx \vee Nx)$

Statement 7 says that either everyone is timid or everyone is nervous. Statement 8 says that everyone is either nervous or timid. Are these logically equivalent? To be equivalent each must imply the other, and for one statement to imply another it must not be possible for the first to be true and the second false. So we ask ourselves, *can* we find a circumstance under which the second is false and the first true?

The only way for statement 8 to be false is for someone to be neither timid nor nervous. But then it can't be the case that everyone is timid *or* that everyone is nervous, and statement 7 is false. So it's not possible for statement 7 to be true and statement 8 false, and the former implies the latter.

Is it possible for statement 7 to be false if statement 8 is true? Yes. Suppose that exactly half the population is timid and exactly half the population is nervous, with no overlapping. Clearly that will make statement 7 false. But statement 8 will be true because everyone is in one or the other of those "halves." So it is possible for statement 8 to be true and statement 7 false. We must conclude that the former does not imply the latter and that the two statements are not logically equivalent.

EXERCISE 8-6

For each pair of statements, decide whether: (a) they are logically equivalent; (b) one implies the other but is not implied by the other; (c) neither implies the other.

1.	$(\exists x)(Fx \cdot \sim Gx)$	$\sim(x)(Fx \supset Gx)$
2.	$(x)(Fx \supset Gx)$	$(x)(\sim Gx \supset \sim Fx)$
3.	$\sim(\exists x)Fx$	$(x) \sim (Fx \cdot Gx)$
4.	$(x)(Fx \supset Gx)$	$(x)Fx \supset (x)Gx$
5.	$(\exists x)Fx \lor (\exists x) \sim Fx$	$(\exists x)(Fx \lor \sim Fx)$
6.	$(x)(Fx \supset Gx)$	$(x)(Gx \supset Fx)$
7.	$(x)(Fx \cdot Gx)$	$(x)Fx \cdot (x)Gx$

MULTIPLY QUANTIFIED STATEMENTS

Statements containing more than one variable, and, therefore, more than one quantifier, vary in difficulty from the quite moderate to the extremely severe. Many interesting statements fall into the first category.

Actually, if one knows how to read the notation, some relational statements are easier to understand than to paraphrase in natural English. For example, suppose that 'Txy' abbreviates 'x is taller than y' and 'Syx' abbreviates 'y is shorter than x'. You may recognize without any trouble the meaning of the following:

1. $(x)(y)(Txy \supset Syx)$

It says, 'For any x and any y, if x is taller than y then y is shorter than x'. If John is taller than Harry, then Harry is shorter than John—and so on and so on. Yes, that's the "sense" of it. But if we try to say it in English, without mentioning names, we probably come up with 'if x is taller than y, then. . . .' or 'if a is taller than b, then. . . .' or 'if this one is taller than that one, then. . . .' What we're really doing in these three cases is to use variables, with the quantifiers left implicit. All that statement 1 does, in effect, is to make the quantifiers explicit and to use a standardized notation.

When, as in the cases following, we do not have to struggle with truth functions, statements about dyadic relationships are easy to translate, if we take care. Thus, if we limit the universe to numbers, and abbreviate 'x is the square of y' by 'Sxy', the meaning of the statement below should emerge as obvious when it is reread in the light of its translations:

2. $(y)(\exists x)Sxy$

'For every number, y, there exists a number, x, such that x is the square of y'. That is, 'For every number there is a number that is its square'. More freely, 'Every number can be squared'.

If we reverse the order of quantifiers in statement 11, we have a quite different statement, and a false one:

3. $(\exists x)(y)Sxy$

'There is a number, x, such that for every number, y, x is the square of y'. Or, 'At least one number is the square of each and every number, including itself'. More freely, 'Every number has the same square'.

If, in statement 2, we reverse the order of the variables in the open sentence, we get:

4. $(y)(\exists x)Syx$

Now we have: Every number is the square of some number (namely, its own square root). Further variations will produce still different propositions; such variations will include the negation of the entire statement, the negation of the open sentence, and the use of either both-universal or both-existential quantifiers.

The next example, while clearing up a possible confusion about universal quantifiers, will introduce an important logical point:

5. $(x)(y)Sxy$

Let 'Sxy' abbreviate 'x is similar to y', and let the universe be restricted to humans. Thus, 'Everyone is similar to everyone'. To *everyone*—not just to everyone *else*. So every individual, if similar to *every* individual, will be similar to himself or herself! Statement 6, which asserts that *every* individual is similar to herself or himself, is implied by statement 5.

6. $(x)Sxx$

What holds for all will, of course, hold for each separately. So if 'd' is 'Daniel', statement 6 logically implies:

7. Sdd

or 'Daniel is similar to Daniel'. If we balk at the proposition that one can be similar to oneself (logicians construe it so but one may think that 'similarity' signifies *some* difference), then we would have to deny statement 5 to avoid its consequences.

Or we can *amend* statement 5, as can be illustrated through a different example. Consider, 'Everyone quarrels with everyone'. Like many textbook examples designed to make a point, the statement is farfetched. But suppose someone did assert it, however perversely, yet did not mean that *everyone* quarrels with herself or himself. "Quarreling with oneself" could then be ruled out by use of a predicate of *identity,* 'x is identical with y', or 'Ixy'. Preserving a "human" universe, we could write:

8. $(x)(y)(\sim Ixy \supset Qxy)$

 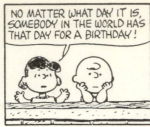  

Charlie Brown hasn't thought about Lucy's observations before. Can you symbolize them using quantificational logic? Are the statements in the first two frames logically equivalent?

© 1962 United Feature Syndicate, Inc.

'For any x and y, if it is *not the case* that x is identical with y, then x quarrels with y'. Short and to the point: 'Everyone quarrels with *everyone else*'.

For a last and more playful example, we ask ourselves just what is meant by saying that a barking dog does not bite. Well, we can begin by noting that this is obviously intended as a universal proposition about *all* barking dogs; that two parties, a dog and a person barked at but not bitten, are involved; and that a third "party," a time factor, needs to be taken into account, because it is certainly not intended that a dog that barks never bites, only that *while* engaged in barking at you, he (or she) is not engaged in biting you.

With dogs, persons, and times we will need three variables. Our quantifiers should all be universal—the proposition not only covers all dogs but (apparently) *any* person and any *time*. Our open sentences will be: 'Dx' for 'x is a dog', 'Py' for 'y is a person', 'Tz' for 'z is a time'; 'Kxyz' for 'x is barking at y at z', and 'Bxyz' for 'x is biting y at z'. (Because our universe must include people, dogs, and points in time, restriction of it would not be helpful.) Now we can write:

9. $(x)(y)(z)(((Dx \cdot Py) \cdot Tz) \supset (Kxyz \supset {\sim} Bxyz))$

And this reads, without too much difficulty, 'For any x, y, and z, if x is a dog and y is a person and z is a time, then, if that dog is barking at that person at that time, that dog is not biting that person at that time'. In effect: we had to have an antecedent to identify the three "parties" involved, after which we tell our story about them.

EXERCISE 8–7   *Define open sentences and individual constants and symbolize. If useful, stipulate a restriction of universe.*

1. Emil is in the tournament and there is at least one player in the tournament whom Emil can beat.
2. All members of the chess team are friends of George.
3. George's friends are all members of the chess team.

4. Everyone has at least one friend.
5. If some residents of Dorm A are women, then not all residents of Dorm A are men.
6. Whatever is greater than something is neither less than nor equal to that thing.
7. Members of the L family greet everyone they meet.
8. Something is identical with something.
9. Nothing is identical with everything.
10. If Sally is older than Winifred, then Winifred is not older than Sally.
11. George is always late for class.
12. Everyone who knows German knows at least one foreign language.
13. Most cigar smokers prefer mild tobaccos.
14. Old wines are not always the best wines.
15. All members of the Dean's List are students with good grades.
16. Members of the L family greet everyone they meet, provided they remember their names.

EXERCISE 8–8   *Give, as closely as possible, colloquial English equivalents for the quantificational statements given below.*

---

1. $(x)(Ax \supset Ex) \supset (\exists x)(Ax \cdot Fx)$
   'Ax' = 'x applied for the job'
   'Ex' = 'x expected that the job demanded a college education'
   'Fx' = 'x was familiar with the writings of Homer'
2. $(x)(y)((Ox \cdot Wyx) \supset Rxy)$
   'Ox' = 'x is a member of the O family'
   'Wyx' = 'y owes x money'
   'Rxy' = 'x remembers the name of y'
3. $(x)(y)((\sim Tx \cdot Ty) \supset \sim Bxy)$
   'Tx' = 'x is in the tournament'
   'Bxy' = 'x has beaten y'
4. $(x)(Wx \supset (\exists y)(My \cdot \sim Lyx))$
   'My' = 'x is a musician'
   'Wx' = 'y is a musical work'
   'Lyx' = 'y likes x'
5. $(x)(y)(((Mx \cdot My) \cdot Kxy) \supset Lxy)$
   'Mx' = 'M is a member of the orchestra'
   'Kxy' = 'x knows y intimately'
   'Lxy' = 'x likes y'

A Problem in Symbolization   The apparently straightforward statements in the cartoon on page 370 actually harbor a surprising number of difficult and interesting logical problems. How should we symbolize these statements? Can they all be true jointly? Does any of them imply any of the others? Do they exhaust the possible viewer responses?

1. *Viewers may find some of this material totally offensive.*

Drawing by Levin; © *1979 The New Yorker Magazine, Inc.*

> **2.** *Some viewers may find all of this material offensive.*
>
> **3.** *Some viewers won't find any of this material offensive at all.*

On the principle of least analysis, we tarry a moment over propositional analysis—but only a moment, for none of these statements is truth functional. (The 'not' in statement 3 is comparable to the 'un-' in the Harriet statement.) The three statements amount to 'p', 'q', 'r', and we don't need a truth table to tell us that they are, truth functionally, logically independent of one another: no conflict (no inconsistency), no implication, and no way to tackle the question of exhaustiveness. Because quantifying terms are present, possibilities for quantificational analysis are open, and we push on.

We encounter a problem immediately: The first statement is ambiguous as to quantity. 'Viewers' is certainly plural, but does it mean 'all' or must we settle for 'at least one'? Our choice will make a difference as we shall see. Following standard logical practice, we opt for the weaker interpretation in the absence of clear indication from the context. To express the first statement, then, still by "least analysis," we will define 'Ax' as 'x is a viewer who may find some of this material totally offensive', quantify existentially, and write:

A. $(\exists x)Ax$

For the second, we define 'Bx' as 'x is a viewer who may find all of this material offensive':

B. $(\exists x)Bx$

For the third, 'Cx', 'x is a viewer who will not find any of this material offensive at all':

C. $(\exists x)Cx$

From 'p', 'q', and 'r' we could not tell whether further analysis would reveal inconsistency among the statements. By rejecting a universal interpretation of the first statement we have virtually decided that issue. A universal proposition can contradict another universal proposition (what one universal asserts of all, the other may deny), and it can contradict an existential proposition (what the universal says does not exist, the existential may say does exist). But with existential propositions only, we can go on and on and on without encountering a contradiction between propositions: 'There are tall people', 'There are people who aren't tall', 'There are mathematicians who sleep eight hours a night', 'There are mathematicians who never sleep', and so forth. (Only for a tiny universe could we reach a limit.) In the case at hand, we should have no difficulty in imagining a television audience divided into three substantial groups, each responding differently to a given program. The only bar to joint truth, then, would be that one or another proposition is self-contradictory. But, if we examine the original statements, we see nothing resembling a contradiction.

None of the symbolic statements implies any of the others, but we may not have analyzed the original statements fully enough to reveal an implication. On the question of "exhaustiveness," our symbolizations are uninformative. So we try for a deeper analysis, and there we run into problems and face hard decisions.

First, how are we to quantify 'some of this material' and 'all of this material'? Does "this material" have "parts" that we can quantify? We can't ignore the problem because right here is one of the items for comparison between our statements. Our choice is to say 'some parts (or segments) of this program', 'all parts (or segments) of this program'. This is somewhat artificial and may not correspond exactly to the meaning of the original, but we do provide ourselves with a way to make the 'some/all' contrasts through quantifiers.

Our second problem is more serious. 'Totally offensive', 'offensive', 'not offensive at all'—these seem to express difference in *degree,* a difference that 'some' and 'all' quantifiers cannot express. What we should do, if we can, is to write our open sentences in a way that allows comparisons. We can accomplish this fairly well by means of two open sentences: 'x will be offended by y' and 'x will be totally offended by y'. In the first statement, both 'offended' and 'totally offended' will apply; in the second the former, and in the third neither.

Deeper yet is our third problem. The first and second statements speak of viewers who *may* be offended or totally offended; the third speaks of viewers who *will not* be offended. Again, we want duplication of terms for the sake of comparison, and in 'may' and 'will' we have two different *types* of verbs. The first indicates possibility or perhaps probability; the second asserts an alleged fact. If we interpret 'may' as 'it is possible that', then we are dealing with a logical operator that is neither truth functional nor quantificational. What does it mean? Logicians tend to treat 'it is possible that' as meaning 'it is not *im*possible that' but, in colloquial speech, 'may' more often means 'it seems rather likely that' or 'the speaker believes it will be the case that'. That the 'may' of an announcement, such as the one in the cartoon, has *any* definite meaning is, to say the least, doubtful. Our imperfect solution to the 'will/may' problem is to standardize to 'will' in all three cases. In favor of this solution is the fact that if a 'will not' is true, then 'may' is false: they have *that* much in common.

Having chosen solutions to our problems we can go on to list open sentences:

> 'Vx' = 'x is a viewer'
> 'Px' = 'x is a part (or segment) of this program'
> 'Oxy' = 'x will be offended by y'
> 'Txy' = 'x will be totally offended by y'

In each case our basic quantification (for 'viewers') will be existential; remembering warnings about "existential conditionals," the reader will anticipate that the main connective in each case will be the dot of conjunction. In each case we need two quantifiers. It is best practice not to introduce a quantifier until needed to bind its variables; in some cases this preserves us from serious errors. So we hold back the 'y' quantifiers until the 'y's show up. Then:

> *A.* $(\exists x)(Vx \cdot (\exists y)(Py \cdot (Oxy \cdot Txy)))$
> *B.* $(\exists x)(Vx \cdot (y)(Py \supset Oxy))$
> *C.* $(\exists x)(Vx \cdot (y)(Py \supset \sim Oxy))$

Reading these into English:

> *A.* *Some viewers will be offended (totally offended)*
>   *by some parts of this program.*
> *B.* *Some viewers will be offended by all parts of this*
>   *program.*
> *C.* *Some viewers will be offended by no parts (or,*
>   *will not be offended by any part) of this program.*

Our aim has been standardization for comparison. By all means, the reader should look back at the originals and form her or his own judgment about the closeness of fit. We would prefer to believe that our symbolic sentences express *exactly the same propositions* as did the cartoon sentences: For, if that is true, then any conclusions we draw about the symbolic sentences will apply to the originals. To the extent that identity of propositions does not hold, we will have to be tentative in such application; and we know that we were uncertain about how to interpret several terms. If we have proved nothing else, we have shown that formal analysis of ordinary language is an art, not a science.

With the reservations indicated, let us examine the results of our latest symbolization. No open sentence is repeated in any statement, so we can rule out self-contradiction. We have already explained that existential propositions don't conflict with each other, so we can assert the consistency of our symbolized statements. Does any imply another? We can see that the persons who are offended by *some* parts (statement A) might also be persons who are offended by *all* parts (statement B). But we cannot *validly infer* from the existence of people who are offended by "some" the existence of people who are offended by "all"; and we can't validly infer the existence of people who are offended "totally" from the existence of people who are, for all we know, merely "offended." So neither A nor B implies the other. Statements A and B assert the existence of people who are offended by some parts or all; statement C asserts the existence of people offended by no parts. Clearly, neither A nor B implies C; nor does C imply either A or B.

Can we say anything about "exhaustiveness"? Can there be a viewer response distinct from those described in the three statements? Yes, there is a possible viewer response that has not received mention: 'offended, and totally offended, by *all* parts', or, '$(\exists x)(Vx \cdot (y)(Py \supset (Oxy \cdot Txy)))$'.

We still have to consider the nice point of what would happen if we construed the first statement universally. As a universal proposition, A would be symbolized as a conditional:

$$(x)(Vx \supset (\exists y)(Py \cdot (Oxy \cdot Txy)))$$

Revised A *is* inconsistent with C. What A says is true of *every* viewer, C says is not true for *some* viewers. We could prove this inconsistency formally by taking the two propositions as premises and deducing an explicit contradiction. The point at which they clash is, of course, 'Oxy' and '~Oxy'. Our division of 'totally offensive' into 'offensive' and 'totally offensive' allowed us to keep the full meaning of the first cartoon statement while providing us with a predicate, 'O', common to both statements, so that we could demonstrate a formal inconsistency.

Our finding of inconsistency points to the following choice: Either the "writer" of the "announcement" (we are not forgetting that it is a cartoon!) contradicted himself, or we were correct in adopting the weaker interpretation as the writer's intention. Earlier we made an "automatic" decision on the principle of 'If in doubt, the weaker'. But, if statement 1 had stood alone, it would not be implausible to take it universally, especially since 'may' softens the claim somewhat ("We could be wrong"). Statement 2 would fit in nicely. What does not fit is the third statement (in effect: "We were wrong"). Might we imagine that the writer of the announcement realized that he had gone too far? Anybody's guess. We mean only to suggest that contradicting oneself is something that goes on all the time, especially when a person wishes to retreat from a too-strong, over-hasty assertion without drawing attention to the fact. If we were in the business of giving advice, we would suggest that "But you just said . . . !" is sometimes best left unsaid.

You are now fully entitled to ask the following question: If the analysis of three "simple" statements, from a cartoon whose meaning any reasonably literate person might grasp, turns out to be so tortuous, what use can such analysis have? Except for a skilled logician, who could no doubt do all this in two minutes, who has the time? Frankly, a reasonably skilled and experienced logician spent some hours working out this analysis—and would never dream of doing that in "real life." What we are up to is this: Knowing one's 'p's and 'q's, or even one's 'x's and 'y's, is not, in itself, of much help if our purpose in studying logic is primarily to improve our ability to state our thoughts clearly, to make a case (an "argument") for what we believe, to recognize quickly just what the point of an argument is, to spot strengths and weaknesses. For that we want, more than anything else, a keener "ear" for the logical words in our language, so that we will notice—when it matters—the presence of an ambiguity, a vagueness, a gap, an inconsistency, *and* also a logical implication, in whatever we are reading or hearing or saying or writing.

When we use our symbolism to try to pin down the meaning of statements by formal analysis, we are obliged to come to grips with some of those "logical

Plenty of quantifying words, logical operators that are neither truth-functional nor quantificational, and a double-'not' that's not exactly a double-negation. Quantification may help you sort out what's being said. Maybe. Try to symbolize the statements in frames 3 and 4 using quantificational logic.

words''—sometimes, even, in their absence. No quantifying word, but some kind of generalization? What kind? How strong? A negating word: Just what does it negate? 'May', 'will'—'might', 'could'—are these words being used synonymously? To mark subtle differences? Or just loosely? 'Some'—is it really being used in a quantifying way? 'Impossible'—logically impossible? physically impossible? unthinkable? We have spoken frequently of our ''intuition'' and have appealed to ''intuitive'' recognition of validity, invalidity, and the like. Experience with logical analysis is, we believe, one way of strengthening the base of our intuition, for our intuitions aren't always right.

SOME GUIDELINES FOR SYMBOLIZING STATEMENTS IN
QUANTIFICATIONAL LOGIC

The following reminders may be of help:

1. *When quantification is universal, a conditional usually follows.*
2. *When quantification is existential, a conjunction usually follows.*
3. *When limiting the universe will eliminate a term from a multi-term argument, do so.*
4. *When practical, symbolize in affirmative form.*
5. *Be careful that the scope of a quantifier is indicated and that all variables are bound.*
6. *Do not give a quantifier more scope than needed to bind its variables. 'If everyone arrives on time, then Billy will be happy' is symbolized correctly as '(x)Ax ⊃ Hb'; '(x)(Ax ⊃ Hb)' makes a different, and stronger, statement.*
7. *In general, follow the principle of least analysis.*

EXERCISE 8–9   *Quantificational treatment may, or may not, make the logic of the following statements clearer. Symbolize them and compare your symbolizations with those of other students. Discuss any differences.*

1. No great advance has ever been made in science, politics, or religion, without controversy.—LYMAN BEECHER
2. If you do not tell the truth about yourself you cannot tell it about other people.—VIRGINIA WOOLF
3. We affirm, as a fundamental principle, that labor, the creator of wealth, is entitled to all it creates.—WENDELL PHILLIPS
4. If my theory of relativity is proven successful, Germany will claim me as a German and France will declare that I am a citizen of the world. Should my theory prove untrue, France will say that I am a German, and Germany will declare that I am a Jew.—ALBERT EINSTEIN
5. All law has for its object to confirm and exalt into a system the exploitation of the workers by a ruling class.—MIKHAIL A. BAKUNIN
6. If the thing believed is incredible, it is also incredible that the incredible should have been so believed.—ST. AUGUSTINE

EXERCISE 8–10   *Reconsider the statements of which you did preliminary analyses in Exercise 1–13. Symbolize each one with as little loss of meaning as possible using the methods of this chapter. Also use the methods of this chapter to try to determine which of the statements (as symbolized) is analytic and which is synthetic.*

SUMMARY

1. Truth-functional logic shows us how to break up compound propositions into simpler propositions; for many arguments, such analysis provides the key to validity. In many other arguments, however, validity depends on the presence of quantifying terms such as 'any', 'every', 'anything', 'everything', 'some', 'none', 'whatever', and 'whenever'. Sometimes two or more such terms interplay in a single statement; sometimes a statement that contains no explicitly quantifying terms is "implicitly" quantified. By quantificational logic, we analyze the internal structure of statements to understand how quantifying terms work; on this basis, in Chapter 9 we will expand our deductive system and prove the validity of many arguments that cannot be identified as valid by propositional logic alone.

2. In its symbolizations, quantificational logic employs the logical operators of truth-functional logic. In addition, quantificational logic employs: the **universal quantifier,** usually '(x)', '(y)', '(z)'; the **existential quantifier,** usually '$(\exists x)$', '$(\exists y)$', '$(\exists z)$'; *individual variables* (usually 'x', 'y', 'z'); *individual constants* ('a' through 't'); and *predicates,* usually abbreviated by the capital letters 'A' through 'Z'.

3. The basic units of quantificational statements are predicates in association with one or more individual variables or individual constants. An **individual**

constant stands for the name or definite description of some individual thing, person, event, number, etc. A **predicate** is an expression that, joined with one or more individual constants, results in a complete statement. A monadic or one-place predicate, joined with an individual constant, constitutes a **singular statement** (e.g., 'Sj' for 'Jim likes strawberries'); a dyadic or two-place predicate, joined with two individual constants, constitutes a **nonquantified relational statement** (e.g., 'Yas' for 'Ann is younger than Sally'); and similarly for more complex relational statements constituted by polyadic or many-place predicates and appropriate individual constants.

4. An individual variable, considered in itself, is merely an 'x' (or a 'y' or 'z') which, when joined with a predicate, functions like the indefinite pronoun 'it'. Such expressions as 'Sx' ('x likes strawberries'), or truth-functional compounds including them, are called **open sentences,** because they are not statements (that is, they have no truth value) but result in singular or relational statements upon substitution of individual constants for the individual variables.

5. Individual variables are said to be **bound** when they lie in the **scope** (indicated when needed by parentheses) of a quantifier of the same letter (e.g., '(x)Sx', '(∃x)Sx', '(x)(y)(Yxy ⊃ ~ Yyx)'). When all variables are bound, the result expresses a quantified (or generalized) statement. No expression including a free variable is a statement.

6. Whatever is true of all individuals in a given universe is true of each considered separately. In logical terminology, a universally quantified statement is true only if each of its instances is true. An instance of a quantified statement is formed by dropping the quantifier and replacing the corresponding variables of the resulting open sentence by a constant that names or describes a member of the universe in question.

7. The basic and most common form of universal statement is the **universal conditional,** constituted by the horseshoe of material implication. The universal conditional approximates in meaning the 'All S are P' statements of traditional logic but does not include the assumption that there are instances of its antecedent, which corresponds to the 'S' of 'All S are P'. If there are no instances of its antecedent, a universal conditional is said to lack **existential import;** logically, it is regarded as true but such truth is "vacuous."

8. Whereas the universal quantifier indicates that everything is such-and-such, the existential quantifier indicates that something, at least one thing, is such-and-such, that is, that there is a such-and-such; or, more formally, that an existentially quantified statement is true if and only if at least one instance of it is true.

9. For any existentially quantified statement, it is possible to write a logically equivalent universally quantified statement, and vice versa. The equivalent statements of opposite quantification have opposite signs before and after. ('Opposite sign' refers to the presence or absence of the negation-operator. Thus, '~(x)Px' ('Not everything is pleasant') is logically equivalent to '(∃x) ~ Px' ('Something is not pleasant').)

10. The basic and most common form of existential statement is the **existential conjunction** (e.g., '(∃x)(Cx · Mx)'). An existential conditional (e.g., '(∃x)(Cx ⊃ Mx)') is usually too weak to be useful, because there are very few

material implications that cannot be asserted to be true of something in the universe. The existential conjunction is the closest quantificational approximation to the 'Some S are P' statements of traditional logic. The existential quantifier can be used also to assert that a universal conditional does have existential import; as, by conjoining '$(\exists x)Cx$' with '$(x)(Cx \supset Mx)$'.

11. Unless a restriction of universe is stipulated, the universal quantifier refers to everything in the universe. Frequently, symbolization of arguments is simplified by restriction of the universe.

CHAPTER NINE

The Predicate Calculus

To apply the methods of quantificational logic to arguments, we need a systematic proof procedure. You may feel that you have firm possession of only a few phrases and a bit of the grammar of this foreign language and are still trying to master the calligraphy. Even so, one has to begin to "speak" a language some time—in this case, try to master the basic moves, try to construct proofs that work. With use, the language and its idioms should become less forbidding.

QUANTIFICATIONAL VALIDITY In quantificational as in propositional logic, if an argument is valid then its premises logically imply its conclusion. Also, the conditional consisting of the premises as antecedent and the conclusion as consequent is logically true. But the reliable truth-table techniques of propositional logic cannot be used. '(x)Ax' logically implies '(∃x)Ax', as we explained in Chapter 8, but from a truth-functional standpoint, the former would be 'p' and the latter 'q' and an argument from 'all' to 'at least one' is *truth-functionally invalid*. The argument from '(x)Ax' to '(∃x)Ax' is, however, *quantificationally valid,* and to prove it formally, as well as to prove more interesting arguments, we need to extend our techniques.

For many types of quantificational argument mechanical procedures exist for proving and disproving validity. Unfortunately, these procedures are difficult to master, and for beginning students they could well be meaningless gymnastics. We shall, instead, carry over the deductive apparatus of the propositional calculus and add to it a small group of rules, five in number. We will preserve the step-by-step procedure of the calculus, so that at every point the logic by which a proof is advancing will be easy to understand.

Our system of rules will be *complete:* every valid quantificational argument will be provable. This broadened system, sometimes called the first-order predicate calculus, will not furnish proofs of invalidity: Just like the propositional calculus, it *lacks* a *decision procedure*. Tantalizingly, it has been proved that, for

This chapter was written by David T. Wieck.

some complex quantificational forms, a decision-procedure is not even possible.[1]

For the elementary problems with which we will mainly deal, you are likely to find that discovery of a correct symbolization is the hardest task. As you begin to acquire skill, the deductions themselves become more and more a game—a mere game when we are solving examples that are found only in logic textbooks or on classroom blackboards, a game with a point when we analyze arguments that might be encountered in the "real world."

INSTANTIATION AND GENERALIZATION
Our basic problem in quantificational deduction is that a statement such as '(x)(Fx ⊃ Qx)' is not a compound of statements; propositionally, it is just 'p'. 'Fx' and 'Qx' are abbreviated open sentences, lacking in truth value; neither 'x is a feline' nor 'x is a quadruped' expresses a statement. To bring propositional rules to bear on such statements, we must prepare the ground.

Let us, for an example, revive the opening argument of the last chapter:

> *All felines are quadrupeds.*
> *All lions are felines and have tufted tails.*
> _____
> ∴*All lions are quadrupeds.*

We have already indicated abbreviations for 'x is a feline' and 'x is a quadruped'; other abbreviations will be obvious:

$$(x)(Fx \supset Qx)$$
$$(x)(Lx \supset (Fx \cdot Tx))$$
$$\therefore (x)(Lx \supset Qx)$$

Familiar with truth-functional logic, we may see that *if* there were no quantifiers, and *if* the open sentences were statements, we would have the following valid truth-functional pattern, readily provable by truth table or the propositional calculus:

$$p \supset q$$
$$r \supset (p \cdot s)$$
$$\therefore r \supset q$$

[1] When we say that the system is complete for quantificational arguments, we mean "complete for all quantifications of the kind we have illustrated." In the first-order predicate logic, we quantify *individual* variables; in the second order predicate logic, *predicate* variables are introduced and quantified.

Unfortunately, the quantificational argument does not consist of statements corresponding to the 'p's and 'q's above, and it does have quantifiers.

We do know, however, that what is true universally, "for any and *every* x," will be true of *each individual* that we single out. Which individual we choose won't matter so we pick one at random and call it 'a'. If our premises are true, then the following "instances" of the premises will be true:

$$Fa \supset Qa$$
$$La \supset (Fa \cdot Ta)$$

We now have truth-functional compounds of singular statements, from which we can deduce validly, in five truth-functional steps,

$$La \supset Qa$$

If our premises are true, their "instantiations" are true, and whatever follows truth functionally from the latter, here 'La ⊃ Qa', is true as well.

Our first *quantificational rule*, called **universal instantiation,** will formally allow us to make such deductions as 'Fa ⊃ Qa' from '(x)(Fx ⊃ Qx)', and 'La ⊃ (Fa · Ta)' from '(x)(Lx ⊃ (Fx · Tx))'. Rules of the propositional calculus will then take us to 'La ⊃ Qa'.

Pleased though we may be at having derived a valid result from our premises, we cannot but be mindful that our aim was to deduce the universal proposition 'All lions are quadrupeds'. As yet we have reached only a proposition about a single individual—that if a is a lion then a is a quadruped.

A second new rule, **universal generalization,** will allow us to achieve our goal. This rule is a bit troublesome. Whereas universal instantiation is a straightforward step of logical implication, universal generalization, which moves from a singular statement to a universal statement, would seem on its face to be totally unacceptable: 'La ⊃ Qa' certainly does not *imply* '(x)(Lx ⊃ Qx)', yet our rule will authorize the inference. How can we justify this strange move? In this way: If what we have deduced about a, that randomly selected individual, is based *solely* on premise information about *all* members of the universe, then what we have concluded about a, namely 'La ⊃ Qa', should hold for *every other* member of the universe, hence for *all*. We don't dare claim that we could repeat the same deduction for every other individual—how could we, if the universe is given as infinite? Our rule rests on the assumption that our selected individual is *completely representative*. We shall have to be very sure, consequently, that we apply the principle of universal generalization only to what we are convinced are thoroughly representative cases; when we present the rule formally, we shall introduce safeguards that guarantee this.

The following, now, will be our full deduction, using the method and rules of the propositional calculus from Chapter 7 with the addition of the two new rules, universal instantiation (U.I.) and universal generalization (U.G.):

1.	*(x)(Fx ⊃ Qx)*	*P.*[2]
2.	*(x)(Lx ⊃ (Fx ·Tx))/*	
	∴(x)(Lx ⊃ Qx)	*P./C.*
3.	*Fa ⊃ Qa*	*U.I., 1*
4.	*La ⊃ (Fa ·Ta)*	*U.I., 2*
→*5.*	*La*	*Assumption*
6.	*Fa ·Ta*	*M.P., 4,5*
7.	*Fa*	*Simp., 6*
8.	*Qa*	*M.P., 3,7*
9.	*La ⊃ Qa*	*C.P., 5−9*
10.	*(x)(Lx ⊃ Qx)*	*U.G., 9*

For arguments containing existential quantifiers, the two rules so far described will not suffice. Such an argument is the following:

All mammals are vertebrates.
Some mammals are lions.

∴**Some vertebrates are lions.**

Once again, if our symbolized argument had no quantifiers, and if the open sentences were statements, we would have a valid truth-functional pattern. The symbolization and its "look-alike" read:

(x)(Mx ⊃ Vx)	***p ⊃ q***
(∃x)(Mx ·Lx)	***p · r***
∴**(∃x)(Vx ·Lx)**	*∴**q · r***

Not only are quantifiers "in our way," and not only do we not have component statements, but we also have two different kinds of quantifiers.

The deduction rules for existential quantifiers have a character just opposite to that of the universal rules previously described. A universal proposition logically implies *any* instance of it but an existential proposition, to be true, need be true of no more than one individual and the proposition gives no information as to *which* individual or individuals fit the description. In the case of mammalian lions we know, as a matter of *fact,* where to look for specimens; zoos are pretty likely places. But as a matter of *logic,* we don't know where to look, and lion-hunting is not logician's work. Logically we cannot treat 'There are mammals who are lions' one bit differently from 'There are prime numbers larger than any prime number *ever* identified', a mathematical truth that excludes our being able to name even one such number. If we could name such a number, then it would have been identified and it would not be such a number—a clear contradiction in terms.

---

[2] Note that we are introducing abbreviations in this chapter for 'Premise' and 'Conclusion' to simplify the writing of proofs.

The constant 'a', which we have attempted to universalize on line 4, is accompanied on line 3 by an existentially derived constant, 'b', that entered the deduction after 'a' had already been instantiated. Proviso II does not allow this.

The reason we must disallow line 4 is that, although a constant introduced by universal instantiation is initially "representative," it can lose that character if it subsequently becomes tied to an existential constant. Line 2 will be true, if our premise is true, no matter what number 'a' abbreviates. But although chosen randomly, 'a' must be a *specific* number—it is not *every* number. Let us say it is seven: then the number 'b' introduced by line 3 must be a square of seven. But now 'a' is no longer representative of all numbers, for not all numbers will have forty-nine as their square. In short, Proviso II prevents universalization when a "representative" constant has been caught in an existential web; the constant can be freed from that web only if its existential companion is once again generalized.

EXERCISE 9–1

1. *Identify which steps violate the rule of universal instantiation; state the violations.*

(a) (x)Fx
     Fa

(b) (x)Fx ⊃ Ga
     Fa ⊃ Ga

(c) (x)(Fx ⊃ Gx)
     Fa ⊃ Gx

(d) (x)(Fx ⊃ Gx)
     Fa ⊃ Ga

(e) ~(x)Fx
     ~Fa

(f) (x)(y)Hxy
     (y)Hay

(g) (x)(y)Hxy
     (x)Hxa

(h) (x) ~ (y)Hxy
     ~(y)Hay

(i) (x)Hxx
     Haa

(j) (x)Hxx
     Hab

---

2. *Identify violations of the rule of universal generalization, and specify the nature of the violation.*

(a) 1. (x)Fx   P.
     2. Fa   U.I., 1
     3. (y)Fy   U.G., 2

(b) 1. (x)Fx   P.
     2. Fa   U.I., 1
     3. (x)Fx   U.G., 2

(c) 1. Fa   P.
     2. (x)Fx   U.G., 1

(d) 1. Fa   Assumption
     2. (x)Fx   U.G.

(e) 1. (x)Fx   P.
    ┌→2. Ga   Assumption
    │ 3. Fa   U.I., 1
    └──────
      4. Ga ⊃ Fa   C.P., 2–3
      5. (x)(Gx ⊃ Fx)   U.G., 4

(f) 1. (∃x)Fx   P.
     2. Fa   E.I., 1
     3. (x)Fx   U.G., 2

(g) 1. (x)(y)Fxy   P.
     2. (y)Fay   U.I., 1
     3. Faa   U.I., 2
     4. (x)Fxx   U.G., 3

(h) 1. (y)(∃x)Hxy   P.
     2. (∃x)Hxa   U.I., 1
     3. Hba   E.I., 2
     4. (y)Hby   U.G., 3

(i) 1. (∃x)(y)Hxy   P.
    2. (y)Hay   E.I., 1
    3. Hab   U.I., 2
    4. (z)Hbz   U.G., 3

(j) 1. (∃x)(y)Hxy   P.
    2. (y)Hay   E.I., 1
    3. Hab   U.I., 2
    4. (∃x)Hxb   E.G., 3
    5. (y)(∃x)Hxy   U.G., 4

3. *Existential instantiation.* From an existentially generalized statement, we may infer a statement from which the initial quantifier has been deleted and the corresponding variables replaced by any individual constant 'a' through 't'. In annotating such a deduction, write 'E.I.' *Proviso:* The constant selected must not appear in any previous line of the deduction or in the conclusion.

Since existential instantiation assigns a name to an unknown individual, we must not assume this individual to be the same as any previously mentioned. The requirement that the constant be completely new to the deduction handles this problem neatly. In addition to preventing universal/existential mixups, it saves us from existential/existential mixups. If one premise says that there are cows and another says that there are barns, and if we assigned the same constant to each, 'Ca' and 'Ba', we could end up, by conjunction and existential generalization, with '(∃x)(Cx · Bx)', 'Some cows are barns', a proposition that would find few defenders. The last phrase in the proviso, 'or in the conclusion', prevents deduction of 'Joe is bald-headed' from 'Someone is bald-headed': we cannot choose 'Joe' as our name in instantiation of the existential proposition.

4. *Existential generalization.* From a statement containing a constant, we may infer an existentially generalized statement in which a quantifier new to the statement has been prefixed and in which the constant is replaced in one or more occurrences by the variable of the new quantifier. In annotating such a deduction, write 'E.G.'

If we now sum up what needs remembering about our first four rules, it turns out that our obligation to put them into "legal" language has given them an appearance much fiercer than the reality. Instantiate from, generalize to, "generalized statements" only; instantiate existentially only to an unused constant (and not one that occurs in the conclusion); generalize universally only after inspecting the history of the constant to be generalized upon. And with respect to universal generalization, we need consult proviso II only if the argument involves mixed-quantifier relational statements.

EXERCISE 9–2

1. *Identify violations of the rule of existential instantiation and specify the nature of the violation.*

(a) 1. (∃x)Fx   P.
    2. Fa   E.I., 1

(b) 1. (∃x)Gx ⊃ Fa   P.
    2. Gb ⊃ Fa   E.I., 1

(c) 1.   ~(∃x)Fx   P.   (d) 1.   (∃x)Fx   P.
     2.   ~Fa   E.I., 1   2.   (x)Gx   P.
                                                          3.   Ga   U.I., 2
                                                          4.   Fa   E.I., 1
(e) 1.   (∃x)Fx   P.   (f) 1.   Ga   P.
     2.   (∃x)Gx   P.   2.   (∃x)Fx   P.
     3.   Fa   E.I., 1   3.   Fa   E.I., 2
     4.   Ga   E.I., 2
(g) 1.   (∃x)Fx/∴Fa   P./C.   (h) 1.   (∃x)(∃y)Fxy   P.
     2.   Fa   E.I., 1   2.   (∃y)Fay   E.I., 1
                                                          3.   Faa   E.I., 2

2. Identify violations of the rule of existential generalization and specify
    the nature of the violation.

(a) Fa ⊃ Fb   (b) Fa ⊃ Fb   (c) Faa
     (∃x)Fx ⊃ Fb   (∃x)(Fx ⊃ Fb)   (∃x)Fxa
(d) Faa   (e) ~Fa
     (∃x)Fxx   (∃x) ~ Fx

EXERCISE 9–3   In the following arguments, 'Ax' is an abbreviation for 'x is an albatross',
                    'Bx' for 'x is a bird', 'Cx' for 'x is a chicken', 'Fxy' for 'x is a friend of y', 'Lxy'
                    for 'x likes y', 'Sxy' for 'x is similar to y'. 'a' stands for 'Albert' and 'g' stands
                    for 'George'. For arguments 7 and 8, assume restriction of the universe to
                    human beings. For each argument, (a) give an English-language reading
                    of the premises and conclusion (or last line of the deduction); (b) identify
                    which deductions are correct and which are incorrect; (c) locate the errors
                    in the incorrect deductions.

1.   1.   (x)Ax ⊃ Bg/∴(x)(Ax ∨ Bx)   P./C.
     2.   Aa   U.I., 1
     3.   Aa ∨ Ba   Add., 2
     4.   (x)(Ax ∨ Bx)   U.G., 3
2.   1.   (x)(Ax ∨ Bx)   P.
     2.   (Aa ∨ Bg) ⊃ (x)Cx/∴(x)(Cx)   P./C.
     3.   Aa ∨ Bg   U.I., 1
     4.   (x)Cx   M.P., 2, 3
3.   1.   (x)(Ax ⊃ Bx)   P.
     2.   (∃x)(Cx ⊃ Ax)/∴(x)(Cx ⊃ Bx)   P./C.
     3.   Ca ⊃ Aa   E.I., 2
     4.   Aa ⊃ Ba   U.I., 1
     5.   Ca ⊃ Ba   H.Syll., 3, 4
     6.   (x)(Cx ⊃ Bx)   U.G., 5
4.   1.   (∃x)Ax   P.
     2.   (∃x)Bx/∴Aa · Ba   P./C.
     3.   Aa   E.I., 1
     4.   Ba   E.I., 2
     5.   Aa · Ba   Conj., 3, 4

5.	1.	(x)(Ax ⊃ Bg)/∴(x)(Ax ⊃ Bx)	P./C.
	2.	Ag ⊃ Bg	U.I., 1
	3.	(x)(Ax ⊃ Bx)	U.G., 2
6.	1.	(∃x)Ax ⊃ (y)By	P.
	2.	(x)Ax/∴(y)By	P./C.
	3.	Aa	U.I., 2
	4.	(∃x)Ax	E.G., 3
	5.	(y)By	M.P., 1, 4
7.	1.	(∃x)(y)Fxy/∴(∃z)Fzz	P./C. (Universe = Human Beings)
	2.	(y)Fay	E.I., 1
	3.	Faa	U.I., 2
	4.	(∃z)Fzz	E.G., 3
8.	1.	(y)(∃x)Lxy/∴(∃x)(y)Lxy	P./C. (Universe = Human Beings)
	2.	(∃x)Lxa	U.I., 1
	3.	Lba	E.I., 2
	4.	(y)Lby	U.G., 3
	5.	(∃x)(y)Lxy	E.G., 4
9.	1.	(x)(Ax ⊃ Bx)/∴(x)Ax ⊃ (x)Bx	P./C.
	2.	(x)Ax	Assumption
	3.	Aa	U.I., 2
	4.	Aa ⊃ Ba	U.I., 1
	5.	Ba	M.P., 3, 4
	6.	(x)Bx	U.G., 5
	7.	(x)Ax ⊃ (x)Bx	C.P., 2–6
10.	1.	(x)(∃y)Sxy	P.
	2.	(x)(y)(Sxy ⊃ Syx)/∴(∃x)(y)Sxy	P./C.
	3.	(∃y)Say	U.I., 1
	4.	Sab	E.I., 3
	5.	(y)(Say ⊃ Sya)	U.I., 2
	6.	Sab ⊃ Sba	U.I., 5
	7.	Sba	M.P., 4, 6
	8.	(y)Sby	U.G., 7
	9.	(∃x)(y)Sxy	E.G., 8

As our last rule, we need a provision for exchanging quantifiers. In Chapter 8 we showed that we are justified in replacing a universal by an existential quantifier, and vice versa, if we change simultaneously the signs of the quantifier. Using the open sentence 'Sx', for example, we listed the following logical equivalences:

$$\text{'}(x)Sx\text{' and '}{\sim}(\exists x) \sim Sx\text{'}$$
$$\text{'}{\sim}(x)Sx\text{' and '}(\exists x) \sim Sx\text{'}$$
$$\text{'}(x) \sim Sx\text{' and '}{\sim}(\exists x)Sx\text{'}$$
$$\text{'}{\sim}(x) \sim Sx\text{' and '}(\exists x)Sx\text{'}$$

Our rule will authorize not only these exchanges but one-step inference of '(x) ∼ (Fx · Gx)' from '∼(∃x)(Fx · Gx)' and all other inferences on the same pattern. Since these are equivalences, the rule will authorize the reverse inference also, but our main use for the rule is to eliminate an initial negation sign to permit instantiation. We can minimize tedious use of **quantifier exchange,** of course, by expressing our premises in affirmative rather than negative form.

5. *Quantifier exchange.* From a universally or existentially generalized statement, or from the negation of either, we may infer a statement with opposite quantifier and with opposite sign preceding and following the quantifier. In annotating such a deduction, write 'Q.E.'

If we wish to instantiate, say, '$\sim(\exists x)(y)Fxy$', we can use Q.E. to move the negation sign in. We could proceed as follows:

1.	$\sim(\exists x)(y)Fxy$	*P.*
2.	$(x) \sim (y)Fxy$	*Q.E., 1*
3.	$\sim(y)Fay$	*U.I., 2*
4.	$(\exists y) \sim Fay$	*Q.E., 3*
5.	$\sim Fab$	*E.I., 4*

QUANTIFICATIONAL ARGUMENT

Quantificational logic incorporates easily—and goes far beyond—the syllogistic logic that was formerly considered to be the very heart of logic. All of the valid syllogisms of the kind discussed in Chapter 5 can be solved by quick quantificational deductions.

If we had dropped the 'tufted tail' clause—it was irrelevant to validity—from our initial quadruped-lion argument, we would have had an example of a classical all-universal syllogism:

>*All felines are quadrupeds.*
>*All lions are felines.*
>_____
>∴*All lions are quadrupeds.*

Its deduction goes as follows:

1.	$(x)(Fx \supset Qx)$	*P.*
2.	$(x)(Lx \supset Fx)/\therefore(x)(Lx \supset Qx)$	*P./C.*
3.	$Fa \supset Qa$	*U.I., 1*
4.	$La \supset Fa$	*U.I., 2*
5.	$La \supset Qa$	*H.Syll., 3,4*
6.	$(x)(Lx \supset Qx)$	*U.G., 5*

The all-universal pattern will handle "negative universals" quite nicely. 'No fish are mammals; all sharks are fish; therefore, no sharks are mammals' will be symbolized:

>$(x)(Fx \supset \sim Mx)$
>$(x)(Sx \supset Fx)$
>_____
>∴$(x)(Sx \supset \sim Mx)$

The deduction will follow exactly the channels of the quadruped-lion deduction. If we had chosen, correctly but unwisely, to write the first premise as '~(∃x)(Fx · Mx)', we would need four steps instead of one to reach 'Fa ⊃ ~ Ma', after which the deduction would be identical.

The famous syllogism form that runs:

> *All humans are mortal.*
> *Socrates is human.*
> _____
> ∴*Socrates is mortal.*

was handled rather inelegantly in the traditional logic by regarding the 'Socrates' sentences as universal propositions about "all" members of a one-member set. In quantificational language, we write simply:

> *(x)(Hx ⊃ Mx)*
> *Hs*
> _____
> ∴*Ms*

Since we know that we want a conclusion about Socrates, we instantiate the universal premise to 'Hs ⊃ Ms', followed by modus ponens, and that is it.

In Chapter 8 we pointed out that a relational treatment of 'child of Harriet' would be necessary for certain arguments. The following is an example:

> *All of Harriet's children are unmarried.*
> *Amy is a daughter of Harriet.*
> *Everyone who is a daughter of someone is a child of*
>   *that person.*
> _____
> *Amy is not married.*

The third premise is necessary to make a connection between the first and second. The delicate point is that 'someone' here means 'anyone'. The statement simply says that, if the relation 'daughter of' holds, the relation 'child of' holds. So:

> 1.   *(x)(Cxh ⊃ ~Mx)*   *P.*
> 2.   *Dah*   *P.*
> 3.   *(x)(y)(Dxy ⊃ Cxy)/∴~Ma*   *P./C.*

The third premise can only be expressed relationally; to get a matchup of the antecedent of the first premise and the consequent of the third, we need a dyadic predicate in both. The deduction itself could hardly be simpler: instantiations and two modus ponens steps:

> 4.   *Cah ⊃ ~ Ma*   *U.I., 1*
> 5.   *(y)(Day ⊃ Cay)*   *U.I., 3*
> 6.   *Day ⊃ Cah*   *U.I., 5*
> 7.   *Cah*   *M.P., 2,6*
> 8.   *~Ma*   *M.P., 4,7*

In choosing our constants for instantiation, we are guided by our sense of who is who and also by our inspection of the premises for linkups between components. Proviso I of the universal generalization rule precludes universalizing of line 8: a constant that appears in an original premise may not be universalized.

We also pointed out in Chapter 8 that some arguments might oblige us to analyze "is married to" as a relational term. Let's imagine that someone says that they've heard that Amy is suing Bert for divorce. The person to whom they relay this rumor replies: It can't be Amy who's suing Bert for divorce; she's one of Harriet's daughters and none of them ever got married. One way to formulate the reply would be the following:

> *Amy is a daughter of Harriet's.*
> *None of Harriet's daughters is married.*
> *No one who is not married to someone can sue that*
>   *person for divorce.*
> _____
> ∴*Amy is not suing Bert for divorce.*

Without the third premise, of course, no deductive link between the other premises and the conclusion would exist; the principle of charity clearly endorses the added premise. In symbolizing we shall weaken 'can sue' to 'is suing', because the latter is all we need, and, more to the point, because the 'suing' clauses in the premise and conclusion must be identical if the deduction is to work. Our open sentences are: 'Dxy' for 'x is a daughter of y'; 'Mxy' for 'x is married to y'; and 'Sxy' for 'x is suing y for divorce'. Our symbolization is:

1. Dah *P.*
2. $(x)(Dxh \supset (y) \sim Mxy)$ *P.*
3. $(x)(y)(\sim Mxy \supset \sim Sxy)/\therefore\sim Sab$ *P./C.*

The courtier has apparently made an inference from the king's remarks. See if you can supply necessary premises and express that inference as an argument from premises to conclusion. Try evaluating two arguments—one with the conclusion 'The king should take the wizard's advice', and the other with the conclusion 'The king should not take the wizard's advice'. Which argument is better?

_____

"The Wizard of Id." by permission of Johnny Hart and Field Enterprises, Inc.

If there is a human being who is freer than I, then I shall necessarily become his slave. If I am freer than any other, then he will become my slave. Therefore equality is an absolutely necessary condition of freedom.
—MIKHAIL A. BAKUNIN

The premises are expressed in terms of 'I' and 'a human being', neither of which occurs in the conclusion; the conclusion speaks of equality and freedom, neither of which occurs in the premises. Is it possible to supply the missing links? How do the terms 'necessary' and 'absolutely necessary' function in this argument? Can you construct a proof of the argument's validity using quantificational logic?

Negative universal propositions—the "shark" was easy by comparison—can give trouble in symbolizing. 'None of Harriet's daughters is married' comes to the same thing as 'All of Harriet's daughters are unmarried'. The symbolization of the third premise is easiest to grasp if it is read as: 'For any x and any y, if it is not the case that x is married to y then it is not the case that x is suing y for divorce'. If one is uncertain about all-universal symbolization—which obviates the need for use of quantifier exchange—one might write the more natural '~(∃x)(∃y)(Sxy · ~Mxy)', that is, 'It is not the case that someone sues someone for divorce but is not married to that person'.

Our problems were all in symbolization, however, and the deduction goes quickly:

4.	*(y)(~May ⊃ ~Say)*	*U.I., 3*
5.	*~Mab ⊃ ~Sab*	*U.I., 4*
6.	*Dah ⊃ (y) ~ May*	*U.I., 2*
7.	*(y) ~ May*	*M.P., 1,6*
8.	*~Mab*	*U.I., 7*
9.	*~Sab*	*MP., 5,8*

EXERCISE 9–4   *Write formal proofs of the following. Of the last eight, a number are most readily solvable by conditional proof.*

1. (x)Tx/∴(∃x)Tx
2. (x)(Tx ⊃ Nx)
   (∃x)Tx/∴(∃x)(Tx · Nx)
3. (x)(Tx ⊃ (Nx ⊃ Cx))/∴(x)((Tx · Nx) ⊃ Cx)
4. (x)(Tx ⊃ Nx)/∴(x)(~Tx ∨ Nx)

 5. (x)(Tx · Nx)/∴(x)Tx · (x)Nx
 6. (x)Tx · (x)Nx/∴(x)(Tx · Nx)
 7. (x)(y)Sxy/∴Sdd
 8. (x)(y)Sxy/∴(∃x)(∃y)Sxy
 9. (x)(y)Sxy/∴(y)(x)Sxy
10. (∃x)(∃y)Sxy/∴(∃x)(∃y)Syx
11. (∃x)Tx/∴~(x)(~Tx · ~ Nx)
12. (∃x)(y)Lxy/∴(y)(∃x)Lxy
13. (x)(Tx ⊃ Nx)/∴(x)Tx ⊃ (x)Nx
14. (x)Tx ∨ (x)Nx/∴(x)(Tx ∨ Nx)
15. (∃x)(Tx ∨ Nx)/∴(∃x)Tx ∨ (∃x)Nx
16. (x)(Cx ⊃ Hx) ⊃ (∃x)Ux
     (x) ~ Ux/∴(∃x)(Cx · ~ Hx)
17. (∃x)(Cx · Hx) ⊃ (x)Ux
     (∃x) ~ Ux/∴(x)(Cx ⊃ ~ Hx)
18. (x)(Fx ⊃ Gx)
     (x)(Gx ⊃ Hx)/∴(∃x)Fx ⊃ (∃x)Hx
19. (x)(y)(Mxy ⊃ ~ Myx)/∴(x) ~ Mxx
20. (x)(y)(Mxy ⊃ ~ Myx)
     (x)(y)(Dxy ⊃ Myx)/∴(x)(y)(Dxy ⊃ ~ Mxy)

ANALYZING ORDINARY LANGUAGE ARGUMENTS

Our last piece of work in this chapter will be to consider the sample arguments carried forward from earlier parts of this book. Before that, some general observations may be helpful.

In analysis of a "natural" argument—as opposed to a "textbook" argument—formal techniques can bear only part of the weight. We have to decide how to "take" certain statements; we must look for rephrasings that will clarify premises and conclusion and make connections between statements and between terms; we have to decide very often whether to settle for an inductive treatment or to try for a deductive treatment; we have to think up, and then choose among, principle of charity amendments. Doing these things well requires imagination; lack of familiarity with the subject matter, or of the context

If blood be shed, let it be our blood. Cultivate the quiet courage of dying without killing. *For man lives freely only by his readiness to die, if need be, at the hands of his brother, never by killing him.*
—MOHANDAS KARAMCHAND GANDHI

Is Gandhi making an argument or merely a series of assertions? If an argument, which are the premises, which the conclusion? By the principle of charity, can you produce a valid argument? Do we need quantificational logic to analyze it?

of an argument, is a serious handicap. As we have said repeatedly, reasonable persons can differ reasonably about the best way to reformulate an argument, and there is such a thing as personal style, even in the working out of deductive proofs. All this said, there are points worth bearing in mind.

By the "principle of least analysis" we look first of all for truth-functional validity. When we have reason to suspect that an argument is valid, but that truth-functional methods don't prove it, or when we think that a propositionally valid interpretation may have been achieved at cost of distortion of the argument, then we should consider quantificational analysis. Sometimes a "background" principle, universal in form, would seem to fill a logical gap: the no-marriage, no-divorce principle we supplied for the Amy-and-Bert argument is a case. Sometimes, one or more premises contain universally quantifying terms that may be a key to validity. Sometimes, also, propositions that do not contain explicitly quantifying terms are implicitly quantificational. 'Geese are fowls' is plainly universal; universal also is 'If a female bear has cubs, it can be dangerous', which looks like, but is not, a truth-functional conditional.

After we have symbolized an argument, a strategy for deduction is essential. "Strategy" means seeing the whole picture, beginning from a perception of what looks like the *pattern* of the argument. Sometimes this is fairly easy, as in the "no divorce" argument, which read:

> 1.   *Dah*   *P.*
> 2. $(x)(Dxh \supset (y) \sim Mxy)$ *P.*
> 3. $(x)(y)(\sim Mxy \supset \sim Sxy)/\therefore \sim Sab$ *P./C.*

We should "see" the universal propositions as possibly producing a hypothetical syllogism, to be followed up by a modus ponens involving the first premise that may (and, in fact, will) yield the conclusion; or else a modus ponens of the first and second premises followed by a modus ponens involving the third. Either of the paths mentioned is a good one for this argument; the point is to *have* a strategy. Trial and error, a poor substitute, is a kind of effort to impose our will on

The peasant does not propose to be lured into committing a crime against the state. How would you formulate (and symbolize) the peasant's reasoning? Does he present a valid argument?

"The Wizard of Id." by permission of Johnny Hart and Field Enterprises, Inc.

Contending for the rights of women, my main argument is built on this simple principle, that if she be not prepared by education to become the companion of man, she will stop the progress of knowledge, for truth must be common to all, or it will be inefficacious with respect to its influence on general practice.
—MARY WOLLSTONECRAFT, VINDICATION OF THE RIGHTS OF WOMEN, 1792.

'Common to all' suggests universal quantification, and 'she' might be seen as shorthand for 'all women'. But the key to good analysis of this argument is careful reformulation into premise/conclusion pattern; for, although you undoubtedly "get the drift," the point the author was seeking to establish in this passage may not be immediately clear. As always, think in terms of "least analysis"; maybe propositional analysis will do justice to the argument.

the stubborn object before us. The search for a strategy means that we are looking to see what that object, perhaps not so stubborn after all, might suggest to us.

Generally, hypothetical syllogism, modus ponens, modus tollens will be at the center of strategy. When the conclusion is a universally quantified conditional, conditional proof is likely to save steps. Even though indirect proof can be used to solve *any* argument, we do not recommend it as a first resort. In the light of strategy, then, we look to "tactics": If we have a good strategy in hand, "tactics" tend to become obvious. The five quantificational rules and propositional rules like simplification and conjunction and transportation and exportation fall into this category. In the example above, universal instantiation leaps to the eye, but our strategy enables us to see immediately which variables should be instantiated to which constants. There are truly hard deductions, but most deductions you are likely to encounter are not nearly so hard as they look.

EXERCISE 9–5

In each of the cases below, if one follows the pattern of the English sentences, it is natural to symbolize the two members of each pair differently. For example, in No. 1 it is natural to symbolize 'Some apples are rotten' as '(∃x)(Ax · Rx)' and 'Some rotten things are apples' as '(∃x)(Rx · Ax)', in each case abbreviating 'x is an apple' as 'Ax' and 'x is rotten' as 'Rx'. On any correct symbolization of each pair, the resulting quantificational statements will be logically equivalent.

For each pair, (a) symbolize, using the abbreviations indicated above, plus 'Fx' for 'x is a fruit' and 'Px' for 'x is a pear'; and (b) show that the members of each pair are logically equivalent by deducing each from the other.

1. a. Some apples are rotten.
   b. Some rotten things are apples.

2. a. Some apples are not rotten.
    b. Some things that are not rotten are apples.
3. a. All apples are fruits.
    b. No nonfruits are apples.
4. a. All apples are fruits.
    b. All nonfruits are nonapples.
5. a. All apples are fruits.
    b. No apples are nonfruits.
6. a. No apples are pears.
    b. No pears are apples.
7. a. It is not the case that all fruits are apples.
    b. Some fruits are not apples.
8. a. All apples are fruits.
    b. It is not the case that some apples are nonfruits.
9. a. No apples are pears.
    b. It is not the case that some apples are pears.
10. a. It is not the case that no fruit are apples.
    b. Some fruit are apples.

EXERCISE 9–6   *For the following arguments, (a) symbolize the premises and conclusion (indicating abbreviations and what they stand for), and (b) deduce the conclusion from the premises.*

---

1. No tomatoes grow on trees, and no squash grow on trees. Since acorns grow on trees, they are neither squash nor tomatoes.
2. Members of the T family speak to everyone whose name they remember; they also gossip about everyone they speak to. Consequently, if any member of the T family remembers anyone's name, they gossip about that person.
3. If someone is injured on the job, every member of group Z is alerted automatically. Felice, who is a member of group Z, has not been alerted. Therefore, no one has been injured on the job.
4. Some three-year-old horses are neither thoroughbreds nor trotters. Only three-year-old thoroughbreds are eligible for the Belmont Stakes. Hence, some three-year-old horses are not eligible for the Belmont Stakes.
5. If the horse that finishes first is disqualified, the second horse is placed first unless it is disqualified also. Since we know that Lazy Bill finished first and was disqualified, and Maizy Dae, who finished second, was not placed first, we can conclude that Maizy Dae was disqualified also.
6. (For the following argument, which is an enthymeme, a 'transitivity premise' must be added—that is, a premise analogous to 'If anything is larger than a second, and the second is larger than the third, then the first is larger than the third'. Supply such a premise.) Ellen runs faster than Harry and Harry runs faster than Joanne. Therefore, Ellen runs faster than Joanne.
7. All human beings are entitled to equal respect. Sally and John are human beings. Sally, therefore, is entitled to as much respect as John.
8. No farmers are executives. Bill is an executive, so he is not a farmer.
9. All beauty contest queens are beautiful and some college graduates are beauty contest queens. Consequently, some college graduates are beautiful.

10. All politicians are liars. Some women are politicians. Thus, it follows that some women are liars.
11. Terriers and poodles are dogs. Cairns are terriers. Therefore, cairns are dogs.
12. Universities are either financially sound or bankrupt. Universities are not all bankrupt. Thus, it follows that there are financially sound universities.

EXERCISE 9–7   (a) *Symbolize the conclusion of each of the following arguments.* (b) *Deduce the conclusion from the symbolized premises. In each case, 'Cx' is an abbreviation for 'x is a cow'; 'Hx' is an abbreviation for 'x has horns', and 'Ux' is an abbreviation for 'x is a unicorn'.*

---

1. Premises: '(x)(Cx ⊃ Hx) ⊃ (∃x)Ux' and '(x) ~ Ux'.
   Conclusion: There are cows that have no horns.
2. Premises: '(∃x)(Cx · Hx)' and '(x) ~ Hx'.
   Conclusion: Everything is a unicorn.
3. Premises: '(∃x)(Cx · Hx) ⊃ (x)Ux' and '(∃x) ~ Ux'.
   Conclusion: All cows are hornless.

EXERCISE 9–8   *The first three of the following arguments need to be reworked, with benefit of the principle of charity, but you should be able to get them into a valid form. Proof of validity will then be easy. The last two are much trickier, and you may want to return to them after studying the next section of the text.*

---

1. Somebody must not have anted up. The pot's a dollar short.
2. I'm sure that John won't be in the tournament. To be eligible, you have to qualify.
3. When experienced gardeners hear of a frost warning, they take precautions. You can count on Jimmy.
4. But I do not think that communism as a belief, apart from overt and illegal actions, can be successfully combatted by police methods, persecution, war, or a mere anti spirit. The only force that can overcome an idea and a faith is another and better idea and faith, positively and fearlessly upheld. (Dorothy Thompson)
5. A Galileo could no more be elected president of the United States than he could be elected Pope of Rome. Both high posts are reserved for men favored by God with an extraordinary genius for swathing the bitter facts of life in bandages of self-illusion. (H. L. Mencken)

ANALYSIS OF SAMPLE ARGUMENTS   Let's turn now to our sample arguments. Of the four, the "Susan" argument especially invites quantificational treatment. The original read as follows:

> **Susan should do well in this logic course, because she always does well in science courses.**

In Chapter 7 the following version was offered:

> *This logic course is a science course.*
> *Susan is taking this logic course.*
> *Susan always does well in science courses.*
> _____
> ∴*Susan will do well in this logic course.*

Although "intuitively" valid, this argument is, propositionally, 'p', 'q', 'r', therefore 's', with no interaction between premises and conclusion, and the argument failed the short truth-table test. Quantificationally, 'always' stands out as a term that should be exploitable. For a reason to be explained, we shall alter the wording slightly:

> *This logic course is a science course.*
> *Susan is taking this logic course.*
> *In all science courses that Susan takes she does*
>   *well.*
> _____
> ∴*Susan does well in this logic course.*

Suppose we now define 'Sx' as 'x is a science course'; 'Tsx' as 'Susan is taking x'; 'Wsx' as 'Susan does well in x'; and 'c' as 'this logic course'. Then we phrase the argument:

1.	*Sc*	*P.*
2.	*Tsc*	*P.*
3.	$(x)((Sx \cdot Tsx) \supset Wsx))/\therefore Wsc$	*P./C.*

We instantiate line 3, replacing 'x' with 'c', conjoin lines 1 and 2, and by modus ponens we have our conclusion.

An alert reader may well suspect a sleight of hand here. Suspicion would focus upon the switch from 'will do well' to 'does well' in the conclusion. (If we did not make the switch, we would not have a matchup of terms—hence no validity.) But the real source of the problem was the third premise. For its "intuitive" validity, the argument depended upon our taking 'always does well' as referring to the future as well as to the past, while, for its apparent "soundness," it depended on our taking the phrase as meaning 'has always done well'. In making a switch in the conclusion, we have brought this ambiguity out into the open.

If the argument were interpreted as predicting a future event on the basis of past events—arguing from 'has done well' to 'will do well'—it would be simply inductive. In seeking to evade the uncertainty of inductive argument, we have created a version of the argument that is vulnerable to the charge that one premise, the third, in fact assumes the truth of the conclusion that the argument purports to prove. How could anyone assert the third premise without already knowing the grade Susan will get in her logic course?

One answer, discussed in Chapter 2, would be an appeal to the principle of induction. By this principle, any inductive argument can be represented properly as a deductive argument if premises are added to the effect that "all similar things behave similarly in similar circumstances" and that such similarities hold in the present case. On such a view, the third premise could be regarded as expressing a judgment that Susan and her science and logic courses fit into "similar things, similar circumstances." As we pointed out in Chapter 2, there are many difficulties with the principle of induction, and we may, besides, consider it exceptionally daring to suppose that all the circumstances relevant to Susan's past success will prevail in the future.

Although our primary goal in the context of formal logic is to assess validity, not to judge soundness, we might well believe that we should consider alternatives that seem less "forced." An obvious way is to go back to the original argument and retrieve the term 'should'. That argument said, 'Susan should do well in this logic course, because she always does well in science courses'. By keeping 'should' in the conclusion, we can moderate the claims we make in the premises. Along these lines, a possible new version is the following:

> *Anyone who has always done well in science*
> *courses should do well in this logic course.*
> *Susan has always done well in science courses.*
> _____
> *∴Susan should do well in this logic course.*

Admittedly, 'should' is a somewhat vague term, but that will not interfere with evaluation for validity. The virtue of 'should' is that it allows that Susan *may not* do well; it is somewhat like saying that Susan is a "good bet" to do well.

Abbreviating 'x has always done well in science courses' by 'Sx', 'x should do well in this logic course' by 'Lx', and 'Susan' by 's', we get an easy deduction of the same form as the argument about the mortality of Socrates:

1.	$(x)(Sx \supset Lx)$	*P.*
2.	*Ss/∴Ls*	*P./C.*
3.	$Ss \supset Ls$	*U.I., 1*
4.	*Ls*	*M.P., 2,3*

This argument is probably fairly close in spirit to the original, but alternative interpretations, some probably superior, could be multiplied. We offer one more, which will prove to be a challenge to our logical skill.

Our new version will combine features of previous interpretations:

> *Susan is taking a logic course.*
> *All logic courses are science courses.*
> *Anyone who has done well in all science courses*
> *they have taken should do well in any given*
> *science course that they now take.*
> *Susan has done well in all the science courses that*
> *she has taken.*
> _____
> *∴Susan should do well in the logic course she is*
> *taking.*

If we read this argument carefully we probably "see" it as valid. Valid it is, but symbolization is not easy. The problem is the third premise in which we have indicated the quantifying terms. To prove validity, we shall be obliged to introduce a quantifier for each of those terms.

The first premise is easy to write. Let 'Lc' be 'c is a logic course' and 'Tsc' be 'Susan is taking c now'. Then:

> *1. Lc · Tsc*

For the second premise, which will be a universal conditional, we need only 'Lx' for 'x is a logic course' and 'Sx' for 'x is a science course'.

> *2.   (x)(Lx ⊃ Sx)*

Now comes our problem, premise 3, in which we must proceed painstakingly, step by step.

We can see that 'anyone' runs through the whole statement, reappearing (twice) as the variable 'they'. Let the 'anyone' quantifier, which will have to govern the entire statement to unify those variables, be '(x)'. With a universal quantifier we look for a conditional structure. So we rephrase in conditional form: For any x, *If* "they" have done well in all science courses "they" have taken, *then* "they" should do well in any given science course that "they" now take. That is, For any x, *If* x has done well in all science courses x has taken, *then* x should do well in any given science course that x now takes. Let us consider next the antecedent of this conditional. It will have its own quantifier. For 'all' we choose '(y)' and rephrase this clause as a universal conditional: For all y, *If* y is a science course, and x has taken y, *then* x has done well in y'. Now for the consequent. 'Any given' is our quantifying term; let it be '(z)'. Again we look for a conditional, and the pattern of the antecedent gives us a model: For all z, *If* z is a science course, and x is taking z now, *then* x should do well in z'.

In possession of the parts, next we put them together:

> **For all x: If (*for all y: if y is a science course and x***
> ***has taken y, then x has done well in y*) then (*for all***
> ***z: if z is a science course and x is taking z, then x***
> ***should do well in z*).**

Our open sentences will be: 'Sy' for 'y is a science course'; 'Txy' for 'x has taken y'; 'Hxy' for 'x has done well in y'; 'Nxz' for 'x is taking z now'; and 'Wxz' for 'x should do well in z'. (By defining 'Sy' we also defined 'Sz' for the consequent.) Now we symbolize, using a bracket to emphasize the sentence structure:

> *3.   (x)[(y)((Sy · Txy) ⊃ Hxy) ⊃ (z)((Sz · Nxz) ⊃ Wxz)]*

With its quantifiers and dyadic predicates and truth functions, premise 3 may look like a monster from outer space. By symbolizing it piece by piece we have tamed it, and the rest of our work will be fairly easy.

If we look back at the argument we are symbolizing, we can see that premise 4 is just a case of the antecedent of premise 3. In writing premise 4, we will simply put 'Susan' in place of the 'anyone' of premise 3:

$$4. \quad (y)((Sy \cdot Tsy) \supset Hsy)$$

We can now look forward to a modus ponens involving premises 3 and 4, after we instantiate premise 3 to the case of Susan. (To have a matchup for modus ponens, we chose the quantifier '(y)' for premise 4.) All that remains is to express our conclusion. Using abbreviations already indicated, we will say it this way: c is a logic course, Susan is taking c now, and Susan will do well in c:

$$\therefore (Lc \cdot Nsc) \cdot Wsc$$

Since '$Lc \cdot Nsc$' is given in premise 1, 'Wsc' is our deductive target.

The proof goes with surprising rapidity, no twists or turns:

1.	$Lc \cdot Nsc$	P.
2.	$(x)(Lx \supset Sx)$	P.
3.	$(x)[(y)((Sy \cdot Txy) \supset Hxy) \supset (z)((Sz \cdot Nxz) \supset Wxz)]$	P.
4.	$(y)((Sy \cdot Tsy) \supset Hsy)/\therefore(Lc \cdot Nsc) \cdot Wsc$	P./C.
5.	$(y)((Sy \cdot Tsy) \supset Hsy) \supset (z)((Sz \cdot Nsz) \supset Wsz)$	U.I., 3
6.	$(z)((Sz \cdot Nsz) \supset Wsz)$	M.P., 4,5
7.	$Lc \supset Sc$	U.I., 2
8.	$(Sc \cdot Nsc) \supset Wsc$	U.I., 6

All that remains is to combine our truth functions: lines 1, 7, and 8:

9.	$Sc \supset (Nsc \supset Wsc)$	Exp., 8
10.	$Lc \supset (Nsc \supset Wsc)$	H.Syll., 7,9
11.	$(Lc \cdot Nsc) \supset Wsc$	Exp., 10
12.	Wsc	M.P., 1,11
13.	$(Lc \cdot Nsc) \cdot Wsc$	Conj., 1,12

Whether this formulation of the "Susan" argument is more or less sound than the simpler and equally valid earlier versions is, of course, debatable. Given a one-premise argument as starting point, as in "real life" we often are, good reasons can usually be found for a number of different interpretations. We have, in the end, a choice between deductive versions, with more and less debatable premises, and inductive versions, with surer premises but weaker premise/conclusion connections.

With respect to the other 'sample arguments' it is not clear that quantification can afford fresh insight. In propositional analysis of the smallpox argument, the following interpretation was shown to be valid by rules of the propositional calculus:

> *Mrs. Parker was infected with the 'Abid' strain of smallpox virus.*
>
> *There was no other possible source of the 'Abid' virus than the downstairs lab.*
>
> *Mrs. Parker had not been in contact with any person or object from the downstairs lab.*
>
> *If Mrs. Parker was infected with the 'Abid' strain of smallpox virus, and there was no other possible source of the 'Abid' virus than the downstairs lab, then either she had been in contact with some person or object from the downstairs lab or she was infected by a virus transmitted through the air from the downstairs lab.*

> ∴*Mrs. Parker was infected by a virus transmitted through the air from the downstairs lab.*

With considerable labor we could reconstruct the second and third premises as universal propositions, employing for that purpose 'there was no' and 'any person or object'. We would gain nothing, for an argument valid propositionally will retain exactly the same propositional structure and remain valid, if its individual propositions are analyzed quantificationally, assuming, of course, that we analyze them in just the same way in each occurrence. The weakness of the argument lay in the uncertainty of the premises, conspicuously the third premise: An inductive interpretation, with premises that claim less, might be more reasonable. But quantificational analysis is unlikely to shed light on that problem.

In the case of the "motel operators" argument also, an interpretation was found that proved to be valid propositionally. Again uselessly, we could interpret every statement but one in universal terms. As in the previous case, the lesson is that one should check an argument truth functionally before going to quantification, where it is much easier to mis-symbolize the argument. We might, however, learn something by considering just the *last* premise and the conclusion:

> *If the motel operators in one Florida town lie about their business, then all motel operators lie about their business.*

> ∴*All motel operators lie about their business.*

Because the antecedent of that premise follows logically from the preceding premises, the conclusion comes by simple modus ponens. The preceding premises were all reasonably plausible factual statements. The premise we have cited must come as a shock but, without it, the conclusion would not follow logically. The effort at deductive analysis, just because it shows the need for such a bold premise, can be credited with having shown thereby the desirability of inductive treatment of the argument.

We might, of course, imagine a premise that would justify that bold premise:

> *Whatever is true of some motel operators is true of*
> *all.*

Intuitively we see that, if this new proposition, however extravagant, is true, then that other premise will be true. But we won't be able to prove logical implication by our predicate calculus. Our new proposition says that whatever characteristic (or property) some motel operators have is a characteristic (or property) of all motel operators. More formally,

> *For any property P, if there is an x such that x is a*
> *motel operator and x is P, then for any x, if x is a*
> *motel operator, x is P.*

We cannot symbolize this properly with the logic we have been studying. 'There is an x' and 'for any x' are in our domain; not so 'for any P'. 'P' would be a *predicate* variable for which our logic does not provide. We are intruding, in fact, into the second-order predicate calculus. Despite the power of the system with which we have been working, there are many arguments that cannot be proved by it or by any formal procedures presented in this book. In compensation, our formal studies make it easier to catch on to the logical sense of statements that we are not in a position to analyze in our system.

Our argument analysis will now end on a more playful note. In previous chapters, various "interpretations" were offered of the cartoon in which a woman remarks to a man, as he enters the apartment door: "No flowers; you want me to think that you don't have a guilty conscience." One of the neater interpretations, propositionally valid, was the following:

> *You didn't bring me any flowers.*
> *If you didn't bring me flowers, then you must have*
> *a guilty conscience.*
> *If you don't bring me flowers, then you want me to*
> *think that you don't have a guilty conscience.*
> *If you want me to think that you don't have a*
> *guilty conscience, then you must have a guilty*
> *conscience.*
> ___
> ∴*You must have a guilty conscience.*

A clever cartoon leaves much to the imagination. Too prosaically, perhaps, one might make up a simple syllogism that is easily shown to be valid:

> *All times you don't bring me flowers are times that*
> *you want me to think that you don't have a*
> *guilty conscience.*

"No flowers. That means you want me to think you haven't got a guilty conscience."

Today is a time that you don't bring me flowers.

∴*Today is a time that you want me to think that you don't have a guilty conscience.*

Abbreviating 'x is a time you don't bring me flowers' as 'Dx', and 'x is a time you want me to think that you don't have a guilty conscience' as 'Gx', and using the constant 't' for 'today', we get:

$$(x)(Dx \supset Gx)$$
$$Dt$$
$$\overline{\qquad}$$
$$\therefore Gt$$

This argument, not valid propositionally, is readily proved valid on the style of the "Socrates" argument or the second "Susan" argument.

Whether we have improved on the results of propositional analysis is an open question; perhaps we should not get unduly serious about a humorous cartoon. So let us end up with an *entirely fresh possibility*: that the woman, rather than *making* an argument, is accusing the man of having committed the fallacy of denying the antecedent! On this interpretation, she *imputes* to him the following reasoning:

Whenever I bring her flowers, she thinks that I have a guilty conscience.
I won't bring her flowers today.

∴*She won't think that I have a guilty conscience today.*

Let 'x is a time I bring her flowers' be abbreviated by 'Fx', 'x is a time that she thinks I have a guilty conscience' by 'Gx', and 'today' by 't'. Now we can write the above argument as follows:

$$(x)(Fx \supset Gx)$$
$$\sim Ft$$
$$\overline{\qquad}$$
$$\therefore \sim Gt$$

Instantiate the universal premise to 'Ft ⊃ Gt': No way will '~Ft' get us to '~Gt'. We have not provided a method for proving invalidity, but the reader should have no difficulty in producing a counterexample, for we have a quantificational case of the classic fallacy of denying the antecedent. As an inductive argument, it would not be entirely implausible, except that the cartoon leads us to believe that the man was dead wrong in thinking that his conclusion would come true.

DEDUCTIVE LOGICS   By completing our survey of quantificational logic we have come now to the limit of our exploration of deductive logic. Beyond it we may pursue the study of formal logic in a number of directions. The second-order predicate calculus, with which we collided briefly, carries us into the study of sets and their properties and relations and toward the realm of mathematical set theory. We can also look into the theory of the logic we have studied—how do we know that our set of deduction rules is complete? Along that trail we arrive eventually at those great problems about formal theories that are associated with the name Gödel. We can also ask what happens if we don't assume that there are only two truth values and don't accept 'p $\lor$ ~ p' as a logical truth. There are, as well, specialized branches of logic that deal with logical operators that are neither truth functional nor quantificational, some of which we have mentioned. And we may also want to look at the relationship between logic and philosophy, subjects which have remained intimately associated throughout their long history. Quantificational logic provides foundation for these further investigations.

EXERCISE 9–9

Reconsider the arguments for which you did preliminary analyses in Exercise 2–9. Find one version of each argument which seems more appropriate for analysis using the methods of the present chapter and carry out such analyses. Compare your analyses here with those of the same arguments which you may have done in Exercises 3–3, 5–10, 7–9, and 10–7.

EXERCISE 9–10

Reconsider the arguments for which you did preliminary analyses in Exercise 2–10. Apply the instructions for Exercise 9–9 to these arguments and compare these analyses with those of the same arguments you might have done in Exercises 3–3, 5–11, 7–10, and 10–8.

SUMMARY

1. By adding five rules to the rules of propositional logic, all of which are carried forward into quantificational logic, it becomes possible to deduce the conclusion of any valid quantificational argument—to show, that is, that a given set of premises logically implies a certain conclusion. The rules are **complete** in the sense of being sufficient for deductive proof of quantificational validity. Unlike propositional logic, however, quantificational logic does not have a universally applicable **decision procedure** capable of proving both validity and invalidity.
2. The rules of propositional logic can be applied to statements only. To carry out quantificational deductions, we made use of the fact that every instance of a true universal proposition is true and that an existential proposition, if true, has at least one true instance. To instances we derive by **instantiation** we can apply propositional rules; from the products of our truth-functional steps, we can derive quantified statements by **generalization.**
3. We may instantiate only from, and generalize only to, **generalized statements.** A statement is *generalized* only if it begins with a quantifier (no negation sign preceding), and only if the entire statement is within the scope of that

quantifier. Neither negated quantified statements nor truth functional compounds of quantified statements count as generalized statements.

4.   Subject to certain restrictions, the rules of instantiation allow us to delete an initial quantifier and to replace the variables of that quantifier by a constant; the rules of generalization, again subject to certain restrictions, allow us to replace a constant by a variable and to prefix the statement with a quantifier of the same variable.

5.   **Universal instantiation** has its justification in the fact that a universally quantified proposition implies *every* instance of it. **Universal generalization** is justified by the fact that, if we have observed the restrictions on application of the rule, the constant generalized upon can be regarded as representative of all members of the universe. **Existential instantiation** is justified by the fact that there must be an individual that fulfills the claims of an existentially quantified statement, if the latter is true; we must simply be careful that the name we give arbitrarily to that individual does not duplicate the name of some other individual mentioned in the deduction. **Existential generalization** is justified by the fact that whatever is true of an individual, considered as such, must also be true of "something," "at least one."

6.   The rule of **quantifier exchange** is a rule of logical equivalence, the basis for which was explained in Chapter 8. Its chief use is to eliminate initial negation signs and permit instantiations.

CHAPTER TEN

Enumerative Induction

Examine each of the following sets of sentences. Assuming ordinary context, each set expresses an argument. In terms of the definitions of 'deductive argument' and 'inductive argument' in Chapter 2, determine which of the arguments is deductive and which is inductive.

1. *Swan A is white.*
   Therefore, some swans are white.

2. *Swan A is white.*
   Swan B is white.
   Swan C is white.
   Therefore, Swan D is white.

3. *All swans are white.*
   Therefore, swan A is white.

4. *Swan A is white.*
   Swan B is white.
   Swan C is white.
   Therefore, all swans are white.

5. *All swans are birds and can swim.*
   All ducks are birds and can swim.
   All seagulls are birds.
   Therefore, all seagulls can swim.

6. *Swan A is a white bird.*
   Therefore, Swan A is a bird.

You are correct if you identified arguments 1, 3, and 6 as deductive arguments and 2, 4, and 5 as inductive arguments. Since we will be considering various types of inductive argument in this and the next two chapters, it is worthwhile to reiterate and expand on the characteristics that distinguish the two different types of argument.

In Chapter 2, a deductive argument was defined as any argument in which the conclusion follows necessarily from the premises, that is, any argument which is such that:

> *If the premises are true, then the conclusion must be*
>   *true; or*
> *The premises provide absolute support for the*
>   *conclusion; or*
> *The conclusion is completely contained in the*
>   *premises.*

In this formal sense of the term, it is redundant to say that an argument is deductively valid; if it is valid, then it must be deductive, and if it is deductive, then it must be valid. It should also be remembered that an argument is not deductive just because someone asserts or intends that the premises provide absolute support for the conclusion. One of the primary values of formal logic is that it gives us procedures for determining which of the many sets of statements that people assert or intend to be valid are, in fact, valid.

Another essential characteristic of a valid deductive argument is that the addition of one or more premises can in no way affect the support that the premises provide for the conclusion. For example, in argument 1, if the premises 'Swan B is black', 'Swan C is beautiful', and 'Swan A is dead' were added to the original argument, it would in no way affect the support that the argument provides for the conclusion 'Some swans are white'. In a valid deductive argument, the truth of the premises guarantees the truth of the conclusion, regardless of any additional premises that may be supplied.

Of course, the validity of a deductive argument is not dependent on the actual truth of the premises; rather it is dependent on the form of the argument, as was pointed out in Chapter 2. Thus, it is possible to have a valid deductive argument with a false premise or premises and a true conclusion. For instance, the premise of argument 3: 'All swans are white', is false, for there are black swans; nevertheless, the conclusion 'Swan A is white' may be true. In other words, the discovery that a premise in a valid deductive argument is false is not sufficient for proving that the conclusion is false, and it in no way affects the validity of the argument. However, if we know that the conclusion of a deductive argument is false, then one or more of its premises must be false. Taking argument 3 again, if Swan A is actually black, the conclusion is false, and so the premise 'All swans are white' must be false.

It should also be remembered from Chapter 2 that an inductive argument is any argument which is not deductive—or to put it in more positive terms, an inductive argument is any set of statements which is such that one of them is supported by (but not implied by) the others. As with deductive arguments, it is irrelevant from the logical point of view whether a particular set of statements has been asserted or intended as an argument by anyone. The only thing that is relevant is the logical relation that actually holds between the statements. Thus, even if someone asserts that a particular set of statements comprises an inductive argument, if the "premises" do not, in fact, provide any support for the "conclusion," then it is not an inductive argument. It is also possible on our definitions for someone to assert that a particular set of statements comprises an inductive argument when, in fact, the premises provide absolute (not just partial) support for the conclusion, in which case it is really a deductive argument. In the remainder of this chapter, we will focus our attention on "real" inductive arguments, that is, arguments in which the premises provide some, but not absolute, support for the conclusion. We will be particularly concerned with identifying criteria for determining the degree of support that a particular set of premises provide for a particular conclusion.

Any argument that is inductive has the basic characteristic that, even if all of its premises are true, it is still possible for the conclusion to be false, because the premises only provide partial support for the conclusion. The partial support that the premises provide for the conclusion can range from almost absolute support at one extreme to almost no support at the other. For example, consider the following argument:

> *Raven 1 is black.*
> *Raven 2 is black.*
> .
> .
> .
> *Raven 10,000 is black.*
> *Therefore, all ravens are black.*

Here the premises provide very strong support for the conclusion. In contrast, the premises in the following example provide almost no support for the conclusion.

> *Beagle 1 lived to be 14 years old.*
> *Beagle 2 lived to be 12 years old.*
> *Beagle 3 lived to be $14\frac{1}{2}$ years old.*
> *Beagle 4 lived to be 13 years old.*
> *Beagle 5 lived to be 9 years old.*
> *Therefore Beagle 6 will live to be 15 years old.*

Of course, neither of these examples is a deductive argument, since neither is such that the premises provide *absolute* support for the conclusion.

Another characteristic that distinguishes deductive from inductive arguments relates to the addition of new premises. Whereas the addition of new premises to a valid deductive argument does not affect the support which the premises provide for the conclusion, adding new premises to an inductive argument may strengthen or weaken the support for the conclusion. For example, if the premise 'Swan D is black' is added to argument 4, then the support which the original premises provide for the conclusion 'All swans are white' is completely destroyed. On the other hand, if the premises 'Swan D is white', 'Swan E is white' . . . 'Swan W is white' are added, then the support for the conclusion is somewhat strengthened.

It is often said that deductive arguments move from the general to the particular, whereas inductive arguments move from the particular to the general. As we noted in Chapter 2, this distinction between the two types of argument is inaccurate. It is possible to have a valid deductive argument with particular premises and a particular conclusion, as in argument 1 at the beginning of this chapter. It is also possible to have a valid deductive argument which moves from general premises to a general conclusion, as in the following example:

> *All fish are animals that live in water.*
> *All bass are fish.*
> *Therefore, all bass are animals that live in water.*

An inductive argument may have particular premises and a particular conclusion, as in argument 2. It is also possible for an inductive argument to have general premises and a general conclusion. For example:

> *All dogs are mammals and are warm-blooded.*
> *All chimpanzees are mammals and are*
> *warm-blooded.*
> *All lions are mammals and are warm-blooded.*
> *All men are mammals and are warm-blooded.*
> *Therefore, all mammals are warm-blooded.*

ENUMERATIVE INDUCTIONS   All the inductive arguments that we have considered so far in this chapter are of a special type known as **enumerative inductions.** An enumerative induction is an argument whose premise(s) comprise a listing of cases concerning either individuals or classes of individuals to support conclusions about individuals or classes of individuals. For example, look at argument 2:

> *Swan A is white.*
> *Swan B is white.*
> *Swan C is white.*
> *Therefore, Swan D is white.*

Here the premises concern individuals, and the conclusion is about an individual. Argument 4 uses the same premises to reach a different conclusion:

> *Swan A is white.*
> *Swan B is white.*

> *Swan C is white.*
> *Therefore, all swans are white.*

In this case, the premises are about individuals, whereas the conclusion is about a class of individuals. Argument 5 has premises of a different sort:

> *All swans are birds and can swim.*
> *All ducks are birds and can swim.*
> *All seagulls are birds.*
> *Therefore, all seagulls can swim.*

Here both the premises and the conclusion are about classes of individuals. Of course, it is also possible to have an enumerative induction in which the premise(s) comprise a listing of cases about a class of individuals offered in support of a conclusion about an individual, as in the following argument:

> *All swans I have seen in the past have been white.*
> *Therefore, the next swan I see will be white.*

(Note that we are considering the naming of a single case or class as a *listing*.)

In this chapter, we will be concerned only with inductive arguments of the enumerative kind, although in the following two chapters we will consider another type of argument known as eliminative induction.

**Types of
Enumerative
Induction** Logicians have traditionally made a distinction between two different kinds of enumerative inductive argument. Argument 4 is an example of the first type and is generally referred to as an **inductive generalization.** As its name suggests, an inductive generalization is *an inductive argument whose conclusion is a universal proposition (that is, a statement about* all *of the members of some class or group), AND at least one of whose premises is such that its falsity could imply the falsity of the conclusion.* (The reason for this "could" qualification will be explained in the section on inductive generalization.) Argument 4 has a universal proposition as its conclusion: 'All swans are white'; and each of the first three premises is such that its falsity implies the falsity of the conclusion (for if Swan A, for instance, is not white, then it follows that not all swans are white).

Any enumerative induction that does not satisfy the criteria for an inductive generalization is commonly referred to as an **induction by analogy.** Argument 2 is clearly an induction by analogy, since its conclusion is not a universal proposition but an individual one about a specific event.

Argument 5 has a universal conclusion: 'All seagulls can swim'; thus it satisfies the first criterion for an inductive generalization. But an examination of the three premises will show that none of them is such that its falsity can possibly imply the falsity of the conclusion. For instance, even if it were shown to be false that all swans can swim, this would at most lessen the probability that all seagulls can swim—it does not prove that it is false that all seagulls can swim.

Both these types of enumerative induction merit closer examination.

INDUCTION BY   When we make an *analogy,* we compare two or more different things
ANALOGY   or ideas by pointing out the ways in which they are similar. Analogies
                        are frequently used by writers to explain new and/or difficult con-
cepts by comparing them to more familiar experiences, as in the following
explanation of light refraction by Isaac Asimov:

> For instance, Huygens' wave theory could explain refraction under certain condi-
> tions. Suppose a straight wave front of light strikes the plane surface of glass
> obliquely. One end of the wave front strikes the glass first, but suppose its progress
> is slowed as it enters the glass. In that case, when the next section of the front hits
> the glass, it has gained on the first section, for the second has been traveling
> through air, while the first has been traveling, more slowly, through glass. As each
> section of the wave front strikes, it is slowed and gained upon by the portion of the
> wave front that has not yet struck. The entire wave front is in this way refracted
> and, in entering the glass, makes a smaller angle with the normal. On emerging from
> the glass, the first section to emerge speeds up again and gains on those portions
> that have not yet emerged. The emerging light takes on its original direction again.
>   An analogy can be drawn between this and a line of marching soldiers leaving a
> paved highway obliquely and entering a plowed field. The soldiers leaving the
> highway are, naturally, slowed down; those first to enter the field are slowed down
> first, and the whole line of soldiers (if they make no effort to correct for the change
> in footing) must alter the direction of march toward the direction of the normal to
> the highway—field interface.[1]

In the excerpt above, the analogy of a line of marching soldiers entering a
plowed field from a highway is used to explain what happens to a wave front of
light as it enters a glass surface from the air. The analogy here is used for
explanatory purposes only; it does not involve an argument, for, although the
two events are compared, no conclusion is drawn.

In daily life, however, we often make inferences that involve analogical judgments. In fact, it is possible to view *all* judgments relating two discrete experiences as being grounded in inductions by analogy, if it is argued that we can
determine only that our present experience is very similar to, somewhat different
from, or very different from previous experiences or abstract concepts which are
used as paradigms or models. For instance, suppose Sue asks Beth if she can
borrow Beth's biology book overnight. Beth lends Sue the book on condition
that she return it by 9:00 the next morning, telling Sue to leave it near the door
to her dormitory room. Beth wakes up at 9:15 the next morning, goes to the
door, opens it, and finds a biology book there. How does Beth *know* that it is her
own book? It looks like her book: Her name is in it; it is underlined in places with
a blue magic marker; there is a coffee stain on the pages dealing with reproduction, left after a long night's study session; and so on. In effect, what Beth is
doing in this situation is making an analogy; she is saying that this book is her
book because it has the same characteristics as her book. Of course, it is highly

[1] Isaac Asimov, *Understanding Physics: Light, Magnetism and Electricity,* (New York:
Signet Books, New American Library, 1966), pp. 62–63.

Notice how people obey traffic laws when there's a patrol car in sight?

That's the idea behind NATO.

Nothing maintains order like the presence of authority.

It keeps children from snitching cookies. Adults from running red lights. And it helps keep peace among nations.

The presence of the North Atlantic Treaty Organization (NATO) has provided security in Europe for 25 years. At the same time, this peace force of 15 allied nations has sought to ease tensions and improve relations between East and West.

Today, from a foundation of strength and in a climate of stability, the East and West can contemplate mutual and balanced force reductions.

Which means more of NATO's resources can be devoted to advancements in economic affairs, science and cultural relations.

That's the idea behind NATO.

April 4th is NATO's 25th anniversary. This week, McDonnell Douglas personnel are observing NATO's founding with a paid holiday for the 11th consecutive year.

MCDONNELL DOUGLAS

Is the analogy being drawn in this ad very strong? What weaknesses or disanalogies can you identify? Is there an argument implicit or explicit in the ad? If so, what is it and how good is it?

McDonnell Douglas Corporation.

unlikely that Sue would have replaced Beth's book with a different one, going through all the trouble to make it appear as if it were Beth's. Nevertheless, Beth has no absolute certainty that it is her book. All that Beth can do and does do is make a comparison between the book she has now and her memory of the book she lent to Sue. Likewise, if you assert that the cover of this book is gray, you could be interpreted as asserting, in effect, that it is sufficiently similar to other things which most people accept as paradigms of grayness (and sufficiently different from things usually called "red," "blue," or "yellow") to justify calling it gray.

Whether it is true that *all* judgments involve the drawing of analogies is open to debate. But certainly many inferences made in daily life are based on analogies between different cases. For instance, a couple might patronize a particular restaurant, inferring that since they had a good meal there the last time, they will have a good meal there this time. A business executive might infer that because a worker was competent at the last task performed, this same worker will do a good job at the next task. A person might buy the latest album

"Some man, that Kissinger . . .
Goes day and night."

Richard Nixon's Secretary of State, Henry Kissinger, had a reputation as a person with seemingly unlimited energy. The humor in the cartoon above makes us recognize the extent to which all of our judgments involve some degree of analogical reasoning.

Stayskal—Chicago Today.

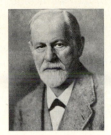

The conscious mind may be compared to a fountain playing in the sun and falling back into the great subterranean pool of the subconscious from which it rises.
—SIGMUND FREUD

Is Freud's analogy plausible? Why or why not? Is it illuminating? Does it in any way constitute an inductive argument? If so, what is the argument?

by the Rolling Stones, assuming that he or she will like it because previously purchased albums by the same group were enjoyable. A farmer who has had previous success with a certain pesticide might infer that the same pesticide will help fight against the insects which are destroying the lettuce crop. And the marijuana user who bought a nickel bag from a particular dealer and who received oregano instead might not return to the same person when making the next purchase, inferring that, if the last batch was a ripoff, so will the next one be. In all these instances, we are dealing with inferences made by means of analogies. None of these examples involves inductive arguments by analogy; they are merely inferences, although for each inference we can construct such an argument as was noted in Chapter 2. Considering the importance of inductions by analogy in everyday life, it is worthwhile to examine the form which such arguments take, as well as the criteria for determining the relative strengths of these arguments.

Consider the following argument:

> *Tim, Sue, Mary, and John are philosophy majors who were enrolled in Professor Wilson's metaphysics course last semester and all of them got A's. So Tom probably got an A, since he is a philosophy major who was in last semester's metaphysics course taught by Professor Wilson.*

To facilitate discussion, it is helpful to formulate the argument in the following way, making all the premises and the conclusion explicit:

> *Tim is a philosophy major who was in Professor Wilson's metaphysics course last semester and got an A.*
> *Sue is a philosophy major who was in Professor Wilson's metaphysics course last semester and got an A.*

> *Mary is a philosophy major who was in Professor*
> *Wilson's metaphysics course last semester and got*
> *an A.*
> *John is a philosophy major who was in Professor*
> *Wilson's metaphysics course last semester and got*
> *an A.*
> *Tom is a philosophy major who was in Professor*
> *Wilson's metaphysics course last semester.*
> *Therefore, Tom got an A.*

Quite clearly, we are dealing with an enumerative induction, for the premises of this argument comprise a listing of cases about individuals. Then, too, we can see that this is an induction by analogy, since the falsity of none of the premises can necessitate the falsity of the conclusion, and the conclusion is not a universal proposition.

The analogy in this particular example involves five persons who are alike in at least two ways: they all (a) are philosophy majors, and (b) were enrolled in Professor Wilson's metaphysics course. Four of them have been observed, and the fifth is being asserted to have (c) received an A grade. If we let *a, b,* and *c* represent the three characteristics respectively, and if we use X_1, X_2, X_3, X_4, and X_5 to stand for Tim, Sue, Mary, John, and Tom, respectively, the argument can be schematized in the following ways:

> X_1 *has* **a, b,** *and* **c.**
> X_2 *has* **a, b,** *and* **c.**
> X_3 *has* **a, b,** *and* **c.**
> X_4 *has* **a, b,** *and* **c.**
> X_5 *has* **a** *and* **b.**
> *Therefore,* X_5 *has* **c.**

or:

> $X_1, X_2, X_3, X_4,$ *and* X_5 *have* **a** *and* **b.**
> $X_1, X_2, X_3,$ *and* X_4 *have* **c.**
> *Therefore,* X_5 *has* **c.**

Note that characteristics *a* and *b* (philosophy major and enrollment in Professor Wilson's metaphysics course) appear only in the premises of the argument, whereas characteristic *c* (the A grade) appears in both the premises and the conclusion. Furthermore, the premises of the argument assert that five of the persons ($X_1 . . . X_5$) are alike in two respects (*a* and *b*) and that four of these persons ($X_1 . . . X_4$) are alike in a third respect (*c*). From the premises, it is inferred that the fifth person (X_5) also shares the third characteristic (*c*).

Of course, not all enumerative inductions by analogy are concerned only with five cases that share three characteristics, nor do all such inductions contain premises about individuals that support a conclusion about individuals. In the following argument, the premise is about a class of individuals, as is the conclusion, and these classes of individuals share only two characteristics.

> *All students in Professor Wilson's metaphysics course*
> *last semester got A's.*
> *Therefore, all students in Professor Wilson's*
> *metaphysics course this semester will get A's.*

This argument certainly qualifies as an enumerative induction, even though its premise lists only one case, concerning one class of individuals, to support a conclusion about another class of individuals. It is also an induction by analogy, for the falsity of its premise does not guarantee the falsity of its conclusion. If the premise statement is false—that is, if some students in Professor Wilson's metaphysics course last semester did not get A's—it is still possible for all the students in his course this semester to get A's.

It is also possible to have an enumerative induction by analogy whose premises are about a class of individuals and whose conclusion is about a particular individual, or vice versa. Furthermore, an induction by analogy may contain premises that involve both a class of individuals and a particular individual, and a conclusion that involves a particular individual. For example, consider the following arguments:

> *Every student in Professor Wilson's metaphysics*
> *course last semester got an A.*
> *Therefore, Tom will get an A in Professor Wilson's*
> *metaphysics course this semester.*

> *Some students in Professor Wilson's metaphysics*
> *course last semester got A's.*
> *Therefore, all students in Professor Wilson's*
> *metaphysics course this semester will get A's.*

> *Every student in Professor Wilson's metaphysics*
> *course last semester got an A.*
> *Bob is a student in Professor Wilson's metaphysics*
> *course this semester.*
> *Therefore, Bob will get an A this semester.*

Notice that, in each argument above, the falsity of the premise(s) could not necessitate the falsity of the conclusion. One might, on an intuitive level, sense that certain of the arguments seem stronger than others, but we will put off our discussion of the relative strength of inductions by analogy until after we have discussed the form of the second type of enumerative induction—inductive generalization.

EXERCISE 10–1

Read each passage below carefully and determine whether it contains an analogical explanation or an analogical argument.

1. Ants are highly organized creatures which go about their task of tunnel construction in a systematic manner. Similarly, the Corps of Engineers who built the subway system in New York City manifested a high degree of organization in the systematic manner in which they approached and performed their task.

2. A particularly troublesome manifestation of the pollution problem called "backwash" has recently been brought to the attention of our citizenry. This phenomenon occurs when the level of pollution becomes so high in an inlet area that the tides cannot carry all the waste material to the sea, thereby causing the pollutants to accumulate in the inlet. This situation is similar to the problem faced by homeowners when they let too much solid waste go down the drain, thereby causing the waste disposal system to back up.

3. The Watergate scandals have brought to light erroneous political thinking concerning campaign spending. In the past, politicians—Republicans and Democrats alike—believed that the more money put into a campaign, the better it would turn out. That's like saying that the more sugar I put into my coffee, the better it will be, just because I happen to like sugar in my coffee. However, we all know that too much sugar will make coffee taste lousy. Politicians long ago should have learned from ordinary experience such as this that too much of a good thing often produces a lousy thing.

4. The computer revolution has arrived, but most people still do not know how a computer works. It works by a process of eliminating possibilities until it comes to the right conclusion. The theory behind it reminds me of my friend's theory of how to find a satisfactory girl at a party. He simply goes from girl to girl, eliminating possibilities until he finds the right one.

5. Many people claim that the scientific method is the basis for all modern technological advances. Using the scientific method, a researcher formulates a hypothesis which conforms to known facts and then devises tests, the results of which either confirm the hypothesis or disconfirm it. In the latter event, the researcher formulates a new hypothesis and tests that. Such a method can be likened to that of a man who kicks a horse to see if this will make it move. If the horse moves, all is well; if not, he tries something else.

6. The waterbed is a new product which has stirred consumer interest. Some people have claimed that it has provided them with comfortable sleep, likening the experience to floating in a quiet pool of water. Others dislike it, because when you sit on it, you sink in. In this respect, it is similar to an old couch that has lost the resiliency of its supporting springs.

7. An accident occurred during yesterday's football practice at school. Chuck ran a pattern toward the goal post and, looking back to catch a pass, lost his sense of direction. As he caught the ball, he turned, ran right into the post, and was knocked on his back. It was like the driver who turned around and ran right into the stopped car in front of him.

8. Chimpanzees are the creatures closest to man in the line of evolution, and for this reason have been the subject of extensive study. It has been observed that when two or more chimpanzees are enclosed in a confined area, the level of tension among the animals increases proportionately to the time element involved; that is, the longer they are confined, the greater the tension. The moral is, don't get stuck in an elevator for any great length of time!

9. In one study, two groups of gorillas were observed. Both were kept in zoos. One group was accessible to the public, whereas the other was kept in a restricted area without access by the public. It was found that the gorillas to which the public had access had unbalanced diets (a result of additional feeding by the public), were overweight, and tended to be sluggish. This study is analogous to a study of two groups of human beings. One group was confined to an institution and had a planned diet. The other group was also confined to an institution but had access to unlimited food. Again, those not restricted from additional eating had unbalanced diets, were overweight, and tended to be sluggish. Consequently, it is evident that strict control of diet is required for any creature to maintain prime physical health and to avoid overweight and sluggishness.

10. Paul was a graduate of Xavier High School, and when subsequently he sought employment, he got the job he wanted. Peter was a graduate of St. Peter's High School, and when subsequently he sought employment, he also got the job he wanted. Jack was a dropout from St. Peter's and did not get the job he wanted. It should be obvious that no matter what high school a person graduates from, so long as he graduates, he will get the job he wants.

INDUCTIVE GENERALIZATIONS

Let us reconsider the argument concerning the students in Professor Wilson's metaphysics class last semester, modifying the conclusion to read as follows:

Tim was a student enrolled in Professor Wilson's metaphysics course last semester and got an A.

Sue was a student enrolled in Professor Wilson's metaphysics course last semester and got an A.

Mary was a student enrolled in Professor Wilson's metaphysics course last semester and got an A.

John was a student enrolled in Professor Wilson's metaphysics course last semester and got an A.

Therefore, all students enrolled in Professor Wilson's metaphysics courses get A's.

Quite clearly, this is an enumerative inductive argument, for its premises consist of a listing of statements about individual cases. It also has a universal proposition as its conclusion, and is such that if any one of the premises is false—that is, if one of the students in question did not get an A—then it necessarily follows that the conclusion of the argument is false. This is an example of an enumerative inductive generalization. Notice that, if the conclusion had been 'All students enrolled in Professor Wilson's metaphysics course *this semester* will get A's' instead of 'All students enrolled in Professor Wilson's metaphysics courses get A's', we would be dealing with an enumerative induction by analogy. The point is significant because it clarifies the difference between the two kinds of inductive argument: In the induction by analogy, the falsity of none of the premises can guarantee the falsity of the conclusion. In the inductive generalization, at least one premise is such that its falsity could imply the falsity of the conclusion.

It must be explained here why the definition of 'inductive generalization' asserts that 'at least one premise is such that its falsity *could* imply the falsity of the conclusion', rather than the more definite '. . . *would* imply. . . .' The reason for this qualification is that an observation statement, such as 'Swan A is white', can be false on *several* different grounds, only one of which is sufficient to falsify a universal conclusion statement such as 'All swans are white'. For example, 'Swan A is white' is false if A is not a swan; but if A is not a swan, the fact that A is not white does not imply that the generalization 'All swans are white' is false. Only if A is a swan, and is also not white, would it follow that 'All swans are white' is false. Any inductive argument with such a conclusion and at least one such premise thus qualifies as an inductive generalization, even though the falsity of the premise does not *always* guarantee the falsity of the conclusion.

If we let X_1 . . . X_4 represent Tim, Sue, Mary, and John, respectively, and let A stand for being a student enrolled in Professor Wilson's metaphysics course and B stand for getting a grade of A in the course, the argument above can be schematized as follows:

> X_1 *is an A and a B.*
> X_2 *is an A and a B.*
> X_3 *is an A and a B.*
> X_4 *is an A and a B.*
> *Therefore, all A's are B's.*

or:

> X_1, X_2, X_3, *and* X_4 *are all A's and B's.*
> *Therefore, all A's are B's.*

In the example above, the argument contained premises about particular individuals that were used to support a conclusion about a whole class of individuals. It is also possible to have an enumerative generalization which contains premises about *classes* of individuals that are used to support a conclusion about a class of individuals. For example, consider the following:

> *All students enrolled in Professor Wilson's*
> *   metaphysics course last semester got A's.*
> *All students enrolled in Professor Wilson's*
> *   metaphysics course the semester before last got*
> *   A's.*
> *All students enrolled in Professor Wilson's*
> *   metaphysics course three semesters ago got A's.*
> *Therefore, all students enrolled in Professor Wilson's*
> *   metaphysics course get A's.*

This, too, is an enumerative generalization, because in this example the falsity of one or more of the premises would guarantee the falsity of the conclusion. Notice that if the conclusion had read 'All students enrolled in Professor Wilson's metaphysics course next semester will get an A', the argument would be an induction by analogy. It is interesting to note that it is impossible to have an inductive generalization with particular premises and a particular conclusion or one which has general premises and a particular conclusion.

Some inductive generalizations have considerable predictive value, but they may also have their drawbacks, as when someone concludes that all Italians (or Poles, or Jews, or blacks, or whites, or members of any other ethnic or racial group) are stupid or untrustworthy, after having had contact with only a few such people. We must therefore establish criteria for determining which inductive arguments are better than others—in other words, criteria of the relative strengths of enumerative inductions.

EXERCISE 10–2   *Determine whether each of the following is an induction by analogy or an inductive generalization.*

---

1. All ants are insects and are social animals. All bees are insects and are social animals. All termites are insects and are social animals. Therefore, all insects must be social animals.
2. All ants are insects and are social animals. All bees are insects and are social animals. All termites are insects and are social animals. All flies are insects. So, all flies are social animals.
3. Rudolf Nureyev was trained by Alexander Pushkin and is a great ballet dancer. So were Mikhail Baryshnikov and Valery Panov, and they're great ballet dancers. Therefore, one may infer that all dancers trained by Alexander Pushkin are great ballet dancers.
4. Susan, Veronica, and Caroline are all intelligent women, and each reads *Ms.* magazine. Betty Ann is also an intelligent woman, so she also reads *Ms.* magazine.
5. All past presidents of the United States were men. Therefore, all future presidents probably will be men.
6. The movie I saw on the late show yesterday was a mystery, and the movie I saw on the late show the night before that was a mystery. Therefore, the movie I will see on tonight's late show will be a mystery.
7. Regina plays football; so do Christine and Judith; so probably all girls play football at some time in their lives.
8. I have been a Yankee baseball fan for many years and have followed seventeen of their players very closely. All seventeen are great hitters, great fielders, and great throwers. It must be that all Yankees can hit, field, and throw well.
9. Earth is a planet and revolves in an elliptical orbit around the sun. Mars is a planet and revolves in an elliptical orbit around the sun. Jupiter is a planet and revolves in an elliptical orbit around the sun. Therefore, all planets revolve in elliptical orbits around the sun.
10. *The Mousetrap* and *Murder on the Orient Express* are both by Agatha Christie. Both are also interesting detective stories. *Murder Ahoy* is by Agatha Christie, so it too is probably an interesting detective story.
11. Ann, Frank, Carol, and Mike are all successful business executives and they all read the *Wall Street Journal*. Consequently, one can infer that all successful business executives read the *Wall Street Journal*.

12. John, Peter, Susan, and Frieda are friends of Bob and graduated from Michigan State, so probably all of Bob's friends are Michigan State graduates.
13. American, Eastern, and Braniff all charge the same coach fare for flights from Chicago to New York. Therefore, all airlines that have flights from Chicago to New York charge the same coach fare.
14. Scott Meredith is the literary agent for Norman Mailer, Gore Vidal, and Jacqueline Susann and all their books sell well. Meredith just took on Spiro Agnew as a client. So, Agnew's book will probably sell well.
15. In Texas, all the roses grow big. In Texas, all the chickens grow big. In Texas, all the boys grow big. In Texas, all the girls grow big. Therefore, in Texas all things grow big.
16. A frog is a warm-blooded mammal.
    A porpoise is a warm-blooded mammal.
    Therefore, all mammals are warm-blooded.
17. Jack couldn't ride the palomino at last year's fair. Bill couldn't ride the palomino at last year's fair. Therefore, no one can ride the palomino at this year's fair.
18. My father always listens to me when I talk to him. My brother, too, always listens to me. My mother always listens to me when I talk to her. Therefore, everybody always listens to me when I talk.

RELATIVE STRENGTH OF ENUMERATIVE INDUCTIONS

We have seen that one of the basic differences between deductive and inductive arguments is that, in a valid deductive argument, the premises provide absolute support for the conclusion whereas, in an inductive argument, they provide support which can range from just less than absolute at one extreme to almost none at the other extreme. Thus, it cannot be said of an inductive argument that it is either good or bad in any absolute sense, as it can be said of a deductive argument that it is valid or invalid. Instead, inductive arguments can be evaluated only in terms of degrees of strength or weakness. It would be convenient if this could be done by means of a single fixed scale, but so far no such system has been devised. Thus, we must evaluate inductive arguments in terms of their *relative* strengths; that is, we must devise criteria for determining whether one inductive argument is stronger or weaker than another. This can be accomplished by seeing how the strength of the argument is affected when we take a fixed set of premises and change the conclusion, when we take a fixed conclusion and modify the premises, and, finally, when both premises and conclusion are changed in certain ways.

Inductive and Deductive Strength

Consider the following inductive arguments. Try to determine which argument is inductively strongest, which is next strongest, and so on.

> *Every student in Professor Wilson's metaphysics course last semester got an A.*
>
> (1) *Therefore, at least one student in Professor Wilson's metaphysics course next semester will get an A.*

Every student in Professor Wilson's metaphysics course last semester got an A.

(2)   Therefore, Herb will get an A in Professor Wilson's metaphysics course next semester.

Every student in Professor Wilson's metaphysics course last semester got an A.

(3)   Therefore, every student in Professor Wilson's metaphysics course next semester will get an A.

Every student in Professor Wilson's metaphysics course last semester got an A.

(4)   Therefore, all students in all of Professor Wilson's metaphysics courses get A's.

Every student in Professor Wilson's metaphysics course last semester got an A.

(5)   Therefore, being a student in Professor Wilson's metaphysics course causes a student to get an A.

You are correct if you concluded that the arguments above are listed in order of decreasing **inductive strength.** On an intuitive level, you can probably see that the argument with statement 1 as its conclusion is stronger (that is, its premises provide stronger support for its conclusion) than the argument with statement 2 as its conclusion. The argument with statement 2 as its conclusion is as strong as, or stronger than, the one with 3 as its conclusion; the one with 3 as its conclusion is stronger than the one with 4 as its conclusion; and the one with 4 as its conclusion is stronger than the one with 5 as its conclusion. The reason for attributing the highest degree of probability to the argument with conclusion 1 is that this conclusion encompasses the broadest range of possibilities. Thus, if any one student in Professor Wilson's metaphysics course next semester gets an A, the conclusion is true. On the basis of the evidence offered in the premise, it is more likely that some one or another of the students in next semester's class will get an A than it is that one specifically named student, such as Herb, will get one; it is at least as likely that Herb will get an A as that every student enrolled in Professor Wilson's metaphysics course next semester will get one; and it is more likely that every student in next semester's course will get an A than it is that all students in all of Professor Wilson's metaphysics courses get A's. Finally, it is more likely that all students in Professor Wilson's course get A's than it is that being a student in the course causes a student to get an A. (Causal statements, such as this last, will be discussed in Chapter 12.)

Note that each of these arguments contains the same premise. Because the premises are identical and the inductive strengths of the arguments are different, the differences in strength must be the result of differences in the conclusions of the arguments. An examination of the conclusion statements in relation to each other will help to clarify the notion of relative strength. Listed without their premises, the conclusion statements are:

(1)   *At least one student in Professor Wilson's metaphysics course next semester will get an A.*

(2)   *Herb will get an A in Professor Wilson's metaphysics course next semester.*

(3)   *Every student in Professor Wilson's metaphysics course next semester will get an A.*

(4)   *All students in all of Professor Wilson's metaphysics courses get A's.*

(5)   *Being a student in Professor Wilson's metaphysics course causes a student to get an A.*

Now, if conclusion 5 is true,[2] then conclusions 4, 3, 2, and 1 must also be true, for conclusion 5 deductively *implies* conclusions 4, 3, 2, and 1. If being a student in Professor Wilson's metaphysics course causes a student to get an A, then it necessarily follows that 'All students in all of Professor Wilson's metaphysics courses get A's' is true, 'Every student in Professor Wilson's metaphysics course next semester will get an A' is true, 'Herb will get an A in Professor Wilson's metaphysics course next semester' is true (assuming, of course, that Herb enrolls in the course), and 'At least one student in Professor Wilson's metaphysics course next semester will get an A' is true. Notice, however, that none of the other conclusions implies conclusion 5. It is possible for any one (or even all) of conclusions 1, 2, 3, and 4 to be true and for conclusion 5 to be false. Similarly, if conclusion 4 is true, then conclusions 3, 2, and 1 must be true, for conclusion 4 implies conclusions 3, 2, and 1. However, conclusion 4 does not imply conclusion 5; that is, it is possible that all students in Professor Wilson's metaphysics classes get A's without it being true that being a student in his class causes a student to get an A. The truth of conclusion 3 implies the truth of conclusions 2 and 1, but neither conclusion 4 nor conclusion 5 is validly deducible from conclusion 3. By the same token, if conclusion 2 is true, conclusion 1 must be

---

[2] As explained in Chapter 2, no statement is a premise or a conclusion in and of itself; it becomes a premise or a conclusion only by being so used in a specific argument. Thus, strictly speaking, we should here talk of 'the statement being used as the conclusion in such-and-such an argument' rather than 'the conclusion statement'. For simplicity, however, we will use the shorter phrasing in our discussion, with the specification here that it should be understood as a shorthand for the more complicated technically precise wording.

true, for conclusion 2 implies conclusion 1, but conclusion 2 does not imply conclusions 3, 4, or 5. Finally, conclusion 1 does not imply any of the other conclusions. If at least one student in Professor Wilson's metaphysics course next semester gets an A, this does not imply that it was Herb who got the A, nor that *every* student got an A, nor that all students in Professor Wilson's metaphysics course get A's, nor that being a student in Professor Wilson's course causes a student to get an A.

All of this can be summed up by saying that the conclusion statements above are arranged in order of increasing **deductive strength.** Statement A is said to be *deductively stronger* than statement B if and only if statement A implies statement B *and* Statement B does not imply statement A. Statement A is said to be *deductively weaker* than statement B if and only if B implies A *and* A does not imply B. Statements A and B are of equal deductive strength if A implies B *and* B implies A. We can conclude, therefore, that the relative strengths of any two or more inductive arguments with the same set of premises are inversely proportional to the deductive strengths of their conclusions. Thus, in our arguments above—all of which have the same premise—we can see that as we move from the argument with conclusion 1 to the argument with conclusion 5, the inductive strength of the arguments decreases, whereas the deductive strength of their conclusions increases. Similarly, as we move from the argument with conclusion 5 to the argument with conclusion 1, the inductive strength of the arguments increases, whereas the deductive strength of the conclusions decreases. It is interesting to note, too, that of the four enumerative inductions (arguments 1–4), the inductive generalization (4) is inductively weaker than any of the inductions by analogy (1–3).

Thus, one way of evaluating the relative inductive strengths of arguments with the same set of premises is in terms of the relative deductive strengths of their conclusions. Another method requires the consideration of what are known as positive and negative analogies. To deal more easily with this method, we must first introduce the notions of observed and unobserved cases.

EXERCISE 10–3   *Place the following arguments in order of decreasing inductive strength on the basis of the relative deductive strength of the various conclusions.*

1. Standard premise for all conclusions that follow:
    Every stone I found yesterday was precious.
    Conclusions:
    a. Therefore, exactly two of the stones I will find today will be precious.
    b. Therefore, every stone I find today will be precious.
    c. Therefore, some stones I will find today will be precious.
    d. Therefore, every stone I find is a precious stone.
    e. Therefore, my finding a stone causes it to be precious.

2. Standard premise for all conclusions that follow:
    All European nations have shown aggressive tendencies in the past.
    Conclusions:
    a. Therefore, Italy will show aggressive tendencies in the future.
    b. Therefore, every European country will show aggressive tendencies in the future.
    c. Therefore, at least one European country will show aggressive tendencies in the future.
    d. Therefore, being a European country causes a country to show aggressive tendencies.
    e. Therefore, all European countries always show aggressive tendencies.

3. Standard premise for all conclusions that follow:
    Every adult member of the Smith's family is a college graduate.
    Conclusions:
    a. Therefore, Mr. and Mrs. Smith's eight-year-old son and twelve-year-old daughter will probably be college graduates.
    b. Therefore, all of Mr. and Mrs. Smith's three children will be college graduates.
    c. Therefore, at least one of Mr. and Mrs. Smith's children probably will be a college graduate.
    d. Therefore, Mr. and Mrs. Smith's eight-year-old son probably will be a college graduate.
    e. Therefore, being a member of the Smith family causes a person to be a college graduate.

4. Standard premise for all conclusions that follow:
    All articles of clothing designed by Pierre Cardin in the past have been expensive.
    Conclusions:
    a. Therefore, being an article of clothing designed by Pierre Cardin causes that article of clothing to be expensive.
    b. Therefore, all articles of clothing designed by Pierre Cardin are expensive.
    c. Therefore, all articles of clothing in Pierre Cardin's new line of evening dresses will be expensive.
    d. Therefore, some articles of clothing in Pierre's Cardin's new lines will be expensive.
    e. Therefore, all articles of clothing in Pierre Cardin's new lines of evening dresses and coats will be expensive.

5. Standard premise for all conclusions that follow:
    Every member of the Jones family has always voted Republican.
    Conclusions:
    a. Therefore, Mr. Jones will vote Republican in the coming election.
    b. Therefore, being a member of the Jones family causes a person to vote Republican.
    c. Therefore, at least one member of the Jones family will vote Republican in the coming election.
    d. Therefore, all members of the Jones family will vote Republican in the coming election.
    e. Therefore, all members of the Jones family will vote Republican in all future elections.

6. Standard premise for all conclusions that follow:
    All persons at Joe's parties in the past have been interesting.
    Conclusions:
    a. Therefore, being at Joe's parties causes a person to be interesting.
    b. Therefore, the first person I talk to at Joe's party tonight will be interesting.
    c. Therefore, some persons at Joe's party tonight will be interesting.

    d.   Therefore, everyone at Joe's party tonight will be interesting.

    e.   Therefore, all persons at Joe's parties are interesting.

7. Standard premise for all conclusions that follow:

All lions observed to date are carnivorous, warm-blooded mammals.

Conclusions:

    a.   Therefore, all lions are carnivorous, warm-blooded mammals.

    b.   Therefore, the very next lion observed will be a carnivorous, warm-blooded mammal.

    c.   Therefore, at least one lion that will be observed in the future will be a carnivorous, warm-blooded mammal.

    d.   Therefore, being a lion causes an animal to be a carnivorous, warm-blooded mammal.

    e.   Therefore, the next six lions observed in the future will be carnivorous, warm-blooded mammals.

8. Standard premise for all conclusions that follow:

All South American countries have had at least one coup d'état in the past fifty years.

Conclusions:

    a.   Therefore, Chile will have a coup d'état in the next fifty years.

    b.   Therefore, every South American country will have a coup d'état in the next fifty years.

    c.   Therefore, at least one South American country will have a coup d'état in the next fifty years.

    d.   Therefore, being a South American country will cause it to have a coup d'état in the next fifty years.

    e.   Therefore, all South American countries have at least one coup d'état every fifty years.

OBSERVED AND UNOBSERVED CASES

In our example of Professor Wilson's logic course, the premises always had the characteristic of describing situations which had presumably already been observed to be the case, while the conclusion referred to something which had apparently not yet been observed. However, strictly speaking, logicians do not consider it relevant to distinguish between observed and unobserved cases. Rather, their only concern is with the logical relationship between the statements in an argument that are designated as premises and the statement that is designated as the conclusion. Thus, it is unnecessary to specify whether the situation described by either a premise or conclusion statement in an inductive argument has been actually observed to be the case.

It is a fact that most enumerative inductions, if they are at all interesting, do involve premises which describe observed cases, while the conclusion involves a prediction—that is, a situation that is yet to be observed. Because it is not always appropriate to use the terms 'premise' and 'conclusion' in talking about inductive arguments, we will use the terms 'observed' and 'unobserved' for simplicity in our discussion of these arguments.

Positive and Negative Analogy

The ways in which the particular individuals or classes of individuals cited in an enumerative induction are *alike* is called a **positive analogy,** while the ways in which they are *different* is called a **negative analogy.** Consider the following argument:

> *Pat's first beagle was a male and lived fourteen*
>   *years.*
> *Pat's second beagle was a male and lived fourteen*
>   *years.*
> *Pat's third beagle was a male and lived fourteen*
>   *years.*
> *Pat's fourth beagle is a male and is presently ten*
>   *years old.*
> *Therefore, Pat's fourth beagle will live fourteen years.*

In this example there is a positive analogy among the observed cases (Pat's first three dogs) with regard to breed (beagle), sex (male), and life span (fourteen years). There is also a positive analogy between the first three cases and the observed features of the fourth case in terms of breed and sex. It can also be reasonably assumed that there is a negative analogy, possibly among the first three cases and certainly between the first three and the fourth case, with regard to the time of their acquisition by Pat. In this induction by analogy, the premises provide at least some support for the conclusion that Pat's fourth beagle will live to the age of fourteen years.

If we were to increase the negative analogy between the observed cases and the unobserved case by making the fourth beagle a female, the resulting inductive argument would be somewhat weaker than the original. As a general rule, we can state that *an enumerative induction becomes weaker as the negative analogy between the observed cases and the unobserved case increases, provided everything else remains the same.*

The following argument is even weaker than the argument in which the fourth beagle is a female, since it has the additional negative analogy that the breed of dog is changed to a collie. It is, of course, also weaker than the original argument.

> *Pat's first dog was a male beagle and lived fourteen*
>   *years.*
> *Pat's second dog was a male beagle and lived*
>   *fourteen years.*
> *Pat's third dog was a male beagle and lived fourteen*
>   *years.*
> *Pat's fourth dog is a female collie and is now ten*
>   *years old.*
> *Therefore, Pat's fourth dog will live fourteen years.*

Although increasing the negative analogy between the observed cases and the unobserved case generally weakens an inductive argument, *increasing the negative analogy among the observed cases will usually strengthen the argument if the unobserved case is left unchanged.* The following modified version of our example illustrates this principle.

Pat's first dog was a male beagle and lived fourteen
* years.*
Pat's second dog was a male pointer and lived
* fourteen years.*
Pat's third dog was a female setter and lived fourteen
* years.*
Pat's fourth dog is a female collie and is now ten
* years old.*
Therefore, Pat's fourth dog will live fourteen years.

The premises in this version clearly provide stronger support for the conclusion than in the previous version. The basic principle at work here is essentially the same as that involved in the concept of "random sampling" used by pollsters and others. For instance, in polling voters about their opinions on a particular social, economic, or political issue, opinion research organizations carefully select the people they interview to get a real cross section of the population in terms of relevant characteristics such as geographical location, annual income, education, age, political and religious affiliations, and occupation. A sample which is restricted to only white, male, blue-collar workers would not provide much support for a conclusion about the preferences of a general population which included such members as women, blacks, and white-collar workers.

Analogy in Inductive   If we took any of the arguments just presented and changed the
Generalizations   conclusion to 'Therefore, all of Pat's dogs will live fourteen years',
this new argument could not be inductively stronger than the origi-
nal, since its conclusion would be deductively stronger than the conclusion of
any of the original arguments. In terms of the relative strengths of inductive

---

ENON, Ohio (AP) — Dairyman Earl E. Chapman says if the government is going to tax property to pay for schools, it ought to tax the knowledge a person gets by going to school.

Chapman said educated people should be taxed on knowledge they use to earn a living, just as his farm is taxed.

"They bought their education just like I buy my land and I pay taxes on the land, but they don't have to pay taxes on their knowledge and that irks me," he said. "I use the land to earn my living and they use their knowledge to earn theirs. If the government can tax my investment, then it should tax their knowledge."

Chapman didn't say how this might be accomplished.

Although it is not an enumerative induction, Mr. Chapman's argument clearly involves analogical reasoning. Evaluate the strength of the analogy he makes, identifying both positive and negative analogies between the two cases.

Today, George Allen starts his fifth year with the Washington Redskins. This time, his contract is for seven years instead of five, but that aside there are a number of very striking parallels, both physical and psychological, between his years with the Rams and with the Redskins, parallels which make one think that if year five at Los Angeles was the end for George Allen and the Rams, then year five at Washington will be, at the very least, the beginning of the end for George Allen and the Redskins.

The most concrete parallels exist in won-lost records. With both teams Allen turned losers into immediate, first year winners: the 4-10 Rams bounced to 8-6 in 1966, the 6-8 Redskins were 9-4-1 in 1971. With both teams, his second year was the best: the 1967 Rams were 11-1-2 and almost got to the Super Bowl, while the 1972 Redskins were 11-3 and did get to the Super Bowl, only to lose to the Dolphins. And a case could even be made that in both cities the second-best Allen teams were his fourth year efforts: the 1969 Rams were 11-3 and won their division, while the 1974 Redskins, though finishing with the same 10-4 record as the 1973 bunch, had the advantage of a healthy Sonny Jurgensen for the playoffs, an advantage, many observers feel, that could have gotten the Redskins perhaps as far as the Super Bowl if George Allen had chosen to use it. He did not.

The prediction in the above analogical enumerative induction turned out to be quite accurate: George Allen's contract with the Washington Redskins was not renewed. Was this just a lucky guess on the part of the authors, or is the argument a good one?

"Is This The End for George Allen?"
WILLIAM GILDEA AND KENNETH IURAN
Wash. Post/Potomac 7/21/75

generalizations, the same relationships obtain regarding positive and negative analogies among observed cases and between observed and unobserved cases. To clarify this, consider the following:

> X_1 *is a sea otter and uses rocks to crack open seashells.*
> X_2 *is a sea otter and uses rocks to crack open seashells.*
> X_3 *is a sea otter and uses rocks to crack open seashells.*
>
> .
> .
> .
>
> X_n *is a sea otter and uses rocks to crack open seashells.*
> *Therefore, all sea otters use rocks to crack open seashells.*

This argument is an inductive generalization, since the falsity of one of its premises could guarantee the falsity of its conclusion. In this example, it is quite obvious that one infers the conclusion 'All sea otters use rocks to crack open seashells' from the fact that each observed case in the premises represents an individual that both was a sea otter and used rocks to crack open seashells. However, there are a number of other relevant characteristics, the specification of which will affect the strength of the argument. For instance, if we learned that all the sea otters cited in the premises were males, observed off the coast of Alaska, and of the species *Lutra canadiens,* the argument as it stands would be seriously weakened. In this instance, there would be a strong positive analogy among the observed cases but a very strong negative analogy between the observed cases and the generalization, which clearly includes female sea otters, those living in other parts of the world as well as off the coast of Alaska, and those of species other than *L. canadiens.* Thus the argument is a relatively weak one because of this relatively strong negative analogy between the observed cases and the generalization. Here, again, as we noted earlier, *the greater the negative analogy between the observed and unobserved cases, the weaker the enumerative induction, other things being unchanged*

If the negative analogy among the observed cases cited in the premises is increased while the generalization remains the same, then the argument becomes stronger. For instance, the negative analogy among the observed cases above would be strengthened if the observed sea otters included males and females, those living in various parts of the world, and members of a number of species. By increasing the negative analogy among the observed cases, we have also increased the positive analogy between observed and unobserved cases. That is, by increasing the negative analogy among observed cases, we have also increased the number of possible unobserved cases (included in the generalization) that would have a positive analogy with the observed cases. Again, as we noted earlier, *the greater the positive analogy between the observed and unobserved cases, the stronger the enumerative induction, other things remaining unchanged.*

Another way in which the original generalization can be made stronger is by narrowing the conclusion. For example, suppose the original argument had read:

> X_1 *is a male sea otter of the species* L. **canadiens**
> *observed off the coast of Alaska, and uses rocks to*
> *crack open seashells.*
> X_2. . . . .
> X_3. . . . .
> .
> .
> .
> X_n. . . . .
> *Therefore, all male sea otters of the species* L.
> **canadiens** *living off the coast of Alaska use rocks*
> *to crack open seashells.*

This argument is certainly stronger than an argument with the same premises but with the conclusion 'All sea otters use rocks to crack open seashells'. By narrowing the conclusion, we have increased the positive analogy between observed and unobserved cases, thereby strengthening the argument. Of course, in doing so we have also narrowed the generalization considerably, and, to some extent, have diminished its usefulness.

Number of Observed Cases Although the intuitively "obvious" principle is generally correct that *the more cases that are observed to support a conclusion, the stronger an inductive argument will be,* there are some significant qualifications of this principle that have to be recognized. One qualification is that as the number of observed cases increases, the inductive support given by *each* additional observed case decreases. For instance, if we are dealing with an argument in which five observed cases are offered in support of the conclusion, and then one hundred more observed cases are added, the strength of the inductive argument will increase greatly. But if we are considering an argument with one thousand observed cases cited in the premises, then an additional one hundred cases will not add as much support to the conclusion as did the additional one hundred cases in the first example.

It must also be recognized that in some cases, an enumerative induction with just a few observed cases, or even one, is not necessarily a weak argument. For instance, suppose you place a magnet near a pile of iron filings and observe that the filings are attracted to the magnet. You might infer, from your observation, that all instances in which a magnet is placed near iron the iron will be attracted to the magnet. An argument corresponding to your inference might read as follows:

> *In this instance, when I placed a magnet near iron,*
> *the iron was attracted to the magnet.*
> *Therefore, in all instances in which a magnet is*
> *placed near iron, the iron will be attracted to the*
> *magnet.*

As it stands, this is a weak induction. But under the principle of charity, the argument might be treated as an enthymeme—that is, an argument in which not all of the premises are explicitly stated. Thus it might be a strong inductive generalization—even though the premise cites only one observed case—depending on other previous inductions or background information which can be added to the premises. You might know, for instance, that nickel, copper, cobalt, silver, gold, and other pure metals each exhibits uniform behavior in the presence of a magnet; that is, some are attracted to it, whereas others are not. Thus, you could reasonably assume that iron, too, will exhibit uniform behavior in the presence of a magnet. When the missing premises based on this background information are supplied, your original argument might read as follows:

> *In past instances, any given pure metal has exhibited*
> *uniform behavior whenever a magnet was placed*
> *near it.*
> *Iron is a pure metal.*

> *In this instance, when I placed a magnet near iron,*
> *the iron was attracted to the magnet.*
> *Therefore, in all instances in which a magnet is*
> *placed near iron, the iron will be attracted to the*
> *magnet.*

The relative strength of this argument can be understood more clearly by comparing it to the argument implicit in the cartoon below. The argument is essentially as follows:

> *When smaller wheel A collided with larger wheel B,*
> *the larger wheel was destroyed.*
> *Smaller wheel C is about to collide with larger wheel*
> *D.*
> *Therefore, larger wheel D will be destroyed.*

In this case, we do not have any theoretical base that can be drawn on to support this induction; indeed, there are many basic general principles which directly contradict the first premise. This argument really involves a possible rejection of a whole set of scientific (and common-sense) theories and laws associated with our normal expectations that larger objects usually suffer less damage when they collide with smaller objects. Thus, when such an anomalous case appears which conflicts with all reasonable expectations, it is usually wise to examine it more carefully to determine whether there is some significant disanalogy involved. For example, in the case of the cartoon, it would be necessary to determine what materials the various wheels might be made of. It could be that, in the first case, the small wheel might be made out of steel and the large one out of brittle rock, while, in the second case, both wheels are made of the same substance. Now the weakness of the argument is not the fact that there is only one observed case but that there is a negative analogy between the observed and unobserved cases as shown here:

> *When small steel wheel A collided with large,*
> *brittle-rock wheel B, the larger (brittle-rock) wheel*
> *was destroyed.*

"B.C." by permission of Johnny Hart and Field Enterprises, Inc.

*Small steel wheel C is about to collide with large
    steel wheel D.
Therefore, larger wheel D will be destroyed.*

In this form, with the extra information about the material out of which the wheels are made now explicit, the weakness of the inductive argument is quite clear.

Just as an enumerative induction with one or a few observed cases in the premise(s) is not necessarily a weak argument, one with a large number of observed cases is not necessarily strong. For instance, suppose you are the Commissioner of Parks in Chicago and you want to find out what percentage of Chicagoans use the city's parks. Suppose, too, that you then send out one of your bright young assistants to do a survey. He goes to five parks and speaks with twenty people in each; each person he speaks to says he uses the park. Based on his over-all sample of one hundred interviews, your bright young assistant returns and informs you that 'All Chicagoans use the city's parks'. Dubious of his findings but not inquiring about his method of research, you tell him to do the survey over. Again, he returns to the five parks, this time interviewing fifty people in each, which gives him a total sample of two hundred and fifty interviews. Again, he discovers that all those interviewed use the parks, and thereby concludes again that all Chicagoans use the city's parks.

Returning with his findings, he reports his conclusion to you and indicates that since the size of his sample is two and one-half times that of his original, there is even greater probability that his conclusion is a good one. This time you inquire about his sampling procedures, and upon finding them out, fire him on the spot. Your bright young assistant could have interviewed a thousand people at each park and he still would have reached the same conclusion. No number of additional observed cases gathered in this way would strengthen the argument. Indeed, the example is a bit absurd, but it points out that the use of a large number of observed cases in the premises of an enumerative induction does not necessarily strengthen the argument. All we can say is that, *generally speaking,* the greater the number of observed cases, the stronger the induction. This is so because *usually,* as we increase the number of observed cases in the premises of an enumerative induction, we also increase the negative analogy among the observed cases. As we noted earlier, the greater the negative analogy among observed cases, the more likely it is that the unobserved case—or generalization—will have a positive analogy to the observed cases, thus increasing the probability of the conclusion and strengthening the enumerative induction.

Relevance   The relevance of the characteristics of the cases being compared or contrasted will affect the strength of an enumerative induction, but determining which characteristics are relevant or irrelevant is not a simple task. For instance, in the argument about Pat's dogs, it is possible that the diet of the animal or certain genetic traits might be as relevant or more relevant to their life span as any of the characteristics considered in the argument. There is no *formal* logical procedure that will guarantee that we have considered all and only the relevant factors in any given case. An individual's personal background of experience and theoretical assumptions will certainly influence her or his judgments as to what should and should not be considered relevant in any case. For instance, a person who has bought three dogs from pet shops, each of which died within two years, might consider the place of purchase relevant to the argument. A believer in astrology might consider the date of purchase and the birth date of the purchaser to be relevant. We will discuss some methods in

How, if at all, can Linus' act of "prophecy" in this cartoon be interpreted as an induction? What would the inductive argument reflecting his reasoning look like? To what extent, if at all, does Lucy's observation confirm Linus' hypothesis or add strength to his induction?

Chapter 12 for determining in a more formal way whether a particular factor we think might be relevant is, in fact, relevant.

In the case of our example of the sea otters and their use of rocks, we must ask ourselves whether it is reasonable to suppose that the species of an animal is relevant to its tool-using behavior. We must usually depend on context and background information to help make such judgments. For instance, in this example, background information about other animal species and their tool-using behavior seems to support the relevance of the two characteristics cited in the argument. It is known, for example, that chimpanzees sometimes strip down grass stems which they use as tools to extract termites from their nests for food; that males of some species of bird present pebbles or other objects to their intended mates; and so on. Then too, information about the environment may help to determine the relevance or irrelevance of particular characteristics in an enumerative induction. If we knew that some species of sea otter live in areas where shellfish are not found, then we might reasonably assume that at least some sea otters do not use rocks to crack open shells—how could they if there are no shellfish present? Background information of this sort would weaken the argument considerably.

EXERCISE 10–4   *Read each argument below carefully. Determine whether the addition of the suggested premise(s) weakens or strengthens the argument in terms of positive and negative analogy, relevance, and/or the number of observed cases.*

---

1. All bees are insects and can fly.
   All flies are insects and can fly.
   All wasps are insects and can fly.
   Therefore, probably all insects can fly.
   a. Add the following premise only: All butterflies are insects and can fly.
   b. Add the following premise only: All moths are insects and can fly.
   c. Add the following premise only: All fleas are insects and do not fly.
   d. Add the following premise only: All spiders are insects and do not fly.
   e. Add premises a and b.
   f. Add premises a, b, and c.

2. The Thomases are Irish Catholic and have always voted Democratic.
   The O'Connors are Irish Catholic and have always voted Democratic.
   The Caseys are Irish Catholic and have always voted Democratic.
   The Flynns are Irish Catholic and have always voted Democratic.
   The Kellys are Irish Catholic.
   Therefore, the Kellys probably have always voted Democratic.
   a. Add the following premise only: Mrs. Kelly's brother was the Republican candidate for mayor last year.
   b. Add the following premise only: The Kellys are registered Democrats.
   c. Add the following premise only: The Kellys are very active in the Democratic party.

    d.   Add the following premise only: The Thomases, O'Connors, Caseys, and Flynns are first-generation immigrants and the Kellys are fifth-generation immigrants.

    e.   Add the following premise only: Ninety-five percent of Irish Catholic voters vote Democrat in every election.

    f.   Add premises a and d.

    g.   Add premises b and e.

    h.   Add premises c and d.

3.   All lions I have observed are cats, warm-blooded, mammals, and carnivorous.
All leopards I have observed are cats, warm-blooded, mammals, and carnivorous.
All panthers I have observed are cats, warm-blooded mammals, and carnivorous.
All cougars I have observed are cats, warm-blooded, and mammals.
Therefore, probably all cougars are carnivorous.

    a.   Add the following premise only: All tigers I have observed are cats, warm-blooded, mammals, and carnivorous.

    b.   Add the following premise only: All types of cat I have observed were in the Kenya Wildlife Reserve.

    c.   Add the following premise only: I have observed only one of each type of cat.

    d.   Add the following premise only: All tabbies I have observed are cats, warm-blooded, mammals, and carnivorous.

    e.   Add premises a and d.

    f.   Add premises b and c.

4.   All bluejays are birds and can fly.
All robins are birds and can fly.
All sparrows are birds and can fly.
All hawks are birds and can fly.
Therefore, all birds can fly.

    a.   Add the following premise only: All seagulls are birds and can fly.

    b.   Add the following premise only: All ostriches are birds and cannot fly.

    c.   Add the following premise only: All pelicans are birds and can fly.

    d.   Add the following premise only: All crows are birds and can fly.

    e.   Add the following premise only: All penguins are birds and cannot fly.

    f.   Add premises a, c, and d.

    g.   Add premises a, c, d, and e.

5.   The Franklins purchased a 1981 Maytag washing machine and have had excellent service.
The Peppers purchased a 1981 Maytag washing machine and have had excellent service.
The Goldslags purchased a 1981 Maytag washing machine and have had excellent service.
The Corleones purchased a 1981 Maytag washing machine. Therefore, the Corleones will probably have excellent service.

    a.   Add the following premise only: The Franklins', Peppers', and Goldslags' washing machines hold twenty-four-pound loads, whereas the Corleones' washing machine holds a sixteen-pound load.

    b.   Add the following premise only: The Franklins, Peppers, and Goldslags all use *White,* the soap powder recommended by the Maytag company, whereas the Corleones use *Wash,* the most inexpensive brand of soap powder.

    c.   Add the following premise only: The Franklins, Peppers, and Goldslags all use a bleach and fabric softener in addition to soap powder, whereas the Corleones do not.

    d.   Add the following premise only: The Petersons purchased a 1981 Maytag washing machine and have had excellent service.

    e.   Add the following premise only: All the washing machines were manufactured at the same plant, tested by the same inspector, and purchased from the same store.

    f.   Add the following premise only: The Corleones' washing machine was a floor model, whereas all the other machines were new and factory sealed.

    g.   Add premises a, c, and d.

    h.   Add premises e and f.

6.   John went to Excel high school and won a scholarship to college.
Mary went to Excel high school and won a scholarship to college.
Peter went to Excel high school and won a scholarship to college.
Frances went to Excel High School and won a scholarship to college.
Susan goes to Excel High School.
Therefore, Susan probably will win a scholarship to college.

    a.   Add the following premise only: John, Mary, Peter, Frances, and Susan each have B+ or better averages.

    b.   Add the following premise only: When John, Mary, Peter, and Frances graduated from Excel High School, the school had a special program preparing students for scholarship examinations; no such program exists now.

    c.   Add the following premise only: John, Mary, Peter, and Frances only won scholarships to the state university; Susan has only applied for a scholarship at Harvard.

    d.   Add the following premise only: John, Mary, and Susan took advanced courses in high school, whereas Peter and Frances did not take advanced courses.

    e.   Add the following premise only: John, Mary, Peter, and Frances scored between 600 and 650 on their college boards, whereas Susan scored between 700 and 750 on her college boards.

    f.   Add premises a, d, and e.

    g.   Add premises b and c.

7.   The Santiagos bought a 1975 Ford Mustang and get about 25 miles to a gallon of gas.
The Prices bought a 1975 Ford Mustang and get about 25 miles to a gallon of gas.
The Thomases bought a 1975 Ford Mustang and get about 25 miles to a gallon of gas.
The Allens bought a 1975 Ford Mustang.
Therefore, the Allens' car gets at least 25 miles to a gallon of gas.

    a.   Add the following premise only: The Judds bought a 1975 Ford Mustang and get about 30 miles to a gallon of gas.

    b.   Add the following premise only: The Martinos bought a 1975 Ford Mustang and get about 10 miles to a gallon of gas.

    c.   Add the following premises only: The Santiagos', Prices', and Thomases' cars are red, and the Allens' car is blue.

    d.   Add the following premise only: All the families bought their cars in the same week from the same dealer.

    e.   Add the following premises only: The Santiagos', Prices', and Thomases' cars do not have air conditioning and power windows and the Allens' car has air conditioning and power windows.

    f.   Add the following premises only: The Santiagos', Prices', and Thomases' cars have six-cylinder engines, and the Allens' car has an eight-cylinder engine.

    g.   Add the following premise only: The Santiagos, Prices, and Thomases use high-octane gas in their cars, and the Allens use regular gas in their car.

    h.   Add premises e and g.

    i.   Add premises a, d, and f.

STATISTICAL INDUCTIONS   We have distinguished two types of enumerative induction: induction by analogy and inductive generalization. Consider the following arguments:

> *Every student in Professor Wilson's metaphysics*
>   *class last semester got an A.*
> *Therefore, every student in Professor Wilson's*
>   *metaphysics class next semester will get an A.*

> *Every student in Professor Wilson's metaphysics*
>   *class last semester got an A.*
> *Therefore, every student in each of Professor Wilson's*
>   *metaphysics classes gets an A.*

The first argument is an induction by analogy, since the falsity of its premise cannot guarantee the falsity of its conclusion. The second argument is an inductive generalization, because the falsity of its premise can guarantee the falsity of its conclusion and, of course, its conclusion is a universal proposition. If we substitute '100 percent' for 'every' in the premises and conclusions the arguments would read as

> *One hundred percent of the students in Professor*
>   *Wilson's metaphysics class last semester got A's.*
> *Therefore, 100 percent of the students in Professor*
>   *Wilson's metaphysics class next semester will get*
>   *A's.*

> *One hundred percent of the students in Professor*
>   *Wilson's metaphysics class last semester got A's.*
> *Therefore, 100 percent of the students in each of*
>   *Professor Wilson's metaphysics classes get A's.*

Both versions carry the same sense as the original arguments: we have merely substituted the numerical value '100 percent' for the word 'every'. The first type of argument above is therefore called a **statistical induction by analogy.** Notice that, as in the inductions by analogy previously discussed, the falsity of its premise cannot guarantee the falsity of its conclusion. The second type is called a **statistical generalization.** As with all inductive generalizations, at least one premise must be such that its falsity could entail the falsity of the conclusion. We can also say that the statistical generalization is inductively weaker than the statistical induction by analogy, since the conclusion of the statistical generalization is deductively stronger than the conclusion of the statistical induction by analogy.

Of course, most statistical inductions—whether they are statistical inductions by analogy or statistical generalizations—do not draw conclusions about 100 percent of the cases. For example:

> *All of the students in Professor Wilson's metaphysics*
> *class last semester got A's.*
> *Therefore, some students in Professor Wilson's*
> *metaphysics class next semester will get A's.*

This argument is inductively stronger than any of the previous arguments in this section. Its strength is the result of the word 'some' (which in logic always means 'at least one'). The statement would be true if *any* one student in the class got an A; but it would also be true if two or three or four or even all of the students got A's. Clearly, given the premise 'All of the students in Professor Wilson's class last semester got A's', it is more probable that at least one student next semester will get an A than it is that all of the students in next semester's class will get A's.

It is possible to remove the vagueness of the word 'some' by replacing it with a number. For example:

> *All of the students in Professor Wilson's metaphysics*
> *class last semester got A's.*
> *Therefore, two students in Professor Wilson's*
> *metaphysics class next semester will get A's.*

If we know that there are only five students registered for next semester's class, the argument might also be written as follows:

> *All of the students in Professor Wilson's metaphysics*
> *class last semester got A's.*
> *Therefore, 40 percent of the students in Professor*
> *Wilson's metaphysics class next semester will get*
> *A's.*

The conclusions of the arguments above—'Two students in Professor Wilson's metaphysics class next semester will get A's' and 'Forty percent of the students in Professor Wilson's metaphysics class next semester will get A's'—are deductively stronger than the conclusion 'Some students in Professor Wilson's metaphysics class next semester will get A's'. This is so because, if two of the students (or 40 percent of the students) in next semester's class get A's, then it must be the case that at least one student next semester will get an A. The conclusions of the two arguments above imply the conclusion 'Some students in Professor Wilson's metaphysics class next semester will get A's', but neither of the numerically precise statements can be deduced from the 'some' statement. Thus, the two arguments above are inductively weaker than the original argument containing the word 'some' in its conclusion because they have the same premises, and the conclusions are deductively stronger.

It is worth noting that the conclusion 'Exactly two students in Professor Wilson's metaphysics class next semester will get A's' is deductively stronger than the conclusion 'At least two students in Professor Wilson's metaphysics class next semester will get A's'. Provided the premise in both arguments remains the same ('One hundred percent of the students in Professor Wilson's metaphysics class last semester got A's'), the argument with the conclusion 'Exactly two students in next semester's class will get A's' is inductively weaker than the argument with the conclusion 'At least two students in next semester's class will get A's'. Clearly, the first conclusion encompasses only one possibility, whereas the second conclusion will be satisfied if two *or more* students in next semester's class get A's. Similarly, the conclusion 'Exactly 40 percent of the students in Professor Wilson's metaphysics class next semester will get A's' is deductively stronger than the conclusion 'At least 40 percent of the students in Professor Wilson's metaphysics class next semester will get A's'. And the argument with the first conclusion ('At least 40 percent . . .') is inductively stronger than the argument with the second conclusion ('Exactly 40 percent . . .').

If we draw the further conclusion 'Tom and Bill will get A's in Professor Wilson's metaphysics class next semester,' this is deductively stronger than the conclusion 'At least two . . .' or 'Exactly two . . .,' for it implies both of them, but is implied by neither. Therefore, the argument with this conclusion is inductively weaker than the others. The probability that *some* two or more students will get A's is clearly greater than that any two *particular* students will get A's.

Of course, it is also possible to have statistical generalizations that argue from less than 100 percent of the cases. For example, consider the following arguments:

> *Sixty percent of the students in Professor Wilson's metaphysics class last semester got A's.*
> *Therefore, 60 percent of all students in each of Professor Wilson's metaphysics classes get A's.*

> *Three students in Professor Wilson's metaphysics class last semester got A's.*
> *Therefore, three students in every metaphysics class taught by Professor Wilson get A's.*

> *Tom was enrolled in Professor Wilson's metaphysics class last semester and got an A.*
> *Sue was enrolled in Professor Wilson's metaphysics class last semester and got an A.*
> *Ann was enrolled in Professor Wilson's metaphysics class last semester and got a B.*
> *Al was enrolled in Professor Wilson's metaphysics class last semester and got a C.*
> *Liz was enrolled in Professor Wilson's metaphysics class last semester and got an A.*
> *Tom, Sue, Al, Ann, and Liz were the only students in Professor Wilson's metaphysics class last semester.*
> *Therefore, 60 percent of all students enrolled in each of Professor Wilson's metaphysics classes get A's.*

From the arguments above, we can see that, while the premises of a statistical generalization may be about individuals and/or classes of individuals, the conclusion is always about a class of individuals. We can see also that numerical values in a statistical generalization can occur in the conclusion or in both premises and conclusion.

Evaluating Statistical Inductions The same criteria that are used to evaluate the strength of enumerative inductions are used to evaluate the strength of statistical inductions, since the latter are merely a type of enumerative induction. Thus, the positive and negative analogies among observed cases and between observed and unobserved cases are important, as is the relevance of the characteristics shared by observed and unobserved cases. The number of observed cases cited is also important. As they stand, none of the statistical inductions above about the students in Professor Wilson's metaphysics class is very strong. Let us consider why this is so, using the following argument:

> *Sixty percent of the students in Professor Wilson's metaphysics class last semester got A's.*
> *Therefore, 60 percent of the students in Professor Wilson's metaphysics class next semester will get A's.*

This argument is inductively weak for several reasons. First, the only positive analogy between the observed case and the unobserved case is that the students are enrolled in a metaphysics course taught by Professor Wilson. Other relevant characteristics are unknown. If we knew, for example, that last semester's class contained five students and that the three students who got A's were senior philosophy majors with 3.8 grade-point indexes and that next semester's class also contains five students, three of whom are senior philosophy majors with 3.8 indexes, then the argument would be stronger than the one above. This is so because the positive analogy between observed and unobserved cases has been increased. However, if the three A students in last semester's class were senior philosophy majors with 3.8 indexes, and the next semester's class contains twenty students, three of whom are senior philosophy majors with 2.0 to 3.0 indexes, then the argument would be weaker than the original. In this instance, the negative analogy between observed and unobserved cases has been increased, thereby weakening the argument inductively.

The relevance of the characteristics shared by observed and unobserved cases is also important when evaluating the relative strength of statistical inductions. For instance, if Professor Wilson is a white Anglo-Saxon Protestant, and all of the students in last semester's class were white Anglo-Saxon Protestants, while all the students in next semester's class are members of other ethnic and racial groups, the argument might be weakened. We say *might* be, because, as we noted earlier, there is no formal logical procedure by which to determine what characteristics are relevant to an enumerative or statistical induction. It may be that ethnicity and race do not affect Professor Wilson's grading or that they affect it significantly; other background information would be necessary to determine whether these characteristics are relevant.

Of course, the number of observed cases also affects the strength of a statistical induction. Consider, for example, the following arguments:

> *Forty percent of the students in Professor Wilson's metaphysics class last semester got A's.*
> *Therefore, 40 percent of the students in Professor Wilson's class next semester will get A's.*

> *In Professor Wilson's metaphysics class three semesters ago, there were twenty students and 40 percent of them got A's.*
> *In Professor Wilson's metaphysics class two semesters ago, there were twenty-five students and 40 percent of them got A's.*
> *In Professor Wilson's metaphysics class last semester, there were ten students and 40 percent of them got A's.*
> *Therefore, in Professor Wilson's metaphysics class next semester, 40 percent of the students will get A's.*

Both arguments contain the same conclusion statement, but the number of observed cases offered in support of the conclusion in the second example is significantly greater than the number offered in the first. In this case, the second argument is inductively stronger than the first argument.

Notice, too, that in the second argument we are dealing with premises each of which refers to a percentage of a class and that the conclusion also refers to a percentage of a class. Such arguments are fairly common and require some additional discussion. Consider the following:

> *Eighty-seven percent of 100 observed Roman Catholics are registered Democrats.*
> *Eighty-four percent of another 100 observed Roman Catholics are registered Democrats.*
> *Eighty-seven percent of another 100 observed Roman Catholics are registered Democrats.*
> *Seventy-three percent of another 100 observed Roman Catholics are registered Democrats.*
> *Therefore, 87 percent of the next group of 100 Roman Catholics observed will be registered Democrats.*

An argument such as the one above is inductively weak, since, in making an inference about a future group of Roman Catholics, it uses the upper limit cited in the observed cases or premises. The following argument based on the same set of premises would be inductively stronger, since its conclusion is deductively weaker than the conclusion in the argument above.

> *Eighty-seven percent of 100 observed Roman*
> *   Catholics are registered Democrats.*
> *Eighty-four percent of another 100 observed Roman*
> *   Catholics are registered Democrats.*
> *Eight-seven percent of another 100 observed Roman*
> *   Catholics are registered Democrats.*
> *Seventy-three percent of another 100 observed*
> *   Roman Catholics are registered Democrats.*
> *Therefore, between 70 percent and 90 percent of the*
> *   next group of 100 Roman Catholics observed will*
> *   be registered Democrats.*

As we can see, this argument is stronger than the first, for the conclusion in the second example is less precise than the conclusion of the first argument; this means that the probability that the conclusion of the second argument will be true is greater than the probability that the conclusion of the first argument will be true. The problem, when dealing with statistical inductions such as those above, is really one of balancing two extremes. The less precise the conclusion, the stronger the inductive support for it. However, very often, when dealing with statistical inductions, we are concerned equally with the precision of the conclu-

---

Carter a one-term president

The United States will have a new president in January 1981.

Ordinarily, we would hesitate to make that flat statement this long before the next presidential election. But all signs point to Jimmy Carter being a one-term president.

Opinion polls show that the major concern of Americans is how far their dollar will go, which isn't very far at all these days. When Carter took office, inflation was at four percent. It's now running at an annual rate of 13 percent.

And the recession that was supposed to have started late last year or early this year, thereby allowing Carter to run as a president who just pulled us out of a recession, is just beginning, and may be worse than predicted. At any rate, it will still be fresh in voters' minds come primary and election days.

Carter's inability to handle inflation and to program the recession for his political benefit shows in the polls. According to the latest Harris Poll, Carter's rating is 75-24 percent negative, the worst for any president in modern times. Even Nixon at his nadir was more highly regarded by the American people as a president.

Carter gets his highest mark for foreign policy, 38 percent positive. But voters don't elect a president because of his foreign policy. They vote for a man because they think he can help their pocketbook.

And this is where the poll is most damaging to Carter. His two lowest positive ratings are for handling the economy, 14 percent, and his anti-inflation program, 13 percent. Both figures are down from the June poll.

Studying these figures, and taking into consideration the attitude of the American electorate, we can come to only one conclusion.

Jimmy Carter has had it.

This editorial was published in July 1979. By the time you are reading it, you should have sufficient information to evaluate it using "hindsight." Considering the time at which it was written, was it a good inductive argument or not, regardless of the actual outcome of the primaries and election? Is the actual outcome at all relevant to the evaluation of the argument? Why or why not?

Troy, N.Y., Times Record.

sion and the inductive strength of the argument. For instance, a politician would not be very satisfied with a public opinion survey that told him he would receive between 30 and 70 percent of the vote on election day. Given normal sampling procedures, an argument with this conclusion would certainly be inductively stronger than an argument with the conclusion that the politician would receive between 50 and 55 percent of the vote, but the politician would clearly be more interested in the argument with the more precise conclusion. Thus, in dealing with statistical inductions that involve percentages about classes, we must find the happy medium; that is, we must seek to determine at what point the argument is sufficiently strong *and* the conclusion is sufficiently precise.

The following rules hold in general for enumerative inductions, statistical as well as absolute, but *there are numerous exceptions, as indicated in the text. In general:*

- *An enumerative induction becomes weaker as the negative analogy between observed and unobserved cases increases, provided that everything else remains the same.*
- *The stronger the positive analogy between the observed and unobserved cases, the stronger the enumerative induction.*
- *Increasing the negative analogy among the observed cases will not usually weaken the argument and it can even strengthen it.*
- *As the number of positive observed cases cited in the premises of an enumerative induction increases, the argument becomes stronger, but the amount of support given by each additional premise is usually less than for previous premises.*
- *Irrelevant characteristics, even if shared by all observed cases, do not contribute to the strength of an enumerative induction.*

EXERCISE 10–5 *Place the following arguments in order of decreasing inductive strength.*

---

1. Standard premise for all conclusions that follow:
   Eighty percent of the 100 fiddler crabs observed dig burrows in the sand.
   Conclusions:
   a. Therefore, 80 percent of all fiddler crabs dig burrows in the sand.
   b. Therefore, at least eight of the next ten fiddler crabs I observe will dig burrows in the sand.

    c. Therefore, exactly 80 percent of the next ten fiddler crabs I observe will dig burrows in the sand.

    d. Therefore, some of the next ten fiddler crabs I observe will dig burrows in the sand.

2. Standard premises for all conclusions that follow:

Sixty percent of 100 observed college graduates earned more than $10,000 a year within two years after graduation.

Fifty-five percent of another 100 observed college graduates earned more than $10,000 a year within two years after graduation.

Sixty-eight percent of another 100 observed college graduates earned more than $10,000 a year within two years after graduation.

Seventy-one percent of another 100 observed college graduates earned more than $10,000 a year within two years after graduation.

Eighty-eight percent of another 100 observed college graduates earned more than $10,000 a year within two years after graduation.

Eighty-three percent of another 100 observed college graduates earned more than $10,000 a year within two years after graduation.

Conclusions:

    a. Therefore, at least 55 percent of the next 100 observed college graduates will earn more than $10,000 a year within two years after graduation.

    b. Therefore, exactly 75 percent of the next 100 observed college graduates will earn more than $10,000 a year within two years after graduation.

    c. Therefore, between 55 and 83 percent of the next 100 observed college graduates will earn more than $10,000 a year within two years after graduation.

    d. Therefore, between 50 and 90 percent of the next 100 observed college graduates will earn more than $10,000 a year within two years after graduation.

    e. Therefore, exactly 60 percent of the next 100 observed college graduates will earn more than $10,000 a year within two years after graduation.

    f. Therefore, at least 71 percent of the next 100 observed college graduates will earn more than $10,000 a year within two years after graduation.

3. Standard premises for all conclusions that follow:

Seventy-eight percent of 100 observed students graduating from law school last year passed the bar examination on the first try.

Seventy-one percent of 100 observed students graduating from law school two years ago passed the bar examination on the first try.

Seventy-three percent of 100 observed students graduating from law school three years ago passed the bar examination on the first try.

Sixty-nine percent of 100 observed students graduating from law school four years ago passed the bar examination on the first try.

Seventy-five percent of 100 observed students graduating from law school five years ago passed the bar examination on the first try.

Conclusions:

    a. Therefore, at least 69 percent of 100 observed students graduating from law school this year will pass the bar examination on the first try.

    b. Therefore, some of 100 observed students graduating from law school this year will pass the bar examination on the first try.

    c. Therefore, exactly 72 percent of 100 observed students graduating from law school this year will pass the bar examination on the first try.

    d. Therefore, between 65 and 80 percent of 100 observed students graduating from law school this year will pass the bar examination on the first try.

    e. Therefore, at least 79 percent of 100 observed students graduating from law school this year will pass the bar examination on the first try.

4. Standard premise for all conclusions that follow:
    Ten percent of the 200 books published by our company last year sold 10,000 copies or more.
    Conclusions:
    a. Therefore, exactly 10 percent of the books published by all companies last year sold 10,000 copies or more.
    b. Therefore, at least ten of the next 100 books our company publishes this year will sell 10,000 copies or more.
    c. Therefore, some of the next 100 books our company publishes this year will sell 10,000 copies or more.
    d. Therefore, exactly ten of the next 100 books our company publishes this year will sell 10,000 copies or more.

5. Standard premises for all conclusions that follow:
    Seventy-five percent of all students entering the university in 1965 graduated in 1969.
    Seventy-nine percent of all students entering the university in 1966 graduated in 1970.
    Eighty-two percent of all students entering the university in 1967 graduated in 1971.
    Seventy-three percent of all students entering the university in 1968 graduated in 1972.
    Eighty percent of all students entering the university in 1969 graduated in 1973.
    Seventy-one percent of all students entering the university in 1970 graduated in 1974.
    Eighty-four percent of all students entering the university in 1971 graduated in 1975.
    Conclusions:
    a. Therefore, at least 80 percent of all students entering the university in 1972 will graduate in 1976.
    b. Therefore, exactly 70 percent of all students entering the university in 1972 will graduate in 1976.
    c. Therefore, at least 70 percent of all students entering the university in 1972 will graduate in 1976.
    d. Therefore, between 60 and 90 percent of all students entering the university in 1972 will graduate in 1976.
    e. Therefore, some students entering the university in 1972 will graduate in 1976.

EXERCISE 10–6   *Read each argument carefully. Determine whether the addition of the suggested premise(s) weakens or strengthens the argument, in terms of positive and negative analogy, relevance, and/or the number of observed cases.*

---

1. Eighty percent of the 100 fiddler crabs I observed dug burrows in the sand.
    Therefore, at least 80 percent of all fiddler crabs dig burrows in the sand.
    a. Add the following premise only: All of the 100 fiddler crabs I observed were from the same location.
    b. Add the following premise only: Eighty-nine percent of the next 100 fiddler crabs I observed dug burrows in the sand.
    c. Add the following premise only: Of the 100 fiddler crabs I observed, 50 percent were males and 50 percent were females.
    d. Add the following premise only: Of the 100 fiddler crabs I observed, 10 were

from Miami, 10 were from New York, 10 were from Maine, 10 were from California, 10 were from Mexico, 10 from England, 10 from France, 10 from China, 10 from Russia, and 10 from Canada.

e. Add the following premise only: All of the fiddler crabs I observed had a disease and died shortly after digging their burrows.

2. Sixty percent of 100 observed college graduates earned more than $10,000 a year within two years after graduation.

Fifty-five percent of another 100 observed college graduates earned more than $10,000 a year within two years after graduation.

Sixty-five percent of another 100 observed college graduates earned more than $10,000 a year within two years after graduation.

Seventy-one percent of another 100 observed college graduates earned more than $10,000 a year within two years after graduation.

Fifty-eight percent of another 100 observed college graduates earned more than $10,000 a year within two years after graduation.

Eighty-three percent of another 100 observed college graduates earned more than $10,000 a year within two years after graduation.

Therefore, between 55 and 83 percent of the next 100 observed college graduates will earn more than $10,000 a year within two years after graduation.

a. Add the following premise only: All of the 100 observed college graduates in each group came from different schools.

b. Add the following premise only: All of the observed college graduates in each group came from the same school.

c. Add the following premise only: All of the observed college graduates in each group were graduated with honors.

d. Add the following premise only: Of the observed college graduates in each group, 50 had a C average, 35 had a B average, 10 had a B+ average, and 5 had an A average.

e. Add the following premise only: All of the observed college graduates in each group earned business degrees.

f. Add the following premise only: Of the 100 observed college graduates in each group, 10 were English majors, 10 were history majors, 10 biology majors, 10 philosophy majors, 10 sociology, 10 political science, 10 premedical, 10 business, 10 engineering, and 10 education.

3. Seventy-five percent of 500 observed students graduating from law school last year passed the bar examination on the first try.

Therefore, at least 75 percent of all students graduating from law school pass the bar examination on the first try.

a. Add the following premise only: All of the 500 observed students graduated from the same law school.

b. Add the following premise only: Of the 500 observed students, 100 had straight-A averages, 100 had B+ averages, 100 had B averages, 100 had C+ averages, and 100 had C averages.

c. Add the following premise only: All of the 500 observed students were on their school law review.

d. Add the following premise only: All of the 500 observed students were males.

4. Forty-one percent of 100 observed families watched "Rhoda" last week.

Thirty-nine percent of 100 observed families watched "Rhoda" two weeks ago.

Fifty percent of 100 observed families watched "Rhoda" three weeks ago.

Forty-six percent of 100 observed families watched "Rhoda" four weeks ago.

Therefore, between 39 and 50 percent of the families to be observed this week will watch "Rhoda."

a. Of the 100 observed families in each group, all of them had their televisions turned on to "Maude" which precedes "Rhoda" on the same channel.
b. The same 100 families constituted the sample each week, but this week a new 100 families will be sampled.
c. Of the 100 observed families in each group, all of them lived in New York City.
d. Of the 100 observed families in each group, all had watched "The Mary Tyler Moore Show" each week for the past two years.
e. Of the 100 observed families in each group, ten lived in New York, ten lived in Philadelphia, ten lived in Atlanta, ten lived in Miami, ten lived in Chicago, ten lived in St. Louis, ten lived in Memphis, ten lived in Akron, ten lived in New Orleans, and ten lived in San Francisco.
f. A new sample of 100 families was used each week.

ANALYSIS OF   One of the basic points being stressed throughout this book is the fact
SAMPLE ARGUMENTS   that most if not all sets of statements intended or asserted as argu-
                          ments in ordinary languages can be subjected to formal analysis in a
variety of different systems of logic, both inductive and deductive. We have already provided a preliminary analysis of four such arguments at the end of Chapter 2, where we saw that each could be interpreted as both deductively valid *and* inductively strong, depending on our interpretation of the given statements and our choice of premises to be added. Let us now return to consider the inductive versions of these arguments in light of our discussion of the formal criteria for evaluating enumerative inductions.

The first argument, concerning Susan's performance in her logic course, was originally expressed as follows:

> **Susan should do well in this logic course, because**
> **she always does well in science courses.**

In this form, these statements already constitute an inductive argument since the one statement, 'She always does well in science courses', provides some, but not absolute, support for the other statement. We saw in our preliminary analysis that there are many ways of interpreting these statements in conjunction with the addition of various possible (but relatively implausible) suppressed premises that can result in apparently valid deductive arguments. We also saw that if the given premise is interpreted as applying only to science courses Susan has taken in the past—which makes it more plausible—several different inductive arguments can be formulated, one of which is the following:

> **This logic course is a science course.**
> **Susan is taking this logic course.**
> **Susan has always done well in science courses in the**
>   **past.**
> **Therefore, Susan will do well in this logic course.**

You should now be able to recognize quickly that insufficient information is provided for this argument to have very much inductive strength. The premise asserting that Susan has always done well in science courses in the past does not really tell us much at all. For example, it does not specify *how many* science courses she has taken nor what the nature of those courses was. It would certainly make some difference if she had taken three science courses or twenty of them. And, as we have seen in this chapter, it is also important to know *what kind* of science courses Susan took so that we can assess the degree of positive and negative analogy among the past cases and between these cases and the present case (this logic course). The premise would be true even if Susan had taken only three science courses—all in geology—but, in such a case, it would provide much less support for the conclusion than if she had taken twenty very different courses, including topology, calculus, set theory, physical chemistry, and molecular biology, where the negative analogy among the observed cases is much greater. The argument would also be relatively strong if Susan had done well in only three courses, all of which are quite similar to logic (e.g., euclidean geometry, set theory, and computer programming) because this would create a strong positive analogy between the observed and unobserved cases.

Thus, as presented, the argument about Susan's grade is inductively weak because so little information is provided in the premise. As we have seen, if the facts underlying this premise were of a certain kind (e.g., many courses similar in various ways to logic), and if they were made explicit, the argument could be made quite strong. But in its present form, we have no basis for assuming anything more than the weakest possible interpretation of this premise, namely that Susan has only taken a few science courses, none of which is very similar to logic.

Our second sample argument (reprinted here) concerning the motel owners provides more of the specific information necessary for evaluating inductive strength. We saw in our preliminary analysis in Chapter 2 that, although it is possible to interpret this as a valid deductive argument, some of the premises that have to be added to do so are not in the least plausible, whereas an inductive interpretation permits somewhat more reasonable premises. We also noted that the conclusion is ambiguous, since it can be read as asserting that all motel owners lie about their business or that most (or many) lie about business. Given the general principle that the weaker the conclusion the stronger the argument, we will focus our analysis on the interpretation which will be strongest, namely that with the conclusion 'Many motel owners lie about their business'. The full argument as worked out in the preliminary analysis in Chapter 2 is as follows:

> *All of the resort motel operators interviewed in one Florida town reported that their business was good.*
> *The parking lots of these motels were practically empty, and the bank reported it had not cashed as many travelers' checks as in previous years.*

Mainstreams

. . . Thoughts on the 10 Greatest Liars

By Edwin A. Roberts, Jr.

It fell to me the other week, in connection with a story assignment, to ask a dozen or so motel operators in a Florida town how business was. They all said business was just fine, the gasoline shortage wasn't hurting them at all, and if they were making any more money the local bank couldn't accommodate their deposits.

Oddly under such happy circumstances, the motel parking lots were practically empty. So I asked an officer of the local bank how the cashing of travelers' checks this year compared to last. As a matter of fact, said the banker, such check cashings were "way below" 1973. This information suggested that the motel operators

Comment

were dissembling, and so I am putting motel owners in resort towns on my list of The 10 Greatest Liars.

Courtesy National Observer, April 6, 1974.

If a motel's parking lot is almost empty and its bank has not cashed many travelers' checks, then the motel's business is not good.
If someone says business is good when it is not, then he is lying.
Therefore, many resort motel owners lie about their business.

The weaknesses of this inductive argument—independent of the questionability of several of the premises—have to do primarily with the very limited kind and quantity of observed cases cited in the first premise. The argument goes from the observation of "twelve or so" motel operators in one town in Florida to a conclusion about thousands of resort motel operators around the entire country. Thus, it violates most of the general principles concerning strong inductions. The positive analogy between the observed cases and unobserved cases is small; the only characteristic they are identified as having in common is being a resort motel operator. The negative analogy among the observed cases is also small; they are all in one town, and there is no indication of any significant differences in terms of the size of the motels, whether or not they are part of a national chain, and so forth. It is also a significant weakening factor that very few cases have been observed at all when a much larger (and broader) sampling would have been possible.

In sum, the evidence provided gives only weak support to the conclusion that many resort motel owners lie about their business and even less support to the stronger conclusion that all resort motel operators are liars.

The third sample argument, that concerning Mrs. Parker's fatal case of smallpox, was one which our preliminary analysis showed to be interpretable in several ways as an inductive argument. But it is interesting to recognize now that none of these is a "pure" form of enumerative induction. The argument qualified as an induction primarily because it was seen that the premises do not provide absolute support for the conclusion, that is, that it is possible to add certain premises which would make the conclusion false. Even though it is not an enumerative induction, the argument is worth taking another look at in this context. Our last formulation of it was as follows:

> *The medical examiners reported that Mrs. Parker was infected with the "Abid" strain of smallpox virus.*
> *A quantity of the "Abid" strain of smallpox virus was being stored in the lab directly below Mrs. Parker's office.*
> *Of all of the millions of cases of smallpox examined over the years, there was only one in which it appeared that the virus was transmitted through the air.*
> *Mrs. Parker was not known to have been in contact with any person or object from the downstairs lab.*
> *Therefore, Mrs. Parker must have been infected by a virus transmitted through the air from the downstairs lab.*

The first premise, to relate properly to the conclusion, needs to be interpreted as the premise of an enthymeme, because we are concerned with Mrs. Parker's illness, not with reports of medical examiners. The necessary argument is an enumerative induction something like the following:

> *In the past, the medical examiners' reports have (usually) been correct.*
> *The medical examiners reported that Mrs. Parker was infected with the "Abid" strain of smallpox virus.*
> *Therefore, Mrs. Parker was infected with the "Abid" strain of smallpox virus.*

The critical point in the general argument is not, however, whether Mrs. Parker had the "Abid" strain of smallpox but whether it was transmitted through the air. The support for this part of the argument is limited to two pieces of evidence—one to the effect that she was not *known* to have been in physical contact with any person or object from the downstairs lab, which was the only *known* source of the virus. It is doubtful that conclusive evidence could be given in support of either of these knowledge claims; it remains *possible* that she was in physical contact with someone or something that was carrying the virus, and it is also possible that there was some other source of the virus. The other essential point concerning the transmission of the virus through the air is the claim that this is possible, based on the one documented case in which it was judged that such transmission had occurred. Given that only one such instance was ever documented out of the millions of cases of smallpox observed over the years, we would need a great deal of additional information about that one case before we could make a judgment as to how much weight it should be given in the evaluation of this argument. If the evidence was indeed strong in that case *and* if there is a strong similarity (i.e., positive analogy) between that case and the present case, then this argument could be relatively strong even though the induction is based on only one observation. But this is only because the argument would then fit the model of Mill's methods for identifying causes, which will be discussed in Chapter 12. For the moment, we can only judge that in its

"No flowers. That means you want me to think you haven't got a guilty conscience."

present form and with the information provided, it is not possible to evaluate this inductive argument as an enumerative induction.

The fourth and final sample argument is that contained in the cartoon. In our preliminary analysis in Chapter 2, we came up with the following possible inductive interpretation of this argument:

> *In the past, whenever you didn't bring me flowers,*
> *you wanted me to think that you didn't have a*
> *guilty conscience.*
> *You didn't bring me flowers.*
> *Therefore, you now want me to think that you don't*
> *have a guilty conscience.*

There appears to be a strong positive analogy between the first premise and the conclusion (or the observed and unobserved cases), so the argument should be relatively strong, but we must qualify our judgment by recognizing that we don't know how many cases are included in the first premise and that there may be special circumstances associated with the present case, which are not specified, that could make it less similar to the previously observed cases then we might normally assume.

If the number of observed cases is large and if there is a strong similarity (positive analogy) between the observed and unobserved cases, then the premises do provide relatively strong inductive support for the conclusion. However, in such circumstances, the first premise becomes less plausible, because it is doubtful that every time the man didn't bring flowers (let's assume a period of several years with at least several visits or numerous homecomings per week) he wanted his wife to think he didn't have a guilty conscience. Thus, as the logical support of the premises for the conclusion increases, the plausibility of the main premise decreases, and all in all the argument is of questionable quality.

EXERCISE 10–7   *Reconsider the arguments for which you did preliminary analyses in Exercise 2–9. Find one version of each argument which seems more appropriate for analysis using the methods of the present chapter and carry out such analyses. Compare your analyses here with those of the same arguments you may have done in Exercises 3–3, 5–10, 7–9, and 9–9.*

EXERCISE 10–8   *Reconsider the arguments for which you did preliminary analyses in Exercise 2–10. Apply the instructions for Exercise 10–7 to these arguments and compare these analyses with those of the same arguments which you might have done in Exercises 3–3, 5–11, 7–10, and 9–10.*

SUMMARY   1.   A deductive argument is any argument such that, if the premises are true, then the conclusion must also be true; that is, the premises provide absolute support for the conclusion; or, in other words, the conclusion is completely contained in the premises. The addition of one or more premises in no way affects the support which the premises provide for the conclusion. Deductive arguments are valid by virtue of their form. A false premise in a valid deductive argument is not sufficient to prove the conclusion false, and it in no way affects the validity of the argument.

2.   An inductive argument is an argument that does not satisfy the definition of a deductive argument as given above. Thus, it is any argument such that, even if all the premises are true, the conclusion may still be false. That is, the premises provide, at most, only partial support for the conclusion; or, in other words, the conclusion is, at most, only partly contained in the premises. The addition of further premises may change the support provided for the conclusion.

3.   An **enumerative induction** is an argument whose premise(s) comprise a listing of cases concerning either individuals or classes of individuals to support conclusions about individuals or classes of individuals. On the basis of the different relationships between the premises and the conclusion, it is possible to distinguish two types of enumerative inductive argument.

4.   An inductive argument, which is such that the falsity of one or more premises may lessen the probability of the conclusion but cannot necessitate the falsity of the conclusion, is an **induction by analogy.** An analogy is a comparison between two or more things or ideas in which similarities are pointed out.

5.   An inductive argument with a universal conclusion, in which at least one of the premises is such that its falsity could necessitate the falsity of the conclusion, is an **inductive generalization.** An inductive generalization may contain premises either about individuals or about classes of individuals, but it cannot possibly have a particular conclusion, regardless of whether the premises are general or particular.

6.   The support the premises provide for the conclusion of an inductive argument can vary from just less than absolute support to no support whatsoever. Inductive arguments can be evaluated only in terms of their relative strengths. The relative strengths of inductive arguments *with the same set of premises* are inversely proportional to the deductive strengths of their conclusions. Of two statements, one is **deductively stronger** than another if and only if the first implies the second and the second does not imply the first. Likewise, of two statements, one is **deductively weaker** than another if and only if the second implies the first and the first does not imply the second. Statements are of equal deductive strength if they imply each other.

7.   The ways in which the individuals or classes of individuals cited in an enumerative induction are alike is called **positive analogy;** the ways in which they are different is called **negative analogy.** Most interesting enumerative inductions involve premises which describe *observed cases* about individuals and/or classes of individuals, and have conclusions concerned with an *unobserved case* about an individual and/or a class of individuals.

8.   In general, an enumerative induction becomes weaker as the negative analogy between observed and unobserved cases increases and provided every-

thing else remains the same. In general, the stronger the positive analogy between observed and unobserved cases, the stronger the enumerative induction, assuming that everything else is unchanged. Increasing the negative analogy among the observed cases in an enumerative induction will not usually weaken the argument; in fact, it may strengthen it, since the greater the negative analogy among the observed cases, the greater the number of possible unobserved cases that would have a positive analogy with the observed cases.

9.   In general, as the number of observed cases mentioned in the premises of an enumerative induction increases, the stronger the argument will be. But as the number of observed cases increases, the inductive support given by *each* additional observed case decreases. However, an enumerative induction with only a few observed cases, or even one, is not necessarily a weak argument. Likewise, an enumerative induction with a large number of observed cases is not necessarily a strong argument.

10.   The relevance of the characteristics being compared or contrasted will affect the strength of an enumerative induction. But determining which characteristics are relevant is not always easy, since there is no formal logical procedure that will enable us to list all the possible relevant factors. To a considerable extent, determining what is relevant depends on an individual's perception rather than on some absolute standard.

11.   A **statistical induction** by analogy is an induction by analogy in which a numerical value appears as the quantifier for the subject term in the premises and/or the conclusion. Similarly, a **statistical generalization** is an inductive generalization in which a numerical value appears as the quantifier for the subject term in the premises and/or the conclusion. Most of the rules that apply to enumerative inductions in general apply also to statistical inductions.

12.   The same criteria that are used to evaluate the relative strengths of enumerative inductions are used to evaluate the relative strengths of statistical inductions. The positive and negative analogies among observed cases and between observed and unobserved cases are important as is the relevance of the characteristics shared by the observed and unobserved cases and the number of observed cases cited. In statistical inductions, the less precise the conclusion, the stronger the inductive support for it. Often a middle point must be reached that provides both a sufficiently strong argument and a sufficiently precise conclusion to be useful for the desired purpose.

13.   It is often asserted that all inductive arguments are grounded in the **principle of induction,** which can be formulated as the assertion that events in the future will resemble events in the past or that unobserved cases will resemble observed cases—in other words, that similar things behave similarly in similar circumstances. The principle of induction was discussed in detail in Chapter 2, and it is of such importance to the topic of this chapter that it should be carefully reviewed now.

14.   It is sometimes argued that, if this principle is considered to be a suppressed premise, all inductive arguments can be reduced to deductive arguments. From a practical point of view, there are several obstacles to this reduction. One is in establishing the truth of the principle of induction itself: Critics maintain that, if we try to do so by the pragmatic argument that it has worked

in the past and therefore will continue to work in the future, we are justifying induction by an inductive argument, so the proof is circular. A second obstacle lies in the problem of resemblance: Do the two cases resemble each other in all relevant ways? One criterion for determining the relevance of a statement is whether its addition to the premises of an argument affects the relative strength of the conclusion. But this criterion also uses an inductive argument to justify the principle of induction. And, finally, even when the principle of induction is added, inductive arguments do not always become deductive, for the addition of more premises can still affect the conclusion.

15.   It has also been argued that there is no way to justify the principle of induction just as there is no way to justify an axiom in mathematics. But such arguments are themselves inductive since they are based on an analogy. They do not prove that the principle of induction *cannot* be justified.

CHAPTER ELEVEN

Scientific Method

It was explained in Chapter 2 how any inductive argument can be reformulated as a valid deductive argument (in the formal logical sense) with the addition of suitably chosen premises such as a general principle of induction. It was also shown that this does not necessarily improve the quality of the argument, since the premises added to make it valid may be anything but well established. In this chapter, we will consider several alternative ways of formulating inductive arguments which *might* be more compelling or at least simpler to evaluate. Although none of these alternatives is "better" in any purely logical sense than the two kinds of induction discussed in the previous chapter, our examination of them will increase our understanding of the nature of inductive reasoning in general.

THE POSSIBLE ELIMINATION OF INDUCTIONS BY ANALOGY

Some logicians have suggested that there is no need to make the distinction—presented as basic in Chapter 10—between inductions by analogy and inductive generalizations. They have argued that it is possible to do away with inductions by analogy, so long as deduction and inductive generalization are available. This claim can be illustrated by examples. Consider the following induction by analogy:

Swan A is white.
Swan B is white.
Swan C is white.
——————————
∴*Swan D is white.*

Now consider the following two-step argument, which consists of an inductive generalization followed by a valid deductive argument, using the generalization as a premise:

Swan A is white.
Swan B is white.
Swan C is white.
——————————
∴*All swans are white.*

> *All swans are white.*
> *D is a swan.*
> ───────────
> *∴D is white.*

In the two-step argument, the same conclusion is ultimately derived from the same initial set of premises as in the original single-step induction by analogy. And it should be clear that a similar two-step generalization/deduction argument can be formulated corresponding to every induction by analogy. If the two-step procedure can be shown to provide a stronger connection between the premises and the final conclusion, it would certainly be a better form to use in presenting inductive arguments. And even if it should turn out to be only strictly equivalent to the one-step method, it might still be considered a better form, since it reduces the basic types of argument from three (deduction, induction by analogy, and inductive generalization) to two.

At first glance the one-step and two-step formulations may appear to be at least logically equivalent, or the two-step method may even appear to be the better of the two alternatives. In point of fact, however, the two methods are not equivalent, and the one-step method is at least as good as, if not better than, the two-step. This is because, insofar as the conclusion in the two-step method is deduced from a generalization which was established by induction, that conclusion can be no more probable than the generalization from which it was deduced. But this means that all conclusions arrived at by means of this method (using the same generalization) would be equally probable; that is, the premises would provide the same support for a number of different conclusions. For example, we could construct the following argument:

> *Swan A is white.*
> *Swan B is white.*
> *Swan C is white.*
> ───────────
> *∴All swans are white.*

> *All swans are white.*
> *At least four swans exist in the universe.*
> ───────────
> *∴At least one swan other than A, B, or C is white.*

This new conclusion receives no more support from the premises in this formulation than did the conclusion of the previous argument—'D is white'. But it should be intuitively clear that, given that three swans have been observed to be white, it is more probable that at least one additional swan will be observed to be white than that a specific other swan (D) will be white—or that all swans are white. These are precisely the points recognized by our distinction between induction by analogy and inductive generalization and also by our rule concerning relative inductive and deductive strengths in arguments with the same premises. Thus, the one-step method, in which the premises lead directly to the conclusion by means of an induction by analogy, is not equivalent to but is stronger than the two-step method, which proceeded by way of the weaker inductive generalization. The one-step method is a "better" method insofar as it is also more in line with our basic intuitions about the relative strengths of inductive arguments, and it allows us to formally identify intuitively apparent differences in inductive strength.

EXERCISE 11–1   *Reformulate each of the following ordinary-language arguments as (a) a one-step argument—that is, an induction by analogy; (b) a two-step argument containing an inductive generalization followed by a valid deductive argument.*

---

1. Frank will win when we play five-card stud [a type of poker]. He's already won at blackjack, seven-card stud, and five-card draw [other types of poker].
2. My mother, father, and both sisters have caught the flu, so I probably will, too.
3. It will rain on Saturday, since it rained on Sunday, Monday, Tuesday, Wednesday, Thursday, and Friday.
4. Swans A, B, C, D, E, F, G, H, I, and J are all white; so probably Swan K is also white.
5. The flood crested in Pittsburgh and Cincinnati earlier this week, so it will crest here in Louisville this week, too.
6. We will probably have a big snow storm this year, since we had big snow storms last year, two years ago, three years ago, and four years ago.
7. The Smiths, Parkers, Roberts, Mitchells, and Conners all own Fisher receiver-amplifiers and get excellent performance. So, probably the Carters who just bought a Fisher receiver-amplifier will get excellent performance.
8. Chimpanzees A, B, C, D, E, and F each engaged in grooming behavior. Consequently, at least one other chimp will engage in grooming behavior.
9. My grandfather, my father, and my older brother went bald before they were thirty years old, so I probably will, too.
10. *Swan Lake,* composed by Tchaikovsky, is a great ballet score. And *The Nutcracker,* also composed by Tchaikovsky, is a great ballet score. *Sleeping Beauty* was composed by Tchaikovsky, so it too must be a great ballet score.
11. Peter, Hans, Maria, Karl, and Karin are all Swiss and speak German. Therefore Antonio, who is Swiss, must speak German.
12. The Rolls-Royce, Volvo, Mercedes-Benz, and Volkswagen are all European-made cars and perform well. The Fiat is a European-made car; consequently, it performs well too.
13. John got As in every course he took in his first, second, third, and fourth semesters in college, so he will get As in every course he takes this semester, which is his fifth.
14. All sea otters observed off the coast of Newfoundland, Washington, Alaska, and Finland use rocks to crack open seashells. Therefore the next sea otter to be observed off the coast of Nova Scotia also uses rocks to crack open seashells.
15. The movie I saw on the "Late Show" yesterday was interesting, and the movie I saw on the "Late Show" the night before that was interesting. Therefore, at least one movie I will see on the "Late Show" in the future will be interesting.
16. Regina is an intelligent woman and reads *Ms.* magazine. Barbara and Johanna are

intelligent women, and they also read *Ms.* magazine. Elizabeth is intelligent, so probably she reads *Ms.* magazine.

17. Italy, Germany, Spain, and France are European countries and have shown aggressive tendencies. Therefore, at least one other European country will probably show aggressive tendencies.

18. There were interesting people at Joe's last three parties, so undoubtedly there will be interesting people at Joe's party tonight.

19. Juan, Kim, Pete, and Michel all attend Princeton and each had combined college board scores over 1100. Five thousand other students go to Princeton, too; therefore, at least one other student's combined college board scores must be over 1100.

THE HYPOTHETICO-DEDUCTIVE METHOD

Although the method of induction by analogy cannot be reduced to the method of inductive generalization, there is another form of inductive reasoning which *is* essentially equivalent to inductive generalization. This method—known as the **hypothetico-deductive method**—is *not* equivalent to and cannot be used as an alternative to the method of induction by analogy. The hypothetico-deductive method is claimed by its proponents to reflect more accurately the way in which people do, in fact, reason, in that it involves a *temporal* sequence of three distinct steps. These steps are:

1. *The formulation of a "hypothetical" generalization.*
2. *The deduction of particular observation statements from this generalization (sometimes in conjunction with other statements).*
3. *The testing of the observation statements to determine whether they confirm or falsify the generalization.*

Formulating a Generalization

The starting point of the hypothetico-deductive method is the formulation of a generalization, in the form of a "working hypothesis." Let us take as an example the generalization 'All sea otters use rocks to crack open seashells', which we discussed in the previous chapter. We are not concerned here with the mental processes by means of which this generalization was reached; our only concern is with the *justification* that can ultimately be provided for it. In other words, it is essentially irrelevant whether a person formulated the hypothesis after observing a thousand sea otters or after experiencing some strange sensations while eating clams. What is of primary importance to the logician is the degree of support which can ultimately be provided for the generalization. The history of science is rich with cases of hypotheses for which a minimal amount of evidence was available at the time they were formulated but for which overwhelming support was obtained afterward. Such experiences are common in everyday life, as well. The logician, as a logician, is not concerned with how the conclusion was arrived at but rather with whether or not the evidence that is ultimately acquired adequately supports it.

Deducing Observation Statements   The second step of the hypothetico-deductive method involves the deduction of particular observation statements from the hypothesized generalization. Given the generalization 'All sea otters use rocks to crack open seashells' as one premise, and conjoining it with other premises, such as 'I will observe several sea otters' and 'Hunters will observe thousands of sea otters off the coast of Alaska this year', a theoretically unlimited number of observation statements can be derived as conclusions, such as the following:

> *All sea otters use rocks to crack open seashells.*
> *Therefore, the next sea otter I observe (X_1) will use rocks to crack open seashells.*
> *Therefore, the twenty-third male sea otter which will be observed by hunters this year off the coast of Alaska (X_2) uses rocks to crack open seashells.*
> *Therefore, the last female sea otter observed by Professor Smith last year off the coast of Alaska (X_3) used rocks to crack open seashells.*
> *Therefore, the next sea otter which will be observed off the coast of Newfoundland (X_4) uses rocks to crack open seashells.*

Note that all of these observation statements are about specific individuals. Although other *generalizations* are also validly deducible from the original hypothesis (for instance, 'All sea otters living off the coast of Denmark use rocks to crack open seashells'), the hypothetico-deductive method is concerned only with deducing statements about specific individuals, the truth or falsity of which can be determined by direct observation.

EXERCISE 11–2   *Below are a generalization and a number of observation statements. None of the observation statements are deducible from this generalization alone. What other generalizations or assumptions would be needed, in addition to the one given, before each observation statement could be validly deduced? Compare your answers with those of your classmates, or discuss the exercise in class.*
Generalization: The earth is spherical rather than flat.
Observation statements:

---

a.   When I stood on the shore and watched a ship sail away, I saw its hull disappear first, and then its superstructure.
b.   The sun rose in the east this morning and set in the west tonight.
c.   In the past in New York City, the day has been longer in summer than in spring or

fall, and has been shorter in winter. In Quito, Ecuador, it has been approximately the same length all year round.

d. My brother, who is 5'11" tall, cast a shadow equal to his own height at noon on September 22 in Venice, Italy. I, who am also 5'11" tall, cast a shadow only 4' long at noon on September 22 in Cairo, Egypt.

e. A ship which set sail in a westerly direction from the Atlantic coast of Africa was able to return to the same spot, all the while continuing to sail in a basically westerly direction.

f. No matter how far west ships sail, they have never yet fallen off the edge of the earth.

Testing the Observation Statements

The third step in the hypothetico-deductive method involves testing the observation statements: that is, making the appropriate observations to determine whether each statement is in fact true or false. In our example above, the person seeking to justify the generalization will note whether the next sea otter he or she observes uses rocks to crack open seashells. If it does not,[1] then he or she will have discovered a disconfirming instance, which in and of itself is sufficient for *proving* that the generalization is false. However, if this sea otter is observed to use a rock to crack open a seashell, the person will deduce another observation statement and proceed to test it. In this instance, he or she might check to see whether a particular male sea otter off the coast of Alaska uses rocks. If it does not, then the generalization has been proved false. But if this male sea otter off the coast of Alaska does use rocks to crack open seashells, then the researcher must continue the process, deducing new observation statements and testing them.

How far should this process of deducing and testing observation statements be carried to provide adequate confirmation of the hypothesized generalization? The process obviously ends as soon as any one of the deduced observation statements is found to be false. If no falsifying instance is found, however, the process could be continued indefinitely. The crucial consideration here is not really how *far* the process should be extended, but rather *how* it should be applied.

One formulation of a basic rule of thumb for the hypothetico-deductive method is that, the greater the effort which is made to find a falsifying instance of the generalization, the greater the probability of its truth (assuming, of course, that no falsifying instances are found). The notion of 'effort' can be made more precise in terms of our example of the sea otter. One person might deduce from the generalization about all sea otters only observation statements about sea otters of a certain kind in a certain location at a certain time. In contrast, a second person might derive observation statements about sea otters of many different

---

[1] Of course, such an observation would not be very easy to make. The researcher would have to make certain that the particular sea otter is being observed every moment from its birth to its death to be entitled to assert that it *never* used a rock to crack open sea shells. It would be much easier, for example, to test an observation statement such as 'This sea otter has a backbone'.

kinds at different locations and at different times. Assuming that all of the observation statements were found to be factually true, it seems intuitively evident that the second person has established the probability of the truth of the generalization to a higher degree than has the first, and it appears reasonable to attribute this increased probability to the increased effort made to find a falsifying instance.

It must be emphasized that we are not concerned with either the physical or the psychological effort expended in the attempt to find a falsifying instance. It

by bernice bede osol

March 26, 1974

YOUR BIRTHDAY

You'll have an opportunity this year to improve your financial position and get a little salted away. Be careful of who you team up with.

ARIES (March 21-April 19) Materially, things look promising today, but there's another situation that will cause frustration due to a companion's opposition.

TAURUS (April 20-May 20) You're likely to have to face some heavy obligations not of your making. Try to have others carry their share.

GEMINI (May 21-June 20) Your interest is not focused where it should be at this time. This could cause future problems. Attend first to priority matters.

CANCER (June 21-July 22) Avoid the company of one in your peer group who is putting pressure on you. This person is much too dictatorial at present.

LEO (July 23-Aug 22) Secondary issues could easily sidetrack you today. Concentrate on goals that contribute to your reputation or career.

VIRGO (Aug 23-Sept 22) This is nt the time to act on financial matter without expert outside advice. Don't rely only on your judgment.

LIBRA (Sept 23-Oct 23) A situation where you share a joint interest requires some adjustments. Bring things out in the open now.

SCORPIO (Oct. 24 - Nov 22) This could be a very trying day workwise. Make some "fun" plans for this evening so your can unwind.

SAGITTARIUS (Nov 23-Dec 21) It's going to take self-discipline to direct your efforts where they belong. Keep your mind on your tasks.

CAPRICORN Dec 22-Jan 19) Tread lightly early in the day. Domestic pressures will still be heavy. Toward late afternoon they'll begin to lift.

AQUARIUS (Jan 20-Feb 19) Don't deal in the realm of ideas. They won't show a profit at this time. Something practical you're involved in will.

PISCES (Feb 20-March 20) Your finances are still up in the air. Your outlay is likely to be greater than your intake. Be very conservative.

Astrology is believed by a surprising number of persons to provide a "scientific" basis for predicting future events. Consider the "predictions" in the above horoscope and determine which of them, if any, could possibly be falsified by observations, and discuss ways in which an astrologer might respond to an apparent observational "refutation."

may have been very difficult and required much psychological effort for the first person in our example to deduce even one observation statement—for instance, if the person had little aptitude for logic or was very tired at the time. Similarly, the second person may have derived the set of diverse observation statements with little or no effort. The same might be true of the testing of the observation statements. It may have taken the first person several weeks of hiking in below-zero weather to reach the one location specified in the observations, while the second person may have simply telephoned colleagues in locations around the world and asked them to make the observations in the areas closest to them. Thus, when we talk of maximizing effort, we are speaking not of physical or psychological effort, but of "logical" effort—which we can define as the effort to deduce and test those observation statements which are *most likely to turn out to be factually false*. This rather vague concept is essentially equivalent to one of the basic concepts that we have already discussed in Chapter 10. To see this more clearly, let us examine the extent to which the hypothetico-deductive method is essentially a reformulation of the method of inductive generalization.

EXERCISE 11–3

Indicate which of the following statements could be confirmed or falsified by direct observation. For those that cannot be, try to suggest observations that could serve to test them. Compare your answers with those of other members of the class.

---

1. This book has 7,439 pages.
2. The moon is 249,172 miles from the earth.
3. This swan is white.
4. The Declaration of Independence was signed on July 4, 1776.
5. An electric current is flowing through this wire.
6. The last page of *Webster's Seventh New Collegiate Dictionary* is 1223.
7. All of the earth's continents once formed a single land mass.
8. Light travels at 186,000 miles per second.
9. Right now I am having the sensation of seeing a solid blue tie.
10. This sculpture is made of an aluminum alloy.
11. Charles I ruled Great Britain from 1625 to 1649.
12. That dog over there is a poodle.
13. I am having a sensation of a red spot here and now.
14. The earth's surface is spreading apart along the Mid-Atlantic Rift.
15. The firemen reached the scene 4 minutes and 32 seconds after the first alarm.
16. The painter of this eleventh-century ikon used a paint made by mixing natural pigments with egg yolk.
17. John, who smokes a pack of cigarettes daily, runs a greater risk of developing cancer than does Ellen, who has never smoked.
18. Tom laughed a lot last week during the movie *Young Frankenstein*.
19. The capital of Corsica is Ajaccio.
20. Most American families own television sets.
21. 2 + 2 = 4.
22. The lights are on in the Oval Office of the White House right now.

23. The *Mona Lisa* is a beautiful painting.
24. The United States is the largest energy consumer in the world.
25. Susan is an M.D.

Hypothetico-Deductive Method and Inductive Generalization   Once the generalization has been hypothesized and the observation statements deduced and confirmed by means of the hypothetico-deductive method, an inductive generalization can be constructed, using the confirmed observation statements as premises and the generalization as conclusion. (Of course, if one of the observation statements has been found to be false, there is no need to deal with inductive arguments, since the falsity of the generalization can be validly *deduced* from the falsity of the observation statement.) Thus we can construct the following inductive argument out of the sea otter example:

> *The sea otter I observed in Australia (X_1) used rocks to crack open seashells.*
> *The twenty-third male sea otter observed by hunters this year off the coast of Alaska (X_2) used rocks to crack open seashells.*
> *The last female sea otter observed by Professor Smith last year off the coast of Alaska (X_3) used rocks to crack open seashells.*
> *The sea otter just observed off the coast of Newfoundland (X_4) used rocks to crack open seashells.*
> *Therefore, all sea otters use rocks to crack open seashells.*

This formulation of the argument brings out the important fact that the rule of thumb for the hypothetico-deductive method (to make the greatest possible logical effort to falsify the generalization) corresponds to a basic criterion for evaluating inductive generalizations—that the greater the negative analogy among observed cases (premises), the stronger the support they are likely to provide for a related generalization. If we have deduced, tested, and found true those observation statements which were most likely to have been false, we have in effect provided the material for constructing an inductive generalization[2] in which the premises provide a high degree of support for the conclusion, since, in such a case, there is almost certain to be a significant negative analogy among the premises. As we saw in Chapter 10, the greater the negative analogy among observed cases, the greater the likelihood that there will be a strong positive

---

[2] This example also helps explain why the hypothetico-deductive method has no formal relation to induction by analogy. Because each observation statement is, in effect, a premise whose falsity can imply the falsity of the hypothesis (conclusion), *every* inductive argument formulated using this procedure must be an inductive generalization.

analogy between the observed and unobserved cases, and, therefore, the argument will have greater inductive strength.

To clarify this point, let us examine the example of the sea otters a bit further. Assume that the first researcher deduced and tested observation statements only about sea otters in Nootka Sound in British Columbia. In this instance, he could formulate the following argument:

> *The first male sea otter I observed in Nootka Sound in 1975 used rocks to crack open seashells.*
>
> .
>
> .
>
> .
>
> *The twenty-third male sea otter I observed in Nootka Sound in 1975 used rocks to crack open seashells.*
> *Therefore, all sea otters use rocks to crack open seashells.*

Clearly, in this argument the premises offer less support for the generalization than do those in the argument cited earlier, which was based on the testing of deduced observation statements about sea otters in a variety of locations at different times. Even if the person in question deduced a hundred or even a thousand more observation statements about sea otters in Nootka Sound using rocks to crack open seashells, tested them, and found them true, the inductive argument that could be constructed on the basis of these tested observation statements would not provide much added support for the generalization, since the negative analogy among the observed cases would not have been significantly increased.

One final comment is called for on the basic nature of the hypothetico-deductive method: The third step of this method has been described in different ways by different philosophers. Some view the essence of this step as being *verification* or confirmation of the generalization, whereas others view it as directed toward *falsification* of the generalization. At the level of the present discussion, this is more or less a distinction without a difference. Because it cannot be known in advance whether the deduced observation statement is true or false, one obviously cannot determine whether it will, in fact, confirm or falsify the generalization until after the observation has been made. As we have already seen, the crucial consideration should be that of increasing the negative analogy among the observed cases. If we increase the negative analogy and then discover that none of the observation statements is factually false, we have provided some confirmation of the generalization. And, of course, if one or more of the observation statements is determined to be, in fact, false, then the generalization has been falsified. Therefore, for present purposes, we need not be too concerned about the question of whether we are seeking to falsify or verify the generalization, inasmuch as in *either* case we should be trying to maximize the negative analogy among the observed cases. The same testing procedure will lead to one or the other result, depending on the outcome of the testing of the deduced observation statements.

EXERCISE 11–4   *For each of the generalizations given below, indicate which of the observation statements are such that if they are false, the generalization must also be false.*

---

1. All professors are intelligent, well-informed college graduates.
   a. Professor Baker is intelligent.
   b. Professor Legrand is a college graduate.
   c. Professor Wheelwright is brilliant.
   d. Professor Rodriguez is well informed and a college graduate.
   e. Professor Thompson is intelligent and well informed.
   f. Every professor whose course I will take next semester will be an intelligent, well-informed college graduate.
2. All Philco black-and-white portable television sets are trouble-free for the first six months.
   a. The Keanes will have no trouble for at least four more months with the Philco black-and-white portable television set they bought two months ago.
   b. Jim will have no trouble before June with the Philco black-and-white portable television set he rented early in December.
   c. The De Carlos will have trouble soon with the Philco black-and-white portable television set they bought six and a half months ago.
   d. Since the Cathode Corner, which sells only new television sets, opened for business just six weeks ago, none of the Philco black-and-white portable television sets it has sold will need repairs until at least four and a half months from now.
   e. If Jay and Laura Wilcox's new Philco black-and-white console television set is delivered next week, as they expect, they will not have any trouble with it for at least six months.
3. When fares on any type of public transportation are increased, the number of people using such transportation decreases immediately.
   a. (Assume that taxi fares have just been raised.) Fewer people will ride taxis today than did so just before the increase.
   b. (Assume that airline fares were raised last year.) Lauren will not travel by air the next time she goes east.
   c. (Assume that airline fares were raised last month, and the number of flights has not been reduced.) The planes will be taking off this month with fewer passengers aboard than before the increase.
   d. (Assume that bus fares are going up tomorrow.) At least one person who rode a bus today will not ride one tomorrow.
   e. (Assume that bus fares are going up tomorrow.) At least one of the people who rode the bus with me today will not do so tomorrow.
   f. (Assume that taxi fares have just been raised.) A lot more people will be riding the buses tomorrow.
4. The area of any rectangle is equal to its length times its width.
   a. This sheet of paper measuring 8 by 11 inches has an area of 88 square inches.
   b. A rectangle 12 inches on each side has an area of 144 square inches.
   c. The Sterns' garden, which is a rectangle measuring 51 by 60 feet, has an area of 340 square yards.

    d.   This corner lot, which measures 105 feet along one street and 75 feet along the other, has an area of 7,875 square feet.

    e.   Dave's new carpet, for which he paid $100 at $5 per square yard (exclusive of taxes), measures 12 by 15 feet.

5.   On the earth's surface, a body of high density (and therefore low air resistance) falls vertically the distance given by the equation "$d = 16t^2$," where "d" is the distance in feet and "t" is the time in seconds.

    a.   When you dropped your logic book out the dormitory window, which is 64 feet above the ground, it took 2 seconds for it to hit the ground.

    b.   When Alice dropped a coconut from her window, which is 100 feet above the ground, it took $2\frac{1}{2}$ seconds for it to fall.

    c.   Your book tumbled end over end as it fell.

    d.   Your book traveled 24 feet during the first second of its fall.

    e.   Sharon threw a pillow out of her window, which is 75 feet above the ground, and it took 3 seconds for it to hit the ground.

    f.   The book and the pillow survived the fall, but the coconut was smashed to bits.

6.   All wild chimpanzees use tools, engage in grooming behavior, and live in social groups. (Assume that it is true that A, B, C, D, E, F, G, and H are wild chimps.)

    a.   Wild Chimp A engaged in grooming behavior.

    b.   Wild Chimp B uses twigs to dig out ants from tree bark.

    c.   Wild Chimp C uses tools.

    d.   Wild Chimps D, E, and F live in the same social group.

    e.   Chimp G is wild, since he uses tools, engages in grooming behavior, and lives in a social group.

    f.   Wild Chimp H lives in a social group.

7.   Every new Volkswagen bug gets at least 20 miles to a gallon of gas during the first six months.

    a.   The Finleys' new Volkswagen bug which they got a month ago will get at least 20 miles to a gallon of gas for at least five more months.

    b.   Since Bugs Unlimited, which sells only new Volkswagen bugs, opened exactly one month ago and it takes exactly one month to receive the car you order, all of the Volkswagen bugs sold there will get at least 20 miles to a gallon of gas for the next six months.

    c.   The Morgansterns' Volkswagen bug which they bought new seven months ago does not get at least 20 miles to a gallon of gas.

    d.   The Bonos' five month old Volkswagen bug will get at least 20 miles to a gallon of gas until September 1, since they received it on May 1.

    e.   The Benvengas bought a new Volkswagen bug three months ago and it gets 40 miles to a gallon of gas.

8.   Whenever the price of a product increases and the supply decreases, fewer persons buy the product.

    a.   The price of color televisions increased and the supply decreased six months ago. Fewer people will buy color televisions now than before the price increase and supply decrease.

    b.   The price of electric knives has just increased and the supply just decreased. Mr. Smith will not buy an electric knife.

    c.   The price of home heating oil has increased and the supply decreased. The people living in Florida are buying less home heating fuel than before the price increased and the supply decreased.

    d.   The price of milk has increased in New York City. Fewer people in New York City will buy milk than before the price of milk increased.

    e.   The supply of milk has decreased in New York City. Fewer people in New York City are buying milk than before the supply of milk decreased.

EXERCISE 11–5   *Formulate three hypotheses—statements of any sort, so long as they can be supported or disproved by evidence. Then give five observation statements for each: three which, if true, would support the hypothesis; and two which, if true, would disprove it.*

EXERCISE 11–6   *Each of the hypotheses given below is followed by five sets of observation statements, all of which are deducible from the hypothesis (sometimes in conjunction with other premises). Assume that all the observation statements have been confirmed. To support each hypothesis, construct five different inductive arguments, using a different set of observation statements for each; then list these arguments in order of decreasing inductive strength.*

1. All people can laugh.
   a.   *i.*   Sergei, a Russian, can laugh.
       ii.   Elena, a Spaniard, can laugh.
       iii.   Muhammed, a Tunisian, can laugh.
       iv.   Vani, a Bantu, can laugh.
       v.   Mikako, a Japanese, can laugh.
   b.   *i.*   Pierre, a Frenchman, can laugh.
       ii.   Elena, a Spaniard, can laugh.
       iii.   Ahmed, an Algerian, can laugh.
       iv.   Muhammed, a Tunisian, can laugh.
       v.   Mario, a Maltese, can laugh.
   c.   *i.*   Hans, a German, can laugh.
       ii.   Asfa, an Ethiopian, can laugh.
       iii.   Su Mei, a Chinese, can laugh.
       iv.   Two Eagles, a Navaho, can laugh.
       v.   Kameha, an Hawaiian, can laugh.
   d.   *i.*   Hans, a German, can laugh.
       ii.   Pierre, a Frenchman, can laugh.
       iii.   Francesca, an Italian, can laugh.
       iv.   Elena, a Spaniard, can laugh.
       v.   Fernando, a Portuguese, can laugh.
   e.   *i.*   Olaf, a Norwegian, can laugh.
       ii.   Pierre, a Frenchman, can laugh.
       iii.   Ahmed, an Algerian, can laugh.
       iv.   Asfa, an Ethiopian, can laugh.
       v.   Vani, a Bantu, can laugh.
2. Pumperup tires have fewer blowouts per thousand miles than Roadmark tires.
   a.   *i.*   On a Model T Ford, a set of Pumperup tires had fewer blowouts per thousand miles than a set of Roadmark tires on the same car.
       ii.   On a Model A Ford, a set of Pumperup tires had fewer blowouts per thousand miles than a set of Roadmark tires on the same car.
       iii.   On a Stanley Steamer, a set of Pumperup tires had fewer blowouts per thousand miles than a set of Roadmark tires on the same car.
   b.   *i.*   On a Model T Ford traveling on asphalt roads, a set of Pumperup tires had

fewer blowouts per thousand miles than a set of Roadmark tires on the same car.

  ii. On a Model A Ford traveling on gravel roads, a set of Pumperup tires had fewer blowouts per thousand miles than a set of Roadmark tires on the same car.

  iii. On a Stanley Steamer traveling on dirt roads, a set of Pumperup tires had fewer blowouts per thousand miles than a set of Roadmark tires on the same car.

  iv. On a Stutz Bearcat traveling across cornfields, a set of Pumperup tires had fewer blowouts per thousand miles than a set of Roadmark tires on the same car.

c. *i.* On a Model T Ford, a set of Pumperup tires had fewer blowouts per thousand miles than a set of Roadmark tires on the same car.

  ii. On a Model A Ford, a set of Pumperup tires had fewer blowouts per thousand miles than a set of Roadmark tires on the same car.

d. *i.* On three different Model T Fords traveling on asphalt roads, sets of Pumperup tires had fewer blowouts per thousand miles than sets of Roadmark tires on the same cars.

  ii. On three different Model A Fords traveling on gravel roads, sets of Pumperup tires had fewer blowouts per thousand miles than sets of Roadmark tires on the same cars.

  iii. On three different Stanley Steamers traveling on dirt roads, sets of Pumperup tires had fewer blowouts per thousand miles than sets of Roadmark tires on the same cars.

  iv. On three different Stutz Bearcats traveling across cornfields sets of Pumperup tires had fewer blowouts per thousand miles than sets of Roadmark tires on the same cars.

e. *i.* On a Model T Ford traveling on asphalt roads, a set of Pumperup tires had fewer blowouts per thousand miles than a set of Roadmark tires on the same car.

  ii. On a Model T Ford traveling on gravel roads, a set of Pumperup tires had fewer blowouts per thousand miles than a set of Roadmark tires on the same car.

  iii. On a Stanley Steamer traveling on asphalt roads, a set of Pumperup tires had fewer blowouts per thousand miles than a set of Roadmark tires on the same car.

  iv. On a Stanley Steamer traveling on gravel roads, a set of Pumperup tires had fewer blowouts per thousand miles than a set of Roadmark tires on the same car.

3. All green plants contain chlorophyll.

 a. *i.* This green oak leaf from New Mexico contains chlorophyll.
  ii. This green sage leaf from Texas contains chlorophyll.
  iii. This green palm frond from Arizona contains chlorophyll.
  iv. This green blade of grass from Colorado contains chlorophyll.
  v. This green grape leaf from southern California contains chlorophyll.

 b. *i.* This green blade of grass from Colorado contains chlorophyll.
  ii. This green tea leaf from Ceylon contains chlorophyll.
  iii. This green algae plant from Lake Erie contains chlorophyll.
  iv. This green coca leaf from Bolivia contains chlorophyll.
  v. This green seaweed plant from off the coast of Vancouver contains chlorophyll.

 c. *i.* This green sage leaf from Texas contains chlorophyll.
  ii. This green violet leaf from New Jersey contains chlorophyll.

   iii. This green tobacco leaf from Kentucky contains chlorophyll.
   iv. This green wheat blade from Minnesota contains chlorophyll.
   v. This green potato leaf from Maine contains chlorophyll.
  d. *i.* This green creeping plant from Arizona contains chlorophyll.
   ii. This green moss plant from northern Alaska contains chlorophyll.
   iii. This green orange leaf from Israel contains chlorophyll.
   iv. This green palm frond from Liberia contains chlorophyll.
   v. This green edelweiss plant from Switzerland contains chlorophyll.
  e. *i.* This green cactus plant from New Mexico contains chlorophyll.
   ii. This green pine needle from Georgia contains chlorophyll.
   iii. This green oak leaf from New York contains chlorophyll.
   iv. This green moss plant from Wisconsin contains chlorophyll.
   v. This green pansy leaf from Oregon contains chlorophyll.

4. All birds have beaks.
  a. *i.* A bluebird observed in Canada had a beak.
   ii. A pigeon observed in New York had a beak.
   iii. A red robin observed in Ireland had a beak.
   iv. A sparrow observed in England had a beak.
   v. A raven observed in Russia had a beak.
  b. *i.* An ostrich observed in Kenya had a beak.
   ii. A bluejay observed in France had a beak.
   iii. A nightingale observed in China had a beak.
   iv. A parrot observed in Argentina had a beak.
   v. A penquin observed in Alaska had a beak.
  c. *i.* A crow observed in New York had a beak.
   ii. A pigeon observed in New York had a beak.
   iii. A finch observed in New York had a beak.
   iv. A swallow observed in New York had a beak.
   v. An oriole observed in New York had a beak.
  d. *i.* A ptarmigan observed in Alaska had a beak.
   ii. A parrot observed in Argentina had a beak.
   iii. A cockatoo observed in Chile had a beak.
   iv. A penquin observed in Canada had a beak.
   v. A seagull observed in Newfoundland had a beak.
  e. *i.* A robin observed in Spain had a beak.
   ii. A sparrow observed in France had a beak.
   iii. A pigeon observed in Italy had a beak.
   iv. A bluejay observed in Portugal had a beak.
   v. An oriole observed in Switzerland had a beak.

5. All dogs are carnivores.
  a. *i.* Frenchie, a miniature poodle, is a carnivore.
   ii. Natasha, a Russian wolfhound, is a carnivore.
   iii. Pierre, a standard poodle, is a carnivore.
   iv. King, a German shepherd, is a carnivore.
   v. Lassie, a collie, is a carnivore.
  b. *i.* Peanut, a Yorkshire terrier, is a carnivore.
   ii. Elizabeth, a cairn terrier, is a carnivore.
   iii. Lad, a Scottish terrier, is a carnivore.
   iv. Charles, a West Highland terrier, is a carnivore.
   v. Sidney, an Australian terrier, is a carnivore.
  c. *i.* Friskie, an Alaskan husky, is a carnivore.
   ii. Saber, a malamute, is a carnivore.
   iii. Chico, a chihuahua, is a carnivore.

    iv.   Sasha, an afghan, is a carnivore.

    v.   Heather, a mixed breed, is a carnivore.

d. *i.*   Lassie, a collie, is a carnivore.

    ii.   Frenchie, a miniature collie, is a carnivore.

    iii.   Lassette, a miniature collie, is a carnivore.

    iv.   Pierre, a standard poodle, is a carnivore.

    v.   BonBon, a toy poodle, is a carnivore.

e. *i.*   King, a German shepherd, is a carnivore.

    ii.   Duke, a German shepherd, is a carnivore.

    iii.   Duchess, a German shepherd, is a carnivore.

    iv.   Princess, a German shepherd, is a carnivore.

    v.   Lady, a German shepherd, is a carnivore.

CRUCIAL EXPERIMENTS   A variation of the hypothetico-deductive method is sometimes cited to characterize the procedure used for distinguishing between two 'competing' theories or generalizations.[3] We can describe this method briefly as follows. Given two logically inconsistent generalizations, that is, two generalizations which are such that it is impossible for both to be true at the same time, it is possible to derive observation statements from these generalizations which are such that a single observation will make one statement false and the other true. Thus, a single observation will force the falsification of one of the generalizations and will provide *some* confirmation of the other.[4] This is sometimes referred to as the **method of crucial experiment** and is often illustrated by examples from the history of science.

One particularly famous and important debate occurred during the sixteenth and seventeenth centuries between the supporters of the "traditional" view (associated with the second century Roman astronomer Ptolemy) that the earth is stationary at the center of the universe, with all other heavenly bodies revolving around it, and the supporters of the "heretical" view of Copernicus, Galileo, and others that it was the sun which is stationary, while all other stars and planets, including the earth, revolve around it.

The historical events surrounding the ultimate acceptance of the Copernican heliocentric theory, and the rejection of the Ptolemaic geocentric account, have sometimes been described as a use of the hypothetico-deductive method to construct a crucial experiment. The two competing hypotheses are essentially the generalizations that all heavenly bodies revolve about a stationary earth, and that all heavenly bodies (including the earth) revolve about a stationary sun.

---

[3] We do not have space to give adequate treatment in this text to the concept of a theory. Since it is generally agreed that one component of any theory is a generalization or a set of generalizations, we can simplify our discussion and focus on this one component for the moment.

[4] Because the hypothetico-deductive method can often be used to *eliminate* at least one of two inconsistent generalizations, it is sometimes referred to as a method of **eliminative induction,** in contrast to the methods of enumerative induction discussed in Chapter 10. More elaborate methods of eliminative induction are discussed in Chapter 12.

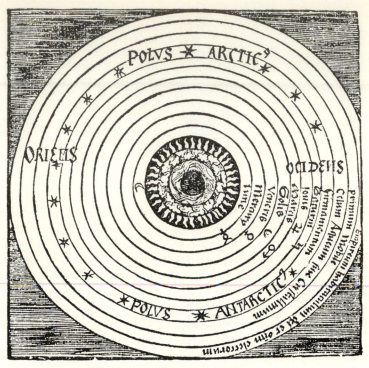

—The Aristotelian scheme of the universe, as portrayed in the middle ages. From within, outwards, (1) Spheres of earth, water, air and fire: these compose the terrestrial region; (2) the planetary spheres carrying Moon, Mercury, Venus, Sun, Mars, Jupiter, Saturn and the fixed stars. Then come (3) the crystalline sphere which provided the rotation of the pole, needed for the precession of the equinoxes (unknown to Aristotle); (4) the first mover, which impels the rest, and (5) the habitation of God and the Saints.

Clearly, the generalizations cannot both be true, although it is possible that both are false.

It should be readily apparent that few, if any, observation statements can be deduced directly from a single generalization such as 'All heavenly bodies revolve about the stationary earth'. For example, the statement 'Mars revolves about the stationary earth' can be deduced from the generalization only in conjunction with the additional premise 'Mars is a heavenly body'. And even a specific statement such as 'Mars revolves around the stationary earth' is not really an observation statement, since it cannot be determined to be true or false on the basis of *direct* observation. However, if we add enough additional assumptions, definitions, generalizations, and other observation statements (all of which are components of the same general theory) as premises in conjunction with our hypothesized generalization, it is possible to deduce an infinite number of observation statements from that generalization. Thus the second step of the

*A seventeenth-century engraving
portraying the Ptolemaic system of the
second century.*

hypothetico-deductive method theoretically could have been carried out, though not quite as easily as was suggested by our example of the sea otters.

The case of the geocentric and heliocentric theories was apparently such that almost all of the observation statements that could be derived from the two competing generalizations and tested at that time were essentially the same. Most observations that would confirm one hypothesis would also confirm the other, and an observation that would falsify one would falsify the other. For instance, both theories gave essentially the same description of the locations of particular bodies at specific times: specifying that an eclipse of the moon would occur at such and such a time, that Mars and Jupiter would be in conjunction at a specific time, and so forth. Of the pairs of observation statements which were such that the observation would confirm one statement and falsify the other, most were such that it was impossible at that time to make the specified observation.

The invention of the telescope around the beginning of the seventeenth century made it possible to test one pair of observation statements. It could be deduced from the geocentric generalization (in conjunction with other compo-

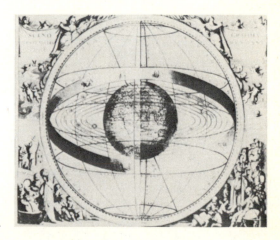

A view of the world in the Middle Ages.

nents of the Ptolemaic theory) that the planet Venus, if it could be viewed at sufficiently close range, would never appear to be more than a fairly thin crescent, rather like the Earth's moon shortly before and after the new moon. On the other hand, it was deduced from the heliocentric generalization (in conjunction with other components of the Copernican theory) that Venus should exhibit all of the phases, "growing" from a crescent to a full circle, waning again to a crescent, and finally vanishing in darkness for a time before reappearing as a crescent, just as the moon does. Telescopic observations made by Galileo in 1609 revealed that Venus does, in fact, exhibit the full set of phases. (Of course, what was directly observed was not Venus itself, but only an image in a telescope. More will be said about this later.)

Since the heliocentric hypothesis was more and more widely accepted after this time, and the geocentric hypothesis was less and less favored, it would seem that this historical case provides a clear instance of a crucial experiment in which

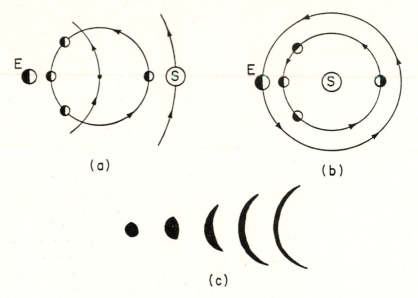

The phases of Venus in (*a*) the Ptolemaic system, (*b*) the Copernican system, and (*c*) as observed with a low-power telescope. In (*a*) an observer on the earth should never see more than a thin crescent of the lighted face. In (*b*) he should see almost the whole face of Venus illuminated just before or after Venus crosses behind the sun. This almost circular silhouette of Venus when it first becomes visible as an evening star is drawn from observations with a low-power telescope on the left of diagram (*c*). The successive observations drawn on the right show how Venus wanes and simultaneously increases in size as its orbital motion brings it closer to the earth.

From T. Kuhn, The Copernican Revolution, *p. 223. Harvard University Press. Reprinted by permission.*

one of two competing generalizations was falsified and the other confirmed by a single observation or set of observations. However, this interpretation of the historical events has been seriously questioned by historians and philosophers of science. They have cited numerous other factors that appear to have played some role in the actual acceptance of the heliocentric theory and the rejection of the geocentric theory. They emphasize that some people had already rejected the geocentric theory even before Galileo's observations, and others did not reject it until one hundred years or more afterwards.

Some of the additional conditions that have been identified as factors in such cases as this one include psychological factors, religious beliefs, aesthetic considerations, and the relationship between theories of astronomy and physics. For instance, so far as psychological factors were concerned, it was considered an attack on the self-esteem of individuals to be told they were not at the center of the universe. In terms of religious beliefs, those who supported the geocentric theory could point to Biblical passages which made reference to the sun's movement, such as prophets who "made the sun stand still." On the other hand, advocates of the heliocentric theory could point to the commonly held beliefs that the sun possessed special powers and was the source of life. From an aesthetic point of view, the heliocentric theory as a whole was simpler and "more elegant" than the geocentric theory. And the physics of the time was unable to explain how it was possible, or what the mechanisms might be, for the earth and other bodies to move in the orbits attributed to them by the heliocentric hypothesis—although the mechanism suggested for the geocentric system had problems as well.

A logical objection can also be raised against the claim that Galileo's observation was an example of a crucial experiment. This objection is grounded in the fact that the falsification of the observation statement about the appearance of Venus does not necessarily falsify the generalization that the earth is stationary at the center of the universe. The observation statement concerning the phases of Venus could be deduced from the geocentric generalization only in conjunction with a set of other statements; therefore, the fact that the deduced observation statement was false could just as reasonably be attributed to one or more of the other statements. The latter could then be modified in such a way that the geocentric generalization could be retained and the true observation statement about the phases of Venus could be deduced from it in conjunction with the new components of the general theory. Also, one could even claim that the statement about the phases of Venus is not really an observation statement, since Venus was not being "directly" observed. On such a view, the *observation* statement would be reduced to a series of statements something like 'I am having the sensation of a yellow disc on a black background here and now' which could then be logically connected to the statement about Venus in a very complex way. This allows additional room for explaining away the "apparent" inconsistency between the generalization and the observation statement, again permitting the retention of both statements.

A theory very much in vogue in the mid-1970s and which is still heard of from time to time is the theory of "biorhythms." This theory holds that every person has three different biorhythm cycles—physical, intellectual, and emotional. The theory asserts that every twenty-three days, our physical capacities go through a full cycle from low to high and back again to low. When a person is at a low point on his or her physical cycle, he or she is not capable of performing various acts as well as when at the peak of a cycle. The intellectual cycle is asserted to be thirty-three days long, and the emotional cycle is twenty-eight days in duration. According to the theory, if two or three of the cycles all hit a low point on a given day, then that person will perform even worse in the affected activities, and, if two or three are at a high point simultaneously, the person is supposed to perform exceptionally well in all areas.

A full-page advertisement that appeared in Sunday newspapers across the country provided the following evidence which was asserted to prove the theory. First, the ad reported that an organization known as the Biorhythm Research Association had studied a "group of celebrities." All the celebrities had one thing in common. They were leading ordinary lives when suddenly they were "skyrocketed to wealth, success, and fame." Three "representative" cases are then cited, one of which is that of Jacqueline Bouvier Kennedy, whose mental and emotional cycles were both at their peaks on May 8, 1952, the day she first met John F. Kennedy. The ad then cites two cases of noncelebrities who also experienced good luck, including that of the Ohio housewife who had a remarkable string of gambling wins during a week when all three of her cycles were at their high points, including winning her office check pool, a number of Bingo games, the superfecta at the racetrack (for $850) and the trifecta and perfecta (for $950).

These "documented cases" are certainly impressive in terms of the dramatic good fortune of the persons cited, but they do not provide much inductive support for any generalization concerning any possible connection between the events and the biorhythm cycles of the individuals. An article in *Psychology Today* presented a critique of the biorhythm theory, one element of which was the citation of several cases where predicted results did not occur. One of these cases was that of baseball player Reggie Jackson's performance in the 1977 World Series. Does this example serve as a "crucial experiment" to falsify the biorhythm theory? How might a proponent of the theory attempt to explain away this apparent counterexample?

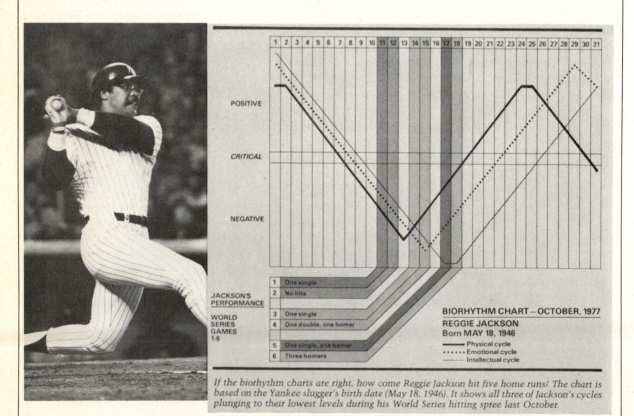

If the biorhythm charts are right, how come Reggie Jackson hit five home runs? The chart is based on the Yankee slugger's birth date (May 18, 1946). It shows all three of Jackson's cycles plunging to their lowest levels during his World Series hitting spree last October.

Logically as well as historically, then, Galileo's experiment was probably not "crucial." The factors which are now believed to have led to the rise of the heliocentric theory and the fall of the geocentric theory are very complex and still not fully understood; but it appears that purely logical factors played a relatively minor role in this (and most other) episodes in the history of science.

This is at best a crude over-simplification of the arguments by which philosophers have attempted to relate the hypothetico-deductive method to science. An adequate treatment of the subject would require an entire book or course on the philosophy of science, and any interested reader is urged to pursue either or both alternatives. However, our present characterization is sufficiently detailed and accurate to permit us to discuss some of the basic relations between formal logic and science.

SCIENTIFIC METHOD   There is little need to state the ways in which science has positively and negatively affected the course of human history. Without science, we would probably still face the threat of plagues such as the ones that killed millions in fourteenth- and fifteenth-century Europe, we would probably be unable to provide food for the world's population, we would be unable to travel around the world at our present speeds, and we would never have made it to the moon and back. By extending man's life span, science has increased the world's population; rapid growth of industrial production has led to environmental problems which have yet to be solved; and there is the overhanging threat that we may wipe ourselves out in one nuclear war. To understand these historical processes and to have some control over our future, we will be well advised to understand, so far as possible, the precise nature of science itself.

Many philosophers and scientists have argued, using concrete historical examples, that the hypothetico-deductive method, or some variation of it, is and should be *the* "scientific method." They have based their argument in support of this recommendation on what they consider to be an accurate description of the way science has functioned to date. In essence, they have argued that science has been very successful during the past several hundred years and is very successful today; that this success resulted from the use of the hypothetico-deductive method (or some variation of it); that, presumably, if this method were to be used in the future, science would continue to be successful; and that, therefore, science should be based on the hypothetico-deductive method.

As we indicated at the end of our discussion of the geocentric-heliocentric debate, there is good reason to doubt the basic premise of the argument just outlined. The history of science is not a sequence of clear-cut, straightforward applications of the hypothetico-deductive method.

In recent years, there has been growing support for alternative theories about the nature of scientific theories, which argue that a scientific theory is much more than a collection of statements of fact and generalizations based on them. One such alternative account asserts that, not only are a person's perceptions (in part, at least) determined by his or her theoretical assumptions, but that a person's

From R. W. Leeper, "A Study of
a Neglected Portion of the Field
of Learning: The Development
of Sensory Organization."
Pedagogical Seminary and
Journal of Genetic Psychology,
1935. 46, 41–75.

theoretical assumptions and perceptions are both determined to some extent by the culture in which the individual was raised. Thus, it is considered possible for two different persons who have different cultural and educational backgrounds to literally *see* different things when presented with what is presumably the "same" stimulus. For instance, look at the drawing in the left margin. Did you see an old woman or a young woman? Or perhaps just a set of black marks on a white background, or black ink on white paper? You may have seen all of these; yet psychologists have found that many people cannot see one or more of them, even though apparently exposed to the same stimuli. These differences in perception have been variously attributed to cultural biases, educational background, and other factors, but they are still not fully understood. In terms of the theories being discussed, such "facts" about perception carry the ultimate implication that "crucial experiments" as described above are impossible, since the proponents of the two competing theories would not necessarily perceive the same things and thus could not even agree as to the truth or falsity of a particular observation statement.

These theories themselves have been the subject of a variety of criticisms and are far from being universally accepted. With regard to the debates over the nature of science and of knowledge in general, the logician can only point out that, since a theory about theories is itself a theory, it must ultimately be a theory about itself. But for the most part, the debates about the nature of science go far beyond the scope of logic and this book. Regardless of which theory about theories in general, and about scientific theories in particular, a person might ultimately accept, there are certain logical relations that will hold in most such theories and that permit the use of the techniques of formal logic. Let us now turn to this subject.

The Role of Logic in Science

Strictly speaking, as we have emphasized throughout this text, logic is essentially concerned with distinguishing valid deductive arguments from invalid ones and relatively strong inductive arguments from relatively weak ones. In addition, logic provides criteria for identifying certain statements which are true or false solely by virtue of their logical form. If we wish to go beyond this—for instance, to determine the meanings of certain ordinary-language sentences (which might be used to express premises or conclusions of certain arguments), or to determine the truth or falsity of statements whose truth or falsity cannot be determined solely on logical grounds—then we will have to resort to extralogical methods and considerations. Within these restrictions, what role can logic play in science?

Given that science is, at least in part, a body of knowledge contained in a set of statements, logic can be used to identify the logical relations among these statements. Many of the statements which comprise the scientific corpus belong to one of two basic types: statements about specific observed or observable individual cases (such as "When dropped from a height of sixteen feet in a vacuum chamber, it took this metal ball precisely 1.004397 seconds to reach the bottom"), and universal generalizations (such as "The distance traversed by a freely falling body is equal to one-half times the gravitational constant times the square of the elapsed time; that is, 's $= \frac{1}{2}$ gt^2' ").

Before proceeding with this brief introductory outline of the role of logic in science, it must be pointed out that, although it is adequate for our present purposes, the distinction between generalizations and observation statements should not be interpreted as being a complete or even correct characterization of the types of statements which comprise the scientific corpus. A statement such as 'Mars rotates in a circular orbit around a stationary earth' is about the behavior of a specific individual entity, but its truth or falsity cannot be tested in as direct a way as can that of a statement such as 'Swan D is white'. Also, statements about what are sometimes referred to as "theoretical entities" (such as the electron in a particular hydrogen atom or Richard Nixon's id) are not such that their truth or falsity can be determined directly. In brief, the distinction between generalizations and observations certainly does not exhaust the kinds of statement which comprise a body of scientific knowledge. Thus, although the present discussion is restricted to the logical relations between generalizations and observation statements, it should be understood that this is for illustrative purposes only and should not be taken as an adequate description of science in general. As the analysis of the kinds of statements becomes more sophisticated and complex, so also does the description of the logical relations among these statements.

Several things can be determined by the logician about such statements and their relations. For one thing, it can be determined whether or not either an individual statement or a generalization is true or false solely by virtue of its logical form (it is generally agreed that no *observation* statement can be true or false solely on logical grounds, and it is widely accepted that few, if any, significant generalizations are true or false on such grounds). More important, the logician can determine whether one statement is validly deducible from one or more other statements; whether two statements are logically inconsistent (that is, whether it is logically impossible for both to be true at the same time); and whether or not one statement provides any inductive support for another.

Perhaps the most significant of these possible contributions by the logician to the scientific enterprise is the determination of the consistency or inconsistency of two or more statements. The question of consistency may arise as between generalizations, between a generalization and an observation statement, or even between two observation statements. It may also arise as between statements in two different theories.[5]

---

[5] A problem has been identified in recent years with respect to determining the consistency or inconsistency of two statements in *competing* scientific systems (or competing systems of any other kind, for that matter). This is the problem of *commensurability* of meanings of the two statements—that is, of whether the two statements are such that they can both be translated into the same formal system without distortion of meaning. If they cannot—that is, if different theories are logically incommensurate—then the use of formal logic must be limited to the study of the logical relations of statements within a particular theory. This issue is related to that of the nature of perception, mentioned briefly in the previous section.

It is generally agreed that inconsistency is undesirable in *any* system, since (for reasons explained in Chapter 7) if a system contains just two inconsistent statements, anything whatsoever can be derived from that system, thus rendering the system essentially useless. The problem that arises, however, when a logical inconsistency is identified within a system, is that of deciding which of the two inconsistent statements to reject. Since, at most, one of the two can be true, we must decide which to hold onto and which to eliminate from the system. But this decision goes beyond the scope of logic proper, and it must be grounded on other, extralogical criteria. If two generalizations are determined to be logically inconsistent—for instance the key generalizations of the Ptolemaic and Copernican theories:

> **All heavenly bodies (including the sun) move around
> the stationary earth.**
> **All heavenly bodies (including the earth) move
> around the stationary sun.**

one might reasonably choose to reject the one whose elimination would cause the least disruption in the rest of the system; but a generally acceptable formal definition of "least disruption" has yet to be formulated. If two observation statements are determined to be inconsistent—for instance, the two statements about the phases of Venus—one might decide which to retain and which to reject on the basis of considerations such as the past reliability of the observers. But this is not an absolute principle. For example, if the observation statement made by a previously reliable observer conflicted with a number of basic widely held beliefs, and the observation statement of an unreliable observer were to support the generally shared beliefs, it would not be unreasonable to accept the unreliable observer's statement, or at least to try to get more information before making a choice. Also, if both observers have been equally reliable, or both observations were made by the same observer, other factors will have to be considered.

Now, if an observation statement is found to be logically inconsistent with a generalization, which should be rejected and why? As we saw in our discussion of the hypothetico-deductive method, the answer is not necessarily "the generalization," although, contrary to the exhortations of some philosophers such as Plato, it probably should not always be "the observation statement" either. There are numerous factors which should be (and which usually are) taken into consideration by scientists in arriving at a decision as to which statement to retain and which to reject. This is equally true in everyday life, for we not infrequently make judgments such as "Gee, I'd have sworn that I saw you at the ball game Thursday, but since you never go to ball games, I must have been mistaken," or "I used to think all college courses were dull and useless, but Dr. Whosit's course sure showed me I was wrong." Thus, again, the question of which of two inconsistent statements to reject and which to retain cannot be answered in terms of purely logical criteria.

These are precisely the kinds of questions philosophers have been trying to answer for over twenty-five hundred years. The questions themselves have not been adequately formulated in the limited space of this chapter and the possible answers have been barely hinted at. The main point we have attempted to make here is that logic in and of itself cannot provide adequate answers to such questions, but yet that the questions cannot even be reliably identified, much less resolved, without some consideration of basic logical issues.

EXERCISE 11–7

1. Construct five cases (giving the complete relevant context) in which it would be reasonable for a person who is confronted with a generalization and an observation statement, which are logically inconsistent, to reject the generalization and retain the observation statement.

2. Construct five cases (giving the complete relevant context) in which it would be reasonable for the person in question 1 to reject the observation statement and retain the generalization.

EXERCISE 11–8

For each of the following cases, discuss ways in which (a) the generalized hypothesis could rationally be retained while rejecting the observation statement, and (b) the hypothesis could be rejected while retaining the observation statement. (c) Which strategy seems most reasonable for the given case? Could a crucial experiment be constructed?

---

1. At one time, it was hoped that a drug known as L-DOPA would cure or at least slow the progression of Parkinson's disease. It had been hypothesized that the disease was caused by a deficiency in the brain of dopamine, a transmitter of nerve messages, and that all persons with a sufficient amount of dopamine would, in effect, not have the disease. L-DOPA has the effect of correcting the dopamine deficiency. The results of recent tests on sixty patients shows that the drug does reduce many of the symptoms of the disease, but the patients using it apparently do not live any longer than the patients who do not use it. (The scientists concluded that this meant that they should reject their hypothesis and look for a new cause of the disease.)

2. It has been hypothesized that lecithin is a "cholesterol fighter"—that is, lecithin causes the cholesterol level in the blood to decrease. In 1956, a study was conducted in which fifteen persons (six other persons were dropped from the study because of allergic reactions) were given six tablespoons of lecithin daily, and the average fall in serum cholesterol was 30 percent. Another study showed that every time an average person eats two eggs (which contain lecithin), the cholesterol level in his or her blood increases.

3. Horoscopes are supposed to be deductions from a complex set of general hypotheses concerning causal relations between the stars, planets, and individual persons. Look up your horoscope in yesterday's paper. Do your experiences of yesterday confirm or refute the astrological hypothesis?

4. James Burnham, a columnist, in the *National Review* (April 27, 1973) wrote the article below entitled "Everyman His Own Teacher." In it he claims that different people have used their observations of the Vietnam war to confirm a multiplicity of conflicting hypotheses. Evaluate this argument.

    We are presently being exhorted by our sages to learn the lessons of Vietnam. "We *must* learn them," they warn us, so that "there will never be another Vietnam," and they generously tick the lessons off for our benefit. Not unexpectedly, each instructor harvests from the Vietnam story the lesson he has sown. To the pacifist, Vietnam has proved that war is wrong; to the isolationists of both the old and new models, that we should steer clear of entanglements beyond our shores; to the fiery chauvinist, that we should have finished things off in a week with a couple of well-placed H-bombs; to the computer strategists, that we failed to understand that the cold war is over; to the New Left theoreticians, that peace can be won only by the overthrow of imperialism; to the Birchites, that U.S. policy is controlled by "them." This Vietnam lesson drawing proves once more, it would seem, that the only thing we learn from history is that we learn nothing from history.

5. A lie-detector expert has hypothesized that plants react to the thoughts of human beings in their vicinity. He claims that these reactions can be registered on lie-detector type devices attached to the plants. He has conducted many tests which he says confirm the hypothesis. However, when repeating the tests for a well-known plant physiologist, no such responses were observed. The lie-detector expert explained that nothing registered because the plants had "fainted" when they sensed that the plant physiologist in her studies used the procedure of incinerating plants and otherwise harming and destroying them.

6. One hypothesis concerning the social cause of unrest and aggression is known as the "twenty-five-year itch hypothesis." This hypothesis maintains that every twenty-five to thirty years the memories of social unrest, war, or aggression die with the generation that was involved in these activities. The young generation is then willing to defy institutions and engage once again in these activities. Asked his opinion of the hypothesis, Herman Kahn, a social commentator and think-tank administrator, said the following: "It is an attractive theory but I don't think it is accurate. I suspect the analogy is drawn from one single instance—the time that elapsed between 1914 and 1939, and I for one would hesitate to generalize from one observation. If one goes further back in history: In the Napoleonic wars, young men in France had been bloodied over and over again but were still willing to go to war. They liked war in some real sense. In America, on the other hand, 25 or 30 years after the Civil War there was no sign of any generational unrest, any thirst for a fresh conflict coming to the surface."

SUMMARY

1. By the addition of suitably chosen premises, any inductive argument can be reformulated as a valid deductive argument; but this does not necessarily improve the quality of the argument, since the premises added are usually weak. However, there are several alternative methods of formulating inductive arguments which some have suggested might improve their logical quality or make them simpler to evaluate.

2. Some argue that the distinction between induction by analogy and inductive generalization is unnecessary, and that only deduction and inductive generalization are needed. They reformulate the single-step induction by analogy into a two-step argument, consisting of an inductive generalization followed by a valid deductive argument. Although the two-step method arrives at the same conclusion from the same set of premises as does the single-step method, the

two are not equivalent. The one-step method is at least as good as, if not better than, the two-step, in that the latter does not recognize differences in the relative inductive strengths of certain arguments.

3. The **hypothetico-deductive method** differs from the more formal mode of enumerative induction presented in Chapter 9, in that it purports to reflect more accurately how people do in fact reason. It involves a temporal sequence of three steps. The first step is the formulation of a generalization in the form of a "working hypothesis." The second step consists of validly deducing observation statements (that is, statements whose truth or falsity can be determined by direct observation) from the generalization. The third step is the testing of the observation statements to determine whether each is, in fact, true or false, for the falsity of an observation statement logically implies the falsity of the generalization from which it was derived.

4. The process of deducing and testing observation statements obviously ends when any one of the deduced observation statements is found to be false. If no falsifying instance is found, the process could be continued indefinitely. A basic rule of thumb is that the greater the "logical effort" expended to deduce and test those observation statements which are most likely to be factually false, the greater the probability that, if they prove to be true, the generalization is true as well.

5. The rule of thumb for the hypothetico-deductive method corresponds to a basic criterion for evaluating inductive generalizations—that the greater the negative analogy among observed cases (premises), the stronger the support they are likely to provide for a related generalization. Some view the second and third steps of this method as being directed toward the *verification* of the generalization, whereas others view them as being directed toward the *falsification* of the generalization.

6. A variation of the hypothetico-deductive method, the method of **crucial experiment,** is sometimes cited to characterize the procedure for choosing between two "competing" theories or generalizations. Given two logically inconsistent generalizations, it is possible to derive observation statements from them which are such that a single observation will make one false and the other true. Thus, a single observation will force the falsification of at least one of the generalizations, and will usually provide at least some confirmation of the other.

7. Many argue that the hypothetico-deductive method, or some variation of it, is and/or should be *the* "scientific method." The argument used to justify the claim that this *should* be so resembles the inductive argument in support of the principle of induction, and is subject to criticisms of circularity. Another difficulty with the argument is that a careful examination of the history of science provides little, if any, evidence that science has in fact developed in this way.

8. An even more serious problem in trying to characterize the nature of science is the apparent fact that the statements of science cannot be neatly and simply categorized as either theoretical statements (or generalizations) or observation statements. There is even the possibility that individuals from different cultures (or with different theoretical training) actually see different things when exposed to the same stimuli. If this is true to any significant extent, then observations would not necessarily provide a basis for resolving theoretical disputes.

9.   Given that science is, at the least, a body of knowledge contained in a set of statements, logic can be used to identify and evaluate the logical relations among these statements. Many scientific statements belong to one of two basic types: statements about specific observable cases and universal generalizations. Logic can be used to determine whether a specific statement is true or false solely by virtue of its logical form. More important, the logician can determine whether one statement is validly deducible from one or more other statements, whether two statements are logically inconsistent, and whether one statement provides any inductive support for another. Perhaps the most significant of these is the determination of inconsistency, since it is generally agreed that inconsistency is undesirable in *any* system. When an inconsistency is found, one must decide which of the two statements to reject, but this decision goes beyond the scope of logic proper. Although logic alone cannot provide adequate answers to many questions concerning what science is and/or should be, the problems cannot be identified, nor adequate solutions provided, without some use of logic.

CHAPTER TWELVE

Mill's Methods

Somewhere in the folklore of most peoples can be found a story more or less like the following: A proud and handsome rooster made it his daily custom, in the cold grey light of early dawn, to fly up to the tallest post of the barnyard fence and crow melodiously, announcing his own magnificence to the clucking accompaniment of his admiring hens below. One day, as he finished his song and stood, crimson-combed head raised high, regally surveying his domain, he saw the sun come up over the eastern hills. "There!" he said to himself, delicately preening a ruffled feather; "Even the sun comes to listen to my splendid crowing." The next day he watched, and again, just as he finished his crowing, the sun rose. This happened day after day, and at last the rooster announced to the assembled hens, "My dears, you are fortunate to be the wives of so great a personage as I. Have you not noticed that it is I who, by my crowing, make the sun rise each day?" All the hens clucked in admiration, save one, who cackled "Nonsense," and turned away to peck at a worm.

The rooster was angry, and flew down from the fencepost to punish her; but she said, "If your crowing really makes the sun rise, then prove it. Tomorrow, do not crow at dawn. If you are right, the sun will not rise, and your glory will then be greater than ever."

The rooster confidently accepted her challenge. The next morning he did not crow, but remained on the ground, strutting about before the hens. The grey light grew as always, and then—just when the rooster, on any other day, would have finished his crowing—the sun rose. A great cackle of laughter burst from the hens, and the humiliated rooster, all his splendid feathers drooping in embarrassment and shame, crept miserably away to hide in the darkest corner of the henhouse.

Master Chanticleer, in this story, fell into an error most of us are prone to. He began with an observation of fact: "I crowed, and the sun came up." After observing that this sequence of events occurred regularly and consistently, he formulated the enumerative generalization: "Every morning I crow, and the sun comes up.'' So far, he was quite correct. His mistake came when he inferred, on the basis of this observed regularity, a causal relationship between the two events: "It is my crowing that causes the sun to come up.'' His ensuing public humiliation stemmed from his failure to recognize an important principle of logic: that no generalization which is arrived at solely by means of enumerative induction is strong enough to support the inference of a causal connection between two or more associated events. That is to say, the fact that Y has always followed X in the past does not prove that X is the *cause* of Y and will continue to always precede Y in the future.

While some purely enumerative inductions are of interest in certain contexts, what people generally look for in their dealings with the world is the stronger connections between events—those which are commonly referred to as *causal* connections. The process involved in the search for causes may be relatively simple, as when a person decides on the basis of a few simple observations that a houseplant is growing spindly *because* it is not getting enough sun. On the other hand, it may be more complex, as when a voter decides to support a particular candidate for office on the basis of her or his belief that the candidate will be able to influence legislation in the right direction; or when a student, desperately needing a good grade, decides to take a course with a teacher who is regarded as undemanding. In all these cases, the person is called upon to make a causal inference, to reason from cause to effect or from effect to cause. We frequently make such inferences without full awareness of the kind of thought processes we are using. In explanation of our judgments, we may say nothing more than "It must not be getting enough light; I'd better move it closer to the window," or "I'm going to vote for Krumholz; she's the only person who can solve the city's problems," or "I think I'll take Schlumbum's course; he's a pushover."

Often, though, one cannot be satisfied with such intuitive, unsystematic methods of causal inference. This is especially so for scientists, who need to make their methods clear and distinct so that others may repeat their experiments and test their conclusions. It is also important, on occasion, for the average person to be able to reason clearly and explicitly about causes. It is this need that has led scientists and philosophers, from the time of Aristotle and before, to investigate the nature of causality.

KINDS OF CAUSE   When people seek to determine the causes of events, it is generally so that the events may be repeated, prevented, or at least predicted, in the future. For example, geologists today are seeking to discover the causes and "early warnings" of earthquakes, since the better these are understood, the greater the chance that earthquakes can be predicted and perhaps even controlled, thus reducing the danger they pose to human life and property. Or, to take a more mundane example, if a bartender mixes a particularly superb cocktail, she will want to know exactly what she did that caused the drink to turn out so well, so that she can do it again later.

When we ask what "causes" a given occurrence, we may mean a number of different things by the word 'cause.' For example, if a glass is dropped at a cocktail party, what causes it to break? Is it the fact that glass is a brittle material? Is it the force with which the glass strikes the floor? Or is it the person who dropped the glass, or another person who bumped into him, thereby knocking the glass out of his hand? Each of these, in its own way, could reasonably be called a cause of the broken glass; but they are not all causes in the same sense. The different answers involve different notions of causality.

Or consider a more serious matter, the case of the Turkish DC-10 airliner that crashed near Paris on March 3, 1974, killing all 346 persons on board. At first the cause seemed a mystery. The plane had taken off for London only a few minutes before, with all systems presumably functioning well. The pilot had sent no word of an emergency before the crash. Some observers reported that the landing gear had been momentarily lowered, as if for an emergency landing, then retracted again, as the plane plunged to earth.

346 DEAD IN DC10 PLANE CRASH
Firemen stand near the fuselage of the Turkish Airlines DC10 jetliner which crashed north of Paris on March 3, 1974. All 346 persons aboard were killed in the worst disaster in civil aviation history.

Wide World Photos.

The principal hypotheses at first were that the crash had been caused by an explosion on board—perhaps a bomb—or by an engine malfunction. One piece of evidence which seemed to support the explosion hypothesis was that six bodies had been found relatively close together, several miles nearer the airport than the crash site. It was suggested that a sudden decompression of the passenger cabin, such as would occur if an explosion breached the cabin wall, could have sucked them out of the plane before the crash. Some anonymous phone calls also alleged sabotage, and Turkish authorities quoted sources which said that certain of the passengers might have been Palestinian guerrillas and guerrilla sympathizers carrying bombs.

The discovery of a cargo-hold door in the same area as the six bodies bolstered the rapid-decompression theory but suggested that the decompression had originated not in the passenger cabin but in the cargo hold. Investigators began examining the door for evidence of burning or chemical deposits, such as might have been left by a bomb. But then it was noted that an earlier incident had occurred, near Windsor, Ontario, in which another DC-10 had lost a cargo door in flight. The resulting sudden decompression of the cargo hold had caused the floor of the passenger cabin to buckle, jamming important control cables. Although in this case the plane had been landed safely, it was clear that a similar accident could have resulted in the March crash.

Further investigation showed that, in the Windsor incident, the cargo door had been improperly latched; that, after that incident, a design change in the latch had been introduced, to prevent improper closing; and that this change had never been made on the airliner involved in the March crash, although company records erroneously showed that it had been made. Together with evidence gathered at the crash site, this information seemed conclusive: The final report of the investigating commission gave the cargo-latch failure as the "sole cause" of the disaster.

In a sense, it *was* the sole cause. There had been no bomb or other sabotage and no engine failure. But why had the cargo door been improperly latched? Even without the design change, it was possible to close it correctly and safely. Had the baggage handlers been careless? Had the flight crew failed to check as they should have? And why had the company records shown the design change as having been made when in fact it had not? Was this the fault of the worker who should have installed the new mechanism? Of the safety inspector who should have checked the installation? Of the plant supervisor? After the Windsor incident, the federal agency responsible for aviation safety had only recommended, not required, the design change. Who was responsible for that decision? And were not all of these people, and their actions or failures to act, in some sense, "causes" of the crash? One might even claim that the cause of the crash was the fact that the plane was in the air. Had it remained on the ground it would not have crashed.

It should be clear from these two examples that the word 'cause' may be used in a number of different senses. Some possible meanings include (1) the preceding events which trigger the event in question (the failure to check the latch, the dropping of the glass, or the bumping-into): this has traditionally been known as the *efficient* cause. It may mean (2) the material out of which a thing is made (such as that which constituted the broken cocktail glass)—traditionally known as the *material* cause. Or it may mean (3) the form of the object involved in the event (the defective design of the latch, the distinctive shape of the glass)—known as the *formal* cause. Still a fourth kind of cause may be the aim or goal of an action (if, as at first suspected, the airliner had been sabotaged, or if the elbow-jogger were trying to embarrass the glass-dropper). This fourth type is known as the *final* or purposive cause. The sort of cause we look for will depend on what we are trying to explain, predict, or control. A manufacturer of glassware might note the shape and the chemical composition of the glass; the hostess at the cocktail party would probably be more concerned about the crowding that made it hard for guests to avoid jostling each other. The airplane manufacturer would certainly be interested in the design of the faulty latch, but the airport maintenance supervisor would be more concerned about the carelessness or lack of comprehension of the cargo handler. And these are not the only possible meanings of 'cause'.

Proximate and Remote Causes   Thus we can see that there are usually many causal factors associated with any given event. When the causes (in the first sense of the term as described above) occur in a temporal sequence, each event producing the next and leading up at last to the event which is to be explained, a causal chain can be said to exist. The "Peanuts" cartoon below provides a good illustration of reasoning involving a causal chain of events.

In this example, Linus is presenting an argument to explain (or defend) his decision to spend his dollar on the salami sandwich instead of the cologne. His primary goal was to make Lucy as happy as possible, and he believed that Lucy would be happier if he were to become a doctor who would help people than if she were to get a bottle of cologne. He then argues that his eating a salami sandwich now would be one link in a causal chain which would ultimately lead to his becoming a doctor. His argument also involves an implicit premise to the effect that, if he hadn't bought the sandwich, he would never become a doctor.

The last event in a causal chain (here, Linus, the doctor, helping the people of the world) is commonly referred to as the **proximate cause**—that is, the one closest to the event whose cause is being considered (in this case, making Lucy happy). It is the proximate cause that is assumed to directly precipitate the caused event. The other links in the chain are the more or less **remote causes.**

How far back we go in analyzing a causal chain depends on our reason(s) for investigating the case in the first place. In the case of the airplane crash, the proximate cause was apparently the failure of the latch. However, the investigators probably would not be satisfied merely with knowing that the latch had failed to lock. It had failed to lock because someone had closed it improperly; it

FEIFFER

Some causal chains seem to involve repeating cycles, as in this analysis of the oil price spiral phenomenon. In such cases, there are not really any proximate or remote causes, and every "effect" is ultimately a "cause" of itself. Can you identify any errors or weaknesses in the above analysis that would offer the possibility of escaping this apparently inescapable cycle?

Field Newspaper Syndicate.

was possible to close it improperly because the recommended change in the mechanism had not been made; the failure to make the change had passed unnoticed because the company's records were wrong; the change had been needed because a faulty design had been approved in the first place; and so on. All these elements were parts of a causal chain leading up to the crash, and the investigator would be interested in discovering as many links in the chain as possible, so that steps could be taken to prevent a recurrence of the final tragedy.

EXERCISE 12–1   *In each of the following paragraphs, determine the proximate and remote causes of the events specified. (Letters identify sentences.)*

---

1. *Event:* Judy's forehead gets cut.
   (a) It was a sunny day, the first in two weeks, so Judy decided to take a drive in her new Alfa Romeo convertible. (b) She settled comfortably into the brown leather driver's seat. (c) Starting the engine, she backed carefully out of the driveway. (d) At first, she drove slowly along the country road, listening to the birds and enjoying the sight of green fields and trees in the late spring sunshine. (e) Gradually, though, her foot pressed more heavily on the accelerator. (f) The car gained speed, and she felt the wind on her face. (g) For a couple of seconds, she closed her eyes and leaned her head back to enjoy the sensation. (h) As she opened her eyes, she saw a moving shape at the edge of the road. (i) Suddenly, a deer dashed in front of the now speeding car. (j) Judy slammed on the brakes and turned the wheel sharply. (k) The car spun halfway round, skidded off the road, and rammed nose-first into a tree. (l) Judy, despite her seat belt, was thrown forward, and her head hit the steering wheel. (m) When she recovered her wits sufficiently to realize what had happened, she began checking herself for injuries. (n) Her forehead felt sticky when she touched it. (o) When she looked in the mirror, she could see a small, bleeding cut, just below the hairline.

2. *Event:* Mrs. Miller's glasses get knocked off.
   (a) Sharon Miller sat on the picnic bench in the backyard of her suburban home. (b) She smiled as she watched the goings-on by the sandbox. (c) Her husband was there, playing ball with their five-year-old son, Glenn. (d) Mr. Miller would gently bounce the big red beach ball on the terrace, and Glenn would spread his arms wide to embrace it. (e) Then Glenn would giggle and, with all the energy of his small body, throw the ball to the ground so it would bounce again for his father to catch. (f) After about five minutes of this, Lou and Alice Porter, the Millers' next-door neighbors, strolled up the driveway with their English sheepdog, Rugg. (g) Sharon waved and called out a greeting. (h) Just at that moment, Rugg spotted the ball and made a dash for it. (i) He made contact with it in midair, but it was much too big for him to get a grip on it. (j) Consequently, it bounced off his nose and hit the corner of the bench where Sharon Miller was sitting. (k) There it bounced again, changed direction, and hit Sharon on the side of the head, knocking her glasses off. (l) Fortunately, the glasses landed on the grass and were undamaged. (m) Sharon laughed, picked them up, and put them back on as she got up to talk with the Porters.

3. *Event:* Susan's new record album by the Grand Funk gets scratched.
   (a) Susan had been saving her lunch money all week so that she could buy the new album by Grand Funk. (b) She could barely sit through her Latin class. (c) When the last bell at Old Bridge High School rang, Susan left the building quickly. (d) She saw a school bus go by, and waved to some of her friends on board. (e) She went to the

Main Street record store. (f) There she found a pile of the new album in the front of the store. (g) She slipped off the top record and went to the cashier. (h) She remarked that the record was already among the top ten. (i) "Four dollars and eighty-nine cents with tax," the cashier said. (j) Susan gave the cashier five singles and waited for her record and change. (k) She then took a bus home. (l) On the way, she read the record jacket notes and looked at the cover design. (m) The song she liked best, having heard the album on the radio, was cut four on side two. (n) When her stop came, she jumped out of her seat and made a fast exit. (o) Down the block, she passed Mr. Langston walking his dog, and greeted him. (p) At home, she rushed into her room. (q) She tossed her coat on the bed. (r) Then she took the record out of its jacket and put on side two. (s) In her rush, she forgot to lift the cueing mechanism. (t) She picked up the playing arm and moved it across to the fourth cut. (u) Then she let it go, and to her horror she saw it drop immediately. (v) It hit the record heavily and then slide across it, making a grinding sound. (w) "Oh, no," she cried. (x) She did so now and put the arm once again above the fourth cut. (z) She lowered the cueing mechanism and the playing arm descended slowly and gracefully. (a') Then she heard loud clicks as the needle hit the scratches on the record.

4. *Event:* Frank scrapes his leg.

(a) Penelope Triscot and her four-year-old son, Frank, were walking through the park. (b) It was a sunny spring afternoon. (c) The temperature was 63°. (d) Mrs. Triscot noticed a group of other parents sitting on benches near the playground area. (e) She recognized some of them as neighbors. (f) Giving her son a little tug on the arm, Mrs. Triscot walked in the direction of the playground area. (g) One neighbor, John Stevenson, suggested that Frank and his daughter, Miriam, might enjoy the slide. (h) Mrs. Triscot thought it would be good fun. (i) She remembered how much she had enjoyed slides when she was a child. (j) She and Frank and John and Miriam walked to the slide. (k) Three other children were just leaving it. (l) Mr. Stevenson lifted the children to the top of the slide and then released them. (m) The children enjoyed the slide down the metal chute. (n) They shouted and laughed as they went down. (o) At the bottom of the slide, Mrs. Triscot caught the children before they fell off the end. (p) At the end of one trip, Miriam fell down and got a big dirt smudge on the seat of her pants. (q) The parents and children had been playing for about five minutes when suddenly Mrs. Triscot heard a scream somewhere behind her. (r) She turned sharply to see what was wrong. (s) A large German shepherd was sniffing at a little girl, who was screaming with fear. (t) Not recognizing the dog, Mrs. Triscot began running to the little girl. (u) Before she had gone more than a few steps, the little girl's mother had seen the situation and reached her child. (v) Then suddenly Mrs. Triscot heard another, familiar voice crying behind her. (w) She turned around and saw Frank on the ground at the foot of the slide, looking up at her and crying. (x) She hurried toward him, picked him up, and he stopped crying almost immediately. (y) Mrs. Triscot looked for bruises and found a small scratch on Frank's left leg.

EXERCISE 12–2　　*The following excerpts are adapted from newspaper reports. Each presents what purports to be a causal chain of events. Try to identify (a) The final event of the causal chain, (b) the proximate cause, and (c) the remote cause(s). Discuss your answers with other members of your class.*

---

1. In 1949, Ivar Hennings, then chairman of the South Bend Bait Company, had a solution to the "threatening" problem of communism. According to Mr. Hennings, "the furnishing of quality tackle would lead to more fishing, which promotes a clean

mind, healthy body, and leaves no time for succumbing to communistic or socialist propaganda—simultaneously building for a better America." Lower taxes would also help to solve the problem, he said. (New York *Times,* May 1, 1974)

2. Discontent has been aggravated by a famine that killed tens of thousands of people last year in rural areas of Ethiopia. This was followed by steep rises in fuel prices caused by the world energy crisis, and by other price increases that have severely pressed both the rural and the urban population. (New York *Times,* February 27, 1974)

3. Freon, a nonflammable hydrocarbon containing fluorine and chlorine, is used as a refrigerant and as a propellant in aerosol spray cans. Some scientists maintain that freon may destroy the earth's ozone radiation shield, which filters out the sun's dangerous ultraviolet rays.

   "Freon itself does not harm the ozone layer, but when it reaches the upper levels of the stratosphere the ultraviolet light of the sun triggers the release of chlorine from freon. Chlorine in turn breaks down the ozone that serves the earth as a shield from most of the sun's ultraviolet light."

   According to Dr. Donald M. Hunten, chairman of a five-member panel of the National Academy of Sciences, which is studying the problem, "Studies have shown that just about all the freon ever used in aerosol spray cans now resides in the earth's atmosphere. The reason is that freon does not dissolve in water and does not combine with anything to drift harmlessly away. The use of freon has grown at a rate of 15 percent per year over the last five years." Hunten maintains that "about 10 percent of the freon released to the atmosphere has already reached the stratosphere, where most of the atmospheric ozone is." (Thomas O'Toole, Washington *Post*)

4. A panel of scientists appointed by the National Research Council supported the theory that the proposed Supersonic Transport (SST) would dangerously deplete the ozone layer.

   "The panel was created to assess the argument that the introduction of oxides of nitrogen into the stratosphere by exhaust from a fleet of about 500 supersonic transports would initiate a series of ozone-depleting chemical reactions.

   "The nitric oxides, this argument goes, would serve as catalysts. That is, they would participate in the reactions but remain afterward to stimulate further reactions in an open-ended manner. The effect would be to convert ozone, whose molecules are formed of three oxygen atoms, into oxygen gas, which consists of paired oxygen atoms. Ozone, in the region between 10 and 30 miles aloft, strongly absorbs the lethal wavelengths of ultraviolet sunlight. The SSTs would operate in the lower part of this region.

   "Last year (1971) Dr. Harold Johnston, a leading authority on atmospheric chemistry at the University of California in Berkeley, contended that within one year the projected SST fleet might halve the amount of ozone in the atmosphere. This, he said, could blind all animals, including human beings, except those remaining indoors or under water." (Walter Sullivan, New York *Times,* November 5, 1972)

5. "The immediate cause of Jackie Robinson's death at age 53 was apparently a heart attack. But to many doctors a more fundamental process was involved: diabetes and its complications.

   "The former Brooklyn Dodger's heart attack, which came after a decade of failing health, was his third since 1968, two of the Manhattan specialists who cared for him said in interviews. These two previous heart attacks had left him with a need for cardiology care to treat his congestive heart failure.

   "The Dodger second baseman had also consulted several other kinds of specialists in the 20 years he knew he had diabetes because during this interval Mr. Robinson had developed most of the conditions that can complicate the endocrine disease. The first black major leaguer lost the sight of one eye and was becoming progressively blind in the other, despite treatments with a laser beam. A week ago today [October 22, 1972], he suddenly lost even more sight from a hemorrhage in his 'good' eye.

"In 1961, his knee, already damaged by arthritis caused by the trauma of sliding around the bases on the playing field, was further injured by a serious infection. The staphylococcal bacteria that caused the knee infection also poisoned his blood system with a near fatal case of septicemia and temporarily threw his diabetes out of control until antibiotics and more insulin helped him recover.

"Mr. Robinson also suffered from burning sensations and other pains in his legs that had resulted from a combination of diabetic damage to the nerves and arteries in his legs. So discomforting were these symptoms, his doctor said, that Mr. Robinson had to give up golf.

"Also, his blood pressure was abnormally high for many years. Though hypertension can be another complication of diabetes, Mr. Robinson's physicians said they considered it an unassociated problem in his case. Cardiologists have reported that hypertension is found with unusually high frequency among blacks." (Lawrence K. Altman, New York *Times*, October 29, 1972. Reprinted by permission)

Causes as Necessary and Sufficient Conditions
We have noted above that the word 'cause' can be understood in a variety of ways—not only as proximate and remote, but as referring to the material or the form of an object, the preceding events, or even the goal or aim of an action.

Unfortunately, the term 'cause' has become too closely associated in most people's minds with only one of the several meanings of the term. People today, on being asked about the cause of something, are apt to think immediately of the proximate *efficient* cause and fail to go any further. And, indeed, many philosophers believe that, in the proper theoretical context, all causes can ultimately be reduced to proximate and remote efficient causes. However, our discussion thus far should be sufficient to show that other kinds of causal explanation (i.e., in terms of material, design, or intent) would normally be regarded as quite legitimate and appropriate in certain contexts without needing to be expressed in terms of efficient causes only.

Because of the tendency to interpret 'cause' as equivalent to 'proximate efficient cause', logicians and others concerned with accurate reasoning find it helpful to use the more neutral term **condition.** We will follow this usage in most of our discussion in the present chapter, speaking not of the causes of an event, but of the conditions under which it takes place. These conditions may be causally related to the event, or they may not: They may be effects of it, or joint effects with it of some other cause, or simply accidents which happened to occur, for no particular ascertainable reason, at the same time. For instance, if a car skids on an icy road and plows into a telephone pole, several associated factors may be noted by the policeman who investigates the accident. The tire treads are worn down; the front wheels are out of alignment; the driver had just been to see his doctor; he was driving fast; a dog ran into the road; someone screamed; a siren sounded nearby; the road is narrow; there was a gusty wind blowing; it was near sunset; and so on. Whether and in what way any of these factors "caused" the accident remains to be determined; but they are all conditions in the presence of which it occurred.

When, as here, we are interested primarily in the determination of *causal* conditions, we must make a distinction between two important types: necessary and sufficient conditions. For the airliner to crash, it had to be in the air. This was a *necessary condition* for the crash—that is, the crash could not have happened without it. However, the plane's mere being in the air was not sufficient by itself to cause the crash; many planes take off and land without crashing. Other conditions—including the faulty latch and the difference in air pressure inside and outside the plane—also had to be present to create a *sufficient condition* for the plane to crash.

A **necessary condition,** then, is one in the absence of which the event *cannot* take place. A **sufficient condition** is one in the presence of which the event is *certain* to take place.

The distinction can be further illustrated by the following example: Without clouds there can be no rain. Therefore, clouds are a necessary condition of rain. If the necessary condition is not present, the event (rain) will certainly not occur. However, even if this necessary condition is present, there is still no guarantee that the event *will* occur. Although there can be no rain when there are no clouds, there may be clouds without rain. Clouds, therefore, do not by themselves constitute a sufficient condition for the occurrence of rain. Other conditions are also necessary. When clouds are present, and when those clouds are beyond a certain saturation point, and when the temperature of the air is above freezing, then rain occurs. These conditions, which, individually, are necessary conditions, together make up a sufficient condition for the occurrence of rain.

Charlie Brown's mistake, for which he is being tormented by his classmates in the "Peanuts" cartoon on p. 500 was that of giving a single proximate necessary condition when the teacher apparently wanted a sufficient (and probably somewhat remote) condition as the appropriate answer. The "correct" answer probably should have included some consideration of the geographical location of the state of Oregon in terms of its proximity to the Pacific Ocean, some mention of the major currents and wind patterns, and even some consideration of the mountain systems in the state.

In the case of rain, the sufficient condition is a **conjunction**—that is, a combination, a joining together—of several necessary conditions. There are other cases in which a necessary condition is a **disjunction** of two or more conditions; that is, the presence of one *or* another (but not all) of several conditions is necessary to produce the caused event. For example, if the police find the dead body of a prominent citizen on the sidewalk below his fifteenth-floor apartment, they are likely to assume that he fell from the window. There are three possibilities as to the proximate cause of the fall: (1) he fell by accident; (2) he was pushed; (3) he jumped. Any one of these three by itself is a sufficient condition of

© 1962 United Feature Syndicate, Inc.

the fall. The necessary condition is a disjunction of all three: The victim could not have fallen unless he *either* jumped *or* was pushed *or* fell by accident.

Whether one looks for the necessary or the sufficient condition(s) in investigating the cause(s) of an event often depends on one's practical aims. If one is trying to *prevent* a certain occurrence, then one will probably search for the necessary condition(s), whose removal will make the recurrence of the event impossible. Thus, suppose a number of thefts have been committed in an office building, and the thieves are believed to be persons who do not legitimately work in the building. One can say that free access by unauthorized persons is (in this case) a necessary condition of the event (theft), so that by removing the condition the management can prevent the event. The management may thus institute a system of door guards and identification badges to keep unauthorized persons out.

Conversely, if one is seeking to *produce* a given event, one seeks the sufficient condition(s). If I wish to attract a certain species of bird to my garden, I may provide a suitable nesting site, or scatter food of which this species is particularly fond, or play a recording of the mating call of the species. Assuming that such birds are in the neighborhood, any one of these actions should be sufficient to produce the event I desire.

Of course, if the sufficient condition is conjunctive, the process may be more involved. A cook, for example, must keep a number of conditions in mind whenever he sets out to prepare a given dish. The correct ingredients; their freshness; their combination in the proper amounts, order, and manner; the proper cooking utensils; and the application of the proper amount of heat for the right amount of time are all necessary conditions. The cook must know not just one of these necessary conditions, but all of them; for, together, they constitute the sufficient condition of success in preparing the dish.

To sum up what we mean by necessary and sufficient conditions, and their relationships to one another:

1. *When we say that A is a necessary condition of B, we mean that it is possible for B to occur if and only if A is present: that is, if A is absent, B cannot occur.*

2. *When we say that A is a sufficient condition of B, we mean that whenever A is present, B is certain to occur.*

3. *A sufficient condition is the conjunction of all of the necessary conditions: that is, if necessary conditions A_1 and A_2 and A_3 are all present together, and they are the only necessary conditions for B, then event B will occur.*

4. *A necessary condition is sometimes a disjunction of several conditions: That is, unless either condition A_1 or A_2 or A_3 is present, necessary condition A is not present and event B cannot occur.*

5. *When an event occurs, it follows by definition that all necessary conditions, and thus at least one sufficient condition, for its occurrence are present.*

6. *Generally, when one is presented with an event and then attempts to reason back to the "cause" to prevent the event, one is looking for a necessary condition. When one is trying to predict whether a given event will occur, or when one is trying to produce the event, one is looking for the sufficient condition.*

EXERCISE 12–3   1.   Assuming ordinary circumstances:
   a.   Is decapitation a sufficient condition for death? A necessary condition for death?
   b.   Is oxygen a sufficient condition for life? A necessary condition for life?
   c.   Is Zulu parentage a sufficient condition for black skin? A necessary condition for black skin?
   d.   Is being female a sufficient condition for having a soprano voice? A necessary condition for having a soprano voice?
   e.   Is spilling a bucket of red paint on the floor a sufficient condition for having red paint on the floor? A necessary condition for having red paint on the floor?

   f.   Is the conjunction of a hamburger, a piece of cheese, and a bun a sufficient condition for the creation of a cheeseburger? A necessary condition for the creation of a cheeseburger?

2.   Read the following paragraph and identify the necessary and sufficient conditions of the event 'Williams won the top prize for the day'. (Letters identify sentences.)

(a) None of the other riders in the rodeo had been able to stay on the fiery little horse, Dynamite, for three minutes; the best time so far was 2:57. (b) In the chute, Williams climbed into Dynamite's saddle. (c) His name was announced as the next rider. (d) Williams boasted to the gate attendant, "You just watch—*I'll* stay on him for at *least* three minutes." (e) The attendant grinned and said, "Yeah, sure, that's what the rest of 'em said." (f) Williams spat on the ground. (g) "Okay," he said, "let's go!" (h) The gate opened, and the horse plunged into the arena. (i) Williams' wife, sitting in the stands, crossed her fingers and watched tensely. (j) Williams gripped the frantically bucking horse with his knees, waving his hat at the crowd with one hand. (k) Suddenly the horse lowered his head and kicked back fiercely, his hind legs going almost straight up in the air. (l) The crowd roared as the clock passed the three-minute mark. (m) Williams tumbled off, landing hard on the packed dirt floor of the arena. (n) Many of the spectators gasped, sure he must have been hurt. (o) Then Williams got up jauntily, and the crowd cheered. (p) The judges certified his time: 3:02. (q) Williams won the top prize for the day.

3.   Scramblex Communications Systems wanted to hire four new management trainees. Eight people answered the personnel director's advertisement. Their qualifications were as shown in the following table:

PERSON	MALE	MATH MAJOR	ENGI-NEERING DEGREE	COMMUNI-CATIONS EXPERIENCE	COMPUTER EXPERIENCE	AGE 23 OR OVER
1	x	x		x		x
2	x	x	x		x	x
3		x	x		x	x
4	x		x	x		x
5	x	x		x		
6	x				x	x
7	x	x	x			
8				x		x

Persons 1, 2, 3, and 6 were hired. What can you identify as probably necessary condition(s) of getting the job? What are the sufficient conditions for getting the job?

4.   Assuming ordinary circumstances:

   a.   Is being eighteen years of age or older a necessary condition for being eligible to vote in a national election? A sufficient condition?

   b.   Is being a male a sufficient condition for being elected president of the United States? A necessary condition?

   c.   Is being a dog a sufficient condition for being a canine? A necessary condition?

   d.   Is the disjunction of being a man, or a woman, or a boy, or a girl a sufficient condition for being human? A necessary condition?

   e.   Is the presence of clouds a necessary condition for a snowfall? A sufficient condition?

   f.   Is being shot with a gun a necessary condition for death? A sufficient condition?

     g. Is the conjunction of an ounce of vodka, six ounces of orange juice, ice cubes, and a glass a sufficient condition for the creation of a screwdriver? A necessary condition?

5. Smart University offered five scholarships to seniors majoring in biology. Ten candidates applied. Their qualifications are shown in the chart below.

STUDENT	OVERALL B AVERAGE	A AVERAGE IN BIOLOGY	FAMILY INCOME UNDER $5,000	RECOMMENDATIONS BY TWO PROFESSORS	BROTHERS OR SISTERS AT THE SCHOOL	INTENTION TO TEACH
1	X	X	X	X		X
2	X	X	X	X	X	X
3	X	X				X
4	X		X	X		X
5	X	X	X	X	X	
6	X	X		X	X	
7	X		X	X		X
8	X				X	
9	X	X		X	X	X
10	X		X	X		X

Students 1, 2, 4, 5, and 7 received the scholarships. What can you identify as probably necessary and/or sufficient conditions of receiving the scholarship?

MILL'S METHODS

John Stuart Mill

Sherlock Holmes, after brilliantly deciphering some puzzling crime, used to favor his doctor friend with a superior smile and remark, "Elementary, my dear Watson—elementary!" He would then proceed to unfold a complicated chain of reasoning that, to ordinary mortals, appeared anything but elementary.

The great detective to the contrary, the process of determining the "cause" of anything is rarely "elementary," especially when inductive reasoning is involved. In the following sections we will discuss a set of inductive methods frequently used for determining necessary and sufficient conditions. They are known as 'Mill's methods', after the nineteenth-century British philosopher, John Stuart Mill, who did much to popularize them. Mill's own formulations of the methods have been superseded by others, but they are still called by the names he used. As with all inductive methods, these can be used only to establish the probability of a statement, not its absolute certainty.

Of the five methods with which Mill's name has become associated, we shall discuss the four most frequently used. It should be emphasized that what follows here is not exactly the way in which Mill presented the methods: We incorporate significant modifications which have been suggested by other logicians in the century since Mill's death. For example, this discussion will be based on the distinction between necessary and sufficient conditions, whereas Mill used the ambiguous notion of causes.

Like the hypothetico-deductive method discussed in Chapter 11, each of Mill's methods involves the formulation of a generalization about what might be necessary and/or sufficient conditions of an event and then the search for disconfirming instances. But, unlike the hypothetico-deductive method, which considers a single generalization, Mill's methods generally require that we begin by hypothesizing several possible conditions for the occurrence of the event.

THE METHOD OF AGREEMENT   The first (and perhaps most frequently used) of the five methods is the **method of agreement.** This method states that if, in every case in which an event or phenomenon occurs, a certain condition is present, and no other factor is common to all occurrences, then that condition is probably a necessary condition of the event or phenomenon. (The event or condition which exists or occurs first is said to be probably the necessary condition of the other.) This method will not by itself aid in the discovery of sufficient conditions.

To take a relatively simple case: Suppose the farmers in a particular region all raise stringbeans. Agents of the government agricultural service notice that the yields of different farms fall into two categories: Half the farms produce twice as many bushels of stringbeans per acre as the other half. The service wants to determine what caused the success of the more productive farmers so as to advise the others on ways to improve their crops. Rainfall, sunlight, and soil quality are approximately the same throughout the region; so, insofar as they are necessary conditions for the production of good crops, they are present already, both on the high-yield and on the low-yield farms. There must be at least one more necessary condition which is present only on the high-yield farms. Someone suggests that a certain type of fertilizer might be that condition, so the agents interview all the high-yield farmers to find out what fertilizers they use. It turns out that four commercial brands of fertilizer are popular with most of the growers using a combination of two or more. The findings are summarized in Figure 12–1, in which 'P' (present) is used to indicate that a particular farmer uses a particular fertilizer, 'A' (absent) that it is not used by that farmer. The table shows that the only fertilizer used by all of the high-yield farmers is Super-X. It therefore appears probable that Super-X (or one of its ingredients) is a necessary condition

FIGURE 12–1
Fertilizer Usage by High-yield Farmers

FERTILIZER USED	FARMER				
	1	2	3	4	5
Greengro	P	P	A	P	A
Bearwell	A	A	P	P	A
Super-X	P	P	P	P	P
Zippp	P	A	P	P	P

for high stringbean production in this region—that is, if Super-X were not present, the high yields would not occur.

The method of agreement has its limitations. If further research were to establish that another farmer (perhaps Farmer 97) used another brand of fertilizer, Formula Z, but did not use Super-X, and got equally high yields, we would have to reject Super-X as a necessary condition in and of itself. However, we could also modify our conclusion to assert that it is probable that a necessary condition is the use of *either* Super-X *or* Formula Z. Again, suppose that the five successful farmers had all used Zippp as well as Super-X. It would then be impossible, using the method of agreement alone, to determine whether the high yield had been caused by the Zippp, the Super-X, or a combination of the two. Also, given that a necessary condition can be a disjunction of conditions, one could conclude that the disjunction of Greengro *or* Zippp is a possible necessary condition. Additional tests would have to be run to rule this out. We must always be aware, therefore, that the use of the method of agreement by itself always exposes us to the risk of premature judgment.

A classic story illustrates the pitfalls of the method of agreement. It concerns the drunkard who reasons on Monday afternoon: "Friday night, I drank rye and soda and got drunk; Saturday night, I drank scotch and soda and got drunk; Sunday night, I drank bourbon and soda and got drunk. I must be getting drunk on soda. So tonight, I'll drink straight gin." In this case, the drinker is bound to discover on the morning after that not enough alternative possibilities were considered. But Monday night's experience by itself will have been sufficient to prove, at any rate, that soda is *not* a necessary condition for getting drunk.

In the case of the stringbean farmers, the necessary condition disclosed by the method of agreement was a positive factor—the presence of Super-X. This is a case, therefore, of positive agreement. Agreement may also be negative, when a necessary condition turns out to be not the presence but the absence of something.

An absent factor has been identified as a necessary condition of rickets, a bone disease that once caused widespread crippling, especially among children in northern Europe.[1] The disease was first noticed in England in the 1650s when the use of soft coal was introduced, and it spread through Europe with the Industrial Revolution (see map of England and Scotland).

Because many of the victims of rickets were poor, dietary deficiency was considered as a possible cause. But a medical study in 1889 made clear that rickets was associated more with city life than with poverty: in the cities, among rich and poor alike, it was more common than in country districts, even though the country diet, at this period, was often poorer.

Confinement was also offered as a tentative explanation. Animals in the London zoo, well cared for and comfortably housed, developed rickets, though

---

[1] The following information is drawn from W. F. Loomis, "Rickets," *Scientific American*, December 1970.

CORRELATION OF RICKETS with industrial areas and smoke from the burning of coal appeared in data assembled in 1889 by the British Medical Association. The map, which shows in gray the principal concentrations of rickets, is based on maps of England and Scotland prepared by the association. Since diets in these areas were in general better than those in poorer surrounding areas, the distribution of rickets is not what one would expect if the disease were of dietary origin. In actuality the cause was smoke that obscured sunlight.

Adapted from Scientific American, Dec. 1970, p. 79.

wild animals never seemed to. Other observations revealed that German babies born in the fall and dying in the spring were more likely to show skeletal evidence of rickets than those born in the spring and dying in the fall; and it was suggested that this was because spring-born infants had more chance of fresh air and exercise.

In 1890 an English medical missionary discovered that rickets was almost totally absent among the Japanese, even those who were poor or undernourished. Subsequent correspondence with colleagues elsewhere revealed that rickets was also rare or unknown in Manchuria and Mongolia, and that, in Java, European children who were suffering from rickets when they arrived recovered in a few months' time without medical treatment. In fact, it appeared, rickets was almost completely a northern European malady; elsewhere it was virtually unknown.

Then rickets did turn out to be prevalent in another area: among well-off Moslems and upper-caste Hindus in Bombay, India. Poor Hindus in the same region, in contrast, rarely developed it, despite their meager diet and abject living conditions.

The common factor in all these cases finally turned out to be an absence of sunlight. Winter sunlight in northern Europe is relatively weak, and the soft coal used in the factories created a heavy, smoky overcast which further obscured it. The industrial poor, who comprised the largest group of sufferers, lived in dark, cramped quarters on dark, narrow streets. Zoo animals in London suffered the effects of the smoke pall; zoo animals in cities with better sunlight remained rickets-free. German children whose rickets had seemed to be associated with confinement also suffered, of course, from lack of sunlight; so did caged puppies in whom rickets was experimentally produced. As for the Hindu and Moslem victims in sun-rich India, they were young mothers and their babies who, in accordance with custom, spent virtually all their time indoors, often in semidarkened rooms. The Hindu poor, like people in Manchuria, Mongolia, and Japan and like Europeans living at a distance from smoky industrial towns, were exposed to adequate amounts of sunlight, and did not develop rickets.

A chart of the findings might look like that in Figure 12–2. As can be seen, the only condition that remained constant for all of the high-rickets groups was the *absence* of sunlight, which could therefore be regarded as a probable necessary condition of the disease. Once this conclusion was reached, steps were taken to eliminate the condition, and the incidence of rickets thereupon decreased, giving proximate additional support to the conclusion.

Actually, the cause (in this case, the relevant necessary condition) of the disease has since been more precisely determined as lack of the hormone calciferol, which is needed for proper bone formation. The human body cannot synthesize calciferol without the aid of ultraviolet radiation, which it normally receives from sunlight. Strictly speaking, therefore, the necessary (and coincidentally, the sufficient) condition of rickets is lack of calciferol, and lack of sunlight is a more remote cause, a link in the causal chain. But it was the

FIGURE 12–2
Conditions Associated with High Incidence of Rickets

HIGH-RICKETS GROUPS	FACTORS CONSIDERED		
	Confinement	Malnutrition	Sunlight
English city poor	A	P	A
English city nonpoor	A	A	A
German fall-born babies	P	A	A
Upper-class Indian Moslems	P	A	A
Upper-caste Hindus	P	A	A
Caged puppies	P	A	A
London zoo animals	P	A	A

discovery of the role of sunlight, through the method of agreement, that pointed the way to fuller knowledge.

Although the method of agreement, when used correctly, can lead to the identification of necessary conditions, this is not a guaranteed way to solve certain kinds of problems. It is true that *if* we eliminate a necessary condition for an event, that event will not occur; but not all conditions are easily removed. For example, the method of agreement was properly applied in the Pogo

Copyright © Selby Kelly, Ex.

cartoon on p. 508 but the necessary condition so identified is clearly not one that can be eliminated. In fact, the necessary condition identified is part of the problem, since polluted air is considered to be undesirable precisely because it interferes with breathing.

THE METHOD OF DIFFERENCE   The **method of difference** can be stated as follows: If the conditions in two cases *appear* to be essentially the same, but the caused event or phenomenon occurs in only one of them, we should look for a condition which exists in this one but not in the other. This condition, when found, will be the probable sufficient condition of the phenomenon. (This method is not adequate for identifying necessary conditions.)

To illustrate this method, Mill suggests the case of a man who is shot in the heart and dies. Here the two cases involve the same individual—the man when alive and the man when dead. Having eliminated all other possible causes of death, we assume that the bullet wound is the sufficient condition, because it is the only circumstance that differs significantly from those present when the victim was alive. (Certainly, the time has changed, but, on the basis of other experience, it can be ruled out as a possible causal factor. A small change in time is a necessary condition of the death only in the trivial and uninteresting sense that no person can be both alive and dead at the same moment—it can in no way be a sufficient condition.)

Let us see how the method of difference applies to the recently proposed theory that music speeds the growth of plants. Is music in fact a sufficient condition for faster growth—that is, does plant growth improve whenever music is present, regardless of other factors?

It is known that many factors contribute to the growth of plants. In testing our hypothesis about music, we must first make sure that all other possibly significant factors—sunlight, temperature, humidity, soil conditions, and so on—are essentially the same for all the plants in the experiment. We then expose one group of plants—the experimental group—to music, but do not expose the other group. The presence or absence of music will be the only variable circumstance in the experiment.

The experiment might begin with the selection of several kinds of house plant: philodendron, kangaroo ivy, purple passion, and asparagus fern. Specimens of each of the four are placed in each of two rooms. The soil for each plant is the same; all of the plants receive the same food and amount of sunlight; the temperature of both rooms is identical, and so on. In room 1, however, classical music is played twenty-four hours a day; in room 2, no music is played. After two months, we measure the growth of the plants. The measurements show that all the plants in room 1 have grown significantly more than those in room 2. We conclude that music probably made the difference.

In this example, the phenomenon (better growth) occurs in one instance, but not in the other. One factor, classical music, was present in one instance but not in the other; all other factors known to be significant were the same for both groups of plants. From this it may reasonably be inferred that classical music is a sufficient condition for better plant growth—provided, of course, that no other differentiating condition slipped past the experimenter's notice. If we assume that none did, the table in Figure 12–3 serves to identify clssical music as a probable sufficient condition of increased plant growth.

FIGURE 12–3
Experimental Factors in Plant Growth

PLANT GROUPS	GROWTH FACTORS PRESENT				
	Optimum sunlight	Optimum temperature	Optimum humidity	Suitable food	Classical music
Room 1	P	P	P	P	P
Room 2	P	P	P	P	A

Having identified classical music as a probable sufficient condition for improved plant growth, we may reasonably conclude that, by adding classical music to a situation which already contains all of the necessary conditions for normal growth, we can induce the plants to grow better.

Again, it is important to note that the method of difference does not provide conclusive proof but only establishes probability. Perhaps further investigation might reveal that the better growth of plants in room 1 was not caused by the music at all. Perhaps the four plants in room 1 happened to be treated at the nursery with a special chemical called Groplant, and those in room 2 were not similarly treated. Such a finding would raise serious questions about the validity of the conclusion that music furthers plant growth. Further tests would have to be made in which the second differentiating factor, Groplant, was either eliminated or administered to all the plants in the experiment.

Another example of the use of the method of difference to determine a sufficient condition is the experiment carried out by Professors Robert Rosenthal and Lenore Jacobson concerning the effects of teacher expectation on pupil achievement. During the heyday of the War on Poverty in the 1960s, it was noted that children from socioeconomically disadvantaged backgrounds generally did less well in school than children of more affluent families. It was widely assumed that the principal cause (or sufficient condition) of these children's academic failure lay in the cultural deprivation arising from their background and environment and that massive programs of remedial instruction, cultural enrichment, and the like could remove the sufficient condition and allow the children to succeed.

Rosenthal and Jacobson hypothesized that—as they put it in a 1968 article describing their experiment—"at least some of the deficiencies . . . might be in the schools, and particularly in the attitudes of teachers toward disadvantaged children."[2] They therefore devised an experiment to test this hypothesis.

Since—if they were correct—disadvantaged children who were failing were doing so, not primarily because of cultural deprivation, but because their teachers expected them to fail, it was necessary to change this expectation, in the case of some children, to an expectation of success without changing any of the other relevant conditions. If, in these circumstances, disadvantaged children did succeed, it could reasonably be supposed that the positive expectations of their teachers provided the sufficient condition for their success; and, therefore, it could also be inferred that the former negative expectations had been a sufficient condition of their failure.

In a certain California elementary school (called Oak School in the report), all the children from kindergarten through fifth grade were given a "Test of Inflected Acquisition." Teachers were told that the test was designed to predict which children would show unusual intellectual growth in the next year or two. In fact, the test was an ordinary standardized intelligence test; the important thing was not what it showed, but what the teachers thought it showed.

The test was given in the spring, and was supposedly sent to Harvard for scoring. In the fall, the teachers were told—casually and as if almost by chance—which of the children could be expected to "spurt" ahead academically in the coming year.

In reality, the names of the "spurters" had been chosen randomly, with no reference to the test. There were four or five of them in each classroom, and they included slow, average, and fast-track learners. Nothing special was done for them; the only way in which, as a group, they differed from their schoolmates was that their teachers had been told they were likely to improve.

Over the next two years, the children were tested three more times. The results showed, interestingly, that both the experimental group (the spurters) and the control group (those not designated as spurters) had made gains in I.Q. But in some grades—particularly the first and second—the gains shown by the spurters far outdistanced those of the control-group children. In these two grades, nearly 80 percent of the spurters gained at least ten points in I.Q., compared with about 50 percent of the control group; over 20 percent of the spurters gained at least thirty I.Q. points, compared with 5 or 6 percent of the control group. It appeared probable, therefore, that, at least in the early grades, the teacher's expectation that a pupil would improve was a sufficient condition for improvement. And, since the children who improved included some from disadvantaged backgrounds, the experiment seemed to show that, contrary to general opinion, the condition of being socioeconomically disadvantaged was *not* a sufficient condition for academic failure.

[2] Robert Rosenthal and Lenore F. Jacobson, "Teacher Expectations for the Disadvantaged." *Scientific American,* April 1968. All information in the following account is drawn from this article.

How does this experiment illustrate use of the method of difference? First, the pupils were divided into two groups corresponding to the two cases of the method of difference. The groups were chosen in such a way that, as groups, they were essentially alike in all characteristics thought to be significant for the phenomenon under study (intellectual improvement). Next, one characteristic or condition (teacher expectation) was changed for the experimental group. The phenomenon of intellectual improvement was then observed to occur to a significantly greater degree in the experimental group than in the control group. This led to the conclusion that the one condition in which the two groups differed was probably a sufficient condition for greater improvement. If, instead, improvement had occurred among the advantaged children and not among the disadvantaged, the socioeconomic difference would have been shown to be a probable sufficient condition.

EXERCISE 12–4   *Which method does the following example illustrate? What is the causal condition? Is it a necessary or a sufficient condition, or both? How can you tell?*

On the morning of November 1, the Jonesburg police department received phone calls from twelve different local merchants. All reported that plate glass windows in their stores had been cracked or broken during the night. It looked like an outbreak of vandalism. Officer Brody investigated the complaints. He found that, while all the windows were badly cracked, there were only two in which pieces of glass had been knocked out and that no merchandise had been taken from any of the stores. Hence theft did not appear to be a motive. Then he tried to establish some pattern of similarity among the stores. They included two supermarkets, one delicatessen, three pharmacies, one shoe store, two small department stores, one hardware store, a sporting-goods store, and a drycleaning establishment. Seven of the proprietors were members of the Rotary Club; one of the seven and one other were Poles (Poles constituted a minority group in Jonesburg, and, in general, were slightly looked down upon). All twelve had been among thirty local merchants who had donated space for a Halloween window-painting competition for local children sponsored by the volunteer fire department. The broken windows were still covered with the colorful pictures, which had been painted directly on the glass.

Officer Brody's wife, a physics teacher at the local high school, finally came up with the solution. There had been a sharp frost on Halloween night. All the affected windows were so located that they had caught the full rays of the early sun the next morning. Because the paint on each was of different colors in different spots, the areas of the glass had expanded at different rates in the sudden warmth, and the strain of the differential expansion had resulted in cracking.

EXERCISE 12–5   *Which of Mill's methods is illustrated by the following examples?*

---

1. In ancient times, men noticed that, if a substance such as meat was kept around for too long, it became infested with maggots or other such insects. From this, a belief

grew up that these creatures were actually produced by the decaying meat. This theory of spontaneous generation—that living organisms can be produced naturally by inanimate matter—was long accepted, until in the nineteenth century Pasteur decided to test it. He placed meat broth in a flask, boiled it to destroy all bacteria, and sealed the flask. After some time he examined the liquid and found it still free of bacteria. Then he left it exposed to the air for a time. In a few hours it contained bacteria and was beginning to decay. Pasteur concluded that the bacteria had entered the broth from the air rather than being spontaneously generated by the broth itself.

2. An examination of patients suffering from a type of blindness called keratitis showed that they had only one thing in common other than the blindness: a deficiency of riboflavin in their diet. The patients were then given large does of riboflavin, and the condition soon cleared up. Therefore, a lack of riboflavin must be the cause of keratitis.

EXERCISE 12–6

In the following problem, identify the causal condition, tell whether it is a necessary or a sufficient condition, and indicate the method used to find it.

On October 23, 1999, a large meteor split apart in the sky over the United States, and pieces of it landed in four different areas of the country. Almost immediately, most of the identifiable pieces were picked up by astronomers and amateur collectors. Early in December, doctors in two of these regions began seeing patients afflicted with a new and unidentified disease. The attacks were invariably severe and almost always brought death within three or four days. Whatever the infection was, the human immune system seemed unable to build up a defense against it. Strict quarantine was imposed on the affected regions, and medical researchers hastily began seeking a cure or a preventive.

Because of the timing, location, and virulence of the outbreaks of disease, and the identity of the first victims (all people who had been in direct contact with the meteoric rock), it was generally assumed that the cause must be associated somehow with the rocks. Cautiously, geologists began assessing their content.

Rock from the first of the affected regions turned out to contain about 20 percent carbon compounds, about 20 percent quartz crystal, about 30 percent various common volcanic minerals, and about 30 percent of an unknown substance, provisionally labeled zeroz. Rock from the other affected region was 30 percent iron and manganese, 40 percent zeroz, and 30 percent quartz crystal. Rock from the two unaffected regions was also checked: The first proved to contain about 40 percent iron, 30 percent other common volcanic minerals, and 30 percent zeroz. Rock from the fourth region was about 10 percent carbon compounds, 70 percent iron and manganese, and 20 percent quartz crystal.

What was the "cause" of the new disease?

THE JOINT METHOD OF AGREEMENT AND DIFFERENCE

We noted, in discussing the method of agreement, that when used by itself it is somewhat weak. It may lead us to identify, as the necessary condition of an event, something which is not really necessary, or it may not give us enough data to allow us to distinguish the necessary condition from accompanying coincidental circumstances. For example, if the successful stringbean farmers had all used Greengro as well as Super-X, we could not be sure, without making additional tests, which fertilizer was responsible for their better crops.

Sometimes we can add the method of difference to the method of agreement by taking away the single circumstance believed to be a necessary condition. If the event then does not occur, our conclusion that we have identified a necessary condition will be strengthened. But it is not always possible to do this. We may not be able to find two instances which are alike in all but this one circumstance, or the circumstance may be one which for some reason cannot be removed. In such a case, we may be able to use what, since Mill, has been called the **joint method of agreement and difference.**

In this method we first use the method of agreement to find a probable necessary condition. We then look for a number of cases in which the phenomenon under study does *not* occur. Without worrying about whether they resemble the first group of cases in all other respects (as we would have to do in using the method of difference), we look only to see if the suspected causal factor is missing. If it is missing from all of them, not only will our belief that this factor is indeed a necessary condition of the phenomenon be further justified, but we will have reason to believe that it may be a sufficient condition as well.

As an example, let us consider again the matter of rickets and its cause. We have described how the use of the method of agreement indicated lack of sunlight as a probable necessary condition of the disease. Now, it would have been possible to set up a method-of-difference experiment, in which two groups of children would have been maintained in precisely the same way, save that one group would have been exposed to sunlight and the other cut off from it. Such an experiment might well have tended to confirm the previous conclusion, but it would also have deliberately exposed half of the children to high risk of a serious and permanently crippling disease. Some other method of checking the conclusion was clearly preferable.

We have already noted that several population groups had been found to be generally free of rickets. These groups, that is, constituted a set of cases in which the phenomenon did not occur. They included, among others, English rural poor, Japanese poor, low-caste Hindus, Manchurians, Mongolians, puppies raised outdoors, and wild animals. When these were rated on the same factors as the rickets groups, it was found that some of the factors were present for each group, but that the only factor common to all of them was the absence of the lack-of-sunlight factor. That is, all the groups which did not tend to develop rickets had a fairly plentiful exposure to sunlight. A table of the findings would look more or less like Figure 12–4.

If this table is compared with that in Figure 12–2, it will be seen that the same factor (sunlight) which was absent for all the high-rickets groups was present for all the low-rickets groups. This not only serves to strengthen the conclusion, already arrived at, that absence of sunlight is a necessary condition of rickets, but implies that it may also be a sufficient condition as well—since, in *every* group for

FIGURE 12–4
Conditions Associated with Low Incidence of Rickets

LOW-RICKETS GROUPS	FACTORS CONSIDERED		
	Confinement	Malnutrition	Sunlight
English rural poor	A	P	P
Japanese poor	A	P	P
Low-caste Hindus	A	P	P
Manchurians	A	P	P
Mongolians	A	A	P
Puppies raised outdoors	A	A	P
Wild animals	A	A	P

which absence of sunlight was found, the incidence of rickets was high, and no other significant conditions appear to have been shared by these groups.

THE METHOD OF CONCOMITANT VARIATIONS

The **method of concomitant variations** is useful when one seeks the cause of changes which occur along a continuum, such as a gradual increase in the divorce rate or an economic decline. It can be stated as follows: If a change in one phenomenon is found to occur every time a certain change in another phenomenon occurs, and if the degree of change in one phenomenon varies consistently with the degree of change in the other, then either: (1) the change in the first phenomenon is the cause of the change in the second; (2) the change in the second phenomenon is the cause of the change in the first; or (3) a third factor is the cause of the change in both.

The word 'concomitant' means 'accompanying' or 'corresponding', and the point of the method of concomitant variations is to find a phenomenon which varies in proportion as the studied phenomenon varies—either at the same time or with a consistent time lag between them.

Statistical studies rely heavily on the method of concomitant variations. Social scientists use it constantly to show relationships between phenomena— unemployment and marriage breakup, slum housing and crime, amount of education and family size, and so on. Certain economic theories are grounded in it in the relations among such things as supply, demand, and price. For instance, if the supply of a commodity remains constant and the demand for it goes up, an economist would expect the price to rise along with the demand. If the demand remains constant but the supply decreases, the price would also be expected to rise. The first of these illustrates *positive* concomitant variation in which both factors vary in the same direction. The second case demonstrates *inverse* variation in which one factor increases as the other decreases.

Medical research, too, employs the method, to show the connection between some particular illness and its suggested cause. An excellent illustration of this is the research on the harmful effects of cigarette smoking. A connection between smoking and cancer was suspected as long ago as 1859, when a French physician noticed that nearly all those of his patients who suffered from cancer of the areas around the mouth were smokers. Almost a century later, after cigarette smoking became increasingly popular, Drs. Alton Ochsner and Michael De Bakey in New Orleans observed that most of their growing number of lung cancer patients were cigarette smokers. Other observations sharpened the suspicion, and eventually some full-scale controlled studies were undertaken. In one of these, a study by Hammond and Horn, a total of 187,783 men were questioned about their past and present smoking habits. These men were then kept track of for nearly four years. During this time, 11,870 of them died, and for each of these the cause of death was recorded.

The findings were quite unequivocal. In Hammond's words, "The total death rate (from all causes of death combined) is far higher among men with a history of regular cigarette smoking than among men who never smoked." Furthermore, "Death rates rose progressively with increasing number of cigarettes smoked per day. . . . The death rate of those who smoked two or more packs of cigarettes a day was approximately two and a quarter times higher than the death rate of men who never smoked." The co-variation of cigarette smoking and death rate, as it appeared in this study, is made very clear in Figure 12–5.

The study also showed that the rates of death from certain diseases varied greatly in accordance with smoking habits. The rate for coronary artery disease

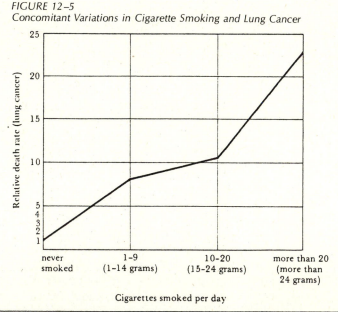

FIGURE 12–5
Concomitant Variations in Cigarette Smoking and Lung Cancer

was 70 percent higher among smokers; that for lung cancer was more than ten times higher. In each case, the death rate rose progressively as the habitual daily number of cigarettes increased; and in each case, also, the death rate for those who had once been smokers but had stopped smoking was lower than that for active smokers but higher than that for those who had never smoked.

In this and similar studies, the method of concomitant variations was used to show a strong probability that cigarette smoking is a cause of certain diseases. Since the frequency of death from such diseases increased as cigarette smoking increased and decreased as cigarette smoking decreased, it was highly likely that one was a cause of the other; and cigarette smoking was more likely to be the cause than the effect. In this case, however, it does not appear that either a necessary or a sufficient condition is involved, since some people with lung cancer and other fatal diseases have never smoked, and some very heavy smokers live very long lives with no such diseases. This is why researchers are looking for more basic "causes" of such deaths—for truly necessary or sufficient conditions.

The relationship between cigarette smoking and lung cancer is a positive one, as the graph shows. In the case of a negative or inverse relationship, such as that of the hypothetical sales estimates shown in Figure 12–6, the curve of the graph slants in the other direction. Here the sales manager for Superlative Widgets,

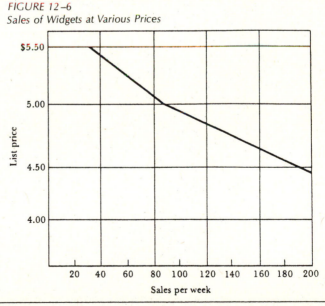

FIGURE 12–6
Sales of Widgets at Various Prices

From Robert Dorfman. The Price System. © 1964. Reprinted by permission of Prentice-Hall, Inc., Englewood Cliffs, New Jersey.

Inc., has calculated how many widgets the company has sold per week at each of several prices. At a price of $5.50, only about thirty were sold; but when the price was lowered to $4.50, weekly sales increased to nearly two hundred. At a price of $5.00, sales reached about eighty per week. Sales at other prices varied more or less consistently along the curve, so the company can now decide on a price which will bring in the best over-all profit.

Sometimes it is hard to tell whether concomitant variations are present or not. For example, psychiatrists Arnold Lieber and Carolyn Sherin conducted a study of possible associations between the cycles of the moon and human emotional disturbance.[3] They obtained homicide records for two counties over periods of fifteen and thirteen years, respectively, and matched the dates of the homicides against the monthly cycle of the moon—new, first quarter, full, and so on. The results are shown in the two graphs in Figure 12–7.

FIGURE 12–7
Homicides in Two U.S. Counties, Plotted in Relation to the Lunar Monthly Cycle

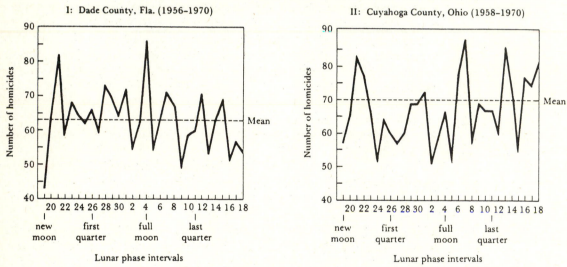

From Arnold L. Lieber, M.D., and Carolyn R. Sherin, Ph.D., "Homicides and the Lunar Cycle: Toward a Theory of Lunar Influence on Human Emotional Disturbance," American Journal of Psychiatry, *July 1972, Vol. 129, pp. 68–77. Copyright 1972, The American Psychiatric Association.*

Here there is no clear relationship, as there was in the case of smoking and lung cancer. However, in both counties the pattern of homicides seems to reach a peak at or just after the full moon. In other respects the two graphs are

[3] Arnold L. Lieber, M.D., and Carolyn R. Sherin, Ph.D., "Homicides and the Lunar Cycle: Toward a Theory of Lunar Influence on Human Emotional Disturbance," *American Journal of Psychiatry,* July 1972.

somewhat different. It is reasonable to suppose, of course, that so complex an event as homicide would be influenced by many conditioning factors, so we would not expect it to vary consistently with any one of these factors alone. Lieber and Sherin, evaluating the data summarized in these graphs and relating it to findings in other studies, concluded that the pattern of homicide in the two counties did, in fact, support their hypothesis of a relation between homicide and the lunar cycle—that is, that underneath all other influential factors, there is a concomitant variation of homicide and the phases of the moon. Other investigators might have interpreted the results differently; for the scientific community in general, the question remains open.

REPLICABILITY AND CONTROLS   There are two fundamental requirements which most scientists (and many others) normally adhere to in applying any of Mill's methods.

      The first is **replicability,** that is, the condition that other persons than the original investigator should be able to carry out the same study in essentially the same way and arrive at the same results. This is basically a theoretical requirement; it is only necessary that the experiment *can* be done by someone else with the same results. In reality, many experiments never are replicated, due to economic and other restrictions; many simply fit in well with researchers' expectations based on general theory-based principles and related observations by others. But many claims which are made by various individuals and which are claimed to be "scientific" are clearly not repeatable and are also in direct conflict with what are considered to be well-established theories. Although this does not prove that the claims are false, it certainly weakens their support for most people, and, at the very least, puts an additional burden of proof on the persons making these claims.

      One example of a nonreplicable experiment is that dealing with the ability of plants to react to thoughts of persons in their vicinity. A researcher claimed that he had attached electronic monitoring devices to the leaves of plants in a special laboratory. He and other persons in the lab would then think either positive thoughts about the plants, or they would think negative thoughts about them (such as about breaking off a leaf or even destroying them). The plants would give off very different electrical signals when the people were thinking bad thoughts than when they were thinking good ones. However, when other researchers tried to do the same experiment, they got the same signals no matter what they were thinking. The original researcher responded that they simply had not replicated his experiment because the people in the lab were not the same ones as when he had run it. He suggested that the plants had sensed that they were genuinely hostile people and that the plants were either too frightened or otherwise upset to give any other responses.

      Other claims are not replicable on more basic grounds. For example, claims about UFOs (unidentified flying objects) and miracles are such that there is no way in which they can be controlled or manipulated as required by any observers, and one cannot even arrange to be in a position to observe such events.

This is also true of large-scale social phenomena for which it is impossible, for political, practical, and other reasons, to replicate the circumstances surrounding an event, such as a major economic depression, a riot, or a war. This is only one reason it is extremely difficult to provide any kind of a reasonable account of the cause—or necessary and sufficient conditions—of such significant events. Another problem also associated with cases of this kind is the problem of controls.

It is very important in using Mill's methods in most cases to have a considerable degree of confidence that all possible relevant factors are known and are being held constant or are varied as we require in the given case. Thus, for example, in using the method of difference, it is necessary to assume that all the factors in all the cases under consideration are the same except for the specific factors which are being considered as possible sufficient conditions. In some cases, we can only examine the cases as carefully as possible and then hope that the various factors have all been recognized and taken into consideration. But in other cases there are more definite steps we can take to make sure that what we have identified is really a necessary or sufficient condition. This is well illustrated by a case from the history of science.

Before the nineteenth century, it was widely believed that there was a kind of spontaneous generation of living creatures analogous to what we know today as a spontaneous generation of fires. In brief, it was believed that, by putting together the proper mix of substances, such as water, air, wood, straw, and salt, under proper conditions for certain periods of time, it was possible to cause the creation of all sorts of animals, including geese, lambs, and frogs. The seventeenth-century Belgain experimenter, van Helmont, designed an experiment which he believed demonstrated that mice would be spontaneously generated from human sweat (e.g., from dirty clothes) and wheat in exactly twenty-one days. He used what appears to be a version of the method of difference, showing that a dirty shirt by itself, and wheat by itself, would not be sufficient, but that the two together are sufficient for producing mice in twenty-one days. What he failed to do was to introduce appropriate controls to rule out other possible factors from coming into play, such as mice being attracted by the wheat and establishing a nest in the dirty shirt. A recent textbook has suggested that appropriate controls would have involved placing the dirty shirt and wheat in a sealed wooden box. (See illustration, "The Origin of Living Things.") The control suggested in this illustration is *not,* however, appropriate. If no mice had been generated in the box after the specified period of time, it could have been argued that other factors such as light and fresh air were also necessary for the spontaneous generation of mice. A better control would have been something like a screen or cage which would not let mice in (or out) but would allow sunlight and air to enter.

In brief, we must always be as careful as possible to make certain that we have adequately considered *all* of the possibly relevant factors in applying Mill's Methods and to try to set up effective **controls** to keep extraneous factors from influencing the results.

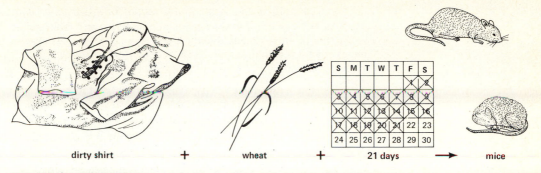

dirty shirt   +   wheat   +   21 days ⟶ mice

VAN HELMONT'S "RECIPE"

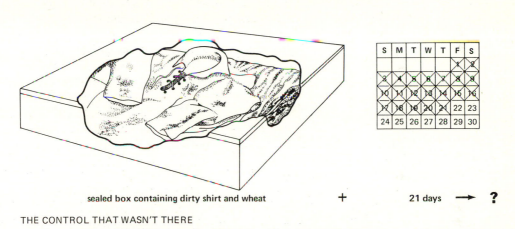

sealed box containing dirty shirt and wheat   +   21 days ⟶ **?**

THE CONTROL THAT WASN'T THERE

From: Biological Sciences—Molecules to Man, *Biological Sciences Curriculum Study (Boston: Houghton Mifflin, 1963).*

EXERCISE 12–7   *Each of the following accounts involves the use of one of Mill's methods. For each, tell (1) which method was used; (2) whether the causal condition discovered was necessary, sufficient, or both.*

---

1.   The Visor Television Company shipped 1,000 portable television sets to a large department store chain. During the next three months, 115 of the sets were returned. In each case, the picture reception was good, but there was no sound. Examining the first group of ten returned sets, a plant inspection supervisor noticed that, in every set, a certain wire to the speaker was improperly soldered. She also noticed that the same person—Bill Evans, a fairly new employee—had done the soldering.

The supervisor inspected the next group of returned sets and found the same improperly soldered wire in each. She concluded that Bill Evans' faulty soldering was the cause of the problem. She returned the sets to Bill with the necessary instructions; later, as other sets with the same defect were returned, she sent these to him as well.

2. It is now generally accepted that the addition of fluorine to drinking water helps to prevent or reduce tooth decay. One of the experiments by which this fact was established was conducted in two communities on the Hudson River. In each community a group of about 1,000 children was chosen; the children were selected so that each of the two groups had about the same number of cavities. Then, for ten years, a small amount of sodium fluoride was added to the water supply of one community; none was added to that of the other. At the end of the ten-year period, the two study groups were checked again, and the group which had received fluoridated water was found to have significantly fewer cavities than the other group. The fluorine was considered the cause of the difference.

3. A sociologist conducted a survey of ten families to determine the relationship, if any, between a family's total income and its expenditures on recreation and entertainment. A summary of the findings appears in the following table:

FAMILY INCOME	APPROXIMATE TOTAL RECREATION AND ENTERTAINMENT EXPENDITURE	
	IN DOLLARS	AS A PERCENTAGE OF TOTAL INCOME
5,000	500	10.0
7,500	650	8.7
12,500	1,100	8.8
17,500	1,450	8.3
22,500	1,600	7.1
27,500	2,000	7.3
32,500	2,300	7.1
42,500	2,800	6.6
75,000	3,600	4.8
100,000	5,500	5.5

4. Professor Stein frowned as he studied the seven Philosophy 104 examination papers spread out on his desk. All seven contained a major error in the third essay question; and all the errors were essentially the same, even to the wording. He examined the papers again. There was a suspicious similarity in some of the correct answers as well. Clearly there had been cheating, either during the examination or before. He looked up his records of the seven students. Two were sophomores, the rest juniors. Furthermore, they were in two different sections of the course, which meant, according to the standard practice at High Rise University, that they had taken the exam in two different rooms. This seemed to rule out collusion during the time of the exam. Someone must have got hold of the questions beforehand and either studied them with the others or prepared a crib sheet which the rest had used. Professor Stein called the office of the Dean of Students and asked to know the residence of the students involved. He found that all seven were members of the very exclusive X Fraternity and lived in its residence. None of the other students in either section of the course was a member of X Fraternity, and there was no indication in the papers that any others had participated in this particular piece of cheating. The professor still had no idea how the questions had been obtained, but he concluded that they had been, quite deliberately, circulated only within X Fraternity.

5. Researchers at the state agricultural laboratories were seeking a means of immunizing poultry against a new virus disease, and had developed several varieties of a vaccine which looked hopeful. To test them, they isolated 500 newly hatched chicks for six days, one day longer than the usual incubation period of the disease. Because none of the chicks became ill, it was clear that they had not contracted the virus, either since hatching or while still in the egg. The chicks were then separated into five groups of 100 each, and each of the first four groups was inoculated with a different one of the four vaccines being tested. The fifth group was given no inoculation. All groups were given the same diet and living conditions. A week later, all 500 chicks were deliberately exposed to the virus. Within ten days, 90 of the chicks in group 5 were dead; 48 of those in group 4; 6 of those in group 3; 59 of those in group 2; and 62 of those in group 1. The researchers concluded that the vaccine given to group 3 furnished a high degree of protection against the virus.

6. Phil and Doris McCabe had never had any particular trouble with their telephone until one fall it went dead three times in two weeks. On each occasion, it came back on by itself in a couple of days. The phone company repairman could find nothing wrong with the instrument or the interior connection, and no one else on the block was having comparable difficulties. The McCabes did not know what to think. Then, a week later, Doris was in the middle of a business call when the phone went dead again. She glared at the receiver, muttered something unladylike, and hung up. Going to the window, she stared out in disgust at the driving November rain. Suddenly she recalled that on each previous occasion when the phone had gone dead, there had also been heavy, driving rain. "I wonder . . .," she said aloud, and made a point of noting that the rain was slanting in from the east, on a fairly strong wind. That night she told Phil her idea. The next day, Saturday, Phil got out the ladder and checked the east wall of the house. Sure enough, high up under the eaves, where the telephone wires from outside were led into the wall, a small patch of insulation on the wires was worn thin and cracked, and the area was still damp from yesterday's rain. A call to the local newspaper office on Monday—by then the phone had turned itself on again—confirmed that on the three earlier occasions the rain had also been driving from the east. Apparently, given the location of the damaged part of the wire, only such a rain could reach the worn spot and penetrate it, thus temporarily short-circuiting the wires.

7. Ed Kolchak, building manager of the New Parkview Apartments, put down the phone and wearily made a note on his desk pad. Then he buzzed the maintenance man on the intercom. "Tim, go up to 16J and check the thermostat. They're having trouble too."

"Another one!" Tim's voice sounded unbelieving. "Mr. Kolchak, this is crazy! How many's that make—nine, no, ten people telling us their heat don't come on right, just since we started up the furnace three days ago. You reckon mebbe somebody dropped a shoe down the duct or something, when they was building this place?"

"Lord only knows. Go on up and see what you can do, anyhow."

"Okay, Mr. Kolchak. But I sure would like to know—" Tim's voice trailed off as he hung up. Ed grinned wryly at the "shoe" hypothesis. There were always bugs in a new building; with luck they'd clear up before really cold weather set in. If not, there would be a lot more complaining tenants.

The next morning, Tim was waiting at the office when Ed came in at 8:30. "Hey, Mr. Kolchak, you know that thermostat business; I got an idea, only I need your okay to check it out."

"What's that?"

"Well, I remembered last night, all of a sudden, that my brother knows a guy that worked on this place when they was building it, so I got his number and called him up, and asked did he know anything funny about the heating system. He says no and wants to know why, so I told him the trouble we was having, and then he says, 'Hey, you know, maybe there is something.' He says, 'Seems to me I remember some guy telling me the contractor had shortchanged them on thermostats, and they was having to go out and buy some somewhere else to get the job done on time. The guy was real sore about it. Maybe it's those odd-lot thermostats that ain't working right.' You reckon we ought to check it, Mr. Kolchak?"

Ed was impressed. "Sure, go ahead. Maybe you're onto something. You have a list of the apartments involved?—Wait a second." His phone was ringing. He picked it up. "Kolchak here—yes—all right, Mr. Lomaki, we'll look into it. Thanks for letting me know. I'll send someone up right away." He hung up. "Add 16M to that list, Tim."

By the end of the day it seemed that Tim's hunch had been right. All of the malfunctioning thermostats had been manufactured by the same company. Tim also checked about twenty apartments where no trouble had been reported and found that only one of their thermostats was of this brand. Clearly, there was a strong probability that a fault in this particular brand of thermostat was the cause of the heating problem, and Ed Kolchak began making arrangements to have the thermostats replaced.

EXERCISE 12–8   *Which of Mill's methods is illustrated by each of the following examples?*

---

1. Two randomly selected troups of people listened to a recorded statement concerning the need for a national compulsory health insurance plan. One group was told that the statement was made by the Surgeon-General, and the other group was informed that it was made by a college student. In the former group, the statement was universally considered persuasive; the second group unanimously found it unpersuasive. (F. S. Haiman, "An Experimental Study of the Effects of Ethos in Public Speaking," *Speech Magazine*, 16 (1949), pp. 190–202.)

2. Scientists were interested in learning why, in some cadavers, rigor mortis sets in soon after death and lasts for a relatively short time, while in others it begins late and lasts for a longer time. Observations showed that, in the cases of late and long rigor mortis, at least one of several conditions was usually present: Either the person had been in good health and well nourished at the time of death, or he had been well rested, or he had been subject to cold temperatures. Early and brief rigor mortis was usually associated with poor nutrition, or physical exhaustion caused by intense exercise, or convulsions brought on by disease. Eventually it was found that the common factor present in all cases of late rigor mortis was a high degree of what Mill called "muscular irritability"—strong reaction of muscles to an electrical impulse. This irritability seemed to be a result of the other conditions noted. The conditions associated with early rigor mortis all resulted in a low degree of muscular irritability. Thus, high muscular irritability at time of death was established as probably the proximate cause of late and prolonged rigor mortis.

EXERCISE 12–9   1. Which of Mill's methods is most appropriate to the following? On the basis of the evidence: (a) What seems to be the "cause" of Mr. Johnson's insomnia; (b) Does it seem to be a necessary condition, a sufficient condition, or both?

Mr. Johnson, a young stockbroker, was suffering from insomnia. To locate the cause of the sleeplessness, he began keeping a list of all the things he did and all the food he ate after arriving home from work. On Monday, he had a dinner of filet of sole, a baked potato, string beans, cole slaw, vanilla ice cream, and coffee with cream. Afterward, he smoked a big cigar. He read part of an exciting novel and then jogged for a mile. Just before going to bed he ate a cream-filled doughnut, kissed his wife, and glanced out the window to notice a brilliant full moon. On Tuesday, he had a meal of steak, mashed potatoes with mushroom gravy, green beans, blueberries and cream, and tea with lemon. Again he smoked a big cigar. He finished reading his novel, watched the later news, kissed his wife, and noticed that the moon was beginning to wane. On Wednesday, he had spaghetti and meatballs, a green salad, and beer, skipped dessert, and smoked a big cigar. He jogged for a mile, watched a mystery show on television, and had a snack of pretzels and coke. Before going to bed he kissed his wife and saw that the moon was still waning. On all three occasions he did not sleep. On Thursday, dinner consisted of veal cutlets, yams, asparagus, apple pie, and a bottle of wine. Afterward he smoked a big cigar. He listened to records, kissed his wife, and saw that the moon was continuing to wane. That night he slept well. On Friday, he ate corned beef and cabbage, mashed potatoes, beets, sliced peaches, and tea with lemon. His wife went out to a late meeting, and he went to bed before she returned. He slept as fitfully as before. On Saturday, he worked outdoors all afternoon, and had a cocktail before dinner. The meal was filet of sole, spaghetti, tortoni, and coffee with cream. He read the latest issue of the *National Geographic*, kissed his wife, ate a jelly doughnut, and did not sleep. On Sunday, he took the family out for a day at the beach with some neighbors. He ate potato chips, hot dogs with sauerkraut and mustard, cotton candy, and beer. At home he watched a horror movie on television, kissed his wife, and was too tired to notice the moon. On Monday, he awoke refreshed from a good night's sleep. For dinner that night, he had meat loaf and mashed potatoes with carrots and peas, a green salad, tea, and a big cigar. Before going to bed he jogged for a mile and kissed his wife. That night he slept well.

2. The table below lists the price–earnings ratio of Dow-Jones Industrial Stocks and the national unemployment rate over a period of nineteen years. Do you agree with Malabre's conclusion? If he is correct, which of Mill's methods is demonstrated by these figures?

YEAR	PRICE–EARNINGS RATIO	UNEMPLOYMENT RATE
1948	7.7	3.4
1949	8.5	5.5
1950	7.7	5.0
1951	10.1	3.0
1952	11.8	2.7
1953	10.3	2.5
1954	14.4	5.0
1955	13.7	4.0
1956	15.0	3.8
1957	12.1	4.3
1958	20.9	6.8
1959	19.8	5.5
1960	19.1	5.6
1961	22.9	6.7
1962	17.4	5.6
1963	18.5	5.7
1964	18.8	5.2
1965	18.1	4.6
1966	13.6	3.8

Analyze the figures (by means of a graph, if possible) and compare your findings with the following statement:

A relative scarcity of manpower, as indicated by a low unemployment rate, has seemed to go hand-in-hand with low price–earnings ratios, while ratios have been high in years that a high unemployment rate indicated free availability of men for industry to hire. (Alfred L. Malabre, *The Wall Street Journal*, August 29, 1967.)

EXERCISE 12–10   *Each of the following illustrates the use of more than one of Mill's methods. Tell which and identify the probable necessary and/or sufficient conditions.*

---

1. An old man was picked up on the streets of Manhattan one morning, clearly in bad shape—rigid with cramps, in a state of shock, and blue around the fingers and lips from a condition known as cyanosis. At the hospital, a tentative diagnosis of gas poisoning was made, and the man was given treatment. After about two hours, his condition began to improve. During the day, ten other men with similar symptoms were admitted at several hospitals in the same area. All were elderly, in poor general health, and semiderelict. All had eaten breakfast that morning at a certain cheap cafeteria, and all but one had had oatmeal, rolls, and coffee. The last had had only oatmeal. All were heavy drinkers.

The first diagnosis was not wholly convincing, for some of the usual symptoms of gas poisoning were missing. Besides, the cafeteria was the only place in which all the men could have been poisoned, and they had been there at times varying from 7 to 10 A.M. If the cafeteria had been full of gas for three hours, there should have been many more victims.

Because all the men had eaten oatmeal, investigators considered food poisoning, but the symptoms were wrong. For one thing, the trouble had started too soon after eating, and too suddenly. Could a drug be involved? A blood test was made, and it showed that the men had, in fact, consumed some sort of drug.

An investigator visited the cafeteria and took samples of everything that would have been used in preparing the men's breakfast—including dry oatmeal, sugar, salt from the small can on the stove, and salt from the big supply can which was used to refill the small one. He also took some saltpetre (sodium nitrate) from a can which stood alongside the salt supply can. Saltpetre looks very much like regular salt. Tests of all these samples were made, and it was discovered that the "salt" in the small can and the "saltpetre" in the second large can were really sodium *nitrite*—a substance which is legally used for some of the same purposes as sodium nitrate, but which is poisonous in more than small quantities. Apparently the cook had inadvertently refilled the small can from the wrong large one, and had consequently used sodium nitrite instead of salt in preparing the oatmeal.

But a test batch of oatmeal showed that the amount of nitrite in a single portion was less than a toxic dose. That explained why none of the other people who had eaten oatmeal that morning had been poisoned. How, then, had these eleven men got enough extra nitrite to make up the difference? A check of the saltshakers on the cafeteria tables revealed that one of them contained a high percentage of nitrite. If the men had sat at that table, if they had used salt—as some people do—instead of sugar on their oatmeal, and if they had each used about a full teaspoon, they would have got a toxic dose of the poison.

By now the men were out of the hospitals and could not be traced, but the explanation seemed reasonable. Still—why would they have put so *much* salt on their oatmeal? Someone remembered that they were all heavy drinkers. Such people usually have a low level of sodium chloride in their blood and tend to eat extra salt to compensate. This seemed to answer the final question. (Adapted from Berton Rouché, *Eleven Blue Men*, N.Y.: Berkley Publishing Corp., 1955.)

2. The Peterson Motor Company began distribution of its new compact car, the Qumquat, in April. Within a month, dealers began receiving complaints about rusty radiators. The complaints came from a wide geographical area, but investigation showed that all the defective cars had been purchased west of the Mississippi, which meant that they had been assembled at the company's western plant in California. Cars produced at the eastern plant, in West Virginia, seemed to be unaffected. Company investigators then checked the production procedures at the California plant, but these revealed nothing to account for the problem. Furthermore, identical procedures were being followed in the West Virginia plant. Cars were taken off the California production line at several stages and tested, but no rust or cause of rust appeared. Finally, someone thought of the fact that, in California, completed cars were stored in an outdoor lot near the ocean for periods up to three weeks before being shipped to the dealers. In West Virginia they were stored indoors. Could the damp salt air in the California lot be the answer? Sample rust-free cars fresh from the California production line were stored in the lot for three weeks, then moved into rented indoor quarters for two months. Other, similar samples were stored indoors for the entire period. Nearly half of the first group developed radiator problems before the end of the testing period, while none of the second group did. The company concluded that the moist salt air in the oceanside lot was indeed the source of the problem, and began making arrangements for indoor storage.

EXERCISE 12–11

Many real-life situations are of such a degree of complexity that Mill's methods can be applied to them only in modified form. The following cases are drawn from newspapers, magazines, and other everyday sources. On the basis of the evidence presented and the conclusions derived: (1) determine which, if any, of Mill's methods was used in that case; (2) indicate what additional evidence, if any, would have (a) strengthened the support for the conclusion, (b) weakened the support for the conclusion, (c) falsified the conclusion; (3) where the term 'cause' is used in the statement of the conclusion, specify whether a necessary or a sufficient condition is more probably meant.

---

1. Dr. Arthur Klatsky conducted a study in which 197 male cardiac patients, each of whom died within twenty-four hours after a heart attack, were compared with a similar group of cardiac patients who did not die of sudden attacks. There turned out to be significantly more current cigarette smokers in the sudden-death group than in the other. No significant difference was found in regard to coffee drinking, heavy aspirin use, or alcohol. The researchers concluded that current cigarette smokers were at substantially greater risk than nonsmokers of sudden death from heart attacks. This would seem to substantiate the contention that cigarette smoking is a cause of sudden cardiac death.

2. It has recently been argued that the cause of crime is not poverty but wealth. Jonathan Quick, in an article in the February, 1974, *Freedom News,* points out that, whereas poverty has not greatly increased in recent years, both crime and the number of very rich people have increased dramatically. He explains this combination of events by suggesting that crime is especially profitable for the rich, who are often in a position to exercise considerable influence over decisions of business and government agencies, and who are seldom punished severely even if they are convicted of crimes. Ambitious members of lower classes, seeing that crime pays for the rich, are led to imitate them so far as they can, thus further increasing the

amount of crime. Therefore, concludes Quick, an effective way to reduce crime is to reduce the number of wealthy people.

3.   Among British and American troops in North Africa during World War II, the incidence of paralytic poliomyelitis was much higher for officers than for men in the lower ranks. Because none of the obvious hypotheses seemed to explain this discrepancy, some rather wild ones were proposed. One of these took note of the fact that most of the officers drank whiskey, whereas most of the other men drank beer, and suggested that this difference was the cause of the different rates of polio.

4.   It is now known that persons who are exposed in infancy to the polio-carrying virus are likely to develop a natural resistance to it, and escape paralysis. Such exposure is more likely in unhygienic surroundings. Since more enlisted men than officers, in the North African group, came from lower-class social backgrounds and were thus likely to have been exposed to such conditions as children, they were less vulnerable to infection in adult life. A similar hypothesis has been proposed to explain the geographical distribution of another disease, multiple sclerosis. MS, as the disease is often known, is more common in the economically advanced parts of the world—particularly northern Europe and the northern parts of the United States—than in many less advanced regions, including southern Europe, southern United States, and South America. It is extremely rare in Japan. In South Africa it is relatively rare among native-born whites and those who immigrated to the country at an early age but more common among those who immigrated after the age of fifteen. In Australia, another country with a high immigration rate, there is no significant difference between immigrant and native-born whites, but there is a higher MS rate in the temperate south than in the more tropical north.

Early exposure to infection appears to be a probable condition in all the low-MS regions—usually, but not always, because of either the poor hygiene associated with economic backwardness or the presence of a tropical climate favorable to the spread of infection. Japan and white South Africa are, of course, neither tropical nor economically backward; but in Japan human excrement was until recently used as a common fertilizer, and in South Africa the majority of white children are cared for by black servants whose own living conditions are poor and primitive. Since Australian whites, as a whole, lack similar close contact with the native population, the immigrant-native difference found in South Africa is not duplicated here. It is therefore hypothesized that MS is a normal virus infection of childhood, and that those who are infected at this time usually develop a natural resistance which protects them from the later effects of the disease.

5.   Some medical researchers have recently found evidence of a possible correlation between beer drinking and certain types of cancer. Drs. James E. Enstrom and Norman E. Breslow compared the 1960 per capita consumption of beer in forty-one states with the mortality rates in those states for 20 types of cancer. They found statistical correlations with at least 7 types, of which the strongest was with cancer of the large intestine and rectum. They emphasized, however, that the presence of a correlation does not, by itself, prove that beer causes cancer.

6.   Doctors have long been puzzled by the occurrence of sudden fatal heart attacks in persons who were, until the attack, in apparently good health. Recent studies by Dr. William A. Greene revealed that, in one group of twenty-six employees of a single company who died of such sudden heart attacks, nearly all had been suffering a period of depression for some time. This depression was then interrupted by some sudden event, usually unpleasant, which made them anxious or angry or otherwise upset their emotional and physical reactions. Usually the heart attacks and death followed shortly thereafter. Greene concluded that the combination of depression and sudden arousal probably contributed importantly to the deaths.

7.   One of the more common signs of heart trouble is the painful condition known as angina pectoris. This is caused by a shortage of oxygenated blood supply to the

heart muscle and can be a forerunner of a damaging or fatal heart attack. The usual treatment for it today is coronary bypass surgery, in which the circulation is shunted around the obstruction in the coronary artery that is directly causing the trouble. Cardiologist Dr. Henry Russek has questioned the value of this, believing that surgery itself entails considerable risk and that effective, less-dangerous treatment with drugs is possible. He treated one group of 102 severe angina patients for six years with a combination of several drugs, and found that their death rate during this period was about the same as that for the general population in the same age range. In contrast, in a talk reported in the March 4, 1974, *Time* magazine, he cited statistics which appeared to show that those who receive coronary bypass surgery have a higher death rate than the general population as well as a high incidence of major nonfatal postoperative complications. He concluded that drug treatment is safer than surgery and at least as effective.

8. A study of regular marijuana smokers by Columbia University researchers indicates that marijuana use may cause a depression of the body's immune system, rendering the user more susceptible to disease. The pertinent evidence was summarized in the March 4, 1974, issue of *Time* magazine as follows:

    Taking T-lymphocytes, or immunologically active white blood cells, from the pot smokers and from healthy, nonsmoking volunteers, the doctors mixed the cells in test tubes with substances known to elicit immune responses. Cells from both groups responded to the foreign substances by multiplying, but those taken from the marijuana users reproduced 40 percent less than those from controls, a result suggesting that regular marijuana users may be more susceptible to disease.

9. Between 1968 and the end of 1972, there were 147 attempts to hijack United States aircraft, and 91 of these were successful. Thirty-one attempts were made in 1972 alone. In 1973 there was only one hijacking—of an Air Force helicopter—and the hijacker was arrested two days later. What caused this abrupt drop? Did potential hijackers suddenly lose interest? Did some secret organization of hijackers send out the word to "lie low"? Was public outrage a factor?

    Early in 1973, President Nixon ordered establishment of the screening procedures now standard at commercial airports, whereby passengers and all their carry-on luggage and other material pass through special X-ray units before boarding their planes. Some people have objected to this procedure on the grounds that it violates their constitutional right to privacy and constitutes an "unwarranted search and seizure." Proponents of the procedure argue that it is the cause of the virtual elimination of hijackings, and that if it were to be discontinued, hijackings would again occur and people would be more seriously inconvenienced or even killed.

10. Recessions cause an increase in deaths from heart disease, kidney failure, and stroke, claims Dr. Harvey Brenner of Johns Hopkins University. Statistics over the past sixty-eight years, he says, show that periods of economic downturn are consistently followed by waves of deaths from all these causes, as well as a rise in infant mortality, and that suicides, murders, and traffic deaths increase during a recession. So do the numbers of patients admitted to mental hospitals. Brenner attributes all these phenomena to the increased stress suffered by individuals at these times whether from unemployment, fear of unemployment, or the struggle to secure basic necessities. He notes that the use of alcohol and tobacco increases during a recession, and holds that these two factors, plus others such as a rise in blood pressure and cholesterol level, are sufficient to cause many of the heart-attack, stroke, and kidney-failure deaths, as well as to increase the number of mothers who give birth to infants unable to survive.

11. In Canada, as in the United States, there has been a trend away from capital punishment, even for convicted murderers. Law-enforcement officials and some others have been worried by this, believing that execution of some criminals

would deter others from committing similar crimes. Among the statistics cited to support this view are the following: in 1963, the first year in which no one was hanged, there were 217 murders in Canada. In 1971, after eight years without a single hanging, there were 426. This data is regarded by many as evidence that abandonment of capital punishment has caused an increase in the murder rate. Therefore, it is claimed, a return to capital punishment would cause a reduction in the number of murders.

12. Mothers in the United States long ago abandoned breast-feeding of their babies in favor of bottle-feeding. Today, many of them are coming back to the breast. But now mothers in underdeveloped countries have begun to adopt bottle-feeding, and nutritional experts are concerned about the possible effects on infants' health. In these countries, cow's milk is often expensive, and packaged formulas are even more so, so a mother may dilute the milk—perhaps with impure water—before giving it to her baby. Or she may prepare a formula wrong, because she does not understand the directions on the package. Furthermore, cow's milk does not contain, as human milk does, precisely the right blend of ingredients for the needs of human babies. Thus a baby may need more cow's milk than human milk to achieve equally good nutrition.

In fact, doctors have noted that, as bottle-feeding has increasingly replaced breast-feeding in many of the underdeveloped countries, babies have begun showing signs of severe malnutrition at earlier and earlier ages. This appears to support the contention that in poor countries bottle-feeding causes an increased level of infant malnutrition.

EXERCISE 12–12

The following account demonstrates use of several of Mill's methods in the development of a scientific theory. Find instances of the methods and show how their findings relate to the final conclusions.

Since World War II, increasing numbers of heroin addicts have died suddenly, in a characteristic fashion, which has generally been attributed to an overdose of the drug. These "overdose" deaths occur very suddenly, they occur very soon after injection of the drug (sometimes even before the needle can be withdrawn), and they are usually accompanied by massive pulmonary edema (filling of the lungs with fluid). Recently, some researchers have challenged the belief that these deaths are caused by heroin overdose and have offered an alternative theory. The case against the overdose theory and for this new theory is well documented in a 1973 book by the editors of *Consumer Reports*. Against the overdose theory, these writers cite the following evidence:

First, the symptoms present in these deaths are not those previously known to be associated with heroin overdose—stupor, lethargy, and prolonged coma, lasting from one to twelve hours before death ensues.

Second, in several studies, heroin addicts have been given quantities of the drug far larger than their usual dosages—in some cases, six to nine times larger—without dying or suffering any serious ill effects.

Third, toxicological examination of tissues and urine from victims, and of syringes and emptied packets found near their bodies, has failed to disclose evidence of abnormally high dosage.

Fourth, other addicts injecting the same dosage at the same time from the same supply are usually unharmed.

Fifth, the victims are usually long-term addicts, who should have a fairly high tolerance for the drug, and not new users, whose tolerance is probably low.

On the basis of such evidence, the authors reject the overdose theory. They then go on to examine other evidence which may suggest an alternative:

First, the timing and increase of these deaths. They were first noted around 1943 and increased fairly slowly at first, then more rapidly, until in 1969 they constituted about 70 percent of all addict deaths in New York City and in 1970 about 80 percent. During the same period, the number of addict deaths from other causes did not significantly increase.

Second, the timing of possibly related events. During World War II, heroin was sometimes unavailable or hard to find; and from this time on, the amount of heroin in a standard New York City bag gradually decreased. Also, after 1939 quinine began to be used to "cut" or adulterate pure heroin; and quinine is capable of producing the symptoms associated with "overdose" deaths.

Third, evidence that the combination of heroin with alcohol or barbiturates may be dangerous. Several deaths (such as that of Janis Joplin) were known to have occurred immediately after an addict injected heroin while under the influence of alcohol or barbiturates. In 1967, toxicological examination revealed the presence of alcohol in about 43 percent of "overdose" deaths in New York City. Hospital personnel were aware that it was dangerous to give standard injections of morphine—which is closely related to heroin—to accident victims who were drunk. British doctors reported that many victims of "overdose" deaths had taken barbiturates with heroin or shortly before.

Fourth, evidence that addicts often use alcohol or barbiturates when they are deprived of heroin. At a clinic in San Francisco, 37 percent of addicts reported using barbiturates during withdrawal; 24 percent reported using alcohol.

Fifth, a 1958 study showing that addicts at that time generally believed it unsafe to combine alcohol or barbiturates with heroin; and the fact that by the 1960s this belief seemed largely to have disapppeared.

Sixth, the fact that "overdose" deaths occurred in Britain, where quinine was not used as an adulterant of heroin.

On the basis of this evidence, the authors concluded that it was probable that the overdose deaths were caused by an acute shock-type reaction to the combination of heroin with a central nervous system depressant such as alcohol or barbiturates. They reasoned that an addict might find himself temporarily unable to obtain heroin, take alcohol or barbiturates to ease withdrawal symptoms, then obtain a supply of heroin and inject it while still under the influence of the depressants. This would create a sufficient condition for the typical "overdose" death and would be consistent with all the known conditions of addict behavior.

SUMMARY

1. No generalization which is arrived at solely by means of an enumerative induction is strong enough to support the inference of a causal connection between two or more associated events.

2. The word 'cause' may be used in a number of different senses. The *efficient* cause is the preceding events which trigger the event in question. The *material* cause is the material out of which a thing is made. The *formal* cause is the form of the object involved in the event. The *final* or purposive cause is the aim or goal of an action.

3. The last event in a causal chain is commonly designated as the **proximate cause**—that is, the one closest to the event whose cause is being sought. It is the proximate cause that is assumed to directly precipitate the caused event. The other links in the causal chain are **remote causes.**

4. Because of the tendency to interpret 'cause' as equivalent to 'proximate efficient cause', or to assume that association of two events necessarily indi-

cates a causal relationship, the neutral term **condition** is useful. There are two types of condition: necessary and sufficient. A **necessary condition** is one in the absence of which the event *cannot* take place. A **sufficient condition** is one in the presence of which the event *is sure to* take place. In some cases, the sufficient condition is a **conjunction**—that is, a combination, a joining together—of several necessary conditions. In other cases, the necessary condition is a **disjunction** of two or more conditions—that is, the presence of one or another (but not necessarily all) of several conditions is necessary to produce the caused event.

5. When an event occurs, it follows by definition that all necessary conditions, and thus at least one sufficient condition, for its occurrence are present. To *prevent* an occurrence, one would search for necessary condition(s); to *produce* it, for sufficient condition(s).

6. Mill's methods are frequently used to determine necessary and sufficient conditions. Each uses a variation of the process of eliminative induction: that is, it considers a number of possibilities, and then eliminates most of them in order to arrive at necessary and/or sufficient condition(s). None of these methods establishes the truth of any proposition absolutely. They merely establish a degree of probability.

7. The **method of agreement** states that if, in every case in which an event occurs, a particular condition is present, and no other factor is common to all occurrences, then that condition is probably a necessary condition of the event.

8. The **method of difference** states that, if the conditions in two cases *appear* to be essentially the same, but the caused event or phenomenon occurs in only one of them, the condition which exists in this one but not in the other is probably the sufficient condition of the phenomenon.

9. In the **joint method of agreement and difference,** the method of agreement is used to find a probable necessary condition. Then a number of cases in which the phenomenon does *not* occur are examined (regardless of whether they resemble the first group of cases in other respects). If the suspected causal factor is missing from all of them, then it is probably a necessary condition of the phenomenon and may be a sufficient condition as well.

10. The **method of concomitant variations** is useful when one seeks the cause of changes which occur along a continuum. It states that if a change in one phenomenon is found to occur *every* time a certain change in another phenomenon occurs, and if the degree of change in one phenomenon varies consistently with the degree of change in the other, then: (1) the change in the first phenomenon is the cause of the change in the second; (2) the change in the second phenomenon is the cause of the change in the first; or (3) a third factor is the cause of the change in both. *Positive* concomitant variation occurs when both factors vary in the same direction. *Inverse* concomitant variation occurs when the factors vary in the opposite direction.

11. Scientists normally apply two additional criteria when using Mill's Methods. One is that studies should be **replicable,** that is, repeatable by other persons with the same results. Special efforts must also be made to establish **controls** to make certain that *only* the factors being considered are, in fact, influencing the outcome of the study.

CHAPTER THIRTEEN

Probability

In Chapters 10, 11, and 12, the word 'probable' has been used frequently. We have said that in an inductive argument the premises provide some, but not absolute, support for the truth of the conclusion. Thus, having observed fifty randomly selected swans and seen that all of them are white, we can reasonably make an enumerative induction to the conclusion that *probably* the next swan we observe will be white, or that *probably* all swans are white. In the discussion of eliminative inductive techniques such as Mill's method of difference, we noted that one can say only that something is the *probable* sufficient condition for the occurrence of an event. For example, knowing that a man was shot through the heart with a bullet, we can infer that the bullet was the probable sufficient condition of his death. We can say only 'probable' since it is possible that the man *may* have died from something else—for example, a heart attack which was the result of uncontrollable fear and rising blood pressure at the sight of a gun pointed at him. Likewise, in respect to scientific theories, one can say only that on the basis of existing evidence, a theory is probably correct or that one theory is more probable than another. Thus, available information suggests that the modern theory that atoms are composed of electrons, neutrons, protons, and other subatomic particles is more probable than the theory of the fifth century (B.C.) Greek philosopher, Democritus, that atoms are solid, indestructible objects which cannot be broken into smaller components.

We are all familiar with other types of probability statement, such as those expressed by the following sentences:

> *The probability of a person picking a heart from a full deck of cards is .25.*
> *The chance that a tossed coin will turn up heads is one in two.*
> *The probability that a marriage will end in divorce is one out of four.*

The probability that a ten-year-old will die before his
or her eleventh birthday is .005.
The odds that the Royals will win the World Series
are 7–5.

The statements of probability expressed by these sentences may be quantitatively more precise than the types mentioned in the first paragraph, but the basic concept of probability involved is no more clear.[1]

How are we to interpret statements of the form 'The probability of X is Y'? It is generally agreed that an adequate definition of the term 'probable', as it is used above, must be given in terms of the processes by means of which the probability is determined. Many such processes have been suggested in the last several centuries. Of these, we shall deal with three which are among the most frequently discussed and debated today. The three theories are quite different from one another, and there is no consensus as to which is the best (or "most probable"?) since each has distinct strengths and weaknesses.

TWO GENERAL PRINCIPLES   It is generally agreed by the proponents of all the competing theories that any adequate theory must satisfy at least two basic requirements.

First, a statement which is absolutely true must be assigned a probability of 1, while a statement which is absolutely false has a probability of 0. Any statement which is neither absolutely true nor absolutely false must have a probability between 0 and 1. For example, the probability that any man will die before his 2,000th birthday is 1, if this is considered to be absolutely certain. But the probability that any man living today died yesterday is 0, insofar as we can agree that this is impossible. And the probability of his surviving for another ten years is a fraction between 0 and 1, depending on his health and other factors. A second requirement is that the sum of the probabilities of any logically inconsistent statements (that is, statements not more than one of which can be true at any given time) must be no greater than 1. For example, not more than one of the statements 'The next card to be drawn from this deck will be an ace'; 'The next card to be drawn from this deck will be an eight'; and 'The next card to be drawn from this deck will be a five' can be true at any given time. (They could all be false.) Thus the sum of the probability that the first is true, the probability that the second is true, and the probability that the third is true cannot be more than 1. So far, all logicians agree. But when one tries to specify the probability of any statement to any degree of precision beyond that imposed by these generally

---

[1] There is a certain ambiguity, which should be noted here, between the probability of a statement (that is, the probability that a statement is true) and the probability of an event. For our purposes, this should not cause any great difficulty, since most statement probabilities can be reformulated as event probabilities, and vice versa. For example, the judgment 'The statement "It will rain tomorrow" is probably true' can be reformulated as the judgment "It will probably rain tomorrow," and vice versa. For the most part, we will be talking in terms of the probability of the occurrence of events, although we could just as well talk about the probability of the truth of statements about these events.

accepted restrictions, the differences among the competing theories become very apparent.

EXERCISE 13–1   *Would the probability of each of the following events be 1, 0, or a fraction in between? If in between, would it be about .5, nearer to 1, or nearer to 0?*

---

1. At least one baby being born tomorrow in New York City
2. The sun rising in the west tomorrow morning
3. The Mississippi River freezing over in July of this year
4. A murder being committed in California next month
5. A particular healthy two-year-old child will die within the next six months.
6. A mugging will be committed in New York City next week.
7. The Arctic ice cap will completely melt in the next year.
8. From this complete deck of ordinary playing cards, the next card I draw will be black.
9. The moon is made of green cheese.
10. A given puppy being male
11. An honor student failing to graduate
12. A nuclear attack on Springfield, Illinois
13. A ninety-two-year-old man dying within the next six years
14. From this container that contains only white balls, the next ball I draw will be white.
15. From this complete deck of ordinary playing cards, the next card I draw will not be black.
16. It will rain somewhere in the world next month.

EXERCISE 13–2   *Can the sum of the probabilities for any of the following pairs of statements be more than 1? Why, or why not?*

---

1. It will rain tomorrow; it will not rain tomorrow.
2. She will be late to this class; she will be on time for this class.
3. It will rain tomorrow; it will be sunny tomorrow.
4. We will go to the game; we will stay home and watch the game on television.
5. It will snow next week; it will not snow at all next week.
6. John will pass biology; John will fail biology.
7. Susan will pass logic this semester; Susan will not pass logic this semester.
8. Mrs. Smith gave birth to a boy yesterday; Mrs. Smith gave birth to a girl yesterday.
9. A Republican will lose the presidential election in 1988; a Democrat will lose the presidential election in 1988.

THREE THEORIES OF PROBABILITY   The three theories of probability that we will consider differ primarily in terms of the assumptions that must underlie the judgment establishing the probability of any statement. The theories are known as the classical (or *a priori*) theory, the relative frequency theory, and the subjective (or personalistic) theory.

The Classical Theory   The process of drawing straws provides a good illustration of the classical (or *a priori*) theory of probability at work. Let us suppose that four starving men stranded on a desert island in the Pacific decide to draw straws to determine which one of them will get to eat the one remaining piece of food. One man holds four straws in his fist, the lucky straw being shorter than the rest. They are arranged so that the man's fingers hide the lower part of the straws, and the exposed portions are all the same length. At the start of the draw, the probability, as determined under the classical theory, that any particular man will receive the short straw is $\frac{1}{4}$ or .25. How was this figure arrived at?

The **classical theory** is based on two assumptions: that all possible events are known, and that the probability of the occurrence of each is equal, unless there is good reason to believe that it is not. The second of these assumptions is generally known as the **principle of indifference.** In the above example, it is assumed that there are only four possible events facing each man—namely, he can draw the short straw or he can draw one of the three long ones. Of these four events, only one may be said to be favorable to the prediction that the individual will draw the short straw. By dividing the number of possible favorable events by the total number of equally possible events, we arrive at the probability that the favorable event will occur. This area can be expressed by the following formula, in which **A** stands for the favorable event, P(**A**) stands for the probability of this event, **m** stands for the number of possible favorable events, and **n** stands for the number of all possible events:

$$P(A) = \frac{m}{n}$$

Substituting figures from the example of the men on the desert island gives us the probability of the favorable event:

P(any particular man drawing the short straw) =
$$\frac{1}{4} = .25$$

Using the same formula, it is easy to see that the probability of picking a red card from a full deck (with no jokers) is .5. Here, the number of possible favorable events is twenty-six, since there are thirteen cards of each suit, and two suits (hearts and diamonds) are red; and the number of all possible events is fifty-two, since there are fifty-two cards in the deck. Using the formula, we can express the probability of drawing a red card as:

P(drawing a red card) $= \frac{26}{52} = \frac{1}{2} = .5$

Critics have challenged the basic assumption of the classical theory that for any given situation, all possible events are being considered. They argue that there are almost always some possible events that we do not take into consideration when computing probabilities. In the case of our men on the desert island,

we assumed that the number of possible events for each man was four. Any one of the men could receive either the short straw or one of the three long straws. But these are not the only outcomes we can conceive of. One or more of the long straws may break off in the man's hand, reducing them to the same length as the short one. In this instance, the chances of drawing a short straw would no longer be $\frac{1}{4}$. Or one or more of the men might fall or be pushed off the island and drown before the draw is finished; help might come in the nick of time; a freighter containing six tons of TV dinners might wash up on the beach. In short, any number of other events might *possibly* occur. Granted, such possibilities as these can usually be ruled out, thereby reducing the number of possible outcomes to finite proportions. Yet, in most situations encountered both in daily life and in scientific research, unanticipated outcomes, relevant to the probability of the occurrence of an event, do continually appear.

Objections have also been raised against the principle of indifference—that is, the assumption that each member of a set of events is equally possible, unless there is good reason to believe otherwise. For example, suppose the holder of the straws is a sleight-of-hand artist, although no one else has any reason to know this. The probability that he will receive the short straw will obviously be greatly increased, while the probability that one of the other three men will receive it will be decreased. Assuming that the sleight-of-hand artist is so clever as to nearly guarantee that he will receive the short straw, then the probability that any one of the other three men will get it is decreased to almost 0. But the classical theory would still show the probability for each man as $\frac{1}{4}$, since there is no good reason to assume otherwise.

Consider another example. What is the probability that the next birth you hear about will be a female birth? According to the classical theory, the probability of this event would be determined by dividing the number of possible favorable events by the number of possible events. In this case, there are only two possible events: the birth of a male or the birth of a female; and only one of these events is favorable. Therefore, it seems obvious that the probability that the next birth you hear about will be that of a female is .5, or one in two. In fact, however, statistics indicate that there are more male births than female births. Many adherents of the classical theory would not consider this statistical evidence significant or relevant—i.e., would believe that it does not provide a "good reason" for not applying the principle of indifference—and would hold that the probability of a female birth is still .5.

A more difficult case for the classical theory is one such as the determination of the probability that a randomly selected ten-year-old child will survive to his or her eleventh birthday. There are only two possible outcomes in this case—the child will either survive or not survive. If the principle of indifference were applied, the probability of survival would be only $\frac{1}{2} = .5$. But there is certainly good reason to believe that today the two outcomes are not equally likely, and that a randomly selected ten-year-old has a much better than even chance of living at least one year. A proponent of the classical theory might well agree that

the principle of indifference should not be applied to this case, but then no further steps could be taken, in terms of this theory, to compute the probability of the event. The classical theorist would simply have to assert that the probability cannot be computed.

But this is precisely the kind of case with which the relative frequency theory is best equipped to deal.

The Relative Frequency Theory   The **relative frequency theory** is based not on an abstract assumption like the principle of indifference but on the direct observation of concrete cases. The theory stipulates that the probability of an event is to be determined by dividing the number of *observed favorable* events by the total number of *observed* events. This may be expressed by the following formula, in which P(A) is the probability of the favorable event **A**, **m** is the number of observed favorable events, and **n** is the total number of observed events:

$$P(A) = \frac{m}{n}$$

How would the relative frequency theory be used to determine the probability that a ten-year-old will not live to his or her eleventh birthday? The researcher, probably an insurance actuary, would observe a sample of, say, 2,000 randomly selected ten-year-olds, and would count the number who die before their eleventh birthday. In this instance, let us say that 10 out of the 2,000 die. Dividing the number of observed deaths among ten-year-olds by the total number of observed cases, the researcher would arrive at the probability that a ten-year-old will not survive to his or her eleventh birthday.

$$P(\textit{ten-year-old not surviving}) = \frac{10}{2000} = .005$$

A proponent of the relative frequency theory can also determine the probability of such events as flipping a coin and coming up with a head, or selecting a heart from a full deck of cards, or throwing a six on a die. However, he does not, as under the classical theory, do this by dividing the number of possible favorable events by the number of possible events; rather, he observes a large sample and divides the number of observed favorable events by the total number of observed events. In such instances, the probability values for such events as determined by the relative frequency method are *usually* fairly close to those for the same events as determined by the classical method. If one were to find a coin for which the probability of heads were determined, by the relative frequency method, to be .75, one would be justified in concluding that the coin was abnormal or even "loaded."

Strictly speaking, there is no single relative frequency theory, but rather a number of different ones. All of them utilize the method outlined above for determining probabilities on the basis of empirical observations; the differences among them result from more subtle technical matters which we cannot go into

here. All the versions have been criticized for one reason or another, and many have been formulated to escape one or more of the weaknesses of earlier versions. No one version is yet recognized as having avoided all possible objections.

One difficulty faced by most versions of the relative frequency theory stems from their assertion that probabilities based on observations of past cases are applicable to future cases only *in the long run.* That is, they hold that it is not proper—in fact, it is meaningless on many accounts—to assign a probability value to a single event, such as getting a head on one particular throw of a coin. To say that the probability of getting a head on the toss of a coin is .5, according to these theorists, is only to say that in the long run, or even in an infinite sequence, half of the tosses will come up heads.

Neither the classical nor the relative frequency theory can deal adequately with complex one-of-a-kind type cases, such as the probability that Tom will get an A in logic this semester. The classical theory is unsatisfactory because the principle of indifference does not apply in Tom's case. The relative frequency theory is also inadequate, because it is not proper to apply this theory to calculating the probability of a particular event, especially one which has the complications that Tom's has (as may be recalled from the account in the Introduction). The proponents of the subjectivist or personalistic theory claim that it can deal much more reasonably with cases of this kind.

The Subjectivist Theory   The **subjectivist theory** defines probabilities as being grounded in the beliefs of individual persons. Thus, in contrast to the classical and relative frequency theories, under the subjectivist theory a variety of different probabilities can be assigned to the same particular event. This is felt by many opponents to constitute a fatal criticism of the theory, but its supporters see it as a strength.

One method suggested by some subjectivists for establishing quantitatively expressed probabilities of events is in terms of betting odds. Thus, if an individual is willing to accept a wager on a particular event at odds of 10 to 1, he is assigning that event the probability figure of $10/(10 + 1) = 10/11$. Or suppose Joe the Pro is willing to bet $6:5$ that the horse Chris E. will win the Derby. This means that he is willing to put up money in the same proportion as his subjective (but in this case "expert") assessment of the chance that the horse will win. The probability assignment of 6/11 to the event of winning the race can be determined from the odds our gambler is willing to give. Joe would compute his probability using the formula:

$$P(\textit{Chris E. will win}) = \frac{6}{6 + 5} = \frac{6}{11}$$

This, of course, is Joe's probability. The bookie down the street is completely free to reject it. If he rejected the odds of $6:5$ that Chris E. would win, but accepted odds of $1:2$, he would have set a probability value of $1/(1 + 2) = 1/3$.

Although this may seem to imply that any probability whatsoever can be assigned to a particular event—which would certainly justify rejection of the subjectivist theory—there are in fact several restrictions which significantly limit us in our assignment of probabilities. First, the general rules mentioned earlier still apply. This means that no event can have a probability greater than 1 and also that the sum of the probabilities of incompatible events cannot be greater than 1. Thus, if one accepts odds of 2 : 1 that a coin will come up heads (that is, assigns a probability of 2/3), one cannot also accept odds of 2 : 1 that the coin will come up tails on the same toss. Secondly, the rules of the probability calculus (to be explained in the next section) must also be observed. A significant feature of the subjectivist theory is that it requires that, so far as possible, all of an individual's beliefs be considered in establishing his probability for a particular event, and the rules of the probability calculus provide a means of doing this.

Philosophers and mathematicians have raised numerous technical objections against the subjectivist theory; many critics believe that the mere fact that different probabilities can be assigned to the same event by different persons (or by the same person at different times) is a sufficient criticism. Still, the theory has considerable appeal, because it allows one to assign probabilities to many events that other theories cannot deal with at all.

EXERCISE 13–3   *Calculate the probability of each of the following, in terms of the theory specified.*

---

1. (Classical theory) In a random draw from a well-shuffled deck of cards without a joker, what is the probability of getting a(n):
   a. ace of spades
   b. red queen
   c. ten
   d. black card
   e. face card (jack, queen, or king)
2. (Classical theory) A blindfolded player picks a ball from an urn. What is the probability that he will get a red ball if the urn contains:
   a. two red, two white, two black, and two blue balls
   b. four black, five white, and six red balls
3. (Classical theory) A charity organization raffled off a wrist watch to raise funds. If 512 chances were sold, what is the probability of winning for a person holding:
   a. one ticket
   b. eight tickets
4. (Relative frequency theory) If the average number of male births in the United States per year is 2,180,000 out of a total of 4,258,000 births, what is the probability that the next baby born will be a boy?
5. (Classical theory) If federal government outlay this year for veterans' benefits and services is $14,000 million out of total federal expenditures of $300,000 million, what is the probability that the next federal dollar spent will benefit a veteran?
6. (Classical theory) The state you are living in holds a weekly lottery. If 525,000 tickets have been sold, what is the probability you will win (a) if you hold two tickets, or (b) if you hold ten tickets?

7. (Relative frequency) If the number of plane crashes among domestic airlines in the United States is 156 out of a total of 342,576 domestic flights, what is the probability that the next domestic flight you take will crash?

8. (Subjectivist theory) A politician believes that the odds are 5 to 1 that he will win a particular election. (a) What is his probability for the event? (b) What is his probability that he will lose the election?

9. (Classical theory) A person is asked to pick a card from a well-shuffled deck of ordinary playing cards without a joker. What is the probability that the person will (a) draw an eight, (b) draw a numbered card (ace, two . . . ten), (c) draw a black picture card (king, queen, or jack), (d) draw a red numbered card, (e) draw the two of diamonds.

10. Of one hundred juniors who took I.Q. tests at City High School last year, 27 had scores between 110 and 118. The scores of the whole group ranged between 102 and 167. If next year's class is similar to this year's class, what is the probability that a randomly selected junior next year will have an I.Q. between 110 and 118? Calculate the answer according to both (a) the relative frequency theory and (b) the classical theory.

11. Three popular racing drivers are among fifteen scheduled to compete in today's stock car race. In the past two years, Jan Alpha has won four out of twelve races. Ben Beta has won seven out of sixteen in the same period. Gail Gamma has been having difficulties and has won only two out of ten. On the basis of this data alone, what is the probability that each will win today's race (a) on the classical theory and (b) on the relative frequency theory?

12. (Subjectivist theory) In a three-horse race, a bookie offers odds of 2 to 5 that the horse Jones Beach will win.
    a. What is his probability for the event?
    b. What is the highest probability he can allow that any other horse will win, and why?
    c. What odds would approximately represent the latter probability?

13. (Subjectivist theory) A stockholder of U.S. Steel believes that the odds are 3 to 2 in favor of prices rising tomorrow.
    a. What is her probability for the event?
    b. What is her probability that the prices will fall?

14. (Subjectivist theory) In early August of 1974, it was generally felt that the odds on President Nixon's impeachment had significantly increased. If a gambler had been offering odds of 5 to 4 for impeachment, and at this point changed them to 9 to 4, what were his old and new probabilities?

15. (Subjectivist theory) A month before the big football game, Benny the Bookie gives odds of 5 to 4 that Team A will defeat Team B. Two weeks before the game, Benny learns that Team B's superstar quarterback has been seriously injured and will play no other games this season. Benny quickly changes his odds, giving new odds of 3 to 1 that Team A will defeat Team B. What was Benny the Bookie's (a) old probability, and (b) new probability that team A will win?

16. (Relative frequency theory) According to actuarial statistics, out of 100,000 newborn females, 800 do not survive to their third birthday. (a) What is the probability that a newborn female will survive to her third birthday? (b) What is the probability that a newborn female will not survive to her third birthday?

17. A man is in a Las Vegas gambling casino, observing a particular roulette wheel. In the past 50 turns of the wheel, the ball has landed on a black number 35 times and on a red number 15 times. (Roulette wheels have an equal number of red and black squares.) What is the probability that on the next turn the ball will land on a red square? (a) Assume the relative frequency theory, and (b) assume the classical theory.

18. (Relative frequency theory) Siamese cats are born either with a bend in the tip of

their tails or with crossed eyes, but not both. Of 75 randomly observed Siamese cats, 45 had bends in the tip of their tails and 30 had crossed eyes. What is the probability that the next Siamese cat you observe (a) will have a bend in the tip of its tail, (b) will have crossed eyes?

19.   (Classical theory) A bag contains 50 jellybeans: 20 licorice, 15 cinnamon, and 15 papaya. What is the probability that a blindfolded child who selected one jellybean from the bag will select a licorice one?

THE PROBABILITY CALCULUS

Thus far we have been discussing only procedures for establishing the probability of a single simple event, and we have found that there is no one generally accepted and universally applicable method for doing this. But we may also wish in certain circumstances to calculate the probabilities of compound events—for example, the probability of getting heads in three consecutive tosses of a coin. The procedures for determining the probabilities of such compound events have been codified in a formal axiom system known as the **probability calculus.** Given the probabilities of the occurrence of each of several simple events, the probability calculus enables us to calculate the probability of their occurring in various combinations.

It is important to note that the probability calculus presupposes that we have some independent procedure for establishing the probabilities of individual events before we attempt to calculate the probability of any combination of these events. The probability of a simple event's occurring by itself is referred to as the **initial probability.** The three theories already discussed are theories for determining the initial probabilities of individual events. As we have seen, the different theories can establish different initial probabilities for the same simple events. But advocates of all three methods accept essentially the same probability calculus, though with some differences in detail.

In the probability calculus, a complex event is viewed as a whole composed of a number of simple events. For example, the complex event of a race horse's winning the Triple Crown is a whole of which the component parts are its winning the Kentucky Derby, then the Preakness, and finally the Belmont Stakes. The complex event of being dealt a royal flush in spades is a whole of which the component parts are being dealt the ace of spades, the king of spades, the queen of spades, the jack of spades, and the ten of spades. The process of calculating the probability of the whole from the probabilities of its parts depends, as we shall see, on understanding the way in which the parts are related. For the sake of simplicity we will use the classical method for determining initial probabilities.

The Restricted Conjunction Rule

The first type of complex event we shall consider is one whose component events are such that the occurrence of one has no effect on the occurrence of any of the others; that is, if one event occurs, the probability of the occurrence of the other event(s) is not changed. Such events are said to be **independent.** For example, suppose two lovers, strolling through a field, each decide to pick a daisy and pull off its petals, to the accompaniment of "he loves me, he loves me not. . . ." Whether they both receive a favorable answer depends on whether the flower each has picked has an odd or an even number of petals. For the present discussion, let us assume that the two conditions are equally possible. We have no reason to believe that the answer one lover receives has any effect on the answer the other lover receives, so the events can be assumed to be independent.

In all, there are four possible outcomes in this situation: First, both lovers may receive unfavorable answers; that is, both may have picked flowers with even numbers of petals. Second, Lover A may receive a favorable answer and Lover B an unfavorable answer. Third, Lover A may receive an unfavorable answer and Lover B a favorable answer. Fourth, both lovers may receive favorable answers. Since each of these outcomes is assumed to be equally possible, the probability (as determined on the classical theory) that the desired outcome will occur is one out of four or 1/4. But this answer may be arrived at in another way. There are only two alternatives open to each lover: a favorable answer or an unfavorable answer. Therefore, each lover's probability of getting a favorable answer is 1/2. This probability value can then be applied to a rule which is used to calculate the probability of the complex event of both lovers' receiving favorable answers. It is called the **restricted conjunction rule,** and it states that:

> *If x and y are independent events, then*
> *P(x and y) = P(x) × P(y).*

In this case, **x** represents the event of Lover A receiving a favorable answer, and **y** represents the event of Lover B receiving a favorable answer. P(**x**) and P(**y**) represent the separate probabilities of each event, whereas P(**x and y**) represents the probability of their occurring together. As we have seen, the probability of **x** is 1/2 and the probability of **y** is 1/2. Therefore:

$$P(x \text{ and } y) = \frac{1}{2} \times \frac{1}{2} = \frac{1}{4} = .25$$

It should be noted that the same rule can be used by other than classical theorists as well; any differences in the final probabilities would result from the use of different initial probabilities. For instance, if an empirical study showed that of 10,000 daisies, 2,500 had an odd number of petals, then the initial probability of a favorable result for one of the lovers might be computed on the relative frequency theory to be 2,500/10,000 = .25. The probability of a favorable result for both would then be .25 × .25 = .0625.

Let us consider a somewhat more complex example. Suppose two men are using a six-shot revolver to play Russian roulette. One of the men places a bullet in one of the six chambers and spins the cylinder. He then points the muzzle of the gun to his temple and pulls the trigger. At this point, there are six (equally probable) events which may occur: namely, the trigger may strike the chamber containing the bullet, or any one of the five empty chambers. Since there are five favorable events and only one unfavorable event, the probability that the man will survive is 5/6. (This of course requires additional assumptions, such as that if the loaded chamber is struck, the bullet will fire, and if it fires it will strike and kill the man, and so on.) What now is the probability that both men will survive one trial? Since it has already been determined that the probability of a single player's surviving his turn is 5/6, this value can be used with the restricted conjunction rule to give the probability that both will survive one round. Thus:

$$P(x \text{ and } y) = \frac{5}{6} \times \frac{5}{6} = \frac{25}{36}$$

Notice that 25/36 is a smaller fraction than 5/6. This means that the probability that both men will survive their first turns is smaller than the probability that either will survive his first turn. The probability of three survivals is 5/6 × 5/6 × 5/6 = 125/216. The fraction is becoming smaller. If a total of four trials are made (two turns each), the probability of four survivals is 5/6 × 5/6 × 5/6 × 5/6 = 625/1296. As the number of trials increases, the numerator of the fraction continues to be multiplied by 5, whereas the denominator is multiplied by 6. As the interval between them gradually widens, the fraction—and the probability that both the players will survive all their turns—approaches, but never reaches, zero.

The General Conjunction Rule Not all complex events have component events which are independent of one another. There are many cases in which one of the component events affects the circumstances of the second event in such a way that the probability of the second is no longer what it would have been if the first event had not occurred. Such events are called **dependent events.** For example, consider the four starving castaways who draw straws to determine which of them will get the last of the food. Whether the draws are considered to be independent or dependent events depends on the manner in which they are carried out. Suppose each of the men were permitted to point to the straw of his choice, whether or not it had been picked by another man, and only after the choices had been made did the straw-holder open his hand to show the results. If the draws were carried out in this fashion, then the component events of each man's selecting a straw would be independent. But it is more likely that each man in turn would draw a straw from the fist of the straw holder. If the draws were conducted in this way, then the composition of the bundle of straws would change as each man took his turn, and, with it, each man's probability of receiving the short straw would also change. Let **w** represent the event of man A receiving it, **x** the event of man B receiving it, **y** the event of man C receiving it, and **z** the event of man D receiving it. The probability of **w** is 1/4. If **w** does not occur, then the probability of **x** becomes 1/3. If **w** and **x** do not occur, the probability of **y** becomes 1/2, and if **w, x,** and **y** do not occur, the probability of **z** becomes 1.

The rule which is used to calculate probability values of the joint occurrence of a number of simple events (whether they are dependent or independent) is called the **general conjunction rule.** It states that:

> *If x and y are any events whatever (either dependent or independent), then*
> $$P(x \text{ and } y) = P(x) \times P(y \text{ given } x).$$

The notation 'P(**y** given **x**)' represents a probability value for the occurrence of the event **y,** given that event **x** has already occurred. For example, on the classical theory, we assign the value 1/10 to the initial probability of choosing a red ball from an urn containing ten balls of ten different colors, and we also assign 1/10 to the initial probability of choosing a yellow ball. However, once the red ball has been chosen, and not replaced, the probability of choosing the yellow ball becomes 1/9, since only 9 balls remain in the urn. Thus the two events are not independent, since the occurrence of one event affects the probability of the occurrence of the other. If P(**x**) is the initial probability of choosing a red ball, and P(**y**) the initial probability of choosing a yellow ball, P(**y** given **x**) is the probability of choosing the yellow ball after the red one has been chosen. By substituting the appropriate values in the general conjunction rule, we can compute the probability of choosing a red and a yellow ball in succession as follows:

$$P(x \text{ and } y) = P(x) \times P(y \text{ given } x) = \frac{1}{10} \times \frac{1}{9} = \frac{1}{90}$$

Consider another example. Suppose there is a jar containing three jellybeans; two are licorice and one is papaya. A child sticks his hand into the jar; what is the probability that he will pick the two licorice jellybeans on two successive tries (provided, of course, that he eats the first one rather than putting it back)? Let **x** represent the event of the child's getting a licorice jellybean on his first try. Since there are three jellybeans, we will assume that there are three equally possible draws. And, since two jellybeans are licorice, two of these draws are favorable. Therefore, the probability of getting a licorice jellybean on the first draw, P(**x**), is 2/3. If **x** occurs, then there will be only two jellybeans left in the jar, one licorice and one papaya. Therefore, the probability of getting a licorice jellybean on the second draw, given that a licorice one was drawn on the first try, is 1/2; or, in terms of the formula, P(**y** given **x**) = 1/2. Using the general conjunction rule, we can calculate that:

$$P(x \text{ and } y) = \frac{2}{3} \times \frac{1}{2} = \frac{2}{6} = \frac{1}{3}$$

Thus the probability that the child will draw two licorice jellybeans in a row is 1/3.

It should be noted that if **x** and **y** are two independent events, then the probability of **y** given that **x** has already occurred is the same as the probability of **y** itself. (This follows directly from the definition of independence.) That is, for independent events **x** and **y**, P(**y** given **x**) = P(**y**).

EXERCISE 13–4   *Calculate the probabilities of the following conjunct events. Give the following information: number of possible favorable events; whether the simple events are dependent or independent; the rule to be applied; the initial probabilities; the probability of the conjunct event; the equation used. Unless otherwise indicated, calculate the initial probabilities by the classical theory.*

1. If a single die is tossed three times, what is the probability that a one will come up on top three times?
2. If three dice are tossed simultaneously, what is the chance that all will come up with fives?
3. Five business executives are going to a convention in Chicago. They are all flying from Louisville, but do not know each other. There are three flights they can conveniently take. Assuming that each does in fact take one of these flights, what is the probability that they will all take the earliest of the three?
4. Three nickels are tossed simultaneously. What is the probability of getting heads on all three?
5. The General Mathematics Examination of the Actuarial Society has seventy multiple-choice questions, with a choice of five answers for each question. If there is only one correct answer for each question, what is the probability that an examinee could get a score of 100 purely by random guessing?
6. Four cards are dealt from a well-shuffled deck without a joker. What is the probability that an ace, a king, a queen, and a jack will be dealt, in that order?
7. A forty-year-old man and his thirty-five-year-old wife have been married for ten years. If the probability that the man will live for another fifteen years is 1/2, and the probability that the wife will live for another fifteen years is 2/3, what is the probability that they will both live until the date of their twenty-fifth wedding anniversary?
8. Carol likes to crochet, but she is totally colorblind. Because of this, she generally keeps her balls of wool in compartments, labeled as to color. Unfortunately, the cat got at the wool and pulled all the balls out onto the floor. There are ten balls, each a different color. What is the probability that the first two balls Carol picks up will be a pink ball and a green ball, in that order?
9. What chance does Carol have to choose a pink, a green, a blue, and a white ball, in that order, in four successive selections?
10. If a four-sided die has sides labeled E, F, N, and U: (a) what is the probability that it will land with the E side up? (b) that the E side will be up after each of three successive tosses?

EXERCISE 13–5   *Calculate the probabilities of the following conjunct events. Provide the following information for each: (a) whether the simple events are dependent or independent; (b) the rule to be applied; (c) the initial probabilities computed using the classical theory; (d) the probability of the conjunct event; (e) the equation used to derive the answer.*

1. If two normal dice are thrown simultaneously, what is the probability they will both turn up with a 1 on their faces?

2. From a well-shuffled ordinary deck of playing cards (without a joker), a person turns over five cards. What is the probability that the cards will be the ace, king, queen, jack, and ten of spades in that order?

3. Assuming that it is equally probable that a person will be born on any particular date and ignoring the complications of a leap year, what is the probability that two randomly selected people were born on October twentieth?

4. There are three urns, each of which contains thirty balls. Urn 1 contains ten white, ten black, and ten red balls. Urn 2 contains fifteen white, five black, and ten red balls. Urn 3 contains twenty white, five black, and five red balls. If a person selects one ball from urn 1, one from urn 2, and one from urn 3 in that order, what is the probability that he will select three black balls?

5. Assuming the same circumstances as in question 4, what is the probability that the person will select a red, white, and black ball in that order?

6. Assuming the same circumstances as in question 4, if a person selected three balls just from urn 1, what is the probability he would select a red, white, and black ball in that order?

7. The Friendly Ripoff Corporation has five employees and offices on the tenth floor of an office building. There are four elevators in the building that are all equally accessible. What is the probability that the five employees of the Friendly Ripoff Corporation took elevator number 1 to the offices on a particular morning?

8. A roulette wheel contains an equal number of black and red numbers. What is the probability that on four successive random spins of the wheel, a black number will turn up each time?

9. There are two well-shuffled decks of playing cards with no jokers. If person A draws a card from one deck and person B draws a card from the other deck, what is the probability that both cards will be spades?

10. There is one well-shuffled deck of playing cards with no jokers. If person A draws a card from the deck and person B draws a second card from the same deck, what is the probability that both cards will be aces?

The Restricted Disjunction Rule

All the situations that have been examined so far have involved conjunctions of simple events—complex events whose component events have occurred jointly; that is, the complex event was said not to occur unless a combination of two or more particular component events occurred in a specific sequence. There are other complex events which are disjunctions—that is, which may be said to occur when *one or more* of several alternative events occur. There are some events which are such that only one can occur: for example, on a given toss a die can come up 1 or 2 or 3 or 4 or 5 or 6, but it cannot have more than one side up after any one throw. Such events are said to be **mutually exclusive.**

To illustrate the method for determining the probability of the occurrence of any one of two or more mutually exclusive events, take the case of identical twins who live together, share a bedroom and a closet, and wear identical clothes. One twin works the day shift and one the night shift. When the night-working twin wakes up, it is pitch dark, and, so as not to disturb her sister's sleep, she dresses without turning on the light. When she goes to the closet to feel around for her shoes, she finds two identical pairs, her sister's and her own. Actually, she does not care whether she chooses her sister's shoes or her own, just so long as she gets a right shoe and a left shoe. What is the probability that the first two shoes she picks up will be a pair?

It is necessary, first, to determine the events that may possibly occur when the night-shift twin takes two shoes from the floor of the closet. There are six alternatives, four of which are favorable: She may get her own left shoe and her own right shoe; her own left shoe and her twin's left shoe; her own left shoe and her twin's right shoe; her own right shoe and her twin's left shoe; her own right shoe and her twin's right shoe; or her twin's left shoe and her twin's right shoe. These six events are mutually exclusive; when the night-shift twin picks up two shoes, the result must be one and only one of these six alternatives.

The rule for calculating the probability of the occurrence of one or another of two or more mutually exclusive events is called the **restricted disjunction rule.** It states that:

> *If x and y are mutually exclusive events, then*
> $P(x \text{ or } y) = P(x) + P(y).$

Clearly, there are four ways the twin might get a pair of shoes and two ways she might get a mismatch. We shall call the four possible events of her getting a pair **w, x, y,** and **z.** Since there are six events in all, and we are assuming that all are equally possible, the initial probability for any one of them is 1/6. According to the formula, then:

$$P(w \text{ or } x \text{ or } y \text{ or } z) = P(w) + P(x) + P(y) + P(z) =$$
$$\frac{1}{6} + \frac{1}{6} + \frac{1}{6} + \frac{1}{6} = \frac{4}{6} = \frac{2}{3}$$

The probability that she will somehow pick up a pair of shoes in the dark, then, is 2/3.

Notice that the probability of joint, or conjunct, occurrences is calculated by *multiplying* the probability values of the component events, whereas the probability of disjunct events is calculated by *adding* their probability values.

The General Disjunction Rule   The components of a disjunction need not be mutually exclusive; that is, it is possible for many events to occur together. For example, to return to our petal-picking lovers, what is the probability that at least one of the two will get a favorable answer? Obviously, the restricted disjunction rule is inapplicable here. The probability of getting a favorable answer from one flower is 1/2, and the probability of getting a favorable answer from the second flower is the same. Nevertheless, the probability of getting one favorable answer in two tries cannot be 1/2 + 1/2 = 1, or certainty. The restricted disjunction rule does not work because the two events are not mutually exclusive. It is possible that both lovers may get favorable answers, or that neither may.

The **general disjunction rule** enables us to calculate the probability of the disjunction of any two or more events whatever—that is, it is not restricted to disjunctions of mutually exclusive events. The rule states that for any events **x** and **y:**

$$P(x \text{ or } y) = P(x) + P(y) - P(x \text{ and } y)$$

where P(**x** and **y**) can be determined using the general conjunction rule.

To illustrate, let us calculate the probability of either getting a head on the first toss of a coin or getting a head on the second toss of the coin. (The 'or' in the general disjunction rule, and in our example, is to be interpreted in the inclusive sense—that is, as 'either **x** or **y** or both.') Using the classical theory to establish the initial probabilities, we find that P(head on the first toss) = 1/2 and P(head on the second toss) = 1/2. Since the two events are independent, P(head on first toss and head on second toss) = 1/2 × 1/2 = 1/4 (by the general conjunction rule). Substituting this value in the general disjunction rule, we get:

$$P(\text{head on first toss or head on second toss}) =$$
$$\frac{1}{2} + \frac{1}{2} - \frac{1}{4} = \frac{3}{4}$$

This can be checked, using the classical theory, by noting that there are only four possible outcomes for the two tosses: heads and heads, heads and tails, tails and heads, and tails and tails. Of the four outcomes, the first three are favorable, and, assuming that all four are equally possible, the probability of obtaining at least one favorable event is 3/4.

It should be noted that the restricted disjunction rule can be immediately derived from the general rule, by virtue of the definition of mutually exclusive events. Since two events are mutually exclusive if and only if it is impossible for both to occur at the same time, it follows that for two mutually exclusive events **x** and **y**, P(**x** and **y**) = 0. This, then, reduces the general rule to:

$$P(x \text{ or } y) = P(x) + P(y) - 0$$

when **x** and **y** are mutually exclusive. And this, in turn, is equivalent to the restricted disjunction rule:

$$P(x \text{ or } y) = P(x) + P(y)$$

For another example, let us return to our jellybean fanatic. For the sake of interest, he has placed his jellybeans in two jars. One jar contains four papaya and four licorice; the other jar contains eight papaya and four licorice. If the boy takes a jellybean from each of the two jars, what is the probability that at least one of the beans will be licorice? To apply the general disjunction rule, let us take **x** to be the event of the choice of licorice from the first jar, **y** the event of the choice of licorice from the second jar. Since the first jar has four licorice out of eight jellybeans, $P(x) = 4/8 = 1/2$. The second jar contains four licorice out of a total of twelve beans, so $P(y) = 4/12 = 1/3$. Since x and y are two independent events, the restricted conjunction rule gives:

$$P(x \text{ and } y) = P(x) \times P(y) = \frac{1}{2} \times \frac{1}{3} = \frac{1}{6}$$

Applying the general disjunction rule with this value inserted, we have:

$$P(x \text{ or } y) = P(x) + P(y) - P(x \text{ and } y) =$$
$$\frac{1}{2} + \frac{1}{3} - \frac{1}{6} = \frac{4}{6} = \frac{2}{3}$$

EXERCISE 13–6

Calculate the probabilities for the following disjunct events. Give the following information for each: number of possible favorable events; whether or not these are mutually exclusive; rule to be applied; initial probability of each favorable event (use the classical theory, when needed, to determine it); where relevant, the value of $P(x \text{ and } y)$; probability of the disjunct event; the equation used to arrive at the answer.

1. A die is tossed. What is the probability that it will turn up (a) either a one or a two; (b) either a one, a two, or a three?
2. A card is drawn at random from a well-shuffled deck without a joker. What is the probability that it will be (a) a king, queen, or jack of clubs; (b) a black face card?
3. The face cards are separated from a standard deck. What is the probability of choosing from this reduced deck (a) either the queen of hearts or the jack of hearts on a single draw; (b) the queen of hearts on either of two draws, if the first card is not replaced in the deck before the second draw?
4. If the probability that a forty-year-old man will survive for another fifteen years is 1/2, and the probability that his wife will do the same is 2/3, what is the probability that at least one of them will survive for another fifteen years?
5. A card is drawn at random from a deck without a joker, and at the same time a coin is flipped. What is the probability that either the king of spades will be drawn or the coin will come up tails?
6. Forty percent of the population of a town have grey hair, and 25 percent have blue eyes. Fifteen percent have both. What is the probability that a randomly selected citizen of the town will have grey hair or blue eyes?
7. Four women are to be seated at a round table. Two of them, June and Jane, are not on speaking terms at the moment. What is the probability that they will be seated next to each other?
8. In a group of one hundred people, seventy are men, and forty of them smoke. Of the thirty women, ten smoke. What is the probability that a randomly selected individual will be a woman or a smoker?

EXERCISE 13–7

Calculate the probabilities for the following disjunct events. Provide the following information for each: (a) whether or not these are mutually exclusive; (b) the rule to be applied; (c) the initial probability of each favorable event (use the classical theory, when needed, to determine it); (d) where relevant, the value of $P(x$ and $y)$; (f) the probability of the disjunct event; (e) the equation used to derive the answer.

1. An urn contains ten black balls, five white balls, six blue balls, five red balls, and four yellow balls. What is the probability that a person will select either a white ball or a blue ball?
2. Two coins are flipped simultaneously. What is the probability that both will come up heads or both will come up tails?
3. If the probability that a ten-year old boy will survive to his twentieth birthday is .90, and the probability that his five-year old sister will survive to her twentieth birthday is .80, what is the probability that either will survive until his or her twentieth birthday?
4. From a standard deck of playing cards without a joker, what is the probability of selecting an ace, or a king, or a queen, or a jack on a single draw?
5. Assuming the same circumstances as in question 4, what is the probability of selecting either the ace of hearts, or the king of hearts, or the queen of hearts, or the jack of hearts on a single draw?
6. Suppose that there are two urns. Urn 1 contains thirty balls, ten of which are black, ten are white, and ten are red. Urn 2 contains thirty balls, five of which are black, fifteen are white, and ten are red. Suppose that person A selects one ball from urn 1, and person B selects one ball from urn 2. What is the probability that at least one of them will select a black ball?
7. Assuming the same circumstances as in question 6, what is the probability that either person A or person B will select a red ball?
8. An urn contains fifty balls, fifteen of which are black, five are white, twenty are red, and ten are yellow. If one ball is selected at random, what is the probability that (a) it will be either white or black, (b) it will be either red or yellow, (c) it will be either black or yellow?

Combining the Rules

As the preceding examples show, there are some complex events for which we must use both conjunction and disjunction rules. Take the boy and the jellybeans again. Suppose that the boy's indulgent parents, seeing how low the supply of beans was growing, have kindly refilled one jar. It now contains forty beans: ten licorice, ten papaya, ten mango, and ten cinnamon. Although the boy likes all these flavors equally, he has an aversion to mixing them. What is the probability that he will get five beans of any one flavor on his first five tries? The four mutually exclusive favorable alternatives here are getting five licorice beans, or five papaya beans, or five mango beans, or five cinnamon beans. The initial probability of the choice of a licorice bean, on the classical theory, is 10/40, since there are ten licorice among the total of forty jellybeans. Assuming that the first one chosen is licorice, the boy now has thirty-nine beans left from which to choose, only nine of which represent favorable outcomes. So the probability of getting a licorice on the second choice, after having gotten a licorice on the first choice, is 9/39. After this there are only thirty-eight beans left, eight of which are licorice. Therefore, the probability of getting a licorice on the third try if the first and second have yielded licorice is 8/38; the probability of getting a licorice on the next try is 7/37; and probability on the fifth try, assuming success in the four previous trials, is 6/36. According to the general conjunction rule, the probability of getting five beans of one particular flavor thus equals:

$$P(\text{five beans of one flavor}) =$$
$$\frac{10}{40} \times \frac{9}{39} \times \frac{8}{38} \times \frac{7}{37} \times \frac{6}{36} = \frac{30{,}240}{78{,}960{,}960}$$

Since the other three favorable alternatives are mutually exclusive (and are being assumed to be all equally probable), the restricted disjunction rule can be used to calculate the probability of getting five jellybeans of any one flavor:

$$P(\text{five licorice beans or five papaya or five mango or}$$
$$\text{five cinnamon}) =$$

$$\frac{30{,}240}{78{,}960{,}960} + \frac{30{,}240}{78{,}960{,}960} + \frac{30{,}240}{78{,}960{,}960} +$$
$$\frac{30{,}240}{78{,}960{,}960} = \frac{120{,}960}{78{,}960{,}960} = \frac{14}{9139}$$

In conclusion, it must be emphasized that the preceding discussion barely scratches the surface of the basic subject matter of probability. Not only have we omitted several significant theories concerning the meaning of, and methods for establishing, initial probabilities, but the three theories we have discussed have been presented only in simplified form, with no treatment of the numerous variations of each of the general types. Similarly, we have described only a few of the most basic and simple concepts and rules of the probability calculus. A full treatment of the probability calculus (even without discussion of the alternative techniques for establishing initial probability) would require a whole book.

EXERCISE 13–8

The following problems require the use of more than one method. Calculate the probabilities, giving the same information as in Exercises 13–4 and 13–6.

---

1. Three dice are tossed on a single throw. What is the probability of (a) three twos; (b) either three twos or three threes?
2. Four cards are dealt from a well-shuffled deck without a joker. What is the probability of getting an ace, a king, a queen, and a jack (a) in spades, in the order given; (b) in any one suit, in the order given; (c) in spades, in any order?

3. A coin purse contains two dimes and three nickels. If you reach in to get change to buy a newspaper, what is the probability that (a) the first two coins you draw out will add up to fifteen cents; (b) the first three coins you draw out will add up to fifteen cents; (c) you will get fifteen cents on either the first two or the first three draws?

SUMMARY

1. An adequate theory of probability must satisfy at least two requirements. First, a statement which is absolutely true has a probability of 1, while a statement which is absolutely false has a probability of 0, and any statement which is neither absolutely true nor absolutely false has a probability between 0 and 1. A second requirement is that the sum of the probabilities of any logically inconsistent statements (that is, statements not more than one of which can be true at any given time) must be no greater than 1.

2. The **classical theory,** or *a priori* theory, of probability is based on two assumptions. The first is that all possible events are known. The second, called the **principle of indifference,** is that the probability of the occurrence of each event is equal to that of the others, unless there is good reason to believe otherwise. The probability that the favorable event will occur is determined by dividing the number of possible favorable events by the total number of equally possible events. This theory cannot be used when statistical or other evidence indicates that not all possible events are equally probable.

3. All of the several versions of the **relative frequency theory** are based on the direct observation of concrete cases. This theory stipulates that the probability of an event is determined by dividing the number of observed favorable events by the total number of observed events. One difficulty faced by most versions of this theory stems from their assertion that probabilities based on observations of past cases are applicable to future cases only in the long run. That is, it is improper, or sometimes even meaningless, to assign a probability value to a single event.

4. The **subjectivist theory** defines probabilities as being grounded in the beliefs of individual persons. Thus, a variety of different probabilities can be assigned to the same particular event. Opponents claim that this is a fatal criticism, but supporters of the theory see it as a strength. One method suggested by some subjectivists for establishing quantitatively expressed probabilities of events is in terms of betting odds.

5. The procedures for determining the probabilities of compound events have been codified in a formal axiom system known as the **probability calculus.** The **initial probability,** determined by one of the above theories, is the probability of a single event's occurring by itself. A **complex event** is a whole composed of a number of simple events.

6. An **independent** complex event is one whose component events are such that the occurrence of one has no effect on the occurrence of the other(s); that is, if one event occurs, the probability of the occurrence of the other event(s) is not changed. The **restricted conjunction rule** states that if **x** and **y** are independent events, then the probability of both **x** and **y** occurring is equal to the probability of **x** occurring multiplied by the probability of **y** occurring.

7. A **dependent** complex event is an event in which one of the components affects the circumstances of the other(s) in such a way that, if one component

occurs, the probability of the other(s) occurring is no longer what it would have been if the first event had not occurred. The **general conjunction** rule is used to calculate probability values of the joint occurrence of a number of simple events (whether dependent or independent). This rule states that if **x** and **y** are any two events whatever, then the probability of their joint occurrence is equal to the probability of **x** occurring multiplied by the probability of **y** occurring, given that **x** has already occurred. The restricted conjunction rule can be derived from the general conjunction rule, since if **x** and **y** are independent events, then the probability of **y**, given that **x** has already occurred, is the same as the probability of **y** itself.

8.   There are some complex events which are disjunctions—that is, which may be said to occur when one or more of several alternative events occur. **Mutually exclusive** events are such that only one can occur. The **restricted disjunction rule** is used to calculate the probability of the occurrence of one or another of two or more mutually exclusive events. This rule states that if **x** and **y** are mutually exclusive events, then the probability that either will occur is equal to the probability of **x** plus the probability of **y**.

9.   The **general disjunction rule** is used to calculate the probability of the disjunction of any two or more events whatsoever; that is, it is not restricted to disjunctions of mutually exclusive events. This rule states that, for any two events **x** and **y**, the probability that at least one will occur is equal to the sum of the initial probabilities of **x** and **y** minus the probability that both **x** and **y** will occur (the probability that both will occur is calculated by the general conjunction rule). The restricted disjunction rule can be derived from the general disjunction rule, since, for mutually exclusive events, the probability that both will occur is 0.

Answers to Odd-Numbered Exercises

EXERCISE 1–2

1. Cognitive: This sentence expresses a factual statement about which it is appropriate to say it is true or false.
3. Noncognitive: This sentence expresses a command not usually considered either true or false.
5. Cognitive 7. Noncognitive 9. Noncognitive
11. Noncognitive 13. Mixed use 15. Noncognitive
17. Mixed use 19. Noncognitive or cognitive (Choice depends on a specific everyday context.)

EXERCISE 1–3

Sample answers for 1 only. A large variety of different correct answers are possible for each exercise.
1. *Cognitive context:* A situation where a person uses this sentence to express the fact that he or she is cold. (I am feeling cold.) *Noncognitive context:* A situation where one person orders another person to close the window of a chilly room.

EXERCISE 1–4

1. Semantically analytic 3. Synthetic
5. Syntactically analytic 7. Semantically analytic
9. Semantically analytic 11. Synthetic
13. Semantically analytic
15. Synthetic, unless the definition of George Washington includes his being the first president, in which case the statement is semantically analytic.
17. Semantically analytic 19. Syntactically analytic
21. Syntactically analytic 23. Syntactically analytic

EXERCISE 1–5

1. Connotative
3. Enumerative, denotative, unless one believes that numbers are nothing more than numerals, in which case it would be an ostensive definition.
5. Connotative, by genus and difference (genus = 'polyhedron')
7. Connotative
9. Connotative, by genus and difference (genus = oak).
11. Enumerative, denotative 13. Synonymous
15. Connotative 17. Operational
19. Enumerative, denotative 21. Operational
23. Connotative

25. Connotative (genus and difference)
27. Synonymous 29. Enumerative (ostensive)
31. Enumerative (denotative) 33. Connotative
35. Connotative (genus and difference)
37. Operational 39. Connotative

EXERCISE 1–6

The following answers are presented only as examples of possible correct answers. Many other answers would also be correct.
1. (a) City. (b) New York, Chicago, Dallas, San Francisco. (denotative definition) (c) An inhabited place having a large size and population.
3. (a) Bug. (b) Beetle, grasshopper, ant, and roach. (c) Any of numerous small invertebrate animals that are more or less segmented and have six legs.
5. (a) Automobile. (b) Buick, Cadillac, and Mercedes-Benz. (c) Usually a four-wheeled vehicle designed for passenger transportation and generally powered by an internal combustion engine using gasoline.
7. (a) Adventure. (b) Climbing Mt. Everest, shooting rapids in a canoe, walking on the moon. (c) An experience offering unusual, exciting, or hazardous circumstances.
9. (a) Drama. (b) *Hamlet, Long Day's Journey into Night,* and *Oedipus Rex.* (c) A theatrical composition or stage representation of a story.

EXERCISE 1–7

1. When one places a piece of iron near an object and the piece of iron is pulled toward the object, the object is a magnet.
3. A substance is flammable if it ignites when a lighted match is placed near it in the presence of oxygen.
5. If you feed a substance to an organism, and the organism dies, the substance is a poison for that organism.
7. Any person who scores over 150 on an IQ test is considered to be a genius.
9. If you hold your finger on the side of an object opposite to your eyes and can still see it clearly, the object is transparent.

EXERCISE 1–8

1. Limited reportive, theoretical   3. Stipulative
5. Limited reportive, theoretical
7. Reportive, legal. (This is not a limited reportive definition since the legal meaning of the word "escrow" is its only meaning.)
9. Precising, possibly also stipulative
11. Persuasive, possibly also reportive
13. Limited reportive, legal
15. Reportive   17. Limited reportive
19. Limited reportive—legal, and persuasive
21. Stipulative

EXERCISE 1–10

1. Noncircularity   3. Clarity   5. Affirmativeness
7. Accuracy (too narrow) though it may be persuasively effective
9. Accuracy (too narrow)
11. Accuracy (too narrow *and* too broad)
13. Clarity   15. Clarity

EXERCISE 1–11

1. Consistent   3. Consistent   5. Inconsistent
7. Consistent   9. Consistent   11. Consistent
13. Inconsistent   15. Consistent

EXERCISE 1–12

1. An apparent disagreement, since both statements may be true simultaneously.
3. An apparent disagreement/verbal; persons A and B are probably using different definitions for the term 'poor'.
5. A real disagreement
7. An apparent disagreement; statement A refers to a perception of the straw, while statement B refers to the way the straw really is.
9. A real disagreement
11. A real disagreement
13. An apparent verbal disagreement; A and B are probably using the term 'masterpiece' differently.
15. An apparent disagreement; it may be true that the sun *looks* as though it revolves and it may also be true that the earth *revolves* about the sun.
17. Most likely an apparent/verbal disagreement with persons A and B having different ideas about what indicates good academic performance.
19. An apparent disagreement

EXERCISE 1–13

1. A implies B.   3. Independent   5. B implies A.
7. Independent   9. A implies B.
11. Logically equivalent   13. Logically equivalent
15. Independent

EXERCISE 2–2

1. (a) Spiders are not insects. (b) Insects have only six legs.
3. (a) Frank could never become a policeman. (b) He is only five feet two inches tall and weighs only 120 lbs.
5. (a) Tom will never be able to climb the face of that cliff. (b) He has no training in rock climbing.
7. (a) Some mammals can fly. (b) Bats can fly.
9. (a) The sum of its (this figure's) interior angles is 540°. (b) This figure is a pentagon.
11. (a) That is not a good French dictionary. (b) It (that French dictionary) does not show how each word should be pronounced.
13. (a) It (coffee) must contain a stimulant. (b) Coffee keeps people awake.
15. (a) It will take two seconds for that rock to fall. (b) It (that rock) is going to fall a distance of sixty-four feet.
17. (a) This solution is an acid. (b) It (this solution) turns litmus paper red.
19. (a) Starvation will inevitably occur somewhere in the world. (b) The expanding world population will eventually increase beyond the capacity of the total world agricultural resources to feed it.
21. (a) Our industrial system will eventually cease to expand. (b) The functioning of an industrial system depends on an abundance of raw materials. Raw materials are running out.
23. (a) He did not commit the crime. (b) The defendant was not present at the scene of the crime.
25. (a) They are responsible. (b) Men are free.
27. (a) No one, including the defendant, could have got off three shots in a span of five seconds. (b) It takes three seconds to operate the bold of this rifle.
29. (a) The statement 'No statement can be proven with absolute certitude' cannot be proved with absolute certitude. (b) No statement can be proved with absolute certitude.

EXERCISE 2–3

1. (a) No. (b) It is a conditional.
3. (a) No. (b) It is a conditional; also 'Give Joan a call' expresses a command.
5. (a) No. (b) 'Since' is probably being used in a temporal sense.
7. (a) No. (b) 'Please don't pick the flowers' expresses a command, not a statement.
9. (a) Yes. (c) Conclusion: You are an idealist. Premise: All Sagittarians are idealists.
11. (a) No. (b) 'Since' is being used in a temporal sense.
13. (a) Yes. (c) Conclusion: Socrates is mortal. Premises: All men are mortal. Socrates is a man.
15. (a) Yes. (c) Conclusion: All our citizens must be allowed to express their opinions freely. Premise: If all

our citizens are not allowed to express their opinions freely, then their freedom of speech will be violated.

17. (a) Yes. (c) Conclusion: It is stored in lead containers. Premise: Hydrofluoric acid dissolves glass.
19. (a) No. (b) 'Since' is being used in a temporal sense.
21. (a) No. (b) This 'if . . . then' sentence is being used to express a conditional statement.
23. (a) Yes. (c) Conclusion: French is called a romance language. Premise: It (French) is derived from Latin.
25. (a) No. (b) 'Since' is used in a temporal sense.
27. (a) No. (b) 'Don't use that book when you write your paper' is a command.
29. (a) Yes. (c) Conclusion: It (this rock) is not quartz. Premises: 'If a rock is quartz, it will scratch glass', *and* 'This rock will not scratch glass'.
31. (a) Yes. (c) Conclusion: I don't think you will agree with his conclusions in *Beyond Freedom and Dignity*. Premise: Skinner is a determinist.
33. (a) No. (b) The passage is exposition; 'Since' is used in the temporal sense.

EXERCISE 2–4

Note that each of these is only one of many possible counterexamples for each argument.

1. If it rains, then the ground will get wet. The ground is wet. Therefore, it rained. (The ground, of course, could be wet because someone hosed it down.)
3. All monkeys are mammals. No men are monkeys. Therefore, no men are mammals.
5. All whales are mammals. An ape is not a whale. Therefore, an ape is not a mammal.
7. Tomato juice is a delicious drink. Coffee is a delicious drink. Therefore, tomato juice-coffee is a delicious drink.
9. No Englishmen are Russians. No Englishmen are Americans. Therefore, all Russians are Americans.
11. If an animal is a mammal, then it bears its young live. A guppy is not a mammal. Therefore, a guppy does not bear its young live. (Guppies, a type of fish, do, in fact, bear their young live.)
13. All chimpanzees are mammals. Some mammals are men. Therefore, some chimpanzees are men.
15. Water extinguishes fires. Water is made of hydrogen and oxygen. Therefore, hydrogen extinguishes fires.

EXERCISE 2–5

Note that for part (b) of the answers in this exercise: Where the argument is deductive, it is so in all cases because the premise(s) provide(s) absolute support for the conclusion. Where the argument is inductive, it is so because the premise(s) do(es) not provide absolute support for the conclusion. For inductive arguments, the answers given in (b) explain why the support is not absolute in each case.

1. Inductive. (b) The fact that the person uttering the argument has not seen a bird that did not fly does not mean that such a bird could not exist. It is possible for the conclusion to be false while the premise is true.
3. (a) Deductive. (b) The conclusion can't possibly be true if both premises are true.
5. (a) Inductive. (b) It is possible for the premises to be true and the conclusion false.
7. (a) Inductive. (b) The truth of the premise does not necessitate the truth of the conclusion.
9. (a) Deductive
11. (a) Inductive. (b) The argument is weakened if a premise is added to the effect that Helen works as a waitress in a truck stop restaurant.
13. (a) Deductive. (b) If the premises are true, the conclusion must be true.
15. (a) Deductive. (b) If the premises are true, the conclusion must be true.
17. (a) Inductive. (b) The argument can be weakened if it is added that Bob's parents both have brown eyes.
19. (a) Inductive. (b) It is possible for the premises to be true and the conclusion false. (This is possibly even a nonargument, since the premises may provide no support whatsoever for the conclusion.)
21. (a) Inductive. (b) Even if the premises are true, it is still possible for the conclusion to be false. Someone who is not a suspect may have committed the crime.
23. (a) Inductive. (b) The premise leaves open the *possibility* that some other species of animal may be observed in the future to be capable of rational thought.
25. (a) Deductive. (b) If the premises are true, the conclusion must be true.

EXERCISE 2–6

1. (a) Yes (b) Yes   3. (a) Yes (b) Yes
5. (a) Yes (b) Yes   7. (a) No (b) No
9. (a) Yes (b) Yes   11. (a) No (b) No
13. (a) No: The second premise is false. (b) No
15. (a) Yes (b) Yes   17. (a) Yes (b) Yes

EXERCISE 2–7

Note that there may be other possibilities for the supplied premise in each answer.

1. Premise: It doesn't have thorns. Conclusion: That is not a rose bush. Supplied premise: All rose bushes have thorns.
3. Premise: The end of a thing is the perfection of life. Conclusion: Death is the perfection of life. Supplied premise: Death is the end of a thing.
5. Premise: This wine is red wine. Conclusion: This wine is not Chablis. Supplied premise: No red wine is Chablis.
7. Premise: Both teams played poorly. Conclusion: The

baseball game was dull. Supplied premise: If both teams play poorly, a baseball game will be dull.

9. Premise: All metaphysicians are eccentric. Conclusion: Karl is eccentric. Supplied premise: Karl is a metaphysician.

11. Premise: Mr. Poindexter did not work for the company. Conclusion: He could not have stolen the money. Supplied premise: If a person did not work for the company, he could not have stolen the money.

13. Premise: All men make mistakes. Conclusion: So does John. Supplied premise: John is a man.

15. Premise: He passed the examination. Conclusion: He must have lied. Supplied premise: If he passed the examination, he must have lied.

17. Premise: Senator Brandt is a major party candidate. Conclusion: He (Senator Brandt) is a Democrat. Supplied premise: All major party candidates are either Republicans or Democrats.

EXERCISE 2–8

Note that there are many other possible answers for (b) and (c) of each answer.

1. (a) Premises: I liked the 1969 Beaujolais wine that I drank, and I liked the 1970 Beaujolais wine that I drank, and I liked the 1971 Beaujolais wine that I drank. Conclusion: I will like the 1972 Beaujolais wine that I am going to drink. (b) I liked the 1967 Beaujolais wine that I drank. (c) I did not like the 1968 Beaujolais wine that I drank.

3. (a) Premise: John has done very well on all of his algebra tests. Conclusion: He will do well on his algebra final today. (b) John studied hard for the final examination in algebra. (c) John did not study at all for his algebra final.

5. (a) Premise: The weatherman says we will have a clear day tomorrow, the same as today. Conclusion: We will be able to see the partial eclipse of the sun. (b) The weatherman's predictions have been correct 90 percent of the time. (c) The weatherman's predictions have been incorrect 90 percent of the time.

7. (a) Premises: I walked under a ladder, and a black cat crossed my path. Conclusion: Something terrible is going to happen to me. (b) All past instances in which I walked under a ladder and a black cat crossed my path are times when something terrible happened to me. (c) All past instances in which I walked under a ladder and a black cat crossed my path are times when something wonderful happened to me.

9. (a) Premises: Most east coast newspaper editors are liberals, and Mr. Harrison is an east coast newspaper editor. Conclusion: Mr. Harrison is probably a liberal. (b) Mr. Harrison is a Democrat. (c) Mr. Harrison has

lived all his life in a small conservative New England town and is editor of the town's only newspaper.

11. (a) Premises: Most members of the Veterans of Foreign Wars condemn draft evaders, and Mr. Robinson is a member of the Veterans of Foreign Wars. Conclusion: He will probably condemn draft evaders. (b) Mr. Robinson always agrees with the opinion of the majority of members of the Veterans of Foreign Wars. (c) Mr. Robinson never agrees with the opinion of the majority of members of the Veterans of Foreign Wars.

13. (a) Premise: Five of the horses I've picked fit the system I've worked out for picking winners. Conclusion: I just know I'm going to win some money at the race track today. (b) My system has worked each time I've used it. (c) My system has never worked in the past.

15. (a) Premise: At the present rate of consumption, the known world petroleum reserves will be exhausted by 2005. Conclusion: The automobile as we know it will eventually have to be replaced with other means of transportation by the year 2020. (b) The rate of consumption will not level off and remain static, but will continue to increase at its present rate so that the known reserves will be exhausted by 1990. (c) It is very probable that a way will be found to produce gasoline and motor oil from other materials, and also that new oil reserves will be discovered.

EXERCISE 3–1

1. False cause 3. False dilemma 5. Division
7. Argument from ignorance 9. False cause
11. Division

EXERCISE 3–2

1. Appeal to authority 3. Begging the question
5. Begging the question 7. Ad hominem (tu quoque)
9. Ad hominem (tu quoque) 11. Hasty generalization
13. Appeal to force 15. Division
17. False dilemma
19. Equivocation (on 'starving') 21. False dilemma
23. Equivocation (on 'difficult to find')
25. Argument from ignorance
27. Equivocation (on 'kill') or ad hominem
29. Ad hominem (abusive)
31. Ad hominem (circumstantial)
33. Equivocation (on 'heavy')
35. Ad populum and false cause
37. Composition 39. Composition 41. False cause
43. Appeal to authority
45. Ad hominem (circumstantial)
47. Ad hominem (tu quoque) 49. Ad populum

51. Ad populum   53.   Ad baculum
55. Appeal to authority   57.   Ad hominem (abusive)
59. False dilemma   61.   Equivocation (on 'rare')
63. False cause or hasty generalization
65. Division   67.   Ad hominem (circumstantial)
69. Hasty generalization

EXERCISE 4–1

1. A 3. O 5. I 7. A 9. O
11. E 13. E 15. E

EXERCISE 4–2

1. (a) All Frenchmen are Europeans. (b) **A** (c) All F are E. (d) All S are P.
3. Some sailors are swarthy persons. (b) **I** (c) Some Sa are Sw. (d) Some S are P.
5. (a) No ponderosas are shrubs. (b) **E** (c) No P are S. (d) No S are P.
7. (a) All kraters are Greek vases. (b) **A** (c) All K are G. (d) All S are P.
9. (a) Some fans are not machines. (b) **O** (c) Some F are not M. (d) Some S are not P.
11. (a) There are two possible interpretations: Some politicians are not dishonest persons, *and* No politicans are dishonest persons, although the lack of context indicates that the weaker **O** statement is more appropriate than the universal negative **E** statement. (b) **O** or **E**. (c) Some P are not D, or No P are D. (d) Some S are not P, or No S are P.
13. (a) Some European families are not families that own an automobile. (b) **O** (c) Some **E** are not **O**. (d) Some S are not P. Alternatively; (a) Some European families are families that do not own an automobile. (b) **I** (c) Some E are N. (d) Some S are P.
15. (a) 'Some paperbacks are inexpensive things, *and* 'Some paperbacks are not inexpensive things', (b) **I, O** (c) Some P are I, *and* Some P are not I. (d) Some S are P *and* Some S are not P.
17. (a) All invited persons are members of the club. (b) **A** (c) All I are M. (d) All P are S.
19. (a) Some college students are students who work part-time to pay for their education. (b) **I** (c) Some C are W. (d) Some S are P.
21. An **I** statement and an **O** statement are expressed by this sentence. **I** statement: (a) Some professional basketball players are persons over six feet four inches tall. (c) Some B are T. (d) Some S are P. **O** statement: (a) Some professional basketball players are not persons over six feet four inches tall. (c) Some B are not T. (d) Some S are not P.

23. (a) All persons who are invited to the party are his friends. (b) A (c) All I are F. (d) All S are P.
25. (a) All persons who were able to get seats are persons who bought tickets in advance. (b) **A** (c) All S are B. (d) All S are P.

EXERCISE 4–3

1. (a) All typewriters are machines that are noisy. (b) All T are N. (c) All S are P.
3. (a) Some dodos are not things which are extinct. (b) Some D are not E. (c) Some S are not P.
5. (a) Some Toyotas are vehicles that get thirty miles to the gallon. (b) Some To are Th. (c) Some S are P.
7. (a) All persons of the class of which yon Cassius is the only member are persons who have a lean and hungry look. (b) All Y are L. (c) All S are P.
9. (a) Some cars are not things having pollution control devices. (b) Some C are not P. (c) Some S are not P.
11. (a) No men are an island. (b) No M are I. (c) No S are P.
13. (a) No seals are animals having a smooth coat of fur. (b) No S are C. (c) No S are P.
15. (a) No persons are things that waved goodbye. (b) No P are G. (c) No S are P.

EXERCISE 4–4

1. (a) Some wines are things made from dandelions. (b) Some W is D. (c) Some S are P.

(d)

3. (a) All beetles are bugs. (b) All B are Bu. (c) All S are P.
(d)

4. 5. (a) No termites are ants. (b) No T are A. (c) No S are P.
(d)

7. (a) Some Arabs are Moslems, *and* some Arabs are not Moslems. (b) Some A are M, *and* Some A are not M. (c) Some S are P, *and* Some S are not P.

(d)

(d)

9. (a) Some dancers are persons who can charleston. (b) Some D are C. (c) Some S are P.

(d)

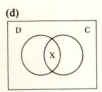

11. (a) All those who attend the Soph-ball are sophomores. (b) All A are S. (c) All S are P.

(d)

13. (a) No persons are people who scored higher than 90 percent on the test. (b) No P are H. (c) No S are P.

(d)

15. (a) All persons who can vote are citizens. (b) All V are C. (c) All P are S.

(d)

17. (a) No thing which is lightning is a thing which strikes twice in the same place. (b) No L is S. (c) No S are P.

(d)

19. (a) Some art collectors are rich persons, *and* Some art collectors are not rich persons. (b) Some A are R *and* Some A are not R. (c) Some S are P, *and* Some S are not P.

(d)

EXERCISE 4–5

Sentences from Exercise 4–1.

1. (a) All typewriters are noisy. (b) All T are N. (c) All S are P.

3. (a) Some dodos are not extinct things. (c) Some D are not E. (c) Some S are not P.

5. (a) Some Toyotas are cars which get thirty miles to the gallon. (b) Some T are C. (c) Some S are P.

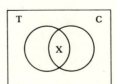

7. (a) All members of the class of which yon Cassius is the only member are people with a lean and hungry look. (b) All C are L. (c) All S are P.

9. (a) Some cars are not things which have pollution control devices; or Some cars are things which do not have pollution control devices. (b) Some C are not P; or Some C are T. (c) Some S are not P; or Some S are P.

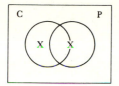 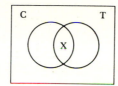

11. (a) No man is an island. (b) No M are I. (c) No S are P.

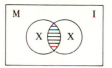

13. (a) No seals are animals having a smooth coat of fur. (b) No S are C. (c) No S are P.

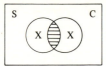

E: No S are C.

15. (a) No persons are persons who waved goodby. (b) No P are W. (c) No S are P.

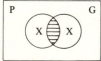

E: No P are W.

Sentences from Exercise 4–2.

1.
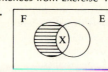
All F are E.

3.
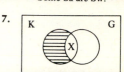
Some Sa are Sw.

5.
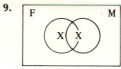
No P are S.

7.
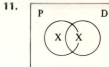
All K are G.

9.
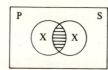
Some F are not M.

11.
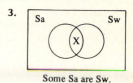
O: Some P are not D.

13.
 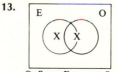
O: Some E are not O.   I: Some E are N.

15.
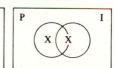 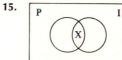
Some P are I.   Some P are not I.

17.

All I are M.

19.

I: Some C are W.

21.
 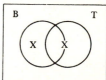
I: Some B are T.   O: Some B are not T.

23.

A: All I are F.

25.

A: All S are B.

EXERCISE 4–6

1. (a) Contrariety (b) False (c) Undetermined
3. (a) Superimplication (b) Undetermined (c) False
5. (a) Superimplication (b) Undetermined (c) False
7. (a) Contrariety (b) False (c) Undetermined
9. (a) Contrariety (b) False (c) Undetermined
11. (a) Subimplication (b) True (c) Undetermined
13. (a) Contradiction (b) False (c) True
15. (a) Contrariety (b) False (c) Undetermined

EXERCISE 4–7

1. (a) Relationship to original statement:
   a. Contrary
   b. Subimplicant
   c. Contradictory
   (b) If original statement is true:
   a. False
   b. True
   c. False
   (c) If original statement is false:
   a. Undetermined
   b. Undetermined
   c. True
3. (a) Relationship to original statement:
   a. Subcontrary
   b. Contradictory
   c. Superimplicant
   (b) If original statement is true:
   a. Undetermined
   b. False
   c. Undetermined
   (c) If original statement is false:
   a. True
   b. True
   c. False
5. (a) Relationship to original statement:
   a. Contrary
   b. Subimplicant
   c. Contradictory
   (b) If original statement is true:
   a. False
   b. True
   c. False
   (c) If original statement is false:
   a. Undetermined
   b. Undetermined
   c. True
7. (a) Relationship to original statement:
   a. Subcontrary
   b. Superimplicant
   c. Contradictory

(b) If original statement is true:
   a. Undetermined
   b. Undetermined
   c. False
(c) If original statement is false:
   a. True
   b. False
   c. True

EXERCISE 4–8

1. (a) Consistent (b) Dependent
3. (a) Consistent (b) Independent
5. (a) Consistent (b) Dependent
7. (a) Consistent (b) Independent
9. (a) Consistent (b) Dependent

EXERCISE 4–9

1. (a) All <u>o</u>aks are non<u>m</u>aples. (b) Equivalent.

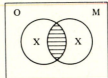 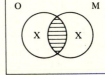

E: No O are M.   A: All O are nonM.

3. (a) No <u>m</u>adrigal <u>s</u>ingers are non<u>m</u>usicians. (b) Equivalent.

A: All S are M.   E: No S are nonM.

5. (a) Some <u>g</u>ifts are not non<u>e</u>xpensive things. (b) Equivalent.

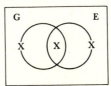 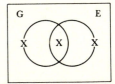

I: Some G are E.   O: Some G are not nonE.

7. (a) All <u>b</u>iscuits are non<u>m</u>uffins. (b) Equivalent.

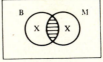

No B are M.   All B are nonM.

9. (a) Some <u>m</u>embers are non<u>l</u>awyers. (b) Equivalent.

 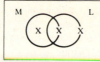

Some M are not L. Some M are nonL.

EXERCISE 4–10

1. (a) All <u>f</u>ish are <u>s</u>almon. (b) Not equivalent.

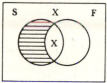

A: All S are F. A: All F are S.

3. (a) Some <u>C</u>alifornians are <u>A</u>mericans. (b) Equivalent.

 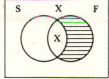

I: Some A are C. I: Some C are A.

5. (a) All <u>w</u>riting instruments are <u>p</u>ens. (b) Not equivalent.

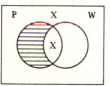 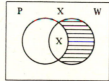

A: All P are W. A: All W are P.

7. (a) No <u>f</u>our-star generals are <u>w</u>omen. (b) Not equivalent.

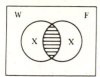

No W are F. No F are W.

9. (a) Some <u>e</u>lected persons are not <u>r</u>epresentatives. (b) Not equivalent.

 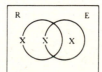

Some R are not E. Some E are not R.

EXERCISE 4–11

1. (a) All non<u>t</u>ools are non<u>h</u>ammers. (b) Equivalent.

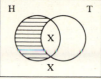 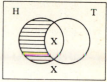

A: All H are T. A: All nonT are nonH.

3. (a) Some <u>a</u>lcoholic beverages are non<u>d</u>rinks. (b) Not equivalent.

I: Some D are nonA. I: Some A are nonD.

5. (a) No non<u>m</u>en are non<u>m</u>ice. (b) Not equivalent.

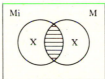 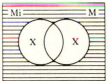

E: No Mi are M. E: No nonM are nonMi.

7. (a) Non non<u>c</u>arnivores are non<u>e</u>lephants. (b) Not equivalent.

No E are C. No nonC are nonE.

9. (a) Some non<u>d</u>eep things are not non<u>k</u>ettles. (b) Equivalent.

Some K are not D. Some nonD are not nonK.

EXERCISE 4–12

1. (a) Obversion (b) True
3. (a) Contradiction (b) False
5. (a) Conversion (b) Undetermined
7. (a) Converse of contradiction (b) Undetermined
9. (a) Converse of obverse of contradication (b) False
11. (a) Contraposition (b) True

EXERCISE 4–12

1. (a) Obversion (b) True
3. (a) Contradiction (b) False
5. (a) Converse (b) True
7. (a) Converse of contradiction (b) False
9. (a) Contraposition of contradiction (b) Undetermined
11. (a) Converse of obverse of contrary (b) False

EXERCISE 4–13

1. (a) Observe (b) True
3. (a) Contradiction (b) False
5. (a) Conversion (b) True
7. (a) Superimplication of converse (b) Undetermined
9. (a) Contraposition of contradiction (b) Undetermined
11. (a) Contraposition (b) Undetermined

EXERCISE 4–14

1. (a) Obverse (b) True
3. (a) Contradiction (b) Undetermined
5. (a) Converse (b) Undetermined
7. (a) Converse of obverse of contradiction (b) False
9. (a) Converse of contradiction (b) Undetermined

EXERCISE 5–1

1. (a) Categorical syllogism. (b) Not in standard form. (c) All bees are things that can sting. Some bees are insects. Therefore, some insects are things than can sting.
3. (a) Not a categorical syllogism. The term "incandescent lights" appears three times and "fluorescent lights" only once.
5. (a) Categorical syllogism. (b) Not in standard form. (c) All drunkards are alcoholics. Some drinkers are drunkards. Therefore, some drinkers are alcoholics.
7. (a) Not a categorical syllogism. Although it is a mediate inference, it has three premises.
9. (a) Not a categorical syllogism. The argument has four different terms.
11. (a) Categorical syllogism. (b) Not in standard form. (c) All communists are Marxists. Some revolutionaries are not Marxists. Therefore, some revolutionaries are not communists.
13. (a) Categorical syllogism. (b) Not in standard form. (c) No kangaroos are soldiers. All generals are soldiers. Therefore, no generals are kangaroos.
15. (a) Not a categorical syllogism. The argument is really an immediate inference (conversion).
17. (a) Not a categorical syllogism. The first premise cannot be put into standard form.
19. (a) Not a categorical syllogism. Immediate inference by contraposition.

EXERCISE 5–2

1. (a) All B are S.
Some B are I.
∴Some I are S.

(b) All $\underline{M}$ are $\underline{P}$.
Some $\underline{M}$ are $\underline{S}$.
∴Some $\underline{S}$ are $\underline{P}$.

5. (a) All D are A.
Some Dr are D.
∴Some Dr are A.

(b) All $\underline{M}$ are $\underline{P}$.
Some $\underline{S}$ are $\underline{M}$.
∴Some $\underline{S}$ are $\underline{P}$.

11. (a) All C are M.
Some R are not M.
∴Some R are not C.

(b) All $\underline{P}$ are $\underline{M}$.
Some $\underline{S}$ are not $\underline{M}$.
∴Some $\underline{S}$ are not $\underline{P}$.

13. (a) No K are S.
All G are S.
∴No G are K.

(b) No $\underline{P}$ are $\underline{M}$.
All $\underline{S}$ are $\underline{M}$.
∴No $\underline{S}$ are $\underline{P}$.

EXERCISE 5–3

1. All-3 **5.** All-1 **11.** AOO-2 **13.** EAE-2

EXERCISE 5–4

Note that each answer is only one of many possible answers.

1. All primates are mammals. Some mammals are aquatic animals. Therefore, some aquatic animals are primates.
3. No horses are flowers. No flowers are animals. Therefore, no horses are animals.
5. All Chicagoans are citizens. Some citizens are New Yorkers. Therefore, some New Yorkers are Chicagoans.
7. No pines are oaks. All pines are trees. Therefore, no trees are oaks.
9. All roses are plants. No roses are trees. Therefore, no trees are plants.
11. No beggars are rich. No millionaires are beggars. Therefore, no millionaires are rich.
13. Some animals are cats. All dogs are animals. Therefore, some dogs are cats.

EXERCISE 5–5

1. Valid
   H = hippies
   L = law-abiding citizens
   P = pot smokers

3. Valid
   Dr = drugs
   Da = dangerous things
   H = hallucinogens

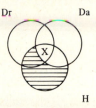

5. Valid
   Dr = drugs
   Da = dangerous things
   H = hallucinogens

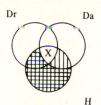

7. Valid
   P = powerful men
   R = reactionaries
   D = dictators

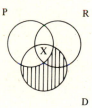

9. Valid
   Standard form:
   All monks are ascetics.
   Some Buddhists are monks.
   Therefore, some Buddhists are ascetics.

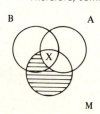

11. Invalid
    Standard form:
    No oak trees are pines.
    All pines are conifers.
    Therefore, no conifers are oak trees.

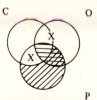

13. Invalid
    Standard form:
    No cats are canines.
    No cats are wolves.
    Therefore, some wolves are canines.

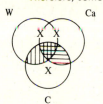

15. Valid
    Standard form:
    No edible things are toadstools.
    Some edible things are mushrooms.
    Therefore, some mushrooms are not toadstools

EXERCISE 5–6

1. Valid
   All P are M.
   No M are S.
   ∴No S are P.

3.   Invalid
No <u>M</u> are <u>P</u>.
<u>All <u>M</u> are <u>S</u>.</u>
∴No <u>S</u> are <u>P</u>.

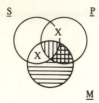

5.   Invalid
Some <u>P</u> are <u>M</u>.
<u>No <u>M</u> are <u>S</u>.</u>
∴Some <u>S</u> are not <u>P</u>.

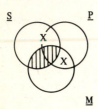

7.   Invalid
Some <u>P</u> are <u>M</u>.
<u>All <u>S</u> are <u>M</u>.</u>
∴Some <u>S</u> are <u>P</u>.

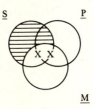

9.   Valid
All <u>M</u> are <u>P</u>.
<u>Some <u>S</u> are <u>M</u>.</u>
∴Some <u>S</u> are <u>P</u>.

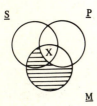

11.   Valid
All <u>P</u> are <u>M</u>.
<u>Some <u>S</u> are not <u>M</u>.</u>
∴Some <u>S</u> are not <u>P</u>.

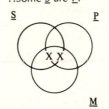

13.   Invalid
Some <u>P</u> are <u>M</u>.
<u>Some <u>S</u> are <u>M</u>.</u>
∴Some <u>S</u> are <u>P</u>.

15.   Valid
No <u>P</u> are <u>M</u>.
<u>All <u>S</u> are <u>M</u>.</u>
∴Some <u>S</u> are not <u>P</u>.

EXERCISE 5–7

1.   (b) Rule two: Illicit major (c) Invalid
3.   (b) Rule three: Negative conclusion without a negative premise. (c) Invalid
5.   (b) Rule 1: Undistributed middle (c) Invalid
7.   (b) Rule 1: Undistributed middle and Rule 2: Illicit minor (c) Invalid
9.   (b) Rule 2: Illicit major (c) Invalid
11.   (a) No trees are things having gangrenous limbs.
All maples are trees.
Therefore, no maples are things having gangrenous limbs.
    (b) No rules violated (c) Valid

13. (a) All sensitive people are people who suffer a lot in life.
    Some intelligent people are sensitive people
    Therefore, some intelligent people are people who suffer a lot in life.
    (b) No rules violated (c) Valid

EXERCISE 5–8

1. All mushrooms are fungi.
   [All toadstools are mushrooms.]
   Therefore, all toadstools are fungi.
3. [No poisonous things are edible things.]
   Some mushrooms are poisonous things.
   Therefore, some mushrooms are not edible things.
   OR
   [No edible things are poisonous things.]
   Some mushrooms are poisonous things.
   Therefore, some mushrooms are not edible things.
5. [All foods that contain a lot of protein are nutritious foods.]
   All soybeans are foods that contain a lot of protein.
   Therefore, all soybeans are nutritious foods.
7. [No things written in foreign languages are under-standable things.]
   All operas are things written in foreign languages.
   Therefore, no operas are understandable things.
   OR
   [No understandable things are things written in foreign languages.]
   All operas are things written in foreign languages.
   Therefore, no operas are understandable things.
9. No reference books are books that can be taken out of the library.
   All foreign-language dictionaries are reference books.
   [Therefore, no foreign-language dictionaries are books that can be taken out of the library.]
   OR
   All foreign-language dictionaries are reference books.
   No reference books are books that can be taken out of the library.
   [Therefore, no books that can be taken out of the library are foreign-language dictionaries.]
11. [All teachers of whom it can be said that all of the students in their class always get good grades are persons who must be terrific teachers.]
    All members of the class of which she is the only member are teachers of whom it can be said that all of the students in their class always get good grades.
    Therefore, all members of the class of which she is the only member are persons who must be terrific teachers.

13. [All movies that have plenty of violence and sex are movies that are sure to make a lot of money.]
    All members of the class of which that movie is the only member are movies that have plenty of violence and sex.
    Therefore, all members of the class of which that movie is the only member are movies that are sure to make a lot of money.
15. [All lawyers are college graduates.]
    All lawyers are members of the American Bar Association.
    Therefore, all members of the American Bar Association are college graudates.
17. [All persons who are members of Phi Beta Kappa are intelligent persons.]
    All members of the class of which Mary is the only member are members of Phi Beta Kappa.
    Therefore, all members of the class of which Mary is the only member are intelligent persons.
19. [All places where I smell smoke are places where there are fires.]
    All members of the class of which this place is the only member are places where I smell smoke.
    Therefore, all members of the class of which this place is the only member are places where there are fires.
21. [All places where grass is growing are places where water must be near.]
    All members of the class of which this place is the only member are places where grass is growing.
    Therefore, all members of the class of which this place is the only member are places where water must be near.
23. [All democratic countries are countries where all citizens can vote.]
    Some countries are not countries where all citizens can vote.
    Therefore, some countries are not democratic countries.

EXERCISE 5–9

Note that the reconstruction of complex and/or invalid sorites can often be facilitated by reconstructing syllogisms for individual stages of the argument starting from the conclusion and working backwards.

1. Valid
   (a) All comets are wanderers in the zodiac.
       No terriers are wanderers in the zodiac.
       _____
       [Therefore, no terriers are comets.]
   (b) All curly-tailed creatures are terriers.
       _____
       Therefore, no curly-tailed creatures are comets.

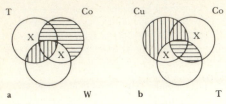

a   b

3. Valid
    (a) All <u>s</u>hade-grown fruit is <u>u</u>nripe fruit.
         No <u>u</u>nripe fruit is <u>w</u>holesome fruit.
         —————————————————————————
    (b) [Therefore, no <u>w</u>holesome fruit is <u>s</u>hade-grown
         fruit.]
         All <u>a</u>pples in this basket are <u>w</u>holesome fruit.
         —————————————————————————
         Therefore, no <u>a</u>pples in this basket are <u>s</u>hade-
         grown fruit.

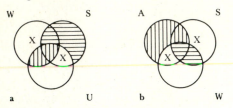

a   b

EXERCISE 6–1

1. (a) Yes (b) Pines are evergreens; 'Oaks are hardwoods'.
    (c) And (d) Yes
3. (a) Yes (b) 'The earth is flat' (c) 'It is not true that'. (d)
    Yes
5. (a) No
7. (a) Yes (b) 'The earth is not flat'. (c) 'You ought to know
    that'. (d) No
9. (a) No
11. (a) Yes (b) 'Joseph came out'; 'He helped me shovel
    snow'. (c) And (d) Yes
13. (a) Yes (b) 'Ronald Reagan is a liberal'; 'Edward
    Kennedy is a conservative' (c) 'And' (d) Yes
15. (a) Yes (b) 'Ronald Reagan is a Republican'; 'Edward
    Kennedy is a Democrat' (c) 'And' (d) Yes
17. (a) No

EXERCISE 6–2

1. A propositional constant is a symbol which represents a
    specific statement found in a compound proposition
    and which remains constant within a given context. A
    propositional variable is a symbol which serves as a
    'blank' in a compound proposition and into which a
    specific proposition may be substituted; the proposi-
    tional variables and logical operators exhibit the propo-
    sitional schema.
3. (a) 'A and B' represents a particular compound proposi-
    tion.

(b) 'p and q' represents an infinite set of compound
    propositions.
5. The formula 'A and B' has a specific truth value because
    it is an abbreviation of a compound proposition con-
    taining propositions about which it is reasonable to say
    that they are true or false.
    The formula 'p and q' does not have a specific truth
    value because p and q do not represent specific propo-
    sitions but merely represent places in a compound
    proposition where statements may be placed.

EXERCISE 6–3

The particular letters used as constants here and in Exercise
6-4 may differ from those chosen by the student, but the
propositions symbolized remain the same.

1. (a) Sense of temporal sequence lost. (b) R · G; R = The
    gunmen <u>r</u>obbed the bank; G = The gunmen made
    their <u>g</u>etaway.
3. (a) Dot cannot properly be used; it does not convey
    the implication that the Oakland Athletics and Los
    Angeles Dodgers played each other in the world
    series.
5. (a) Dot cannot properly be used; it loses the essential
    meaning of 'rock and roll'.
7. (a) Dot cannot properly be used; it loses the essential
    meaning of 'ball and chain'.
9. (a) Dot cannot suitably be used; loss of essential
    meaning of 'hit-and-run accident'.
11. (a) Dot cannot suitably be used: loss of time-sequence.
13. (a) No significant meaning loss. (b) G · M; G =
    'George is a character in Albee's *Who's Afraid of
    Virginia Woolf?*'; M = 'Martha is a character in Albee's
    Who's Afraid of Virginia Woolf?'

EXERCISE 6–4

1. (a) R · B (b) R = 'roses are red'; B = 'violets are blue'.
    (c) No meaning loss.
3. (a) R · L (b) R = 'it rained today'; L = 'the mailman
    was late'. (c) Loss of a suggestion of possible causal
    connection.
5. (a) ~H (b) H = 'hickory is a soft wood' (c) No loss of
    meaning.
7. (a) K · C (b) K = 'Joyce needs a <u>k</u>itchen table for her
    apartment'; C = 'Joyce needs some <u>c</u>hairs for her
    apartment'. (c) None
9. (a) Not adequately translatable.
11. (a) M ≡ E (b) M = 'Oil and water will <u>m</u>ix'; E = Oil
    and water are <u>e</u>mulsified.' (c) Loss of suggestion of
    causal sequence.
13. (a) <u>E</u> ≡ P (b) E = 'A total <u>e</u>clipse of the sun occurs'; P =
    The moon is <u>p</u>ositioned directly between the earth and
    the sun'. (c) <u>S</u>uggestion of causal connection is lost.

15. (a) E ≡ ~P (b) P = 'Sugar is a protein'. (c) None

17. (a) F ≡ G (b) F = 'this object will float'; G = 'its specific gravity is less than 1.0' (c) Loss of a suggestion of causal connection.

19. (a) E ≡ S (b) E = 'A geometrical figure is an equilateral'; S = 'All its (the geometrical figure's) sides have the same length'. (c) None

21. (a) T ⊃ P (b) T = 'I will take the job'; P = 'It (the job—pays well'. (c) None

23. (a) J ⊃ V (b) J = 'An American president's last name was Johnson'; V = 'He (the American president) was vice-president before he was president'. (c) None

25. (a) W · G (b) W = 'Most swans are white'; G = 'Some swans are gray'. (c) 'Although' connotes an exception to the rule

27. C ≡ P (b) C = 'a conjunction is true'; P = 'both its component propositions are true'.

29. (a) S ⊃ L (b) S = 'the stock market fails'; L = 'many people will lose fortunes'. (c) Loss of suggestion of causal connection

31. (a) C ∨ D (b) C = 'he came after I left'; D = 'he didn't come at all'. (c) Loss of suggestion that he was expected to come, and/or that probably he didn't come

33. (a) P ⊃ S (b) P = 'you will pass this exam'; S = 'you study hard'. (c) Loss of suggestion of causal connection

35. (a) R · C (b) R = 'it did not rain'; C = 'the clouds were dark and ominous'. (c) Loss of suggestion that the failure to rain was contrary to normal expectations.

EXERCISE 6–5

1. (S · R) ∨ D   **3.** S ∨ (R · D)   **5.** S · (R · D)
7. ~(W ⊃ H)   **9.** W ⊃ ~H)   **11.** ~W ⊃ H
13. C · ~M   **15.** ~C · ~M   **17.** ~(C · ~M)
19. (S · H) ⊃ ~C   **21.** S ⊃ (~H ∨ ~C)
23. S ⊃ (H ⊃ ~C)   **25.** B ⊃ (D · P)
27. B ⊃ (D ∨ P)   **29.** (K · M) ∨ H
31. K ∨ (M · H)   **33.** ~(K ∨ (M · H))
35. ~((K · M) ∨ H)   **37.** K ∨ (M · ~H)
39. ~K · (M ∨ H)

EXERCISE 6–6

1.

p	q	p · ~ q	
T	T	F	F
F	T	F	F
T	F	T	T
F	F	F	T
		(2)	(1)

3.

p	q	p ⊃ ~ q	
T	T	F	F
F	T	T	F
T	F	T	T
F	F	T	T
		(2)	(1)

5.

p	q	~ p · ~ q		
T	T	F	F	F
F	T	T	F	F
T	F	F	F	T
F	F	T	T	T
		(1)	(2)	(1)

7.

p	q	~ (p ⊃ q)	
T	T	F	T
F	T	F	T
T	F	T	F
F	F	F	T
		(2)	(1)

9.

p	q	p ∨ ~ q	
T	T	T	F
F	T	F	F
T	F	T	T
F	F	T	T
		(2)	(1)

11.

p	q	~ (~ p ∨ q)		
T	T	F	F	T
F	T	F	T	T
T	F	T	F	F
F	F	F	T	T
		(3)	(1)	(2)

13.

p	q	(p · q) ≡ p	
T	T	T	T
F	T	F	T
T	F	F	F
F	F	F	T
		(1)	(2)

15.

p	q	(p · q) ⊃ q	
T	T	T	T
F	T	F	T
T	F	F	T
F	F	F	T
		(1)	(2)

17.

p	q	r	(p ∨ q) ⊃ r	
T	T	T	T	T
F	T	T	T	T
T	F	T	T	T
F	F	T	F	T
T	T	F	T	F
F	T	F	T	F
T	F	F	T	F
F	F	F	F	T
			(1)	(2)

19.

p	q	r	~ (p · q) ⊃ ~ r			
T	T	T	F	T	T	F
F	T	T	T	F	F	F
T	F	T	T	F	F	F
F	F	T	T	F	F	F
T	T	F	F	T	T	T
F	T	F	T	F	T	T
T	F	F	T	F	T	T
F	F	F	T	F	T	T
			(3)	(2)	(4)	(1)

21.

p	q	r	((p ∨ q) · p) ⊃ r		
T	T	T	T	T	T
F	T	T	T	F	T
T	F	T	T	T	T
F	F	T	F	F	T
T	T	F	T	T	F
F	T	F	T	F	T
T	F	F	T	T	F
F	F	F	F	F	T
			(1)	(2)	(3)

23.

p	q	r	(~ (p ∨ ~ q) · p) ⊃ r				
T	T	T	F	T	F	F	T
F	T	T	T	F	F	F	T
T	F	T	F	T	T	F	T
F	F	T	F	T	T	F	T
T	T	F	F	T	F	F	T
F	T	F	T	F	F	F	T
T	F	F	F	T	T	F	T
F	F	F	F	T	T	F	T
			(3)	(2)(1)		(4)	(5)

25.

p	q	((p ⊃ q) · ~ q) ⊃ ~ p				
T	T	T	F	F	T	F
F	T	T	F	F	T	T
T	F	F	F	T	T	F
F	F	T	T	T	T	T
		(2)	(3)	(1)	(4)	(1)

27.

p	q	~ (p · q) ≡ (~ p ∨ ~ q)					
T	T	F	T	T	F	F	F
F	T	T	F	T	T	T	F
T	F	T	F	T	F	T	T
F	F	T	F	T	T	T	T
		(3)	(2)	(4)(1)		(2)(1)	

29.

p	q	r	((p · q) ⊃ r) ≡ (p ⊃ (q ⊃ r))
T	T	T	T T T T T
F	T	T	F T T T T
T	F	T	F T T T T
F	F	T	F T T T T
T	T	F	T F T F F
F	T	F	F T T T F
T	F	F	F T T T T
F	F	F	F T T T T
			(1) (2) (3) (2) (1)

EXERCISE 6–7

1. (a) Equivalent

p	q	p · q	~ (~p ∨ ~q)
T	T	T	T F F F
F	T	F	F T T F
T	F	F	F F T T
F	F	F	F T T T
		(3)	(1) (2) (1)

3. (a) Equivalent

(b)

p	q	~p · q	~ (p ∨ ~q)
T	T	F F	F T F
F	T	T T	T F F
T	F	F F	F T T
F	F	T F	F T T
		(1) (2)	(3) (2) (1)

5. (a) Not equivalent

(b)

p	q	~ (p ∨ q)	~p ∨ q
T	T	F T	F T
F	T	F T	T T
T	F	F T	F F
F	F	T F	T T
		(3) (2)	(1) (2)

7. (a) Equivalent

(b)

p	q	p ⊃ q	~p ∨ q
T	T	T	F T
F	T	T	T T
T	F	F	F F
F	F	T	T T
			(1) (2)

9. Equivalent

p	q	~p ≡ q	p ≡ ~q
T	T	F F	F F
F	T	T T	T F
T	F	F T	T T
F	F	T F	F T
		(1) (2)	(2) (1)

11. Equivalent

p	q	~ (p ⊃ q)	p · ~q
T	T	F T	F F
F	T	F T	F F
T	F	T F	T T
F	F	F T	F T
		(2) (1)	(2) (1)

13. Not equivalent

p	q	~ (p ∨ q)	~p ∨ ~q
T	T	F T	F F F
F	T	F T	T T F
T	F	F T	F T T
F	F	T F	T T T
		(2) (1)	(1) (2) (1)

EXERCISE 6–8

1. (a) Contingent

(b)

p	q	p ⊃ q
T	T	T
F	T	T
T	F	F
F	F	T

3. (a) Contingent

(b)

p	p ⊃ ~ p
T	F F
F	T T
	(2) (1)

5. (a) Tautology

(b)

p	q	p ⊃ (p ∨ q)
T	T	T T
F	T	T T
T	F	T T
F	F	T F
		(2) (1)

7. (a) Contradiction

(b)

p	q	((p ⊃ q) · ~ q) · p
T	T	T F F F
F	T	T F F F
T	F	F F T F
F	F	T T T F
		(2) (3)(1) (4)

9. Tautology

p	q	(p ⊃ q) ≡ (~ p ∨ q)
T	T	T T F T
F	T	T T T T
T	F	F T F F
F	F	T T T T
		(2) (3)(1)(2)

11. (a) Contradiction

(b)

p	q	(p ⊃ q) ≡ (p · ~ q)
T	T	T F F F
F	T	T F F F
T	F	F F T T
F	F	T F F T
		(2) (3)(2)(1)

13. (a) Contradiction

(b)

p	q	((p ⊃ q) · p) · ~ q
T	T	T T F F
F	T	T F F F
T	F	F F F T
F	F	T F F T
		(2) (3) (4)(1)

15. (a) Contingent

(b)

p	q	(p ∨ ~ p) ⊃ (p · ~ q)
T	T	T F F F F F
F	T	T T F F F F.
T	F	T F T T T
F	F	T T F F T
		(2)(1) (3) (2)(1)

17. (a) Contradiction

(b)

p	q	~ (p ⊃ q) ≡ (~ p ∨ q)
T	T	F T F F T
F	T	F T F T T
T	F	T F F F F
F	F	F T F T T
		(3) (2) (4)(1) (2)

EXERCISE 7-1

Note that the letters used in the following abbreviations are arbitrary and may not match those letters you selected. In all cases, however, make certain that you have provided a dictionary indicating which letter stands for which proposition.

1. **R** = It is raining. **W** = The ground gets wet.

  (a) R ⊃ W
     R
  ∴W

  (b) p ⊃ q
     p
  ∴q

3. **C** = There are clouds in the sky. **S** = The sun is shining.

  (a) C ∨ S
    ~S
  ∴C

  (b) p ∨ q
    ~q
  ∴p

5. **S** = That artifact is from the <u>S</u>tone Age. **M** = That artifact is made of <u>m</u>etal.

(a) S ⊃ ~M
    M
    ∴~S

(b) p ⊃ ~q
    q
    ∴~p

7. **D** = All <u>d</u>ogs are carnivores. **F** = <u>F</u>ido is a carnivore.

(a) D ⊃ F
    ~F
    ∴~D

(b) p ⊃ q
    ~q
    ∴~p

9. **W** = This chair is made of <u>W</u>alnut. **M** = This chair is made of <u>M</u>ahogany. **T** = This chair is made of <u>T</u>eakwood.

(a) (W ∨ M) ∨ T
    ~W
    ∴M ∨ T

(b) (p ∨ q) ∨ r
    ~p
    ∴q ∨ r

11. **N** = That glass you are holding contains <u>n</u>itroglycerin. **D** = You are <u>d</u>ropping the glass. **E** = The nitroglycerin will <u>e</u>xplode.

(a) (N · D) ⊃ E
    N · D
    ∴E

(b) (p · q) ⊃ r
    p · q
    ∴r

13. **S** = We are going to the <u>s</u>tate park for a picnic. **J** = We will take <u>J</u>ohnny along. **B** = We will take <u>B</u>illy along.

(a) S ⊃ (J ∨ B)
    S
    ∴J ∨ B

(b) p ⊃ (q ∨ r)
    p
    ∴q ∨ r

15. Using the same propositional constants as in 13:

(a) (S · J) ⊃ B
    S · J
    ∴B

(b) (p · q) ⊃ r
    p · q
    ∴r

17. Using the same propositional constants as in 13:

(a) (S ∨ J) ⊃ P
    J
    ∴P

(b) (p ∨ q) ⊃ r
    q
    ∴r

19. **T** = You put <u>t</u>opspin on the cue ball. **F** = The cue ball will <u>f</u>ollow the six ball into the pocket. **S** = You will <u>s</u>cratch.

(a) T ⊃ (F · S)
    T
    ∴F · S

(b) p ⊃ (q · r)
    p
    ∴(q · r)

21. **R** = We are having a heavy <u>r</u>ain. **O** = The sewers will be <u>o</u>verloaded. **F** = The basement will <u>f</u>lood.

(a) R ⊃ O
    O ⊃ F
    R
    ∴F

(b) p ⊃ q
    q ⊃ r
    p
    ∴r

23. **S** = It is <u>s</u>nowing. **F** = Sleet is <u>f</u>alling. **R** = We will go sled <u>r</u>iding.

(a) S ⊃ R
    S ∨ F
    ~R
    ∴F

(b) p ⊃ q
    p ∨ r
    ~q
    ∴r

25. **R** = It is <u>r</u>aining. **W** = The <u>w</u>ind is blowing. **T** = Water will get in the <u>t</u>ent.

(a) (R · W) ⊃ T
    R
    W
    ∴T

(b) (p · q) ⊃ r
    p
    q
    ∴r

27. **F** = Snow is <u>f</u>alling. **C** = It is getting <u>c</u>old. **S** = My car will <u>s</u>tart.

(a) F ⊃ C
    C ⊃ ~S
    F
    ∴~S

(b) p ⊃ q
    q ⊃ ~r
    p
    ∴~r

29. **P** = <u>P</u>eter is playing piano. **B** = <u>B</u>ob is playing bass. **D** = <u>D</u>on is playing drums. **C** = Our regular <u>c</u>ombo is here.

(a) (P · B · D) ⊃ C
    ~C
    ∴~P ∨ ~B ∨ ~D

(b) (p · q · r) ⊃ s
    ~s
    ∴~p ∨ ~q ∨ ~r

31. **E** = The statement under discussion is an <u>e</u>quivalence. **I** = The statement under discussion contains an <u>i</u>mplication. **D** = The statement under discussion is a <u>d</u>isjunction.

(a) E ⊃ I
    D ∨ E
    ~D
    ∴I

(b) p ⊃ q
    r ∨ p
    ~r
    ∴q

33. **C** = The statement under discussion is a <u>c</u>onjunction. **D** = The statement under discussion is a <u>d</u>isjunction. **I** = The statement under discussion is an <u>i</u>mplication.

(a) C ∨ D
    C ∨ I
    D ⊃ ~I
    ∴C

(b) p ∨ q
    p ∨ r
    q ⊃ ~r
    ∴p

35. **T** = The statement is a <u>t</u>ruth-functional proposition. **C** = The statement is a <u>c</u>ommand. **P** = The statement is a compound <u>p</u>roposition. **L** = The statement contains a <u>l</u>ogical operator.

(a) T ∨ C
    T ⊃ P
    P ⊃ L
    ~C
    ∴L

(b) p ∨ q
    p ⊃ r
    r ⊃ s
    ~q
    ∴s

37. **Y** = The Cheshire cat is yellow. **C** = The Cheshire cat is colored. **V** = The Cheshire cat is visible. **R** = The Cheshire cat is real.

   (a) Y ⊃ C
       C ⊃ V
       V ⊃ R
       ~R
       ∴~Y

   (b) p ⊃ q
       q ⊃ r
       r ⊃ s
       ~s
       ∴~p

39. Using the same propositional constants as in 37:

   (a) R ∨ ~V
       V ∨ ~C
       C ∨ ~Y
       Y
       ∴R

   (b) p ∨ ~r
       q ∨ ~r
       r ∨ ~s
       s
       ∴p

41. **H** = Herb is a Hoosier. **B** = Herb is a Buckeye. **I** = Herb is from Indiana. **O** = Herb is from Ohio. **A** = Herb is a U.S. citizen.

   (a) H ⊃ I
       B ⊃ O
       (I ∨ O) ⊃ C
       H ∨ B
       ∴C

   (b) p ⊃ q
       r ⊃ s
       (q ∨ s) ⊃ t
       p ∨ r
       ∴t

43. **R** = We will have red wine for dinner. **W** = We will have white wine for dinner. **B** = We will have roast beef for dinner. **S** = We will have fillet of sole for dinner. **F** = We will have fruit salad for dessert.

   (a) R ∨ W
       B ⊃ R
       B ∨ S
       S ⊃ F
       ~R
       ∴S · (W · F)

   (b) p ∨ q
       r ⊃ p
       r ∨ s
       s ⊃ t
       p
       ∴s · (q · t)

45. **P** = Preston is a member of the safari club. **Q** = Quincy is a member of the safari club. **R** = Randolph is a member of the safari club. **S** = Stuart is a member of the safari club. **T** = Trumbull is a member of the safari club.

   (a) (P ⊃ Q) ∨ (R ⊃ S)
       (P ⊃ R) · (T ⊃ ~S)
       P
       ∴Q · (R · T)

   (b) (p ⊃ q) ∨ (r ⊃ s)
       (p ⊃ r) · (t ⊃ ~s)
       p
       ∴q · (r · t)

EXERCISE 7–2

1. Valid

p	q	p · q	p
T	T	T	T
F	T	F	F
T	F	F	T
F	F	F	F

3. Invalid

p	q	q ⊃ p	~q ⊃ ~p
T	T	T	F T F
F	T	F	F T T
T	F	T	T F F
F	F	T	T T F

5. Valid

p	q	(p ⊃ q)	⊃	(p ∨ q)	(p ∨ q)	⊃	(q ∨ p)
T	T	T	T	T	T	T	T
F	T	T	T	T	T	T	T
T	F	F	T	T	T	T	T
F	F	T	F	F	F	T	F

7. Valid

p	q	p ∨ q	~p	q
T	T	T	F	T
F	T	T	T	T
T	F	T	F	F
F	F	F	T	F

9. Invalid

p	q	p ∨ q	q
T	T	T	T
F	T	T	T
T	F	T	F
F	F	F	F

11. Valid

p	q	p	q	p · q
T	T	T	T	T
F	T	F	T	F
T	F	T	F	F
F	F	F	F	F

13. Invalid

p	q	r	p⊃q	p⊃r	q∨r
T	T	T	T	T	T
F	T	T	T	T	T
T	F	T	F	T	T
F	F	T	T	T	T
T	T	F	T	F	T
F	T	F	T	T	T
T	F	F	F	F	F
F	F	F	T	T	F

19. Valid

p	q	r	[p	⊃	(q · r)]	[(q ∨ r)	⊃	~p]	~	p
T	T	T	T	T	T	T	F	F	F	T
F	T	T	F	T	T	T	T	T	T	F
T	F	T	T	F	F	T	F	F	F	T
F	F	T	F	T	F	T	T	T	T	F
T	T	F	T	F	F	T	F	F	F	T
F	T	F	F	T	F	T	T	T	T	F
T	F	F	T	F	F	F	T	F	F	T
F	F	F	F	T	F	F	T	T	T	F

15. Valid

p	q	r	p⊃q	p∨r	~r	q
T	T	T	T	T	F	T
F	T	T	T	T	F	T
T	F	T	F	T	F	F
F	F	T	T	T	F	F
T	T	F	T	T	T	T
F	T	F	T	F	T	T
T	F	F	F	T	T	F
F	F	F	T	F	T	F

21. Invalid

p	q	r	p⊃q	p⊃r	~r	~q
T	T	T	T	T	F	F
F	T	T	T	T	F	F
T	F	T	F	T	F	T
F	F	T	T	T	F	T
T	T	F	T	F	T	F
F	T	F	T	T	T	F
T	F	F	F	F	T	T
F	F	F	T	T	T	T

17. Valid

p	q	r	p⊃q	q⊃r	p⊃r
T	T	T	T	T	T
F	T	T	T	T	T
T	F	T	F	T	T
F	F	T	T	T	T
T	T	F	T	F	F
F	T	F	T	F	T
T	F	F	F	T	F
F	F	F	T	T	T

23. Valid

p	q	r	p⊃q	p∨r	~q	r
T	T	T	T	T	F	T
F	T	T	T	T	F	T
T	F	T	F	T	T	T
F	F	T	T	T	T	T
T	T	F	T	T	F	F
F	T	F	T	F	F	F
T	F	F	F	T	T	F
F	F	F	T	F	T	F

25. Invalid

p	q	r	~q	q ⊃ r	r
T	T	T	F	T	T
F	T	T	F	T	T
T	F	T	T	T	T
F	F	T	T	T	T
T	T	F	F	F	F
F	T	F	F	F	F
T	F	F	T	T	F
F	F	F	T	T	F

27. Invalid

p	q	p ⊃ q	~p	~q
T	T	T	F	F
F	T	T	T	F
T	F	F	F	T
F	F	T	T	T

29. Valid

p	q	r	p ⊃ q	r · p	q ∨ r
T	T	T	T	T	T
F	T	T	T	F	T
T	F	T	F	T	T
F	F	T	T	F	T
T	T	F	T	F	T
F	T	F	T	F	T
T	F	F	F	F	F
F	F	F	T	F	F

31. Valid

p	q	r	(p · q)	⊃	p	·	~r	~q
T	T	T	T	T		F	F	F
F	T	T	F	T		F	F	F
T	F	T	F	T		F	F	T
F	F	T	F	T		F	F	T
T	T	F	T	F		T	T	F
F	T	F	F	T		F	T	F
T	F	F	F	T		T	T	T
F	F	F	F	T		F	T	T

33. Invalid

p	q	r	p ⊃	(q ⊃ r)	p ⊃ q	q ⊃ r
T	T	T	T	T	T	T
F	T	T	T	T	T	T
T	F	T	T	T	F	T
F	F	T	T	T	T	T
T	T	F	F	F	T	F
F	T	F	T	F	T	F
T	F	F	T	T	F	T
F	F	F	T	T	T	T

35. Valid

p	q	r	~p	⊃	(q · r)	~r	p
T	T	T	F	T	T	F	T
F	T	T	T	T	T	F	F
T	F	T	F	T	F	F	T
F	F	T	T	F	F	F	F
T	T	F	F	T	F	T	T
F	T	F	T	F	F	T	F
T	F	F	F	T	F	T	T
F	F	F	T	F	F	T	F

37. Valid

p	q	r	s	p ⊃ q	p ⊃ (q ⊃ r)	(q ⊃ r)	q ⊃ (r ⊃ s)	(r ⊃ s)	p ⊃ s
T	T	T	T	T	T	T	T	T	T
F	T	T	T	T	T	T	T	T	T
T	F	T	T	F	T	T	T	T	T
F	F	T	T	T	T	T	T	T	T
T	T	F	T	T	F	F	T	T	T
F	T	F	T	T	T	F	T	T	T
T	F	F	T	F	T	T	T	T	T
F	F	F	T	T	T	T	T	T	T
T	T	T	F	T	T	T	F	F	F
F	T	T	F	T	T	T	F	F	T
T	F	T	F	F	T	T	T	F	F
F	F	T	F	T	T	T	T	F	T
T	T	F	F	T	F	F	T	T	F
F	T	F	F	T	T	F	T	T	T
T	F	F	F	F	T	T	T	T	F
F	F	F	F	T	T	T	T	T	T

39. Invalid

p	q	r	(~p ∨ q)	(~p∨q) ⊃ r	~ r	~ p
T	T	T	F T	T	F	F
F	T	T	T T	T	F	T
T	F	T	F F	T	F	F
F	F	T	T T	T	F	T
T	T	F	F T	F	T	F
F	T	F	T T	F	T	T
T	F	F	F F	T	T	F
F	F	F	T T	F	T	T

EXERCISE 7–3

Note that any of the following rows will prove the argument schema invalid.

1.

p	q	r	p ⊃ q	q ⊃ r	q ∨ r
F	F	F	F T F	F T F	F F F

3.

p	q	r	p ⊃ (q · r)	~ p	~ r
F	T	T	F T TTT	T	F
F	F	T	F T FFT	T	F

5.

p	q	r	p	q	p ∨ r	r
T	T	F	T	T T	T T F	F

7.

p	q	r	p ⊃ q	p ∨ r	q ⊃ ~ r
T	T	T	T **T** T	T **T** T	T F **F** T
F	T	T	F **T** T	F **T** T	T F **F** T

9.

p	q	r	p ⊃ (q ∨ r)	~ q	r ⊃ p
F	F	T	**T** T	**T**	**T**

11.

p	q	r	s	p ⊃ (q ∨ r)	q ⊃ s	p	r ⊃ s
T	F	T	F	**T** T	**T**	T	**F**

13.

p	q	r	p ⊃ (q ⊃ r)	p	r
T	F	F	T **T** F T F	T	F

15.

p	r	s	t	(p ⊃ r) · (s ⊃ t)	r ∨ t	p ∨ s
F	T	F	T	F T T **T** F T T	T **T** T	F **F** F
F	T	F	F	F T T **T** F T F	T **T** F	F **F** F
F	F	F	T	F T F **T** F T T	F **T** T	F **F** F

17.

p	q	r	s	p ⊃ q	r ⊃ s	(p ∨ q) ⊃ (r · s)
T	T	F	T	**T**	**T**	T **F** F
F	T	F	T	**T**	**T**	T **F** F
T	T	F	F	**T**	**T**	T **F** F
F	T	F	F	**T**	**T**	T **F** F

EXERCISE 7–4

Each proof below and in the exercises which follow is only one of many possible correct proofs.

1.
1. p ∨ ~q — Premise
2. r ⊃ q — Premise
3. ~p ∴ ~r — Premise/conclusion
4. ~q — D. Syll., 1,3
5. ~r — M.T., 2,4

3.
1. (p ∨ q) ⊃ r — Premise
2. p/∴r — Premise/conclusion
3. p ∨ q — Add., 2
4. r — M.P., 1,3

5.
1. p — Premise
2. q ⊃ r — Premise
3. s ⊃ t — Premise
4. p ⊃ (q · s)/∴r · t — Premise/conclusion

	5. q · s	M.P., 1,4	
	6. q	Simp., 5	
	7. r	M.P., 2,6	
	8. s	Simp., 5	
	9. t	M.P., 3,8	
	10. r · t	Conj., 7,9	
7.	1. p ⊃ ~r	Premise	
	2. q ⊃ r	Premise	
	3. p/∴~q	Premise/conclusion	
	4. ~r	M.P., 1,3	
	5. ~q	M.T., 2,4	
9.	1. (p · q) ⊃ (r · s)	Premise	
	2. (r · s) ⊃ (t · u)/∴(p · q) ⊃ (t · u)	Premise/conclusion	
	3. (p · q) ⊃ (t · u)	H. Syll., 1,2	
11.	1. p	Premise	
	2. (p · q) ⊃ r	Premise	
	3. s ⊃ (p ⊃ q)	Premise	
	4. s/∴r	Premise/conclusion	
	5. p ⊃ q	M.P., 3,4	
	6. q	M.P., 1,5	
	7. p · q	Conj., 1,6	
	8. r	M.P., 2,7	
13.	1. (p ⊃ q) ⊃ (r ⊃ s)	Premise	
	2. (t ⊃ u) ∨ (p ⊃ q)	Premise	
	3. ~(r ⊃ s)/∴t ⊃ u	Premise/conclusion	
	4. ~(p ⊃ q)	M.T., 1,3	
	5. t ⊃ u	D. Syll., 2,4	
15.	1. p · s	Premise	
	2. (p ∨ r) ⊃ (p ⊃ q)	Premise	
	3. s ⊃ t/∴q · t	Premise/conclusion	
	4. p	Simp., 1	
	5. p ∨ r	Add., 4	
	6. p ⊃ q	M.P., 2,5	
	7. q	M.P., 4,6	
	8. s	Simp., 1	
	9. t	M.P., 3,8	
	10. q · t	Conj., 7, 9	
17.	1. p ⊃ q	Premise	
	2. q ⊃ r	Premise	
	3. p/∴p · r	Premise/conclusion	
	4. p ⊃ r	H. Syll., 1,2	
	5. r	M.P., 3,4	
	6. p · r	Conj., 3,5	
19.	1. (p ⊃ q) · (r ⊃ s)	Premise	
	2. (q ⊃ t) · (s ⊃ u)	Premise	
	3. p ∨ r/∴t ∨ u	Premise/conclusion	
	4. q ∨ s	Dil., 1,3	
	5. t ∨ u	Dil., 2,4	
21.	1. ~p	Premise	
	2. (~p ∨ ~q) ⊃ ~(r ⊃ s)	Premise	
	3. (r ⊃ s) ∨ (t ⊃ s)	Premise	

	4. ~s/∴~t	Premise/conclusion	
	5. ~p ∨ ~q	Add., 1	
	6. ~(r ⊃ s)	M.P., 2,5	
	7. t ⊃ s	D. Syll., 3,6	
	8. ~t	M.T., 4,7	
23.	1. p	Premise	
	2. (p ∨ q) ⊃ (r · s)	Premise	
	3. (s ∨ t) ⊃ ~u	Premise	
	4. r ⊃ q/∴q · ~u	Premise/conclusion	
	5. p ∨ q	Add., 1	
	6. r · s	M.P., 2,5	
	7. r	Simp., 6	
	8. q	M.P., 4,7	
	9. s	Simp., 6	
	10. s ∨ t	Add., 9	
	11. ~u	M.P., 3,10	
	12. q · ~u	Conj., 8,11	
25.	1. p	Premise	
	2. q	Premise	
	3. ((p ∨ r) · (q ∨ s)) ⊃ ((p · q) ⊃ (q ⊃ s))	Premise	
	4. (s ∨ r) ⊃ t/∴t ∨ r	Premise/conclusion	
	5. p ∨ r	Add., 1	
	6. q ∨ s	Add., 2	
	7. (p ∨ r) · (q ∨ s)	Conj., 5,6	
	8. (p · q) ⊃ (q ⊃ s)	M.P., 3,7	
	9. p · q	Conj., 1,2	
	10. q ⊃ s	M.P., 8,9	
	11. s	M.P., 2,10	
	12. s ∨ r	Add., 11	
	13. t	M.P., 4,12	
	14. t ∨ r	Add., 13	
27.	1. p	Premise	
	2. p ⊃ q	Premise	
	3. (p · q) ⊃ (r · s)/∴s ∨ t	Premise/conclusion	
	4. q	M.P., 1,2	
	5. p · q	Conj., 1,4	
	6. r · s	M.P., 3,5	
	7. s	Simp., 6	
	8. s ∨ t	Add., 7	
29.	1. p	Premise	
	2. (p ∨ q) ⊃ (r · s)	Premise	
	3. s ⊃ t/∴t ∨ u	Premise/conclusion	
	4. p ∨ q	Add., 1	
	5. r · s	M.P., 2,4	
	6. s	Simp., 5	
	7. t	M.P., 3,6	
	8. t ∨ u	Add., 7	
31.	1. (p ∨ q) ⊃ (r ∨ s)	Premise	
	2. (r ∨ s) ⊃ (t ∨ u)	Premise	
	3. (t ∨ u) ⊃ (v ∨ w)	Premise	
	4. ~(v ∨ w)/∴~(p ∨ q)	Premise/conclusion	

5.	~(t ∨ u)	M.T., 3,4
6.	~(r ∨ s)	M.T., 2,5
7.	~(p ∨ q)	M.T., 1,6

EXERCISE 7–5

1.	1. ~p/∴~(p · q)	Premise/conclusion
	2. ~p ∨ ~q	Add., 1
	3. ~(p · q)	De. M., 2
3.	1. p	Premise
	2. ~q ⊃ ~p/∴q	Premise/conclusion
	3. p ⊃ q	Trans., 2
	4. q	M.P., 1,3
5.	1. p	Premise
	2. q ∨ (r · s)	Premise
	3. ~q ∨ ~p/∴s	Premise/conclusion
	4. ~~p	D.N., 1
	5. ~q	D. Syll., 3,4
	6. r · s	D. Syll., 2,5
	7. s	Simp., 6
7.	1. q ⊃ ~p	Premise
	2. p/∴~q	Premise/conclusion
	3. ~~p	D.N., 2
	4. ~q	M.T., 1,3
9.	1. ~r · ~s	Premise
	2. (p ∨ q) ⊃ (r ∨ s)/∴~(p ∨ q)	Premise/conclusion
	3. ~(r ∨ s)	De M., 1
	4. ~(p ∨ q)	M.T., 2,3
11.	1. p ⊃ (q ⊃ r)	Premise
	2. ~r/∴~(p · q)	Premise/conclusion
	3. (p · q) ⊃ r	Exp., 1
	4. ~(p · q)	M.T., 2,3
13.	1. ~p	Premise
	2. ~(p · q) ⊃ (~p ⊃ r)∴r	Premise/conclusion
	3. ~p ∨ ~q	Add., 1
	4. ~(p · q)	D.M., 3
	5. ~p ⊃ r	M.P., 2,4
	6. r	M.P., 1,5
15.	1. ~(p ∨ q)	Premise
	2. r ⊃ p	Premise
	3. s ⊃ q/∴~(r ∨ s)	Premise/conclusion
	4. ~p · ~q	D.M., 1
	5. ~p	Simp., 4
	6. ~r	M.T., 2,5
	7. ~q	Simp., 4
	8. ~s	M.T., 3,7
	9. ~r · ~s	Conj., 6,8
	10. ~(r ∨ s)	D.M., 9
17.	1. ~r · ~s	Premise
	2. (p ∨ q) ⊃ (r ∨ s)/∴~q ∨ t	Premise/conclusion
	3. ~(r ∨ s)	DeM., 1
	4. ~(p ∨ q)	M.T., 2,3
	5. ~p · ~q	DeM., 4

	6. ~q	Simp., 5
	7. ~q ∨ t	Add., 6
19.	1. ~r · ~s	Premise
	2. (p ∨ q) ⊃ (r ∨ s)/∴~(p · q)	Premise/conclusion
	3. ~(r ∨ s)	DeM., 1
	4. ~(p ∨ q)	M.T., 2,3
	5. ~p · ~q	DeM., 4
	6. ~p	Simp., 5
	7. ~p ∨ ~q	Add., 6
	8. ~(p · q)	DeM., 7
21.	1. ~(p ∨ ~p)	Premise
	2. (p · ~q) ⊃ (p ⊃ r)	Premise
	3. r ⊃ s/∴p ⊃ s	Premise/conclusion
	4. ~q · ~~p	De. M., 1
	5. ~q · p	D.N., 4
	6. p · ~q	Comm., 5
	7. p ⊃ r	M.P., 2,6
	8. p ⊃ s	H. Syll., 3,7
23.	1. ~(p ⊃ q)	Premise
	2. p ⊃ r	Premise
	3. s ⊃ q/∴~(r ⊃ s)	Premise/conclusion
	4. ~~(p · ~q)	Impl., 1
	5. p · ~q	D.N., 4
	6. p	Simp., 5
	7. r	M.P., 2,6
	8. ~q	Simp., 5
	9. ~s	M.T., 3,8
	10. r · ~s	Conj., 7,9
	11. ~~(r · ~s)	D.N., 10
	12. ~(r ⊃ s)	Impl., 11
25.	1. p	Premise
	2. q/∴p ≡ q	Premise/conclusion
	3. q ∨ ~p	Add., 2
	4. ~p ∨ q	Comm., 3
	5. p ⊃ q	Impl., 4
	6. p ∨ ~q	Add., 1
	7. ~q ∨ p	Comm., 6
	8. q ⊃ p	Impl., 7
	9. (p ⊃ q) · (q ⊃ p)	Conj., 5,8
	10. p ≡ q	Equiv., 9
27.	1. ~p ∨ q	Premise
	2. (p ⊃ q) ⊃ (p ⊃ r)	Premise
	3. p/∴r	Premise/conclusion
	4. p ⊃ q	Impl., 1
	5. p ⊃ r	M.P., 2,4
	6. r	M.P., 3,5
29.	1. ~(p · ~q)	Premise
	2. (p ⊃ q) ⊃ (p ⊃ r)/∴p ⊃ r	Premise/conclusion
	3. p ⊃ q	Impl., 1
	4. p ⊃ r	M.P., 2,3
31.	1. p · (q ∨ r)	Premise
	2. ~(p · r)/∴q	Premise/conclusion
	3. (p · q) ∨ (p · r)	Dist., 1

	4.	p · q	D. Syll., 2,3
	5.	q	Simp., 4
33.	1.	(p · q) ⊃ r	Premise
	2.	(p · r) ⊃ q	Premise
	3.	p/∴r ≡ q	Premise/conclusion
	4.	p ⊃ (q ⊃ r)	Exp., 1
	5.	p ⊃ (r ⊃ q)	Exp., 2
	6.	q ⊃ r	M.P., 3,4
	7.	r ⊃ q	M.P., 3,5
	8.	(r ⊃ q) · (q ⊃ r)	Conj., 6,7
	9.	r ≡ q	Equiv., 8
35.	1.	~p ∨ (q · r)	Premise
	2.	r ⊃ p/∴p ≡ r	Premise/conclusion
	3.	(~p ∨ q) · (~p ∨ r)	Dist., 1
	4.	~p ∨ r	Simp., 3
	5.	p ⊃ r	Impl., 4
	6.	(p ⊃ r) · (r ⊃ p)	Conj., 2,5
	7.	p ≡ r	Equiv., 6

EXERCISE 7–6

1.	1.	p ⊃ q/∴p ⊃ (p · q)	Premise/conclusion
	2.	p	Assumption
	3.	q	M.P., 1,2
	4.	p · q	Conj., 2,3
	5.	p ⊃ (p · q)	C.P., 2–4
3.	1.	(p ∨ q) ⊃ (r · s)	Premise
	2.	~r/∴~s ⊃ ~q	Premise/conclusion
	3.	~s	Assumption
	4.	~s ∨ ~r	Add., 3
	5.	~r ∨ ~s	Comm., 4
	6.	~(r · s)	De. M., 5.
	7.	~(p ∨ q)	M.T., 1,6
	8.	~p · ~q	DeM., 7
	9.	~q	Simp., 8
	10.	~s ⊃ ~q	C.P., 3–9
5.	1.	p ⊃ (q ⊃ r)/ ∴(~r · s) ⊃ (q ⊃ ~p)	Premise/ conclusion
	2.	~r · s	Assumption
	3.	~r	Simp., 2
	4.	(p · q) ⊃ r	Exp., 1
	5.	~(p · q)	M.T., 3,4
	6.	~p ∨ ~q	DeM., 5
	7.	~q ∨ ~p	Comm., 6
	8.	q ⊃ ~p	Impl., 7
	9.	(~r · s) ⊃ (q ⊃ ~p)	C.P., 2–8
7.	1.	p ⊃ (q ⊃ r)/∴(p · q) ⊃ r	Premise/conclusion
	2.	p · q	Assumption
	3.	p	Simp., 2
	4.	q ⊃ r	M.P., 1,3
	5.	q	Simp., 2
	6.	r	M.P., 4,5
	7.	(p · q) ⊃ r	C.P., 2–6

9.	1.	q ⊃ r/∴p ⊃ (q ⊃ (r ∨ s))	Premise/conclusion
	2.	p	Assumption
	3.	q	Assumption
	4.	r	M.P., 1,3
	5.	r ∨ s	Add., 4
	6.	q ⊃ (r ∨ s)	C.P., 3–5
	7.	p ⊃ (q ⊃ (r ∨ s))	C.P., 2–6
11.	1.	(p ∨ q) ⊃ (r ≡ s)	Premise
	2.	~(~s · p)	Premise
	3.	~t ⊃ ~r/∴p ⊃ (t · r)	Premise/conclusion
	4.	p	Assumption
	5.	p ∨ q	Add., 4
	6.	r ≡ s	M.P., 1,5
	7.	(r ⊃ s) · (s ⊃ r)	Equiv., 6
	8.	~~s ∨ ~p	DeM., 2
	9.	s ∨ ~p	D.N., 8
	10.	~~p	D.N., 4
	11.	s	D. Syll., 9,4
	12.	s ⊃ r	Simp., 7
	13.	r	M.P., 12,11
	14.	~~r	D.N., 13
	15.	~~t	M.T., 3,14
	16.	t	D.N., 15
	17.	t · r	Conj., 16,13
	18.	p ⊃ (t · r)	C.P., 4–17
13.	1.	~p ⊃ (q ⊃ r)	Premise
	2.	s ⊃ q/∴s ⊃ (~p ⊃ r)	Premise/conclusion
	3.	s	Assumption
	4.	~p	Assumption
	5.	q	M.P., 2,3
	6.	q ⊃ r	M.P., 1,4
	7.	r	M.P., 6,5
	8.	~p ⊃ r	C.P., 4–7
	9.	s ⊃ (~p ⊃ r)	C.P., 3–8
15.	1.	(p · q) ⊃ r/∴p ⊃ (q ⊃ r)	Premise/conclusion
	2.	p	Assumption
	3.	q	Assumption
	4.	p · q	Conj., 2,3
	5.	r	M.P., 1,4
	6.	q ⊃ r	C.P., 3–5
	7.	p ⊃ (q ⊃ r)	C.P., 2–6
17.	1.	p · (q ∨ r)/∴~q ⊃ (p · r)	Premise/conclusion
	2.	~q	Assumption
	3.	q ∨ r	Simp., 1
	4.	r	D. Syll., 2,3
	5.	p	Simp., 1
	6.	p · r	Conj., 4,5
	7.	~q ⊃ (p · r)	C.P., 2–6
19.	1.	s/∴p ⊃ (q ⊃ (r ⊃ s))	Premise/conclusion
	2.	p	Assumption

3.	q	Assumption
4.	r	Assumption
5.	s	Premise 1
6.	r ⊃ s	C.P., 4–5
7.	q ⊃ (r ⊃ s)	C.P., 3–6
8.	p ⊃ (q ⊃ (r ⊃ s))	C.P., 2–7

EXERCISE 7–7

1.
1.	~q ⊃ (~p · r)	Premise
2.	~r/∴q	Premise/conclusion
3.	~q	Assumption
4.	~p · r	M.P., 1,3
5.	r	Simp., 4
6.	r · ~r	Conj., 2,5
7.	q	I.P., 3–6

3.
1.	p ∨ (q · r)	Premise
2.	p ∨ t	Premise
3.	t ⊃ ~(q · r)/∴p	Premise/conclusion
4.	~p	Assumption
5.	q · r	D. Syll., 1,4
6.	t	D. Syll., 2,4
7.	~(q · r)	M.P., 3,6
8.	(q · r) · ~(q · r)	Conj., 5,7
9.	p	I.P., 4–8

5.
1.	(p ⊃ q) · (r ⊃ s)	Premise
2.	(q ∨ s) ⊃ t	Premise
3.	~t/∴~(p ∨ r)	Premise/conclusion
4.	~~(p ∨ r)	Assumption
5.	p ∨ r	D.N., 4
6.	q ∨ s	Dil., 1,5
7.	t	M.P., 2,6
8.	t · ~t	Conj., 7,3
9.	~(p ∨ r)	I.P., 4–8

7.
1.	p ⊃ (q ⊃ r)	Premise
2.	~s ⊃ (p ∨ r)	Premise
3.	p ⊃ q/∴s ∨ r	Premise/conclusion
4.	~(s ∨ r)	Assumption
5.	~s · ~r	DeM., 4
6.	~s	Simp., 5
7.	p ∨ r	M.P., 2,6
8.	~r	Simp., 5
9.	p	D.S., 7,8
10.	q	M.P., 3,9
11.	q ⊃ r	M.P., 1,9
12.	r	M.P., 10,11
13.	r · ~r	Conj., 8,12
14.	s ∨ r	I.P., 4–13

9.
1.	(p · q) ⊃ r	Premise
2.	~p ⊃ r	Premise
3.	q/∴r	Premise/conclusion
4.	~r	Assumption
5.	~(p · q)	M.T., 1,4
6.	~p ∨ ~q	DeM., 5
7.	~~q	D.N., 3
8.	~p	D. Syll., 6,7
9.	r	M.P., 2,8
10.	r · ~r	Conj., 4,9
11.	r	I.P., 4–10

11.
1.	p · q	Premise
2.	~(p ⊃ q)/∴r ⊃ s	Premise/conclusion
3.	~(r ⊃ s)	Assumption
4.	q	Simp., 1
5.	~~(p · ~q)	Impl., 3
6.	p · ~q	D.N., 5
7.	~q	Simp., 6
8.	q · ~q	Conj., 4,7
9.	r ⊃ s	I.P., 3–8

13.
1.	p ⊃ (q ∨ ~(r ∨ s))	Premise
2.	~r ⊃ s/∴~q ⊃ ~p	Premise/conclusion
3.	~(~q ⊃ ~p)	Impl., 1
4.	~p ∨ (q ∨ ~(r ∨ s))	Impl., 1
5.	(~p ∨ q) ∨ ~(r ∨ s)	Assoc., 4
6.	~~r ∨ s	Impl., 2
7.	r ∨ s	D.N., 6
8.	~(p ⊃ q)	Trans., 3
9.	~(~p ∨ q)	Impl., 8
10.	~(r ∨ s)	D. Syll., 9,5
11.	(r ∨ s) · ~(r ∨ s)	Conj., 7,10
12.	~q ⊃ ~p	I.P. 3–11

EXERCISE 8–1

1. Tj ⊃ Sj
3. Indeterminate. False
5. (a) and (e)
7. False. Indeterminate. False. Indeterminate
9. (c) is a singular statement; (a) and (d) are universally quantified statements; (b) is an open sentence. Reasons: (c) contains just one constant, 'a', and no variables; in (a) and (d) all variables are bound; in (b) 'x' is not bound in its last occurrence.

EXERCISE 8–2

1. (a,c) Yes (b,d,e,g,h) No (f) Monadic
3. (a,b,c,d,e,h) No (f) Monadic (g) 'x' and 'y' are free.
5. (a,b) Yes (c,d,e,g) No (f) Monadic (h) 'a' is a constant.
7. (a,d) Yes (c,e,g) No. (b) 'Bg' is singular but statement as a whole is not. (f) Monadic (h) 'g' is a constant.
9. (a,e) Yes (b,g,h) No (c) '(∃x)Bx' is existentially quantified but statement as a whole is not. (d) '(x)Ax' is universally quantified but statement as a whole is not. (f) Monadic

EXERCISE 8–3

1. x is a three-lane highway, *and* x is dangerous.
3. x is a sentence, *and* x expresses a proposition (*or* x is a sentence, *and* y is a proposition, *and* x expresses y).
5. x is an open sentence, x becomes a statement, y is a free variable of x, z is the name of an individual, *and* y is replaced by z.
7. x is greater than y, x is less than y, *and* x is equal to y.
9. x is a vertebrate, *and* x is an animal.
11. x is a player of the first rank, *and* x entered the tournament.
13. x is a player in the tournament, *and* Emil can beat x.

EXERCISE 8–4

1. No one who eats meat is a vegetarian.
3. Nothing is a unicorn.
5. Nothing is both circular and square.
7. If someone is absent then not everyone is present.
9. Everything that John learned proved useful.
11. If everything is a form of energy then something is a form of energy.
13. Every integer is either odd or even.

EXERCISE 8–5

1. Cx = x is a centipede; Mx = x is a mammal. (x)(Cx ⊃ ~Mx) ⊃ (x)(Mx ⊃ ~Cx).
3. Px = x is a proposition; Ex = x is expressible by a sentence. (x)(Px ⊃ Ex).
5. Tx = x is a three-lane highway; Dx = x is dangerous. (x)(Tx ⊃ Dx).
7. Jx = x does his job; Px = x is a plan of ours; Wx = x will work out; w = Walter. Jw ⊃ (x)(Px ⊃ Wx).
9. Px = x is a player in the tournament; Fx = x is a former champion. (∃x)(Px · Fx).
11. Fx = x is a friend of Eliot's; Dx = x lives in Detroit; j = Jerry. Fj ⊃ Dj.
13. Ax = x is an argument; Vx = x is valid; Tx = x is truth-functionally valid. (∃x)(Ax · (Vx · ~ Tx)).
15. Ex = x is an expression; Cx = x contains free variables; Sx = x is a statement. (x)((Ex · Cx) ⊃ ~Sx).
17. Cx = x is a piece of cheap goods in the store; Sx = x is shoddily made; Dx = is defective (x)(Cx ⊃ (Sx ∨ Dx)).
19. Ax = x is an actor; Wx = x is an award winner; Cx = x is an Academy Award winner. (∃x)(Ax · (Wx · ~Cx)).

EXERCISE 8–6

1, 2, 5, 7: in each case, logically equivalent. 3,4: in each case, the first statement implies the second, but the second doesn't imply the first. 6: neither implies the other.

EXERCISE 8–7

1. Tx = x is a player in the tournament; Byx = y can beat x; e = Emil. Te · (∃x)(Tx · Bex).
3. Fx = x is a friend of George; Cx = x is a member of the chess team. (x)(Fx ⊃ Cx). *Or:* Fxy = x is a friend of y; Cx = x is a member of the chess team; g = George. (x)(Fxg ⊃ Cx).
5. Ax = x is a resident of Dorm A; Wx = x is a woman; Mx = x is a man. (∃x)(Ax · Wx) ⊃ ~ (x)(Ax ⊃ Mx).
7. Lx = x is a member of the L family; Gxy = x greets y; Mxy = x meets y. (x)(Lx ⊃ (y)(Mxy ⊃ Gxy)).
9. Ixy = x is identical with y. ~(∃x)(y)Ixy.
11. Cx = x is a class of George's; Lx = George is always late for x. (x)(Cx ⊃ Lx).
13. Cx = x is a cigar smoker; Mx = x prefers mild tobaccos. (∃x)(Cx · Mx).
15. Dx = x is a member of the Dean's List; Gx = x has good grades. (x)(Dx ⊃ Gx).

EXERCISE 8–8

1. If every applicant expected that the job demanded a college education, then some applicants were familiar with the writings of Homer.
3. No one who is not in the tournament has beaten anyone who is.
5. All members of the orchestra who know each other intimately like each other.

EXERCISE 9–1

1. (b) '(x)Fx ⊃ Ga' is not a generalized statement. (c) 'x' is not replaced in all occurrences and is free in the second line. (e) '~(x)Fx' is not a generalized statement. (g) '(y)' is not the initial quantifier. (j) 'x' has not been replaced uniformly.

EXERCISE 9–2

1. (b) and (c), statements instantiated-from are not generalized statements. (d) Violates new-constant requirement. (e) Line 4 violates new-constant requirement (line 3 is correct). (f) Violates new-constant requirement. (g) 'a' appears in the conclusion to be proved. (h) Line 3 violates new-constant requirement (line 2 is correct).

EXERCISE 9–3

1. (a) If everything is an albatross, then George is a bird. Therefore, everything is either an albatross or a bird. (b) Incorrect (c) Line 2 is incorrect; the statement on line 1 is not a generalized statement.
3. (a) Everything that is an albatross is a bird. Something either is not a chicken or is an albatross. Therefore, everything that is a chicken is a bird. (b) Incorrect (c)

The constant 'a', generalized upon by line 6, originated by E.I. (violation of proviso I, U.G. rule). Note that, although premises and conclusion are factually true, the argument is invalid.

5. If anything is an albatross, George is a bird. Therefore, all albatrosses are birds. (b) Incorrect (c) Line 3 violates proviso I, U.G. rule ('g' originated in a premise).

7. (a) Someone is a friend of everyone. Therefore, someone is a friend to herself or himself. (b) Correct

9. (a) All albatrosses are birds. Therefore, if everything is an albatross then everything is a bird. (b) Correct

EXERCISE 9–4

1.
1. $(x)Tx$ — P.
2. Ta — U.I., 1
3. $(\exists x)Tx$ — E.G., 2

3.
1. $(x)(Tx \supset (Nx \supset Cx))$ — P.
2. $Ta \supset (Na \supset Ca)$ — U.I., 1
3. $(Ta \cdot Na) \supset Ca$ — Exp., 2
4. $(x)((Tx \cdot Nx) \supset Cx)$ — U.G., 3

5.
1. $(x)(Tx \cdot Nx)$ — P.
2. $Ta \cdot Na$ — U.I., 1
3. Ta — Simp., 2
4. Na — Simp., 2
5. $(x)Tx$ — U.G., 3
6. $(x)Nx$ — U.G., 4
7. $(x)Tx \cdot (x)Nx$ — Conj., 5,6

7.
1. $(x)(y)Sxy$ — P.
2. $(y)Sdy$ — U.I., 1
3. Sdd — U.I., 2

9.
1. $(x)(y)Sxy$ — P.
2. $(y)Say$ — U.I., 1
3. Sab — U.I., 2
4. $(x)Sxb$ — U.G., 3
5. $(y)(x)Sxy$ — U.G., 4

11.
1. $(\exists x)Tx$ — P.
2. Ta — E.I., 1
3. $\sim\sim Ta$ — D.N., 2
4. $\sim\sim Ta \lor \sim\sim Na$ — Add., 3
5. $\sim(\sim Ta \cdot \sim Na)$ — DeM., 4
6. $(\exists x) \sim (\sim Tx \cdot \sim Nx)$ — E.G., 5
7. $\sim(x)(\sim Tx \cdot \sim Nx)$ — Q.E., 6

13.
1. $(x)(Tx \supset Nx)$ — P.
2. $(x)Tx$ — Assumption
3. Ta — U.I., 2
4. $Ta \supset Na$ — U.I., 3
5. Na — M.P., 3,4
6. $(x)Nx$ — U.G., 5
7. $(x)Tx \supset (x)Nx$ — C.P., 2–6

15.
1. $(\exists x)(Tx \lor Nx)$ — P.
2. $\sim(\exists x)Tx$ — Assumption
3. $(x) \sim Tx$ — Q.E., 2

4. $Ta \lor Na$ — E.I., 1
5. $\sim Ta$ — U.I., 3
6. Na — D. Syll., 4,5
7. $(\exists x)Nx$ — E.G., 6
8. $\sim(\exists x)Tx \supset (\exists x)Nx$ — C.P., 2–7
9. $\sim\sim(\exists x)Tx \lor (\exists x)Nx$ — Impl., 8
10. $(\exists x)Tx \lor (\exists x)Nx$ — D.N., 9

17.
1. $(\exists x)(Cx \cdot Hx) \supset (x)Ux$ — P.
2. $(\exists x) \sim Ux$ — P.
3. $\sim(x)Ux$ — Q.E., 2
4. $\sim(\exists x))Cx \cdot Hx$ — M.T., 1,3
5. $(x) \sim (Cx \cdot Hx)$ — Q.E., 4
6. $\sim(Ca \cdot Ha)$ — U.I., 5
7. $\sim(Ca \cdot \sim\sim Ha)$ — D.N., 6
8. $Ca \supset \sim Ha$ — Impl., 7
9. $(x)(Cx \supset \sim Hx)$ — U.G., 8

19.
1. $(x)(y)(Mxy \supset \sim Myx)$ — P.
2. $(y)(May \supset \sim Mya)$ — U.I., 1
3. $Maa \supset \sim Maa$ — U.I., 2
4. $\sim Maa \lor \sim Maa$ — Impl., 3
5. $\sim Maa$ — Taut., 4
6. $(x) \sim Mxx$ — U.G., 5

EXERCISE 9–5

1. (a) a. $(\exists x)(Ax \cdot Rx)$
   b. $(\exists x)(Rx \cdot Ax)$
(b) 1. $(\exists x)(Ax \cdot Rx) / \therefore (\exists x)(Rx \cdot Ax)$
   — Premise/conclusion
   2. $Aa \cdot Ra$ — E.I., 1
   3. $Ra \cdot Aa$ — Comm., 2
   4. $(\exists x)(Rx \cdot Ax)$ — E.G., 3
Same strategy for deducing a from b.

3. (a) a. $(x)(Ax \supset Fx)$
   b. $(x)(\sim Fx \supset \sim Ax)$
(b) 1. $(x)(Ax \supset Fx) / \therefore (x)(\sim Fx \supset \sim Ax)$
   — Premise/conclusion
   2. $Aa \supset Fa$ — U.I., 1
   3. $\sim Fa \supset \sim Aa$ — Trans., 3
   4. $(x)(\sim Fx \supset \sim Ax)$ — U.G., 3
Same strategy for deducing a from b.
But if alternatively:
(a) a. $(x)(Ax \supset Fx)$
   b. $\sim(\exists x)(\sim Fx \cdot Ax)$
(b) 1. $(x)(Ax \supset Fx) / \therefore \sim(\exists x)(\sim Fx \cdot Ax)$
   — Premise/conclusion
   2. $Aa \supset Fa$ — U.I., 1
   3. $\sim(Aa \cdot \sim Fa)$ — Impl., 2
   4. $\sim(\sim Fa \cdot Aa)$ — Comm., 3
   5. $(x)\sim(\sim Fx \cdot Ax)$ — U.G., 4
   6. $\sim(\exists x)(\sim Fx \cdot Ax)$ — Q.E., 5
For deducing a from b, use Q.E., U.I., Comm., Impl., and U.G. in that order.

5. (a) a. $(x)(Ax \supset Fx)$
    b. $\sim(\exists x)(Ax \cdot \sim Fx)$
  (b) Same as 3, variant.
7. (a) a. $\sim(x)(Fx \supset Ax)$
    b. $(\exists x)(Fx \cdot \sim Ax)$
  (b)
  1. $\sim(x)(Fx \supset Ax)/\therefore(\exists x)(Fx \cdot \sim Ax)$
     Premise/conclusion
  2. $(\exists x)\sim(Fx \supset Ax)$ O.E., 1
  3. $\sim(Fa \supset Aa)$ E.I., 2
  4. $\sim\sim(Fa \cdot \sim Aa)$ Impl., 3
  5. $Fa \cdot \sim Aa$ D.N., 4
  6. $(\exists x)(Fx \cdot \sim Ax)$ E.G., 5

For deducing a from b: E.I., D.N., Impl., E.G., and Q.E. in that order.

9. (a) a. $(x)(Ax \supset \sim Px)$
    b. $\sim(\exists x)(Ax \cdot Px)$

EXERCISE 9–6

1. (a) 'Gx' = 'x grows on trees'; 'Tx' = 'x is a tomato'; 'Sx' = 'x is a squash'; 'Ax' = 'x is an acorn'.
  1. $(x)(Gx \supset \sim Tx)$ Premise
  2. $(x)(Gx \supset \sim Sx)$ Premise
  3. $(x)(Ax \supset Gx)/\therefore(x)(Ax \supset \sim(Tx \lor Sx))$
     Premise/conclusion
  (b) 4. $Ga \supset \sim Ta$ U.I., 1
  5. $Ga \supset \sim Sa$ U.I., 2
  6. $Aa \supset Ga$ U.I., 3
  $\rightarrow$ 7. Aa Assmption
  8. Ga M.P., 6,7
  9. $\sim Ta$ M.P., 4,8
  10. $\sim Sa$ M.P., 5,8
  11. $\sim Ta \cdot \sim Sa$ Conj., 9, 10
  12. $\sim(Ta \lor Sa)$ DeM., 11
  13. $Aa \supset \sim(Ta \lor Sa)$ C.P., 7–12
  14. $(x)(Ax \supset \sim(Tx \lor Sx))$ U.G., 12

But if symbolized as:
  1. $(x)(Gx \supset \sim(Tx \lor Sx))$ Premise
  2. $(x)(Ax \supset Gx)/\therefore(x)(Ax \supset \sim(Tx \lor Sx))$
     Premise/conclusion
then deduction may be accomplished by U.I. (repeated), H. Syll., and U.G.

3. (a) 'Jx' = 'x is injured on the job'; 'Zx' = 'x is a member of group Z'; 'Ax' = 'x is alerted automatically'; 'f' = 'Felice'.
  1. $(\exists x)Jx \supset (x)(Zx \supset Ax)$ Premise
  2. $Zf \cdot \sim Af/\therefore\sim(\exists x)Jx$ Premise/conclusion
  (b) 3. $\sim\sim(\exists x)Jx$ Assumption
  4. $(\exists x)Jx$ D.N. 3
  5. $(x)(Zx \supset Ax)$ M.P., 1,3
  6. $Zf \supset Af$ U.I., 4
  7. $\sim(Zf \cdot \sim Af)$ Impl., 5
  8. $\sim(\exists x)Jx$ I.P., 3–7

Alternatively:
  3. $\sim\sim(Zf \cdot \sim Af)$ D.N., 2
  4. $\sim(Zf \supset Af)$ Impl., 3
  5. $(\exists x)\sim(Zx \supset Ax)$ E.G., 4
  6. $\sim(x)(Zx \supset Ax)$ Q.E., 5
  7. $\sim(\exists x)Jx$ M.T., 1,6

5. (a) 'Fx' = 'x finishes first'; 'Dx' = 'x is disqualified'; 'Sy' = 'y finishes second'; 'Py' = 'y is placed first'; 'b' = 'Lazy Bill'; 'm' = 'Maizy Dae'.
  1. $(\exists x)(Fx \cdot Dx) \supset (y)((Sy \cdot \sim Dy) \supset Py)$
     Premise
  2. $Fb \cdot Db$ Premise
  3. $Sm \cdot \sim Pm/\therefore Dm$ Premise/conclusion
  (b) 4. $(\exists x)(Fx \cdot Dx)$ E.G., 2
  5. $(y)((Sy \cdot \sim Dy) \supset Py)$ M.P., 1,4
  6. $(Sm \cdot \sim Dm) \supset Pm$ U.I., 5
  7. $\sim Pm$ Simp., 3
  8. $\sim(Sm \cdot \sim Dm)$ M.T., 6,7
  9. $Sm \supset Dm$ Impl., 8
  10. Sm Simp., 3
  11. Dm M.P., 9,10

On the alternative correct symbolization of premise 1 as '$(x)((Fx \cdot Dx) \supset (y)((Sy \cdot \sim Dy) \supset Py))$', U.I. would immediately yield '$(Fb \cdot Db) \supset (y)((Sy \cdot \sim Dy) \supset Py)$', with M.P. following to arrive at line 5 in the deduction above.

7. (a) 'Hx' = 'x is a human being'; 'Rxy' = 'x is entitled to as much respect as y'; 's' = 'Sally'; 'j' = 'John'.
  1. $(x)(y)((Hx \cdot Hy) \supset Rxy)$ Premise
  2. $Hs \cdot Hj/\therefore Rsj$ Premise/conclusion
  (b) 3. $(y)((Hs \cdot Hy) \supset Rsy)$ U.I., 1
  4. $(Hs \cdot Hj) \supset Rsj$ U.I., 2
  5. Rsj M.P., 2,4

9. (a) 'Qx' = 'x is a beauty queen'; 'Bx' = 'x is beautiful'; 'Gx' = 'x is a college graduate'.
  1. $(x)(Qx \supset Bx)$ Premise
  2. $(\exists x)(Gx \cdot Qx)/\therefore(\exists x)(Gx \cdot Bx)$
     Premise/conclusion
  (b) 3. $Ga \cdot Qa$ E.I., 2
  4. $Qa \supset Ba$ U.I., 1
  5. Ga Simp., 3
  6. Qa Simp., 6
  7. Ba M.P., 4,7
  8. $Ga \cdot Ba$ Conj., 5,8
  9. $(\exists x)(Gx \cdot Bx)$ E.G., 9

11. (a) 'Tx' = 'x is a terrier'; 'Px' = 'x is a poodle'; 'Dx' = 'x is a dog'; 'Cx' = 'x is a Cairn'.
  1. $(x)((Tx \lor Px) \supset Dx)$ Premise
  2. $(x)(Cx \supset Tx)/\therefore(x)(Cx \supset Dx)$
     Premise/conclusion
  (b) 3. $(Ta \lor Pa) \supset Da$ U.I., 1
  4. $Ca \supset Ta$ U.I., 2
  5. $\sim Ca \lor Ta$ Impl., 4

6. (~Ca ∨ Ta) ∨ Pa	Add., 5
7. ~Ca ∨ (Ta ∨ Pa)	Assoc., 6
8. Ca ⊃ (Ta ∨ Pa)	Impl., 7
9. Ca ⊃ Da	H.S., 3,8
10. (x)(Cx ⊃ Dx)	U.G., 9

EXERCISE 9–7

1. (a) (∃x)(Cx · ~Hx)

   (b)

1. (x)(Cx ⊃ Hx) ⊃ (∃x)Ux	Premise
2. (x)~Ux/∴(∃x)(Cx · ~Hx)	Premise/conclusion
3. ~(∃x)Ux	Q.E., 2
4. ~(x)(Cx ⊃ Hx)	M.T., 1,3
5. (∃x)~(Cx ⊃ Hx)	Q.E., 4
6. ~(Ca ⊃ Ha)	E.I., 5
7. ~~(Ca · ~Ha)	Impl., 6
8. Ca · ~Ha	D.N., 7
9. (∃x)(Cx · ~Hx)	E.G., 8

3. (a) (x)(Cx ⊃ ~Hx)

   (b)

1. (∃x)(Cx · Hx) ⊃ (x)Ux	Premise
2. (∃x)~Ux/∴(x)(Cx ⊃ ~Hx)	Premise/conclusion
3. ~(x)Ux	Q.E., 2
4. ~(∃x)(Cx · Hx)	M.T., 1,3
5. (x)~(Cx · Hx)	Q.E., 4
6. ~(Ca · Ha)	U.I., 5
7. ~(Ca · ~~Ha)	D.N., 6
8. Ca ⊃ ~Ha	Impl., 7
9. (x)(Cx ⊃ ~Hx)	U.G., 8

EXERCISE 9–8

1. On the principle of least analysis, quantification can be avoided. 'If the pot's a dollar short, somebody did not ante up. The pot's a dollar short. Therefore, somebody did not ante up'.

3. One reformulation would be: Everyone who is an experienced gardener and hears of a frost warning takes precautions. Jimmy is an experienced gardener. If Jimmy hears of a frost warning he will take precautions. Abbreviating 'x is an experienced gardener' by 'Gx', 'x hears of a frost warning' by 'Wx', 'x takes precautions' by 'Px', and 'Jimmy' by 'j', we get: '(x)((Gx · Wx) ⊃ Px)', 'Gj'; therefore, 'Wj ⊃ Pj'. Proof takes just three steps: instantiation to 'j,' exportation, and modus ponens.

EXERCISE 10–1

1. Explanation 3. Argument 5. Explanation
7. Explanation 9. Argument

EXERCISE 10–2

1. Inductive generalization
3. Inductive generalization

5. Induction by analogy
7. Inductive generalization
9. Inductive generalization
11. Inductive generalization
13. Inductive generalization
15. Inductive generalization
17. Induction by analogy

EXERCISE 10–3

1. c, a, b, d, e   3. c, d, a, b, e   5. c, a, d, e, b
7. c, b, e, a, d

EXERCISE 10–4

1. (a) Strengthens by increasing the number of observed cases and increasing the negative analogy among them. (b) Strengthens by increasing the number of observed cases and increasing the negative analogy among them. (c) Destroys the argument by providing a counterexample. (d) Destroys the argument by providing a counterexample. (e) Strengthens the argument by increasing the number of observed cases and increasing the negative analogy among them. (f) Destroys the argument by providing a counterexample.

3. (a) Strengthens by increasing the number of observed cases and increasing the negative analogy among them. (b) Weakens by increasing the positive analogy among the observed cases, *if* the location of the cats is considered to be relevant. (c) Weakens by presumably reducing the number of observed cases. (d) Strengthens by increasing the number of observed cases and increasing the negative analogy among them. (e) Strengthens by increasing the number of observed cases. (f) Weakens by both increasing the positive analogy among the observed cases and decreasing the number of observed cases.

5. (a) Weakens by increasing the negative analogy between the observed and unobserved cases. (b) Weakens by increasing the negative analogy between the observed and unobserved cases, if one considers the type of soap powder used relevant. (c) Weakens by increasing the negative analogy between observed and unobserved cases, if one considers the type of bleach and fabric softener relevant. (d) Strengthens by increasing the number of observed cases. (e) Strengthens by increasing the positive analogy among observed cases and between observed and unobserved cases, if one considers the plant of manufacture, the inspector, and place of purchase relevant. (f) Weakens by increasing the negative analogy between observed and unobserved cases, if one considers the fact that the Corleones' washing machine was a floor model relevant.

(g) Weakens by increasing the negative analogy between the observed and unobserved cases, if one considers the size of the machine, and the use of a certain type of soap powder, bleach, and softener relevant. (h) Strengthens by increasing the positive analogy between observed and unobserved cases and increasing the number of observed cases.

7. (a) Increases the negative analogy among the observed cases and between the observed and unobserved cases; strengthens the argument that the Allens will get *at least* 25 miles to a gallon of gas (but would weaken an argument that they will get *exactly* 25 miles per gallon). (b) Weakens by decreasing the positive analogy between the observed and unobserved cases. (c) No effect, since color is presumably not relevant to mileage per gallon. (d) Strengthens by increasing the positive, *if* analogy between the observed and unobserved cases, if the dealer and the date of purchase are considered relevant to mileage per gallon. (e) May strengthen by increasing the negative analogy between the observed and unobserved cases. (f) Weakens by increasing the negative analogy between the observed and unobserved cases. (g) Weakens by increasing the negative analogy between observed and unobserved cases, *if* the octane level is considered relevant to mileage per gallon. (h) Weakens by increasing the negative analogy between observed and unobserved cases. (i) Strengthens the argument that the Allens will get *at least* 25 miles to a gallon of gas, even though the negative analogy between observed and unobserved cases is increased.

EXERCISE 10–5

1. d, b, c, a   3. b, a, d, e, c   5. e, d, c, a, b

EXERCISE 10–6

1. (a) Weakens by decreasing the negative analogy among the observed cases. (b) Strengthens by increasing the number of observed cases. (c) Strengthens by increasing the negative analogy among the observed cases. (d) Strengthens by increasing the negative analogy among the observed cases. (e) Weakens by increasing the positive analogy among the observed cases, *if* the specified characteristics are considered relevant. (f) Weakens by increasing the positive analogy among the observed cases.

3. (a) Weakens by increasing positive analogy among observed cases and increasing negative analogy between observed and unobserved cases. (b) Strengthens by increasing the negative analogy among observed cases. (c) Weakens by increasing positive analogy among observed cases and increasing negative analogy

between observed and unobserved cases. (d) Weakens by increasing positive analogy among observed cases, if one considers the sex of the students relevant.

EXERCISE 11–1

1. (a)   Frank has won at blackjack.
          Frank has won at seven-card stud.
          Frank has won at five-card draw.
          ∴Frank will win at five-card stud.

    (b)   Frank has won at blackjack.
          Frank has won at seven-card stud.
          Frank has won at five-card draw.
          ∴Frank always wins at all kinds of poker.
          Five-card stud is a kind of poker.
          Frank will play five-card stud.
          ∴Frank will win at five-card stud.

3. (a)   It rained on Sunday.
          It rained on Monday.
          It rained on Tuesday.
          It rained on Wednesday.
          It rained on Thursday.
          It rained on Friday.
          ∴It will rain on Saturday.

    (b)   It rained on Sunday.
          It rained on Monday.
          It rained on Tuesday.
          It rained on Wednesday.
          It rained on Thursday.
          It rained on Friday.
          ∴It rains every day.
          Saturday is a day.
          ∴It will rain on Saturday.

5. (a)   The flood crested in Pittsburgh this week.
          The flood crested in Cincinnati this week.
          ∴The flood will crest in Louisville this week.

    (b)   The flood crested in Pittsburgh this week.
          The flood crested in Cincinnati this week.
          ∴The flood is cresting in all cities on the Ohio River this week.
          Louisville is a city on the Ohio River.
          ∴The flood will crest in Louisville this week.

7. (a)   The Smiths own a Fisher receiver-amplifier and get excellent service.
          The Parkers own a Fisher receiver-amplifier and get excellent service.
          The Roberts own a Fisher receiver-amplifier and get excellent service.
          The Mitchells own a Fisher receiver-amplifier and get excellent service.

The Conners own a Fisher receiver-amplifier and get excellent service.
The Carters just bought a Fisher receiver-amplifier.
∴The Carters will get excellent service.

(b) The Smiths own a Fisher receiver-amplifier and get excellent service.
The Parkers own a Fisher receiver-amplifier and get excellent service.
The Roberts own a Fisher receiver-amplifier and get excellent service.
The Mitchells own a Fisher receiver-amplifier and get excellent service.
The Conners own a Fisher receiver-amplifier and get excellent service.
∴All persons who own Fisher receiver-amplifiers always get excellent service
The Carters just bought a Fisher receiver-amplifier.
∴The Carters will get excellent service.

9. (a) My grandfather went bald before he was thirty years old.
My father went bald before he was thirty years old.
My older brother went bald before he was thirty years old.
∴I will go bald before I am thirty years old.

(b) My grandfather went bald before he was thirty years old.
My father went bald before he was thirty years old.
My older brother went bald before he was thirty years old.
∴All males in my family go bald before they are thirty years old.
I am a male in my family.
∴I will go bald before I am thirty years old.

11. (a) Peter is Swiss and speaks German.
Hans is Swiss and speaks German.
Maria is Swiss and speaks German.
Karl is Swiss and speaks German.
Karin is Swiss and speaks German.
∴Antonio, who is Swiss, must speak German.

(b) Peter is Swiss and speaks German.
Hans is Swiss and speaks German.
Maria is Swiss and speaks German.
Karl is Swiss and speaks German.
Karin is Swiss and speaks German.

∴All who are Swiss speak German.
Antonio is Swiss.
∴Antonio must speak German.

13. (a) John got A's in every course he took in his first semester in college.
John got A's in every course he took in his second semester in college.
John got A's in every course he took in his third semester in college.
John got A's in every course he took in his fourth semester in college.
∴John will get A's in every course he takes in this, his fifth semester in college.

(b) John got A's in every course he took in his first semester in college.
John got A's in every course he took in his second semester in college.
John got A's in every course he took in his third semester in college.
John got A's in every course he took in his fourth semester in college.
∴John gets A's in all his courses in every semester in college.
This is John's fifth semester in college
∴John will get A's in every course he takes in this, his fifth semester in college.

15. (a) The movie I saw on the "Late Show" yesterday was interesting.
The movie I saw on the "Late Show" the night before that was interesting.
I will see many more movies on the "Late Show" in the future.
∴At least one movie I will see on the "Late Show" in the future will be interesting.

(b) The movie I saw on the "Late Show" yesterday was interesting.
The movie I saw on the "Late Show" the night before that was interesting.
∴All movies I see on the "Late Show" are interesting.
I will see many movies on the "Late Show" in the future.
∴At least one movie I will see on the "Late Show" in the future will be interesting.

17. (a) Italy is a European country and has shown aggressive tendencies.
Germany is a European country and has shown aggressive tendencies.

Spain is a European country and has shown aggressive tendencies.

France is a European country and·has shown aggressive tendencies.

∴At least one other European country will show aggressive tendencies.

(b)   Italy is a European country and has shown aggressive tendencies.

Germany is a European country and has shown aggressive tendencies.

Spain is a European country and has shown aggressive tendencies.

France is a European country and has shown aggressive tendencies.

∴All European countries show aggressive tendencies.

Several other European countries exist.

∴At least one other European country will show aggressive tendencies.

19. (a)   Juan attends Princeton and had combined college board scores over 1100.

Kim attends Princeton and had combined college board scores over 1100.

Pete attends Princeton and had combined college board scores over 1100.

Michel attends Princeton and had combined college board scores over 1100.

Five thousand other students attend Princeton.

∴At least one other Princeton student had combined college board scores over 1100.

(b)   Juan attends Princeton and had combined college board scores over 1100.

Kim attends Princeton and had combined college board scores over 1100.

Pete attends Princeton and had combined college board scores over 1100.

Michel attends Princeton and had combined college board scores over 1100.

∴All students who attend Princeton have combined college board scores over 1100.

Tony attends Princeton.

∴Tony had combined college board scores over 1100.

EXERCISE 11–4

1. a, b, d, e, f.   **3.**   a, c, d.   **5.**   a, b.
7.   a, b, d, e.

EXERCISE 11–5

Sample answer: Hypothesis: All planets in the solar system have satellites. *Supporting observation statements:* (a) The earth has one satellite, the moon. (b) Mars has two satellites. (c) Jupiter has twelve satellites. *Disconfirming observation statements:* (d) Mercury has no satellites. (e) Pluto has no satellites.

EXERCISE 11–6

1.   *Inductive argument:*
(a)   Sergei, a Russian, can laugh.
Elena, a Spaniard, can laugh.
Muhammed, a Tunisian, can laugh.
Vani, a Bantu, can laugh.
Mikako, a Japanese, can laugh.
∴All people can laugh.
(b, c, d, e) These arguments take the same form as (a). *Order of decreasing inductive strength:* c, a, e, b, d.

3.   *Inductive argument:*
(a) This green oak leaf from New Mexico contains chlorophyll.
This green sage leaf from Texas contains chlorophyll.
This green palm frond from Arizona contains chlorophyll.
This green blade of grass from Colorado contains chlorophyll.
This green grape leaf from southern California contains chlorophyll.
∴All green plants contain chlorophyll.
(b, c, d, e) These arguments take the same form as (a). *Order of decreasing inductive strength:* b, d, e, c, a.

5.   *Inductive argument:*
(a)   Frenchie, a miniature poodle, is a carnivore.
Natasha, a Russian wolfhound, is a carnivore.
Pierre, a standard poodle, is a carnivore.
King, a German shepard, is a carnivore.
Lassie, a collie, is a carnivore.
∴All dogs are carnivores.
Arguments b, c, d, and e take the same form as argument a. *Order of decreasing inductive strength:* c, a, d, b, e.

EXERCISE 12–1

1.   *Proximate:* l. *Remote:* a, b, c, e, g, i, j, k
3.   *Proximate:* v. *Remote:* a through u, except b, d, h, l, o, q.

EXERCISE 12–3

1. a. Sufficient but not necessary. b. Necessary but not sufficient. c. Sufficient but not necessary. d. Neither necessary nor sufficient e. Sufficient but not necessary. f. Both necessary and sufficient.

3. *Necessary conditions:* age 23 or over, and the disjunction of previous communications experience and previous computer experience. However, this combination is not a sufficient condition as is shown by the fact that it was fulfilled by persons 4 and 8, who were not hired.

5. Probably an over-all B average, family income under $5,000, and recommendations by two professors are necessary conditions for the scholarship. The conjunction of these three necessary conditions cannot be taken to be the sufficient condition, since student 10 satisfied all three conditions but did not receive the scholarship.

EXERCISE 12–4

Method of agreement. The proximate condition of cracking was probably the differential expansion, and the condition of this was the conjunction of sudden change in temperature, eastward exposure, and the presence of the varicolored paints on the glass. Since cracking occurred *only* where these conditions were present, the expansion and the conjunction which produced it were necessary conditions. They would not be shown to be sufficient conditions unless it could be demonstrated that cracking occurred in *every* case in which they were present.

EXERCISE 12–5

1. Method of difference. Since the only significant condition in which the contaminated broth differed from the uncontaminated was that of exposure to ordinary air (and to whatever microorganisms it contained), this exposure was established as probably a sufficient condition of the contamination.

EXERCISE 12–6

The necessary condition is probably the conjunction of crystal and zeroz—an answer arrived at by use of the method of agreement. (Of course, in real life it is highly unlikely that the different samples would vary as much as in this imaginary case.)

EXERCISE 12–7

1. Method of agreement: the only structural flaw common to all the malfunctioning sets was the improperly soldered wire. Therefore the presence of this improperly soldered wire was probably a necessary condition for this particular type of malfunction.

3. Method of concomitant variations: expenditure in dollars varies positively with total income, and expenditure as a percentage of income varies inversely (though not perfectly so) with total income. It would not be unreasonable to conclude from this evidence that an increase in income is a necessary condition for an increase in expenditure on recreation and entertainment.

5. Method of difference: The various groups of chicks differed only in the substance with which they were inoculated (or not inoculated), and their subsequent death rates from the virus. Therefore, since the death rate of group 3 was markedly lower than that of any other group, the vaccine given to this group was probably a sufficient condition of the lower death rate. Vaccines 1, 2, and 4 were also sufficient conditions for lowering the death rate, although they were less effective than vaccine 3.

7. Joint method: the suspect brand of thermostat was present in every case in which the heating system malfunctioned and absent in almost every case in which it failed to malfunction. Therefore this brand of thermostat was probably a necessary condition of the malfunction. Because at least one such thermostat, however, was not associated with a malfunction, the sufficient cause was possibly not the thermostat itself but some flaw which was present in most if not all of the individual thermostats of this brand.

EXERCISE 12–8

1. This may have been either method of difference or joint method. If the random selection process resulted in two groups which, *as groups,* were alike in all relevant respects save the one experimental difference, this represents use of the method of difference. If, as seems more likely with the fairly small groups of people involved, there were other possibly significant differences among them, it represents use of the joint method.

EXERCISE 12–9

1. Joint method. (a) Caffeine is the condition associated with Mr. Johnson's insomnia (it is present in coffee, tea, and coke, but not in the other foods or beverages consumed). (b) Caffeine is probably a necessary condition (insomnia occurred *only* when caffeine was present) and also a sufficient condition (insomnia occurred *whenever* caffeine was present).

EXERCISE 12–10

1. Method of agreement and method of difference. The successive findings that all the men were heavy

drinkers, that they had all eaten at the same cafeteria, that they had all eaten oatmeal, and that they had all consumed a drug were important steps in leading investigators to the probable source of the poisoning and proved to be, in this particular case, necessary though not sufficient conditions. Working from these clues, and from the symptoms, the investigators eliminated one after another possible alternative explanation (gas poisoning, food poisoning) which failed to account for all the circumstances, until they arrived at one which could successfully explain all the known facts. The presence of the sodium nitrite in the oatmeal and in the salt-shaker, together with the other known conditions and the likelihood that the men had salted their oatmeal from that shaker, constituted what appeared to be sufficient condition for the poisonings. That is, probably the *only* significant difference between the poisoning victims and others who had eaten at the cafeteria that morning was that the victims had all both eaten the contaminated oatmeal and salted it heavily from the contaminated shaker, while the others had not fulfilled both these conditions. In effect, the investigators were assuming that use of the method of difference, had it been possible to check all the details, would have supported this conclusion.

EXERCISE 12–11

1. (1) Method of difference: presumably the sudden-death victims, as a group, did not differ in other significant respects from the cardiac patients who did not die.
   (2) (a) The argument would be strengthened if studies of larger groups—say 1,000 or 10,000—of cardiac patients showed similar discrepancies beween the smoking habits of those who did and those who did not suffer sudden cardiac death. (b) The argument would be weakened if it were shown that most of the cigarette smokers among the sudden-death victims had been heavy smokers for ten years or more. (This might, however, provide strong evidence that prolonged heavy smoking is a cause of sudden cardiac death) (c) It is doubtful that there is any single piece of evidence that would completely falsify the conclusion—or completely prove the truth of it.
   (3) "Cause" is here being used to refer to a sufficient condition. The fact that some nonsmokers are also victims of sudden cardiac death is good evidence that there are other causes as well—that is, that smoking is not a necessary condition.

3. (1) Probably joint method. In the high-polio group, there was a general pattern, or condition, of

drinking whiskey but not beer. In the lower ranks, this condition was reversed. Since other conditions (quality of living quarters, type of duty, and so on) were probably not always the same for the two groups, the method of difference cannot be used in this case.
   (2) (a) The argument would be strengthened if it were found that in *every* case of paralytic polio, the affected individual had drunk whiskey and had not drunk beer, or if studies among other population groups in other parts of the world showed a similar pattern. (b) The argument would be weakened if it were shown that certain other possibly relevant conditions were consistently different for the two groups: for instance, that all the officers, and *only* the officers, had eaten food from a particular source or had attended training sessions at a particular place. (c) The conclusion would be falsified if a high-polio group were discovered in which beer rather than whiskey was the usual drink.
   (3) "Cause" is here being used to refer to a necessary condition, which may also be a sufficient condition. However, the evidence does not permit a conclusion as to whether the significant condition is the drinking of whiskey, or the nondrinking of beer or both.

5. (1) Method of concomitant variations: The rate of mortality from these types of cancer varied in accordance with the per capita consumption of beer from one state to another.
   (2) (a) The argument would be strengthened if records of the individuals who died of these types of cancer showed that a high percentage of them were indeed beer drinkers. (b) The argument would be weakened if comparison of a group of the cancer victims with an otherwise similar group of nonvictims showed no significant difference in beer-drinking habits. (c) The conclusion that beer causes cancer would be falsified only if it could be shown that no beer drinker had ever had cancer.
   (3) "Cause" is here being used to refer to a sufficient condition.

7. (1) Method of difference: As a group, the angina patients who received drug treatment apparently differed only in this respect from the angina patients who received surgery; yet the caused event—lowered death rate—was present in the first group and not in the second.
   (2) (a) The argument would be strengthened if a larger study group, or one followed for a longer time, showed the same results; or if each drug patient

were paired with a surgery patient essentially similar to him in all other respects, and the results still showed lower death rates for the drug patients. (b) The argument would be weakened if it were shown that the drug patients, as a group, suffered from less-severe angina than the surgery patients, or from less-severe advanced coronary obstruction. (c) There does not seem to be any one item that could completely falsify the conclusion, given accuracy of the research data.

(3) "Cause" here is being used to refer to a sufficient condition: The drug treatment is presented as a sufficient condition for the lowered death rate.

9. (1) Method of difference: The institution of screening was presumably the only change in significant conditions between 1972 and 1973.

(2) (a) The argument would be strengthened if the institution of similar procedures in several other countries were followed by a similar drop in hijackings, or if the procedures were eliminated here and hijackings did, in fact, increase significantly. (b) The argument would be weakened if it were found that at least some potential hijackers knew of an easy way to smuggle weapons past the screening equipment but had not done so, or if it turned out that there had in reality been thirty or more attempted hijackings in 1973, but that the knowledge of these had been kept secret. (c) No observations could completely falsify the conclusion.

(3) "Cause" is here being used to refer to a sufficient condition.

11. (1) Joint method: when the condition (capital punishment) is present, the supposed effect (low murder rate) is also present; when the supposed effect is absent, so also is the condition.

(2) (a) The argument would be strengthened if reinstitution of capital punishment were followed by a significant drop in the murder rate. (b) The argument would be weakened if it were shown that some other possibly significant condition had also changed during the time when capital punishment was suspended, or that the rise in numbers of murders was about in proportion to the rise in numbers of the general population, so that the murder rate had remained about the same. (c) The conclusion would be falsified if reinstitution of capital punishment were followed by an increase in the murder rate.

(3) "Cause" is here probably being used to refer to a necessary condition and possibly also a sufficient one.

EXERCISE 13–1

1. Very close to 1
3. Very close to 0
5. Almost 0
7. Almost 0
9. 0 or at least very near to 0
11. Close to 0
13. Close to 1.
15. About .5

EXERCISE 13–2

1. No—logically inconsistent
3. Yes—logically consistent (both could happen at different times).
5. No—logically inconsistent.
7. No—logically inconsistent
9. Yes—logically consistent (Both Republican and Democratic candidates may lose, and an Independent may win.)

EXERCISE 13–3

1. (a) $\frac{1}{52}$ (b) $\frac{1}{26}$ (c) $\frac{1}{13}$ (d) $\frac{1}{2}$ (e) $\frac{3}{13}$
3. $\frac{1}{512}$ (b) $\frac{1}{64}$
5. $\frac{7}{150}$
7. $\frac{156}{342,826}$ or $\frac{1}{2196}$ assuming that it is permissible to apply the relative frequency definition to single cases.
9. (a) $\frac{4}{52}$ or $\frac{1}{13}$ (b) $\frac{40}{52}$ or $\frac{10}{13}$ (c) $\frac{6}{52}$ or $\frac{3}{26}$ (d) $\frac{20}{52}$ or $\frac{5}{13}$ (e) $\frac{1}{52}$
11. (a) $\frac{1}{3}$ for each, if we feel justified in applying the principle of indifference. If we feel that the probability for each driver is not the same, we cannot use the classical theory. (b) The probabilities cannot be computed on the relative frequency theory, since we are not told how the three drivers have fared in races *against each other,* and against the rest of today's field of 15. We have only each driver's won-lost record to go on.
13. (a) $.6 \left(\frac{3}{2+3} = \frac{3}{5} = .6 \right)$
(b) Undetermined: they might fall, or they might stay the same.
15. (a) $\frac{5}{4+5} = \frac{5}{9} =$ about .55.
(b) $\frac{3}{3+1} = \frac{3}{4} =$ about .75
17. (a) $\frac{15}{50} = \frac{3}{10} = .3$ assuming that probabilities can be computed for single cases. (b) $\frac{1}{2} = .5$
19. $\frac{20}{50} = \frac{2}{5} = .4$

EXERCISE 13–4

1. One possible favorable event; independent; restricted conjunction rule. Initial probability of each simple

event: $\frac{1}{6}$. Probability of conjunct event: $\frac{1}{216}$. Equation:

$P(x \ \& \ y \ \& \ z) = P(x) \times P(y) \times P(z)$

$$= \frac{1}{6} \times \frac{1}{6} \times \frac{1}{6} = \frac{1}{216}$$

3. One possible favorable event; independent; restricted conjunction rule. Initial probability of each simple event: $\frac{1}{3}$. Probability of conjunct event: $\frac{1}{243}$. Equation:

$P(v \ \& \ w \ \& \ x \ \& \ y \ \& \ z) =$
$= P(v) \times P(w) \times P(x) \ g \ P(y) \times P(z) =$

$$= \frac{1}{3} \times \frac{1}{3} \times \frac{1}{3} \times \frac{1}{3} \times \frac{1}{3} = \frac{1}{243}$$

5. One possible favorable event; independent; restricted conjunction rule. Initial probability of each simple event: $\frac{1}{5}$. Probability of conjunct event: $(\frac{1}{5})^{70}$. Equation: $P(x_1 \ \& \ x_2 \ \& \ \ldots \ x_{70}) = P(x_1) \times P(x_2) \times \ldots \ P(x_{70}) = (\frac{1}{5})^{70}$ (The denominator would be astronomical; even $5^{10} = 9,756,625$; so the probability would be infinitesimally small.)

7. One possible favorable event; independent; restricted conjunction rule. Initial probabilities of simple events: $\frac{1}{2}$ and $\frac{2}{3}$. Probability of conjunct event: $\frac{1}{3}$. Equation:

$P(x \ \& \ y) = P(x) \times P(y) = \dfrac{1}{2} \times \dfrac{2}{3} = \dfrac{2}{6} = \dfrac{1}{3}$

9. One possible favorable event; dependent; general conjunction rule. Initial probability of each simple event: $\frac{1}{10}$. Probability of conjunct event: $\frac{1}{5040}$. Equation: $P(w \ \& \ x \ \& \ y \ \& \ z) = P(w) \times P(x \text{ given } w) \times P(y \text{ given } w \ \& \ x) \times P(z \text{ given } w, x, \ \& \ y)$

$$= \frac{1}{10} \times \frac{1}{9} \times \frac{1}{8} \times \frac{1}{7} = \frac{1}{5040}$$

EXERCISE 13–5

1. (a) Independent (b) Restricted conjunction rule (c) Initial probability of each simple event is $\frac{1}{6}$. (d) $\frac{1}{36}$.

   (e) $P(x \text{ and } y) = P(x) \times P(y) = \dfrac{1}{6} \times \dfrac{1}{6} = \dfrac{1}{36}$

3. (a) Independent (b) Restricted conjunction rule (c) Initial probability of each simple event is $\frac{1}{365}$. (d) $\frac{1}{133,225}$
   (e) $P(x \text{ and } y) = P(x) \times P(y)$

$$= \frac{1}{365} \times \frac{1}{365} = \frac{1}{133,225}$$

5. (a) Independent (b) Restricted conjunction rule (c) Initial probability of drawing a red ball from urn 1 is $\frac{1}{3}$, of drawing a white ball from urn 2 is $\frac{1}{2}$, and of drawing a black ball from urn 3 is $\frac{1}{6}$. (d) $\frac{1}{36}$
   (e) $P(x \text{ and } y \text{ and } z) = P(x) \times P(y) \times P(z)$

$$= \frac{1}{3} \times \frac{1}{2} \times \frac{1}{6} = \frac{1}{36}$$

7. (a) Independent (b) Restricted conjunction rule (c) Initial probability for each person is $\frac{1}{4}$. (d) $\frac{1}{1024}$
   (e) $P(v \text{ and } w \text{ and } x \text{ and } y \text{ and } z)$
   $= P(v) \times P(w) \times P(x) \times P(y) \times P(z)$

$$= \frac{1}{4} \times \frac{1}{4} \times \frac{1}{4} \times \frac{1}{4} \times \frac{1}{4} = \frac{1}{1029}$$

9. (a) Independent (b) Restricted conjunction rule (c) Initial probability of each simple event is $\frac{1}{4}$. (d) $\frac{1}{16}$

   (e) $P(x \text{ and } y) = P(x) \times P(y) = \dfrac{1}{4} \times \dfrac{1}{4} = \dfrac{1}{16}$

EXERCISE 13–6

1. (a) Two possible favorable events; mutually exclusive; restricted disjunction rule. Initial probability of each simple event: $\frac{1}{6}$. Probability of disjunct event: $\frac{1}{3}$ or about .33. Equation:

$P(x \text{ or } y) = P(x) + P(y) = \dfrac{1}{6} + \dfrac{1}{6} = \dfrac{2}{6} = \dfrac{1}{3}$

   (b) Three possible favorable events; mutually exclusive; restricted disjunction rule. Initial probability of each simple event: $\frac{1}{6}$. Probability of disjunct event: $\frac{1}{2}$ or .5. Equation:
   $P(x \text{ or } y \text{ or } z) = P(x) + P(y) + P(z)$

$$= \frac{1}{6} + \frac{1}{6} + \frac{1}{6} = \frac{3}{6} = \frac{1}{2}$$

3. (a) Two possible favorable events; mutually exclusive; restricted disjunction rule. Initial probability of each simple event: $\frac{1}{12}$. Probability of disjunct event: $\frac{1}{6}$ or about .166. Equation:

$P(x \text{ or } y) = P(x) + P(y) = \dfrac{1}{12} + \dfrac{1}{12} = \dfrac{2}{12} = \dfrac{1}{6}$

   (b) Two possible favorable events; mutually exclusive; restricted disjunction rule. Initial probabilities of simple events: $\frac{1}{12}$ (first draw) and $\frac{1}{11}$ (second draw). Probability of disjunct event: $\frac{23}{132}$ or about .175. Equation:

$P(x \text{ or } y) = P(x) + P(y) = \dfrac{1}{12} + \dfrac{1}{11} = \dfrac{23}{132}$

5. Two possible favorable events; not mutually exclusive; general disjunction rule. Initial probabilities of simple events: $\frac{1}{52}$ and $\frac{1}{2}$. $P(x \ \& \ y) = \frac{1}{104}$. Probability of disjunct event: $\frac{53}{104}$ or about .51. Equation:
   $P(x \text{ or } y) = P(x) + P(y) - P(x \ \& \ y)$

$$= \frac{1}{52} + \frac{1}{2} - \frac{1}{104} = \frac{53}{104}$$

7. Two possible favorable events (June may be seated at Jane's right or at Jane's left); mutually exclusive; restricted disjunction rule. Initial probability of each simple event: $\frac{1}{3}$. Probability of disjunct event: $\frac{2}{3}$ or about .67. Equation:

$P(x \text{ or } y) = P(x) + P(y) = \dfrac{1}{3} + \dfrac{1}{3} = \dfrac{2}{3}$

EXERCISE 13–7

1. (a) Mutually exclusive events (b) Restricted disjunction rule (c) Initial probability of drawing a white ball is $\frac{5}{30}$, of drawing a blue ball is $\frac{6}{30}$. (d) Not relevant (e) $\frac{11}{30}$

   (f) $P(x \text{ or } y) = P(x) + P(y) = \frac{5}{30} + \frac{6}{30} = \frac{11}{30}$

3. (a) Not mutually exclusive (b) General disjunction rule (c) Initial probability of boy living to his twentieth birthday is $\frac{9}{10}$, of girl living to her twentieth birthday is $\frac{8}{10}$. (d) $P(x \text{ and } y) = P(x) \times P(y) = \frac{9}{10} \times \frac{8}{10} = \frac{72}{100}$. (e) $\frac{98}{100}$ or .98

   (f) $P(x \text{ or } y) = P(x) + P(y) - P(x \text{ and } y)$

   $= \frac{9}{10} + \frac{8}{10} - \frac{72}{100} = \frac{170}{100} - \frac{72}{100} = \frac{98}{100} = .98$

5. (a) Mutually exclusive (b) Restricted disjunction rule (c) Initial probability of each simple event is $\frac{1}{52}$. (d) Not relevant (e) $\frac{1}{13}$

   (f) $P(w \text{ or } x \text{ or } y \text{ or } z) = P(w) + P(x) + P(y) + P(z)$

   $= \frac{1}{52} + \frac{1}{52} + \frac{1}{52} + \frac{1}{52} = \frac{4}{52} = \frac{1}{13}$

7. (a) Not mutually exclusive (b) General disjunction rule (c) Initial probability of selecting a red ball from urn 1 is $\frac{1}{3}$, from urn 2 is $\frac{1}{3}$. (d) $P(x \text{ and } y) = P(x) \times P(y) = \frac{1}{3} \times \frac{1}{3} = \frac{1}{9}$. (e) $\frac{5}{9}$

   (f) $P(x \text{ or } y) = P(x) + P(y) - P(x \text{ and } y)$

   $= \frac{1}{3} + \frac{1}{3} - \frac{1}{9} = \frac{2}{3} - \frac{1}{9} = \frac{5}{9}$

EXERCISE 13–8

1. (a) Conjunction; one possible favorable event (all twos); independent; restricted conjunction rule. Initial probability of each simple event: $\frac{1}{6}$. Probability of conjunct event: $\frac{1}{216}$, or about .0045. Equation:

   $P(x \& y \& z) = P(x) \times P(y) \times P(z)$

   $= \frac{1}{6} \times \frac{1}{6} \times \frac{1}{6} = \frac{1}{216}$

   (b) Conjunction (from 1a) and disjunction; two possible favorable events; mutually exclusive; restricted disjunction rule. Initial probability of each conjunct event: $\frac{1}{216}$ (from 1a). Probability of disjunct event: $\frac{1}{108}$ or about .009. Equation:

   $P(x \text{ or } y) = P(x) + P(y) = \frac{1}{216} + \frac{1}{216} = \frac{2}{216} = \frac{1}{108}$

3. (a) Conjunction and disjunction; two possible favorable events (drawing a dime and then a nickel or a nickel and then a dime). Initial probabilities of simple events: $\frac{2}{5}$ and $\frac{3}{5}$. Probability of disjunct event: $\frac{3}{5}$.

   Probability of first possible favorable event (drawing a dime and then a nickel): dependent simple events; general conjunction rule. Equation:

   $P(x \& y) = P(\text{dime} \& \text{nickel})$

   $= P(\text{dime}) \times P(\text{nickel given dime on first draw})$

   $= \frac{2}{5} \times \frac{3}{4} = \frac{6}{20} = \frac{3}{10}$

   Probability of second possible favorable event (drawing a nickel and then a dime): dependent simple events; general conjunction rule. Equation:

   $P(x \& y) = P(\text{nickel and dime})$

   $= P(\text{nickel}) \times P(\text{dime given nickel on first draw})$

   $= \frac{3}{5} \times \frac{2}{4} = \frac{6}{20} = \frac{3}{10}$

   Probability of disjunction (either dime and nickel or nickel and dime): mutually exclusive events; restricted disjunction rule. Equation:

   $P(x \text{ or } y) = P(\text{dime and nickel or nickel and dime})$

   $= \frac{3}{10} + \frac{3}{10} = \frac{6}{10} = \frac{3}{5}$

   (b) Conjunction; one possible favorable event (three nickels); dependent; general conjunction rule. Initial probability of each simple event: $\frac{3}{5}$. Probability of conjunct event: $\frac{1}{10}$ or .1. Equation:

   $P(x \& y \& z) = P(x) \times P(y \text{ given } x) \times P(z \text{ given } x \& y)$

   $= \frac{3}{5} \times \frac{2}{4} \times \frac{1}{3} = \frac{6}{60} = \frac{1}{10}$

   (c) Disjunction; three possible favorable events; mutually exclusive; restricted disjunction rule. Initial probabilities of simple events: $\frac{3}{10}, \frac{3}{10}, \frac{1}{10}$. Probability of disjunct event: $\frac{7}{10}$. Equation:

   $P(x \text{ or } y \text{ or } z) = P(x) + P(y) + P(z)$

   $= \frac{3}{10} + \frac{3}{10} + \frac{1}{10} = \frac{7}{10}$

Index

Numbers in **boldface** indicate pages on which the term or concept is defined.

Answers to Even-Numbered Exercises

for

LOGIC second edition

Robert Baum Rensselaer Polytechnic Institute

Holt, Rinehart and Winston New York Chicago San Francisco
Dallas Montreal Toronto

ISBN: 0-03-056878-1
Copyright © 1981 by Holt, Rinehart and Winston
All rights reserved
Printed in the United States of America
Published simultaneously in Canada
1 2 3 4   005   9 8 7 6 5 4 3 2 1

Answers to Even-Numbered Exercises

EXERCISE 1–2

2. Mixed use: This sentence may express a value judgment favoring Hitler's defeat, or it may represent an emotional expression of fact.
4. Noncognitive: Although this sentence may reflect a value judgment, the command that it expresses would not ordinarily be considered either true or false.
6. Cognitive
8. Noncognitive
10. Cognitive
12. Noncognitive
14. Cognitive
16. Mixed use
18. Noncognitive or cognitive*
20. Mixed use

EXERCISE 1–3

Sample answers for 1 and 2 only. A large variety of different correct answers are possible for each exercise.

2. *Cognitive context:* George was seen with Barbara, and this sentence is used by the person who saw them to express the statement, "George, I saw you with Barbara last night."
   Noncognitive context: A person may suspect that George was seen with Barbara and is using this sentence to inquire into the grounds of the suspicion.

EXERCISE 1–4

2. Synthetic, 'unless revolves around earth' is part of the definition of 'moon,' in which case it is semantically analytic.
4. Synthetic
6. Semantically analytic
8. Syntactically analytic
10. Synthetic; Although, by definition, all bachelors are men, there may in fact be no men who are or exist as bachelors.
12. Synthetic; Although liars do not always tell the truth, it must be proved that some of them never tell the truth.
14. Syntactically analytic: One could argue the definition

* Choice depends on a specific everyday context.

of death in an effort to show that John is neither dead nor nondead.
16. Syntactically analytic
18. Synthetic
20. Synthetic, unless the definition of 'coral snakes' includes the trait of being poisonous, in which case the statement is semantically analytic.
22. Semantically analytic
24. Synthetic

EXERCISE 1–5

2. Synonymous
4. Enumerative, ostensive
6. Operational
8. Connotative, by genus and difference (genus = 'letter of the Hebrew alphabet').
10. Synonymous
12. Operational
14. Connotative, by genus and difference (genus = 'lizard')
16. Synonymous
18. Enumerative, ostensive
20. Connotative
22. Enumerative (denotive)
24. Synonymous
26. Enumerative (ostensive)
28. Connotative
30. Connotative (genus and difference)
32. Connotative (genus and difference)
34. Enumerative (ostensive)
36. Enumerative (denotative)
38. Synonymous
40. Operational

EXERCISE 1–6

2. (a) Film. (b) *Casablanca, 2001: A Space Odyssey, Last Tango in Paris, Play it Again, Sam* (denotative definition). (c) A representation of a story or series of events by means of a series of pictures projected on a screen in rapid succession, usually with accompanying sound.
4. (a) Feline. (b) Tabby, Siamese, Persian, Angora. (c) A

domesticated carnivorous animal kept as a pet or for catching mice and rats.

6. (a) Conflict. (b) Punic, Crusades, Napoleonic, Franco-Prussian, Spanish-American, Korean. (c) State of open and armed conflict occurring between two or more factions and usually involving many human casualties.

8. (a) Liberty. (b) Having a voice in the government, choice of personal lifestyle, speaking or writing as one pleases. (c) The ability to exercise one's will as one sees fit and being free of political or personal restraint.

10. (a) Autocrat. (b) Caligula, Ivan the Terrible, Adolf Hitler. (c) A ruler who disregards the needs or wishes of those he rules and who imposes his will and demands out of self-interest.

EXERCISE 1–7

2. If you place an object in water, and it does not sink to the bottom it is buoyant.

4. If you place a person with a disease in close and prolonged contact with a group of people, and many persons in the group catch the same disease shortly thereafter, the disease is contagious.

6. If you divide a number by two and the quotient is a whole number, the original number is an even number.

8. If a piece of blue litmus paper is placed in a substance and the paper turns red, the substance is an acid.

10. Any assemblage of words and/or sentences which serve to explain the meaning of a word, object, or idea.

EXERCISE 1–8

2. Precising
4. Persuasive
6. Stipulative and limited reportive, theoretical
8. Persuasive
10. Limited reportive, theoretical
12. Persuasive
14. Precising
16. Limited reportive, theoretical
18. Precising and persuasive
20. Limited reportive, theoretical
22. Reportive

EXERCISE 1–10

2. Clarity and accuracy (too broad)
4. Accuracy
6. Noncircularity
8. Accuracy (too broad)

10. Noncircularity
12. Accuracy (too broad)
14. Accuracy (too narrow, it excludes the British penny), clarity

EXERCISE 1–11

2. Logically inconsistent
4. Logically consistent
6. Logically consistent
8. Logically consistent
10. Logically inconsistent
12. Logically consistent
14. Logically inconsistent

EXERCISE 1–12

2. An apparent disagreement; these statements represent the personal viewpoints of two individuals and, as such, may both be true.

4. An apparent disagreement/verbal, since different definitions of 'impeach' are being used.

6. Possibly an apparent disagreement, verbal; the father and son are using different meanings for music by the Rolling Stones. However, the father may be saying 'I don't like that music,' and the son may be saying 'I like it,' in which case it is an apparent nonverbal disagreement.

8. A real disagreement
10. A real disagreement
12. A real disagreement
14. A real disagreement, unless A and B are using different definitions of "same person."
16. A real disagreement
18. An apparent verbal disagreement where persons A and B use different definitions of 'a well-educated person'.
20. Most likely an apparent verbal disagreement with persons A and B using different definitions for the term 'conservative'.

EXERCISE 1–13

2. Independent
4. Logically equivalent
6. Independent
8. Logically equivalent
10. Independent
12. Independent
14. Independent

EXERCISE 2–2

2. (a) Y = 2. (b) X + Y = 6 × 4.

4. (a) This cannot be Pinot Chardonnay. (b) It is red wine.

6. (a) He (the defendant) is not guilty. (b) The defendant is insane.

8. (a) He (Mr. Scott) is a lawyer. (b) Mr. Scott is a judge.

10. (a) The Vietnam War was futile. (b) Neither side really won.

12. (a) It (the flu) can't be cured with antibiotics. (b) The flu is caused by a virus.

14. (a) Tom will not be able to go to the New Year's Eve party at the club. (b) He (Tom) is not a member.

16. (a) The housing bill will never come to a vote on the floor of Congress. (b) The opposition has enough votes to kill it (the housing bill) in committee.

18. (a) Composers do not have to be able to hear music to write it. (b) Beethoven was deaf.

20. (a) This flint knife . . . has to be older than 2500 B.C. (b) It was found three layers below the layer we dated at 2500 B.C.

22. (a) Not even an infinitely powerful being could make a square circle. (b) A square circle is a logical contradiction.

24. (a) We can expect the home opener to be cancelled. (b) It is raining and has been for most of the past two days.

26. (a) Plastics are becoming more expensive. (b) Oil is becoming more expensive. Plastics are made from oil.

28. (a) This chair is not made of oak, walnut, or willow. (b) Oak is a coarse-grained wood. Walnut is a dark-colored wood. Willow is not a very strong wood. This chair is strong and made of light-colored, fine-grained wood.

30. (a) It (a body) cannot travel faster than the speed of light. (b) As a body approaches the speed of light, its mass becomes infinite. An infinite source (of energy) would be needed to accelerate it.

EXERCISE 2–3

2. (a) Yes. (c) Conclusion: That could not have been Helen you met last night. Premise: Helen has short brown hair.

4. (a) No. (b) The portion of the sentence preceeding 'because' is probably expressing a command; therefore, it is not a statement.

6. (a) No. (b) This is probably expressing the causal statement "His company's bankruptcy caused him to loose all his money."

8. (a) Yes. (c) Conclusion: Spiders are not insects. Premise: Insects have only six legs.

10. (a) No. (b) There are no premise or conclusion indicators, and only one thought is being expressed.

12. (a) No. (b) There are no premise and conclusion indicators, and only one thought is being expressed.

14. (a) No. (b) This 'if . . . then' sentence is being used to express a conditional statement.

16. (a) Yes. (c) Conclusion: This white crystalline substance is not sugar. Premises: If sugar is placed in water it will dissolve, *and* This white crystalline substance did not dissolve when I placed it in water.

18. (a) Yes. (c) Conclusion: Logic is distinct from psychology. Premise: Logic deals with prescriptive laws whereas psychology deals with descriptive laws.

20. (a) Yes. (c) Conclusion: It could not have rained. Premise: The streets are completely dry.

22. (a) Yes. (c) Conclusion: President Nixon was impeachable. Premise: He (President Nixon) was involved in obstruction of justice.

24. (a) No. (b) 'Because' is used in a causal sense.

26. (a) No. (b) 'Since' is used in a temporal sense.

28. (a) Yes. (b) Conclusion: It (this rock) will scratch glass. Premises: 'If a rock is quartz, it will scratch glass', *and* 'This rock is made of quartz'.

30. (a) Probably. (c) Conclusion: The United States has always been governed by a president, congress, and Supreme Court. Premise: That is the form of government specified in the Constitution. But this might also be interpreted as a causal statement.

32. (a) No. (b) This is exposition which is probably suggesting the cause of Lake Erie's death.

34. (a) No. (b) The passage is exposition.

EXERCISE 2–4

Note that each of these is only one of many possible counterexamples for each argument.

2. Some men are tall. Some men are short. Therefore, some men are tall and short.

4. All violets are plants. All trees are plants. Therefore, all violets are trees.

6. Some men are six feet tall. Gloria Steinem is six feet tall. Gloria Steinem is a man.

8. All governors are politically powerful. Lyndon B. Johnson was politically powerful. Therefore, Lyndon B. Johnson was a governor.

10. If an animal is a mammal, then it bears its young live. A guppy bears its young live. Therefore, a guppy is a mammal.

12. If it is raining, then it is cloudy. It is not raining. Therefore, it is not cloudy.

14. Some Englishmen are dentists. Winston Churchill was an Englishman. Therefore, Winston Churchill was a dentist.

EXERCISE 2–5

Note that for part (b) of the answers in this exercise: Where the argument is deductive, it is so in all cases because the premise(s) provide(s) absolute support for the conclusion. Where the argument is inductive, it is so because the premise(s) do(es) not provide absolute support for the conclusion. For inductive arguments, the answers given in (b) explain why the support is not absolute in each case.

2. (a) Deductive. (b) If the premises are true, the conclusion must be true.

4. (a) Deductive. (b) If the premise is true, then the conclusion must be true.

6. (a) Inductive. (b) The argument can be weakened if it is added that a Sagittarian is one born between November 23 and December 21.

8. (a) Inductive. (b) The argument can be weakened if it is pointed out that John just ate ten pizzas, fifteen pickles, and seven pies.

10. (a) Deductive

12. (a) Inductive. (b) The conclusion can be false even though the premise is true.

14. (a) Inductive. (b) It is possible for the premises to be true and the conclusion false. For example, the person to whom the letter was sent may be away on vacation or may not have bothered to write.

16. (a) Inductive. (b) A number of other things might have happened to Spot—he might have lost his way; he might have been kidnapped; he might have been found by someone, and so forth. It is possible for the premises to be true and the conclusion false.

18. (a) Inductive. (b) It is possible for the conclusion to be false, even though the premises are true. The premise "Most supporters of Barry Goldwater are conservatives" leaves open the possibility that some supporters may not be conservatives.

20. (a) Deductive. (b) If the premises are true, the conclusion must be true.

22. (a) Inductive. (b) The argument is weakened if the electric company's estimates of power needs in the past have all been very inaccurate. Also, if the conclusion is interpreted as a command, then this collection of sentences does not express an argument.

24. (a) Inductive. (b) It is possible for the conclusion to be false, even if the premise is true.

EXERCISE 2–6

2. (a) No: Both premises are false. (b) No

4. (a) No: The first premise is false. (b) No

6. (a) No (b) No

8. (a) No (b) No

10. (a) Yes (b) Yes

12. (a) No (b) No

14. (a) No: The second premise is false. (b) No

16. (a) No: The second premise may or may not be true. (b) No

18. (a) Yes (b) Yes

EXERCISE 2–7

Note that there may be other possibilities for the supplied premise in each answer.

2. Premise: All politicians are corrupt. Conclusion: There is no reason to vote. Supplied premise: If all politicians are corrupt, then there is no reason to vote.

4. Premise: Birds have feathers. Conclusion: Bats are not birds. Supplied premise: No bats have feathers.

6. Premise: Gregory is not a Turkish Cypriot. Conclusion: He (Gregory) is a Greek Cypriot. Supplied premise: All Cypriots are either Turkish or Greek.

8. Premise: She has no experience. Conclusion: Susan will not get the job. Supplied premise: All persons with no experience are persons who will not get the job.

10. Premise: All trees are plants, and All oaks are trees. Conclusion: All oaks are living things. Supplied premise: All plants are living things.

12. Premise: He just received a pay raise. Conclusion: He must be competent at his job. Supplied premise: If a person receives a pay raise, he must be competent at his job.

14. Premise: He told lies about me. Conclusion: Peter is not my friend. Supplied premise: All persons who tell lies about me are not my friend.

16. Premise: The litmus paper we placed in it did not turn red. Conclusion: This liquid is not acid. Supplied premise: If litmus paper is placed in acid, it will turn red.

18. Premise: If the demand for sugar exceeds the supply, the price of sugar will go up. Conclusion: The price of sugar has gone up. Supplied premise: The demand for sugar exceeds the supply.

EXERCISE 2–8

Note that there are many other possible answers for (b) and (c) of each answer.

2. (a) Premises: The guests our family has to dinner always like my mother's pot roasts, and The Karlans are coming to dinner, and My mother is serving pot roast. Conclusion: The Karlans will like her pot roast. (b) My mother says she has purchased an especially good cut of meat this time. (c) The Karlans are vegetarians.

4. (a) Premise: All swans observed to date have been white. Conclusion: The chances are that any swans observed in the future will be white. (b) Ten thousand swans have been observed to date. (c) Ten swans have been observed to date.

6. (a) Premise: Sluggo Jones has hit more home runs this season than any other player on the team. Conclusion: He (Sluggo Jones) is likely to hit a home run today. (b) Sluggo Jones has already hit four home runs this season off the opposing team's starting pitcher. (c) Sluggo Jones has a sprained wrist.

8. (a) Premise: The polls say 52 percent of the voters favor the mayor for reelection. Conclusion: No runoff will be necessary. (b) The polls have never been wrong in the past. (c) The polls have never been correct in the past.

10. (a) Premises: The life expectancy of someone your age is 70 years, and Your health has been better than average. Conclusion: You will live to be at least 70 years of age. (b) You eat good food, exercise properly, and get frequent medical checkups. (c) You just came in contact with someone who has an incurable, highly contagious, and fatal disease.

12. (a) Premises: It's not supposed to rain. Enough people to make two teams have promised to come. We reminded them to bring their gloves and bats and balls. Conclusion: We should have a good baseball game at the picnic. (b) Everyone who promised to come to the picnic loves to play baseball. (c) Most people who promised to come to the picnic promised the same thing last year and did not show up.

14. (a) Premises: There has been an outbreak of the Asian flu in the United States this month, and I have had a flu vaccination, and You have not had a flu vaccination. Conclusion: You are more likely to catch the flu than I am. (b) Your father and your sister already have the flu. (c) Studies have shown that the flu vaccination is not very effective in preventing a person from catching the flu.

EXERCISE 3–1
2. Hasty generalization
4. Argument from ignorance
6. Composition
8. False dilemma
10. Argument from ignorance
12. Composition

EXERCISE 3–2
(Other fallacies, particularly the irrelevant conclusion, may be found in the same exercises.)
2. Hasty generalization
4. Straw person
6. Argument from ignorance
8. Ad populum

10. Composition
12. Equivocation (on 'life' of mosquitoes and of humans)
14. Equivocation (on 'meteoric') or appeal to authority
16. Appeal to force
18. Equivocation (on 'straight line')
20. Division
22. Amphiboly
24. Begging the question
26. Ad baculum (from force)
28. False cause
30. Equivocation (on 'well done')
32. Ad hominem (abusive)
34. Appeal to authority
36. Ad hominem (circumstantial)
38. Ad populum
40. Ad baculum
42. Amphiboly
44. Begging the question
46. False dilemma
48. Ad hominem (tu quoque)
50. Ad hominem (circumstantial)
52. Amphiboly ('avoid _____' in the first instance means 'avoid eating _____')
54. Division
56. Ad baculum
58. Ad hominem combined with argument from ignorance
60. Division
62. Hasty generalization
64. Ad hominem (circumstantial)
66. False cause
68. Straw person
70. Begging the question

EXERCISE 4–1
2. I
4. E
6. A
8. E
10. I
12. A
14. O

EXERCISE 4–2
2. (a) No dogs that are Lassie are cocker spaniels. (b) E (c) No L are C. (d) No S are P.
4. (a) Some records are things costing less than five dollars. (b) I (c) Some R are F. (d) Some S are P.
6. (a) Some hives are not things having bees. (b) O (c) Some H are not B. (d) Some S are not P. or (a) Some hives are things that don't have bees. (b) I (c) Some H are B. (d) Some S are P.

8. (a) Some P̲anama hats are things made in E̲cquador. (b) **I** (c) Some P are E. (d) Some S̲ are P̲.

10. (a) All m̲en are t̲ool-making animals. (b) **A** (c) All M are T. (d) All S̲ are P̲.

12. (a) No m̲ussels are m̲ammals. (b) **E** (c) No Mu are Ma. (d) No S̲ are P̲.

14. (a) All members of the class of which B. F. S̲kinner is the only member are b̲ehavioral scientists. (b) **A** (c) All S are B. (d) All S̲ are P̲.

16. (a) No w̲ars are things that are h̲ealthy for children and other living things. (b) **E** (c) No W are H. (d) No S̲ are P̲.

18. (a) All nona̲utomotive unions are unions that have s̲ettled their strikes, *and* No a̲utomotive unions are unions that have s̲ettled their strikes. (b) **A, E** (c) All non-A are S, *and* No A are S. (d) All non-S̲ are P̲, *and* No S̲ are P̲.

20. (a) All peacemakers are b̲lessed people. (b) **A** (c) All P are B. (d) All S̲ are P̲.

22. (a) All r̲oads to success are roads that involve h̲ard work. (b) **A** (c) All R are H. (d) All S̲ are P̲.

24. This exceptive sentence expresses an A statement and an E statement. A statement: (a) All things that are d̲eath and taxes are c̲ertain things. (c) All D are C. (d) All S̲ are P̲. **E** statement: (a) No things that are not d̲eath and taxes are c̲ertain things. (c) No non-D are C. (d) No non-S̲ are P̲.

EXERCISE 4–3

2. (a) Some d̲octors are s̲urgeons. (b) Some D are S. (c) Some S̲ are P̲.

4. (a) No n̲ewspapers are things that are r̲ed. (b) No N are R. (c) No S̲ are P̲.

6. (a) All t̲riangles are polygons that have three s̲ides. (b) All T are S. (c) All S̲ are P̲.

8. (a) No g̲uitars are things which have more than t̲welve strings. (b) No G are T. (c) No S̲ are P̲.

10. (a) Some F̲renchmen are persons who are P̲arisiens. (b) Some F are P. (c) Some S̲ are P̲.

12. (a) All s̲eals are animals having a smooth c̲oat of fur. (b) All S are C. (c) All S̲ are P̲.

14. (a) Some d̲olphins are not animals that are c̲etaceans. (b) Some D are not C. (c) Some S̲ are not P̲.

EXERCISE 4–4

2. (a) No B̲eatles are b̲ugs. (b) No B are Bu. (c) No S̲ are P̲.
(d)

4. (a) All o̲aks are h̲ardwoods. (b) All O are H. (c) All S̲ are P̲.

(d)

6. (a) Some n̲ebulae are not galaxies. (b) Some N are not G. (c) Some S̲ are not P̲.

(d)

8. (a) All h̲arpies are m̲ythological creatures. (b) All H are M. (c) All S̲ are P̲.

(d)

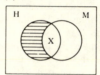

10. (a) Some people in the world are not people who have enough to e̲at. (b) Some P are not E. (c) Some S̲ are not P̲.

(d)

12. (a) No b̲ehaviorists are persons who t̲olerate idle speculation. (b) No B are T. (c) No S̲ are P̲.

(d)

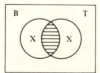

14. (a) Some persons at the M̲ardi Gras are persons who were d̲runk, *and* Some persons at the M̲ardi Gras are not persons who were d̲runk. (b) Some M are D, *and*

Some M are not D. (c) Some S̲ are P̲, and Some S̲ are not P̲.

(d)   **(d)**

16. (a) All those i̲nvited to the picnic are f̲reshmen. (b) All I are F. (c) All S̲ are P̲.

(d)

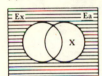

18. (a) All nonex̲ceptive statements are e̲asy to translate into standard form sentences, *and* No exc̲eptive statements are e̲asy statements to translate into standard form sentences. (b) All nonEx are Ea, *and* No Ex are Ea. (c) All non-S̲ are P̲ and No S̲ are P̲.

(d)

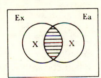

20. (a) Some B̲eetles are not automobiles that have b̲ugs. (b) Some B are not Bu. (c) Some S̲ are not P̲.

(d)

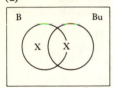

EXERCISE 4–5
Sentences from Exercise 4–1.

2. (a) Some d̲octors are s̲urgeons. (b) Some D are S. (c) Some S̲ are P̲.

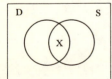

I: Some D are S.

4. (a) No n̲ewspapers are r̲ed things. (b) No N are R. (c) No S̲ are P̲.

E: No N are R.

6. (a) All t̲riangles are polygons having three s̲ides. (b) All T are S. (c) All S̲ are P̲.

A: All T are S.

8. (a) No guitar is an instrument having more than t̲welve strings. (b) No G are T. (c) No S̲ are P̲.

E: No G is T.

10. (a) Some F̲renchmen are P̲arsiens. (b) Some F are P. (c) Some S̲ are P̲.

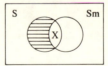

I: Some F are P.

12. (a) All s̲eals are animals having a s̲mooth coat of fur. (b) All S are Sm. (c) All S̲ are P̲.

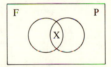

H: All S are Sm.

14. (a) Some d̲olphins are not animals which are c̲etaceans. (b) Some D are not C. (c) Some S̲ are not P̲. (a) Some d̲olphins are a̲nimals which are cetaceans. (b) Some D are A. (c) Some S̲ are P̲.

C: Some D are not C.   I: Some D are C.

EXERCISE 4–5

Sentences from Exercise 4–2.

2.

E: No L are C.

4.
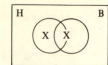
I: Some R are F.

6.
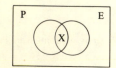
Some H are not B.

8.

Some P are E.

10.

All: M are T.

12.

E: No Mu are Ma.

14.

A: All S are B.

16.
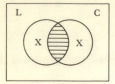
E: No W are H.

18.
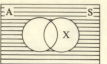
All nonA are S.   No A are S.

20.

A: All P are B.

22.
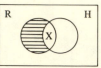
A: All R are H.

24.
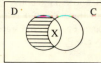
All D are C.   E: No nonD are C.

EXERCISE 4–6

2. (a) Subcontrariety (b) Undetermined (c) True
4. (a) Contradiction (b) False (c) True
6. (a) Contradiction (b) False (c) True
8. (a) Superimplication (b) Undetermined (c) False
10. (a) Subimplication (b) True (c) Undetermined
12. (a) Subcontrariety (b) Undetermined (c) True
14. (a) Subimplication (b) True (c) Undetermined

EXERCISE 4–7

2. (a) Relationship to original statement:
    a. Contradictory
    b. Subimplicant
    c. Contrary
  (b) If original statement is true:
    a. False
    b. True
    c. False
  (c) If original statement is false:
    a. True
    b. Undetermined
    c. Undetermined
4. a. Relationship to original statement:
    a. Contradictory
    b. Superimplicant
    c. Subcontrary

(b) If original statement is true:
    a. False
    b. Undetermined
    c. Undetermined

(c) If original statement is false:
    a. True
    b. False
    c. True

6. (a) Relationship to original statement:
    a. Contradictory
    b. Subimplicant
    c. Contrary

(b) If original statement is true:
    a. False
    b. True
    c. False

(c) If original statement is false:
    a. True
    b. Undetermined
    c. Undetermined

EXERCISE 4–8

2. (a) Consistent (b) Dependent
4. (a) Inconsistent (b) Dependent
6. (a) Consistent (b) Independent
8. (a) Consistent (b) Dependent
10. (a) Inconsistent (b) Dependent

EXERCISE 4–9

2. (a) Some books are not nondictionaries. (b) Equivalent.

    I: Some B are D.   O: Some B are not nonD.

4. (a) Some of Shakespeare's works are nonplays. (b) Equivalent.

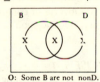

    O: Some S are not P.   I: Some S are nonP.

6. (a) No senators are nonpoliticians. (b) Equivalent.

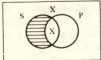

    All S are P.   No S are nonP.

8. (a) Some vampire bats are not nondangerous animals.
(b) Equivalent.

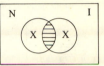

    Some V are D.   Some V are not nonD.

10. (a) All numbers are nonintegers. (b) Equivalent.

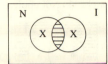

    No N are I.   All N are nonI.

EXERCISE 4–10

2. (a) No auks are gnus. (b) Equivalent.

    E: No G are A.   E: No A are G.

4. (a) Some ballads are not songs. (b) Not equivalent.

    O: Some S are not B.   O: Some B are not S.

6. (a) All vipers are asps. (b) Not equivalent.

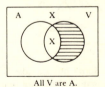

    All A are V.   All V are A.

8. (a) Some marble things are tables. (b) Equivalent.

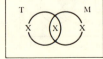
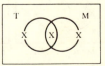

    Some T are M.   Some M are T.

10. (a) No beneficial things are pollutants. (b) Equivalent.

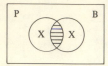

EXERCISE 4–11

2. (a) No nonpens are nonpencils. (b) Not equivalent.

E: No Pc are P.   E: No nonP are nonPc.

4. (a) Some nonFords are not noncars. (b) Equivalent.

O: Some C are not F.   O: Some nonF are not nonC.

6. (a) All nongraduates of Harvard are nonmembers. (b) Equivalent.

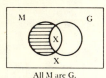

All M are G.   All nonG are nonM.

8. (a) Some nonvaluable objects are nonbicycles. (b) Not Equivalent.

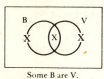

Some B are V.   Some nonV are nonB.

10. (a) Some non-(good obligations) are non-(unpleasant obligations). (b) Not equivalent.

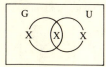

Some U are G.   Some nonG are nonU.

EXERCISE 4–12

2. (a) Contrariety (b) False
4. (a) Subimplication (b) True
6. (a) Converse of contrary (b) False
8. (a) Converse of subimplicant (b) True
10. (a) Contrapositive of subimplicant (b) Undetermined
12. (a) Contrapositive of contrary (b) Undetermined

EXERCISE 4–12

2. (a) Contrariety (b) False
4. (a) Subimplication (b) True
6. (a) Converse of contrary (b) Undetermined
8. (a) Converse of subimplicant (b) Undetermined
10. (a) Obverse—subimplication—converse (b) True
12. (a) Contraposition (b) Undetermined

EXERCISE 4–13

2. (a) Subcontrariety (b) Undetermined
4. (a) Superimplication (b) Undetermined
6. (a) Contradiction of conversion (b) False
8. (a) Contraposition of superimplicant (b) Undetermined
10. (a) Subcontrary of converse (b) Undetermined
12. (a) Contrary of superimplicant of converse. (b) Undetermined

EXERCISE 4–14

2. (a) Subcontrary (b) False
4. (a) Superimplication (b) Undetermined
6. (a) Converse of obverse (b) True
8. (a) Obverse of contradiction (b) False
10. (a) Contraposition of contradiction (b) False

EXERCISE 5–1

2. (a) Categorical syllogism. (b) Standard form.
4. (a) Categorical syllogism. (b) Standard form.
6. (a) Categorical syllogism. (b) Not in standard form. (c) All documentaries are educational things. Some films are documentaries. Therefore, some films are educational things.
8. (a) Not a categorical syllogism. The first premise cannot be put into standard form.
10. (a) Categorical syllogism. (b) Not in standard form. (c) No squares are conic sections. All hyperbolas are conic sections. Therefore, no hyperbolas are squares.
12. (a) Categorical syllogism. (b) Not in standard form. (c) No substances dangerous to human health are substances that should be allowed. Some food additives are substances dangerous to human health. Therefore,

some food additives are not substances that should be allowed.

14. (a) Categorical syllogism. (b) Not in standard form. (c) All bees are things that can sting. Some insects are bees. Therefore, some insects are things that can sting.

16. (a) Categorical syllogism. (b) Not in standard form. (c) No toadstools are edible things. Some edible things are mushrooms. Therefore, some mushrooms are not toadstools.

18. (a) Categorical syllogism. (b) Not in standard form. (c) Some mayors are not Democrats. All mayors are respectable citizens. Therefore, some respectable citizens are not Democrats.

20. (a) Not a categorical syllogism. Immediate inference by conversion.

EXERCISE 5–2

2. (a) All V are L.
All S are V.
∴All S are L.

(b) All M are P.
All S are M.
∴All S are P.

4. (a) No S are M.
All H are M.
∴No H are S.

(b) No P are M.
All S are M.
∴No S are P.

6. (a) All D are E.
Some F are D.
∴Some F are E.

(b) All M are P.
Some S are M.
∴Some S are P.

10. (a) No S are C.
All H are C.
∴No H are S.

(b) No P are M.
All S are M.
∴No S are P.

12. (a) No D are Al.
Some Ad are D.
∴Some Ad are not Al.

(b) No M are P.
Some S are M.
∴Some S are not P.

14. (a) All B are S.
Some I are B.
∴Some I are S.

(b) All M are P.
Some S are M.
∴Some S are P.

16. (a) No T are E.
Some E are M.
∴Some M are not T.

(b) No P are M.
Some M are S.
∴Some S are not P.

18. (a) All M are R.
Some M are not D.
∴Some R are not D.

(b) All M are P.
Some M are not S.
∴Some S are not P.

EXERCISE 5–3

2. AAA-1
4. EAE-2
6. AII-1
10. EAE-2
12. EIO-1

14. AII-1
16. EIO-4
18. AOO-3

EXERCISE 5–4

Note that each answer is only one of many possible answers.

2. Some animals are dogs.
No dogs are cats.
Therefore, some cats are not animals.

4. Some reptiles are not extinct species.
All dinosaurs are reptiles.
Therefore, some dinosaurs are not extinct species.

6. All lilacs are plants.
All roses are plants.
Therefore, all roses are lilacs.

8. All Chinese are Orientals.
Some Indians are Orientals.
Therefore, some Indians are Chinese.

10. All men are featherless animals.
All men are bipeds.
Therefore, all bipeds are featherless animals.

12. Some animals are dangerous things.
No animals are hydrogen bombs.
Therefore, some hydrogen bombs are not dangerous things.

14. All tennis players are human beings.
Some women are not tennis players.
Therefore, some women are not human beings.

EXERCISE 5–5

2. Valid
L = law-abiding citizens.
H = hippies
P = pot smokers

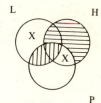

4. Invalid
Dr = drugs
Da = dangerous things
H = hallucinogens

6. Invalid

D = dictators
R = reactionaries
P = powerful men

8. Invalid

Standard form:

Some actors are egoists.
Some actors are rich persons.
Therefore, some rich persons are egoists.

10. Invalid

Standard form:

All monks are ascetics.
Some Buddhists are not monks.
Therefore, some Buddhists are not ascetics.

12. Invalid

Standard form:

All roses are flowers.
All zinnias are flowers.
Therefore, all zinnias are roses.

14. Valid

Standard form:

No edible things are toadstools.
Some edible things are mushrooms.
Therefore, some mushrooms are not toadstools.

EXERCISE 5–6

2. Valid

No P are M.
All S are M.
∴No S are P.

4. ·Valid

No M are P.
Some M are S.
∴Some S are not P.

6. Invalid

All M are P.
No S are M.
∴No S are P.

8.   Valid
Some M̲ are P̲.
All M̲ are S̲.
∴Some S̲ are P̲.

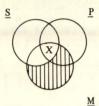

10.   Invalid
All P̲ are M̲.
Some M̲ are not S̲.
∴Some S̲ are not P̲.

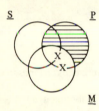

12.   Invalid
Some M̲ are P̲.
Some S̲ are M̲.
∴Some S̲ are P̲.

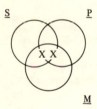

14.   Valid
No P̲ are M̲.
Some M̲ are S̲.
∴Some S̲ are not P̲.

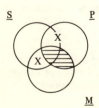

EXERCISE 5–7

2.   (b) No rules violated (c) Valid
4.   (b) Rule two: Illicit minor (c) Invalid
6.   (b) Rule two: Illicit major (c) Invalid
8.   (b) No rules violated (c) Valid
10.   (b) Rule three: Fallacy of two negative premises (c) Invalid
12.   (a) No primates are unicellular organisms.
          All amoebae are unicellular organisms.
          Some amoebae are not primates
       (b) No rules violated (c) Valid
14.   (a) All human beings are persons who make mistakes.
          Jane is a human being.
          Therefore, Jane is a person who makes mistakes.
       (b) No rules violated (c) Valid

EXERCISE 5–8

2.   [No elected officials are appointed officials.]
       Some judges are appointed officials.
       Therefore, some judges are not elected officials.
       OR
       [No appointed officials are elected officials.]
       Some judges are appointed officials.
       Therefore, some judges are not elected officials.
4.   No soaps are detergents.
       All detergents are cleansing agents.
       [Therefore, some cleansing agents are not soaps.]
6.   [All liquors are bourbons.]
       All whiskeys are liquors.
       Therefore, some whiskeys are bourbons.
8.   All people who jog five miles every day are people who are in good physical condition.
       Some people are people who jog five miles every day.
       [Therefore, some people are people who are in good physical condition.]
10.   [All substances that may cause cancer are substances which should be banned from use as food additives.]
       All cyclamates are substances which may cause cancer.
       Therefore, all cyclamates are substances which should be banned from use as food additives.
12.   [All rare things are valuable things.]
       All diamonds are rare things.
       Therefore, all diamonds are valuable things.
14.   [All persons who can practice law are persons who have passed the bar examination.]
       No members of the class of which Jack is the only member are persons who passed the bar examination.
       No members of the class of which Jack is the only member are persons who can practice law.
16.   [All persons who cook well are connoisseurs of good food.]

All members of the class of which Ed is the only member are persons who cook well.

Therefore, all members of the class of which Ed is the only member are connoisseurs of good food.

18. [All things which increase in value are good investments.]
Some paintings are things which increase in value.
Therefore, some paintings are good investments.

20. [All basketball players are persons who must be over six feet tall.]
All members of the class of which Willis Reed is the only member are basketball players.
Therefore, all members of the class of which Willis Reed is the only member are persons who must be over six feet tall.

22. [All car owners are persons who have drivers' licenses.]
No members of the class of which John is the only member are persons who have drivers' licenses.
Therefore, no members of the class of which John is the only member are car owners.

24. [All items that require much labor are expensive items.]
Some handmade items are items that require much labor.
Therefore, some handmade items are expensive items.

EXERCISE 5–9

Note that the reconstruction of complex and/or invalid sorites can often be facilitated by reconstructing syllogisms for individual stages of the argument starting from the conclusion and working backwards

2. Not valid: First stage violates rule two: Illicit major and rule three: Negative premises
(a) Some officers are not creatures that waltz.
No ducks are creatures that waltz.

(b) [Therefore, no ducks are officers.]
All creatures that are my poultry are ducks.

Therefore, no creatures that are my poultry are officers.

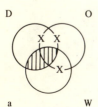

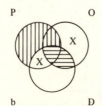

4. Valid
(a) All really well-informed people are people who are good company.
No people who think too much of themselves are people who are good company.

(b) [Therefore, no people who think too much of themselves are really well-informed people.]
All showy talkers are people who think too much of themselves.

Therefore, no showy talkers are really well-informed people.

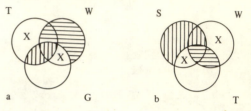

EXERCISE 6–1

2. (a) Yes (b) 'Oaks are evergreens'; 'Pines are hardwoods'. (c) 'And' (d) Yes

4. (a) Yes (b) 'ice melts at 32° Fahrenheit' (c) 'it is not the case that' (d) Yes

6. (a) Yes (b) 'the sky is blue'; 'the grass is green' (c) 'and' (d) Yes

8. (a) Yes (b) 'Thomas Jefferson was the second president of the United States' (c) 'it is not true that' (d) Yes

10. (a) No

12. (a) No

14. (a) Yes (b) 'Ronald Reagan is a Republican'; 'Edward Kennedy is a Conservative' (c) 'Or' (d) Yes

16. (a) No

18. (a) Yes (b) 'Maureen is not coming to dinner'; 'She has to stay home and study'. (c) Because (d) No

EXERCISE 6–2

2. (a) 'p and q' contains the propositional variables p and q. (b) 'A and B' contains the propositional constants A and B.

4. (a) 'A and B' normally has a determinate truth value. (b) 'p and q' normally does not have a truth value.

EXERCISE 6–3

The particular letters used as constants here and in Exercise 6–4 may differ from those chosen by the student, but the propositions symbolized remain the same.

2. (a) No significant meaning lost. (b) M · G; M = The gunmen covered their faces with masks; G = The gunmen wore gloves.

4. (a) No significant meaning lost. (b) A · D; A = The Oakland Athletics is a baseball team; D = The Los Angeles Dodgers is a baseball team.

6. (a) Possible loss of temporal sequence, but this is not clear without more contextual information. (b) S · M; S = The band played Stardust; M = The band played Moon River.

8. (a) Some meaning loss: original sentence implies connection—perhaps causal—between cloudy weather and cool weather. (b) Cl; Co; Cl = 'the weather will be cloudy tomorrow'; Co = 'the weather will be cool tomorrow'.

10. (a) No significant meaning loss. (b) L · B; L = 'Jim mailed a letter'; B = 'Jim bought some books'.

12. (a) Dot cannot properly be used; it does not convey implication that they are quarreling with each other.

14. (a) Loss of suggestion that it is an accomplishment to score 20 points in only one half of a game. (b) S · P; S = Kareem Abdul-Jabbar scored 20 points; P = Kareem Abdul-Jabbar played only half the game.

EXERCISE 6–4

2. (a, b) As in 7 (c) Loss of meaning: 'yet' implies apparent surprise that both are not the same color.

4. (a) Y ⊃ E (b) Y = 'I give you one'; E = 'everybody will want one' (c) Loss of suggestion of causal connection and temporal sequence.

6. (a) S ∨ W (b) S = 'It is snowing in Detroit'; W = 'The weather report is inaccurate'. (c) None

8. (a) A ∨ F (b) A = 'Thoreau was an American'; F = 'Thoreau was a Frenchman' (c) No significant meaning loss.

10. (a) A · S (b) A = 'Athens was a city-state in ancient Greece'; S = 'Sparta was a city-state in ancient Greece'. (c) None

12. (a) E ⊃ D (b) E = 'A total eclipse of the sun occurs'; D = 'The sky darkens'. (c) Causal implications of the original are lost.

14. D · ~S (b) D = 'His battery went dead'; S = 'His car would start'. (c) Sense of temporal sequence is lost.

16. (a) S ⊃ D (b) S = 'this lump of sugar is placed in water'; D = 'it will dissolve'. (c) Loss of a suggestion of causal connection and also of temporal sequence.

18. (a) W ∨ T (b) W = 'you left the window open'; T = 'the thermostat is turned down too low'. (c) Loss of the suggestion that the room is cold.

20. (a) ~R (b) R = 'All triangles are right triangles'. (c) None

22. (a) T ≡ P (b) T = 'I will take the job'; P = 'It (the job) pays well'. (c) None

24. (a) B ∨ S (b) B = 'Carl drinks bourbon'; S = 'Carl drinks scotch'. (c) None

26. (a) ~D (b) D = 'Plato was Aristotle's disciple' (c) No significant meaning loss

28. (a) S ⊃ L (b) S = 'the stock market fails'; L = 'many people will lose fortunes'. (c) Loss of suggestion of causal connection

30. (a) T ∨ B (b) T = 'Candles can be made of tallow'; B = 'Candles can be made of beeswax'. (c) None

32. (a) S ⊃ P (b) S = 'you study hard'; P = 'you will pass this exam'. (c) Loss of suggestion of causal connection

34. (a) P ≡ S (b) as in 16 (c) Loss of suggestion of causal connection.

EXERCISE 6–5

2. S · (R ∨ D)
4. (S ∨ R) · D
6. (S · R) · D
8. ~W ⊃ H
10. W ⊃ ~H
12. ~ (C · M)
14. ~C · M
16. ~(~C · ~M)
18. ~(~C · M)
20. S ⊃ (H · ~C)
22. S ⊃ (H ∨ C)
24. (S ∨ H) ⊃ ~C
26. B · (D ⊃ P)
28. (B ∨ D) ⊃ P
30. K · (M ∨ H)
32. K · ~(M ∨ H)
34. ~ (K · (M ∨ H))
36. K ∨ ~(M · H)
38. K ∨ ~(M · ~H)
40. ~K · ~(~M ∨ ~H)

EXERCISE 6–6

	p	q		~p · q
2.				
	T	T	F	F
	F	T	T	T
	T	F	F	F
	F	F	T	F
			(1)	(2)

4.

p	q	~p ⊃ q	
T	T	F	T
F	T	T	T
T	F	F	T
F	F	T	F
		(1)	(2)

14.

p	q	(p · q) ⊃ p	
T	T	T	T
F	T	F	T
T	F	F	T
F	F	F	T
		(1)	(2)

6.

p	q	~(p · q)	
T	T	F	T
F	T	T	F
T	F	T	F
F	F	T	F
		(2)	(1)

16.

p	q	r	(p · q) ⊃ r	
T	T	T	T	T
F	T	T	F	T
T	F	T	F	T
F	F	T	F	T
T	T	F	T	F
F	T	F	F	T
T	F	F	F	T
F	F	F	F	T
			(1)	(2)

8.

p	q	~ (p · ~ q)		
T	T	T	F	F
F	T	T	F	F
T	F	F	T	T
F	F	T	F	T
		(3)	(2)	(1)

18.

p	q	r	(p ⊃ q) ⊃ r	
T	T	T	T	T
F	T	T	T	T
T	F	T	F	T
F	F	T	T	T
T	T	F	T	F
F	T	F	T	F
T	F	F	F	T
F	F	F	T	F
			(1)	(2)

10.

p	q	~(p ∨ q)	
T	T	F	T
F	T	F	T
T	F	F	T
F	F	T	F
		(2)	(1)

20.

p	q	r	~ (p · ~ q) ⊃ ~ r				
T	T	T	T	F	F	F	F
F	T	T	T	F	F	F	F
T	F	T	F	T	T	T	F
F	F	T	T	F	T	F	F
T	T	F	T	F	F	T	T
F	T	F	T	F	F	T	T
T	F	F	F	T	T	T	T
F	F	F	T	F	T	T	T
			(3)	(2)	(1)	(4)	(1)

12.

p	q	~ (~ p ∨ ~ q)			
T	T	T	F	F	F
F	T	F	T	T	F
T	F	F	F	T	T
F	F	F	T	T	T
		(3)	(1)	(2)	(1)

22.

p	q	r	((p ∨ ~q) · p) ⊃ r			
T	T	T	T	F	T	T
F	T	T	F	F	F	T
T	F	T	T	T	T	T
F	F	T	T	T	F	T
T	T	F	T	F	T	F
F	T	F	F	F	F	T
T	F	F	T	T	T	F
F	F	F	T	T	F	T
			(2)	(1)	(3)	(4)

24.

p	q	r	~(~(p ∨ ~q) · p) ⊃ r					
T	T	T	T	F	T	F	F	T
F	T	T	T	T	F	F	F	T
T	F	T	T	F	T	T	F	T
F	F	T	T	F	T	T	F	T
T	T	F	T	F	T	F	F	F
F	T	F	T	T	F	F	F	F
T	F	F	T	F	T	T	F	F
F	F	F	T	F	T	T	F	F
			(5)	(3)	(2)	(1)	(4)	(6)

26.

p	q	(p ⊃ q) ≡ (~q ⊃ ~p)				
T	T	T	T	F	T	F
F	T	T	T	F	T	T
T	F	F	T	T	F	F
F	F	T	T	T	T	T
		(2)	(3)	(1)	(2)	(1)

28.

p	q	~(p · q) ≡ (~p · q)				
T	T	F	T	T	F	F
F	T	T	F	T	T	T
T	F	T	F	F	F	F
F	F	T	F	F	T	F
		(3)	(2)	(4)	(1)	(2)

30.

p	q	r	((~p · q) ⊃ ~r) ≡ (~p ⊃ (q ⊃ ~r))
T	T	T	F F T F T F T F F
F	T	T	T T F F T T F F F
T	F	T	F F T F T F T T F
F	F	T	T F T F T T T T F
T	T	F	F F T T T F T T T
F	T	F	T T T T T T T T T
T	F	F	F F T T T F T T T
F	F	F	T F T T T T T T T
			(1) (2) (3)(1) (4) (1) (3) (2)(1)

EXERCISE 6–7

2. (a) Equivalent

(b)

p	q	p	·	~q	~	(~p ∨ q)	
T	T	F	F		F	F	T
F	T	F	F		F	T	T
T	F	T	T		F	T	F
F	F	F	T		F	T	T
			(2)	(1)	(3)	(1)	(2)

8. Not equivalent

p	q	~	(p ≡ q)	~p	≡	~q
T	T	F	T	F	T	F
F	T	T	F	T	F	F
T	F	T	F	T	F	T
F	F	F	T	T	T	T
		(2)	(1)	(1)	(2)	(1)

4. (a) Not equivalent

(b)

p	q	~	(p · q)	~p	·	~q
T	T	F	T	F	F	F
F	T	T	F	T	F	F
T	F	T	F	F	F	T
F	F	T	F	T	T	T
		(2)	(1)	(1)	(2)	(1)

10. Not equivalent

p	q	~	(p ⊃ q)	~p	⊃	~q
T	T	F	T	F	T	F
F	T	F	T	T	F	F
T	F	T	F	F	T	T
F	F	F	T	T	T	T
		(2)	(1)	(1)	(2)	(1)

6. Equivalent

p	q	p	≡	q	~p	≡	~q
T	T		T		F	T	F
F	T		F		T	F	F
T	F		F		F	F	T
F	F		T		T	T	T
			(1)		(1)	(2)	(1)

12. (a) Not equivalent

(b)

p	q	~	(p ⊃ q)	p	∨	~q
T	T	F	T		T	F
F	T	F	T		F	F
T	F	T	F		T	T
F	F	F	T		T	T
		(3)	(2)		(2)	(1)

14. (a) Equivalent

(b)

p	q	~ (p · ~q)	·	~ (q · ~p)	p ≡ q
T	T	T F F	T	T F F	T
F	T	T F F	F	F T T	F
T	F	F T T	F	T F F	F
F	F	T F T	T	T F T	T
		(3) (2)(1)	(4)	(3) (2)(1)	

EXERCISE 6–8

2. (a) Tautology

(b)

p	p ⊃ p
T	T
F	T

4. (a) Tautology

(b)

p	q	(p · q) ⊃ p
T	T	T T
F	T	F T
T	F	F T
F	F	F T
		(1) (2)

6. (a) Contingent

(b)

p	q	(p ∨ ~p) ⊃ (p ∨ q)
T	T	T F T T
F	T	T T T T
T	F	T F T T
F	F	T T F F
		(2)(1) (3) (2)

8. (a) Contingent

(b)

p	q	((p ⊃ q) · ~q) ∨ p
T	T	T F F T
F	T	T F F F
T	F	F F T T
F	F	T T T T
		(2) (3)(1) (4)

10. (a) Contingent

(b)

p	q	(p ⊃ q) ≡ (~p · q)
T	T	T F F F
F	T	T T T T
T	F	F T T F
F	F	T F T F
		(2) (3)(1)(2)

12. (a) Contingent

(b)

p	q	((p ⊃ q) · p) · q
T	T	T T T
F	T	T F F
T	F	F F F
F	F	T F F
		(1) (2) (3)

14. (a) Tautology

(b)

p	q	((p ⊃ q) · p) ⊃ q
T	T	T T T
F	T	T F T
T	F	F F T
F	F	T F T
		(1) (2) (3)

16. (a) Contradiction

(b)

p	(p ∨ ~p) ⊃ (p · ~p)
T	T F F F F
F	T T F F T
	(2)(1) (3) (2)(1)

18. (a) Tautology

(b)

p	q	(~p ⊃ q) ≡ (p ∨ q)
T	T	F T T T
F	T	T T T T
T	F	F T T T
F	F	T F T F
		(1) (2) (3) (2)

EXERCISE 7–1

Note that the letters used in the following abbreviations are arbitrary and may not match those letters you selected. In all cases, however, make certain that you have provided a dictionary indicating which letter stands for which proposition.

2. R = It <u>r</u>ains. W = The ground is getting <u>w</u>et.

  (a)   R ⊃ W   (b)   p ⊃ q

         ~W   ~q

      ∴~R   ∴~p

4. P = The television set is <u>p</u>lugged in. W = The television set is <u>w</u>orking.

  (a)   ~P ∨ ~W   (b)   ~p ∨ ~q

         P   p

      ∴~W   ∴~q

6. D = All <u>d</u>ogs are carnivores. F = <u>F</u>ido is a carnivore.

  (a)   D ⊃ F   (b)   p ⊃ q

         D   p

      ∴F   ∴q

8. L = The <u>l</u>aw of noncontradiction holds. T = Logical <u>t</u>hought is possible.

  (a)   ~L ⊃ ~T   (b)   ~p ⊃ ~q

         T   q

      ∴L   ∴p

10. D = The gross national product has <u>d</u>ecreased for three straight quarters. R = The country is in a <u>r</u>ecession. U = <u>U</u>nemployment is high.

  (a)   D ⊃ R   (b)   p ⊃ q

         D · U   p · r

      ∴R   ∴q

12. F = The <u>f</u>use blows. B = There is an electric <u>b</u>lackout. O = The appliances in the kitchen will <u>o</u>perate.

  (a)   (F ∨ B) ⊃ ~O   (b)   (p ∨ q) ⊃ ~r

         B   q

      ∴~O   ∴~r

14. S = We are going to the <u>s</u>tate park for a picnic. J = We will take <u>J</u>ohnny along. B = We will take <u>B</u>illy along.

  (a)   S ⊃ (J · B)   (b)   p ⊃ (q · r)

         S   p

      ∴J · B   ∴q · r

16. Using the same propositional constants as in 14:

  (a)   (S ∨ J) ⊃ B   (b)   (p ∨ q) ⊃ r

         S   p

      ∴B   ∴r

18. H = Harry needs <u>h</u>elp painting. W = Joan will take time off from <u>w</u>ork. P = Tom will <u>p</u>ostpone writing his <u>p</u>aper.

  (a)   H ⊃ (W ∨ P)   (b)   p ⊃ (q ∨ r)

         H   p

      ∴W ∨ P   ∴q ∨ r

20. R = It is <u>r</u>aining. S = It is <u>s</u>nowing. F = Sleet is <u>f</u>alling.

  (a)   R ∨ (S ∨ F)   (b)   p ∨ (q ∨ r)

         ~R   ~p

      ∴S ∨ F   ∴q ∨ r

22. S = It is <u>s</u>nowing. F = Sleet is <u>f</u>alling. R = We will go sled <u>r</u>iding.

  (a)   S ∨ F   (b)   p ∨ q

         S ⊃ R   p ⊃ r

         ~F   ~q

      ∴R   ∴r

24. F = Sleet is <u>f</u>alling. R = We will go sled <u>r</u>iding. H = We will stay at <u>h</u>ome.

  (a)   F ⊃ ~R   (b)   p ⊃ ~q

         R ∨ H   q ∨ r

         F   p

      ∴H   ∴r

26. R = It is <u>r</u>aining. C = It is getting <u>c</u>old. S = My car will <u>s</u>tart.

  (a)   R ⊃ (C ⊃ ~S)   (b)   p ⊃ (q ⊃ ~r)

         R · C   p · q

      ∴~S   ∴~r

28. P = <u>P</u>eter is playing piano. B = <u>B</u>ob is playing bass. D = <u>D</u>on is playing drums. C = Our regular <u>c</u>ombo is here.

  (a)   ((P · B) · D) ⊃ C   (b)   ((p · q) · r) ⊃ s

         P   p

         B   q

         D   r

      ∴C   ∴s

30. Using the same propositional constants as in 28:

  (a)   (P · (B · D)) ∨ ~C   (b)   (p · (q · r)) ∨ ~s

         C   s

      ∴P · (B · D)   ∴p · (q · r)

32. E = The statement under discussion is an <u>e</u>quivalence. I = The statement under discussion contains an <u>i</u>mplication. D = The statement under discussion is a <u>d</u>isjunction.

  (a)   D ∨ E   (b)   r ∨ p

         E ⊃ I   p ⊃ q

         ~I   ~q

      ∴D   ∴r

34. T = The statement under discussion is a <u>t</u>ruth-functional proposition. C = The statement under discussion is a <u>c</u>ommand. P = The statement under discussion is a compound <u>p</u>roposition. L = The statement under discussion contains a <u>l</u>ogical operator.

  (a)   T ∨ C   (b)   p ∨ q

         T ⊃ P   p ⊃ r

         P ⊃ L   r ⊃ s

         ~L   ~s

      ∴C   ∴q

36. Y = The Cheshire cat is <u>y</u>ellow. C = The Cheshire cat is <u>c</u>olored. **V** = The Cheshire cat is <u>v</u>isible. **R** = The Cheshire cat is <u>r</u>eal.

(a) **Y ⊃ C**
    C ⊃ V
    V ⊃ R
    Y
    ∴**R**

(b) p ⊃ q
    q ⊃ r
    r ⊃ s
    p
    ∴s

38. Using the same propositional constants as in argument 36:

(a) **R ∨ ~V**
    V ∨ ~C
    C ∨ ~Y
    ~R
    ∴**~Y**

(b) p ∨ ~q
    q ∨ ~r
    r ∨ ~s
    ~p
    ∴~s

40. **A** = Plato was an <u>A</u>thenian. **P** = Descartes was a <u>P</u>arisian. **G** = Plato spoke <u>G</u>reek. **F** = Descartes spoke <u>F</u>rench.

(a) **A ∨ P**
    A ⊃ G
    P ⊃ F
    ~P
    ∴**G**

(b) p ∨ q
    p ⊃ r
    q ⊃ s
    ~q
    ∴r

42. **P** = <u>P</u>ete can come tonight. **G** = <u>G</u>ary can come tonight. **R** = <u>R</u>alph can come tonight. **S** = <u>S</u>am can come tonight. **T** = <u>T</u>ed can come tonight.

(a) **P ⊃ (G ∨ R)**
    G ⊃ S
    S ⊃ T
    P ⊃ ~T
    P
    ∴**R**

(b) p ⊃ (q ∨ r)
    q ⊃ s
    s ⊃ t
    p ⊃ ~t
    p
    ∴r

44. **P** = <u>P</u>reston is a member of the Safari Club. **Q** = <u>Q</u>uincy is a member of the Safari Club. **R** = <u>R</u>andolph is a member of the Safari Club. **S** = <u>S</u>tuart is a member of the Safari Club. **T** = <u>T</u>rumbull is a member of the Safari Club.

(a) **P ∨ Q**
    (Q ∨ R) ⊃ ~S
    S ∨ (T · ~R)
    ~P
    ∴**Q · T**

(b) p ∨ q
    (q ∨ r) ⊃ ~s
    s ∨ (t · ~r)
    ~p
    ∴q · t

EXERCISE 7–2

2. Valid

p	q	(Premise) q ⊃ p	(Conclusion) ~p ⊃ ~q
T	T	T	F T F
F	T	F	T F F
T	F	T	F T T
F	F	T	T T T

4. Valid

p	q	(Premise) p ⊃ q	(Conclusion) p ⊃ (p · q)
T	T	T	T T
F	T	T	T F
T	F	F	F F
F	F	T	T F

6. Invalid

p	q	(Premise) q ⊃ p	(Conclusion) p ⊃ (p · q)
T	T	T	T T
F	T	F	T F
T	F	T	F F
F	F	T	T F

8. Invalid

p	q	(Premise) p ∨ q	(Premise) p	(Conclusion) ~q
T	T	T	T	F
F	T	T	F	F
T	F	T	T	T
F	F	F	F	T

10. Valid

p	q	(Premise) p	(Conclusion) p ∨ q
T	T	T	T
F	T	F	T
T	F	T	T
F	F	F	F

12. Invalid

p	q	r	(Premise) q ∨ r	(Premise) p ⊃ q	(Conclusion) p ⊃ r
T	T	T	T	T	T
F	T	T	T	T	T
T	F	T	T	F	T
F	F	T	T	T	T
T	T	F	T	T	F
F	T	F	T	T	T
T	F	F	F	F	F
F	F	F	F	T	T

14. Invalid

p	q	r	p ⊃ (⊃)	~q	(q · r)	∨ p (∨)	~ q
T	T	T	F	F	T	T	F
F	T	T	T	F	T	T	F
T	F	T	T	T	F	T	T
F	F	T	T	T	F	F	T
T	T	F	F	F	F	T	F
F	T	F	T	F	F	F	F
T	F	F	T	T	F	T	T
F	F	F	T	T	F	F	T

(Premise) p ⊃ ~q (Premise) (q · r) ∨ p (Conclusion) ~ q

16. Invalid

p	q	r	p ⊃ (⊃)	(q ⊃ r)	~r	∨ (∨)	~q	p
T	T	T	T	T	F	F	F	T
F	T	T	T	T	F	F	F	F
T	F	T	T	T	F	T	T	T
F	F	T	T	T	F	T	T	F
T	T	F	F	F	T	T	F	T
F	T	F	T	F	T	T	F	F
T	F	F	T	T	T	T	T	T
F	F	F	T	T	T	T	T	F

(Premise) p ⊃ (q ⊃ r) (Premise) ~r ∨ ~q (Conclusion) p

18. Valid

p	q	r	s	(p ⊃ q)	·	(r ⊃ s)	(p ⊃ q)
T	T	T	T	T	T	T	T
F	T	T	T	T	T	T	T
T	F	T	T	F	F	T	F
F	F	T	T	T	T	T	T
T	T	F	T	T	T	T	T
F	T	F	T	T	T	T	T
T	F	F	T	F	F	T	F
F	F	F	T	T	T	T	T
T	T	T	F	T	F	F	T
F	T	T	F	T	F	F	T
T	F	T	F	F	F	F	F
F	F	T	F	T	F	F	T
T	T	F	F	T	T	T	T
F	T	F	F	T	T	T	T
T	F	F	F	F	F	T	F
F	F	F	F	T	T	T	T

(Premise) (p ⊃ q) · (r ⊃ s) (Conclusion) (p ⊃ q)

20. Valid

p	q	r	(Premise) p ⊃ q	(Premise) q ⊃ r	(Premise) ~r	(Conclusion) ~p
T	T	T	T	T	F	F
F	T	T	T	T	F	T
T	F	T	F	T	F	F
F	F	T	T	T	F	T
T	T	F	T	F	T	F
F	T	F	T	F	T	T
T	F	F	F	T	T	F
F	F	F	T	T	T	T

22. Invalid

p	q	r	(Premise) p ⊃ q	(Premise) p ∨ r	(Premise) ~p	(Conclusion) q
T	T	T	T	T	F	T
F	T	T	T	T	T	T
T	F	T	F	T	F	F
F	F	T	T	T	T	F
T	T	F	T	T	F	T
F	T	F	T	F	T	T
T	F	F	F	T	F	F
F	F	F	T	F	T	F

24. Invalid

p	q	r	(Premise) p ⊃ (q ⊃ r)		(Premise) p ⊃ q	(Conclusion) r
T	T	T	T	T	T	T
F	T	T	T	T	T	T
T	F	T	T	T	F	T
F	F	T	T	T	T	T
T	T	F	F	F	T	F
F	T	F	T	F	T	F
T	F	F	T	T	F	F
F	F	F	T	T	T	F

26. Invalid

p	q	r	(p · q)	⊃	(p ∨ r)	p ∨ r	p · q
			(Premise)			(Premise)	(Conclusion)
T	T	T	T	T	T	T	T
F	T	T	F	T	T	T	F
T	F	T	F	T	T	T	F
F	F	T	F	T	T	T	F
T	T	F	T	T	T	T	T
F	T	F	F	T	F	F	F
T	F	F	F	T	T	T	F
F	F	F	F	T	F	F	F

28. Valid

p	q	r	p ⊃ q	q ⊃ r	p	r
			(Premise)	(Premise)	(Premise)	(Conclusion)
T	T	T	T	T	T	T
F	T	T	T	T	F	T
T	F	T	F	T	T	T
F	F	T	T	T	F	T
T	T	F	T	F	T	F
F	T	F	T	F	F	F
T	F	F	F	T	T	F
F	F	F	T	T	F	F

30. Invalid

p	q	r	p ⊃ (q ⊃ r)	q ⊃ r	q ⊃ (p ⊃ r)	p ⊃ r	(p ∨ q) ⊃ r	r
			(Premise)		(Premise)		(Conclusion)	
T	T	T	T	T	T	T	T	T
F	T	T	T	T	T	T	T	T
T	F	T	T	T	T	T	T	T
F	F	T	T	T	T	T	F	T
T	T	F	F	F	F	F	T	F
F	T	F	T	F	T	T	T	F
T	F	F	T	T	T	F	T	F
F	F	F	T	T	T	T	F	T

32. Valid

p	q	r	(Premise) p ⊃ q	(Premise) ~(q · ~r)	(Conclusion) p ⊃ r
T	T	T	T	T F F	T
F	T	T	T	T F F	T
T	F	T	F	T F F	T
F	F	T	T	T F F	T
T	T	F	T	F T T	F
F	T	F	T	F T T	T
T	F	F	F	T F T	F
F	F	F	T	T F T	T

34. Valid

p	q	r	(Premise) p ⊃ (q ⊃ r)	(Premise) p ⊃ q	(Conclusion) p ⊃ r
T	T	T	T T	T	T
F	T	T	T T	T	T
T	F	T	T T	F	T
F	F	T	T T	T	T
T	T	F	F F	T	F
F	T	F	T F	T	T
T	F	F	T T	F	F
F	F	F	T T	T	T

36. Valid

p	q	r	(Premise) p ∨ (~q · r)	(Premise) q ⊃ ~p	(Conclusion) ~q
T	T	T	T F F	F F	F
F	T	T	F F F	T T	F
T	F	T	T T T	T F	T
F	F	T	T T T	T T	T
T	T	F	T F F	F F	F
F	T	F	F F F	T T	F
T	F	F	T T F	T F	T
F	F	F	F T F	T T	T

38. Valid

p	q	r	(Premise) (p ∨ q) ⊃ (p · q)	(Premise) ~(p · q)	(Conclusion) ~(p ∨ q)
T	T	T	T T T	F T	F T
F	T	T	T F F	T F	F T
T	F	T	T F F	T F	F T
F	F	T	F T F	T F	T F
T	T	F	T T T	F T	F T
F	T	F	T F F	T F	F T
T	F	F	T F F	T F	F T
F	F	F	F T F	T F	T F

40. Invalid

p	q	r	s	(Premise) (p · q) ⊃ (r ∨ s)	(Premise) r ⊃ p	(Premise) ~r ∨ ~s	(Premise) q	(Conclusion) p ⊃ s
T	T	T	T	T T T	T	F F F	T	T
F	T	T	T	F T T	F	F F F	T	T
T	F	T	T	F T T	T	F F F	F	T
F	F	T	T	F T T	F	F F F	F	T
T	T	F	T	T T T	T	T T F	T	T
F	T	F	T	F T T	T	T T F	T	T
T	F	F	T	F T T	T	T T F	F	T
F	F	F	T	F T T	T	T T F	F	T
T	T	T	F	T T T	T	F T T	T	F
F	T	T	F	F T T	F	F T T	T	T
T	F	T	F	F T T	T	F T T	F	T
F	F	T	F	F T T	F	F T T	F	T
T	T	F	F	T F F	T	T T T	T	F
F	T	F	F	F T F	T	T T T	T	T
T	F	F	F	F T F	T	T T T	F	F
F	F	F	F	F T F	T	T T T	F	T

EXERCISE 7–3

Note that any of the following rows will prove the argument schema invalid.

	p	q	r	p ⊃ q	q ⊃ r	r ⊃ p
2.	F	F	T	F T F	F T T	F F
	F	T	T	F T T	T T T	T F
						T F F

4.

p	q	r	s	p ⊃ (q ∨ r)	(q · r) ⊃ s	p ⊃ s
T	F	T	F	T T F T T	F F T T F	T F F
T	T	F	F	T T T T F	T F F T F	T F F

6.

p	q	r	p ⊃ q	p ∨ r	q
F	F	T	F T F	F T T	F

8.

p	q	r	p ⊃ q	p ∨ r	q ∨ ~r
F	F	T	F T F	F T T	F F F T

10.

p	q	r	p ⊃ (q ∨ r)	(q · r) ⊃ ~p	~p
T	F	T	T T F T T	F F T T F T	F T
T	T	F	T T T T F	T F F T F T	F T

12.

p	q	r	s	(p · q) ⊃ r	r ⊃ s	(p · s) ⊃ q	~r ∨ q
F	F	T	T	F F F T T	T T T	F F T T F	F T F F

14.

p	q	r	p ⊃ q	q ⊃ r	p · r
F	F	T	F T F	F T T	F F T
F	F	F	F T F	F T F	F F F
F	T	T	F T T	T T T	F F T

16.

p	q	r	(p ⊃ q) ∨ (q ⊃ r)	p ∨ q	q · r
T	F	F	T F F T F T F	T T F	F F F
T	F	T	T F F T F T T	T T F	F F T
T	T	F	T T T T T F F	T T T	T F F
F	T	F	F T T T T F F	F T T	T F F

18.

p	q	r	s	t	p ⊃ ((q · r) ∨ (s · t))	q ⊃ ~(s · t)	p ⊃ ~(q · r)
T	T	T	F	T	T T T T T T F F T	T T T F F T	T F F T T T
T	T	T	T	F	T T T T T T T F F	T T T T F F	T F F T T T
T	T	T	F	F	T T T T T T F F F	T T T F F F	T F F T T T

EXERCISE 7–4

Each proof below and in the exercises which follow is only one of many possible correct proofs.

2.	1.	p ∨ q	Premise
	2.	q ⊃ r	Premise
	3.	~p/∴r	Premise/conclusion
	4.	q	D. Syll., 1,3
	5.	r	M.P., 2,4
4.	1.	p	Premise
	2.	(p ⊃ q) · (r ⊃ s)/∴q ∨ s	Premise/conclusion
	3.	p ∨ r	Add., 1
	4.	q ∨ s	Dil., 2,3
6.	1.	p ⊃ (q · r)	Premise
	2.	p/∴r	Premise/conclusion
	3.	q · r	M.P., 1,2
	4.	r	Simp., 3
8.	1.	p ⊃ ~r	Premise
	2.	q ∨ r	Premise
	3.	p/∴q	Premise/conclusion
	4.	~r	M.P., 1,3
	5.	q	D.S., 2,4
10.	1.	(p · q) ⊃ (r · s)	Premise
	2.	(r · s) ⊃ (t · u)	Premise
	3.	p · q/∴t · u	Premise/conclusion
	4.	(p · q) ⊃ (t · u)	H.Syll., 1,2
	5.	t · u	M.P., 3,4
12.	1.	p ⊃ q	Premise
	2.	~p ⊃ (q ⊃ r)	Premise
	3.	r ⊃ s	Premise
	4.	~q/∴q ⊃ s	Premise/conclusion
	5.	~p	M.T., 1,4
	6.	q ⊃ r	M.P., 2,5
	7.	q ⊃ s	H. Syll., 3,6
14.	1.	(p ⊃ q) ∨ (r ⊃ s)	Premise
	2.	(r ⊃ s) ⊃ (t ⊃ u)	Premise
	3.	q ⊃ r	Premise
	4.	~(t ⊃ u)/∴p ⊃ r	Premise/conclusion
	5.	~(r ⊃ s)	M.T., 2,4
	6.	p ⊃ q	D. Syll., 1,5
	7.	p ⊃ r	H. Syll., 3,6
16.	1.	(p · q) ⊃ (r · s)	Premise
	2.	(r · s) ⊃ (t · u)	Premise
	3.	p · q/∴u	Premise/conclusion
	4.	(p · q) ⊃ (t · u)	H. Syll., 1,2
	5.	t · u	M.P., 3,4
	6.	u	Simp., 5
18.	1.	p ⊃ q	Premise
	2.	q ⊃ r	Premise
	3.	~r/∴~r · ~p	Premise/conclusion
	4.	p ⊃ r	H. Syll., 1,2
	5.	~p	M.T., 3,4
	6.	~r · ~p	Conj., 3,5

20.	1.	p	Premise
	2.	p ⊃ q	Premise
	3.	(p · q) ⊃ (r · s)/∴r · s	Premise/conclusion
	4.	q	M.P., 1,2
	5.	p · q	Conj., 1,4
	6.	r · s	M.P., 3,5
22.	1.	~p · ~q	Premise
	2.	(~p · ~s) ⊃ ~(r ∨ t)	Premise
	3.	(r ∨ t) ∨ (r ⊃ s)	Premise
	4.	s ⊃ q/∴r ⊃ s	Premise/conclusion
	5.	~p	Simp., 1
	6.	~q	Simp., 1
	7.	~s	M.T., 4,6
	8.	~p · ~s	Conj., 5,7
	9.	~(r ∨ t)	M.P., 2,8
	10.	r ⊃ s	D. Syll., 3,9
24.	1.	p	Premise
	2.	~q	Premise
	3.	((p ∨ r) · ~q) ⊃ (r · ~s)	Premise
	4.	t ⊃ s	Premise
	5.	r ∨ t/∴r	Premise/conclusion
	6.	p ∨ r	Add., 1
	7.	(p ∨ r) · ~q	Conj., 2,6
	8.	r · ~s	M.P., 3,7
	9.	~s	Simp., 8
	10.	~t	M.T., 4,9
	11.	r	D. Syll., 5,10
26.	1.	p	Premise
	2.	p ⊃ q	Premise
	3.	(p · q) ⊃ (r · s)/∴s	Premise/conclusion
	4.	q	M.P., 1,2
	5.	p · q	Conj., 1,4
	6.	r · s	M.P., 3,5
	7.	s	Simp., 6
28.	1.	p	Premise
	2.	(p ∨ q) ⊃ (r · s)	Premise
	3.	s ⊃ t/∴t	Premise/conclusion
	4.	p ∨ q	Add., 1
	5.	r · s	M.P., 2,4
	6.	s	Simp., 5
	7.	t	M.P., 3,6
30.	1.	p ⊃ q	Premise
	2.	q ⊃ r	Premise
	3.	r ⊃ s	Premise
	4.	~s/∴~p	Premise/conclusion
	5.	~r	M.T., 3,4
	6.	~q	M.T., 2,5
	7.	~p	M.T., 1,6
32.	1.	(p ∨ q) ⊃ (r ⊃ s)	Premise
	2.	p ⊃ r	Premise
	3.	p/∴s	Premise/conclusion
	4.	r	M.P., 2,3

5.	p ∨ q	Add., 3
6.	r ⊃ s	M.P., 1,5
7.	s	M.P., 4,6

EXERCISE 7–5

2.
1. ~p · ~q — Premise
2. (p ∨ q) ∨ (r ∨ s)/∴r ∨ s — Premise/conclusion
3. ~(p ∨ q) — D.M., 1
4. r ∨ s — D. Syll., 3

4.
1. p — Premise
2. ~p ∨ q — Premise
3. q ≡ r/∴r — Premise/conclusion
4. p ⊃ q — Impl., 2
5. q — M.P., 1,4
6. (q ⊃ r) · (r ⊃ q) — Equiv., 3
7. q ⊃ r — Simp., 6
8. r — M.P., 5,7

6.
1. p ∨ q — Premise
2. (q ∨ p) ⊃ (r ∨ s) — Premise
3. (s ∨ r) ⊃ ~q/∴p — Premise/conclusion
4. q ∨ p — Comm., 1
5. r ∨ s — M.P., 2,4
6. s ∨ r — Comm., 5
7. ~q — M.P., 3,6
8. p — D. Syll., 1,7

8.
1. p ∨ (q ∨ r) — Premise
2. (p ∨ q) ⊃ ~s — Premise
3. ~r/∴~s — Premise/conclusion
4. (p ∨ q) ∨ r — Assoc., 1
5. p ∨ q — D. Syll., 3,4
6. ~s — M.P., 2,5

10.
1. ~r · ~s — Premise
2. (p ∨ q) ⊃ (r ∨ s)/∴~p · ~q — Premise/conclusion
3. ~(r ∨ s) — DeM., 1
4. ~(p ∨ q) — M.T., 2,3
5. ~p · ~q — DeM., 4

12.
1. ~p — Premise
2. ~q — Premise
3. ~(p ∨ q) ⊃ (p ∨ r)/∴r — Premise/conclusion
4. ~p · ~q — Conj., 1,2
5. ~(p ∨ q) — De. M., 4
6. p ∨ r — M.P., 3,5
7. r — D. Syll., 1,6

14.
1. ~r — Premise
2. (p · q) ⊃ (r · s)/∴~p ∨ ~q — Premise/conclusion
3. ~r ∨ ~s — Add., 1
4. ~(r · s) — De. M., 3
5. ~(p · q) — M.T., 2,4
6. ~p ∨ ~q — De. M., 5

16.
1. ~r · ~s — Premise
2. (p ∨ q) ⊃ (r ∨ s)/∴~q — Premise/conclusion
3. ~(r ∨ s) — DeM., 1
4. ~(p ∨ q) — M.T., 2,3
5. ~p · ~q — DeM., 4
6. ~q — Simp., 5

18.
1. ~r · ~s — Premise
2. (p ∨ q) ⊃ (r ∨ s)/∴~q · ~r — Premise/conclusion
3. ~(r ∨ s) — DeM., 1
4. ~(p ∨ q) — M.T., 2,3
5. ~p · ~q — DeM., 4
6. ~q — Simp., 5
7. ~r — Simp., 1
8. ~q · ~r — Conj., 6,7

20.
1. ~r ∨ ~s — Premise
2. (r · s) ⊃ (p · q)/∴q ∨ t — Premise/conclusion
3. ~(r · s) — DeM., 1
4. p · q — M.P., 2,3
5. q — Simp., 4
6. q ∨ t — Add., 5

22.
1. p ⊃ q — Premise
2. (r ∨ s) ⊃ p — Premise
3. (~p ∨ q) ⊃ s/∴q — Premise/conclusion
4. ~p ∨ q — Impl., 1
5. s — M.P., 3,4
6. s ∨ r — Add., 5
7. r ∨ s — Comm., 6
8. p — M.P., 2,7
9. q — M.P., 1,8

24.
1. ~(p · q) — Premise
2. (p ⊃ ~q) ⊃ (~(p · q) ⊃ r)/∴r — Premise/conclusion
3. ~p ∨ ~q — D.M., 1
4. p ⊃ ~q — Impl., 3
5. ~(p · q) ⊃ r — M.P., 2,4
6. r — M.P., 1,5

26.
1. ~p ∨ q — Premise
2. (p ⊃ q) ⊃ (p ⊃ r)/∴p ⊃ r — Premise/conclusion
3. p ⊃ q — Impl., 1
4. p ⊃ r — M.P., 2,3

28.
1. ~p ∨ q — Premise
2. (p ⊃ q) ⊃ (p ⊃ r) — Premise
3. p/∴q · r — Premise/conclusion
4. p ⊃ q — Impl., 1
5. p ⊃ r — M.P., 2,4
6. r — M.P., 3,5
7. q — M.P., 3,4
8. q · r — Conj., 6,7

30.
1. p · ~r — Premise
2. (p ⊃ q) ⊃ (p ⊃ r)/∴p · ~q — Premise/conclusion
3. ~~(p · ~r) — D.N., 1
4. ~(p ⊃ r) — Impl., 3

    5. ~(p ⊃ q)   M.T., 2,4
    6. ~~(p · ~q)   Impl., 5
    7. p · ~q   D.N., 6

32. 1. p · (q ∨ r)   Premise
     2. ~p/∴q   Premise/conclusion
     3. (p · q) ∨ (p · r)   Dist., 1
     4. ~p ∨ ~r   Add., 2
     5. ~(p · r)   DeM., 4
     6. p · q   D. Syll., 3,5
     7. q   Simp., 6

34. 1. (p · q) ≡ (r ∨ s)   Premise
     2. r/∴p · r   Premise/conclusion
     3. ((p · q) ⊃ (r ∨ s)) · ((r ∨ s) ⊃ (p · q))
                           Equiv., 1
     4. (r ∨ s) ⊃ (p · q)   Simp., 3
     5. r ∨ s   Add., 2
     6. p · q   M.P., 4,5
     7. p   Simp., 6
     8. p · r   Conj., 2,7

EXERCISE 7–6

2. 1. (p ⊃ q) · (r ⊃ s)/∴(p ∨ r) ⊃ (q ∨ s)
                           Premise/conclusion
    →2. p ∨ r   Assumption
     3. q ∨ s   Dil., 1,2
     4. (p ∨ r) ⊃ (q ∨ s)   C.P., 2-3

4. 1. (p ∨ q) ⊃ r/∴((r ∨ s) ⊃ t) ⊃ (p ⊃ t)
                           Premise/conclusion
    →2. (r ∨ s) ⊃ t   Assumption
     →3. p   Assumption
      4. p ∨ q   Add., 3
      5. r   M.P., 1,4
      6. r ∨ s   Add., 5
      7. t   M.P., 2,6
     8. p ⊃ t   C.P., 3-7
     9. ((r ∨ s) ⊃ t) ⊃ (p ⊃ t) C.P., 2-8

6. 1. q/∴p ⊃ (p · q)   Premise/conclusion
    →2. p   Assumption
     3. p · q   Conj., 1,2
     4. p ⊃ (p · q)   C.P., 2-3

8. 1. p ⊃ (q ⊃ r)   Premise
     2. p ⊃ q/∴p ⊃ r   Premise/conclusion
    →3. p   Assumption
     4. q ⊃ r   M.P., 1,3
     5. q   M.P., 2,3
     6. r   M.P., 4,5
     7. p ⊃ r   C.P., 3-6

10. 1. p ⊃ r/∴p ⊃ (q ⊃ (r ∨ s)) Premise/conclusion
    →2. p   Assumption
     →3. q   Assumption
      4. r   M.P., 1,2
      5. r ∨ s   Add., 4
     6. q ⊃ (r ∨ s)   C.P., 3-5
     7. p ⊃ (q ⊃ (r ∨ s))   C.P., 2-6

12. 1. ~p ∨ ~(q · r)/∴q ⊃ (r ⊃ ~p)
                           Premise/conclusion
    →2. q   Assumption
     →3. r   Assumption
      4. q · r   Conj., 2,3
      5. ~~(q · r)   D.N., 4
      6. ~p   D. Syll., 1,5
     7. r ⊃ ~p   C.P., 3-6
     8. q ⊃ (r ⊃ ~p)   C.P., 2-7

14. 1. p ⊃ q/∴(p · r) ⊃ q   Premise/conclusion
    →2. p · r   Assumption
     3. p   Simp., 2
     4. q   M.P., 1,3
     5. (p · r) ⊃ q   C.P., 2-4

16. 1. (p · q) ∨ (r · s)/∴~p ⊃ (r · s) Premise/conclusion
    →2. ~p   Assumption
     3. ~p ∨ ~q   Add., 2
     4. ~(p · q))   DeM., 3
     5. r · s   D. Syll., 1,4
     6. ~p ⊃ (r · s)   C.P., 2-5

18. 1. r ≡ s   Premise
     2. p ∨ r/∴~p ⊃ (r · s) Premise/conclusion
    →3. ~p   Assumption
     4. r   D. Syll., 2,3
     5. (r ⊃ s) · (s ⊃ r)   Equiv., 1
     6. r ⊃ s   Simp., 5
     7. s   M.P., 4,6
     8. r · s   Conj., 4,7
     9. ~p ⊃ (r · s)   C.P., 3-8

20. 1. r/∴p ⊃ (p ∨ q)   Premise
    →2. p   Assumption
     3. p ∨ q   Add., 1
     4. p ⊃ (p ∨ q)   C.P., 2-3

EXERCISE 7–7

2. 1. p ⊃ (q · r)   Premise
     2. ~q/∴~p   Premise/conclusion
    →3. ~~p   Assumption
     4. p   D.N., 3
     5. q · r   M.P., 1,4
     6. q   Simp., 5
     7. q · ~q   Conj., 2,6
     8. ~p   I.P., 3-7

4.
1.	$(r \lor q) \supset p$	Premise
2.	$p \supset (s \cdot t)$	Premise
3.	$\sim s \lor \sim t / \therefore \sim (r \lor q)$	Premise/conclusion
→4.	$\sim\sim(r \lor q)$	Assumption
5.	$r \lor q$	D.N., 4
6.	p	M.P., 1,5
7.	$s \cdot t$	M.P., 2,6
8.	$\sim(s \cdot t)$	DeM., 3
9.	$(s \cdot t) \cdot \sim(s \cdot t)$	Conj., 7,8
10.	$\sim(r \lor q)$	I.P., 4-9

6.
1.	$p \lor q$	Premise
2.	$p \lor \sim q / \therefore p$	Premise/conclusion
→3.	$\sim p$	Assumption
4.	q	D. Syll., 1,3
5.	$\sim q$	D. Syll., 2,3
6.	$q \cdot \sim q$	Conj., 4,5
7.	p	I.P., 3-6

8.
1.	$\sim p \supset q$	Premise
2.	$\sim(\sim p \cdot q) / \therefore p$	Premise/conclusion
→3.	$\sim p$	Assumption
4.	q	M.P., 1,3
5.	$\sim\sim p \lor \sim q$	DeM., 2
6.	$p \lor \sim q$	D.N., 5
7.	$\sim q$	D. Syll., 3,6
8.	$q \cdot \sim q$	Conj., 4,7
9.	p	I.P., 3-8

10.
1.	$p \equiv q$	Premise
2.	$\sim r \lor p / \therefore r \supset q$	Premise/conclusion
→3.	$\sim(r \supset q)$	Assumption
4.	$\sim\sim(r \cdot \sim q)$	Impl., 3
5.	$r \cdot \sim q$	D.N., 4
6.	r	Simp., 5
7.	$\sim q$	Simp., 5
8.	$(p \supset q) \cdot (q \supset p)$	Equiv., 1
9.	$p \supset q$	Simp., 8
10.	$\sim p$	M.T., 7,9
11.	$\sim r$	D. Syll., 2,10
12.	$r \cdot \sim r$	Conj., 6,11
13.	$r \supset q$	I.P., 3-12

12.
1.	$\sim p \supset (q \cdot r)$	Premise
2.	$\sim r / \therefore p$	Premise/conclusion
→3.	$\sim p$	Assumption
4.	$q \cdot r$	M.P., 1,3
5.	r	Simp., 4
6.	$r \cdot \sim r$	Conj., 2,5
7.	p	I.P., 3-6

14.
1.	$(p \lor q) \supset (r \supset \sim s)$	Premise
2.	$(s \lor t) \supset (p \cdot r) / \therefore \sim s$	Premise/conclusion
→3.	$\sim\sim s$	Assumption
4.	s	D.N., 3
5.	$s \lor t$	Add., 4
6.	$p \cdot r$	M.P., 2,5

7.	p	Simp., 6
8.	$p \lor q$	Add., 7
9.	$r \supset \sim s$	M.P., 1,8
10.	r	Simp., 6
11.	$\sim s$	M.P., 9,10
12.	$s \cdot \sim s$	Conj., 4,11
13.	$\sim s$	I.P., 3-12

EXERCISE 8–1

2. $(x)(Tx \supset Sx)$
4. True. Indeterminate
6. 'n' = 'my next door neighbor'; 'Tn. ~ Sn'
8. True, for the universe of mammals; false, for the universe of living things.

EXERCISE 8–2

2. (a,c,h) Yes (d,e,g) No (b) 'Ba' is singular but statement as a whole is not. (f) Monadic
4. (a,b,c,d,e,h) No (f) Monadic (g) 'y' is free.
6. (a,d) Yes (b,c,e,g,h) No (f) Dyadic
8. (a,d) Yes (b,c,e,g,h) No (f) Monadic
10. (a,b,h) Yes (c,d,e,g) No (f) Dyadic

EXERCISE 8–3

2. x is a proposition, *and* x is expressible by a sentence (*or* x is a proposition, *and* y is a sentence, *and* x is expressible by y).
4. x is an expression, *and* x contains free variables, *and* x is a statement (*or* x is an expression, y is a free variable, x contains y, *and* x is a statement).
6. x is an argument, x is valid, *and* x is truth-functionally valid.
8. x is a book, *and* x is hardbound.
10. x is a universally quantified statement, x is true, y is an instance of x, *and* y is true.
12. x is a piece of cheap goods in the store, x is shoddily made, *and* x is defective.
14. x is an actor, x is an award winner, *and* x is an Academy Award winner.

EXERCISE 8–4

2. Not everything that grows in my yard is a weed.
4. Someone is both a physicist and a musician.
6. Everything that is for sale is too expensive.
8. No one who is a child of Harriet's is married.
10. Someone who is a child of Harriet's is not married.
12. Something is a canine and a dog.

EXERCISE 8–5

2. Bx = x is a book; Hx = x is hardbound. ~(x)(Bx ⊃ Hx).

4. Ax = x is an atheist; Gx = x believes in God. (x)(Ax ⊃ ~Gx).

6. Ix = x is an impulsive person; Mx = x makes good decisions. (∃x)(Ix.Mx).(∃x)(Ix.~Mx).

8. Lx = x enjoyed the lecture; universe, persons. (∃x)Lx.(∃x)~Lx.

10. Hx = x is a human; Mx = x is a mammal. (x)(Hx ⊃ Mx).

12. Dx = x lives in Detroit; Mx = x lives in Michigan; universe, persons. (x)(Dx ⊃ Mx). If universe not restricted, add Px = x is a person: (x)(Px ⊃ (Dx ⊃ Mx)).

14. Tx = x is a three-lane highway; Dx = x is dangerous. (x)(Tx ⊃ Dx).

16. Px = x is a player of the first rank; Tx = x entered the tournament. (x)(Tx ⊃ Px); *or* (x)(~Px ⊃ ~Tx).

18. Hx = x is human; Ax = x is alive. (x)(Hx ⊃ (Ax ∨ ~Ax)).

EXERCISE 8–6

1, 2, 5, 7: in each case, logically equivalent. 3, 4: in each case, the first statement implies the second, but the second doesn't imply the first. 6: neither implies the other.

EXERCISE 8–7

2. Cx = x is a member of the chess team; Fx = x is a friend of George. (x)(Cx ⊃ Fx). *Or:* Cx = x is a member of the chess team; Fxy = x is a friend of y; g = George. (x)(Cx ⊃ Fxg).

4. Fyx = y is a friend of x. Universe, people. (x)(∃y)Fyx.

6. Gxy = x is greater than y; Lxy = x is less than y; Exy = x is equal to y. (x)(y)(Gxy ⊃ (~Lxy · ~Exy)).

8. Ixy = x is identical with y. (∃x)(∃x)Ixy.

10. Oxy = x is older than y. Osw ⊃ ~Ows.

12. Gx = x knows German; Fx = x knows at least one foreign language. (x)(Gx ⊃ Fx). *Or:* Kxy = x knows y; Fy = y is a foreign language; g = the German language. (x)(Kxg ⊃ (∃y)(Fy · Kxy)).

14. Ox = x is an old wine; Bx = x is one of the best wines. ~(x)(Ox ⊃ Bx).

16. Lx = x is a member of the L family; Gxy = x greets y; Mxy = x meets y; Rxy = x remembers y's name. (x)(Lx ⊃ (y)((Mxy · Rxy) ⊃ Gxy))).

EXERCISE 8–8

2. Every member of the 0 family remembers the name of anyone who owes money to him or her.

4. There is no music that all musicians like.

EXERCISE 9–1

2. (c) 'a' originated in a premise. (d) 'a' originated in an undischarged assumption. (f) 'a' originated by E.I. (h) Violates proviso II.

EXERCISE 9–2

2. (a) '(∃x)Fx ⊃ Fb' is not a generalized statement.

EXERCISE 9–3

2. (a) Everything is either an albatross or a bird. If Albert is an albatross or George is a bird, then everything is a chicken. Therefore, everything is a chicken. (b) Incorrect (c) On line 3, 'x' is not replaced uniformly.

4. (a) Something is an albatross. Something is a bird. Therefore, something is both a bird and an albatross. (b) Incorrect (c) Line 4 violates the new-constant requirement for E.I.

6. (a) If something is an albatross, then everything is a bird. Everything is an albatross. Therefore, everything is a bird. (b) Correct

8. (a) Everyone likes someone. Therefore, someone likes everyone. (b) Incorrect (c) Line 4 violates proviso II of U.G. rule.

10. (a) Everything is similar to something. If anything is similar to a second thing, then the second is similar to the first. Therefore, something is similar to everything. (b) Incorrect (c) Line 8 violates proviso I, U.G. rule ('b' originated by E.I.).

EXERCISE 9–4

2.
1.	(x)(Tx ⊃ Nx)	P.
2.	(∃x)Tx	P.
3.	Ta	E.I., 2
4.	Ta ⊃ Na	U.I., 1
5.	Na	M.P., 3,4
6.	Ta · Na	Conj., 3,4
7.	(∃x)(Tx · Nx)	E.G., 6

4.
1.	(x)(Tx ⊃ Nx)	P.
2.	Ta ⊃ Na	U.I., 1
3.	~Ta ∨ Na	Impl., 2
4.	(x)(~Tx ∨ Nx)	U.G., 3

6.
1.	(x)Tx · (x)Nx	P.
2.	(x)Tx	Simp., 1
3.	(x)Nx	Simp., 1
4.	Ta	U.I., 2
5.	Na	U.I., 3
6.	Ta · Na	Conj., 4,5
7.	(x)(Tx · Nx)	U.G., 6

8.
1.	(x)(y)Sxy	P.
2.	(y)Say	U.I., 1

3. Sab   U.I., 2
4. (∃y)Say   E.G., 3
5. (∃x)(∃y)Sxy   E.G., 4

10. 1. (∃x)(∃y)Sxy   P.
2. (∃y)Say   E.I., 1
3. Sab   E.I., 2
4. (∃y)Syb   E.G., 3
5. (∃x)(∃y)Syx   E.G., 4

12. 1. (∃x)(y)Lxy   P.
2. (y)Lay   E.I., 1
3. Lab   U.I., 2
4. (∃x)Lxb   E.G., 3
5. (y)(∃x)Lxy   U.G., 4

14. 1. (x)Tx ∨ (x)Nx   P.
2. ~Ta   Assumption
3. (∃x)~Tx   E.G., 2
4. ~(x)Tx   Q.E., 3
5. (x)Nx   D. Syll., 1,4
6. Na   U.I., 5
7. ~Ta ⊃ Na   C.P., 2-6
8. ~~Ta ∨ Na   Impl., 7
9. Ta ∨ Na   D.N., 8
10. (x)(Tx ∨ Nx)   U.G., 9

16. 1. (x)(Cx ⊃ Hx) ⊃ (∃x)Ux   P.
2. (x)~Ux   P.
3. ~(∃x)Ux   Q.E., 2
4. ~(x)(Cx ⊃ Hx)   M.T., 1,3
5. (∃x)~(Cx ⊃ Hx)   Q.E., 4
6. ~(Ca ⊃ Ha)   E.I., 5
7. ~(~Ca ∨ Ha)   Impl., 6
8. ~~Ca · ~Ha   DeM., 7
9. Ca · ~Ha   D.N., 8
10. (∃x)(Cx · ~Hx)   E.G., 9

18. 1. (x)(Fx ⊃ Gx)   P.
2. (x)(Gx ⊃ Hx)   P.
3. (∃x)Fx   Assumption
4. Fa   E.I., 3
5. Fa ⊃ Ga   U.I., 1
6. Ga ⊃ Ha   U.I., 2
7. Fa ⊃ Ha   H. Syll., 5,6
8. Ha   M.P., 4,7
9. (∃x)Hx   E.G., 8
10. (∃x)Fx ⊃ (∃x)Hx   C.P., 3-9

20. 1. (x)(y)(Mxy ⊃ ~Myx)   P.
2. (x)(y)(Dxy ⊃ Myx)   P.
3. (y)(May ⊃ ~Mya)   U.I., 1
4. Mab ⊃ ~Mba   U.I., 3
5. (y)(Day ⊃ Mya)   U.I., 2
6. Dab ⊃ Mba   U.I., 5
7. ~~Mba ⊃ ~Mab   Trans., 4
8. Mba ⊃ ~Mab   D.N., 7
9. Dab ⊃ ~Mab   H. Syll., 6,8

---

10. (y)(Day ⊃ ~May)   U.G., 9
11. (x)(y)Dxy ⊃ ~Mxy)   U.G., 10
(Alternatively: by C.P.)

EXERCISE 9–5

2. (a) a. (∃x)(Ax · ~Rx)
b. (∃x)(~Rx · Ax)
(b) For both deductions, the same strategy as in 1 is used.
4. (a) a. (x)(Ax ⊃ Fx)
b. (x)(~Fx ⊃ ~Ax)
(b) Same as 3.
6. (a) a. (x)(Ax ⊃ ~Px)
b. (x)(Px ⊃ ~Ax)
(b) Same as 3, with negation signs to be dealt with.
But if alternatively:
(a) a. ~(∃x)(Ax · Px)
b. ~(∃x)(Px · Ax)
(b) 1. ~(∃x)(Ax · Px)/∴~(∃x)(Px · Ax)   Premise/conclusion
2. (x) ~ (Ax · Px)   Q.E., 1
3. ~(Aa · Pa)   U.I., 2
4. ~(Pa · Aa)   Comm., 3
5. (x) ~ (Px · Ax)   U.G., 4
6. ~(∃x)(Px · Ax)   Q.E., 5
Similarly for deducing a from b.
8. (a) a. (x)(Ax ⊃ Fx)
b. ~(∃x)(Ax ⊃ Fx)
(b) 1. (x)(Ax ⊃ Fx)/∴~(∃x)(Ax ⊃ Fx)   Premise/conclusion
2. Aa ⊃ Fa   U.I., 1
3. ~(Aa · ~Fa)   Impl., 2
4. (x) ~ (Ax · ~Fx)   U.G., 3
5. ~(∃x)(Ax · ~Fx)   Q.E., 4
For deducing a from b: Q.E., U.I., Impl., U.G. in that order.
10. (a) a. ~(x)(Fx ⊃ ~Ax)
b. (∃x)(Fx · Ax)
(b) Same strategies as for 7, with need for repeated D.N.

EXERCISE 9–6

2. (a) 'Tx' = 'x is a member of the T family'; 'Rxy' = 'x remembers the name of y'; 'Sxy' = 'x speaks to y'; 'Gxy' = 'x gossips about y'.
1. (x)(y)(Tx ⊃ (Rxy ⊃ Sxy))   Premise
2. (x)(y)(Tx ⊃ (Sxy ⊃ Gxy))/
∴(x)(y)(Tx ⊃ (Rxy ⊃ Gxy))
Premise/conclusion

(b) 3. (y)(Ta ⊃ (Ray ⊃ Say))   U.I., 1
    4. Ta ⊃ (Rab ⊃ Sab)   U.I., 3
    5. (y)(Ta ⊃ (Say ⊃ Gay))   U.I., 2
    6. Ta ⊃ (Sab ⊃ Gab)   U.I., 5
    7. Ta   Assumption
    8. Rab ⊃ Sab   M.P., 4,7
    9. Sab ⊃ Gab   M.P., 6,7
    10. Rab ⊃ Gab   H. Syll., 8,9
    11. Ta ⊃ (Rab ⊃ Gab)   C.P., 7-10
    12. (y)(Ta ⊃ (Ray ⊃ Gay))   U.G., 11
    13. (x)(y)(Tx ⊃ (Rxy ⊃ Gxy))   U.G., 12

4. (a) 'Yx' = 'x is a three-year-old horse'; 'Tx' = 'x is a thoroughbred'; 'Sx' = 'x is a standardbred'; 'Bx' = 'x is eligible for the Belmont Stakes'.
    1. (∃x)(Yx · (~Tx · ~Sx))   Premise
    2. (x)(Bx ⊃ (Yx · Tx))/∴(∃x)(Yx · ~Bx)   Premise/conclusion
(b) 3. Ya · (~Ta · ~Sa)   E.I., 1
    4. ~Ta · ~Sa   Simp., 3
    5. ~Ta   Simp., 4
    6. ~Ta ∨ ~Ya   Add., 5
    7. ~Ya ∨ ~Ta   Comm., 6
    8. ~(Ya · Ta)   DeM., 7
    9. Ba ⊃ (Ya · Ta)   U.I., 2
    10. ~Ba   M.T., 8,9
    11. Ya   Simp., 3
    12. Ya · ~Ba   Conj., 10,11
    13. (∃x)(Yx · ~Bx)   E.G., 12

6. (a) 'Feh' = 'Ellen runs faster than Harry'; 'Fhj' = 'Harry runs faster than Joanne'.
    1. Feh · Fhj   Premise
    2. (x)(y)(z)((Fxy · Fyz) ⊃ Fxz)/∴Fej   Premise/conclusion
(b) 3. (y)(z)((Fey · Fyz) ⊃ Fez)   U.I., 2
    4. (z)((Feh · Fhz) ⊃ Fez)   U.I., 3
    5. (Feh · Fhj) ⊃ Fej   U.I., 4
    6. Fej   M.P., 1,5

8. (a) 'Fx' = 'x is a farmer'; 'Ex' = 'x is an executive'; 'b' = 'Bill'.
    1. (x)(Fx ⊃ ~Ex)   Premise
    2. Eb/∴~Fb   Premise/conclusion
(b) 3. Fb ⊃ ~Eb   U.I., 1
    4. ~~Eb   D.N., 2
    5. ~Fb   M.T., 3,4

10. (a) 'Px' = 'x is a politician'; 'Lx' = 'x is a liar'; 'Wx' = 'x is a woman'.
    1. (x)(Px ⊃ Lx)   Premise
    2. (∃x)(Wx · Px)/∴(∃x)(Wx · Lx)   Premise/conclusion
(b) 3. Wa · Pa   E.I., 2
    4. Pa ⊃ La   U.I., 1
    5. Pa · Wa   Comm., 3
    6. Pa   Simp., 5
    7. La   M.P., 4,6
    8. Wa   Simp., 3
    9. Wa · La   Conj., 8,7
    10. (∃x)(Wx · Lx)   E.G., 9

12. (a) 'Ux' = 'x is a university'; 'Tx' = 'x is financially sound'; 'Bx' = 'x is bankrupt'.
    1. (x)(Ux ⊃ (Tx ∨ Bx))   Premise
    2. (∃x)(Ux · ~Bx)/∴(∃x)(Tx · Ux)   Premise/conclusion
(b) 3. Ua · ~Ba   E.I., 2
    4. Ua ⊃ (Ta ∨ Ba)   U.I., 1
    5. Ua   Simp., 3
    6. Ta ∨ Ba   M.P., 4,5
    7. ~Ba · Ua   Comm., 3
    8. ~Ba   Simp., 7
    9. Ba ∨ Ta   Comm., 6
    10. Ta   D.S., 9,8
    11. Ta · Ua   Conj., 10,5
    12. (∃x)(Tx · Ux)   E.G., 11

EXERCISE 9–7
2. (a) (x) Ux
(b) 1. (∃x)(Cx · Hx)   Premise
    2. (x) ~ Hx/∴(x)Ux   Premise/conclusion
    3. ~(x)Ux   Assumption
    4. Ca · Ha   E.I., 1
    5. ~Ha   U.I., 2
    6. Ha   Simp., 4
    7. Ha · ~Ha   Conj., 5,6
    8. (x)Ux   I.P., 3-7

EXERCISE 9–8
2. The following can easily be shown to be valid: No one who cannot qualify is eligible for the tournament. No one who is not eligible will be in the tournament. John cannot qualify. Therefore, John will not be in the tournament. Abbreviating 'x can qualify' as 'Qx', 'x is eligible for the tournament' as 'Ex', 'x will be in the tournament' as 'Tx', and 'John' as 'j', we get: '(x)(~Qx ⊃ ~Ex)', '(x)(~Ex ⊃ ~Tx)', '~Qj'; therefore, '~Tj'. Instantiation of the universal propositions to 'j', followed by two modus ponens (or hypothetical syllogism and modus ponens) produces the conclusion.

EXERCISE 10–1
2. Explanation
4. Explanation
6. Explanation
8. Argument
10. Argument

EXERCISE 10–2

2. Induction by analogy
4. Induction by analogy
6. Induction by analogy
8. Inductive generalization
10. Induction by analogy
12. Inductive generalization
14. Induction by analogy
16. Inductive generalization
18. Inductive generalization

EXERCISE 10–3

2. c, a, b, e, d
4. d, c, e, b, a
6. c, b, d, e, a
8. c, a, b, e, d

EXERCISE 10–4

2. (a) Weakens by increasing the negative analogy between observed and unobserved cases, if one considers the information about Mrs. Kelly's brother-in-law relevant. (b) Strengthens, if one considers party registration relevant. (c) Strengthens, if one considers party involvement relevant. (d) Weakens by increasing negative analogy between observed and unobserved cases, if one considers the generational history of the families relevant. (e) Strengthens by increasing the number of observed cases and increasing the negative analogy among the observed cases. (f) Weakens, if one considers the information about Mrs. Kelly's brother-in-law and the generational histories of the families relevant. (g) Strengthens, if one considers party registration and political activity relevant. (h) Strengthens, if one considers political activity and the generational histories of the families relevant.

4. (a) Strengthens by increasing the number of observed cases and increasing the negative analogy among them. (b) Destroys the argument by providing a counterexample. (c) Strengthens by increasing the number of observed cases and increasing the negative analogy among them. (d) Strengthens by increasing the number of observed cases and increasing the negative analogy among them. (e) Destroys the argument by providing a counterexample. (f) Strengthens by increasing the number of observed cases and increasing the negative analogy among them. (g) Destroys the argument by providing a counterexample.

6. (a) Strengthens by increasing the positive analogy between observed and unobserved cases. (b) Weakens by increasing the negative analogy between the observed and unobserved case, if one considers the special program relevant. (c) Weakens by increasing the negative analogy between observed and unobserved cases, if one considers the colleges applied to relevant. (d) Strengthens by increasing negative analogy among observed cases. (e) Strengthens by increasing the positive analogy between observed and unobserved cases, if one interprets this information as 'all of them scored better than 600'. Otherwise, it would have to be viewed as weakening the argument, because it would appear that the negative analogy between observed and unobserved cases is increased. (f) Strengthens by increasing positive analogy between observed and unobserved cases, if one considers grades, college board scores and advances courses relevant. (g) Weakens by increasing negative analogy between observed and unobserved cases.

EXERCISE 10–5

2. a, d, f, c, b, e
4. c, b, d, a

EXERCISE 10–6

2. (a) Strengthens by increasing the negative analogy among the observed cases. (b) Weakens by increasing the positive analogy among the observed cases. (c) Weakens by increasing the positive analogy among the observed cases. (d) Strengthens by increasing the negative analogy among the observed cases. (e) Weakens by increasing the positive analogy (or decreasing the negative analogy) among the observed cases. (f) Strengthens by increasing the negative analogy among the observed cases.

4. (a) Weakens by increasing the positive analogy among observed cases and increasing the negative analogy between observed and unobserved cases, if one considers watching the same station relevant. (b) Weakens by increasing the positive analogy among observed cases and increasing the negative analogy between observed and unobserved cases. (c) Weakens by increasing the positive analogy among observed cases and increasing the negative analogy between observed and unobserved cases, if one considers the location of the viewers in the sample relevant. (d) Weakens by increasing the positive analogy among observed cases and increasing the negative analogy between observed and unobserved cases, if one considers watching "The Mary Tyler Moore Show" relevant. (e) Strengthens by increasing negative analogy among observed cases and increasing positive analogy between observed and unobserved cases, if one considers the location of the viewers in the samples relevant. (f) Strengthens by

increasing the negative analogy among observed cases and increasing positive analogy between observed and unobserved cases.

EXERCISE 11–1

2. (a) My mother has caught the flu.
My father has caught the flu.
My first sister has caught the flu.
My second sister has caught the flu.
∴I will catch the flu.

(b) My mother has caught the flu.
My father has caught the flu.
My first sister has caught the flu.
My second sister has caught the flu.
∴Everyone in our family is catching the flu.
I am a member of our family.
∴I will catch the flu.

4. (a) Swan A is white.
Swan B is white.
Swan C is white.
Swan D is white.
Swan E is white.
Swan F is white.
Swan G is white.
Swan H is white.
Swan I is white.
Swan J is white.
∴Swan K is white.

(b) Swan A is white.
Swan B is white.
Swan C is white.
Swan D is white.
Swan E is white.
Swan F is white.
Swan G is white.
Swan H is white.
Swan I is white.
Swan J is white.
∴All swans are white.
K is a swan.
∴Swan K is white.

6. (a) We had a big snow storm last year.
We had a big snow storm two years ago.
We had a big snow storm three years ago.
We had a big snow storm four years ago.
∴We will have a big snow storm this year.

(b) We had a big snow storm last year.
We had a big snow storm two years ago.
We had a big snow storm three years ago.
We had a big snow storm four years ago.
∴We have big snow storms every year.
This year is a year.
∴We will have a big snow storm this year.

8. (a) Chimp A engaged in grooming behavior.
Chimp B engaged in grooming behavior.
Chimp C engaged in grooming behavior.
Chimp D engaged in grooming behavior.
Chimp E engaged in grooming behavior.
Chimp F engaged in grooming behavior.
Many chimps in addition to A, B, C, D, E, and F exist.
∴At least one chimp other than A, B, C, D, E, or F will engage in grooming behavior.

(b) Chimp A engaged in grooming behavior.
Chimp B engaged in grooming behavior.
Chimp C engaged in grooming behavior.
Chimp D engaged in grooming behavior.
Chimp E engaged in grooming behavior.
Chimp F engaged in grooming behavior.
∴All chimps engage in grooming behavior.
Many chimps besides A, B, C, D, E, and F exist.
∴Many chimps besides A, B, C, D, E, and F will engage in grooming behavior.

10. (a) *Swan Lake* was composed by Tchaikovsky and is a great ballet score.
The Nutcracker was composed by Tchaikovsky and is a great ballet score.
Sleeping Beauty is a ballet score composed by Tchaikovsky.
∴*Sleeping Beauty* is a great ballet *score*.

(b) *Swan Lake* was composed by Tchaikovsky and is a great ballet score.
The Nutcracker was composed by Tchaikovsky and is a great ballet score.
∴All ballet scores composed by Tchaikovsky are great ballet scores.
Sleeping Beauty is a ballet score composed by Tchaikovsky.
∴*Sleeping Beauty* is a great ballet score.

12. (a) This Rolls-Royce is a European-made car and performs well.

This Volvo is a European-made car and performs well.

This Mercedes-Benz is a European-made car and performs well.

This Volkswagen is a European-made car and performs well.

∴This Fiat, which is a European-made car, performs well.

(b) This Rolls-Royce is a European-made car and performs well.

This Volvo is a European-made car and performs well.

This Mercedes-Benz is a European-made car and performs well.

This Volkswagen is a European-made car and performs well.

∴All European-made cars perform well.

This Fiat is a European-made car.

∴This Fiat performs well.

14. (a) All sea otters observed off the coast of Newfoundland use rocks to crack open seashells.

All sea otters observed off the coast of Washington use rocks to crack open seashells.

All sea otters observed off the coast of Alaska use rocks to crack open seashells.

All sea otters observed off the coast of Finland use rocks to crack open seashells.

∴The next sea otter to be observed off the coast of Nova Scotia uses rocks to crack open seashells.

(b) All sea otters observed off the coast of Newfoundland use rocks to crack open seashells.

All sea otters observed off the coast of Washington use rocks to crack open seashells.

All sea otters observed off the coast of Alaska use rocks to crack open seashells.

All sea otters observed off the coast of Finland use rocks to crack open seashells.

∴All sea otters use rocks to crack open seashells.

At least one sea otter will be observed off the coast of Nova Scotia.

∴The next sea otter to be observed off the coast of Nova Scotia uses rocks to crack open seashells.

16. (a) Regina is an intelligent woman and reads *Ms.* magazine.

Barbara is an intelligent woman and reads *Ms.* magazine.

Johanna is an intelligent woman and reads *Ms.* magazine.

Elizabeth is an intelligent woman.

∴Elizabeth reads *Ms.* magazine.

(b) Regina is an intelligent woman and reads *Ms.* magazine.

Barbara is an intelligent woman and reads *Ms.* magazine.

Johanna is an intelligent woman and reads *Ms.* magazine.

∴All women who are intelligent read *Ms.* magazine.

Elizabeth is an intelligent woman.

∴Elizabeth reads *Ms.* magazine.

18. (a) There were interesting people at Joe's last party.

There were interesting people at Joe's party before last.

There were interesting people at Joe's party before the last two.

Joe is having another party tonight.

∴There will be interesting people at Joe's party tonight.

(b) There were interesting people at Joe's last party.

There were interesting people at Joe's party before last.

There were interesting people at Joe's party before the last two.

∴There are interesting people at all of Joe's parties.

Joe is having another party tonight.

∴There will be interesting people at Joe's party tonight.

EXERCISE 11–4

2. a, d, and e.
4. a, b, c.
6. a, c, f.
8. a, c.

EXERCISE 11–5

Sample answer: Hypothesis: All planets in the solar system have satellites. *Supporting observation statements:* (a) The earth has one satellite, the moon. (b) Mars has two satellites. (c) Jupiter has twelve satellites. *Disconfirming observation statements:* (d) Mercury has no satellites. (e) Pluto has no satellites.

EXERCISE 11–6

Inductive argument:

2. (a)   On a Model T Ford, a set of Pumperup tires had fewer blowouts per thousand miles than a set of Roadmark tires on the same car.

   On a Model A Ford, a set of Pumperup tires had fewer blowouts per thousand miles than a set of Roadmark tires on the same car.

   On a Stanley Steamer, a set of Pumperup tires had fewer blowouts per thousand miles than a set of Roadmark tires on the same car.

   ∴Pumperup tires have fewer blowouts per thousand miles than Roadmark tires.

   (b, c, d, e) These arguments take the same form as (a). *Order of decreasing inductive strength:* d, b, e, a, c.

   Inductive argument:

4. (a)   A bluebird observed in Canada had a beak.
   A pigeon observed in New York had a beak.
   A red robin observed in Kentucky had a beak.
   A sparrow observed in England had a beak.
   A raven observed in Russia had a beak.

   ∴All birds have beaks.

   Arguments b, c, d, and e take the same form as argument a. *Order of decreasing inductive strengths:* b, a, d, e, c.

EXERCISE 12–1

2. *Proximate:* k. *Remote:* a, c, d, e, f, h, i, j.

4. *Proximate:* t. *Remote:* a through s except b, c, i, k, n, p. Note that, in both examples, it might be possible to give a justification for considering one or more of the excluded events as remote causes.

EXERCISE 12–3

2. *Necessary conditions:* a, b, h, j, l, p. *Sufficient conditions:* the conjunction of a, l, p. (Sentence g would also be included in both lists, if Williams' words were necessary for getting the gate opened.)

4. a. Necessary but not sufficient. b. Neither necessary nor sufficient. c. Sufficient but not necessary. d. Sufficient but not necessary (hermaphrodites are neither men nor women). e. Necessary but not sufficient. f. Neither necessary nor sufficient. g. Sufficient but not necessary (one could use more or less than six ounces of orange juice).

EXERCISE 12–4

Method of agreement. The proximate condition of cracking was probably the differential expansion, and the condition of this was the conjunction of sudden change in temperature, eastward exposure, and the presence of the varicolored paints on the glass. Since cracking occurred *only* where these conditions were present, the expansion and the conjunction which produced it were necessary conditions. They would not be shown to be sufficient conditions unless it could be demonstrated that cracking occurred in *every* case in which they were present.

EXERCISE 12–5

2. Method of agreement, then method of difference. The finding that riboflavin deficiency was present in all cases of keratitis established that substance as probably a necessary condition of the disease. The fact that, for each patient, the elimination of that one condition sufficed to cure the disease established the deficiency as probably a sufficient cause of keratitis.

EXERCISE 12–6

The necessary condition is probably the conjunction of crystal and zeroz—an answer arrived at by use of the method of agreement. (Of course, in real life it is highly unlikely that the different samples would vary as much as in this imaginary case.)

EXERCISE 12–7

2. Method of difference: the only differences between the two groups, as groups, were the presence or absence of fluorine in the drinking water, and the subsequent difference in number of cavities. Therefore the presence of fluorine was probably a sufficient condition for the reduction in numbers of cavities.

4. Joint method: the suspicious error was present on all the papers of X Fraternity students, and absent from the paper of all students who were not members of X Fraternity. Therefore being a member of X Fraternity was probably a necessary condition for making this particular error on the exam, though it was probably not a sufficient condition.

6. Joint method: the only known factor common to all occasions on which the phone died was the presence of a heavy, driving rain from the east. Consequently, such a rain was probably a necessary condition of this particular pattern of telephone malfunction. Also, given that probably no other factor changed when it was not raining hard from the east, it was probably also a sufficient condition. A more immediate (or less remote) "cause" of the malfunction was the accumulation of moisture in the defective wire.

EXERCISE 12–8

2. If we regard late and early rigor mortis as two fairly well-defined and opposing characteristics (as Mill here did), this is an illustration of the joint method. The cases of late rigor mortis varied in many respects but were alike in the presence of high muscular irritability; the cases of early rigor mortis also varied among themselves, but were alike in the absence of high muscular rigidity.

However, both the degree of irritability and the timing and duration of rigor mortis probably vary along a continuum. Therefore, the precise measurements (if we had them available) would probably show concomitant variations as well.

EXERCISE 12–9

2. This represents use of the method of concomitant variations. There is a *slight* (though far from wholly convincing) degree of association between the two sets. For example, the two years when the price-earnings ratio was highest (1958 and 1961) were also the years of highest unemployment rate. Also, for the first ten years of the period, the average of both price-earnings ratio and unemployment was distinctly lower than for the remaining nine years. Additionally, the most substantial single rise in the price-earnings ratio (from 1957 to 1958) was accompanied by a drop in unemployment, and the sharpest single drop (from 1965 to 1966) was accompanied by a drop in unemployment. Thus, the figures can be interpreted to suggest that concomitant variations *may* be present. More recent figures, however, have tended to disconfirm this hypothesis.

EXERCISE 12–10

2. The method of agreement indicated California origin as probably a necessary condition of the rusty radiators. The method of difference eliminated production error as a factor by failing to disclose any differences in production procedure between the eastern and western plants. Also, because rust did not appear after any specific production stage, the method of difference appeared to rule out any such stage as a sufficient condition. With production eliminated as a causal factor, the salt-air hypothesis was checked and confirmed by means of an experiment utilizing the method of difference, which established exposure to damp salt air as probably a sufficient condition of the rusty radiators.

EXERCISE 12–11

2. (1) Method of concomitant variations. Since the number of rich people and the rate of crime have both increased during the same period, it is assumed that one of the changes is probably the cause of the other. In this instance, the concomitant variation is positive.

(2) (a) The argument would be strengthened if it could be shown that the two factors consistently varied, not only in the same direction, but also at similar rates: for instance, that a 10 percent increase in the number of rich people was accompanied or soon followed by twice as large an increase in crime as a 5 percent increase in rich people. (b) The argument would be weakened if it were found that one or more other possibly significant factors also varied concomitantly with the crime rate—for example, that the number of people on welfare also increased. It would also be weakened if the relative rates of increase in the two factors already considered were widely disproportionate (contrary to the situation proposed in answer 2a). (c) Again, assuming the truth of the basic data (that both wealth and crime have increased during the same period), it is difficult to suggest any one piece of evidence that would absolutely falsify the conclusion.

(3) 'Cause' is certainly not being used here to refer to a necessary condition, since there is no suggestion that crime occurs only in the presence of wealth. It may be intended to refer to a sufficient condition, but this seems somewhat doubtful, since Quick is at pains to point out an intermediate element in the evidence—namely, that, for the rich, crime pays. It might thus be argued that, for Quick, the sufficient condition of crime is not the existence of wealth but the conjunction of wealth with the existence of a society in which the wealthy can profit from crime.

4. (1) This appears to be an application of the joint method. In all the low-MS populations, conditions are favorable for infection in early childhood; no other condition appears to be common to all these populations. This condition is absent in all high-MS populations.

(2) (a) The argument would be strengthened if studies of MS victims and nonvictims *within* any one of these countries or regions showed a similar pattern of early exposure for the nonvictim, early protection for the victim. (b) The argument would be weakened if it were shown that a region of high childhood exposure—such as China, where, as in Japan, human excrement has traditionally been used for fertilizer—had a high rate of MS. (c) The conclusion would be falsified if MS were shown to be caused by a hereditary genetic factor or by a

virus incapable of transmission by means of body wastes. But this can be done only at a relatively abstract theoretical level. It is not clear which, if any, observations would falsify the hypothesis.

(3) 'Cause' is here being used to refer to a necessary condition. Widespread exposure to infection at an early age is seen as probably a necessary condition of a low MS rate; widespread protection from infection at an early age is seen as probably a necessary condition for a high MS rate; but neither is thereby shown to be a sufficient condition.

6. (1) Possible method of agreement: The suggested condition was present in nearly all the cases studied, and it was apparently the only condition (or at least the only one thought likely to be significant) which was present in nearly all. It must be presumed that there is a more-proximate cause of these deaths, which is itself caused by conditions other than depression, since not all of the twenty-six victims had this common history.

(2) (a) The argument would be strengthened if all of the victims had undergone physical examinations shortly before suffering their heart attacks and had shown no medical warning signs of impending heart trouble. (b) The argument would be weakened if all of the victims were shown to have been exposed to a particular and unusual industrial chemical or other possibly hazardous working condition shortly before death. (c) It is not likely, given accuracy of the initial data, that any single item of evidence would completely falsify the conclusion.

(3) 'Cause' is here being used to refer to a necessary condition. Presumably there were other employees who also experienced the sequence of depression and arousal but did not suffer heart attacks; thus, the condition cannot be regarded as sufficient.

8. (1) Method of difference, assuming that the two groups, as groups, differed only in respect to the use or nonuse of marijuana. The experimental conditions were the same for cells taken from both groups.

(2) (a) The argument would be strengthened if a follow-up study showed that the smokers did, in fact, suffer from a higher disease rate than the nonsmokers, or if studies of larger groups showed similar laboratory results. (b) The argument would be weakened if it were shown that the smokers, as a group, tended to eat less well, get less rest, or otherwise take poorer care of their general health than the nonsmokers. (c) The experiment could be invalidated if it were found that the cultural me-

dium used for cells from the smokers had accidentally been contaminated with a substance inhibiting cell reproduction, but even this would not prove the conclusion to be false.

(3) 'Cause' is here being used to refer to a sufficient condition.

10. (1) Method of concomitant variations: a downturn in the economy is consistently accompanied, or followed at fairly predictable intervals, by rises in the incidence of certain other phenomena.

(2) (a) The argument would be strengthened if were found that all or most of the victims had lost their jobs or otherwise suffered loss of income during the recession. (b) The argument would be weakened if it were found that stress did not, in general, contribute to the likelihood of a heart attack, stroke, or kidney failure. (c) It seems unlikely that any single piece of evidence would completely falsify the conclusion.

(3) 'Cause' is here being used to refer to a sufficient condition. Note, however, that a causal chain intervenes between the recession and the heart attack or other proximate cause of death. The recession itself is a fairly remote sufficient condition.

12. (1) Concomitant variations: The average age of malnutrition symptoms has declined concomitantly with the rise of the trend to bottle-feeding.

(2) (a) The argument would be strengthened if studies of two groups of children, known to be alike in all significant respects except that one group was breast-fed and the other bottle-fed, showed earlier or more severe malnutrition in the bottle-fed group. (b) The argument would be weakened if it were shown that the bottle-fed children, as a group, and breast-fed children in the same societies showed no difference in malnutrition levels in the two groups. (c) The conclusion cannot be totally falsified.

(3) 'Cause' is here being used to refer to a sufficient condition.

14. (1) Method of difference: the swine, as groups, were presumably alike in all significant respects save the controlled difference in diet.

(2) (a) The argument would be strengthened if similar studies using other animals showed similar effects. (b) The argument would be weakened if the diet containing the "trans" fatty element were shown to contain, as well, some other possibly active element not present in the diet of the other groups. The conclusion also would be seriously weakened if a similar study using whole margarine, instead of the "trans" fatty element alone, showed no

significantly higher degree of arterial damage in the margarine group than in the other groups. (c) The conclusion cannot be falsified in any absolute sense.

(3) 'Cause' is here being used to refer to a sufficient condition.

EXERCISE 13–1

2. Very close to 0
4. Very close to 1
6. Nearer to 1
8. Nearer to .5
10. About .5
12. Near 0
14. 1
16. 1 or at least very near to 1

EXERCISE 13–2

2. No—logically inconsistent
4. No—logically inconsistent
6. Yes—logically consistent (John may take the course two different semesters, failing the first and passing the second.)
8. Yes—logically consistent (she could have had a multiple birth—twins, triplets, etc.)

EXERCISE 13–3

2. (a) $\frac{1}{4}$ or .25 (b) $\frac{2}{5}$ or .4
4. $\frac{2,180,000}{4,258,000} = \frac{1090}{2129} =$ about .51
6. (a) 2/525,000 or 1/262,500 (b) 10/525,000 or 1/52,500
8. (a) $\frac{5}{1+5} = \frac{5}{6} = .83.$ (b) Assuming that there is no probability of a tie, the odds of losing are .17 or 1 to 5.
10. (a) M = 27 n = 100 P(A) = $\frac{27}{100}$ or .27 (b) $\frac{9}{66}$ or about .13 (For each student there are 9 favorable events—scores between 110 and 118—and 66 total possible events—scores between 102 and 167, if we assume strict similarity of the two classes.)
12. (a) $\frac{2}{5+2} = \frac{2}{7}$ or about .28 (b) about .72 (because .72 + .28 = 1.0, the maximum permissible figure) (c) 7 to 3 $\left(.72 = \text{about } \frac{7}{10} = \frac{7}{3+7}\right)$
14. *Old:* $\frac{5}{4+5} = \frac{5}{9} =$ about .55;

   New: $\frac{9}{4+9} = \frac{9}{13} =$ about .69
16. (a) 99,200/100,000 = .992 (b) 800/100,000 = 8/1000 = .008 assuming that probabilities can be computed for single cases.

18. (a) $\frac{45}{75} = \frac{3}{5} = .6$ (b) $\frac{30}{75} = \frac{2}{5} = .4$ assuming that probabilities can be computed for single cases.

EXERCISE 13–4

2. One possible favorable event; independent; restricted conjunction rule. Initial probability of each simple event: $\frac{1}{6}$. Probability of conjunct event: $\frac{1}{216}$. Equation: P(x & y & z) = P(x) × P(y) × P(z)

$$= \frac{1}{6} \times \frac{1}{6} \times \frac{1}{6} = \frac{1}{216}$$

4. One possible favorable event; independent; restricted conjunction rule. Initial probability of each simple event: $\frac{1}{2}$. Probability of conjunct event: $\frac{1}{8}$. Equation: P(x & y & z) = P(x) × P(y) × P(z)

$$= \frac{1}{2} \times \frac{1}{2} \times \frac{1}{2} = \frac{1}{8}$$

6. One possible favorable event; dependent; general conjunction rule. Initial probability of each simple event: $\frac{4}{52}$. Probability of conjunct event: 32/812,175. Equation:

P(w & x & y & z) = P(w) × P(x given w)
   × P(y given w & x) × P(z given w, x, & y)

$$= \frac{4}{52} \times \frac{4}{51} \times \frac{4}{50} \times \frac{4}{49} = \frac{256}{6,497,400} = \frac{32}{812,175}$$

8. One possible favorable event; dependent; general conjunction rule. Initial probability of each event: $\frac{1}{10}$. Probability of conjunct event: $\frac{1}{90}$. Equation:

$$P(x \& y) = P(x) \times P(y \text{ given } x) = \frac{1}{10} \times \frac{1}{9} = \frac{1}{90}$$

10. (a) $\frac{1}{4}$ (b) One possible favorable event; independent; restricted conjunction rule. Initial probability of each simple event: $\frac{1}{4}$. Probability of conjunct event: $\frac{1}{64}$. Equation:

P(x & y & z) = P(x) × P(y) × P(z)

$$= \frac{1}{4} \times \frac{1}{4} \times \frac{1}{4} = \frac{1}{64}$$

EXERCISE 13–5

2. (a) Dependent (b) Restricted conjunction rule (c) Initial probability of each simple event is $\frac{1}{52}$.
   (d) 1/311,875,200
   (e) P(v and w and x and y and z)
      = P(v) × P(w given v)
      × P(x given w and v)
      × P(y given x and w and v)
      × P(z given y and x and w and v)

$$= \frac{1}{52} \times \frac{1}{51} \times \frac{1}{50} \times \frac{1}{49} \times \frac{1}{48} = \frac{1}{311,875,200}$$

4. (a) Independent (b) Restricted conjunction rule (c) Initial probability of selecting a black ball from urn 1 is $\frac{1}{3}$; from urns 2 and 3 the initial probability is $\frac{1}{6}$ (d) $\frac{1}{108}$

(e) $P(x \text{ and } y \text{ and } z) = P(x) \times P(y) \times P(z)$

$$= \frac{1}{3} \times \frac{1}{6} \times \frac{1}{6} = \frac{1}{108}$$

6. (a) Dependent (b) General conjunction rule (c) Initial probability of drawing a red ball is $\frac{1}{3}$, of drawing a white ball after a red ball is $\frac{10}{29}$, and of drawing a blue ball after a red ball and then a white ball is $\frac{10}{28}$. (d) $\frac{100}{2436}$ or about .04

(e) $P(x \text{ and } y \text{ and } z)$

$= P(x) \times P(y \text{ given } x) \times P(z \text{ given } y \text{ and } x)$

$$= \frac{10}{30} \times \frac{10}{29} \times \frac{10}{28} = \frac{1000}{24,360} = \frac{100}{2436}$$

8. (a) Independent (b) Restricted conjunction rule (c) Initial probability of each simple event is $\frac{1}{2}$. (d) $\frac{1}{16}$

(e) $P(w \text{ and } x \text{ and } y \text{ and } z) =$

$P(w) \times P(x) \times P(y) \times P(z) = \frac{1}{2} \times \frac{1}{2} \times \frac{1}{2} \times \frac{1}{2} = \frac{1}{16}$

10. (a) Dependent (b) General conjunction rule (c) Initial probability of drawing the first ace is $\frac{1}{13}$, of drawing the second ace is $\frac{3}{51}$. (d) $\frac{1}{221}$

(e) $P(x \text{ and } y) = P(x) \times P(y)$

$$= \frac{1}{13} \times \frac{3}{51} = \frac{3}{663} = \frac{1}{221}$$

EXERCISE 13–6

2. (a) Two possible favorable events; mutually exclusive; restricted disjunction rule. Initial probability of each simple event: $\frac{1}{52}$. Probability of disjunct event: $\frac{3}{52}$ or about .058. Equation:

$P(x \text{ or } y \text{ or } z) = P(x) + P(y) + P(z)$

$$= \frac{1}{52} + \frac{1}{52} + \frac{1}{52} = \frac{3}{52}$$

(b) Six possible favorable events; mutually exclusive; restricted disjunction rule. Initial probability of each simple event: $\frac{1}{52}$. Probability of disjunct event: $\frac{3}{28}$ or about .115. Equation:

$P(u \text{ or } v \text{ or } w \text{ or } x \text{ or } y \text{ or } z)$

$= P(u) + P(v) + P(w) + P(x) + P(y) + P(z)$

$$= \frac{1}{52} + \frac{1}{52} + \frac{1}{52} + \frac{1}{52} + \frac{1}{52} + \frac{1}{52} = \frac{6}{52} = \frac{3}{52}$$

4. Two possible favorable events: not mutually exclusive; general disjunction rule. Initial probabilities of simple events: $\frac{1}{2}$ and $\frac{2}{3}$. $P(x \& y) = \frac{1}{3}$. Probability of disjunct event: $\frac{5}{6}$ or about .833. Equation:

$P(x \text{ or } y) = P(x) + P(y) - P(x \& y) = \frac{1}{2} + \frac{2}{3} - \frac{1}{3} = \frac{5}{6}$

6. Possible favorable events = 50 percent of total population; not mutually exclusive; general disjunction rule. Initial probabilities of simple events: .4 (gray hair) and .25 (blue eyes). $P(x \& y) = .15$. Probability of disjunct event: .5. Equation:

$P(x \text{ or } y) = P(x) + P(y) - P(x \& y) =$

$$.4 + .25 - .15 = .5$$

8. (a) 1/999,999. This is, of course, a simple event, not a disjunction. (b) Two possible favorable events; mutually exclusive; restricted disjunction rule. Initial probability of each simple event: 1/999,999. Probability of disjunct event: 2/999,999. Equation:

$P(x \text{ or } y) = P(x) + P(y)$

$$= \frac{1}{999,999} + \frac{1}{999,999} = \frac{2}{999,999}$$

(c) Four possible favorable events; mutually exclusive; restricted disjunction rule. Initial probability of each simple event: 1/999,999. Probability of disjunct event: 4/999,999. Equation:

$P(w \text{ or } x \text{ or } y \text{ or } z)$

$$= P(w) + P(x) + P(y) + P(z)$$

$$= \frac{1}{999,999} + \frac{1}{999,999} + \frac{1}{999,999}$$

$$+ \frac{1}{999,999} = \frac{4}{999,999}$$

10. Seventy possible favorable events; not mutually exclusive; general disjunction rule. Initial probabilities of simple events: $\frac{3}{10}$ (woman) and $\frac{1}{2}$ (smoker). $P(x \& y) = \frac{1}{10}$. Probability of disjunct event: $\frac{7}{10}$ or .7. Equation:

$P(x \text{ or } y) = P(x) + P(y) - P(x \& y)$

$$= \frac{3}{10} + \frac{1}{2} - \frac{1}{10} = \frac{7}{10}$$

EXERCISE 13–7

2. (a) Not mutually exclusive (b) Restricted disjunction rule (c) Initial probability of both coming up heads (by restricted conjunction rule) is $\frac{1}{2} \times \frac{1}{2}$ or $\frac{1}{4}$. (d) Not relevant. (e) $\frac{3}{4}$ or .75 (f) $P(x \text{ or } y) = P(x) + P(y) - P(x \text{ and } y) =$

$$\frac{1}{2} + \frac{1}{2} - \frac{1}{4} = \frac{3}{4}$$

4. (a) Mutually exclusive (b) Restricted disjunction rule (c) Initial probability of each simple event is $\frac{4}{52}$ or $\frac{1}{13}$. (d) Not relevant (e) $\frac{4}{13}$ or about .31

(f) $P(w \text{ or } x \text{ or } y \text{ or } z) =$

$P(w) + P(x) + P(y) + P(z)$

$$= \frac{1}{13} + \frac{1}{13} + \frac{1}{13} + \frac{1}{13} = \frac{4}{13}$$

6. (a) Not mutually exclusive (b) General disjunction rule (c) Initial probability of drawing black ball from urn 1 is $\frac{1}{3}$, from urn 2 is $\frac{1}{6}$. (d) $P(x \text{ or } y) = P(x) \times P(y) = \frac{1}{3} \times \frac{1}{6} = \frac{1}{18}$. (e) $\frac{4}{9}$

(f) $P(x \text{ or } y) = P(x) + P(y) - P(x \text{ and } y)$

$$= \frac{1}{3} + \frac{1}{6} - \frac{1}{18} = \frac{3}{6} - \frac{1}{18} = \frac{8}{18} = \frac{4}{9}$$

8a. (a) Mutually exclusive events (b) Restricted disjunction rule (c) Initial probability of selecting a white ball is $\frac{5}{50}$ or $\frac{1}{10}$, of selecting a black ball is $\frac{15}{50}$ or $\frac{3}{10}$. (d) Not relevant (e) $\frac{4}{10}$ or .40

(f) $P(x \text{ or } y) = P(x) + P(y) = \frac{1}{10} + \frac{3}{10} = \frac{4}{10}$

8b. (a) Mutually exclusive events (b) Restricted disjunction rule (c) Initial probability of selecting a red ball is $\frac{20}{50}$ or $\frac{2}{5}$, of selecting a yellow ball is $\frac{10}{50}$ or $\frac{1}{5}$. (d) Not relevant (e) $\frac{3}{5}$ or .60

(f) $P(x \text{ or } y) = P(x) + P(y) = \frac{2}{5} + \frac{1}{5} = \frac{3}{5}$

8c. (a) Mutually exclusive (b) Restricted disjunction rule (c) Initial probability of selecting a black ball is $\frac{3}{10}$, of selecting a yellow ball is $\frac{1}{5}$. (d) Not relevant (e) $\frac{1}{2}$ or .5

(f) $P(x \text{ or } y) = P(x) + P(y) = \frac{3}{10} + \frac{1}{5} = \frac{5}{10} = \frac{1}{2}$

10. (a) Not mutually exclusive events (b) General disjunction rule (c) Initial probability of one adult member in the family is $\frac{1}{2}$, of three school-aged children in the family is $\frac{3}{5}$. (d) $P(x \text{ and } y) = P(x) \times P(y) = \frac{1}{2} \times \frac{3}{5} = \frac{3}{10}$. (e) $\frac{4}{5}$ or .80

(f) $P(x \text{ or } y) = P(x) + P(y) - P(x \text{ and } y)$

$$= \frac{1}{2} + \frac{3}{5} - \frac{3}{10} = \frac{11}{10} - \frac{3}{10} = \frac{8}{10} = \frac{4}{5}$$

EXERCISE 13–8

2. (a) Conjunction; one possible favorable event; dependent; general conjunction rule. Initial probability of each simple event: $\frac{1}{52}$. Probability of conjunct event: 1/6,497,400 or about .00000015. Equation:

$P(w \& x \& y \& z)$

$= P(w) \times P(x \text{ given } w) \times P(y \text{ given } w \& x)$
$\quad \times P(z \text{ given } w, x, \& y)$

$$= \frac{1}{52} \times \frac{1}{51} \times \frac{1}{50} \times \frac{1}{49} = \frac{1}{6,497,400}$$

(b) Disjunction; four possible favorable events; mutually exclusive; restricted disjunction rule. Initial probability of each conjunct event: 1/6,497,400. Probability of disjunct event: 1/1,624,350 or about .0000006. Equation:

$P(w \text{ or } x \text{ or } y \text{ or } z)$

$$= P(w) + P(x) + P(y) + P(z)$$

$$= \frac{1}{6,497,400} + \frac{1}{6,497,400} + \frac{1}{6,497,400}$$

$$+ \frac{1}{6,497,400} = \frac{4}{6,497,400} = \frac{1}{1,624,350}$$

(c) Conjunction; twenty-four possible favorable events; dependent; general conjunction rule. Initial probability of each simple event: $\frac{4}{52}$—i.e., P(any one of the four on the first draw). Probability of conjunct event: 1/270,725.

$P(w) = \frac{4}{52}$

$P(x \text{ given } w) = $ P(any one of the four on the second draw given that one of the four was drawn on the first draw) $= \frac{3}{51}$

$P(y \text{ given } w \& x) = $ P(any one of the four on the third draw, given that two of the four were drawn on the first two draws) $= \frac{2}{50}$

$P(z \text{ given } w, x, \& y) = $ P(any one of the four on the fourth draw, given that three of the four were drawn on the first three draws) $= \frac{1}{49}$

$P(w \& x \& y \& z) = P(w) \times P(x \text{ given } w) \times P(y \text{ given } w \& x) \times P(z \text{ given } w, x, \& y)$

$$= \frac{4}{52} \times \frac{3}{51} \times \frac{2}{50} \times \frac{1}{49} = \frac{24}{6,497,400} = \frac{1}{270,725}$$

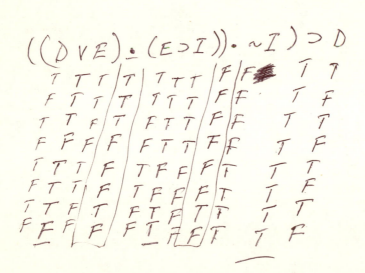

ISBN 0 03 056878 1